The Conflict
of Interpretations

Northwestern University
STUDIES IN *Phenomenology &*
Existential Philosophy

Paul Ricoeur

Edited by

The Conflict
of Interpretations

Essays in Hermeneutics

DON IHDE

Northwestern University Press

Evanston   1 9 7 4

Published in French under the title *Le Conflit des interprétations: Essais d'herméneutique,* copyright © 1969 by Editions du Seuil, Paris.

Contents

[vii]

Editor's Introduction

I

THE VECTORS AND LINES OF FORCE of Paul Ricoeur's thought stand out in bolder contrast in *The Conflict of Interpretations* than in the more systematic works of the same period. The twenty-two essays which appear here, most for the first time in English translations, span the period 1960–69, during which time *The Symbolism of Evil* (1960) and *Freud and Philosophy* (1965) also appeared. But the shorter form of the theses elaborated here are often not only more concise statements of themes also found in the systematic works but stand out in stronger and more explicit terms. Moreover, the hints of new directions and increasingly of problems which will appear in Ricoeur's forthcoming *Poetics of the Will* begin to surface.

At first this collection of essays is striking in its diversity: structuralism and linguistic analysis, hermeneutics and phenomenology, psychoanalysis and the question of the subject, religion and faith, are all discussed. This is more than a concrete testimonial to Ricoeur's catholicity of interests. For, upon closer reading, the same systematic and dialectically critical thinking which has become Ricoeur's hallmark in contemporary philosophy shows itself.[1]

The guiding thread which unites these diverse interests and which holds the clue for the direction of Ricoeur's thought is the

1. See Don Ihde, *Hermeneutic Phenomenology: The Philosophy of Paul Ricoeur* (Evanston, Ill.: Northwestern University Press, 1971).

[ix]

question of *hermeneutics*, interpretation. The hermeneutic question, in very recent years, has come into its own as a *philosophic* question linked both to what has been the overriding concern of philosophers in the twentieth century—the philosophy of language—but also to what is now emerging as a new interest in the foundations of the human or social sciences.

Nor can these two questions be separated. *Man is language*, as both Ricoeur and Heidegger are fond of saying. Language as "institution" is already a social phenomenon. Thus, even though seemingly distant, the questions of the structure or logic of language remain subterraneously linked to questions of sociality and human historicality. One could build a case that those philosophies of language which have emerged in Anglo-American circles have sometimes tended to treat language as if it were a kind of self-generating computing "machine" which contains a certain series of finite laws which in turn produce proper sentences almost without the intervention of the human speaker.

On the other hand, expressing this argument in its most extreme form, Continental thinkers have sometimes tended to think of language too exclusively as the act of a speaker, an expression of a subject. This is particularly the case in the giving of an implicit, if not explicit, privilege to the "bringing-to-speech" of novel discourse.

It is almost as if a certain "Cartesian" split had occurred at the English Channel, with linguistic "mechanists" holding the day on one side and linguistic "spiritualists" holding the day on the other. That too gross characterization, of course, no longer obtains today. In Germany there is a revival of interest in analytic and even neopositivistic concerns, while in the United States the impact of hermeneutics has begun to be felt, especially in the philosophy of the social sciences.

But Ricoeur in his own way also seeks to span this set of linked but unresolved tendencies in the philosophy of language. And it is in the hermeneutic question that he finds a certain key toward the resolution of the relation between "speech act" and the "logic" or structure of language. In *The Conflict of Interpretations* it remains the case that the influences of linguistic analysis remain on the fringes. His more recent studies of Wittgenstein, particularly in relation to a certain parallelism with the development of phenomenology, are not included, nor are the even more recent studies of metaphor. But nevertheless, there are background references to Austin, Strawson, and Wittgenstein. What can be noted here, though, is a deeper sympathy for ordinary-language philosophies than for the formalistic approaches to language. Austin's appreciation of the extraordinary wealth of ordinary language, Strawson's use of a "descriptive" metaphysics, and Wittgenstein's noting of the complicated flexibility of language in the notion of language games strike immediate response for phenomenological thought in its own nonreductive tendencies.

But the stronger influence here is that of structuralism. In part this is natural, for France has been the center of much of the structuralist interest and conflict. Ricoeur plays the role of a rigorous but friendly critic to Lévi-Strauss in the Parisian climate. The success of the *Esprit* editions on structuralism, which sold out and sold out again on reprinting, testify to this strong current of structuralist thought in France (see, in this volume, "Structure and Hermeneutics" and "Structure, Word, Event").

On one level, that of the dialectic of a phenomenological focus with a body of "objectivist" theory as a counterfocus, Ricoeur's debate with and use of structuralism follow a pattern of thought already well established as a working habit. Structuralist linguistics is questioned carefully and analyzed in terms of both operational and foundational presuppositions. Ricoeur grants, with a preliminary charity not often found in more polemical or radical thinkers of the phenomenological tradition, that there is a certain necessity to the "objectivism" of structuralism, precisely in order to establish language as an "object" and structuralist analysis as a "science."

But this idealization of language into a system operating according to structural laws pays a price. This price is that it can deal with language only at a certain *level* and only within a certain set of presuppositionally prescribed *limits*. Thus, as Ricoeur contends in "Structure, Word, Event," structural linguistics begins with the supposition that language may be treated as a corpus, a closed and already constituted system (synchrony takes precedence over diachrony). Then, within this assumed closure of language, structural linguistics may begin to establish units (analysis of parts), note oppositions (binary relations), and establish a calculus of elements and their possible relations.

Ricoeur points out that such a set of operational presuppositions is implicitly a reductionist move from the start. Not only does it deliberately suppress the diachronic to the synchronic, which is to subsume history to structure, but it deliberately reads out of consideration the speaking subject. The act of speaking, in one sense the fulfillment of language, is excluded from the start and, within the strictest confines of a structuralist analysis, cannot be reintroduced. In this, structuralist linguistics is yet another triumph of a "Cartesian" science. For it is only by exiling the "body" from the "soul," "language" from "speech," that a "Cartesian" science is established. Language as a system of inter-related units is not only idealized under the presuppositions of structuralism but operates as a kind of "idealism," i.e., as a system of internal relations.

It is at this juncture, however, that Ricoeur differentiates his basically phenomenological stance from that of both Merleau-Ponty and Heidegger. Merleau-Ponty, before Ricoeur, entered into the debate with structuralism. He, too, recognized the implicit reductionism of a system of signs which reads the subject out of the field of language. His response, too, was dialectical, but, according to Ricoeur, too directly so (cf. "The Question of the Subject: The Challenge of Semiology"). At least in the *Phenomenology of Perception*, Merleau-Ponty's response was that of reinstating the primacy of the speaker. The embodied subject is primordially an expressive subject. The chapter dealing with language and speech there is titled "The Body as Expression and Speech." And the privileged illustrations are those which point up "first words," a certain coming-into-speech of initial discourse such as that of the "first man," the child with first words, the creative speaker, such as poet or artist. The countermovement in Merleau-Ponty tends toward a phenomenology of speech in contrast to a system of language.

Heidegger, according to Ricoeur, opts for an even more radical "ontology of understanding," which, in effect, transforms the whole question of speech and language (see "Existence and Hermeneutics"). It is a route which forces, as Ricoeur says, a choice between a fundamental ontology and contemporary epistemology. And while Ricoeur does not close the door on the radical Heideggerian strategy, his objection to both Merleau-Ponty and Heidegger is that both, in effect, close off the possibility of debate with and use of the linguistic sciences. Thus in a sense Ricoeur's more indirect, more dialectical route is also more "conservative." It is only *through* contemporary epistemology and a theory of hermeneutics that one will be able to deal with structuralism or any of the current linguistic disciplines. Ricoeur's approach is one of attaining ontology by degrees, through methodological considerations.

But the use of approximations hides another key to Ricoeur's development of hermeneutic phenomenology. It is through the development of a theory of the *levels* of language that structuralism and the other linguistic disciplines are both located and limited. A "higher" level locates and limits a "lower"-level investigation. But what must be noted is that the "lower" level does not in the process lose any of its claim to a proper domain of validity or even of a certain "universality."

Semiotics, the linguistic disciplines which operate at the level of language as "objectified," constitute the lowest, but also the necessary, level of language as structure. The semiotic constitution of language is the finitude of language. Moreover, there is a certain "universality" even here, for whatever is expressed is expressed within the limits or structures of the system of signs. This is the case whether one speaks a simple declarative statement or a primitive confession of evil, to which Ricoeur gives privileged status in his own analysis of symbols as the location of the fullness of language.

Yet, in spite of the necessity and universality of the finite structure of language, there is also an *infinite* focus in the dialectic of levels. Language at its highest level is *open*. This is revealed in simple speech, which, while activating the "mechanism" of the system, also *says*. Here is event, choice, the new, the referential, the discursive. (That is why Chomskyan "generative grammar" poses a challenge to structuralism. For the simple fact that any normal speaker of a language can immediately understand a new sentence, one never uttered before, must necessarily pose an enigma for any absolute structuralism of pure difference or of pure "internal relations.")

This dialectic of finite-infinite, closed-open, in relation to language and speech recalls a similar pattern of thought developed earlier in *Fallible Man*. There the infinity of "verb," or word act, was mediated and located through the finitude of perspective. The significative situation of man is primordially both perception and language, a seeing and a saying. Now, within language itself, the finitude of structure mediates the infinity of event.

But just as in *Fallible Man* there was a "third term" which unites the foci of the dialectic, so now within the region of language there is a "third term" which is *word itself*. Word is both system and act, structure and history. And in a sense this most obvious, most familiar phenomenon of language and speech poses itself late only because it was too obvious to begin with. Yet the obvious is not the simple. For word within itself is already *polysemic,* as Ricoeur underlines. Within itself word poses itself with a certain potential for opacity, which is also its richness.

Moreover, although every word is already latently rich in polysemy, for Ricoeur the hermeneutics of language centers upon certain privileged words, those of the *symbolic word.* Hermeneutics becomes primarily, under Ricoeur's use, the interpretation and investigation of those words which have a certain type of multiple sense.

The location of the hermeneutic problem for Ricoeur takes its specific shape in words which have symbolic significance, which have a "metaphorical" structure. And although the formula varies from time to time, the form it takes in "Existence and Hermeneutics," an article which Ricoeur claims is a very important statement of his position, indicates the outline of the hermeneutic problem. *"I define 'symbol' as any structure of meaning in which a direct, primary, literal sense designates in addition another sense which is indirect, secondary, and figurative and which can be apprehended only through the first."*

In turn, the hermeneutic task is that of deciphering this multiple significance. *"Interpretation . . . is the work of thought which consists in deciphering the hidden meaning in the apparent meaning, in unfolding the levels of meaning implied in the literal meaning."* Here hermeneutics makes contact with its older exegetical traditions in the task of deciphering *texts.*

The text, in this case, is not, however, the simple narrative or descriptive treatise but is a text in which there is some analogical or allegorical significance. Thus the surface meaning may "hide" or "conceal" or at least "contain" a less obvious depth meaning which is nevertheless dependent upon the surface literal meaning. The *work* of the hermeneut is to discover and explicate that significance.

But this textual model for the hermeneutic task becomes, in Ricoeur's thought, much more than a matter of textual interpretation or exegesis alone. It is the case, of course, that, before becoming a philosophical problem as such, hermeneutics was a religio-theological problem. The development of types of exegesis and textual analysis which were interested in the symbolic in Ricoeur's sense has had a long history in biblical interpretation. But Ricoeur's aim is to *graft* hermeneutics to a *phenomenological philosophy.* This is his version of a *hermeneutic phenomenology.*

There are three aspects to this "graft" of hermeneutic problems and textual paradigms to a phenomenological methodology which are of interest in pointing up the development of Ricoeur's hermeneutic phenomenology. First, in some of the earlier essays in *The Conflict of Interpretations,* those surrounding the period of the *Symbolism of Evil,* Ricoeur tends to stick much more closely to the notion of a textual analysis of symbolic discourse. In both parts of the "Hermeneutics of Symbols and Philosophical Reflection," Ricoeur is concerned with working out the methodological grounds for a theory of analogous meaning. Here phenomenology enters as a version of a comparativist strategy and as a means of "recovering" the intentionalities of symbolic expressions, i.e., of unlayering the experiential significations of these expressions. Thus the constellation of meaning surrounding the various confessions (*l'aveu*) of the experience of evil are explored. At a higher level—the insertion of symbolic words into myths—a system of meanings is discerned and hermeneutics also becomes the explication of the forms of the great cultural-religious myths.

However, the second step in expanding the graft of hermeneutics to phenomenology toward a "hermeneutic philosophy of existence," as Ricoeur calls his project, begins to occur in a much more radical form in the period which surrounds the time of *Freud and Philosophy.* There remains a "textual" element. The Freudian interpretation of dreams, of art works, of jokes, is read by Ricoeur as a type of hermeneutics. It is an interpretation which deals with the *expressions* of the patient; thus its therapy works within the domain of the verbal. The psychoanalyst must interpret the dream "text" and the "text" of the joke or the slip of the tongue. Freudian hermeneutics remains within the world of language.

But, at the same time, the object of the analysis is no longer a text as such but is the human *subject.* And it is precisely at this juncture that Ricoeur's own radicalization of phenomenology begins to emerge. The transference which occurs may be put analogously: *the subject becomes, under a hermeneutic analysis, "like" a text.* But in Ricoeur's sense the *subject as text* is a text that is symbolic and, therefore, calls for a work of deciphering. It is at this juncture that the two figures who dominate the foreground of much of *The Conflict of Interpretations* become contextually understandable. What is needed is a means of interpretation which takes into account the hidden meaning of the text-self.

These two figures are Freud and Hegel. Moreover, in Ricoeur's treatment of these two dominant figures, each becomes a kind of inversion of the other. They belong together as founders of related *hermeneutics of suspicion*. What they have in common is a mistrust and suspicion of (immediate) consciousness. Through them an attack is made upon (immediate) subjectivity, particularly in its direct or Cartesian form.

Ricoeur sees in both Freud and Hegel a hermeneutics which deliberately displaces the immediacy of consciousness and which in turn reveals a stratum of significance within the subject which was hitherto unsuspected (at least by the subject himself). The functional similarity of the Freudian and Hegelian hermeneutics lies in their respective strategies of the dispossession of immediacy.

Freud's detour from immediacy, justified by the vast and complicated theory of the unconscious, provides a way into hidden significances which the persistent narcissism of self-bewitchment keeps from the subject. This detour, *regressive* toward the childhood of the self, gradually unlayers the archaic sediments of the constitution of the subject. Freud's psychoanalysis provides an *archaeology* of the subject. Hegel's *direction* of interpretation is inverse to that of Freud. It is the *progression* of becoming aware which provides, according to Ricoeur, a *teleology* of the spirit. But this teleology, too, displaces immediacy through a dialectic of unfolding meanings. In the march of the "figures" of the Spirit, the hidden truth of a previous meaning is revealed only in and through the transcending of the previous meaning. Thus the Hegelian teleology is a *progressive* interpretation. Progression and regression are inversions of the same problematic.

This is not to say that Ricoeur repeats Freud and Hegel. To the contrary, the phenomenological dialectic which he employs also serves to *demythologize* both Freud and Hegel. Ricoeur rejects the "realism" of the Freudian unconscious, just as he rejects the "idealism" of the Absolute Idea in Hegel. In this sense Ricoeur remains radically phenomenological in his rigorous rejection of metaphysics, of reification, of closure.

What is accepted fits, however, under the notion of an analysis of the subject as text. The "unconscious" and the configuration of future possibilities of "spirit" function as the hidden depth meaning of a text which the hermeneutics of suspicion allows to emerge. Thus the necessity of the wager of suspicion concerning "false consciousness" appears only after the risk of suspicion has been taken.

But now a question is raised concerning phenomenology itself. At least there is a question which must confront phenomenology interpreted as a method which deals with consciousness directly and which continues any pretension to consciously control its meanings. The hermeneutics of suspicion enters into the dialectical pattern with that of phenomenology, and phenomenology must stand "humiliated" in the confrontation. But at a deeper level this chastisement is also a recovery from within phenomenology itself. For in spite of Husserl's surface language of egology, of transcendental idealism, of solipsism, the subject, even in the Husserlian sense, does not know itself directly. Rather, it knows itself only in correlation with and through the mirror of the World. The other reveals me to myself in a way which radically modifies any naïve or direct self-knowledge.

Thus, out of a dialectic of phenomenology with an other there comes a further radicalization of phenomenology. But, in the process, phenomenology, under Ricoeur's use, takes on a different significance. If the iconoclastic and suspicious hermeneutics of false consciousness are the counterparts of phenomenology, then phenomenology becomes in contrast an implicit *hermeneutics of belief*.

It is at this juncture that the third aspect of the graft of hermeneutics to phenomenology begins to take specific shape. Insofar as the origin and model for hermeneutics come out of the biblical tradition, its problem includes the question of faith. The hermeneutics of belief in Ricoeur's use of it is already latently religious in intention. Hidden in the hermeneutic problem, now linked to an understanding of phenomenology itself, is the question of faith.

With the question of faith in the background, the dialectic of hermeneutics which emerges is one which counterplays those interpretations of meanings which demythize the existential *cum* religious significations with those which seek a "recovery" of "forgotten" significations. The counterpart of suspicion is a latent belief in Ricoeur's version of a hermeneutic phenomenology.

But once phenomenology has passed through the chastisement of a suspicious hermeneutic, there is no recovery of simple faith; if faith is to survive, it must be an informed, critical faith. Thus, once again, a type of "third term" is sought. Its model is that of a type of *demythologization*. Demythologization is a process of interpretation which accepts the loss of all pretensions to direct "rationality" in symbolic discourse, but at the same time this loss is seen as the way toward a freeing, a recovery, of the symbolic-existential dimension. Symbolic word is a word which opens, which explores the possibilities of mankind in relation to the sacred.

That is also why, ultimately, Hegel must take precedence over Freud, why teleology surpasses archaeology in relation to the subject. The displacement of immediacy does not become an excuse for either a return to prephenomenological objectivism or for a closure upon the subject. It becomes the radicalization of belief itself.

It will not be missed that *The Conflict of Interpretations* contains Ricoeur's most explicitly religious themes and questions to date. Moreover, the section on religion and faith carries the most recently dated (1968–69) articles of this book. But, while this is so, and may even be disappointing to philosophers more interested in questions of language and culture, what Ricoeur does with the question of faith needs to be looked at carefully.

For what happens with the question of faith is similar to what happens with both psychoanalysis and the Hegelian dialectic. Even while Freud and Hegel dominate the foreground, while they are taken into a dialogue with Ricoeur to the point of being incorporated into the very heart of a dialectical hermeneutic, the result for an "orthodox" Freudian or an "orthodox" Hegelian cannot help but be disquieting. For, in the process, both Freud and Hegel are seriously demythologized and transformed. A Freud in effect without an unconsciousness or a Hegel without an Absolute Idea is after all not the same as before. In fact, what seemed to be either foundation or goal in the respective justifying metaphysics is now removed through hermeneutics.

Returning to the graft of the hermeneutic problem to a phenomenological methodology, we find that the question which arises is one directed toward what is included in Ricoeur's version of a "new phenomenology" of which he speaks. The graft, in Ricoeur's case, bears evidence of a previous graft, perhaps old enough not always to be noticed: the graft of the question of faith to the hermeneutic problem itself. This may be noted by attending to three facets of the question of faith, which now undergoes its own process of demythologization in a "new phenomenology."

First, there is and has been from the outset a certain suspicion and a use of phenomenology to demythologize *theology*. For Ricoeur, theology begins too late. Already in the *Symbolism of Evil*, what is taken as more fundamental, more primitive for phenomenology are the primary expressions of evil. These primary or archaic and metaphorical symbols are "closer" to the things themselves than theology. Theology is at best a third-level elaboration of such symbols (symbols are primary, myths are already secondary, and theology is tertiary). Thus, methodologically, what is needed prior to theology is the recovery of the primitive intentionalities found in the expressions of the experience of evil. But in addition to the "distance" of theology from these primary expressions, theology may also hide essential dimensions of this experience in a pseudorationality, an implicit gnosis. Thus for a second reason theology is methodologically demythologized.

In the present essays there are some attempts to recover this primary sense through a critique of theology (see "Original Sin: A Study in Meaning" and "Interpretation of the Myth of Punishment"), but it remains the case that there is a negative tone regarding theology. But this critique is not simply due to Ricoeur; it lies in the heart of phenomenology. Theology is to "religious" phenomena what metaphysics is to "scientific" phenomena, and to get to the phenomena calls for a radical undercutting of currently taken-for-granted presuppositions encased in currently sedimented theologies.

This is not to say that Ricoeur does this in the same way that Husserl would. The Husserlian language of getting back to the "things themselves" is considerably misleading in that it appears to be a quest for some pure or simple "given." But there is no pure "given"—although that is a *second* lesson and not the first lesson of phenomenology in action. The language of "givenness" or even of "pregivenness" is heuristic. It is a means of creating a different perspective from which to view things, a deliberate forcing of issues such that current sediments are stirred up in order to discover *other possibilities.*

Ricoeur has recognized this from the beginning. In relation to the archaic man who utters his confession of the experience of evil, Ricoeur does not find some privileged romantic access to the sacred but an already "fallen" situation in which the expression is more an unfulfilled intention than an indication of access to the sacred. But it is in the lack of fulfillment that the question of possibility is raised.

A second step in the demythologization of faith itself through hermeneutics occurs in the dialectic of the counterparts, a hermeneutics of suspicion and the hermeneutics of belief. Instructive in this regard is the often repeated treatment of the father figure (see "Fatherhood: From Phantasm to Symbol"). Ricoeur applies the dialectic of a Freudian regressive and demythizing analysis to the father figure first. Thus the father figure must be recognized as relating to both punishment and consolation in terms of the desires and the immaturity of the subject, and this deep-seated and archaic constellation undergoes a radical demythization and even rejection. But in a second interpretation, progressive under the sign of Hegel, the father figure becomes "identified" with the son in a play and counterplay like that of the master-slave relationship in the *Phenomenology of Mind*. Here the fate of the father "becomes" that of the son. But the "third term" is one which existentializes this dialectic. For what the demythization of the father reveals when it is coupled to the development of the identity of the father in the son is the question of *being-toward-death*. And although Ricoeur does not use such explicitly Heideggerian language, the dialectic of approximations leads to this same question.

It is in the unique way that Ricoeur answers the question of facing death revealed through the demythologization of the symbol that he is differentiated from Heidegger. And it is here that a third step is taken. From the demythologization of theology through the demythologization of the symbol Ricoeur moves to a more radical stage in respect to faith itself. Faith, too, must undergo criticism (see "Religion, Atheism, and Faith" and "Freedom in the Light of Hope"). Although the Freud-Hegel dialectic need not be followed in detail, faith is seen to conceal within itself a dimension of primitive immaturity with respect to the recalcitrant narcissism of the subject. Without acceptance of the death of the father and, by extension, even ultimately without some sense of the death of God, maturity cannot come to humankind. Thus Ricoeur makes contact with the contemporary strands of the "death of God" and "secular" theologies. Through a hermeneutic critique *the question of faith itself is displaced.*

This displacement now applies to the "second naïveté," spoken of earlier by Ricoeur. Contemporary man is not primarily a man of faith, and the chastisement of the hermeneutics of belief by the hermeneutics of suspicion must be genuine. But the "third term" which appears through the displacement is in keeping with the very early sense of an "ontology of affirmation" that Ricoeur once sought. For what displaces faith is *hope*. Ricoeur recognizes that hope has rarely been made central in theology— but that is what he proposes.

The emergence of hope as a central religious notion echoes, not the foreground figures of Freud and Hegel, though the open-ended Hegel of Ricoeur's interpretation remains important, but the background figure of Kant. Kant has always served as a figure of *limitation* for Ricoeur; and it may now be recalled that it was Kant who defined the religious question solely in terms of "What can I hope for?" Furthermore, it is the Kant of *Religion within the Limits of Reason Alone*. This preference on Ricoeur's part, however, does not stem from a mere preference for "rationalism" but from the needs imposed by a demythologized, chastised faith.

Faith is displaced from the center, and under the displacement a number of other shifts occur as well. Immediacy is displaced, and with it the pretension of the subject to self-determination. This has been a constant in Ricoeur's philosophy, but now immediacy is also linked to the sense of the present which is displaced for the sake of the *future*. Theologically, this is to displace the God who is for the God who is to come. There is a lateral displacement as well, in that emphasis upon the individual is displaced by an emphasis upon the social.

In his earlier works Ricoeur often began with and gave a privileged weighting to what he called the "ethical view of the world." For example, in the analysis of the cultural-religious myths, the role of the Adam figure in the only truly anthropological myth was a role dominated by this "ethical view." With the displacement of faith by hope, Ricoeur now speaks of a "new ethics" in accordance with hope.

> This . . . trait of freedom in the light of hope removes us . . . from the existential interpretation that is too much centered on the present decision; for the ethics of mission . . . a new ethics [which] marks the linkage of freedom to hope . . . has communitarian, political, and even cosmic implications which the existential decision, centered on the personal interiority, tends to hide. A freedom open to the new creation is in fact less centered on subjectivity, on personal authenticity, than on social and political justice; it calls for a reconciliation which itself demands to be inscribed in the recapitulation of all things.

The future, now clearly weighted under the sign of the promise, is an eschatological response to the question of being-toward-death. "It is the meaning of my existence in the light of the Resurrection . . . ; *hermeneutics of religious freedom is an interpretation of freedom in conformity with the Resurrection in terms of promise and hope*." This response to being-toward-death is "in spite of" death.

xxii / CONFLICT OF INTERPRETATIONS

This affirmation is not justified, however, by any of the counterparts of hermeneutic phenomenology in Ricoeur's sense, for its "logic," which Ricoeur calls the "logic of superabundance," does not rest on the precedence of structure over history but on the precedence of the future, of history to come, over the present. However, the hope that is central is a hope engendered through the very opening provided by hermeneutic phenomenology in its uncovering of *possibilities:*

> We would call freedom in the light of hope the "passion for the possible"; this formula, in contrast to all wisdom of the present, to all submission to necessity, underscores the imprint of the promise of freedom. Freedom entrusted to the "God who comes" is open to the radically new; it is the creative imagination of the possible.

There is in this displacement of faith from the center through hope, which takes its place, an anticipation of what Ricoeur's *Poetics of the Will* must be. Hope is the "answer" to evil; and the "logic" of hope must be a renewal of contemporary eschatology in which the symbols of hope are elicited from a progressive interpretation of polysemic word. Hidden in the present is the promise of the future.

There are two extremely suggestive hints concerning the shape and direction of faith demythologized and the task to come which Ricoeur has lately termed a "post-Hegelian Kantianism." The first regards a direction which arises out of Ricoeur's central theology of hope.

> Faith justifies the man of the *Aufklärung,* for whom, in the great romance of culture, evil is a factor in the education of the human race, rather than the puritan, who never succeeds in taking the step from condemnation to mercy and who thus remains within the ethical dimension and never enters into the perspective of the Kingdom to come.

Eschatology takes precedence over ethics in the "new ethics."

As for philosophy's task, its shape retains the constant echo of Hegel, who gives to Ricoeur's hermeneutic phenomenology its open and ongoing dialectical character:

> What [is demanded] of the philosopher is nothing else but this: to undertake again, with renewed energy, the task assumed in the last century by Hegel, of a dialectical philosophy which would take up the diversity of the schemes of experience and reality into a systematic unity. Now, it is indeed with renewed energy that we must take up this task once again, if it is true that, on the one hand, the unconscious ought to be assigned another place than

the categories of reflective philosophy and that, on the other hand, hope is destined to open what system tends to close up. That is the task. But who today could assume it?

To the contemporary ear these themes must indeed sound strange. In contrast to tones of alienation, anomie, and despair, Ricoeur proclaims a revival of hope even to the extent of echoing the Enlightenment. In contrast to the increase in belief in the essential finitude of the earth and its life, Ricoeur announces that his thought will turn to a "logic of superabundance" which operates "in spite of" the present outlook. For here is what may be called a *new rationalism* in its echo of progressivist thought, almost forgotten.

Perhaps this is prophecy, the announcement of a turning of the time. In Kazantzakis' *Last Temptation of Christ,* prophecy is characterized as the wisdom which sees that things will return to a forgotten way; and to announce this at the right moment is to be prophetic. But it must also be recalled that this observation is made cynically by Judas. The prophecy which notes only a return of eternal reaction and response is not historical but ahistorical, in that it takes place in a secret view of the Whole, a totality which is ever the same.

Ricoeur struggles mightily against such a closure of history. His philosophy, shaped by a version of a quasi-Hegelian dialectic, rejects any premature closure upon an Absolute Idea. Instead, hope directed to the God to come *functions* as the unfulfilled intention of the dialectic. But Hegel usually has his revenge upon those who follow him. In this respect, Ricoeur, like Marx before him, implicitly claims history to have a direction which is fulfilled in a surplus.

What is unsaid, however, is that faith, hidden within hope, remains. For if the hermeneutics of history was strictly the phenomenological discovery of the vastness of the possible, then here there must be a second step, which remains unjustified by the passion for the possible. Were the phenomenological discovery of the possible the "last word" of Ricoeur's hermeneutics, the conclusion would have to be that history is open and therefore unpredictable by reason of the very essence of possibility. Thus while the historical essence of sociality and human history does indeed hold the possibility of discontinuities, among those discontinuities must also be the possibility of a "logic of scarcity" and an "economy of loss" unless the irruptions of genuine history are subterraneously guided by a God not yet come but who remains the secret of the future.

Faith thus remains hidden within hope, for it is not just any possible which history may reveal, but certain possibilities, those which respond to and fulfill hope. In this respect Ricoeur stands a second time in contrast to the existential theories, which nevertheless remain in the same register. There is a sense in which the existential philosophies have also too soon believed a determination of the possible in terms of a secretly accepted metaphysics. The "meaninglessness" of a universe untuned to man's desires echoed in Camus and Sartre is an existential version of the highly pervasive physicalist metaphysics of the twentieth century. Ricoeur, in contrast, revives a historical theology which sees the openness of the historical moving in a different direction.

But a question remains: does a radical phenomenology of history take yet a third direction, a direction which remains truer to the "passion for the possible"? For Ricoeur the burden of proof to be demonstrated in his promised *Poetics* must be one which at one and the same time preserves the openness of genuine history while making the case for hope.

II

RICOEUR'S MASSIVE BIBLIOGRAPHY—which now consists of over three hundred items—combined with his regular appearance in translation, has posed a continual problem. More than most, Ricoeur has had to find English expression through multiple translators whose tastes and abilities have varied widely. In the present case we have utilized a small number of extant translations and have used a team of Ricoeur readers for the rest. This necessarily poses a problem for the consistent use of terms. We have tried to attain as much consistency as possible, using in some cases already established conventions from earlier translations and in some cases a conformity with Northwestern University Press style for its phenomenology series. But even simple words sometimes pose problems. For example, *instance* in Freudian contexts (reflecting Freud's term *Instanz*) is translated as "agency," while, in the context of structural linguistics, it is translated as "instance," following Benveniste's translator. The same double context occurs in the use of *parole,* which in its theological context means "word," connoting that which comes to man, while in a linguistic context it is "speech," which is an act of man speaking. Ricoeur's use of multiple contexts, from Hegel studies to structural linguistics to analytic philosophy, complicates the issue. In the main we have tried to let the context decide and have explained the problems in footnotes.

A further difficulty was introduced by the fact that Ricoeur, in preparing these collected essays—in their French versions—for his French publisher, made a number of revisions in essays that had previously appeared in English translation. Discrepancies between the published versions of these essays and the texts that appear here are thus due in part to Ricoeur's own revisions and in part to our desire to achieve a consistent terminology throughout the book.

IT IS OUR HOPE that this long process of minute decisions will result in a further appreciation of the power of Ricoeur's careful thought as it probes crucial issues in twentieth-century philosophy. In Ricoeur one finds a mind which is both open and fastidious, searching and reasoned. The crossroads of the contemporary search for a deeper rationality meet in *The Conflict of Interpretations*. And, if there is no closure or resolution of the conflicting interpretations, that, too, is a reflection of the position of the thinker in the present.

DON IHDE

State University of New York
Stony Brook
December, 1973

The Conflict
of Interpretations

To Enrico Castelli

Existence and Hermeneutics

MY PURPOSE HERE is to explore the paths opened to contemporary philosophy by what could be called the graft of the *hermeneutic problem* onto the *phenomenological method*. I shall limit myself to a brief historical reminder before undertaking the investigation as such, an investigation which should, at least at its close, give an acceptable sense to the notion of *existence*— a sense which would express the renewal of phenomenology through hermeneutics.

I. THE ORIGIN OF HERMENEUTICS

THE HERMENEUTIC PROBLEM arose long before Husserl's phenomenology; this is why I speak of grafting and, properly, must even say a late grafting.

It is useful to recall that the hermeneutic problem was first raised within the limits of *exegesis*, that is, within the framework of a discipline which proposes to understand a text—to understand it beginning with its intention, on the basis of what it attempts to say. If exegesis raised a hermeneutic problem, that is, a problem of interpretation, it is because every reading of a text always takes place within a community, a tradition, or a living current of thought, all of which display presuppositions and exigencies—regardless of how closely a reading may be tied to the *quid*, to "that in view of which" the text was written. Thus, based on philosophical principles in physics and in ethics, the

Translated by Kathleen McLaughlin.

[3]

reading of Greek myths in the Stoic school implies a hermeneutics very different from the rabbinical interpretation of the Torah
in the Halakah or the Haggadah. In its turn, the apostolic generation's interpretation of the Old Testament in the light of the
Christic event gives quite another reading of the events, institutions, and personages of the Bible than the rabbinical interpretation.

In what way do these exegetic debates concern philosophy?
In this way: that exegesis implies an entire theory of signs and
significations, as we see, for example, in Saint Augustine's *De
doctrina christiana*. More precisely, if a text can have several
meanings, for example a historical meaning and a spiritual
meaning, we must appeal to a notion of signification that is
much more complex than the system of so-called univocal signs
required by the logic of argumentation. And finally, the very
work of interpretation reveals a profound intention, that of overcoming distance and cultural differences and of matching the
reader to a text which has become foreign, thereby incorporating
its meaning into the present comprehension a man is able to
have of himself.

Consequently, hermeneutics cannot remain a technique for
specialists—the *technē hermēneutikē* of those who interpret
oracles and marvels; rather, hermeneutics involves the general
problem of comprehension. And, moreover, no noteworthy interpretation has been formulated which does not borrow from
the modes of comprehension available to a given epoch: myth,
allegory, metaphor, analogy, etc. This connection between interpretation and comprehension, the former taken in the sense
of textual exegesis and the latter in the broad sense of the clear
understanding of signs, is manifested in one of the traditional
senses of the word "hermeneutics"—the one given in Aristotle's
Peri hermēneias. It is indeed remarkable that, in Aristotle, *hermēneia* is not limited to allegory but concerns every meaningful
discourse. In fact, meaningful discourse is *hermēneia*, "interprets" reality, precisely to the degree that it says "something *of*
something." Moreover, discourse is *hermēneia* because a discursive statement is a grasp of the real by meaningful expressions, not a selection of so-called impressions coming from the
things themselves.

Such is the first and most primordial relation between the
concept of interpretation and that of comprehension; it relates
the technical problems of textual exegesis to the more general
problems of meaning and language.

But exegesis could lead to a general hermeneutics only by means of a second development, the development of classical philology and the *historical sciences* that took place at the end of the eighteenth century and the start of the nineteenth century. It is with Schleiermacher and Dilthey that the hermeneutic problem becomes a philosophic problem. The title of the present section, "The Origin of Hermeneutics," is an explicit allusion to the title of Dilthey's famous essay of 1900. Dilthey's problem, in the age of positivistic philosophy, was to give to the *Geisteswissenschaften* a validity comparable to that of the natural sciences. Posed in these terms, the problem was epistemological; it was a question of elaborating a critique of historical knowledge as solid as the Kantian critique of the knowledge of nature and of subordinating to this critique the diverse procedures of classical hermeneutics: the laws of internal textual connection, of context, of geographic, ethnic, and social environments, etc. But the resolution of the problem exceeded the resources of mere epistemology. An interpretation, like Dilthey's, bound to information fixed by writing is only a province of the much vaster domain of understanding, extending from one psychic life to another psychic life. The hermeneutic problem is thus seen from the perspective of psychology: to understand, for a finite being, is to be transported into another life. Historical understanding thus involves all the paradoxes of historicity: how can a historical being understand history historically? These paradoxes, in turn, lead back to a much more fundamental question: in expressing itself, how can life objectify itself, and, in objectifying itself, how does it bring to light meanings capable of being taken up and understood by another historical being, who overcomes his own historical situation? A major problem, which we will find again at the close of our investigation, is thus raised: the problem of the relationship between force and meaning, between life as the bearer of meaning and the mind as capable of linking meanings into a coherent series. If life is not originally meaningful, understanding is forever impossible; but, in order for this understanding to be fixed, is it not necessary to carry back to life itself the logic of immanent development which Hegel called the *concept*? Do we not then surreptitiously provide ourselves with all the resources of a philosophy of the spirit[1] just when we are

1. [Throughout this book we have translated Ricoeur's "*esprit*" (Hegel's "*Geist*") as "spirit" rather than "mind," and in harmony with this the title of Hegel's work will appear in the text as *The Phenomenology of the Spirit.*—EDITOR.]

formulating a philosophy of life? Such is the major difficulty which justifies our search for a favorable structure within the domain of *phenomenology* or, to return to our initial image, for the young plant onto which we can graft the hermeneutic slip.

II. GRAFTING HERMENEUTICS ONTO PHENOMENOLOGY

THERE ARE TWO WAYS to ground hermeneutics in phenomenology. There is the short route, which I shall consider first, and the long route, the one I propose to travel. The short route is the one taken by an *ontology of understanding*, after the manner of Heidegger. I call such an ontology of understanding the "short route" because, breaking with any discussion of *method*, it carries itself directly to the level of an ontology of finite being in order there to recover *understanding*, no longer as a mode of knowledge, but rather as a mode of being. One does not enter this ontology of understanding little by little; one does not reach it by degrees, deepening the methodological requirements of exegesis, history, or psychoanalysis: one is transported there by a sudden reversal of the question. Instead of asking: On what condition can a knowing subject understand a text or history? one asks: What kind of being is it whose being consists of understanding? The hermeneutic problem thus becomes a problem of the Analytic of this being, Dasein, which exists through understanding.

Before saying why I propose to follow a more roundabout, more arduous path, starting with linguistic and semantic considerations, I wish to give full credit to this ontology of understanding. If I begin by giving due consideration to Heidegger's philosophy, it is because I do not hold it to be a contrary solution; that is to say, his Analytic of Dasein is not an alternative which would force us to choose between an ontology of understanding and an epistemology of interpretation. The long route which I propose also aspires to carry reflection to the level of an ontology, but it will do so by degrees, following successive investigations into semantics (in part III of this essay) and reflection (part IV). The doubt I express toward the end of this section is concerned only with the possibility of the making of a direct ontology, free at the outset from any methodological requirements and consequently outside the circle of interpretation whose theory this ontology formulates. But it is the *desire* for this ontology which animates our enterprise and which keeps it from sinking into either a linguistic philosophy like Wittgenstein's or a reflective philosophy of the neo-Kantian sort. My problem will be exactly this: what happens to an epistemology of interpretation, born of a reflection on exegesis, on the method of history, on psychoanalysis, on the phenomenology of religion, etc., when it is touched, animated, and, as we might say, inspired by an ontology of understanding?

Let us then take a look at the requirements of this ontology of understanding.

In order to thoroughly understand the sense of the revolution in thought that this ontology proposes, we must in one leap arrive at the end of the development running from Husserl's *Logical Investigations* to Heidegger's *Being and Time*, prepared to ask ourselves later what in Husserl's phenomenology seems significant in relation to this revolution in thought. What must thus be considered in its full radicalness is the reversal of the question itself, a reversal which, in place of an epistemology of interpretation, sets up an ontology of understanding.

It is a question of avoiding every way of formulating the problem *erkenntnistheoretisch* and, consequently, of giving up the idea that hermeneutics is a *method* able to compete on an equal basis with the method of the natural sciences. To assign a method to understanding is to remain entangled in the presuppositions of objective knowledge and the prejudices of the Kantian theory of knowledge. One must deliberately move outside the enchanted circle of the problematic of subject and object and question oneself about being. But, in order to question oneself about being in general, it is first necessary to question oneself about that being which is the "there" of all being, about Dasein, that is, about that being which exists in the mode of understanding being. Understanding is thus no longer a mode of knowledge but a mode of being, the mode of that being which exists through understanding.

I fully accept the movement toward this complete reversal of the relationship between understanding and being; moreover, it fulfills the deepest wish of Dilthey's philosophy, because for him life was the prime concept. In his own work, historical understanding was not exactly the counterpart of the theory of nature; the relationship between life and its expressions was rather the common root of the double relationship of man to nature and of man to history. If we follow this suggestion, the problem is not to strengthen historical knowledge in the face of physical knowledge but to burrow under scientific knowledge, taken in all its generality, in order to reach a relation between historical being and the whole of being that is more primordial than the subject-object relation in the theory of knowledge.

If the problem of hermeneutics is posed in these ontological terms, of what help is Husserl's phenomenology? The question invites us to move from Heidegger back to Husserl and to reinterpret the latter in Heideggerian terms. What we first encounter on the way back is, of course, the later Husserl, the Husserl of the *Crisis;* it is in him first of all that we must seek the phenomenological foundation of this ontology. His contribution to hermeneutics is twofold. On the one hand, it is in the last phase of phenomenology that the critique of "objectivism" is carried to its final consequences. This critique of objectivism concerns the hermeneutic problem, not only indirectly, because it contests the claim of the epistemology of the natural sciences to provide the only valid methodological model for the human sciences, but also directly, because it calls into question the Diltheyan attempt to provide for the *Geisteswissenschaften* a method as objective as that of the natural sciences. On the other hand, Husserl's final phenomenology joins its critique of objectivism to a positive problematic which clears the way for an ontology of understanding. This new problematic has as its theme the *Lebenswelt*, the "life-world," that is, a level of experience anterior to the subject-object relation, which provided the central theme for all the various kinds of neo-Kantianism.

If, then, the later Husserl is enlisted in this subversive undertaking, which aims at substituting an ontology of understanding for an epistemology of interpretation, the early Husserl, the Husserl who goes from the *Logical Investigations* to the *Cartesian Meditations,* is held in grave suspicion. It is he, of course, who cleared the way by designating the subject as an intentional pole, directed outward,[2] and by giving, as the correlate of this subject,

2. [The French term used here to describe the subject is *porteur de visée,* which in turn renders the German *die Meinung,* employed frequently by Husserl. The French substantive (*visée*) and verb (*viser*) are often translated in English as "intention" and "to intend," respectively. When asked about his use of the term, Ricoeur himself stressed the outward directedness of intention, the fact that the subject points toward or aims at its object. Indeed, in expressions such as *visée intentionnelle* he makes it impossible to view *visée* and *intention* as completely equivalent terms. In the present essay (and elsewhere in the book, as well—ED.) *visée* and *viser* have been rendered variously by "directed outward," "aim," and "intention," according to the context in which they appear.—TRANSLATOR.]

not a nature but a field of meanings. Considered retrospectively from the point of view of the early Husserl and especially from the point of view of Heidegger, the early phenomenology can appear as the very first challenge to objectivism, since what it calls phenomena are precisely the correlates of intentional life. It remains, nevertheless, that the early Husserl only reconstructed a new idealism, close to the neo-Kantianism he fought: the reduction of the thesis of the world is actually a reduction of the question of being to the question of the sense of being; the sense of being, in turn, is reduced to a simple correlate of the subjective modes of intention [*visée*].

It is thus finally against the early Husserl, against the alternately Platonizing and idealizing tendencies of his theory of meaning and intentionality, that the theory of understanding has been erected. And if the later Husserl points to this ontology, it is because his effort to reduce being failed and because, consequently, the ultimate result of phenomenology escaped the initial project. It is in spite of itself that phenomenology discovers, in place of an idealist subject locked within its system of meanings, a living being which from all time has, as the horizon of all its intentions, a world, the world.

In this way, we find delimited a field of meanings anterior to the constitution of a mathematized nature, such as we have represented it since Galileo, a field of meanings anterior to objectivity for a knowing subject. Before objectivity, there is the horizon of the world; before the subject of the theory of knowledge, there is operative life, which Husserl sometimes calls anonymous, not because he is returning by this detour to an impersonal Kantian subject, but because the subject which has objects is itself derived from this operative life.

We see the degree of radicality to which the problem of understanding and that of truth are carried. The question of historicity is no longer the question of historical knowledge conceived as method. Now it designates the manner in which the existent "is with" existents. Understanding is no longer the response of the human sciences to the naturalistic explanation; it involves a manner of being akin to being, prior to the encounter with particular beings. At the same time, life's ability to freely stand at a distance in respect to itself, to transcend itself, becomes a structure of finite being. If the historian can measure himself against the thing itself, if he can compare himself to the known, it is because both he and his object are historical. Making this historical character explicit is thus prior to any methodology.

What was a limit to science—namely, the historicity of being
—becomes a constituting element of being. What was a paradox—namely, the relation of the interpreter to his object—
becomes an ontological trait.

Such is the revolution brought about by an ontology of understanding. Understanding becomes an aspect of Dasein's "project"
and of its "openness to being." The question of truth is no longer
the question of method; it is the question of the manifestation of
being for a being whose existence consists in understanding being.

However great may be the extraordinarily seductive power of
this fundamental ontology, I nevertheless propose to explore
another path, to join the hermeneutic problem to phenomenology
in a different manner. Why this retreat before the Analytic of
Dasein? For the following two reasons. With Heidegger's radical
manner of questioning, the problems that initiated our investigation not only remain unresolved but are lost from sight. How, we
asked, can an organon be given to exegesis, to the clear comprehension of texts? How can the historical sciences be founded in
the face of the natural sciences? How can the conflict of rival
interpretations be arbitrated? These problems are not properly
considered in a fundamental hermeneutics, and this by design:
this hermeneutics is intended not to resolve them but to dissolve
them. Moreover, Heidegger has not wanted to consider any particular problem concerning the understanding of this or that being. He wanted to retrain our eye and redirect our gaze; he
wanted us to subordinate historical knowledge to ontological understanding, as the derived form of a primordial form. But he
gives us no way to show in what sense historical understanding,
properly speaking, is derived from this primordial understanding.
Is it not better, then, to begin with the derived forms of understanding and to show in them the signs of their derivation? This
implies that the point of departure be taken on the same level on
which understanding operates, that is, on the level of language.

The first observation leads to the second: if the reversal
from epistemological understanding to the being who understands is to be possible, we must be able to describe directly—
without prior epistemological concern—the privileged being of
Dasein, such as it is constituted in itself, and thus be able to
recover understanding as one of these modes of being. The difficulty in passing from understanding as a mode of knowledge
to understanding as a mode of being consists in the following:
the understanding which is the result of the Analytic of Dasein is

precisely the understanding through which and in which this being understands itself as being. Is it not once again *within language* itself that we must seek the indication that understanding is a mode of being?

These two objections also contain a positive proposition: that of substituting, for the short route of the Analytic of Dasein, the long route which begins by analyses of language. In this way we will continue to keep in contact with the disciplines which seek to practice interpretation in a methodical manner, and we will resist the temptation to separate *truth*, characteristic of understanding, from the *method* put into operation by disciplines which have sprung from exegesis. If, then, a new problematic of existence is to be worked out, this must start from and be based on the semantic elucidation of the concept of interpretation common to all the hermeneutic disciplines. This semantics will be organized around the central theme of meanings with multiple or multivocal senses or what we might call symbolic senses (an equivalence we will justify in due time).

I will indicate immediately how I intend to reach the question of existence by the detour of this semantics. A purely semantic elucidation remains suspended until one shows that the understanding of multivocal or symbolic expressions is a moment of *self*-understanding; the *semantic* approach thus entails a *reflective* approach. But the subject that interprets himself while interpreting signs is no longer the *cogito*: rather, he is a being who discovers, by the exegesis of his own life, that he is placed in being before he places and possesses himself. In this way, hermeneutics would discover a manner of existing which would remain from start to finish a *being-interpreted*. Reflection alone, by suppressing itself as reflection, can reach the ontological roots of understanding. Yet this is what always happens in language, and it occurs through the movement of reflection. Such is the arduous route we are going to follow.

III. The Level of Semantics

It is first of all and always in language that all ontic or ontological understanding arrives at its expression. It is thus not vain to look to semantics for an *axis* of reference for the whole of the hermeneutic *field*. Exegesis has already accustomed us to the idea that a text has several meanings, that these meanings overlap, that the spiritual meaning is "transferred" (Saint Augustine's *translata signa*) from the historical or literal meaning because of the latter's surplus of meaning. Schleiermacher and Dilthey have also taught us to consider texts, documents, and manuscripts as expressions of life which have become fixed through writing. The exegete follows the reverse movement of this objectification of the life-forces in psychical connections first and then in historical series. This objectification and this fixation constitute another form of meaning transfer. In Nietzsche, values must be interpreted because they are expressions of the strength and the weakness of the will to power. Moreover, in Nietzsche, life itself is interpretation: in this way, philosophy itself becomes the interpretation of interpretations. Finally, Freud, under the heading of "dream work," examined a series of procedures which are notable in that they "transpose" (*Entstellung*) a hidden meaning, submitting it to a distortion which both shows and conceals the latent sense in the manifest meaning. He followed the ramifications of this distortion in the cultural expressions of art, morality, and religion and in this way constructed an exegesis of culture very similar to Nietzsche's. It is thus not senseless to try to zero in on what could be called the *semantic node* of every hermeneutics, whether general or individual, fundamental or particular. It appears that their common element, which is found everywhere, from exegesis to psychoanalysis, is a certain architecture of meaning, which can be termed "double meaning" or "multiple meaning," whose role in every instance, although in a different manner, is to show while concealing. It is thus within the semantics of the shown-yet-concealed, within the semantics of multivocal expressions, that this analysis of language seems to me to be confined.

Having for my part explored a well-defined area of this semantics, the language of avowal, which constitutes the *symbolism of evil*, I propose to call these multivocal expressions "symbolic." Thus, I give a narrower sense to the word "symbol" than authors who, like Cassirer, call symbolic any apprehension of reality by means of signs, from perception, myth, and art to science; but I give it a broader sense than those authors who, starting from Latin rhetoric or the neo-Platonic tradition, reduce the symbol to analogy. *I define "symbol" as any structure of signification in which a direct, primary, literal meaning designates, in addition, another meaning which is indirect, secondary, and figurative and which can be apprehended only through the first*. This circumscription of expressions with a double meaning properly constitutes the hermeneutic field.

In its turn, the concept of interpretation also receives a distinct meaning. I propose to give it the same extension I gave to the symbol. *Interpretation, we will say, is the work of thought which consists in deciphering the hidden meaning in the apparent meaning, in unfolding the levels of meaning implied in the literal meaning.* In this way I retain the initial reference to exegesis, that is, to the interpretation of hidden meanings. Symbol and interpretation thus become correlative concepts; there is interpretation wherever there is multiple meaning, and it is in interpretation that the plurality of meanings is made manifest.

From this double delimitation of the semantic field—in regard to symbols and in regard to interpretation—there results a certain number of tasks, which I shall only briefly inventory.

In regard to symbolic expressions, the task of linguistic analysis seems to me to be twofold. On the one hand, there is the matter of beginning an enumeration of symbolic forms which will be as full and as complete as possible. This inductive path is the only one accessible at the start of the investigation, since the question is precisely to determine the structure common to these diverse modalities of symbolic expression. Putting aside any concern for a hasty reduction to unity, this enumeration should include the cosmic symbols brought to light by a phenomenology of religion—like those of Van der Leeuw, Maurice Leenhardt, and Mircea Eliade; the dream symbolism revealed by psychoanalysis—with all its equivalents in folklore, legends, proverbs, and myths; the verbal creations of the poet, following the guideline of sensory, visual, acoustic, or other images or following the symbolism of space and time. In spite of their being grounded in different ways—in the physiognomical qualities of the cosmos, in sexual symbolism, in sensory imagery—all these symbolisms find their expression in the element of language. There is no symbolism before man speaks, even if the power of the symbol is grounded much deeper. It is in language that the cosmos, desire, and the imaginary reach expression; speech is always necessary if the world is to be recovered and made hierophany. Likewise, dreams remain closed to us until they have been carried to the level of language through narration.

This enumeration of the modalities of symbolic expression calls for a criteriology as its complement, a criteriology which would have the task of determining the semantic constitution of related forms, such as metaphor, allegory, and simile. What is the function of analogy in "transfer of meaning"? Are there ways other than analogy of relating one meaning to another meaning? How can the dream mechanisms discovered by Freud be integrated into this symbolic meaning? Can they be superimposed on known rhetorical forms like metaphor and metonymy? Do the mechanisms of distortion, set in motion by what Freud terms "dream work," cover the same semantic field as the symbolic operations attested to by the phenomenology of religion? Such are the structural questions a criteriology would have to resolve.

This criteriology is, in turn, inseparable from a study of the operations of interpretation. The field of symbolic expressions and the field of the operations of interpretation have in fact been defined here in terms of each other. The problems posed by the symbol are consequently reflected in the methodology of interpretation. It is indeed notable that interpretation gives rise to very different, even opposing, methods. I have alluded to the phenomenology of religion and to psychoanalysis. They are as radically opposed as possible. There is nothing surprising in this: interpretation begins with the multiple determination of symbols —with their overdetermination, as one says in psychoanalysis; but each interpretation, by definition, reduces this richness, this multivocity, and "translates" the symbol according to its own frame of reference. It is the task of this criteriology to show that the form of interpretation is relative to the theoretical structure of the hermeneutic system being considered. Thus, the phenomenology of religion deciphers the religious object in rites, in myth, and in faith, but it does so on the basis of a problematic of the sacred which defines its theoretical structure. Psychoanalysis, on the contrary, sees only one dimension of the symbol: the dimension in which symbols are seen as derivatives of repressed desires. Consequently, it considers only the network of meanings constituted in the unconscious, beginning with the initial repression and elaborated by subsequent secondary repressions. Psychoanalysis cannot be reproached for this narrowness; it is its *raison d'être*. Psychoanalytic theory, what Freud called his metapsychology, confines the rules of decipherment to what could be called a semantics of desire. Psychoanalysis can find only what it seeks; what it seeks is the "economic" meaning of representations and affects operating in dreams, neuroses, art, morality, and religion. Psychoanalysis will thus be unable to find anything other than the disguised expressions of representations and affects belonging to the most archaic of man's desires. This example well shows, on the single level of semantics, the fullness of a philosophical hermeneutics. It begins by an expanding investigation into symbolic forms and by a comprehensive analysis of symbolic structures. It proceeds by the confrontation of hermeneutic styles and by the critique of systems of interpretation, carrying the diversity of hermeneutic methods back to the structure of the corresponding theories. In this way it prepares itself to perform its highest task, which would be a true arbitration among the absolutist claims of each of the interpretations. By showing in what way each method expresses the form of a theory, philosophical hermeneutics justifies each method within the limits of its own theoretical circumscription. Such is the critical function of this hermeneutics taken at its purely semantic level.

Its multiple advantages are apparent: First of all, the semantic approach keeps hermeneutics in contact with methodologies as they are actually practiced and so does not run the risk of separating its concept of truth from the concept of method. Moreover, it assures the implantation of hermeneutics in phenomenology at the level at which the latter is most sure of itself, that is, at the level of the theory of meaning developed in the *Logical Investigations*. Of course, Husserl would not have accepted the idea of meaning as irreducibly nonunivocal. He explicitly excludes this possibility in the First Investigation, and this is indeed why the phenomenology of the *Logical Investigations* cannot be hermeneutic. But, if we part from Husserl, we do so within the framework of his theory of signifying expressions; it is here that the divergence begins and not at the uncertain level of the phenomenology of the *Lebenswelt*. Finally, by carrying the debate to the level of language, I have the feeling of encountering other currently viable philosophies on a common terrain. Of course, the semantics of multivocal expressions opposes the theories of metalanguage which would hope to remake existing languages according to ideal models. The opposition is as sharp here as in regard to Husserl's ideal of univocity. On the other hand, this semantics enters into a fruitful dialogue with the doctrines arising from Wittgenstein's *Philosophical Investigations* and from the analysis of ordinary language in the Anglo-Saxon countries. It is likewise at this level that a general hermeneutics rejoins the preoccupations of modern biblical exegesis descending from Bultmann and his school. I see this general hermeneutics as a contribution to the grand philosophy of language which we lack today. We have at our disposal today a symbolic logic, a science of exegesis, an anthropology, and a psychoanalysis; and, for the first time perhaps, we are capable of encompassing as a single question the reintegration of human discourse. The progress of these dissimilar disciplines has at once made manifest and worsened the dislocation of this discourse. The unity of human speech is the problem today.

IV. THE LEVEL OF REFLECTION

THE PRECEDING ANALYSIS, dealing with the semantic structure of expressions with double or multiple meanings, is the narrow gate through which hermeneutic philosophy must pass if it does not want to cut itself off from those disciplines which, in their method, turn to interpretation: exegesis, history, and psychoanalysis. But a semantics of expressions with multiple meanings is not enough to qualify hermeneutics as philosophy. A linguistic analysis which would treat these significations as a whole closed in on itself would ineluctably set up language as an absolute. This hypostasis of language, however, repudiates the basic intention of a sign, which is to hold "for," thus transcending itself and suppressing itself in what it intends. Language itself, as a signifying milieu, must be referred to existence.

By making this admission, we join Heidegger once again: what animates the movement of surpassing the linguistic level is the desire for an ontology; it is the demand this ontology makes on an analysis which would remain a prisoner of language.

Yet how can semantics be integrated with ontology without becoming vulnerable to the objections we raised earlier against an Analytic of Dasein? The intermediary step, in the direction of existence, is reflection, that is, the link between the understanding of signs and self-understanding. It is in the self that we have the opportunity to discover an existent.

In proposing to relate symbolic language to self-understanding, I think I fulfill the deepest wish of hermeneutics. The purpose of all interpretation is to conquer a remoteness, a distance between the past cultural epoch to which the text belongs and the interpreter himself. By overcoming this distance, by making himself contemporary with the text, the exegete can appropriate its meaning to himself: foreign, he makes it familiar, that is, he makes it his own. It is thus the growth of his own understanding of himself that he pursues through his understanding of the other. Every hermeneutics is thus, explicitly or implicitly, self-understanding by means of understanding others.

So I do not hesitate to say that hermeneutics must be grafted onto phenomenology, not only at the level of the theory of meaning expressed in the *Logical Investigations*, but also at the level of the problematic of the *cogito* as it unfolds from *Ideen I* to the *Cartesian Meditations*. But neither do I hesitate to add that the graft changes the wild stock! We have already seen how the introduction of ambiguous meanings into the semantic field forces us to abandon the ideal of univocity extolled in the *Logical Investigations*. It must now be understood that by joining these multivocal meanings to self-knowledge we profoundly transform the problematic of the *cogito*. Let us say straight off that it is this internal reform of reflective philosophy which will later justify our discovering there a new dimension of existence. But, before saying how the *cogito* is exploded, let us say how it is enriched and deepened by this recourse to hermeneutics.

Let us in fact reflect upon what the self of self-understanding signifies, whether we appropriate the sense of a psychoanalytic interpretation or that of a textual exegesis. In truth, we do not know beforehand, but only afterward, although our desire to understand ourselves has alone guided this appropriation. Why is this so? Why is the self that guides the interpretation able to recover itself only as a result of the interpretation?

There are two reasons for this: it must be stated, first, that the celebrated Cartesian *cogito*, which grasps itself directly in the experience of doubt, is a truth as vain as it is invincible. I do not deny that it is a truth; it is a truth which posits itself, and as such it can be neither verified nor deduced. It posits at once a being and an act, an existence and an operation of thought: I am, I think; to exist, for me, is to think; I exist *insofar as* I think. But this truth is a vain truth; it is like a first step which cannot be followed by any other, so long as the *ego* of the *ego cogito* has not been recaptured in the mirror of its objects, of its works, and, finally, of its acts. Reflection is blind intuition if it is not mediated by what Dilthey called the expressions in which life objectifies itself. Or, to use the language of Jean Nabert, reflection is nothing other than the appropriation of our act of existing by means of a critique applied to the works and the acts which are the signs of this act of existing. Thus, reflection is a critique, not in the Kantian sense of a justification of science and duty, but in the sense that the *cogito* can be recovered only by the detour of a decipherment of the documents of its life. Reflection is the appropriation of our effort to exist and of our desire to be by means of the works which testify to this effort and this desire.

The *cogito* is not only a truth as vain as it is invincible; we must add, as well, that it is like an empty place which has, from all time, been occupied by a false *cogito*. We have indeed learned, from all the exegetic disciplines and from psychoanalysis in particular, that so-called immediate consciousness is first of all "false consciousness." Marx, Nietzsche, and Freud have taught us to unmask its tricks. Henceforth it becomes necessary to join a critique of false consciousness to any rediscovery of the subject of the *cogito* in the documents of its life; a philosophy of reflection must be just the opposite of a philosophy of consciousness.

A second reason can be added to the preceding one: not only is the "I" able to recapture itself only in the expressions of life that objectify it, but the textual exegesis of consciousness collides with the initial "misinterpretation" of false consciousness. Moreover, since Schleiermacher, we know that hermeneutics is found wherever there was first misinterpretation.

Thus, reflection must be doubly indirect: first, because existence is evinced only in the documents of life, but also because consciousness is first of all false consciousness, and it is always necessary to rise by means of a corrective critique from misunderstanding to understanding.

At the end of this second stage, which we have termed the reflective stage, I should like to show how the results of the first stage, which we termed the semantic stage, are consolidated.

During the first stage, we took as a fact the existence of a language irreducible to univocal meanings. It is a fact that the avowal of guilty consciousness passes through a symbolism of the stain, of sin, or of guilt; it is a fact that repressed desire is expressed in a symbolism which confirms its stability through dreams, proverbs, legends, and myths; it is a fact that the sacred is expressed in a symbolism of cosmic elements: sky, earth, water, fire. The philosophical use of this language, however, remains open to the logician's objection that equivocal language can provide only fallacious arguments. The justification of hermeneutics can be radical only if one seeks in the very nature of reflective thought the principle of a logic of double meaning. This logic is then no longer a formal logic but a transcendental logic. It is established at the level of conditions of possibility: not the conditions of the objectivity of a nature, but the conditions of the appropriation of our desire to be. It is in this sense that the logic of the double meaning proper to hermeneutics can be called transcendental. If the debate is not carried to this level, one will quickly be driven into an untenable situation; in vain will one attempt to maintain the debate at a purely semantic level and to make room for equivocal meanings alongside univocal meanings, for the theoretical distinction between two kinds of equivocalness—equivocalness through a surplus of meaning, found in the exegetic sciences, and equivocalness through the confusion of meanings, which logic chases away—cannot be justified at the level of semantics alone. Two logics cannot exist at the same level. Only a problematic of reflection justifies the semantics of double meaning.

V. The Existential Level

At the end of this itinerary, which has led us from a problematic of language to a problematic of reflection, I should like to show how we can, by retracing our steps, join a problematic of existence. The ontology of understanding which Heidegger sets up directly by a sudden reversal of the problem, substituting the consideration of a mode of being for that of a mode of knowing, can be, for us who proceed indirectly and by degrees, only a horizon, an aim rather than a given fact. A separate ontology is beyond our grasp: it is only within the movement of interpretation that we apperceive the being we interpret. The ontology of understanding is implied in the methodology of interpretation, following the ineluctable "hermeneutic circle" which Heidegger himself taught us to delineate. Moreover, it is only in a conflict of rival hermeneutics that we perceive something of the being to be interpreted: a unified ontology is as inaccessible to our method as a separate ontology. Rather, in every instance, each hermeneutics discovers the aspect of existence which founds it as method.

This double warning nevertheless must not deter us from clearing the ontological foundations of the semantic and reflective analysis which precedes it. An implied ontology, and even more so a truncated ontology, is still, is already, an ontology.

We will follow a track open to us, the one offered by a

philosophical reflection on psychoanalysis. What can we expect from the latter in the way of a fundamental ontology? Two things: first, a true dismissal of the classical problematic of the subject as consciousness; then, a restoration of the problematic of existence as desire.

It is indeed through a critique of consciousness that psychoanalysis points to ontology. The interpretation it proposes to us of dreams, fantasies, myths, and symbols always contests to some extent the pretension of consciousness in setting itself up as the origin of meaning. The struggle against narcissism—the Freudian equivalent of the false *cogito*—leads to the discovery that language is deeply rooted in desire, in the instinctual impulses of life. The philosopher who surrenders himself to this strict schooling is led to practice a true ascesis of subjectivity, allowing himself to be dispossessed of the origin of meaning. This abandonment is of course yet another turn of reflection, but it must become the real loss of the most archaic of all objects: the self. It must then be said of the subject of reflection what the Gospel says of the soul: to be saved, it must be lost. All of psychoanalysis speaks to me of lost objects to be found again symbolically. Reflective philosophy must integrate this discovery with its own task; the self [le moi] must be lost in order to find the "I" [le je]. This is why psychoanalysis is, if not a philosophical discipline, at least a discipline for the philosopher: the unconscious forces the philosopher to deal with the arrangement of significations on a level which is set apart in relation to the immediate subject. This is what Freudian topography teaches: the most archaic significations are organized in a "place" of meaning that is separate from the place where immediate consciousness reigns. The realism of the unconscious, the topographic and economic treatment of representations, fantasies, symptoms, and symbols, appears finally as the condition of a hermeneutics free from the prejudices of the ego.

Freud invites us, then, to ask anew the question of the relationship between signification and desire, between meaning and energy, that is, finally, between language and life. This was already Leibniz' problem in the *Monadology*: how is representation joined to appetite? It was equally Spinoza's problem in the *Ethics*, Book III: how do the degrees of the adequation of ideas express the degrees of the *conatus*, of the effort which constitutes us? In its own way, psychoanalysis leads us back to the same question: how is the order of significations included within the order of life? This regression from meaning to desire is the indication of a possible transcendence of reflection in the direction of existence. Now an expression we used above, but whose meaning was only anticipated, is justified: by understanding ourselves, we said, we appropriate to ourselves the meaning of our desire to be or of our effort to exist. Existence, we can now say, is desire and effort. We term it effort in order to stress its positive energy and its dynamism; we term it desire in order to designate its lack and its poverty: Eros is the son of Poros and Penia. Thus the *cogito* is no longer the pretentious act it was initially—I mean its pretension of positing itself; it appears as *already* posited in being.

But if the problematic of reflection can and must surpass itself in a problematic of existence, as a philosophical meditation on psychoanalysis suggests, it is always in and through interpretation that this surpassing occurs: it is in deciphering the tricks of desire that the desire at the root of meaning and reflection is discovered. I cannot hypostasize this desire outside the process of interpretation; it always remains a being-interpreted. I have hints of it behind the enigmas of consciousness, but I cannot grasp it in itself without the danger of creating a mythology of instinctual forces, as sometimes happens in coarse conceptions of pschoanalysis. It is behind itself that the *cogito* discovers, through the work of interpretation, something like an *archaeology of the subject*. Existence is glimpsed in this archaeology, but it remains entangled in the movement of deciphering to which it gives rise.

This decipherment, which psychoanalysis, understood as hermeneutics, compels us to perform, other hermeneutic methods force us to perform as well, although in different ways. The existence that psychoanalysis discovers is that of desire; it is existence as desire, and this existence is revealed principally in an archaeology of the subject. Another hermeneutics—that of the philosophy of the spirit, for example—suggests another manner of shifting the origin of sense, so that it is no longer behind the subject but in front of it. I would be willing to say that there is a hermeneutics of God's coming, of the approach of his Kingdom, a hermeneutics representing the prophecy of consciousness. In the final analysis, this is what animates Hegel's *Phenomenology of the Spirit*. I mention it here because its mode of interpretation is diametrically opposed to Freud's. Psychoanalysis offered us a regression toward the archaic; the phenomenology of the spirit offers us a movement in which each figure finds its meaning, not in what precedes but in what follows.

Consciousness is thus drawn outside itself, in front of itself, toward a meaning in motion, where each stage is suppressed and retained in the following stage. In this way, a teleology of the subject opposes an archaeology of the subject. But what is important for our intention is that this teleology, just like Freudian archaeology, is constituted only in the movement of interpretation, which understands one figure through another figure. The spirit is realized only in this crossing from one figure to another; the spirit is the very dialectic of these figures by means of which the subject is drawn out of his infancy, torn from his archaeology. This is why philosophy remains a hermeneutics, that is, a reading of the hidden meaning inside the text of the apparent meaning. It is the task of this hermeneutics to show that existence arrives at expression, at meaning, and at reflection only through the continual exegesis of all the significations that come to light in the world of culture. Existence becomes a self—human and adult—only by appropriating this meaning, which first resides "outside," in works, institutions, and cultural monuments in which the life of the spirit is objectified.

It is within the same ontological horizon that the phenomenology of religion—both Van der Leeuw's and Mircea Eliade's—would have to be interrogated. As phenomenology it is simply a description of rite, of myth, of belief, that is, of the forms of behavior, language, and feeling by which man directs himself toward something "sacred." But if phenomenology can remain at this descriptive level, the reflective resumption of the work of interpretation goes much further: by understanding himself in and through the signs of the sacred, man performs the most radical abandonment of himself that it is possible to imagine. This dispossession exceeds that occasioned by psychoanalysis and Hegelian phenomenology, whether they are considered individually or whether their effects are combined. An archaeology and a teleology still unveil an *arché* and a *telos* which the subject, while understanding them, can command. It is not the same in the case of the sacred, which manifests itself in a phenomenology of religion. The latter symbolically designates the alpha of all archaeology, the omega of all teleology; this alpha and this omega the subject would be unable to command. The sacred calls upon man and in this call manifests itself as that which commands his existence because it posits this existence absolutely, as effort and as desire to be.

Thus, the most opposite hermeneutics point, each in its own way, to the ontological roots of comprehension. Each in its own way affirms the dependence of the self upon existence. Pscho-analysis shows this dependence in the archaeology of the subject, the phenomenology of the spirit in the teleology of figures, the phenomenology of religion in the signs of the sacred.

Such are the ontological implications of interpretation.

The ontology proposed here is in no way separable from interpretation; it is caught inside the circle formed by the conjunction of the work of interpretation and the interpreted being. It is thus not a triumphant ontology at all; it is not even a science, since it is unable to avoid the *risk* of interpretation; it cannot even entirely escape the internal warfare that the various hermeneutics indulge in among themselves.

Nevertheless, in spite of its precariousness, this militant a truncated ontology is qualified to affirm that rival hermeneutics are not mere "language games," as would be the case if their absolutist pretensions continued to oppose one another on the sole level of language. For a linguistic philosophy, all interpretations are equally valid within the limits of the theory which founds the given rules of reading. These equally valid interpretations remain language games until it is shown that each interpretation is grounded in a particular existential function. Thus, psychoanalysis has its foundation in an archaeology of the subject, the phenomenology of the spirit in a teleology, and the phenomenology of religion in an eschatology.

Can one proceed any further? Can these different existential functions be joined in a unitary figure, as Heidegger tried to do in the second part of *Being and Time*? This is the question the present study leaves unresolved. But, if it remains unresolved, it is not hopeless. In the dialectic of archaeology, teleology, and eschatology an ontological structure is manifested, one capable of reassembling the discordant interpretations on the linguistic level. But this coherent figure of the being which we ourselves are, in which rival interpretations are implanted, is given nowhere but in this dialectic of interpretations. In this respect, hermeneutics is unsurpassable. Only a hermeneutics instructed by symbolic figures can show that these different modalities of existence belong to a single problematic, for it is finally through the richest symbols that the unity of these multiple interpretations is assured. These symbols alone carry all the vectors, both regressive and progressive, that the various hermeneutics dissociate. True symbols contain all hermeneutics, those which are directed toward the emergence of new meanings and those which are directed toward the resurgence of archaic fantasies.

It is in this sense, beginning with our introduction, that we have insisted that existence as it relates to a hermeneutic philosophy always remains an interpreted existence. It is in the work of interpretation that this philosophy discovers the multiple modali-ties of the dependence of the self—its dependence on desire glimpsed in an archaeology of the subject, its dependence on the spirit glimpsed in its teleology, its dependence on the sacred glimpsed in its eschatology. It is by developing an archaeology, a teleology, and an eschatology that reflection suppresses itself as reflection.

In this way, ontology is indeed the promised land for a phi-losophy that begins with language and with reflection; but, like Moses, the speaking and reflecting subject can only glimpse this land before dying.

PART I

Hermeneutics and Structuralism

Structure and Hermeneutics

THE SUBJECT of the present conference[1] is hermeneutics and tradition. It is notable that what comes into question under both headings is a certain manner in which time is lived and used: the time of transmission and the time of interpretation.

We have the feeling—and it remains a feeling so long as it has not been sufficiently established—that these two temporalities concern each other, mutually relate to each other. We feel that interpretation has a history and that this history is a segment of tradition itself. Interpretation does not spring from nowhere; rather, one interprets in order to make explicit, to extend, and so to keep alive the tradition itself, inside which one always remains. It is in this sense that the time of interpretation belongs in some way to the time of tradition. But tradition in return, even understood as the transmission of a *depositum,* remains a dead tradition if it is not the continual interpretation of this deposit: our "heritage" is not a sealed package we pass from hand to hand, without ever opening, but rather a treasure from which we draw by the handful and which by this very act is replenished. Every tradition lives by grace of interpretation, and it is at this price that it continues, that is, remains living.

However, the inner connection of these two temporalities is not visible. How does interpretation enter into the time of tradition? Why does tradition live only in and through the time of interpretation?

Translated by Kathleen McLaughlin.
1. [This essay was originally a paper presented before the International Congress of Philosophy (Rome, 1963).]

I intend to look for a third temporality, a profound time which would be inscribed in the fullness of meaning and which would make the intersection of these two temporalities possible. This time would be the time of meaning itself; it would be like a temporal charge, initially carried by the advent of meaning. This temporal charge would allow for both a sedimentation in a deposit and a clarification in an interpretation; in short, it would permit the struggle between these two temporalities, one transmitting, the other renewing.

But where do we look for this time of meaning, and, in particular, how do we reach it?

My working hypothesis is that this temporal charge has something to do with the semantic constitution of what in my two previous papers delivered before this body[2] I have called the symbol and which I have defined by the power of the double meaning. The symbol, I said, is constituted from a semantic perspective such that it provides a meaning by means of a meaning. In it a primary, literal, worldly, often physical meaning refers back to a figurative, spiritual, often existential, ontological meaning which is in no way given outside this indirect designation. The symbol invites us to think, calls for an interpretation, precisely because it says more than it says and because it never ceases to speak to us. My problem today is to elicit the temporal import of this semantic analysis. Between the surplus of meaning and the temporal charge, there must be an essential relation. It is this essential relation which is at issue in the present paper.

One more particular: I have called this study the time of symbols and not the time of myths.[3] As I stated in a previous study, the myth in no way exhausts the semantic constitution of the symbol. I want to recall here the principal reasons why the myth should be subordinated to the symbol. First of all, the myth is a form of narration: it recounts the events of the beginning and the end inside a fundamental time—"In those times . . . ." This referential time adds a new dimension to the historicity which charges the symbolic meaning and so must be treated as a specific problem. Second, the relation of myth to rite and to the complex of institutions of a particular society places the myth in the social web and, up to a certain point, masks the temporal potential of the symbols put into play. The

2. See "The Hermeneutics of Symbols and Philosophical Reflection," Parts I and II, below.
3. [Original title: "Symbolique et temporalité."]

importance of this distinction will be shown later; the determined social function of the myth does not, to my mind, exhaust
the fullness of meaning of the symbolic base, which another
mythical constellation can use again in another social context.
Finally, the literary ordering of the myth implies a beginning
of rationalization which limits the signifying power of the symbolic base. Rhetoric and speculation already begin to fix the
symbolic base; there is no myth without a hint of mythology.
For all these reasons—the arrangement in narrative form, the
relation to rite and to a determined social function, mythological
rationalization—the myth is no longer at the level of the symbolic base and of the hidden time which we are seeking to un-
earth. For my part I have shown this in the symbolism of evil.
The symbols embraced by the avowal of evil appeared to me to
fall into three signifying levels: the primary symbolic level of the
stain, of sin, of guilt; the mythical level of the great narratives
of the Fall or the Exile; and the level of the mythological dog-
matisms of Gnosticism and original sin. It appeared to me, in
putting this dialectic of the symbol in motion—based solely, it
is true, on Semitic and Hellenic traditions—that the store of
meaning of primary symbols was richer than that of mythical
symbols and even more so than that of rationalizing mythologies.
From symbol to myth and to mythology, one goes from a hidden
time to an exhausted time. It seems, then, that tradition, to the
extent to which it descends the slope from symbol to dogmatic
mythology, places itself on the trajectory of this exhausted time.
It is transformed into heritage and into sediment at the same
time that it is rationalized. This process is evident when one
compares the great Hebraic symbols of sin to the fantastic
constructions concerning original sin of Gnosticism and also
Christian anti-Gnosticism, which is only a reply to Gnosticism
on the same semantic level. A tradition exhausts itself by
mythologizing the symbol; a tradition is renewed by means of
interpretation, which reascends the slope from exhausted time
to hidden time, that is, by soliciting from mythology the symbol
and its store of meaning.

But what can be said about this fundamental time in regard
to the double time of tradition and interpretation? And, in
particular, how can it be reached?

This study intends to propose a means of indirect access, a
detour: I will start with the structuralist notions of synchrony
and diachrony, in particular as they appear in Lévi-Strauss's
Structural Anthropology. It is not at all my intention to oppose

hermeneutics to structuralism, the historicity of the one to the diachrony of the other. Structuralism is part of science, and I do not at present see any more rigorous or more fruitful approach than the structuralist method at the level of comprehension which is its own. The interpretation of symbols is worthy of being called a hermeneutics only insofar as it is a part of self-understanding and of the understanding of being; outside this effort of appropriating meaning, it is nothing. In this sense hermeneutics is a philosophical discipline. To the extent to which the aim of structuralism is to put at a distance, to objectify, to separate out from the personal equation of the investigator the structure of an institution, a myth, a rite, to the same extent hermeneutics buries itself in what could be called "the hermeneutic circle" of understanding and of believing, which disqualifies it as science and qualifies it as meditating thought. There is thus no reason to juxtapose two ways of understanding; the question is rather to link them together as the objective and the existential (or *existentiell!*). If hermeneutics is a phase of the appropriation of meaning, a stage between abstract and concrete reflection, if hermeneutics is thought recovering meaning suspended within a system of symbols, it can encounter the work of structural anthropology only as its support and not as its contrast. One appropriates only what has first been held at a distance and examined. It is this objective examination, put to work in the concepts of synchrony and diachrony, that I want to perform in the hope of leading hermeneutics, through the discipline of objectivity, from a naïve to a mature comprehension.

It does not seem expedient to start with *The Savage Mind* but to proceed to it, for *The Savage Mind* represents the final stage in a gradual process of generalization. Initially, structuralism made no claim of defining the entire constitution of thought, even in its savage state, but rather of delineating a well-defined group of problems which have, one might say, an affinity for the structural treatment. *The Savage Mind* represents the reaching of a kind of limit, a terminal systematization which calls too hastily for the positing of a false alternative, the choice between several ways of understanding, between several kinds of intelligibility. I stated that this was absurd *in principle;* to avoid falling into the trap *in fact,* structuralism must be treated as an explanation which is at first limited and then extended by degrees, following the guideline of the problems themselves. The consciousness of the validity of a method is never separable from the consciousness of its limits. It is in order to give full measure to this method, and especially to allow myself to be instructed by it, that I will seize hold of it in its movement of expansion, starting with an indisputable core, rather than taking it at its final stage, past a certain critical point where, perhaps, it loses the sense of its limits.

I. THE LINGUISTIC MODEL

AS WE KNOW, structuralism proceeds by applying a linguistic model to anthropology and to the human sciences in general. In the beginnings of structuralism, we find first Ferdinand de Saussure and his *Course in General Linguistics* and then the properly phonemic orientation of Trubetskoy, Jakobson, and Martinet. With them we witness a reversal of the relations between system and history. For historicism, understanding is finding the genesis, the previous form, the sources, and the sense of the evolution. With structuralism, what is first given as intelligible are the arrangements, the systematic organizations in a given state. Ferdinand de Saussure begins to introduce this reversal by making a distinction, within human language in general, between language and speech. If by "language" one understands the set of conventions adopted by a social body to allow individuals to exercise language, and by "speech" the very activity of speaking subjects, this principal distinction gives us access to three rules whose generalization outside the initial domain of linguistics we will follow later.

First of all, we must look at the very idea of system. Separated from speaking subjects, a language presents itself as a system of signs. Of course Ferdinand de Saussure is not a phonologist; his concept of the linguistic sign as the relation between the sonorous signifier and the conceptual signified is more a semantic than a phonemic distinction. Nevertheless, what seemed to him to constitute the object of a linguistic science is the system of signs which arise from the mutual determination of the sonorous chain of the signifier and the conceptual chain of the signified. In this mutual determination, what counts are not the terms, considered individually, but the differential variations; it is the differences of sound and meaning and the relations of the one to the other which constitute the system of signs of a language. One then understands that each sign is arbitrary, insofar as it represents an isolated relation of a meaning and a sound, and that all the signs of a language form a system: ". . . in language there are only differences." [4]

This governing idea commands the second theme which specifically concerns the relation of diachrony to synchrony. Indeed, the system of differences appears only on the axis of coexistences, which is wholly distinct from the axis of successions. In this way a synchronic linguistics is born as a science of states in their systematic aspects, distinct from a diachronic linguistics or a science of evolutions applied to the system. As one sees, history is secondary and figures as an alteration of the system. Moreover, in linguistics these alterations are less intelligible than the states of the system: de Saussure writes that "never is the system modified directly. In itself it is unchangeable; only certain elements are altered without regard for the solidarity that binds them to the whole" (p. 84). History is responsible for disorders rather than for meaningful changes. De Saussure says it well: "[synchrony] is a relation between simultaneous elements, [diachrony is] an event" (p. 91). From this point on, linguistics is synchronic first, and diachrony itself is intelligible only as the comparison of states of anterior and posterior systems; diachrony is comparative, and in this it depends on synchrony. Finally, events are apprehended only when they have been realized in a system, that is, by receiving from the system an aspect of regularity; the diachronic datum is the innovation which arises from speech (whether from one or several is of no matter) but which has become "a fact of language" (p. 98).

It will be the central issue of our reflection to know how far the linguistic model of the relations between synchrony and diachrony leads us to a clear understanding of the historicity proper to symbols. Let us say straight off that the critical point will have been reached when we are confronting a true tradition, that is, a series of interpreting recoveries which can no longer be considered the intervention of disorder in a system state.

Please understand me well: I do not attribute to structuralism, like some of its critics, a pure and simple opposition between diachrony and synchrony. Lévi-Strauss, in this respect, is right to oppose to his detractors Jakobson's great article on the

---

4. Ferdinand de Saussure, *Course in General Linguistics*, trans. Wade Baskin (New York, 1966), p. 120.

"Principles of Historical Phonetics," where the author explicitly distinguishes between synchrony and statics.[5] What is important is the subordination, not the opposition, of diachrony to synchrony; it is this subordination which is questioned in hermeneutic comprehension, that diachrony is meaningful only through its relation to synchrony and not the inverse.

But there is a third principle, which no less involves our problem of interpretation and of the time of interpretation. It has been pointed out in particular by phonologists, but it is already present in the Saussurean opposition between language and speech. This third principle is that linguistic laws designate an unconscious level and, in this sense, a nonreflective, nonhistorical level of the mind. This unconscious is not the Freudian unconscious of instinctual, erotic drives and its power of symbolization; it is more a Kantian than a Freudian unconscious, a categorial, combinative unconscious. It is a finite order or the finitude of order, but such that it is unaware of itself. I call it a Kantian unconscious, but only as regards its organization, since we are here concerned with a categorial system without refer ence to a thinking subject. This is why structuralism as philosophy will develop a kind of intellectualism which is fundamentally antireflective, anti-idealist, and antiphenomenological. Moreover, this unconscious mind can be said to be homologous to nature; perhaps it even is nature. We will come back to this when we study *The Savage Mind*. Yet, as early as 1956, referring to the rule of economy in Jakobson's explanation, Lévi-Strauss wrote: "the assertion that the most parsimonious explanation also comes closest to the truth rests, in the final analysis, upon the identity postulated between the laws of the universe and those of the human mind."[6]

This third principle concerns us no less than the second, for it establishes between the observer and the system a relationship which is itself nonhistorical. Understanding is not seen here as the recovery of meaning. In contrast to what is stated by Schleiermacher in *Hermeneutik und Kritik* (1828), by Dilthey in his important article "Die Entstehung der Hermeneutik" (1900), and by Bultmann in *Das Problem der Hermeneutik* (1950), there is no "hermeneutic circle"; there is no historicity

5. Roman Jakobson, "Principien der historischen Phonologie," *Travaux du Cercle linguistique de Prague*, IV (1931).
6. Claude Lévi-Strauss, *Structural Anthropology*, trans. Claire Jacobson and Brooke Grundfest Schoepf (New York, 1963), p. 89.

to the relation of understanding. The relation is objective, independent of the observer. This is why structural anthropology is science and not philosophy.

II. THE TRANSPOSITION OF THE LINGUISTIC MODEL IN
Structural Anthropology

ONE CAN FOLLOW this transposition in Lévi-Strauss's work by examining methodological articles published in *Structural Anthropology*. Mauss had already said: "Sociology would certainly have progressed much further if it had everywhere followed the lead of the linguists."[7] But it is the phonemic revolution in linguistics that Lévi-Strauss considers the true point of departure:

> Not only did it renew linguistic perspectives; a transformation of this magnitude is not limited to a single discipline. Structural linguistics will certainly play the same renovating role with respect to the social sciences that nuclear physics, for example, has played for the physical sciences. In what does this revolution consist, as we try to assess its broadest implication? N. Trubetzkoy, the illustrious founder of structural linguistics, himself furnished the answer to this question. In one programmatic statement, he reduced the structural method to four basic operations. First, structural linguistics shifts from the study of *conscious* linguistic phenomena to the study of their *unconscious* infrastructure; second, it does not treat *terms* as independent entities, taking instead as its basis of analysis the *relations* between terms; third, it introduces the concept of *system*—"Modern phonemics does not merely proclaim that phonemes are always part of a system; it *shows* concrete phonemic systems and elucidates their structure"—; finally, structural linguistics aims at discovering *general laws*, either by induction "or . . . by logical deduction, which would give them an absolute character" (p. 33).[8]

Kinship systems provide Lévi-Strauss with the first rigorous analogue of phonemic systems. These are indeed systems established at the unconscious level of the mind; they are, moreover, systems in which oppositional pairs and differential elements in general are alone meaningful (father-son, the mater-

---

7. In an article written in 1945; cited by Lévi-Strauss, pp. 31–32.
8. The quotations are from N. Trubetskoy, "La Phonologie actuelle," *Psychologie du langage* (Paris, 1933).

nal uncle and his sister's son, husband-wife, brother-sister). Consequently, the system operates not on the level of the terms but on that of the pairs of relations. (This brings to mind the elegant and convincing solution to the problem of the maternal uncle in *Structural Anthropology;* see esp. pp. 42–43, 46–47). Finally, these are systems which are most readily intelligible from a synchronic perspective: the systems are constructed without regard to history, although they do include a diachronic dimension, since the kinship structures connect a series of generations.[9]

Now, what authorizes this initial transposition of the linguistic model? Essentially this: kinship is itself a system of communication; by virtue of this it is comparable to language.

> The kinship system is a language; but it is not a universal language, and a society may prefer other modes of expression and action. From the viewpoint of the anthropologist this means that in dealing with a specific culture we must always ask a preliminary question: Is the system systematic? Such a question, which seems absurd at first, is absurd only in relation to language; for language is the systematic system par excellence; it cannot but signify, and exists only through signification. On the contrary, this question must be rigorously examined as we move from the study of language to the consideration of other systems which also claim to have semantic functions, but whose fulfillment remains partial, fragmentary, or subjective, like, for example, social organization, art, and so forth (pp. 47–48).

This text proposes, then, that we arrange social systems in diminishing order, "but with an increasing rigor,"[10] beginning with the system of signification par excellence, language. If kinship is the closest analogue, it is because, like language, it is "an arbitrary system of representations, not the spontaneous development of a real situation" (p. 50). But this analogy appears only if the organization is based on elements which form

9. See p. 47: "Kinship is not a static phenomenon; it exists only in self-perpetuation. Here we are not thinking of the fact that in most kinship systems the initial disequilibrium produced in one generation between the group that gives the woman and the group that receives her can be stabilized only by counter-prestations in following generations. Thus, even the most elementary kinship structure exists both synchronically and diachronically." This remark must be compared to the one we made above concerning diachrony in structural linguistics.

10. [While the English translation (p. 48) reads: "this question must be rigorously examined," the actual French text is: "la question doit être examinée avec une rigueur croissante" (*Anthropologie structurale* [Paris, 1958], p. 58).—TRANS.]

an alliance and not a biological modality: marriage rules represent "so many different ways of insuring the circulation of women within the social group or of substituting the mechanism of a sociologically determined affinity for that of a biologically determined consanguinity" (p. 60). Considered in this way, these rules make kinship

> . . . a kind of language, a set of processes permitting the establishment, between individuals and groups, of a certain type of communication. That the mediating factor, in this case, should be the *women of the group*, who are *circulated* between clans, lineages, or families, in place of the *words of the group*, which are circulated between individuals, does not at all change the fact that the essential aspect of the phenomenon is identical in both cases (p. 61).

The entire program of *The Savage Mind* is contained here, and the very principle of generalization is already postulated; I will limit myself to citing the following text, which dates from 1945:

> . . . the question must be raised whether the different aspects of social life (including even art and religion) cannot only be studied by the methods of, and with the help of concepts similar to those employed in linguistics, but also whether they do not constitute phenomena whose inmost nature is the same as that of language. . . .
>
> How can this hypothesis be verified? It will be necessary to develop the analysis of the different features of social life, either for a given society or for a complex of societies, so that a deep enough level can be reached to make it possible to cross from one to the other; or to express the specific structure of each in terms of a sort of general [code] language, valid for each system separately and for all of them taken together. It would thus be possible to ascertain if one had reached their inner nature and to determine if this pertained to the same reality (p. 62).

It is indeed in the idea of a general language, or code, understood in the sense of a formal correspondence between specified structures, and so in the sense of structural homology, that the essential element of this structural comprehension is concentrated. This understanding of the symbolic function can alone be said to be strictly independent of the observer: "We thus find in language a social phenomenon that manifests both independence of the observer and long statistical runs" (p. 57). Our problem will be to know how an objective comprehension which decodes can work with a hermeneutic comprehension which deciphers, that is, which assumes the meaning as its own at the same time that it grows from the sense it deciphers. A remark by Lévi-Strauss puts us, perhaps, on the trail; the author notes that "the original impulse" (p. 62) to exchange women perhaps reveals, by rebounding on the linguistic model, something about the origin of all language:

> As in the case of women, the original impulse which compelled men to exchange words must be sought for in that split representation that pertains to the symbolic function. For, since certain terms are simultaneously perceived as having a value both for the speaker and the listener, the only way to resolve this contradiction is in the exchange of complementary values, to which all social existence is reduced (*ibid.*).

Is this not to say that structuralism comes into play only against the already existing background of "a split representation that pertains to the symbolic function"? Does this not call for another kind of understanding, which aims at the split itself and is the basis for any exchange? Wouldn't the objective science of exchange be an abstract segment in the full understanding of the symbolic function, which basically would be semantic understanding? For the philosopher, structuralism's *raison d'être* would then be to rebuild this full understanding, but only after having first stripped it, objectified it, and replaced it with structural understanding. Thus mediated by the structural form, the semantic base would become accessible to an understanding which, although more indirect, would be more certain.

Let us suspend this question until the end of this study, and let us follow instead the thread of analogies and of generalization.

At first, Lévi-Strauss's generalizations are most prudent and are tempered by precautions (see, e.g., pp. 64–65). The structural analogy between other social phenomena and language, considered in its phonemic structure, is actually very complex. In what sense can one say that their "nature is the same as that of language" (p. 62)? Equivocalness is hardly a consideration when the signs of exchange are not themselves elements of discourse; thus one will say that men exchange women *as* they exchange words. The formalization which brought out the structural homology is not only legitimate but very enlightening. Things become more complicated in art and religion; here we no longer have only "a kind of language," as in the case of marriage rules and kinship systems, but rather a signifying discourse erected on the foundation of language, considered as an instrument of communication. The analogy is shifted inside language and from this moment on refers to the structure of this or that particular discourse in relation to the general structure of a language. It is thus not certain *a priori* that the relation between diachrony and synchrony, valid in general linguistics, rules the structure of particular discourses in an equally dominant fashion. The things said do not necessarily have an architecture similar to that of language viewed as a universal instrument of speaking. All that one can assert is that the linguistic model directs the investigation toward articulations which are similar to its own, that is, toward a logic of oppositions and correlations, that is to say, finally, toward a system of differences. After speaking about language as a diachronic condition of culture, insofar as it is the vehicle of instruction or education, Lévi-Strauss states:

> . . . from a much more theoretical point of view, language can be said to be a condition of culture because the material out of which language is built is of the same type as the material out of which the whole culture is built: logical relations, oppositions, correlations, and the like. Language, from this point of view, may appear as laying a kind of foundation for the more complex structures which correspond to the different aspects of culture (pp. 68–69).

But Lévi-Strauss must grant that the correlation between culture and language is not sufficiently justified by the universal role of language in culture:

> But we have not been sufficiently aware of the fact that *both* language and culture are the products of activities which are basically similar. I am now referring to this uninvited guest which has been seated during this conference beside us and which is the *human mind* (p. 71).

The third party called upon here occasions some serious problems; for the mind comprehends the mind, not only by the analogy of structure, but by recovering and continuing individual discourses. Now, nothing guarantees that this understanding arises from the same principles as those of structural linguistics. The structuralist enterprise thus seems to me to be perfectly legitimate and shielded from all criticism as long as it remains conscious of its conditions of validity and thus of its limits. One thing is certain under any hypothesis: the correlation must be sought, not between "language and behavior, but (between) two parallel ways of categorizing the same data" (p. 72). On this condition, but on this condition alone, "anthropology will become a general theory of relationships. Then it will be possible to analyze societies in terms of the differential features characteristic of the systems of relationships which define them" (pp. 95–96).

My problem at this point becomes more precise: what is the place of "a general theory of relationships" inside a general theory of meaning?[11] In questions of art and religion, what does one understand when one understands the structure? And how does structural comprehension instruct hermeneutic comprehension, directed toward a recovery of signifying intention?

It is here that our problem of time can provide a good touchstone. We are going to follow the course of the relationship between diachrony and synchrony in this transposition of the linguistic model and will confront it with what we know from elsewhere about the historicity of sense in the case of symbols for which we possess clear temporal sequences.

III. *The Savage Mind*

With *The Savage Mind*,[12] Lévi-Strauss proceeds to a bold generalization of structuralism. Certainly, nothing authorizes us to conclude that the author no longer envisages any collaboration with other modes of understanding, nor can it be said that structuralism no longer recognizes any boundaries. It is not all thought that falls under its grasp, but a level of thought, the level of

11. Lévi-Strauss can allow this question, since he poses it very well himself: "So the conclusion which seems to me the most likely is that some kind of correlation exists between certain things on certain levels, and our main task is to determine what these things are and what these levels are" (p. 79). In an answer to Haudricourt and Granai, Lévi-Strauss seems to agree that there is a zone of optimal validity for a general theory of communication: "This endeavor is possible on three levels, since the rules of kinship and marriage serve to insure the circulation of women between groups, just as economic rules serve to insure the circulation of goods and services, and linguistic rules the circulation of messages" (p. 83). The author's warnings against the excesses of American metalinguistics are also to be noted (pp. 73, 84–85).

12. English trans., Chicago: University of Chicago Press, 1966.

savage thought. Nevertheless, the reader who goes from *Structural Anthropology* to *The Savage Mind* is struck by the change in the approach and in the tone. One no longer proceeds by degrees, from kinship to art or religion; what becomes the object of investigation is rather an entire level of thought, considered globally. Moreover, this level of thought is itself held to be the nondomesticated form of thought, which is one. There are no savages as opposed to civilized people, no primitive mentality, no savage thought; there is no longer any absolute exoticism. Beyond the "totemic illusion," there is only a savage mind, and this thought is not anterior to logic. It is not prelogical but homologous to logical thought—homologous in the strong sense: the ramifications of its classifications, the refinement of its nomenclatures, are classifying thought itself, but operating, as Lévi-Strauss says, at another strategic level, at the sensory level. Savage thought is thought which orders but which does not think itself. In this it does indeed conform to the conditions of structuralism mentioned above: an unconscious order—an order conceived as a system of differences—an order capable of being treated objectively, independently of the observer. As a result, arrangements at an unconscious level are alone intelligible; understanding does not consist in taking up anew signifying intentions, reviving them through a historical act of interpretation which would itself be inscribed within a continuous tradition. Intelligibility is attributed to the code of transformations which assure correspondences and homology between arrangements belonging to different levels of social reality (clan organization, nomenclatures and classifications of animals and plants, myths and arts, etc.). I will characterize the method in one word: it is the choice of syntax over semantics. To the extent to which it is a wager made with coherence, this choice is perfectly legitimate. Unfortunately, it lacks reflection on its conditions of validity, on the price to be paid for this type of comprehension, in short, a reflection on limits, which did, however, appear from time to time in previous works.

For my part, I find it striking that all the examples were taken from the geographical area which was that of so-called totemic thought and never from Semitic, pre-Hellenic, or Indo-European thought; and I wonder what is implied in this initial limitation of the ethnographic and human material. Hasn't the author stacked the deck by relating the state of the savage mind to a cultural area—specifically, that of the "totemic illusion"—where the arrangements are more important than the contents, where thought is actually *bricolage*,[13] working with a heterogeneous material, with odds and ends of meaning? Never in this book is the question raised concerning the unity of mythical thought. It is taken for granted that the generalization includes all savage thought. Now, I wonder whether the mythical base from which we branch—with its Semitic (Egyptian, Babylonian, Aramaic, Hebrew), proto-Hellenic, and Indo-European cores—lends itself so easily to the same operation; or rather, and I insist on this point, it surely lends itself to the operation, but does it lend itself entirely? In the examples of *The Savage Mind*, the insignificance of the contents and the luxuriance of the arrangements seem to me to constitute an extreme example much more than a canonical form. It happens that a part of civilization, precisely the part from which our culture does not proceed, lends itself better than any other to the application of the structural method transposed from linguistics. But that does not prove that structural comprehension is just as enlightening elsewhere and, in particular, just as self-sufficient. I spoke above of the price to be paid: this price—the insignificance of the contents—is not a high price with the totemists, the counterpart being so great, that is, the great significance of the arrangements. Totemic thought, it seems to me, is precisely the one that has the greatest affinity to structuralism. I wonder whether its example is . . . exemplary or whether it is not exceptional.[14]

13. [In *The Savage Mind*, Lévi-Strauss defines this term in the following manner: "In its old sense the verb 'bricoler' applied to ball games and billiards, to hunting, shooting and riding. It was however always used with reference to some extraneous movement: a ball rebounding, a dog straying or a horse swerving from its direct course to avoid an obstacle. And in our own time the 'bricoleur' is still someone who works with his hands and uses devious means compared to those of a craftsman" (pp. 16–17). Because this term has no precise equivalent in English, we shall follow the lead of the English translation and use the French word.— TRANS.]

14. We find some indications of this in *The Savage Mind:* ". . . few civilizations seem to equal the Australians in their taste for erudition and speculation and what sometimes looks like intellectual dandyism, odd as this expression may appear when it is applied to people with so rudimentary a level of material life. . . . Granting that Australia has been turned in on itself for hundreds of thousands of years, that theorizing and discussion was all the rage in this closed world and the influence of fashion often paramount, it is easy to understand the emergence of a sort of common philosophical and sociological style along with methodically studied variations on it, even the most minor of which were pointed out for favorable or adverse comment" (pp. 89–90).

And toward the end of the book: "There is a sort of fundamental antipathy between history and systems of classification. This perhaps explains what one is tempted to call the 'totemic void,' for in the bounds

There perhaps exists another pole of mythical thought where syntactical organization is weaker, the connection to ritual less marked, the relation to social classifications more tenuous, and where, on the contrary, the semantic richness allows an indefinite number of historical recoveries in more varied social contexts. At this other pole of mythical thought, concerning which I shall later give examples taken from the Hebraic world, structural comprehension is perhaps less important, in any case less exclusive, and more explicitly requires being joined to a hermeneutic comprehension, which endeavors to interpret the contents themselves, so as to prolong their existence and thereby to incorporate what in these contents is efficacious for philosophical reflection.

It is here that I will take as touchstone the question of time, which set our meditation in movement. *The Savage Mind* draws all of its consequences from the linguistic concepts of synchrony and diachrony and elicits from them a general conception of the relationships between structure and event. The question is to know whether this same relation is found to be identical through the entire range of mythical thought.

Lévi-Strauss delights in repeating a statement of Boas: ". . . it would seem that mythological worlds have been built up, only to be shattered again, and that new worlds were built from the fragments" (p. 21).[15] This statement had already served as epigraph to one of the articles collected in *Structural Anthropology* (p. 206). It is this inverse relationship between the synchronic solidity and the diachronic fragility of mythological universes that Lévi-Strauss illuminates through the comparison to *bricolage*.

The *bricoleur*, in contrast to the engineer, works with a material he has not produced with its present use in mind; he works with a limited and varied repertory which forces him to work, as one says, with the means at hand. This repertory is made up of the remains of previous constructions and destructions; it represents the contingent state of instrumentality at a

of the great civilizations of Europe and Asia there is a remarkable absence of anything which might have reference to totemism, even in the form of remains. The reason is surely that the latter have elected to explain themselves by history and that this undertaking is incompatible with that of classifying things and beings (natural and social) by means of finite groups" (p. 232).

15. This remark is taken from Boas' Introduction to James Teit, "Traditions of the Thompson River Indians of British Columbia," *Memoires of the American Folklore Society*, VI (1898), 18.

given moment. The *bricoleur* works with signs which have already been used and which thus act as a "preconstraint" in regard to new reorganizations. Like *bricolage,* the myth "addresses [it]self to a collection of oddments left over from human endeavours, that is, only a sub-set of the culture" (*The Savage Mind,* p. 19). In terms of event and structure, of diachrony and synchrony, mythical thought forms a structure from the remains and the debris of events. By building its palaces from the odds and ends of anterior social discourse, it offers an inverse model of science, which gives the form of a new event to its structures:

> Mythical thought, that "bricoleur," builds up structures by fitting together events, or rather the remains of events, while science, "in operation" simply by virtue of coming into being, creates its means and results in the form of events, thanks to the structures which it is constantly elaborating and which are its hypotheses and theories (p. 22).

Of course, Lévi-Strauss opposes myth and science only to bring them back together, for, he says:

> Mythical thought for its part is imprisoned in the events and experiences which it never tires of ordering and re-ordering in its search to find them a meaning. But it also acts as a liberator by its protest against the idea that anything can be meaningless with which science at first resigned itself to a compromise (*ibid.*).

But it remains that the sense is on the side of the current arrangement, of synchrony. This is why these societies are so vulnerable to events. As in linguistics, the event is threatening, or at least upsetting, and in any case is a purely contingent interference (hence demographic upheavals—wars, epidemics—which alter the established order): "the synchronic structures of so-called totemic systems [are] extremely vulnerable to the effects of diachrony. . . ." (p. 67). The myth's instability thus becomes a sign of the primacy of synchrony. This is why so-called totemism is "a grammar fated to degenerate into a lexicon" (p. 232).

> The classification tends to be dismantled like a palace swept away upon the flood, whose parts, through the effect of currents and stagnant waters, obstacles and straits, come to be combined in a manner other than that intended by the architect. In totemism, therefore, function inevitably triumphs over structure. The problem it has never ceased presenting to theorists is that of the

relation between structure and event. And the great lesson of totemism is that the form of the structure can sometimes survive when the structure itself succumbs to events (*ibid.*).

Mythical history is itself in the service of the struggle of structure against events and represents an effort of societies to annul the disturbing action of historical factors; it represents a tactic of annulling history, of deadening the effect of events. Thus, by making history and its nontemporal model reciprocal reflections, by situating the ancestor outside of history and by making history a copy of the ancestor, "diachrony, in some sort mastered, collaborates with synchrony without the risk of further conflicts arising between them" (p. 236). It is the function of ritual to join this past that is outside of time to the rhythm of life and the seasons and to the chain of generations. Rites "pronounce on diachrony but they still do so in terms of synchrony since the very fact of celebrating them is tantamount to changing past into present" (p. 237).

It is in this perspective that Lévi-Strauss interprets the *churinga*—objects in stone or in wood or pebbles representing the ancestor's body—as the confirmation of "the diachronic essence of diachrony at the very heart of synchrony" (*ibid.*). He finds in them the same savor of historicity that we find in our archives: the being-incarnate of eventfulness, pure history confirmed at the heart of the classificatory mind. In this way mythical history is itself enlisted in the work of rationality:

> . . . so-called primitive peoples have managed to evolve not unreasonable methods for inserting irrationality, in its dual aspect of logical contingence and emotional turbulence, into rationality. Classificatory systems thus allow the incorporation of history, even and particularly that which might be thought to defy the system (p. 243).

IV. THE LIMITS OF STRUCTURALISM?

I HAVE INTENTIONALLY FOLLOWED in Lévi-Strauss's work the series of transpositions from the linguistic model to its ultimate generalization in *The Savage Mind*. The consciousness of the validity of a method, I stated in the beginning, is inseparable from the consciousness of its limits. These limits appear to me to be of two kinds: on the one hand, it seems to me that the passage to *the* savage mind is made by favor of an example that is already too favorable, one which is perhaps an exception rather than an example. On the other hand, the passage from a structural science to a structuralist philosophy seems to me to be not very satisfying and not even very coherent. These two extreme passages, whose effects reinforce each other, give the book a singular character, at once seductive and provoking, which distinguishes it from the preceding ones.

Is the example exemplary, I asked above. While I was reading *The Savage Mind* of Lévi-Strauss, I was also involved in Gerhard von Rad's remarkable book, *Theology of the Historical Traditions of Israel,* the first volume of his *Theology of the Old Testament.*[16] Here we find ourselves confronting a theological conception exactly the inverse of that of totemism and which, because it is the inverse, suggests an inverse relationship between diachrony and synchrony and raises more urgently the problem of the relationship between structural comprehension and hermeneutic comprehension.

What is decisive in understanding the core of meaning of the Old Testament? Not nomenclatures or classifications, but founding events. If we limit ourselves to the theology of the Hexateuch, the signifying content is a kerygma, the sign of the action of Jahweh, constituted by a complex of events. It is a *Heilgeschichte.* The first sequence is given in the series: deliverance from Egypt, crossing the Red Sea, the revelation on Sinai, wandering in the desert, reaching the Promised Land, etc. A second nucleus is formed around the theme of Israel as the chosen people and the Davidic mission; finally, a third nucleus of sense is established after the catastrophe: the destruction appears here as a fundamental event opening upon the unresolved alternatives of the promise and the threat. The method of understanding to be applied to this complex of events consists in recreating the *intellectual activity* born of this historical faith and unfolding within a confessional framework which is often in the form of a hymn and always a cultural manifestation. Gerhard von Rad says it very well: "Historical investigation searches for a critically assured minimum—the kerygmatic picture tends towards a theological maximum" (p. 108). Now, it is indeed an intellectual activity which presided over this elaboration of traditions and led to what we now call Scripture. Gerhard

16. Gerhard von Rad, *Theology of the Old Testament,* Vol. I: *Theology of the Historical Traditions of Israel* (London, 1962), translated from the German by D. M. G. Stalker.

von Rad shows how, starting from a minimal confession, a gravitational field was constituted for diverse traditions, belonging to different sources, transmitted by different groups, tribes, or clans. Thus Abraham's saga, that of Jacob, that of Joseph, belonging to cycles of different origins, were in some sense taken into and internalized by the primitive core of the confession of faith celebrating the historical action of Yahweh. As we see, we can speak here of a primacy of history, and this in multiple senses: in a first sense, a basic sense, since all Yahweh's relations to Israel are signified through and in events without any trace of speculative theology—but also in two other senses, which we stated at the beginning. The theological work upon these events is in effect itself an ordered history, an interpreting tradition. The reinterpretation, for each generation, of the foundation of traditions confers a historical character upon this understanding of history and gives rise to a development possessing a signifying unity which cannot be projected into a system. We are confronting a historical interpretation of the historical; the very fact that here sources are juxtaposed, schisms maintained, and contradictions exposed has a profound sense: the tradition corrects itself through additions, and these additions themselves constitute a theological dialectic.

It is remarkable, moreover, that through this work of reinterpreting its own traditions Israel assumed an identity which is itself historical, because critical work shows that there was probably no unity in Israel before the regrouping of the clans, after settlement, in a kind of amphictyony. By interpreting its history historically, by elaborating this history as a living tradition, Israel projected itself into the past as a single people, to whom occurred, as to an indivisible totality, the deliverance from Egypt, the revelation on Sinai, the wandering in the desert, and the gift of the Promised Land. The single theological principle toward which the entire thought of Israel tends is then: this was Israel, the people of God, which always acts as a unit and which God treats as a unit. But this identity is inseparable from an endless search for a meaning to history and in history: "this Israel, of which the Old Testament presentations of history have so much to say, is the object of faith, and the object of a history constructed by faith" (p. 118).

The three historicities are linked in the following way. After the historicity of the founding events—or *hidden time*, after the historicity of the living interpretation of sacred writers—which constitutes *tradition*, we now have the historicity of understanding, the *historicity of hermeneutics*. Gerhard von Rad uses the word *Entfaltung*, "unfolding" or "development," to designate the task of a theology of the Old Testament which respects the threefold historical character of the *heilige Geschichte* (the level of the founding events), the *Überlieferungen* (the level of constituting traditions), and finally the identity of Israel (the level of constituted tradition). This theology must respect the precedence of event over system:

> Hebrew thinking is thinking in historical traditions; that is, its main concern is with the proper combination of traditions and their theological interpretation, and in the process historical grouping always takes precedence over intellectual and theological grouping (p. 116).

Gerhard von Rad concludes his methodological chapter in these terms:

> But it would be fatal to our understanding of Israel's witness if we were to arrange it from the outset on the basis of theological categories which, though current among ourselves, have absolutely nothing to do with those on whose basis Israel herself allowed her theological thinking to be ordered (p. 121).

From this moment on, "retelling" (*wiedererzählen*) remains the most legitimate form of discourse on the Old Testament. The *Entfaltung* of hermeneutics is the repetition of the *Entfaltung* which presided over the elaboration of the traditions of the biblical base.

What are the results of this for the relations between diachrony and synchrony? One thing struck me concerning the great symbols of Hebrew thought which I dealt with in *The Symbolism of Evil*, and concerning myths—for example, those of the Creation and the Fall—built on the primary symbolic level: these symbols and these myths do not exhaust their meaning in arrangements homologous to social arrangements. I do not say that they do not lend themselves to the structural method; I am even convinced of the contrary. I say that the structural method does not exhaust their meaning, for their meaning is a reservoir of meaning ready to be used again in other structures. You might say this to me: it is precisely this revising which constitutes *bricolage*. Not at all: *bricolage* works with debris; in *bricolage* the structure saves the event; the debris plays the role of a preconstraint, of a message already transmitted. It has the inertia of something presignified: the reuse of biblical symbols in our cultural domain rests, on the contrary, on a semantic richness, on a surplus of what is signified, which opens toward new interpretations. If one considers from this perspective the series constituted by the Babylonian narrations of the Flood and by the chain of rabbinical and Christological reinterpretations, it is immediately evident that these renewals represent the inverse of *bricolage*. One can no longer speak of utilizing remains in structures where syntax is of more weight than semantics; we must speak, rather, of utilizing a surplus, which itself orders, as an initial giving of sense, the rectifying intentions of a properly theological and philosophical character which are applied to this symbolic base. In these ordered series, starting from a network of signifying events, it is the initial *surplus* of meaning which *motivates* tradition and interpretation. This is why, in this case, one must speak of semantic regulation by the content and not simply of structural regulation, as in the case of totemism. The structuralist explanation triumphs in synchrony ("The system is given, synchronically . . ." [*The Savage Mind*, p. 66]). This is why it is at ease with those societies where synchrony is strong and diachrony disturbing, as in linguistics.

I recognize full well that structuralism does not confront this problem empty-handed, and I admit that "if the structural orientation survives the shock, it has, after each upheaval, several means of re-establishing a system, which may not be identical with the earlier one but is at least formally of the same type" (p. 68). In *The Savage Mind* one finds examples of such a remodeling or perseverance of the system:

> If, for the sake of argument, we suppose an initial point at which the set of systems was precisely adjusted, then this network of systems will react to any change affecting one of its parts like a motor with a feed-back device: governed (in both senses of the word) by its previous harmony, it will direct the discordant mechanism towards an equilibrium which will be at any rate a compromise between the old state of affairs and the confusion brought in from outside (p. 68).

Thus the structural regulation is much closer to the phenomenon of inertia than to the living reinterpretation which seems to us to characterize true tradition. It is because semantic regulation proceeds from the excess of potential meaning over its use and function inside the given synchronic system that the hidden time of symbols can carry the twofold historicity—of tradition, which transmits and sediments the interpretation, and of interpretation, which maintains and renews the tradition.

If our hypothesis is valid, the remodeling of structures and the overdetermination of contents are two different conditions of diachrony. One might ask if this is not the combination, in different degrees and perhaps in inverse proportions, of those two general conditions which allow individual societies—according to a remark of Lévi-Strauss himself—to "work out a single scheme which allowed them to combine the standpoint of structure with that of event" (p. 70). But when this combination is built, as was stated above, on the model of a feedback mechanism, it is just a "compromise between the old state of affairs and the confusion brought in from outside" (p. 68). Tradition betrothed to duration and capable of being reincarnated in different structures depends more, it seems to me, on the overdetermination of the contents than on the remodeling of the structures.

This discussion leads us to question the adequacy of the linguistic model and the import of the ethnological submodel borrowed from the system of denominations and classifications commonly termed totemic. This ethnological submodel has a privileged position in relation to totemism. The same requirement of differential variation dwells in both of them. What structuralism elicits from both are "codes suitable for conveying messages which can be transposed into other codes, and for expressing messages received by means of different codes in terms of their own system" (p. 75). But if it is true, as the author sometimes admits, that "in the bounds of the great civilizations of Europe and Asia there is a remarkable absence of anything which might have reference to totemism, even in the form of remains" (p. 232), has one the right, at the risk of falling into a "totemic illusion" of a new kind, to identify, with *the* savage mind in general, a type which is perhaps exemplary only because it occupies an extreme position in a chain of mythical types, which would have to be understood by the other pole as well? I would be willing to think that in the history of humanity the exceptional survival of Jewish kerygma in constantly changing sociocultural contexts represents the other pole, exemplary of mythical thought as well because it is an extreme.

In this chain of types, thus bounded by their two poles, temporality—that of tradition and that of interpretation—has a different aspect according to whether synchrony takes the lead over diachrony or the opposite. At one extreme, that of the totemic type, we have a broken temporality, which verifies Boas' assertion rather well: "it would seem that mythological worlds have been built up, only to be shattered again, and that new worlds were built from the fragments" (p. 21; cf. *Structural Anthropology*, p. 206). At the other extreme, where we find the kerygmatic type, we have a temporality governed by the continual reappraisal of meaning inside an interpreting tradition.

If this is so, can one even continue to speak of myth without the risk of equivocalness? One can indeed grant that in the totemic model, where structures are more important than contents, the myth tends to be identified with an "operator," with a "code" which governs a system of transformation. This is how Lévi-Strauss defines it:

> The mythical system and the modes of representation it employs serve to establish homologies between natural and social conditions or, more accurately, it makes it possible to equate significant contrasts found on different planes: the geographical, meteorological, zoological, botanical, technical, economic, social, ritual, religious, and philosophical (*The Savage Mind*, p. 93).

The myth's function, thus presented in terms of structure, appears in synchrony; its synchronic solidity is indeed the inverse of the diachronic fragility which Boas' statement recalled.

In the kerygmatic model the structuralist explanation is doubtless enlightening, as I will attempt to show in my conclusion, but it represents a secondary level of expression, subordinated to the surplus of meaning found in the symbolic substratum. Thus the Adamic myth is second in relation to the elaboration of the symbolic expressions of the pure and the impure, of wandering and exile, formed at the level of cultic and penitential experience. The richness of this symbolic substratum appears only in diachrony. The synchronic point of view reaches, then, only the current social function of the myth, more or less comparable to the totemic operator, which earlier assured the convertibility of afferent messages at each level of cultural life and assured the mediation between nature and culture. Structuralism is undoubtedly still valid (the proof of its fruitfulness is respect to our cultural areas still remains to be given; to this end, the example of the Oedipus myth in *Structural Anthropology*, pp. 213–19, is very promising). While the structuralist explanation seems to encompass almost everything when synchrony takes the lead over diachrony, it provides us only a kind of skeleton, whose abstract character is apparent, when we are faced with an overdetermined content, a content which does not cease to set us thinking and which is made explicit only through the series of recoveries by which it is both interpreted and renewed.

I should like now to say a few words about the second crossing of the limit we mentioned above, the passage from a structural science to a structuralist philosophy. Structural anthropology seems to me to be convincing as long as it understands itself as the extension, by degrees, of an explanation which was first successful in linguistics, then in systems of kinship, and finally extending, little by little, by the play of affinities with the linguistic model, to all forms of social life. By the same token, it seems to me suspect when it sets itself up as a philosophy. An order posited as unconscious can never, to my mind, be more than a stage abstractly separated from an understanding of the self by itself; order in itself is thought located outside itself. Of course, "the day may come when all the available documentation on Australian tribes is transferred to punched cards, and with the help of a computer their entire techno-economic, social, and religious structures can be shown to be like a vast group of transformations" (*The Savage Mind*, p. 89). Indeed, this day may come, but on the condition that thought does not become alienated from itself in the objectivity of the codes. If the decoding is not the objective stage of the deciphering and the latter an existential—or *existentiell*—episode of the comprehension of self and of being, structural thought remains a thought which does not think itself. In return, it is up to a reflective philosophy to understand itself as a hermeneutics, so as to create the receptive structure for a structural anthropology. In this respect, it is the function of hermeneutics to make the understanding of the other—and of his signs in various cultures—coincide with the understanding of the self and of being. Structural objectivity can then appear as an abstract moment—and validly abstract— of the appropriation and the recognition through which abstract reflection becomes concrete reflection. At the limit, this appropriation and this recognition would consist in a total recapitulation of all the signifying contents in a knowledge of self and of being, as Hegel attempted—in a logic which would be that of contents, not that of syntaxes. It goes without saying that we can produce only fragments, known to be partial, of this exegesis of self and of being. But structural comprehension is no less partial, in the sense that it does not proceed from a recapitulation of the signified but only reaches its "logical level . . . by semantic impoverishment" (p. 105).

Lacking this receptive structure, which for my part I conceive as the mutual joining of reflection and hermeneutics, structuralist philosophy seems to me to be condemned to oscillate between several rough outlines of philosophies. It could be called at times a Kantianism without a transcendental subject, even an absolute formalism, which would found the very correlation between nature and culture. This philosophy is motivated by the consideration of the duality of "true models of concrete diversity: one on the plane of nature, namely that of the diversity of species, and the other on the cultural plane provided by the diversity of functions" (p. 124). The principle of the transformations can then be sought in a combination, in a finite order or in the finitude of order, more fundamental than each of the models. All that is said of the "unconscious teleology, which, although historical, completely eludes human history" (p. 252) corroborates this view. This philosophy would make the linguistic model an absolute, following its gradual generalization. "For language," the author declares,

> does not consist in the analytical reason of the old style grammarians nor in the dialectic constituted by structural linguistics nor in the constitutive dialectic of individual *praxis* facing the practico-inert, since all three presuppose it. Linguistics thus presents us with a dialectical and totalizing entity but one outside (or beneath) consciousness and will. Language, an unreflecting totalization, is human reason which has its reasons and of which man knows nothing (p. 252).

But what is language if not an abstraction of the speaking being? Here one objects that "his discourse never was and never will be the result of a conscious totalization of linguistic laws" (*ibid.*). We answer by saying that linguistic laws are not what we attempt to totalize in order to understand ourselves; rather, we are concerned with the meaning of the words, for which linguistic laws serve as the instrumental mediation, forever unconscious. I seek to understand myself by taking up anew the meaning of the words of all men; it is on this plane that hidden time becomes the historicity of tradition and of interpretation.

But at other moments the author invites us to "recognize the system of natural species and that of manufactured objects as two mediating sets which man employs to overcome the opposition between nature and culture and think of them as a whole" (p. 127). He holds that structures precede practices, but he allows that praxis precedes structures. Henceforth, it appears that the structures are the superstructures of this praxis, which, for Lévi-Strauss as for Sartre, "constitutes the fundamental totality for the sciences of man" (p. 130).[17] Besides the outline of a transcendentalism without a subject, we thus find in *The Savage Mind* the sketch of a philosophy in which structure plays the role of mediator, placed "between *praxis* and practices" (p. 130). But it cannot stop there, under the penalty of conceding to Sartre all that was refused him by refusing to sociologize the *cogito* (p. 249). This sequence: *praxis–structure–practices* allows one at least to be a structuralist in ethnology and a Marxist in philosophy. But what kind of Marxism is this?

There is, in fact, in *The Savage Mind* the sketch of a very different philosophy, where the order is the order of things and a thing itself. A meditation on the notion of "species" naturally leads in this direction: isn't the species—that of vegetable and animal classifications—a "presumptive objectivity"? "[The] diversity of species furnishes man with the most intuitive picture at his disposal and constitutes the most direct manifestation he can perceive of the ultimate discontinuity of reality. It is the sensible expression of an objective coding" (p. 137). It is indeed the privilege of the notion of species to "furnish a mode of sensory apprehension of a combination objectively given in nature, and that the activity of the mind, and social life itself, do no more than borrow it to apply it to the creation of new taxonomies" (*ibid.*).

Perhaps the consideration of the notion of structure alone prevents us from going beyond a "reciprocity of perspectives, in which man and the world mirror each other" (p. 222). It seems, then, to be by an unjustified *coup de force* that, after having pushed the pendulum to the side of the primacy of praxis over structural mediations, one stops it at the other pole and declares

17. See also pp. 130–31: "Marxism, if not Marx himself, has too commonly reasoned as though practices followed directly from *praxis*. Without questioning the undoubted primacy of infrastructures, I believe that there is always a mediator between *praxis* and practices, namely the conceptual scheme by the operation of which matter and form, neither with any independent existence, are realized as structures, that is as entities which are both empirical and intelligible. It is to this theory of superstructures, scarcely touched on by Marx, that I hope to make a contribution. The development of the study of infrastructures proper is a task which must be left to history—with the aid of demography, technology, historical geography and ethnography. It is not principally the ethnologist's concern, for ethnology is first of all psychology."

"the ultimate goal of the human sciences to be not to constitute but to dissolve man . . . , [to be] the reintegration of culture in nature and finally of life within the whole of its physico-chemical conditions" (p. 247). "As the mind too is a thing, the functioning of this thing teaches us something about the nature of things: even pure reflection is in the last analysis an inter-nalization of the cosmos" (p. 248 n.). The final pages of the book would have us understand that we must look for the principle of the mind's functioning as a thing in "a universe of information where the laws of savage thought reign once more" (p. 267).

Such are the structuralist philosophies among which struc-tural science does not allow us to choose. But would it not be just as much in keeping with the teachings of linguistics if one held that language, and all the mediations for which it serves as a model, was the unconscious instrument by means of which a speaking subject can attempt to understand being, beings, and himself?

V. Hermeneutics and Structural Anthropology

In concluding, I want to return to the initial question: in what sense are structural considerations today a necessary stage of any hermeneutic comprehension? More generally, how are hermeneutics and structuralism joined, one to the other?

1. I would first like to dissipate a misunderstanding that the previous discussion may occasion. By suggesting that myth-ical types form a chain in which the "totemic" type would form one extreme and the "kerygmatic" type another extreme, I ap-pear to have gone back on my initial statement, according to which structural anthropology is a scientific discipline and hermeneutics a philosophical discipline. This is not the case. To distinguish two submodels is not to say that one is dependent on structuralism and that the other would come under the direct jurisdiction of a nonstructural hermeneutics. I only wish to show that the totemic submodel better tolerates a structuralist explanation which is all-inclusive because totemism is, among all the mythical types, the one which has the greatest affinity for the initial linguistic model. In the kerygmatic type, however, the structuralist explanation—which generally has not yet been attempted—more clearly refers to another way of apprehending meaning. But the two ways of understanding are not species,

opposing one another on the same level inside the common genus of comprehension; this is why they require no methodological *eclecticism*. I want, then, before attempting some exploratory remarks concerning their connection, to stress one last time their unevenness. The structuralist explanation bears (1) on an unconscious system which (2) is constituted by differences and oppositions (by signifying variations) (3) independently of the observer. The interpretation of a transmitted sense consists in (1) the conscious recovery of (2) an overdetermined symbolic substratum by (3) an interpreter who places himself in the same semantic field as the one he is understanding and thus enters the "hermeneutic circle."

This is why the two ways of revealing time are not on the same level; it is only by reason of a provisional dialectic concern that we spoke of the priority of diachrony over synchrony. Truly speaking, the expressions "diachrony" and "synchrony" must be reserved for the explanatory schema in which synchrony forms a system and diachrony forms a problem. I will reserve the term "historicity"—historicity of tradition and historicity of interpretation—for any understanding which implicitly or explicitly knows itself to be on the road of the philosophical understanding of self and of being. In this sense, the Oedipus myth arises from hermeneutic understanding when the myth is understood and taken up again—as was already the case for Sophocles—as a primordial appeal for meaning, giving rise to a meditation on self-recognition, the struggle for truth, and "tragic knowledge."

2. The joining of these two comprehensions raises more problems than their differentiation. The question is too new to allow us to go beyond exploratory remarks. Can the structuralist explanation, we might ask first, be separated from *all* hermeneutic comprehension? Doubtless it can be, insofar as the function of myth is exhausted in the establishment of homologous relations between the significant contrasts located on several levels of nature and culture. But then doesn't hermeneutic comprehension have recourse to the very constitution of the semantic field where the homologous relations are operating? This brings to mind Lévi-Strauss's important remark concerning the "split representation that pertains to the symbolic function" (*Structural Anthropology*, p. 62). The "contradiction" of this sign can be neutralized, he said, only "in the exchange of complementary values, to which all social existence is reduced" (*ibid.*). In this remark I see the indication of a path to follow, leading to the union of hermeneutics and structuralism, which would in no

way be an eclecticism. I know full well that the split at issue here is the split that engenders the function of sign in general and not the double meaning of the symbol as we understand it. But what is true of the sign in its primary sense is even truer of the double meaning of symbols. The comprehension of this double meaning, an essentially hermeneutic comprehension, is always presupposed by the comprehension of "the exchange of complementary values" (*ibid.*) put into operation by structuralism. A careful examination of *The Savage Mind* suggests that at the base of structural homologies one can always look for semantic analogies which render comparable the different levels of reality whose convertibility is assured by the "code." The "code" presupposes a correspondence, an affinity of the contents, that is, a cipher.[18] Thus, in interpreting the rites of eagle-hunting in the Hidatsa tribe (pp. 52–53), the constitution of the high-low pair, from which are formed all the differences, including the maximum differences between the hunter and his game, provides a mythological typology only on the condition of an implicit comprehension of the surcharge of sense of the high and the low. I grant that in the systems studied here this affinity of the contents is in some sense residual—residual, but not null. This is why structural comprehension is never without a degree of hermeneutic comprehension, even if the latter is not thematized. A good example to consider is the homology between marriage rules and food prohibitions (pp. 100–108); the analogy between eating and marrying, between fasting and chastity, constitutes a metaphorical relation anterior to the operation of transformation. Here, too, structuralism is not at a loss: it too speaks of metaphor (p. 105), but in order to formalize it into a

18. The value of ciphers is first perceived in feelings. Reflecting on the aspects of concrete logic, Lévi-Strauss shows that they "can be observed in the course of ethnographic enquiry. Both an affective and intellectual aspect become apparent" (*The Savage Mind*, p. 37). Taxonomy unfolds its logic against the background of a feeling of kinship between men and beings: "This disinterested, attentive, fond and affectionate lore acquired and transmitted through the attachments of marriage and upbringing" (*ibid.*) the author finds also in circus people and the employees of zoological gardens (p. 38). If "taxonomy and warmest affection" (*ibid.*) are the common emblem of the so-called primitive and of the zoologist, is it not necessary to distinguish this comprehension from feeling? Moreover, the comparisons, correspondences, associations, blendings, and symbolizations which occupy the following pages (pp. 38–44) and which the author does not hesitate to compare to hermeticism and emblematicism, places correspondences—the cipher—at the origin of the homologies between differential variations belonging to different levels, thus to the origin of the code.

conjunction by complementarity. It nevertheless remains that here the apprehension of similitude precedes formalization and founds it. This is why this similitude must be reduced in order to bring out the structural homology:

> The connection between them is not casual but metaphorical. Sexual and nutritional relations are at once associated even today. . . . But how is this fact and its universality to be explained? Here once again the logical level is reached by semantic impoverishment: the lowest common denominator of the union of the sexes and the union of the eater and eaten is that they both effect a *conjunction by complementarity* (pp. 105–6).

It is always at the price of such a semantic impoverishment that the "logical subordination of resemblance to contrast" (p. 106) is obtained. Here psychoanalysis, taking up the same problem, will follow, instead, the thread of analogical cathexes and will take sides with a semantics of contents and not with a syntax of arrangements.[19]

3. The joining of a philosophically oriented interpretation to the structural explanation must now be taken in the other sense; I let it be understood from the beginning that the latter was today the necessary detour, the stage of scientific objectivity along the path of recovering meaning. In a statement which is symmetrical to, and the inverse of, the preceding one, I assert that there is no recovery of meaning without some structural comprehension. Why? We can once more consider the example

---

19. A notable consequence follows the intolerance of the logic of contrasts in regard to universality: totemism—although termed "so-called totemism"—is resolutely preferred to the logic of sacrifice (pp. 223–28), whose "fundamental principle is that of substitution" (p. 296), that is, something foreign to the logic of totemism, which "consists in a network of differentiation between terms posited as discontinuous" (*ibid.*). Sacrifice appears then as "an *absolute* or *extreme* operation which relates to an *intermediary* object," the victim (p. 225). Why extreme? Because the sacrifice *breaks* the relation between man and the divinity by destroying it, in order to release the concession of grace which *will fill* the void. Here the ethnologist no longer describes, he judges: "The system of sacrifice, on the other hand, makes a non-existent term, divinity, intervene; and it adopts a conception of the natural series which is false from the objective point of view, for, as we have seen, it represents it as continuous" (pp. 227–28). Between totemism and sacrifice, it must be said: "one is true, and the other is false. Rather, to put it precisely, the classificatory systems belong to the levels of language: they are codes which, however well or badly made, aim always to make sense. The system of sacrifice, on the other hand, represents a private discourse wanting in good sense for all that it may be frequently pronounced" (p. 228).

of Judeo-Christian symbolism, this time no longer in its origin but at its extreme point of development, that is, at a point where it manifests both its greatest exuberance, its greatest intemperance, and its highest organization—in the twelfth century; of this century, so rich in explorations of every kind, Father Chenu has given us an authoritative description in his work *Théologie au XII° siècle.*[20] This symbolism is expressed alike in the Quest of the Grail, in the stone images and animal forms worked into the porches and cornices, in the allegorizing exegesis of Scripture, in rite and in speculations about liturgy and the sacraments, in meditations on the Augustinian *signum* and the Dionysian *symbolum,* and on the *analogia* and *anagogē* which follow from them. Between the cathedral as a book of stone images and the entire literature of the *Allegoriae* and the *Distinctiones* (those rich storehouses of the relations among meanings, grafted onto the words and the invocations of Scripture) there is a unity of intention which constitutes what the author himself calls a "symbolic mentality" (chap. VII) at the origin of "symbolic theology" (chap. VIII). Now, what *holds together* the multiple and exuberant aspects of this mentality? The people of the twelfth century "did not confuse," the author says, "either levels or objects; rather, they benefited on these diverse levels from a common denominator in the subtle play of analogies, in accordance with the mysterious relation of the physical world to the sacred world" (p. 160). This problem of the "common denominator" is unavoidable if one considers that an isolated symbol has no meaning; or rather, an isolated symbol has too much meaning; *polysemy* is its law: "the fire warms, illuminates, purifies, burns, regenerates, consumes; it signifies concupiscence as well as the Holy Spirit" (p. 184). It is in an economy of the whole that differential values are separated out and polysemy is dammed up. It was in this search for a "mystical coherence of the economy" (*ibid.*) that the symbolists of the Middle Ages were involved. In nature everything is a symbol, certainly; but for the man of the Middle Ages nature speaks only when revealed by a historical typology instituted in the confrontation of the two Testaments. The "mirror" (*speculum*) of nature becomes a "book" only in contact with the Book, that is, with an exegesis instituted within an ordered community. Thus, the symbol symbolizes only in an "economy," a *dispensatio,* an *ordo.* It is on this condition that Hugues de Saint-Victor could define it thus:

20. M.-D. Chenu, *La Théologie au XII° siècle* (Paris, 1957), pp. 159–210.

"symbolum est collatio, id est coaptatio, visibilium formarum ad demonstrationem rei invisibilis propositarum" ("a symbol is a bringing together, that is, a harmonizing of visible forms for the purpose of demonstrating things that have been stated about what is invisible"). We see that this "demonstration" is incompatible with a logic of propositions, which supposes definite concepts (concepts bounded by a notional and univocal contour), notions that signify something because they signify *one* thing; but this is not our concern here. What does concern us is the fact that it is only in an economy of the whole that this *collatio et coaptatio*—this bringing together and relating—can understand itself as a relation and can claim the rank of *demonstratio*. Here I reiterate Edmond Ortigues's thesis in *Le Discours et le symbole:* "A single term can be imaginary if one considers it absolutely, and symbolic if one understands it as a differential value, correlative to other terms which limit it reciprocally" (p. 194). "As one approaches the material imagination, the differential function diminishes, and one tends toward equivalences; as one approaches the formative elements of society, the differential function diminishes, and one tends toward distinctive valences" (p. 197). In this respect the stone figures and the animal forms of the Middle Ages are very close to images. This is indeed why they join, by means of their imaginary pole, images drawn from an undifferentiated substratum, imagery which can be Cretan as easily as Assyrian and which appears in turn exuberant in its variations and stereotyped in its conception. But if this system of stone figures and animal forms belongs to the same economy as allegorizing exegesis and speculation on signs and symbols, it is because the unlimited potential of the signification of images is differentiated by the operations of language which in fact constitute its exegesis. What then takes the place of polymorphic, naturalistic symbolism and dams up its wild proliferations is a typology of history exercised within the framework of the ecclesiastical community, in connection with a cult, a ritual, etc. It is by interpreting accounts, by deciphering a *Heilgeschichte,* that the exegete attributes to the image-maker a principle of choice in the exuberances of the imagery. It must then be said that the symbolic does not reside in this or that symbol and even less so in their abstract repertory. This repertory will always be too poor—for it is always the same images which return; and it will always be too rich—for each symbol signifies potentially all the others. The symbolic is rather between the symbols, as relation and as the economy of their relating. This system of symbolics is nowhere more apparent than in Christianity, where the natural symbolism is at once freed and ordered entirely in the light of the Word, made explicit only in a Recitative. There is no natural symbolism, no abstract or moralizing allegorism (the allegorism always being the counterpart of the symbolism, not only its requital but its fruit—to such an extent does the symbol consume its own physical, sensible, visible basis) without a historical typology. The symbolic resides, then, in this ordered play of natural symbolism, of abstract allegorism, and of historical typology: signs of nature, figures of virtues, Christ's acts, are mutually interpreted in this dialectic of the mirror and the book which is continued in every creature.

These considerations constitute the exact counterpart of the preceding remarks: no structural analysis, we said, without a hermeneutic comprehension of the transfer of sense (without "metaphor," without *translatio*), without that indirect giving of meaning which founds the semantic field, which in turn provides the ground upon which structural homologies can be discerned. In the language of our mediaeval symbolists—a language coming from Augustine and Denis and adapted to the exigencies of a transcendental object—what is primary is the translation, the transfer from the visible to the invisible by means of an image borrowed from sensible realities; what is primary is the semantic constitution under the form of the "similar-dissimilar" at the root of symbols or figures. Starting from this, a syntax of the arrangements of signs on multiple levels can be abstractly elaborated.

But, in turn, neither is there any hermeneutic comprehension without the support of an economy, of an order in which the symbol signifies. Taken by themselves, symbols are threatened by their oscillation between sinking into the imaginary and evaporating in allegorism; their richness, their exuberance, their polysemy expose naïve symbolists to intemperance and to complacency. What Saint Augustine in the *De doctrina christiana* already called *verborum translatorum ambiguitates*,[21] what we call simply equivocalness in regard to the demand for univocity in logical thought, makes symbols symbolize only within wholes which limit and link their significations.

Henceforth, the understanding of structures is no longer outside an understanding whose task would be to *think* by start-

21. Cited by Chenu, p. 171.

ing from symbols; today this understanding of structures is the necessary intermediary between symbolic naïveté and hermeneutic comprehension.

It is with this remark, which leaves the last word to the structuralist, that I should like to end, so that both our attention and our expectation remain open in his behalf.

The Problem of Double Meaning
as Hermeneutic Problem
and as Semantic Problem

THIS PRESENTATION is intended to be interdisciplinary in scope. I will attempt to study several ways of approaching a single problem, symbolism, and to reflect upon the signification of the diversity of these approaches. I like to grant philosophy the role of arbitrator, and I have previously attempted to arbitrate the conflict of several hermeneutics in modern culture: the hermeneutics which demystifies and the hermeneutics which recovers meaning.[1] This is not the problem that I intend to take up again here; rather, I wish to consider a different problem, occasioned by a different kind of split. The approaches to symbolism which I propose to bring face to face represent different *strategic levels*. I will consider two and even a third strategic level and will take hermeneutics as a single strategic level, that of *texts*. This level will be confronted with the semantics of linguists, but this semantics itself includes two different strategic levels. First is the level of *lexical* semantics, which is often called simply "semantics" (for example, by Stephen Ullmann or P. Guiraud). It is maintained at the level of words or, rather, as Ullmann proposes, of names, of the process of nomination or denomination. But before our eyes a *structural* semantics is being constituted as well, characterized, among other things, by a change of level and a change of unit, by the passage from molar units of communication, such as words and

Translated by Kathleen McLaughlin.
1. See *La Symbolique du mal* (Paris: Aubier, 1960). English translation by Emerson Buchanan, *The Symbolism of Evil* (Boston: Beacon Press, 1969).

[62]

a fortiori texts, to molecular units, considered to be the basic structures of signification.

I propose to examine what becomes of our problem of symbolism when it is transferred from one level of consideration to the other. Certain problems which I had the opportunity to discuss under the title "Structure and Hermeneutics" [2] will turn up again, but perhaps under more favorable conditions; for the risk of conflict that occurs at the same level between a *philosophy* of interpretation and a structural *science* can be averted by a method which places at different levels of realization the meaning effects being considered.

Broadly speaking, I want to show that the change of scale of the problem causes the appearance of the atomic *constitution* which alone permits a scientific treatment of the problem; the path of *analysis,* the decomposition into smaller units, is the very path of science, as one sees in the use of the analytic process in automatic translation. In turn, I would also like to show that the reduction to simple elements sanctions the elimination of a fundamental function of symbolism which can appear only at the higher level of *manifestation* and which places symbolism in relation with reality, with experience, with the world, with existence (I am intentionally leaving the choice open among these terms). In short, I would like to establish that the way of analysis and the way of synthesis do not coincide, are not equivalent: by way of analysis one discovers the *elements* of signification, which no longer have any relation to the things said; by way of synthesis is revealed the function of signification, which is to *say* and finally to *"show."*

I. THE HERMENEUTIC LEVEL

IN ORDER TO CARRY OUT OUR INQUIRY, it is important to be sure that it is the same problem which is treated on three different levels. This problem I have termed the problem of *multiple meaning.* By this I designate a certain meaning effect, according to which one expression, of variable dimensions, while signifying one thing at the same time signifies *another* thing without ceasing to signify the first. In the proper sense of

2. See, above, "Structure and Hermeneutics."

the word, it is the allegorical function of language (*all-ēgoreō:* "while saying one thing to say another thing").

What defines hermeneutics, at least in relation to the other strategic levels which we are going to consider, is first of all the length of sequences with which it works and which I call texts. It was first in the exegesis of biblical texts and then secular ones that the idea of a hermeneutics, conceived as a science of the rules of exegesis, was constituted. Here the notion of text has a precise and limited meaning. Dilthey, in his great article "Die Entstehung der Hermeneutik," said: "We call exegesis or interpretation the art of comprehending vital manifestations fixed in a durable fashion"; and again: "The art of comprehending gravitates around the interpretation of human testimonies preserved by writing"; and yet again: "We call exegesis, interpretation, the art of comprehending the written manifestations of life." Now, in addition to a certain length in relation to the minimal sequences with which the linguist likes to work, the text includes the internal organization of a work, a *Zusammenhang,* an internal connection. The first achievement of modern hermeneutics was to posit as a rule that one proceed from the whole to the part and the details, to treat, for example, a biblical pericope as a linking or—to use Schleiermacher's terms—as the relationship between an internal form and an external form.

For the interpreter, it is the text which has a multiple meaning; the problem of multiple meaning is posed for him only if what is being considered is a whole in which events, persons, institutions, and natural or historical realities are articulated. It is an entire "economy," an entire signifying whole, which lends itself to the transfer of meaning from the historical to the spiritual level. In the entire mediaeval tradition of the multiple meanings of Scripture, it is through great wholes that the quadruple meaning is articulated.[3]

Today this problem of multiple meaning is no longer simply the problem of exegesis in the biblical or even in the secular sense of the word; it is rather an interdisciplinary problem, which I wish to consider first on a single strategic level, on a homogeneous plane—that of the text. The phenomenology of religion, after the fashion of Van der Leeuw and, to a certain extent, after the fashion of Eliade, Freudian and Jungian psychoanalysis (I am not distinguishing between them here), literary criticism ("New" or not), allows us to generalize the

3. H. de Lubac, *L'Exégèse médiévale: Les quatre sens de l'Ecriture,* 4 vols. (Paris, 1953–65).

notion of text to signifying wholes of a different degree of complexity than that of sentences. I will consider here only one example, sufficiently removed from biblical exegesis so as to give an idea of the fullness of the hermeneutic field. The dream is treated by Freud as a *narration,* which can be extremely brief but which always has an internal multiplicity; according to Freud, it is a question of substituting for this narration, unintelligible at the first hearing, a more meaningful text, which would be to the first as the latent is to the patent. There is thus a vast area of double meaning, whose internal connections clearly set forth the diversity of hermeneutics.

Now, what causes the diversity of these various hermeneutics? For one thing, they reflect differences in technique: psychological decipherment is one thing, biblical exegesis is another. The difference here depends on the internal rules of interpretation; it is an epistemological difference. But these differences of technique in turn refer back to different intents concerning the function of interpretation: it is one thing to use hermeneutics as a weapon of suspicion against the "mystification" of false consciousness; it is another thing to use it as a preparation for a better understanding of what once made sense, of what once was said.

Now, the very possibility of divergent and rival hermeneutics—on the level of technique and on the level of intent—is related to a fundamental condition which, to my mind, characterizes the entire strategic level of the various hermeneutics, and it is this fundamental condition which now holds our attention. It consists in the following: that symbolics is the means of expressing an extralinguistic reality. This is of the greatest importance for the subsequent confrontation; anticipating an expression which will take on its precise meaning only on another strategic level, I will say that in hermeneutics there is no closed system of the universe of signs. While linguistics moves inside the enclosure of a self-sufficient universe and encounters only intrasignificant relations—relations of mutual interpretation between signs (to use the vocabulary of Charles Sanders Peirce)—hermeneutics is ruled by the open state of the universe of signs.

My aim is to show that this rule of the open state is connected to the very scale on which interpretation, understood as exegesis, operates and that the closing of the linguistic universe is accomplished only by a change of scale and by the consideration of small signifying units.

What do we mean here by "open state"? In each hermeneutic discipline, interpretation is at the hinge between linguistics and nonlinguistics, between language and lived experience (of whatever kind). What causes the specific character of various hermeneutics is precisely that this *grip* of language on being and of being on language takes place according to different modes. Thus, dream symbolism can in no way be a simple play of meanings, referring back and forth among themselves; it is the milieu of expression where desire is uttered. For my part, I have proposed the notion of a semantics of desire in order to designate this interweaving of two kinds of relations: relations of force, expressed in a dynamics, and relations of meaning, expressed in an exegesis of meaning. Symbolism occurs because what is symbolizable is found initially in nonlinguistic reality, which Freud terms instinct, considered in its affective and representative agents. It is these emissaries and their derivatives that are revealed and hidden in the meaning effects we call symptoms, dreams, myths, ideals, illusions. Far from moving in a closed linguistic circle, we are ceaselessly at the juncture of the erotic and the semantic. The power of the symbol is due to the fact that double meaning is the mode in which the very ruse of desire is expressed.

The same thing is true at the other end of the hermeneutic scale: if there is some sense in speaking of a hermeneutics of the sacred, it lies in the degree to which the double meaning of a text which, for example, in telling me about the Exodus, opens onto a certain state of wandering which is lived existentially as a movement from captivity to deliverance. Under the summons of a word which gives what it ordains, the double meaning aims here at deciphering an existential movement, a certain ontological condition of man, by means of the surplus of meaning attached to the event which, in its literalness, is situated in the observable historical world. Here, double meaning is the means of detecting a condition of being.

In this way, symbolism, taken at the level of manifestation in texts, marks the breakthrough of language toward something other than itself—what I call its *opening*. This breakthrough is *saying;* and saying is showing. Rival hermeneutics conflict not over the structure of double meaning but over the mode of its opening, over the finality of showing. This is the strength and the weakness of hermeneutics; its weakness because, taking language at the moment when it escapes from its enclosure, it takes it at the moment when it also escapes a scientific treatment, which can begin only by postulating the closed system of the signifying universe. All other weaknesses flow from this one, and first and foremost the conspicuous weakness of delivering hermeneutics over to the warfare of rival philosophical projects. But this weakness is also its strength, because the place where language escapes from itself and escapes us is also the place where language comes to itself, the place where language is *saying.* Whether I understand the relation of showing-hiding as a psychoanalyst or as a phenomenologist of religion (and I think that today these two possibilities must be assumed together), the understanding is in each case like a force which *discovers,* which manifests, which brings to light, a force which language utilizes and becomes itself. Then language becomes *silent* before what it says.

I will venture to summarize this in a few words: the sole philosophical interest in symbolism is that it reveals, by its structure of double meaning, the equivocalness of being: "Being speaks in many ways." Symbolism's *raison d'être* is to open the multiplicity of meaning to the equivocalness of being.

The remainder of this investigation aims at discovering why this grip on being is related to the scale of discourse which we have called the text and which is realized as dream or hymn. This is something we do not know yet but will learn through comparisons with other approaches to the problem of double meaning, where the change of scale will be marked at once by progress toward scientific rigor and by the disappearance of this ontological function of language which we have called *saying.*

II. LEXICAL SEMANTICS

THE FIRST CHANGE OF SCALE is the one which makes us consider *lexical units.* Part of the Saussurean heritage is on this level, but only part of it. Indeed, we shall later consider the work that begins with the application of phonological analysis to semantics and which, to do this, requires a much more radical change of scale, since the lexemes, as they are called, are still on the level of the manifestation of discourse, as were the large units we considered earlier. Nevertheless, a certain kind of description and even a certain explanation of symbolism can be carried out at this first level.

First, a description. The problem of multiple meaning can in fact be limited in lexical semantics to polysemy, that is, to the possibility for a name (I am adopting S. Ullmann's terminology)[4] to have more than one meaning. It is possible to describe this meaning effect in the Saussurean terms of "signifier" and "signified" (Ullmann's "name" and "sense"). Thus, the relation to the thing is already excluded, although Ullmann does not make a final choice between the illustration in Ogden Richard's "basic triangle"—symbol-referent-reference—and the Saussurean analysis into two levels. (Later we will see why: the closed system of the linguistic universe is not yet complete at this level.)

We will continue the description in Saussurean terms, distinguishing a "synchronic" definition and a "diachronic" definition of double meaning. The synchronic definition: in a given state of language, the same word has several meanings; strictly speaking, polysemy is a synchronic concept. In diachrony, multiple meaning is called a change of meaning, a transfer of meaning. Of course, the two approaches must be combined in order to take a global view of the problem of polysemy at the lexical level; for in polysemy, changes of meaning are considered in their synchronic dimension, that is to say, the old and the new are contemporaneous in the same system. Moreover, these changes of meaning are to be taken as guides in disentangling the synchronic skein. A semantic change, in turn, always appears as an alteration in a preceding system; if one does not know the place of a meaning in a system state, one has no notion of the nature of the change which affects the value of this meaning.

Finally, we can extend the description of polysemy further along Saussurean lines by considering the sign no longer as the internal relation between a signifier and a signified, between a name and a meaning (this was necessary in order to formally define polysemy), but in its relation to other signs. This recalls the principle of the *Course in General Linguistics*:[5] treat signs as differences within a system. What becomes of polysemy if we place it in this perspective, which is that of structural linguistics? Some light is shed initially on what can be called the functional character of polysemy. But this is only an initial clarification, for we remain on the level of language [*la langue*], while the symbol is a function of speaking [*la parole*], that is, an expres-

4. Stephen Ullmann, *The Principles of Semantics* (New York: Philosophical Library, 1957).

5. Ferdinand de Saussure, *Course in General Linguistics,* trans. Wade Baskin (New York: Philosophical Library, 1959).

sion in discourse. But, as Godel has shown in the *Sources manuscrites du "Cours de linguistique générale,"* [6] as soon as one considers the "mechanism of language," one remains in an intermediate position between system and execution. It is at the level of the mechanism of language that the rule of ordered polysemy, which is that of ordinary language, is discovered. This phenomenon of ordered or limited polysemy is at the crossroads of two processes: the first originates in the sign, considered as "accumulative intention." Left to itself, it is a process of expansion which continues to the point of a surplus charge of meaning (overload), as we see in certain words which, because they signify too many things, cease to signify anything, or in certain traditional symbols which have taken on so many contradictory values that they tend to neutralize one another (the fire that burns and warms, the water that both quenches thirst and drowns). In contrast, there is also a process of limitation exercised by the rest of the semantic field and first of all by the structuring of certain organized fields, like those studied by Jost Trier, the author of the theory of semantic fields. Here we are still on Saussurean ground, for a sign does not have, or is not, a fixed signification but a value in opposition to other values; it results from the relation between an identity and a difference. This regulating, which arises from the conflict between the semantic expansion of signs and the limiting action of the field, is similar in its effects to the organization of a phonological system, although it differs profoundly from the latter in its mechanism. In fact, the difference between the organization of a semantic field and that of a phonological system is considerable. Far from having a merely differential, and hence oppositional, function, the values are also cumulative; and this makes polysemy one of the prime problems in semantics, perhaps the central one. Here we touch upon what is specific to the semantic level and what allows the phenomenon of double meaning. Urban has remarked that what makes language an instrument of knowledge is precisely the fact that a sign can indicate one thing without ceasing to indicate another thing and thus that, in order to have an expressive value in regard to the second, it must be constituted as a sign of the first. And he added this: "The 'accumulated intention' of words is the fruitful source of ambiguity, but it is also the

6. Robert Godel, *Sources manuscrites du "Cours de linguistique générale" de Ferdinand de Saussure* (Geneva and Paris: Droz-Minard, 1957).

source of that analogous predication through which alone the symbolic power of language comes into being." [7]

Urban's penetrating remark gives us a glimpse of what could be called the functionality of polysemy. What appeared to us at the level of texts as a particular sector of discourse, namely, the sector of plurivocity, now seems to us to be grounded in a general property of lexical units, namely, to function as accumulators of meaning, as a switch operating between the old and the new. It is in this way that double meaning can take on an expressive function with regard to realities signified in an indirect manner. But how does this occur?

Here again Saussure can guide us by means of his distinction between two axes of speech [*langage*] function (actually, here he is no longer speaking of language [*langue*] as a system of signs at a given moment but of the mechanism of language or discourse, which goes along with speaking [*la parole*]). In the spoken chain, he remarked, signs are in a double relation: in a syntagmatic relation, which links opposing signs in a relation *in praesentia*, and in an associative relation, which compares signs which are similar and thus have the capacity to be substituted for one another, but compares them only in a relation *in absentia*. This distinction, as we know, has been revived by Roman Jakobson,[8] who formulates it in similar terms: the "concatenation relation" and the "selection relation." This distinction is of great importance for the investigation of the problem of semantics in general and of symbolism in particular. Indeed, it is the combined play of these two axes—concatenation and selection—that makes up the relation between syntax and semantics.

Now, with Jakobson, we have assured a linguistic status not only for semantics but for symbolism as well. The axis of substitutions is in fact the axis of similarities, while the axis of concatenations is the axis of contiguities. It is thus possible to make correspond to the Saussurean distinction a distinction formerly confined to rhetoric, the distinction between metaphor and metonymy; or, rather, it is possible to assign to the polarity of metaphor and metonymy the more general functional sense of a polarity between two processes and to speak of the metaphoric process and the metonymic process.

7. Ullmann, *Principles of Semantics*, p. 117.
8. Roman Jakobson, *Essais de linguistique générale* (Paris: Editions de Minuit, 1963), chap. 2.

Here we touch a root of the same process of symbolization which earlier we reached directly as an effect of the text. Here we grasp its mechanism in what we can now call an effect of context. Let us look once more at the functioning of ordered polysemy, which we considered earlier with field theory at the level of language. Then it was a question of limited polysemy; ordered polysemy is properly a meaning effect produced in discourse. When I speak, I realize only a part of the potential signified; the rest is erased by the total signification of the sentence, which operates as the unit of speaking. But the rest of the semantic possibilities are not canceled; they float around the words as possibilities not completely eliminated. The context thus plays the role of filter; when a single dimension of meaning passes through by means of the play of affinities and reinforcements of all analogous dimensions of other lexical terms, a meaning effect is created which can attain perfect univocity, as in technical languages. It is in this way that we make univocal statements with multivocal words by means of this sorting or screening action of the context. It happens, however, that a sentence is constructed so that it does not succeed in reducing the potential meaning to a monosemic usage but maintains or even creates a rivalry among several ranges of meaning. Discourse can, by various means, realize *ambiguity,* which thus appears as the combination of a lexical fact—polysemy—and a contextual fact—the possibility allowed to several distinct or even opposed values of a single name to be realized in the same sequence.

Let us take our bearings at the end of this second part. What have we gained by transposing in this way onto the lexical level problems encountered on the hermeneutic level? What have we gained, and what have we lost?

We have certainly gained a more precise knowledge of symbolism: it now appears to us to be a meaning effect, observable on the level of discourse but constructed on the base of a more elementary function of signs. This function was in turn traced back to the existence of an axis of language other than the linear axis, along which are found the successive and contiguous series arising from syntax. Semantics and, in particular, the problems of polysemy and metaphor assumed their rightful place in linguistics. By receiving a determined linguistic status, the process considered receives a functional value. Polysemy is thus not in itself a pathological phenomenon, nor is symbolism an ornament of language; polysemy and symbolism are part of the constitution and the functioning of *all* language.

Such are the achievements in the area of description and function, but the inclusion of our problem on the linguistic level has another side as well: semantics can indeed be included in linguistics, but at what price? At the price of keeping the analysis within the enclosure of the linguistic universe. This we have not made apparent, but we see it clearly if we include some traits of Jakobson's analysis omitted in the previous account. In order to justify the intrinsically linguistic character of semantics, Jakobson compares Saussure's views on associative relations (in his terms, the axis of substitutions) to the views of Charles Sanders Peirce on the remarkable power of signs to be mutually interpreted. This is a notion of interpretation that has nothing in common with exegesis: every sign, according to Peirce, requires, in addition to two protagonists, an interpretant. The function of the interpretant is filled by another sign or group of signs which develops the meaning of the first sign and which can be substituted for the sign being considered. This notion of an interpretant, in Peirce's sense, joins the Saussurean notion of a substitutive group, but at the same time it reveals the place of this notion inside an intralinguistic play of relations. Every sign, we say, can be translated by another sign in which it is developed more fully; this includes definitions, equational predications, circumlocutions, predicative relations, and symbols. But by saying this, what have we done? We have resolved a semantical problem by means of the metalinguistic function, that is, according to another of Jakobson's studies, which deals with the multiple functions included in communication, by means of a function that relates a sequence of discourse to the code and not to the referent. That this is the case is evident in the fact that when Jakobson advocates the structural analysis of the metaphoric process (which, we will remember, has been assimilated to the group of operations which utilize resemblances on the axis of substitutions), it is as a metalinguistic operation that he develops his analysis of the metaphoric process. It is insofar as the signs intersignify among themselves that they enter into relations of substitution and so make the metaphoric process possible. In this way, semantics and its problem of multiple meaning remain inside the closed system of language. It is not by chance that the linguist here invokes the logician: "Symbolic logic," notes Jakobson, "has not ceased to remind us that linguistic meanings constituted by the system of analytic relations of one expression to

other expressions does not presuppose the presence of things." [9]
There is no better way of stating that a more rigorous treatment
of the problem of double meaning has been paid for by abandoning its aim toward things. At the end of part I, we said that the
philosophical import of symbolism is that in symbolism the
equivocalness of being is conveyed by means of the multivocity
of our signs. We now know that the science of this multivocity—
the science of linguistics—requires that we remain within the
enclosure of the universe of signs. Does this not indicate a
particular relation between the *philosophy* of language and the
science of language, between hermeneutics as philosophy and
semantics as science?

This is an articulation we will specify by a new change of
scale—to structural semantics as it is practiced not only in applied linguistics (for example, in automatic translation) but also
in theoretical linguistics, in all the work that is today included
under the heading of structural semantics.

III. Structural Semantics

Three methodological choices, according to Grei-
mas,[10] direct structural semantics. From the outset this discipline
adopts the axiom of the closed state of the linguistic universe.
By virtue of this axiom, semantics is governed by the metalinguistic operations of translating one order of signs into another
order of signs. But while in Jakobson the relation between the
structures of the language object and those constituted by
metalanguage is unclear, here the hierarchical levels of language
are very clearly articulated. First, there is the language object,
then the language in which the elementary structures of the
preceding level are described, next the language in which the
operant concepts of this description are elaborated, and finally
the language in which we state axioms and define the preceding
levels. By means of this clear view of the hierarchical levels
of language within the enclosure of linguistics, the postulate
of this science is better illustrated, namely, that the structures
built on the metalinguistic level are the same as the structures
which are immanent in language. The second postulate or

9. *Ibid.*, p. 42.
10. A. J. Greimas, *La Sémantique structurelle* (Paris: Larousse, 1966).

methodological choice concerns the change of strategic level of the analysis; one takes as a reference not words (lexemes) but underlying structures, constituted wholly for the needs of analysis.

I can give here only a minimal idea of this enterprise; it is a question of working with a new unit of value, the seme, which is always found in a relation of binary opposition of the type long-short, breadth-depth, etc., but at a more basic level than lexical units. No seme, no semic category, even if its denomination is borrowed from ordinary language, is identical to a lexeme appearing in discourse. We are no longer dealing with object terms but with relations of conjunction and disjunction: disjunction into two semes (for example, masculine-feminine), conjunction under a single trait (for example, gender). Semic analysis consists in establishing for a group of lexemes the hierarchical tree of conjunctions and disjunctions which constitute it entirely. We can see the advantage of this analysis for applied linguistics: binary relations can be calculated in a system of base 1 (0,1), and the conjunctions-disjunctions lend themselves to processing by machines of a cybernetic type (open circuit, closed circuit).

But this analysis benefits theory as well, for semes are units of meaning constructed from their relational structures alone. The ideal is to reconstruct the whole lexical level from a much smaller number of these elementary structures of meaning. If it were successful—this is not a superhuman endeavor—the object terms would be defined wholly, in an exhaustive analysis, as a collection of semes containing only conjunctions-disjunctions and hierarchies of relations—in short, as semic systems.

The third postulate is that the units which we know as lexemes in descriptive linguistics and which we employ as words in discourse belong to the level of the *manifestation of discourse* and not to the level of *immanence*. Words—to use ordinary language—have a mode of presence other than the mode of existence of these structures. This point is of the greatest importance for our investigation, for what we considered as multiple meaning and as symbolic function is a "meaning effect" which is manifested in discourse but whose principle is situated at a different level.

The entire effort of structural semantics will be to reconstruct, bit by bit, the relations that allow us to account for these meaning effects, following an increasing complexity. I will retain here only two points of this reconstruction. First, it is possible to take up once more, with an unequaled degree of precision and rigor, the problem of multiple meaning, taken as a lexical property, and the problem of symbolic function in units greater than words, let us say, in sentences. Structural semantics attempts to account for the semantic richness of words by means of a highly original method which consists in matching the variants of meaning to classes of contexts. The variants of meaning can then be analyzed in a fixed nucleus, which is common to all the contexts, and in contextual variables. If we place this analysis inside the framework of operational language, by reducing lexemes to a collection of semes, we can then define the variable meaning effects of a word as derivatives of semes—or of sememes—arising from the conjunction of a semic nucleus and of one or several contextual semes, which are themselves semic classes corresponding to contextual classes.

What was necessarily imprecise in our preceding analysis, namely, the notion of semantic possibility, now takes on a precise analytic character. We can transcribe every meaning effect into formulas containing only conjunctions, disjunctions, and hierarchical relations and can thus localize precisely the contextual variable which brings about the meaning effect. Likewise we can account, with a much greater degree of precision and rigor, for the role played by the context, which we first described in rather vague terms as a screening action or as the play of affinities between certain dimensions of meaning of the various words in a sentence. We can now speak of a sorting among contextual variables; to employ Greimas's example, in "The dog barks," the contextual variable "animal" common to "dog" and to "barks" allows us to eliminate the meanings of the word "dog" that would refer not to an animal but to a thing[11] and, likewise, the meanings of the word "barks" that might, for example, apply to a man. The sorting action of the context thus consists in a reinforcement of semes on the basis of reiteration.

As we see in this analysis of contextual function, we find once more the same problems we dealt with in the second part, but they are now approached with a precision that an analytical instrument alone can provide. The theory of context is, in this respect, quite striking; by making the stability of the meaning in a sentence depend on the reiteration of the same semes, we can rigorously define what can be termed the isotopy of a

---

11. [Here, Ricoeur's example is an idiomatic usage of the French word *chien* in the expression *le chien du fusil,* "the hammer of a gun."— TRANS.]

discourse, that is, its elaboration at a homogeneous level of meaning; we can say that "The dog barks" is a statement about an animal.

It is starting from this concept of the isotopy of discourse that the problem of symbolism can also be studied with the same analytical methods. What happens in the case of an equivocal or plurivocal discourse? The following: the isotopy of discourse is not assured by the context; rather, the context, instead of filtering a series of isotopic sememes, allows the development of several semantic series belonging to discordant isotopies.

It seems to me that the conquest of this deliberately and radically analytic level allows us to better understand the relations between the three strategic levels which we have successively occupied. We worked first as exegetes with vast units of discourse, with texts, then as lexical semanticians with the meaning of words, i.e., with names, and then as structural semanticians with semic constellations. Our change of level has not been in vain; it marks an increase in rigor and, if I may say so, in scientific method. We have progressively approached the Leibnizian ideal of a universal characteristic. It would be false to say that we have eliminated symbolism; rather, it has ceased to be an enigma, a fascinating and possibly mystifying reality, to the extent that it invites a twofold explanation. It is first of all situated in relation to multiple meaning, which is a question of lexemes and thus of language. In this respect, symbolism in itself possesses nothing remarkable; all words used in ordinary language have more than one meaning. Bachelard's "fire" is no more extraordinary in this respect than any word in the dictionary. Thus the illusion that the symbol must be an enigma at the level of words vanishes; instead, the possibility of symbolism is rooted in a function common to all words, in a universal function of language, namely, the ability of lexemes to develop contextual variations. But symbolism is related to discourse in another way as well: it is in discourse and nowhere else that equivocalness exists. Discourse thus constitutes a particular meaning effect: planned ambiguity is the work of certain contexts and, we can now say, of texts, which construct a certain isotopy in order to suggest another isotopy. The transfer of meaning, the metaphor (in the etymological sense of the word), appears again, but this time as a change of isotopy, as the play of multiple, concurrent, superimposed isotopies. The notion of isotopy has thus allowed us to assign the place of metaphor in language with greater precision than did the notion of the axis of substitutions, borrowed by Jakobson from Saussure.

But then, I ask you, does the philosopher not find his stake in the question at the end of this journey? Can he not legitimately ask why in certain cases discourse cultivates ambiguity? The philosopher's question can be made more precise: ambiguity, to do what? Or rather, *to say what?* We are brought back to the essential point here: the closed state of the linguistic universe. To the extent that we delved into the density of language, moved away from its level of manifestation, and progressed toward sublexical units of meaning—to this very extent we realized the closed state of language. The units of meaning elicited by structural analysis signify nothing; they are only combinatory possibilities. They say nothing; they conjoin and disjoin.

There are, then, two ways of accounting for symbolism: by means of what constitutes it and by means of what it attempts to say. What constitutes it demands a structural analysis, and this structural analysis dissipates the "marvel" of symbolism. That is its function and, I would venture to say, its mission; symbolism works with the resources of all language, which in themselves have no mystery.

As for what symbolism attempts to say, this cannot be taught by a structural linguistics; in the coming and going between analysis and synthesis, the going is not the same as the coming. On the return path a problematic emerges which analysis has progressively eliminated. Ruyer has termed it "expressivity," not in the sense of expressing emotion, that is, in the sense in which the speaker expresses himself, but in the sense in which language expresses something, says something. The emergence of expressivity is conveyed by the heterogeneity between the level of discourse, or level of manifestation, and the level of language, or level of immanence, which alone is accessible to analysis. Lexemes do not exist only for the analysis of semic constellations but also for the synthesis of units of meaning which are understood immediately.

It is perhaps the emergence of expressivity which constitutes the marvel of language. Greimas puts it very well: "There is perhaps a mystery of language, and this is a question for philosophy; there is no mystery in language." I think we too can say that there is no mystery in language; the most poetic, the most "sacred," symbolism works with the same semic variables as the most banal word in the dictionary. But there is a mystery *of* language, namely, that language speaks, says something, says something about being. If there is an enigma of symbolism, it resides wholly on the level of manifestation, where the equivocalness of being is spoken in the equivocalness of discourse.

Is not philosophy's task then to ceaselessly reopen, toward the being which is expressed, this discourse which linguistics, due to its method, never ceases to confine within the closed universe of signs and within the purely internal play of their mutual relations?

Structure, Word, Event

THE AIM OF THIS COMMENTARY is to return the current discussion on structuralism to its place of origin—the science of language or linguistics. There we will have an opportunity to shed light on the debate and at the same time move beyond it. For it is there that we can glimpse the validity of structural analysis and the limits of this validity.

1. I wish to show that the type of intelligibility that is expressed in structuralism prevails in every case in which one can: (a) work on a corpus already constituted, finished, closed, and, in that sense, dead; (b) establish inventories of elements and units; (c) place these elements or units in relations of opposition, preferably binary opposition; and (d) establish an algebra or combinatory system of these elements and opposed pairs.

The aspect of language which lends itself to this inventory I will designate *a language* [*langue*]; the inventories and combinations which this language yields I will term *taxonomies;* and the model which governs the investigation I will call *semiotics.*

2. I next wish to show that the very success of this undertaking entails (as a counterpart) an elimination from structural thinking of any understanding of the acts, operations, and processes that constitute discourse. Structuralism leads to thinking in an antinomic way about the relation between language and speech. I will make the *sentence* or *utterance* [*énoncé*] the pivot of this second investigation. I will call *semantics* the model which governs our understanding of the sentence.

Translated by Robert Sweeney. This translation appeared originally in *Philosophy Today*, Volume XII, no. 2/4 (Summer, 1968), pages 114-29, and is reproduced here by permission of *Philosophy Today*.

3. Lastly, I would like to make a survey of inquiries that henceforth will escape the structuralist model—at least in the form defined below in Part I—and which will proclaim a new understanding of operations and processes; this new understanding will be situated beyond the antinomy between structure and event, between system and act, to which our structuralist investigation will have led us.

In this context I will have something to say about Chomsky's linguistics, known as "generative grammar," which signals the end of structuralism conceived of as a science of taxonomies, closed inventories, and already settled combinations.

But above all I would like to sketch out a reflection on the *word,* which is the place in language where this exchange between structure and event is constantly produced. Hence the title of my exposition, in which the word has been placed as a third term between the structure and the event.

Such an investigation presupposes a quite fundamental notion: that language is composed of a hierarchy of levels. All linguists say this, but many weaken their affirmation by submitting all the levels to the same method, for example, to the method which has succeeded on the phonological level, where one is actually dealing with limited and closed entities, with entities defined by the single test of commutation, with relations of binary opposition, and finally with rigorous combinations between discrete units. The problem is to know whether all the levels are homologous. My whole study will rest on the idea that the passage to the new unit of discourse constituted by the sentence or utterance represents a break, a mutation, in the hierarchy of levels. Moreover, I shall not exhaust the question of levels; I shall even suggest at the end that there are perhaps other strategic levels, such as the text, whose internal linking requires another sort of intelligibility than the sentence and the word in sentence position. It is with these larger units of order of the text that an ontology of the *logos* or of saying would find its place; if language has some hold on being, it is on the level of manifestation or efficiency, the laws of which are original with respect to previous levels.

In short, the linking of methods, points of view, and models is a consequence of the hierarchy of levels in the work of language.

I. THE PRESUPPOSITIONS OF STRUCTURAL ANALYSIS

I WILL CONCERN MYSELF less with the results than with the presuppositions which constitute linguistic theory, in the epistemologically strong meaning of the word theory. Saussure, the founder of modern linguistics, noted these presuppositions but stated them in a language that often remained considerably behind the new conceptualization that he introduced; it is Louis Hjelmslev who theorized about these presuppositions in his *Prolegomena to a Theory of Language,* published in 1943. He is the first to have enunciated them in a treatment [*discours*] that is entirely homogeneous with its object. Let us enumerate these presuppositions:

1. Language is an object for an empirical science; empirical is taken here in the modern sense; it designates not solely the role and primacy of observation but also the subordination of inductive operations to deduction and the calculus.

This possibility of constituting language as a specific object of a science was introduced by Saussure himself in his famous distinction between a language [*la langue*] and speech [*la parole*]. By relegating to speech the psychophysiological execution, the individual performance, and the free combinations of discourse, Saussure reserves to a language the rules constituting the code, the institution that is valid for the linguistic community, the collection of entities among which the choice of the free combinations of discourse takes place. Thus, a homogeneous object is isolated: everything which concerns a language falls, in effect, within the same domain, while speech is dispersed among the domains of psychophysiology, psychology, sociology and does not seem to be able to constitute the unique object of a specific discipline.

2. Within a language itself we must still distinguish between a science of states of system, or synchronic linguistics, and a science of changes, or diachronic linguistics. Here again Saussure led the way by declaring emphatically that the two approaches cannot be conducted simultaneously and that, moreover, it is necessary to subordinate the second to the first. Pushing Saussure's thesis to its most radical form, Hjelmslev says: "Behind every process one should be able to find a system." This second presupposition opens up a new range of intelligibility: change, considered as such, is unintelligible. We understand it only as

the passage from one state of system to another, which is what the word diachrony signifies; it is therefore to the system, that is, to the arrangement of elements in a simultaneous grouping, that we give priority in understanding.

3. In a state of system there are no absolute terms, only relations of mutual dependence. As Saussure expressed it, "language is not a substance but a form."[1] And, if the intelligible form par excellence is opposition, then, again with Saussure, "in language there are only differences" (p. 120). This means that we need not consider the meanings attached to isolated signs as labels in a heteroclite nomenclature; what we are to consider are only the relative, negative, oppositive values of signs with respect to each other.

4. The collection of signs must be maintained as a closed system in order to submit it to analysis. This is evident on the level of phonology, which establishes the finite inventory of phonemes of a given language; but it is true also on the lexical level, which, as we can see in a unilingual dictionary, is immense but not infinite. But we can understand it better if we succeed in substituting, for this practically innumerable list, the finite inventory of subsigns that underlie our lexicon and beginning from which one could reconstitute the immense richness of real lexicons. Finally, it is useful to recall that syntax is constituted by a finite system of forms and rules. If we add that, on a still higher level, linguistics always operates on a finite corpus of texts, we can formulate in a general fashion the axiom of closure that governs the work of analysis. Working thus at the interior of a closed system of signs, linguistics can consider that the system that it analyzes has no outside but only internal relations. It is in this way that Hjelmslev defines structure: *an autonomous entity of internal dependencies.*

5. The definition of the sign which satisfies these four presuppositions breaks entirely with the naïve idea that the sign is made to stand for a thing. If we have correctly separated language from speech, the states of system from the history of changes, the form from the substance, and the closed system of signs from all references to a world, we must define the sign not only by its relation of opposition to all other signs of the same level but also in itself as a purely internal or immanent difference. It is in this sense that Saussure distinguishes the sig-

1. Ferdinand de Saussure, *Course in General Linguistics*, trans. Wade Baskin (New York: Philosophical Library, 1959), p. 122.

nifying and the signified, and Hjelmslev, expression and content. This presupposition could be placed first, as Saussure does in his *Course in General Linguistics;* but, in the logical order of presuppositions, this definition of the sign serves only to sanction the set of anterior axioms. Under the rule of the closure of the universe of signs, the sign is either a difference between signs or a difference, internal to each sign, between expression and content. This two-sided reality falls entirely within the linguistic closure.

Structuralism can thus be defined as the complete awareness of the exigencies contained in this series of presuppositions. Of course, Saussure does not use the word "structure" but the word "system." The word "structure" appeared only in 1928 at the First International Congress of Linguists at the Hague, in the form "structure of a system." The word "structure" would appear then as a specification of the system and would designate the restrictive combinations, highlighted against the whole field of the possibilities of articulation and combination, which create the individual configuration of a language. But in the form of the adjective "structural," the word has become synonymous with system. The structural point of view is thus globally opposed to the genetic point of view. It gathers together at the same time the idea of synchrony (the priority of the state of a language over its history), the idea of organism (a language as a unity of wholes enveloping parts), and finally the idea of combination or of the combinatory (a language as a finite order of discrete units). Thus, from the expression "structure of a system," we have passed to the adjective "structural," to define the point of view which contains these diverse ideas, and finally to "structuralism," to designate the investigations which take the structuralist point of view as a working hypothesis, indeed as ideology and polemic.

II. Speech as Discourse

The triumph of the structural point of view is at the same time a triumph of the scientific enterprise. By constituting the linguistic object as an autonomous object, linguistics constitutes itself as science. But at what cost? Each of the axioms we have listed is both a gain and a loss.

The act of speaking is excluded not only as exterior execution, as individual performance, but as free combination, as producing new utterances. Now this is the essential aspect of language—properly speaking, its goal.

At the same time, history is excluded, and not simply the change from one state of system to another but the production of culture and of man in the production of his language. What Humboldt called production and what he opposed to the finished work is not solely diachrony, that is, the change and passage from one state of system to another, but rather the generation, in its profound dynamism, of the work of speech in each and every case.

The structural point of view also excludes, along with free combination and generation, the primary intention of language, which is to say something about something; speaker and hearer understand this intention immediately. For them language aims at something, or, more exactly, it has a double direction: an ideal direction (to say something) and a real reference (to say about something). In this movement, language leaps across two thresholds: the threshold of ideality of meaning and, beyond this meaning, the threshold of reference. Across this double threshold and by means of this movement of transcendence, language *"means"* [*veut dire*]; it has taken hold of reality and expresses the hold of reality on thought. Meillet already spoke of this: in language we must consider two things, its immanence and its transcendence. Today we would say: its immanent structure and the level of manifestation, where its effects of meaning are offered to the bite of the real. It is necessary then to balance the axiom of the closure of the universe of signs by attention to the primary function of language, which is to *say*. In contrast to the closure of the universe of signs, this function constitutes its openness or its opening.

These considerations—still general and unanalyzed—lead us to question the whole first supposition of the science of language, namely, that language is an object for an empirical science. That language is an object goes without saying, so long as we maintain the critical awareness that this object is entirely defined by the procedures, methods, presuppositions, and finally the structure of the theory which governs its constitution. But if we lose sight of this subordination of object to method and to theory, we take for an absolute what is only a phenomenon. Now the experience which the speaker and listener have of language comes along to limit the claim to absolutize this object. The experience we have of language reveals something of its mode of being which resists this reduction. For us who speak, language is not an object but a mediation. Language is that through which, by means of which, we express ourselves and express things. Speaking is the act by which the speaker overcomes the closure of the universe of signs, in the intention of saying something about something to someone; speaking is the act by which language moves beyond itself as sign toward its reference and toward what it encounters. Language seeks to disappear; it seeks to die as an object.

An antinomy begins to show itself here: on the one hand, structural linguistics starts from a decision of an epistemological character, viz., to remain inside the closure of the universe of signs. By virtue of this decision, the system has no outside; it is an autonomous entity of internal dependencies. But this is a methodological decision which does violence to linguistic experience. The task is then, on the other hand, to reclaim for the understanding of language what the structural model excluded and what perhaps is language itself as act of speech, as saying. It is necessary here to resist any intimidation, the veritable terrorism, which some nonlinguists impose, on the basis of a model naïvely extrapolated from the conditions of its functioning. The appearance of a "literature" which takes its own operations as its theme introduces the illusion that the structural model exhausts the understanding of language. But a "literature" thus conceived is itself an exception in the field of language; it includes neither science nor poetry, which in different ways take up the vocation of language as saying. The conjunction of structural linguistics and of a "literature" of the same name should itself be considered as a quite contingent event and as having very limited importance. The claim of some to demystify, as they put it, speech and saying ought itself to be demystified, as being noncritical and naïve.

Our task appears to me to be rather to go all the way with the antinomy, the clear conception of which is precisely the ultimate result of structural understanding. The formulation of this antinomy is today the condition for the return to an integral understanding of language; *to think* language should be to think the unity of that very reality which Saussure has disjoined, the unity of language and speech.

But how? The danger here is to set up a phenomenology of speech in opposition to a science of language, at the risk of falling again into psychologism or mentalism, from which structural linguistics has rescued us. To think correctly the antinomy between language and speech, it would be necessary to be able to produce the act of speech in the very midst of language, in the fashion of a setting-forth of meaning, of a dialectical production, which makes the system occur as an act and the structure as an event.

And this promotion, this production, this advance can be thought, if we undertake a precise understanding of the hierarchical levels of language.

We have said nothing about this hierarchy so long as we have simply superimposed two levels of articulation: phonological articulation and lexical articulation (indeed three levels, if we add syntactical articulation). We have not yet got beyond the point of view according to which a language is a taxonomy, a body of already emitted texts, a repertory of signs, an inventory of units, and a combinatory system of elements. The hierarchy of the levels of language includes something more than a series of articulated systems: phonological, lexical, and syntactic. We actually change levels when we pass from the units of a language to the new unit constituted by the sentence or the utterance. This is no longer the unit of a language, but of speech or discourse. By changing the unit, one also changes the function, or rather, one passes from structure to function. We then have the opportunity of encountering language as saying.

The new unit which we shall now consider is in no way semiological—if by this we understand everything concerning the relations of internal dependence between signs or components of signs. This large unit is properly semantic, if we take this word in its strong sense, which is not solely to signify in general but to say something, to refer the sign to the thing.

The utterance or sentence includes all the traits that underlie the antinomy between structure and event. By its own characteristics, the sentence attests that this antinomy does not oppose language to something other than itself but traverses it at its center, at the heart of its own accomplishment.

1. For discourse has an *act* as its mode of presence—the instance of discourse (Benveniste),[2] which, as such, is of the nature of an event. To speak is a present event, a transitory, vanishing act. The system, in contrast, is atemporal because it is simply potential.

---

2. ". . . we shall call 'instances of discourse' . . . the discrete and always unique acts by which a language is actualized in speech by a speaker" (Emile Benveniste, *Problems in General Linguistics,* trans. Mary E. Meek, Miami Linguistics Series, no. 8 [Coral Gables: University of Miami Press, 1971], p. 217).

2. Discourse consists in a series of *choices* by which certain meanings are selected and others excluded. This choice is the counterpart of a corresponding trait of the system—constraint.

3. These choices produce *new* combinations: to emit new sentences, to understand such sentences—such is the essence of the act of speaking and of comprehending speech. This production of new sentences in virtually infinite number has as its counterpart the finite and closed collection of signs.

4. It is in the instance of discourse that language has a reference. To speak is to say something about something. It is here that we again encounter Frege and Husserl. In his famous article "Über Sinn und Bedeutung" (expressions which Peter Geach and Max Black have translated as "sense" and "reference"), Frege showed precisely that the aim of language is double: the aim of an ideal sense or meaning (that is, not belonging to the physical or psychic world) and the aim of reference. If the meaning can be called inexistent, insofar as it is a pure object of thought, it is the reference—*Bedeutung*—which roots our words and sentences in reality. "We expect a reference of the proposition itself: it is the exigency of truth (*das Streben nach Wahrheit*) which drives (*treibt*) us to advance (*vordringen*) toward the reference." This advance of (ideal) meaning toward the (real) reference is the very soul of language. Husserl does not say anything different in his *Logical Investigations:* the ideal meaning is a void and an absence which demand to be fulfilled. By such fulfilling, language comes into its own, that is to say, dies to itself. Whether we distinguish, with Frege, between *Sinn* and *Bedeutung* or, with Husserl, between *Bedeutung* and *Erfüllung,* what we thus articulate is a signifying intention that breaks the closure of the sign, which opens the sign onto the other, in brief, which constitutes language as a saying, a saying something about something. The moment when the turning from the ideality of meaning to the reality of things is produced is the moment of the transcendence of the sign. This moment is contemporaneous with the sentence. It is on the level of the sentence that language says something; short of it, it says nothing at all. In fact, the double articulation of Frege is the source of predication, insofar as "to say something" designates the ideality of meaning and "to say about something" designates the movement of meaning to the reference.

It is not necessary, therefore, to oppose two definitions of the sign, the one as internal difference of the signifying and the signified, the other as external reference of sign to thing. There is no need to choose between these two definitions. One relates to the structure of the sign in the system, the other to its function in the sentence.

5. The last trait of the instance of discourse: the event, choice, innovation, reference also imply a specific manner of designating the subject of discourse. Someone speaks to someone —that is the essence of the act of communication. By this trait, the act of speech is opposed to the anonymity of the system. There is speech wherever a subject can take up in an act, in a single instance of discourse, the system of signs which a language puts at his disposal. This system remains potential as long as it is not actualized, realized, operated by someone who, at the same time, addresses himself to another. The subjectivity of the act of speech is from the beginning the intersubjectivity of an allocution.

Thus it is at the same level and in the same instance of discourse that language has a reference and a subject,[3] a world and an audience. It is not surprising, then, that reference to the world and self-reference are excluded together by structural linguistics as not constitutive of the system as such. But this exclusion is only the presupposition that must be set up in order to constitute a science of articulations. It no longer operates when it is a matter of attaining the level of effecting speech, where a speaker realizes his signifying intention relative to a situation and to an audience. Allocution and reference merge with act, event, choice, innovation.

III. STRUCTURE AND EVENT

HAVING ARRIVED AT THIS POINT, we might be tempted to let ourselves be split apart by the antinomy. Doubtless structuralism leads to that. But this journey by way of antinomy is not in vain: it constitutes the first level—the properly dialectical level—of a constituting thought. That is why, in a first phase, nothing else can be done than to reinforce this antinomy of the systematic and the historical and to oppose, term for term, the "event-ual" to the potential, choice to constraint, innovation to institution, reference to closure, allocution to anonymity.

3. The *subjective* implications of the instance of discourse are developed further in "The Question of the Subject: The Challenge of Semiology"; see below, pp. 236 ff.

But in a second phase it is necessary to explore new ways, to try to find new models of intelligibility, where the synthesis of the two points of view would be thinkable once again. It is a matter then of finding instruments of thought capable of mastering the phenomenon of language, which is neither structure nor event but the incessant conversion of one into the other in discourse.

This problem concerns language as syntax and as semantics. I will speak only briefly to the first point, reserving a return to it for a later study, and nothing of the second; for it is with it that I reach the problem aimed at by the title of this study: structure, *word*, event.

1. It is in the order of *syntax* that poststructuralist linguistics is now making spectacular progress. The Chomsky school in the United States is currently working on the notion of "generative grammar." Turning its back on the taxonomies of the original structuralism, this new linguistics concerns itself from the beginning with the sentence and the problem posed by the production of new sentences. At the beginning of *Current Issues in Linguistic Theory* Chomsky writes:

> The central fact to which any significant linguistic theory must address itself is this: a mature speaker can produce a new sentence of his language on the appropriate occasion, and other speakers can understand it immediately, though it is equally new to them. Most of our linguistic experience, both as speakers and hearers, is with new sentences; once we have mastered a language, the class of sentences with which we can operate fluently and without difficulty or hesitation is so vast that for all practical purposes (and, obviously, for theoretical purposes), we can regard it as infinite. Normal mastery of a language involves not only the ability to understand immediately an indefinite number of entirely new sentences, but also the ability to identify deviant sentences and, on occasion, to impose an interpretation on them . . . ; it is clear that a theory of language that neglects this "creative" aspect of language is of only marginal interest.[4]

A new concept of structure is thus required to take into account what Chomsky calls the grammar of a language. He defines it in these terms: "Grammar is a device which specifies the infinite set of well-formed sentences and assigns to each of these one or more structural descriptions" (*ibid.*, p. 9). Thus the

4. Noam Chomsky, *Current Issues in Linguistic Theory* (New York: Humanities Press, 1964), pp. 7–8.

traditional structural description, which is concerned with dead inventories, is the result of the assignment of a dynamic rule of generation which undergirds the competence of the reader [*lecteur*]. Chomsky continually opposes a generative grammar to the inventories of elements characteristic of the taxonomies favored by the structuralists. And we are led back to the Cartesians (Chomsky's latest book is titled *Cartesian Linguistics*) and to Humboldt, for whom language is not a product but production, generation.

In my understanding, this new conception of structure as a regulated dynamism will overcome the original structuralism. It will overcome it by integrating it, by situating it exactly at its own level of validity. I will return to this problem in a later study. But I wish to speak now of someone who has a real kinship with this new development in linguistics. I have in mind the great but too little recognized French linguist, Gustave Guillaume. Guillaume's theory of morphological systems—that is, the parts of speech—is a kind of generative grammar. His studies on the article and on the tenses of the verb show how the task of discourse is to put words in a sentence position. What we call parts of speech—the categories of noun, verb, etc.—have as their function to complete, to terminate, to close the word in such a way as to insert it into the sentence, into discourse. By placing the word in a sentence position, the system of categories allows our words and our discourse to be applied to reality. More particularly, the noun and the verb are parts of speech thanks to which our signs are in a certain sense "returned to the universe" under the aspect of space and of time. By completing the word as noun and verb, these categories render our signs capable of grasping the real and keep them from closing up in the finite, closed order of a semiology.

But morphology fulfills this function only because the science of discourse and of systems such as those of the article, the verb, etc., is a science of operations and not a science of elements. And let no one raise the charge of mentalism. This accusation, which inhibits too many investigators, is valid against a psychologism of the image and of the concept, against the claim of psychic contents accessible to introspection alone. It is foolish when directed against operations. Here, too, it is necessary to know how to escape more or less terroristic prohibitions.

More than anything else, recourse to Guillaume at this point in our investigation helps break down a prejudice and bridge a lacuna. The prejudice is this: we readily think of syntax as the most interior form of language, as the completion of the self-sufficiency of language. Nothing is more false. Syntax does not assure the division of language, which has already been accomplished by the constitution of the sign in the closed and taxonomic system. Because it relates to discourse and not to language, syntax is on the path of the return of the sign toward reality. That is why the parts of speech, such as the noun and the verb, mark the endeavor of language to apprehend reality under its spatial and temporal aspects: what Gustave Guillaume calls "returning the sign to the universe." This shows that a philosophy of language must not simply account for the distance and the absence of the sign from reality (Lévi-Strauss). One can hold to this point of view as long as one considers the closed system of discrete units which compose a language; it no longer suffices when one approaches discourse in act. It would appear then that the sign is not only that which is lacking to things, it is not simply absent from things and other than them; it is what wishes to be applied, in order to express, grasp, apprehend, and finally to show, to manifest.

That is why a philosophy of language need not be limited to the conditions of possibility of a semiology: to account for the absence of the sign from things, the *reduction* of relations of nature and their mutation into signifying relations suffices. It is necessary in addition to satisfy conditions of possibility of discourse insofar as it is an endeavor, renewed ceaselessly, to express integrally the thinkable and the sayable in our experience. Reduction—or any act comparable to it by reason of its negativity—no longer suffices. Reduction is only the inverse, the negative side, of a wanting-to-say which aspires to become a wanting-to-show.

Whatever may be the fate of Chomsky's work in France and of the assistance that Gustave Guillaume can offer toward its assimilation, the philosophical interest of this new phase of linguistic theory is evident: a new relation, of a nonantinomic character, is in process of being instituted between structure and event, between rule and invention, between constraint and choice, thanks to dynamic concepts of the type *structuring operation* and no longer *structured inventory*.

I hope that anthropology and the other human sciences will know how to draw the consequences of this, as they are doing now with the original structuralism at the moment when its decline is beginning in linguistics.

2. I would like to sketch a parallel overcoming of the

antinomy of structure and event in the *semantic* order. It is here that I again meet my problem of the word.

The word is much more and much less than the sentence. It is much less, because there is not yet any word before the sentence. What is there before the sentence? Signs, that is, differences in the system, values in the lexicon. But there is not yet any meaning, any semantic entity. Insofar as it is a difference in the system, the sign says nothing. That is why it is necessary to say that in semiology there is no word but only relative, differential, oppositive values. In this respect, Hjelmslev is right: if we remove from semiology the substance of sounds and of meanings, such as they are, each of them, accessible to the feeling of speakers, it is necessary to say that phonetics and semantics do not belong to semiology. Each of them relates to *usage* or *use*, not to the *schema*. Now the schema alone is essential to a language. Usage or use is at the intersection of language and speech. We must conclude that the word names at the same time that the sentence says. It names in sentence position. In the dictionary, there is only the endless round of terms which are defined circularly, which revolve in the closure of the lexicon. But then someone speaks, someone says something. The word leaves the dictionary; it becomes word at the moment when man becomes speech, when speech becomes discourse and discourse a sentence. It is not by chance that, in German, *Wort*—"word"— is also *Wort*, "speech" (even if *Wort* and *Wort* do not have the same plural). Words are signs in speech position. Words are the point of articulation between semiology and semantics, in every speech event.

Thus the word is, as it were, a trader between the system and the act, between the structure and the event. On the one hand, it relates to structure, as a differential value, but it is then only a semantic potentiality; on the other hand, it relates to the act and to the event in the fact that its semantic actuality is contemporaneous with the ephemeral actuality of the utterance.

But it is here also that the situation is reversed. The word, I have said, is less than the sentence in that its actuality of meaning is subject to that of the sentence. But it is more than the sentence from another point of view. The sentence, we have seen, is an event; as such, its actuality is transitory, passing, ephemeral. But the word survives the sentence. As a displaceable entity, it survives the transitory instance of discourse and holds itself available for new uses. Thus, heavy with a new use-value—as

minute as this may be—it returns to the system. And, in returning to the system, it gives it a history.

To explain this process, I shall again take up the analysis of
the problem of polysemy that I have elsewhere[5] attempted to understand directly, but without yet making use of the distinction
that I now perceive between a semiology, or science of signs in
systems, and a semantics, or a science of usage, of the use of
signs in sentence position. The phenomenon of polysemy is in-
comprehensible if we do not introduce a dialectic between sign
and use, between structure and event. In purely synchronic
terms, polysemy signifies that at a given moment a word has
more than one meaning, that its multiple meanings belong to the
same state of system. But this definition lacks the essential point,
which concerns not the structure but the process. There is a
process of naming, a history of usage, which has its synchronic
projection in the form of polysemy. Now this process of the
transfer of meaning—of metaphor—supposes that the word is a
cumulative entity, capable of acquiring new dimensions of meaning without losing the old ones. It is this cumulative metaphorical process which is projected over the surface of the system as
polysemy.

Now what I here call projection is only one case of the return
of the event to the system. It is the most interesting and perhaps
the most fundamental case, if it is true, as has been said, that
polysemy is the pivot of semantics. It is the most interesting because we there come marvelously upon what I have called the
exchanges between the structure and the event. In fact this process presents itself as a convergence of two distinct factors, a factor of expansion and, at the limit, of surcharge. By virtue of the
cumulative process which I was speaking of, the word tends to be
charged with new use-values, but the projection of this cumulative process into the system of signs implies that the new meaning finds its place within the system. The expansion—and, if the
case obtains, the surcharge—is arrested by the mutual limitation
of signs within the system. In this sense we can speak of a limiting action of the field, opposed to the tendency to expansion,
which results from the cumulative process of the word. Thus is
explained what one could call a regulated polysemy, which is the
law of our language. Words have more than one meaning, but
they do not have an infinity of meanings.

5. See above, "The Problem of Double Meaning."

This example shows how semantic systems differ from semiological systems. The latter can be treated without any reference to history; they are atemporal systems because they are potential. Phonology gives the best illustration of this. Only the binary oppositions between distinct units play a role. In semantics, in contrast, the differentiation of meanings results from the equilibrium between two processes, a process of expansion and a process of limitation, which force words to shape themselves a place amid others, to hierarchize their use-values. This process of differentiation is irreducible to a simple taxonomy. Regulated polysemy is of the panchronic order, that is, both synchronic and diachronic to the degree that a history projects itself into states of systems, which henceforth are only instantaneous cross-sections in the process of meaning, in the process of nomination.

We then understand what happens when the word reaches discourse along with its semantic richness. All our words being polysemic to some degree, the univocity or plurivocity of our discourse is not the accomplishment of words but of contexts. In the case of univocal discourse, that is, of discourse which tolerates only one meaning, it is the task of the context to hide the semantic richness of words, to reduce it by establishing what Greimas calls an isotopy, that is, a frame of reference, a theme, an identical topic for all the words of the sentence (for example, if I develop a geometrical "theme," the word "volume" will be interpreted as a body in space; if the theme concerns the library, the word "volume" will be interpreted as designating a book). If the context tolerates or even preserves several isotopies at the same time, we will be dealing with an actually symbolic language, which, in saying *one* thing, says something *else*. Instead of sifting out one dimension of meaning, the context allows several to pass, indeed, consolidates several of them, which run together in the manner of the superimposed texts of a palimpsest. The polysemy of our words is then liberated. Thus the poem allows all the semantic values to be mutually reinforced. More than one interpretation is then justified by the structure of a discourse which permits multiple dimensions of meaning to be realized at the same time. In short, language is in celebration [*en fête*]. It is indeed in a structure that this abundance is ordered and deployed, but the structure of the sentence does not, strictly speaking, create anything. It collaborates with the polysemy of our words to produce this effect of meaning that we call symbolic discourse, and the polysemy of our words itself results from the

concurrence of the metaphorical process with the limiting action
of the semantic field.

Thus the exchanges between structure and event, between
system and act, do not cease to be complicated and renewed. It is
clear that the installation of one or several isotopies is the work
of sequences much longer than the sentence and that it would be
necessary, to pursue this analysis, to change once more the level
of reference, to consider the *linking of a text:* dream, poem, or
myth. It is at this level that I would again encounter my problem
of hermeneutics. But it is in the complex unit of the word, it
seems to me, that everything is played out. It is there that the exchange between genesis and structure is read clearly. But to interpret correctly this *work* of language, it is necessary to learn
again to think like Humboldt in terms of process rather than system, of structuration rather than structure.

The word has appeared to me to be the point of crystalliza-
tion, the tying-together of all the exchanges between structure
and function. If it has this virtue of forcing us to create new
models of intelligibility, it is because it is itself at the intersection
of language and speech, of synchrony and diachrony, of system
and process. In rising from system to event, in the instance of
discourse, it brings structure to the act of speech. In returning
from the event to the system, it brings to the system the contingency and disequilibrium without which it could neither
change nor endure; in short, it gives a "tradition" to the structure, which, in itself, is outside of time.

I will stop here. But I would not wish to leave the impression
that the phenomenon of language has been exhausted; other approaches remain possible. I have just made an allusion to the
level of the text and to the strategy of exegesis which corresponds to this further level of organization. By going further in
the same direction, one would meet the problems posed by Heidegger concerning the ontology of language. But these problems
would demand not only a change of level but a change of approach. Heidegger does not proceed according to the ascending
order that we have followed, which is a progressive order from
elements to structures, then from structures to process. He follows another order—perfectly legitimate in itself—which consists in beginning from spoken being, from the ontological
weight of established languages such as that of the thinker, the
poet, the prophet. Thus involved with the language which thinks,
he is on the way toward speaking: *Unterwegs zur Sprache.*

For perhaps we are always on the way toward language, although language itself may be the way. I will not take this Heideggerian way toward language, but let me say in conclusion that I have not closed it, even if I have not explicitly opened it. I have not closed it, in that our own progress has consisted in passing from the closure of the universe of signs to the openness of discourse. There would then be new scope for a meditation on the "word." For there are great words, powerful words—Mikel Dufrenne speaks magnificently of them in his *Poétique:* by means of the process of naming, these words capture some aspect of being, by a kind of violence that delimits the very thing that the word opens up and uncovers. These are the great words of the poet, of the thinker. They point out, they let be, that which surrounds their enclosure. But if this ontology of language cannot become our theme, by reason of the procedure of this study, at least it can be glimpsed as the horizon of this investigation. Considered against this horizon, our investigation would appear to be prompted and guided by a conviction, namely, that the essential aspect of language begins beyond the closure of signs. We restrict ourselves within the closure of signs whenever we descend toward the elements, inventories, and nomenclatures and reach the underlying combinatory functions. In effect, the more we distance ourselves from the level of manifestation, in order to immerse ourselves in the thickness of language in the direction of sublexical units, the more we realize the closure of language. The units that we uncover by analysis signify nothing. They are simply combinatory possibilities. They say nothing, they are limited to conjoining and disjoining. But in the movement of going and coming between analysis and synthesis, the return is not equivalent to going. On the return, in ascending from the elements toward the entire text and poem, there emerges, at the juncture of the sentence and the word, a new problematic which tends to eliminate structural analysis. This problematic, proper to the level of discourse, is that of saying. The upsurge of saying into our speaking is the very mystery of language. Saying is what I call the openness, or better, the opening-out, of language.

You have fathomed that the greatest opening-out belongs to language in celebration.

PART II

Hermeneutics and Psychoanalysis

Consciousness and
the Unconscious

FOR SOMEONE TRAINED in phenomenology, existential philosophy, linguistic or semiological methods, and the revival of Hegel studies, the encounter with psychoanalysis constitutes a considerable shock, for this discipline affects and questions anew not simply some particular theme within philosophical reflection but the philosophical project as a whole. The contemporary philosopher meets Freud on the same ground as Nietzsche and Marx. All three rise before him as protagonists of suspicion who rip away masks and pose the novel problem of the lie of consciousness and consciousness as a lie. This problem cannot remain just one among many, for what all three generally and radically put into question is something that appears to any good phenomenologist as the field, foundation, and very origin of any meaning at all: consciousness itself. What in one sense is a foundation must appear to us in a different sense as a prejudice, the prejudice of consciousness. This situation is comparable to Plato's in *The Sophist*, where he begins as a follower of Parmenides and an advocate of the immutability of being but is eventually compelled by the enigma of error and false opinion not only to give nonbeing the rights to the city as one of "the most all-embracing of genera" but even to admit that "the question of being is just as obscure as that of nonbeing." We must be reduced to a similar admission: *The question of consciousness is just as obscure as that of the unconscious.*

It is in this mood of suspicion as to consciousness' claim to original self-knowledge that a philosopher may enter into the

Translated by Willis Domingo.

company of psychiatrists and psychoanalysts. Anyone who arrives at the correlation between consciousness and the unconscious must first have crossed the arid zone of a double confession: "I cannot understand the unconscious from what I know about consciousness or even preconsciousness," and "I no longer even understand what consciousness is." This is the essential benefit of what is most antiphilosophical, antiphenomenological, about Freud, namely, the topographical and economic point of view as it is applied to the psychic apparatus as a whole, such as we find in the famous metapsychological article devoted to "The Unconscious." [1] Only from this phenomenological distress will we become aware of questions such as might become phenomenological once again, as, for example: How must I rethink and reground the concept of consciousness in such a way that the unconscious can be its *other* and consciousness can be fit for the sort of other that we call the unconscious?

A second question might be: How can we also bring to bear a *critique* (in the Kantian sense of the term as a reflection on the conditions and limits of something's validity) on those "models" which the psychoanalyst who wishes to take account of the unconscious must constitute? It is an urgent task to find such an epistemology for psychoanalysis. Unlike twenty years ago, we can no longer rest content to distinguish method and doctrine. Now we know that in the humane sciences "theory" is not a contingent addition but in fact constitutes their very object. It is "constitutive." The unconscious as something real is inseparable from the topographic, dynamic, and economic models by which psychoanalytic theory is organized. "Metapsychology," to use Freud's own term, is indeed the doctrine of psychoanalysis, but it is so only in that it makes the constitution of the object possible. In this case doctrine is method.

And a third: Following the revision of the concept of consciousness imposed by the science of the unconscious, and after the critique of the "models" of the unconscious, what is at stake is the possibility of a *philosophical anthropology* which can take up the dialectic between consciousness and the unconscious. What world view and vision of man will make this possible? What must man be to assume the responsibility of sound thought and yet be susceptible of falling into insanity, to be obligated by his humanity to strive for greater and greater consciousness and

1. *SE*, Vol. XIV. [*SE* will be used throughout to refer to the Standard Edition of Freud's works: *The Complete Psychological Works of Sigmund Freud*, ed. James Strachey (London, 1927–31).]

yet remain a product of topographic or economic models insofar as "the id speaks through him"? What new vision of human fragility—and, even more radically, of the paradox of responsibility vs. fragility—is required by the sort of thought which has allowed itself to be decentered from consciousness through reflecting on the unconscious?

I. The Crisis of the Notion of Consciousness

The substance of my first point can be summarized in two propositions: (1) Immediate consciousness does involve a type of certainty, but this certainty does not constitute true self-knowledge. (2) All reflection points back to the unreflected with the intention of escaping from itself, but the unreflected is no longer able to constitute a true knowledge of the unconscious.

These two propositions constitute what I have just called the admission of phenomenological distress before the problem posed by the unconscious. Even the simple advance from the first to the second leads to a threshold of failure: the threshold of reflective noncomprehension of the unconscious.

1. There is indeed an immediate certainty to consciousness, and this certainty is impregnable. It is the type articulated by Descartes in Part I, art. 9, of the *Philosophical Writings*:

> By the term *conscious experience* (*cogitationis*) I understand everything that takes place within ourselves so that we are aware of it (*nobis consciis*). . . . And so not only acts of understanding, will, and imagination, but even sensations are here to be taken as experience (*cogitare*).[2]

Although this certainty is unquestionable as certainty, it can be doubted as truth. We have come to realize that the profoundest depths of the life of intentionality can possess other meanings besides this immediate one. The most distant, general, and, we must admit, the most abstract of possibilities, that of the unconscious, is written into the initial gap between the certainty and the true knowledge of consciousness. This knowledge is not given; it must be sought and found. The self-adequation which we could call self-consciousness in the strong sense of the word comes not at the beginning but at the end. It is a limit-idea—a

2. [Translated by G. E. M. Anscombe and Peter Geach (London: Nelson, 1966).]

limit-idea which Hegel called absolute knowledge. Whether or not we believe that absolute knowledge can be spoken of and articulated, we can in any event agree with the assertion that it is the terminal and not the initial situation of consciousness. It is, moreover, the conclusion of a philosophy of *spirit*,[3] not of *consciousness*. Whatever may be thought of Hegelianism and the chances for its success, Hegel does show that an individual consciousness cannot be equated with its own content. Idealism is impossible for individualized consciousness, and in this sense Hegel's critique of individualized consciousness and its claims to be equated with its own content is in exact symmetry with the Freudian critique of consciousness based on experience with analysis. For inverse and yet coinciding reasons, Hegel and Freud say the same thing. For both, consciousness is what cannot totalize itself, and this is why a philosophy of consciousness is impossible.

2. This first negative consideration calls forth a second. Husserlian phenomenology also began with a critique of reflective consciousness and introduced the theme, which has since become well known, of the prereflective and unreflected. It is the inestimable value, however negative in the long run, of Husserlian phenomenology as a whole to have established the fact that any investigation into "constitution" refers to something pregiven or preconstituted. But Husserl's phenomenology is incapable of taking the failure of consciousness all the way. It remains within the circle of correlations between noesis and noema and can make room for the notion of the unconscious only by way of the theme of "passive genesis."

The failure of the reflective approach to consciousness must be brought to a conclusion. The unconscious which is involved in the phenomenological method's theme of the unreflected remains "capable of becoming conscious." It is reciprocal to consciousness as a field of inattention or as an implicit consciousness in relation to explicit consciousness. This is the theorem of *Ideen I*. It belongs to the essence of consciousness to never be entirely explicit, but always related to implicit consciousness. All the facts which made the elaboration of the concept of consciousness necessary, however, are not included in this theorem. *That* is our threshold. *That* is why it is necessary to take account of "models" which must necessarily appear as "naturalistic" to

3. [Here, as elsewhere in this book, the Hegelian *Geist* is translated as "spirit."—TRANS.]

phenomenology. It is at this point that Freudian realism is the necessary stage to bring the failure of reflective consciousness to its completion. As we shall see at the end, this failure is neither fruitless nor utterly negative. For, aside from its pedagogical or didactic value and its potentiality for preparing us to understand the lessons of Freudianism, this failure begins a process of converting consciousness in such a way as to understand the necessity of letting go all avarice with regard to itself, including that subtle self-concupiscence which may be what is narcissistic in the immediate consciousness of life. Through this failure, consciousness discovers that its immediate self-certainty was mere presumption and thus gains access to *thought,* which is no longer the attention consciousness pays to itself so much as to *saying,* or rather to what is said in the saying.

II. CRITIQUE OF FREUDIAN CONCEPTS

FOR THESE REASONS a critique of the realist concepts in Freud's metapsychology must be completely nonphenomenological. No phenomenology of consciousness can provide the rules for this critique, since that would be regressive. The "topography" in the famous article entitled "The Unconscious" is remarkable in that it disqualifies from the start any phenomenological reference and thus represents a necessary and necessarily corrective stage for any form of thought which will allow itself to be dislodged from self-certainty. Politzer's critique, for example, went wrong in remaining imprisoned in an idealism of sense. A critique of Freudian realism must be epistemological in the Kantian sense of a "transcendental deduction" whose task is to justify the use of a concept through its ability to organize a new field of objectivity and intelligibility. It seems to me that if more attention had been paid to that irreducible difference between an epistemological critique and a phenomenology of immediate consciousness, we would have been spared a good many scholastic discussions on the nature of the unconscious. Kant teaches us to join empirical realism with transcendental (which does not imply subjective or psychological) idealism in the realm of the concepts of physics.

First, empirical realism: This means that metapsychology is not a mere additional or optional construction but rather belongs to what Kant would call determinant judgments of experience.

Hence psychoanalytic method and doctrine cannot be distinguished. The topographic model is a valuable discovery, since it is the condition for the possibility of a real decipherment, which (as Lévi-Strauss reminds us in *Structural Anthropology*) attains a reality by the same right as the stratigraphy and archaeology. This is how I understand Laplanche's assertion—in many respects so disturbing—that the unconscious is finite. I take it to mean that, once finished, an analysis ends up with certain signifiers and not with others. That is the condition for a "terminable analysis," and in this sense a realism of the unconscious is the correlate of terminable analysis. The analysis of Philip's dream, for example, finishes with the facticity of *this* particular linguistic chain and no other. Let me state clearly at this point, however, that the reality of this realism is one which *can* be known. It is not unknowable. Freud is very helpful in this respect. For him, the knowable is not an instinct (*Trieb*)[4] in its being as instinct; it is rather the representation by which instincts are represented.

> Even in the unconscious . . . an instinct cannot be represented otherwise than by an idea. If the instinct did not attach itself to an idea or manifest itself as an affective state, we could know nothing about it. When we nevertheless speak of an unconscious instinctual impulse or of a repressed instinctual impulse, the looseness of phraseology is a harmless one. We can only mean an instinctual impulse the ideational representative of which is unconscious, for nothing else comes into consideration.[5]

Psychoanalysis has nothing to do with something unknowable, for it *can* know the unconscious precisely on account of its empirical realism, although it does so only through "ideational representatives." In this sense we must point out that Freud's empirical realism is one of unconscious representation, in relation to which the instincts themselves remain an unknowable x factor.

4. [Originally the Freudian term *Trieb* was rendered as "instinct" in French as well as in English. Because Freud does use *Instinkt*, however, in a distinctly different sense from *Trieb*, recent French writers in the fields of psychoanalysis and philosophy have begun to translate *Trieb* as *pulsion*, which is closer to the original German sense of "drive" or "impulse." Although the *SE* translation as "instinct" will be retained here, it should be remembered that the French term is *pulsion* in every case. Cf. Laplanche and Pontalis, *Vocabulaire de la psychanalyse* (Paris: Presses Universitaires de France, 1971), s.v. "Pulsion."—TRANS.]

5. *Papers on Metapsychology*, SE, XIV, 177.

The transition from the "topographic" to the "economic" viewpoint in the rest of the article (*ibid.*, pp. 178 ff.) brings about no radical change. The whole theory of cathexis, anti-cathexis, and withdrawal of cathexis by which "the system Pcs. protects itself from the pressure upon it of the unconscious idea" (p. 181) unfolds on the level of this representational realism. "Repression is essentially a process affecting ideas on the border between the system Ucs. and Pcs. (Cs.)" (p. 180).[6]

It is because Freud's analytical investigation foregoes any attempt to attain the being of instincts and remains within the limits of their conscious or unconscious representation that it does not get trapped in a realism of the unknowable. As opposed to that of the Romantics, the Freudian unconscious can in essence be known because the instinct's "ideational representatives" remain on the level of the signified and are permissibly homogeneous with the empire of speech. That is why Freud can write this surprising text:

> Like the physical, the psychical is not necessarily in reality what it appears to us to be. We shall be glad to learn, however, that the correction of internal perception will turn out not to offer such great difficulties as the correction of external perception—that internal objects are less knowable than the external world (p. 171).

Such is Freud's empirical realism. Its nature is fundamentally the same as the empirical realism of physics. It designates the "internal object" as something *knowable*.

By the same token, however, we can see how this empirical realism is directly related to a transcendental idealism in a purely epistemological and in no way subjectivist sense of the term. This transcendental idealism means that the "reality" of the unconscious exists only as a reality which has been *diagnosed*. The unconscious can be defined *only* in terms of its relations with the Cs.-Pcs. system (pp. 190 ff.):

> The Ucs. is alive and capable of development and maintains a number of other relations with the Pcs., amongst them that of cooperation. In brief, it must be said that the Ucs. is continued into what are known as derivatives, that it is accessible to the impressions of life, that it constantly influences the Pcs. and is even, for its part, subjected to influences from the Pcs. (p. 190).

6. [Cs. = consciousness; Ucs. = the unconscious; Pcs. = preconsciousness.]

We might say that psychoanalysis is "the study of the derivatives of the Ucs." (p. 190). Freud describes these "derivatives" as "*qualitatively* [belonging] to the system Pcs., but *factually* to the Ucs. Their origin is what decides their fate" (p. 191). We must thus conclude that the unconscious exists and is just as real as physical objects and yet that its existence is merely relative to the "derivatives" which represent it and make it appear in the field of consciousness.

What, then, is the meaning of this *relativity* which allows us to speak of transcendental idealism and empirical realism at the same time? In the first sense, one can say that the unconscious is relative to the system by which it is deciphered or decoded. But this meaning should be correctly understood. It does not mean that the unconscious is something projected by the hermeneut, in a vulgarly psychologistic sense. We should rather say that the reality of the unconscious is constituted in and by hermeneutics in an epistemological and transcendental sense. It is in the very movement by which the "derivative" reascends to its unconscious "origin" that the concept of Ucs. and its empirical reality are constituted. We are not asserting a relativity to consciousness or a subjective relativity, therefore, but rather the purely epistemological relativity between the psychic object which has been discovered and the hermeneutic constellation composed of symptoms, interpretative models, and the analytical method. From the first relativity, which will be called "objective" because it involves a relation to the rules of analysis and not to the personality of the analyst, we can derive a second type, which can be called "intersubjective relativity" and whose decisive trait is that the facts which the analysis attributes to the unconscious are *meaningful for another*. The role of the witness-consciousness, i.e., the psychoanalyst's own, has not received enough attention in the constitution of the unconscious as a reality. The unconscious has generally been defined within the limits of its relationship to the consciousness in which it is "contained." The role of the other consciousness is considered to be accidental rather than essential and is reduced to a relationship of therapy. But it is essential to the unconscious to be an object elaborated by someone other through a hermeneutics which its own consciousness cannot perform alone. In other words, the relationship which the unconscious and its witness-consciousness maintain is not merely therapeutic; it is also a diagnostic relationship. It was in this sense that I said that the unconscious is a diagnosed reality. That assertion is essential in determining the objective significance of assertions about the unconscious. First, it is only for someone other that I even *possess* an unconscious. *In the end,* of course, that makes no sense unless I can reaffirm the meanings which the other elaborates about and for me. Yet that stage of the search for meaning in which I dispossess myself of my own consciousness for the benefit of another person is fundamental for the *constitution* of that psychic region that we call the unconscious. We define both the validity and the limits of all assertions about the reality of the unconscious by referring it from the start, and on essential and non-accidental grounds, first to the hermeneutic method and then to a different hermeneutic witness-consciousness. In short, we exercise a *critique* of the concept of the unconscious, in the wide sense of the term critique, i.e., as a justification of the concept's meaningful significance and a rejection of all claims to extend the concept beyond the limits of its validity. We can say, therefore, that the unconscious is an object in the sense that it is "constituted" by the totality of hermeneutic procedures by which it is deciphered. Its being is not absolute but only relative to hermeneutics as method and dialogue. This is why we should not see in the unconscious some fanciful reality with the extraordinary ability of thinking in place of consciousness. The unconscious must be made relative, but in this way it is no different from the physical object whose reality is relative to the set of scientific procedures by which it is constituted. Psychoanalysis depends upon the same "rationalistic approach" as the natural sciences. Only with respect to these first two meanings of the term can we speak of it in a third sense, of a relativity to the analyst's own personality. But this third sense no longer defines the epistemological constitution of the notion of the unconscious so much as the specific circumstances surrounding each case of decipherment and its irrevocable imprint from the language of transference. What is manifested here is the precarious position and even the failure of analysis rather than its intention and true meanings. For the opponents of psychoanalysis this is the only relativity. They consider the unconscious as no more than a projection on the part of the analyst with the complicity of his patient. Only therapeutic success can guarantee to us that the unconscious is not an invention of psychoanalysis in this purely subjective sense.

These reflections on the relativity of the notion of the unconscious seem to me to be necessary in order to rid Freudian realism of the sort of naïve realism which would project back into the unconscious a fully elaborated meaning such as had been progressively constituted in the course of the hermeneutic relationship as opposed to empirical realism in the sense in which I have used the term, namely, as an assertion of the reality of the instincts as something which can be known by way of their ideational representations. Against this naïve realism we must continually emphasize that the unconscious does not think. Freud himself *never* makes the unconscious think, and in this respect the discovery of the term *Es* or id was a stroke of genius. Ucs. is the id and nothing but the id. Freudian realism is a realism of the id in its ideational representations and not a naïve realism of unconscious meaning. By a strange reversal, naïve realism would end up by giving consciousness to the unconscious and would thus produce the monster of an idealism of unconscious consciousness. This fanciful idealism would never be anything more than an idealism of meaning as projected into a thinking *thing*.

Hence a sort of continual alternation is necessary between empirical realism and transcendental idealism. The first must be maintained against all the claims of immediate consciousness to true self-knowledge, the second against all fanciful metaphysics which would attribute self-consciousness to this unconscious which is always "constituted" by the set of hermeneutic processes by which it is deciphered.

III. CONSCIOUSNESS AS A TASK

AT THE BEGINNING OF THIS DISCUSSION I spoke of the phenomenologist's distress before the unconscious and pointed out that consciousness is just as obscure as the unconscious. Should we then conclude that nothing further can be said about consciousness? Not at all. Everything that can be said about consciousness after Freud seems to me to be contained in the following formula: Consciousness is not a given but a *task*. What meaning can we give to this task at the present state of our knowledge about the unconscious? By posing such a question we acquire a knowledge of the unconscious which is no longer *realist* so much as it is *dialectical*, not so much a type of knowledge which belongs to analysis as something which belongs to the layman and the philosopher. Our question is the following: What is the meaning of the unconscious for a being whose task is consciousness? This question is related to a second: What is consciousness as a task for a being who is somehow bound to those factors, such as repetition and even regression, which the unconscious represents for the most part?

It is to this dialectical inquiry that I would now like to turn, without in any way attenuating its painful alternations, which seem to me to be inevitable and even necessary. Even in the immediately preceding analysis we could not avoid this alternation between consciousness and unconscious. What led us to the threshold of the unconscious was the discovery of the unreflected element in the reflected. But the realism of the unconscious is what disabused us of the prejudice of consciousness and forced us to put it, not at the origin, but at the end.

I will now resume at the pole of consciousness. Since Freud, it has become necessary to speak of consciousness only in terms of *epigenesis*. That is, the question of consciousness seems to me to be bound to the other question of how a man leaves his childhood behind and becomes an adult. While strictly reciprocal, this other question reverses the question asked by the analyst, who shows man as *subject* to his childhood. The bleak vision which he proposes of consciousness as subject to the three masters of the Id, the Superego, and Reality defines the task of consciousness in an obverse sense and the route of epigenesis as a negative.

Yet we run the risk of falling back into an introspective psychology by simply uttering the phrase "consciousness as epigenesis." Thus I think we should at this point reject entirely any psychology of consciousness whatsoever. Frail attempts to elaborate the notion of consciousness on the basis of a "conflict-free sphere," such as those of Hartmann and his followers, seem to me to belong to just such a psychology of consciousness. I believe that we should, rather, deliberately confront Freudian psychoanalysis with a method related to Hegel's in the *Phenomenology of Spirit*. Such a method is not a refined form of introspection, for Hegel does not present his succession of spiritual "figures" as a mere extension of immediate consciousness. His genesis is not a genesis of or in consciousness but a genesis of the spirit in discourse. The only forms which would be irreducible to Freud's key signifiers—the Father, the Phallus, Death, the Mother—in which, psychoanalysis teaches us, all other chains of signifiers are anchored, must be similar to those marked out in the *Phenomenology of Spirit*. I will argue, therefore, that man becomes an adult only by becoming capable of new key signifiers which are similar to the moments of the spirit in Hegelian phenomenology and regulate spheres of meaning which are absolutely irreducible to Freudian hermeneutics.

Consider the well-known and much discussed example of the master-slave relationship in Hegel. This is not at all a dialectic of consciousness. What is at stake here is the birth of the Self or, in Hegelian terms, the passage out of desire as desire for another into *Anerkennung* or *mutual recognition*. What happens in this process? Nothing less than the birth of the Self through a diremption of consciousness. There had been no Self before this dialectic (and even, as de Waehlens has pointed out, nothing like death, in the sense of human death, before the Self).

The stages of this mutual recognition bring us across "regions" of human meaning which are essentially nonsexual. I emphasize "essentially"; and, although I will deal with the secondary libidinal cathexis of these interhuman relationships when I alternate back to the unconscious, these spheres of meaning, on a primary level and in their essential constitution, are not *constituted* by this libidinal cathexis. Let me distinguish three spheres of meaning, therefore, which can briefly be subsumed into the trilogy of possession, power, and value [*avoir, pouvoir, et valoir*].

By relations of possession I understand those interhuman relations which are involved with work and appropriation in a situation of "scarcity"—which, so far, is the only situation we have known in human conditions involving possession. When such relations occur, we see the birth of new, purely human, and nonbiological feelings. These feelings originate not from biological life but from reflection within human affectivity upon a new realm of objects and a specifically "economic" objectivity where man appears as capable of an "economics." By the same token he becomes capable of feelings relative to possession and capable also of a new type of alienation, essentially nonlibidinal, of the sort described by the young Marx and which in *Capital* will become the "fetish" of merchandise converted into money. This is the economic alienation which, as he shows, is able to generate "false consciousness" and "ideological" thought. It is in this way that, in the same movement, man becomes adult and capable of adult alienation. But, more important, we note that the source of the proliferation of these feelings, passions, and alienation is in new and different objects, such as exchange values, monetary signs, and structures and institutions. We can claim, therefore, that man becomes self-conscious to the degree that he lives this economic objectivity as a new modality of subjectivity and enters into specifically human "feelings" which are relative to the availability of goods as products of labor and appropriation, while he turns himself into their expropriated appropriator. It is this new objectivity which generates instincts, representations, and affects. This is why the claim cannot be made, for example, that the mother is an economic reality; for not only is she not edible (as has already been pointed out), but also, even if she were, she would still not figure into relations of economic objectivity, which are bound to work, exchange, and appropriation.

We should also examine the sphere of power in terms of objectivity and the feelings and forms of alienation it engenders, for this sphere is also constituted in an objective structure. In fact, here is where Hegel begins to use the term *objective spirit* in order to describe the appropriate structures and institutions for the inscription and generation of the relationship of ordering and obeying which is essential to political power. As we see at the beginning of Hegel's *Philosophy of Right*, any specific "consciousness" which corresponds to this political sphere does so to the degree that man generates himself as a specifically spiritual will [*vouloir*] by entering into the relationship of ordering and obeying. Here also consciousness increases reciprocally to an increase in "objectivity." Ambition, intrigue, submission, and responsibility are the appropriate human "feelings" which are organized around the "object," power. They are also its specific types of alienation and as such have already been provisionally described by the ancients in the figure of the "tyrant." Plato shows quite well how the illnesses of the soul manifested in the figure of the tyrant proliferate from a center which he calls *dynamis* or power [*puissance*] and spread as far as the region of language in the form of "flattery." This is why the "tyrant" calls upon the "sophist." We can conclude from all this that man possesses consciousness insofar as he is capable of entering into the political problematic of power and begins to have feelings which gravitate around it and to run the risk of its accompanying pitfalls. In this way a genuinely adult sphere of guilt is born, for power leads to madness, as both Plato and Alain have pointed out. Power is a good example of how a psychology of consciousness does no more than trail behind in subjective reflection as a shadow of the series of figures man passes through as he generates economic and then political objectivity.

The same can be said of the third specifically human sphere of meaning, the sphere of *value*, whose movement can be understood in the following way. The constitution of the Self is not limited to the economic or political sphere but continues in the region of culture. Here also, "psychology" grasps only a shadow or outline, which is present in all men, of what it means to be esteemed, approved, and recognized as a person. My existence for myself depends utterly on this self-constitution in the opinion of others. My Self—if I dare say so—is received from the opinions of others, who consecrate it. This mutual constitution of individual subjects is guided, however, by new figures, which we might call "objective" in a different sense. Institutions do not always correspond to these human figures, and yet they can be sought out in works of art and literature. It is in this new sort of objectivity that the search for human possibilities is pursued. Even when Van Gogh, for example, paints a chair, he portrays man and projects a figure or image of man as the owner of the world represented. Cultural background is what gives these "images" of man the density of "things," makes them exist between and among men and incarnates them in "works." By the mediation of works and cultural monuments such as these, human *dignity* and self-esteem are constituted. Finally, this is also the level at which man is capable of alienation, self-degradation, ridicule, and self-annihilation.

Such, it seems to me, is the exegesis of "consciousness" that might be devised by rejecting a psychology of consciousness and turning to a reflective method whose point of departure is in the objective movement of the figures of man. It is this objective movement which Hegel calls spirit, and subjectivity can be derived from it precisely through reflection in such a way that the self-constitution of subjectivity and the generation of objectivity are simultaneous.

As we can see, this indirect and mediate approach on the part of consciousness has nothing to do with immediate self-presence or self-certainty.

The question toward which this entire essay has been heading is now ripe. What happens to the Freudian unconscious when a different counterpart than a transparent, immediately self-certain consciousness is given to it? What happens to the realism of the unconscious when it is put into a dialectical relationship with the mediate apperception of self-consciousness? We might distinguish two moments in this dialectic. First, we can understand it as a relation of *opposition* and can contrast the regressive procedure of Freudian analysis with the progressive procedure of Hegelian synthesis. As we shall see, however, this point of view remains abstract and needs to be surpassed, although it is, of course, necessary to spend enough time within such a dialectic before earning the right to surpass it. But toward what? We will speak about this later and in an admittedly very rudimentary way, for I admit that I find it extremely difficult to see clearly the second moment which will concretize the dialectic.

Hence, my comparison of the procedure of analysis toward the unconscious with that of synthesis toward consciousness will be only provisional.

I will begin with the following formula. Consciousness is a movement which continually annihilates its starting point and can guarantee itself only at the end. In other words, it is something that has meaning only in later figures, since the meaning of a given figure is deferred until the appearance of a new figure. Thus the fundamental meaning of the moment of consciousness called stoicism in the *Phenomenology of Spirit* is not revealed until the arrival of skepticism, since it itself reveals the absolute unimportance of the relative positions held by Master and Slave before the abstract thought of freedom. The same is true for all the spiritual figures. We can say in a very general way that an understanding of consciousness always moves backwards. Is this not the key to the dialectic between consciousness and the unconscious? The fundamental meaning of the unconscious is in fact that an understanding always comes out of *preceding* figures, whether one understands this priority in a purely temporal and factual or symbolic sense. Man is the only being who is subject to his childhood. He is that being whose childhood constantly draws him backwards. The unconscious is thus the principle of all regressions and all stagnations. Even if we underplay the much too historical character of this interpretation and interpret the unconscious as a set of key meanings which are always already there, we remain faced with a *symbolic* antecedence. The fact that primary repression precedes secondary repression and that key meanings precede any temporally interpreted events brings us back to a more symbolic sense of antecedence but one which continues to provide to the inverse order of consciousness the guarantee we have been looking for. We can say, therefore, in very general terms that consciousness is the order of the terminal, the unconscious that of the primordial.

The above formula allows us to return to a point which I mentioned earlier and left hanging, namely, that of the intersection of two ways of explaining a single experience. I alluded to the possibility of interpreting political relationships, for example, both by the figures of a phenomenology of spirit and by the libidinal cathexis spoken of by Freud in his *Group Psychology and the Analysis of the Ego*. The two explanations are so far from being mutually exclusive that they can even be superimposed on each other. On the one hand, we can say, as we did above, that political relationships are not constituted from primordial instinctual relationships but from the objectivity of power and the feelings and passions which come out of it. On the other hand, however, we must admit that none of the figures of a phenomenology of spirit escape libidinal cathexis and thus the regressive attraction of the instincts. In this way the Freudian interpretation of the leader as someone whose charisma comes from a homosexual libidinal cathexis is fundamentally true. Although that does not mean that politics is sexual, it does imply that such politics is inauthentically political because it is a transfer to the political sphere of human relations which have been generated in the libidinal sphere. In this sense, analysis will always be correct in mistrusting political passion and seeing in it an escape or disguise. An integral genesis of political relationships from the sphere of instinct, however, will never succeed. The most we can say is that if the so-called political vocation were a mere libidinal cathexis of the figure of the chief, it would be destroyed by a psychoanalysis of the political militant. At the same time, however, the way would be opened for authentic political vocations, which would resist any libidinal reduction and show themselves to be genuinely inspired by the specifically political problems. This is the meaning of Plato's observation in the *Republic* that "the true magistrate—the philosopher—governs without passion." We can reconsider in a similar way the relations of possession, which can then be read either from the viewpoint of the anal stage of development and man's relation to his body, etc., or from that of work. These two geneses, however, do not operate on the same level. While one explains only a play of masks and substitutes and in the end is limited to "false consciousness," the other is constitutive. Let us pause for a moment with an example borrowed from the domain of culturally created symbols and use this example in an attempt to outline the dialectical opposition of the two types of hermeneutics of symbols, the one oriented toward the discovery of figures to come (i.e., the hermeneutics of consciousness) and the other toward preceding forms (i.e., the hermeneutics of the unconscious).

Sophocles' *Oedipus Rex* gives us the opportunity to grasp the interaction of the two different types of hermeneutics. How can we understand this tragedy? It can be interpreted in two ways, first, as Freud did, in *The Interpretation of Dreams,* by regression to an original complex, which would, of course, be the Oedipus complex, and second by a progressive synthesis toward a problematic which ceases to have anything in common with the Oedipus complex. According to Freud, the play's hold over the spectator does not come from the conflict between destiny and liberty, which is the interpretation of classical aesthetics, but from the nature of *this particular* destiny which unawares we recognize as our own. Freud writes, "His destiny moves us only because it might have been ours—because the oracle laid the same curse upon all of us before our birth as upon him";[7] and, later on, "King Oedipus . . . merely shows us the fulfillment of our own childhood wishes" (*ibid.*) Our pity and terror, the famous tragic *phobos,* is merely an expression of the violence of our own repression before this manifestation of our impulses.

This reading is possible, illuminating, and necessary, but there is a second possible reading which is not so much concerned with the drama of incest and patricide *which actually took place* as with the tragedy of truth. It deals, not with Oedipus' relation to the Sphinx, but with his relation to the seer. The objection will be made that the latter relationship is the analytic relationship itself. Did Freud himself not say,

> The action of the play consists in nothing other than the process of revealing, with cunning delays and ever-mounting excitement—a process that can be likened to the work of a psychoanalysis—that Oedipus himself is the murderer of Laius, but further that he is the son of the murdered man and of Jocasta (*ibid.,* pp. 261–62).

But we must not stop here. Sophocles' creation is not some sort of machine for reliving the Oedipus complex by the two processes of a fictional realization of compromise to satisfy the id and an exemplary punishment to satisfy the superego. Through the repetition and anamnesis of what took place the tragic poet creates a second problematic: the tragedy of self-consciousness. A second-degree drama, which points toward *Oedipus at Colonus,* is intertwined with the first, while Oedipus himself takes on a second and specifically adult guilt, namely, that of his own justice. When, in the beginning of the tragedy, he

---

7. *The Interpretation of Dreams, SE,* IV, 261.

pronounces a curse upon the unknown bearer of pollution who is the cause of the plague, he utterly ignores the fact that he could also be that individual and thus condemns himself. What follows is merely the progress toward destruction of that presumptuous consciousness which had assumed its own innocence. Thus Oedipus' pride must be broken through suffering. In a sense, this second-degree drama remains part of the primary tragedy, since the punishment of the guilty party completes the crime; but the process of crime and punishment develops a secondary drama which *is* the tragedy itself. Oedipus' zeal for the truth, which sets the search for the guilty party into motion, is impure. It is the presumption of the *king*. Oedipus' zeal belongs to the greatness of the *king*. It is the presumption of a man who considers himself unaffected by the truth and is related to that of Prometheus. His is the zeal of ignorance. Tiresias alone represents the power of truth. Oedipus is still only the *hybris* of truth, and this *hybris* is what is really the minister of its own condemnation. The guilt of this *hybris* is expressed in Oedipus' outburst of anger against Tiresias. This is not sexual guilt but the anger of ignorance. Admittedly, Oedipus' anger is expressed through his effort to clear himself of a primary crime of which he is not guilty. But the specific guilt, which is internal to the drama of truth, requires a specific unveiling, which is represented by the figure of the "seer." Thus Tiresias and not Oedipus is the center from which the truth proceeds. Oedipus is only the *king*, and this is why the tragedy is that of Oedipus *Rex* and not Oedipus the incestuous patricide. In this respect Oedipus represents human greatness. His vanity must be revealed by a figure who, in a sense, possesses the view of the whole. This figure, related to that of the fool in Elizabethan tragedy, is not tragic in himself but rather expresses the irruption of comedy in the midst of tragedy. This figure of the seer is called by Sophocles himself "the power of truth," a power which Oedipus will eventually acquire through suffering. The connection between Oedipus' anger and the power of truth is the core of the real Oedipus tragedy, and it expresses the problem of light, whose symbol is Apollo, and not that of sex. We might say that it is the same Apollo who calls upon Oedipus to know himself and urges Socrates to examine himself and other men and to say that an unexamined life is not worth living. If that is the case, Oedipus' self-punishment also belongs to the two intertwined dramas. Oedipus' act of putting out his eyes is a perfect example of self-punishment, self-cruelty, and the extreme point of masochistic conduct. In one sense that is true, and the chorus will not hesitate to interpret it as such. Later even the aged Oedipus will repent of that new violence as his ultimate guilt. But just as the tragedy of truth belongs to and yet escapes the sexual tragedy, the meaning of Oedipus' punishment turns out to be twofold as well. It belongs equally to the drama of self-knowledge and takes its meaning from the relationship between Oedipus and Tiresias. Tiresias is the seer, but blind. Oedipus sees with his eyes, but his understanding is blind. When he loses his sight, he receives vision. Punishment as masochistic conduct has become the night of meaning, understanding, and will. "Stop wanting to be always the master," cries Creon, "for all that your former victories have brought you has not always been of use to you." External destiny has been internalized, and the condemned man has become, like Tiresias, the blind seer. The inferno of truth is the blessing of vision. This is the ultimate meaning of the tragedy, but it is not yet uncovered in *Oedipus Rex*. It will remain hidden until Oedipus has completely internalized not only the meaning of his birth but also that of his anger and self-punishment. But at that moment he will pass beyond even death, for death remains the curse of life and the supreme threat for an unpurified existence.

Thus there are indeed two types of hermeneutics. One is oriented toward the resurgence of archaic symbols and the other toward the emergence of new symbols and ascending figures, all absorbed into the final stage, which, as in the *Phenomenology of Spirit*, is no longer a figure but knowledge. We are told that the second type consists in filling in the lacunae in a discontinuous text and that the first is concerned less with reestablishing a mutilated text than with forming new thoughts on the basis of the archaic symbol. The duality in hermeneutic methods thus brings to light a corresponding duality in the symbols themselves. In a sense, a single symbol possesses two vectors. On the one hand, it is a *repetition* (in all the temporal and atemporal meanings of this term) of our childhood. On the other, it *explores* our adult life. "O my prophetic soul," as Hamlet says. In this second form the symbol is an indirect discourse on our most radical possibilities, and in relation to these possibilities it is prospective. Culture is nothing else than this epigenesis or orthogenesis of the "images" of man's becoming adult. The creation of "works," "monuments," and cultural "institutions" is not something projected by a human symbolizing power which is brought to light by regressive analysis. It is the emergence of a *Bildung*. As a way of denoting these symbolic emergences which mark out the promotion of self-consciousness, I will speak not only of their "projective" function but of what might be called their "formative" function, whereby symbols express by promoting what they express. This is how they are *paideia,* education, *eruditio,* or *Bildung.* They are *open* to what they have disclosed. It is in this sense that culture or *Bildung* is not a dream. Dreams disguise, while the work of culture uncovers and reveals.

What is the effect of this dialectic of two hermeneutics and two ways of symbolizing upon the dialectic between the conscious and the unconscious that we are aiming at? As long as we remain within the perspective of an opposition between the two, consciousness and the unconscious will answer to two inverse interpretations, progressive and regressive. We might say that consciousness is history, while the unconscious is fate. It is the hinterside fate of childhood and of symbols already there and reiterated, the fate of the repetition of the same themes on different helices of a spiral. And yet man has a responsibility to grow out of his childhood and shatter the process of repetition by constituting ahead of himself a contrasting history of hitherside forms through eschatology. The unconscious is the origin or genesis, while consciousness is the end of time or apocalypse. But we remain in an abstract opposition. We must therefore understand that, although opposed, the system of hitherside figures and that of figures which always refer to a previously given symbolism are *the same.* This is not easy to understand, and I myself do so only with difficulty. We can at least say, however, that, at the point we have reached, the great temptation would be to declare that the unconscious explains the lower, inferior, and nocturnal part of man and is the Passion of the Night, while consciousness expresses the higher, superior, daylight part of man and is the Law of the Day. The danger would thus be in taking comfort in an easy eclecticism in which consciousness and the unconscious would be vaguely complementary. This sort of compromise is a caricature of the dialectic, but it will not be entirely exorcised unless we can understand that the two types of hermeneutics, that of the Day and that of the Night, are the same. We cannot simply add up Hegel and Freud and give to each a half of man. Just as we must say that everything about man is equally physiological and sociological, so we must also say that the two readings in question cover exactly the same field. For a Hegelian everything is in the series of spiritual figures, including what Hegel calls the discourse of the spirit, which each of us interiorizes as consciousness. And I also admit that, for a Freudian, everything, including the Master-Slave dialectic, is in the overdetermination of fundamental symbols. The relation between the analyst and his patient is a perfect realization of this dialectic, and treatment can be interpreted as a struggle for recognition based on a nonreciprocal and inegalitarian situation. Are "being" and "having" spoken of in analysis? Of course: having and not having the phallus, losing it by agreeing not to have it in fact, is the very model of having, etc. In this sense, Hegel's and Freud's two imperialisms are complete and without compromise. The best proof of this is that everything that can be said about the one can also be said about the other. Do not both the *Phenomenology of Spirit* and analytical anamnesis finish with a return to the immediate? Conversely, is not psychoanalysis' regression to the archaic a new march to the future? Is not the therapeutic situation in itself a prophecy of freedom? This is why the Freudian can always say that the interpretation of *Oedipus Rex* in other than psychoanalytic terms expresses no more than the resistance of the self-proclaimed hermeneut to analysis itself. For this reason we must enter into the most complete opposition between consciousness as history and the unconscious as fate if we wish to acquire the right to overcome this opposition and understand the identity of the two opposed systematics, one of which is a synthesis of consciousness, the other an analysis of the unconscious. But neither their opposition nor their identity gives us the right to eclecticism. Three cups of the unconscious, two tablespoons of preconsciousness, and a pinch of consciousness is not our recipe at any price. Eclecticism is always the enemy of the dialectic.

Consider the path we have taken. We began from the failure of a phenomenology of consciousness and argued that immediate consciousness possesses certainty but not truth. The unreflected field to which reflection points is not the unconscious. Such a failure led us to examine the validity of a realism of the unconscious; this appeared "well grounded" and related to a transcendental idealism which would prevent us from making the unconscious think. Then we were forced to surpass this realism of the unconscious, according to which consciousness is merely one "area" in the Freudian topography. Next we attempted to conceive consciousness by way of and against the unconscious and conversely, according to Kant's opposition of negative magnitudes. We remained at this stage the longest. In order to sustain our enterprise, we entirely rejected a psychology of consciousness which would have led us back to a pre-Freudian as well as a pre-Husserlian position. We were guided rather by a phenomenology of spirit in the Hegelian sense of the term. The "consciousness" to which the unconscious is *other* is not self-presence or the apperception of some content but the *ability to retravel the journey of the figures of the spirit*. The hermeneutics of these figures by way of the symbols in which they were born appears to us as the real partner of regressive hermeneutics, whose meaning is revealed when in its turn it finds *its own other* in the progressive hermeneutics of the phenomenology of spirit. Now we discover the unconscious as the other of its other, as a destiny, opposed to any progressive history oriented toward the future totality of the spirit. Finally, we have left unanswered the question of the fundamental identity of these two hermeneutics—an identity which leads us to say that a phenomenology of spirit and an archaeology of the unconscious speak not of two halves of man but each one of the whole of man.

If all this is true, finite consciousness is perhaps no more than the way, open to a limited and mortal destiny, of living the identity between spirit, considered in its essential figures, and the unconscious, grasped in its key meanings. When we understand this identity between the progression of figures of the spirit and the regression toward the key meanings of the unconscious, we will also understand Freud's well-known saying "Wo es war, soll ich werden"—"Where id was, there ego shall be."

Psychoanalysis and the Movement of Contemporary Culture

A QUESTION AS IMPORTANT as that which concerns the place of psychoanalysis in the movement of contemporary culture demands that we be limited in our approach and yet try to reveal what is essential. Our exposition must be limited if it is going to allow for discussion and verification, but revelatory in order to give an idea of the scope of the cultural phenomenon which psychoanalysis represents for us. Such an approach might be a rereading of Freud's texts *on* culture, and indeed these essays attest to the fact that psychoanalysis does not concern itself with culture for merely accessory or indirect reasons. Far from being a mere explanation of the refuse of human existence and the darker side of man, it shows its real intentions when it breaks out of the limited framework of the therapeutic relationship between the analyst and his patient and rises to the level of a hermeneutics of culture. This first part of our demonstration is essential to the argument we eventually want to establish, namely, that psychoanalysis takes part in the contemporary cultural movement by acting as a hermeneutics of culture. In other words, psychoanalysis marks a change *of* culture because its interpretation of man bears in a central and direct way *on* culture as a whole. It makes interpretation into a moment of culture; it changes the world by interpreting it.

First of all, therefore, we should demonstrate that psychoanalysis is an interpretation of culture *as a whole*. We are not saying that it is an exhaustive explanation; later we will say that its viewpoint is limited and even that it has not yet found

Translated by Willis Domingo.

its proper place among all the various interpretations of culture
—which implies that the meaning of psychoanalysis remains in
suspense and its place undecided. This interpretation, however,
is not limited on the side of its object, man, which it tries to
grasp as a totality. It is limited only by its point of view; and it
is this point of view which we must understand and locate. I
would even say, as Spinoza does when he speaks of divine attributes as "infinite in one genus," that psychoanalysis is a total
interpretation in one genus and in this way is itself an event in
our culture.

Now we miss this unity of viewpoint on the part of psychoanalysis when we consider it to be a branch of psychiatry which
has been progressively extended from individual to social psychology and then to art, morality, and religion. It was, of course,
toward the end of Freud's life that his great texts on culture
began to appear. *The Future of an Illusion* dates from 1927,
Civilization and Its Discontents from 1930, *Moses and Monotheism* from the period 1937–39. These, however, do not represent
simply a belated extension of individual psychology to a sociology of culture. By 1908 Freud had written "Creative Writers and
Daydreaming." "Delusions and Dreams in Jensen's *Gradiva*"
dates from 1907, *Leonardo da Vinci and a Memory of His Childhood* from 1910, *Totem and Taboo* from 1913, "Thoughts for
the Times on War and Death" from 1915, "The Uncanny" from
1919, "A Childhood Recollection from *Dichtung und Wahrheit*"
from 1917, "The Moses of Michelangelo" from 1914, *Group
Psychology and the Analysis of the Ego* from 1921, "A Seven-
teenth-Century Demonological Neurosis" from 1923, and
"Dostoevsky and Parricide" from 1928. The great "invasions"
into the domains of aesthetics, sociology, ethics, and religion are
therefore strictly concurrent with texts as important as *Beyond
the Pleasure Principle, The Ego and the Id,* and, above all, the
great *Papers on Metapsychology.* The truth is that psychoanalysis
disrupts traditional divisions, however justified these may be by
methodologies belonging to other disciplines. It applies the
single viewpoint of its topographic, economic, and genetic
"models" (the unconscious) to these separate domains. This
unified viewpoint is what makes psychoanalytic interpretation
both universal and limited. It is universal because it can legitimately be applied to humanity as a whole, but limited because it
does not extend beyond the validity of its model or models. For
example, Freud always objected to the distinction between psychological and sociological domains and constantly asserted the

fundamental analogy between individual and group—an analogy which he never tried to prove by speculating about the "being" of the psychism or the "being" of the group. He simply let it be assumed by applying the same genetic and topographic-economic models to all cases. Yet Freud never claimed to give exhaustive explanations. He merely carried explanation by way of origins and the economy of instincts to its most extreme consequences. "I cannot speak of everything at the same time," he insists; "my contribution is modest, partial, and limited." Such reservations are not mere stylistic parries but express the conviction of an investigator who realizes that his explanation gives him a view which is limited as a result of his angle of vision but which gives onto the totality of the human phenomenon.

I. A Hermeneutics of Culture

A purely historical study of the evolution of Freud's thought on culture should begin with *The Interpretation of Dreams*, for here is where Freud, in an interpretation of Sophocles' *Oedipus Rex* and Shakespeare's *Hamlet*, posited once and for all the unity of literary creation, myths, and dream distortion. All succeeding developments are contained in this seed. In "Creative Writers and Daydreaming" Freud states his basic argument that the barely perceptible transitions from the nocturnal dream to play and then to humor, fantasy, the daydream, and finally to folklore, legends, and genuine works of art leads us to suspect that creativity results from the same dynamism and involves the same economic structure as the phenomena of compromise and substitutive satisfaction which he had already developed for the interpretation of dreams and the theory of neurosis. But he cannot go further in this essay because he lacks a clear vision of a *topography* of the various agencies of the psychic apparatus and an *economy* of cathexes and anticathexes which would allow him to relocate aesthetic pleasure in the dynamics of culture as a whole. For this reason we will, in the space of this brief article, turn to an interpretation that is more systematic than historical and go straight to the texts which give a synthetic definition of culture. It is from this central problematic that a general theory of "illusion" can be developed and a place be found for Freud's previous aesthetic writings, whose meaning remains in suspense as long as the special domain of the phenomenon of culture is not perceived. Aesthetic "seduction" and religious "illusion" are to be taken together as the opposite poles of an investigation into compensation, itself one of the tasks of culture.

The same is true of Freud's richer writings, such as *Totem and Taboo,* in which he reinterprets by means of psychoanalysis the results of early twentieth-century ethnography on the totemic origins of religion and the sources of our ethical imperative in archaic taboos. These *genetic* studies can also be reconsidered in the wider framework of a topographic-economic interpretation. Similarly, in *The Future of an Illusion* and *Moses and Monotheism* Freud himself points out that such an explanation deals only with a partial phenomenon, i.e., an archaic form of religion, and not with religion as such. The key to a rereading of Freud's work which would be more systematic than historical lies in subordinating all partial and "genetic" interpretations to a topographic-economic interpretation, since this alone confers unity of perspective. This second preliminary remark confirms our first one. What anchors the genetic explanation in the topographic-economic explanation is the theory of illusion, for here is where we find the repetition of the archaic as a "return of the repressed." If this is the case—a point which can be verified only in practice—the following systematic order becomes necessary. We must descend from the whole to the parts, from the central economic function of culture to the particular functions of religious "illusion" and aesthetic "seduction"—and from economic to genetic explanation.

1. *An Economic Model of the Phenomenon of Culture*

What, then, is culture as such? We can define it first of all in a negative way by saying that Freud does not distinguish between civilization and culture. This refusal to accept an almost classical distinction is in itself very illuminating. There is no separation between the utilitarian enterprise of dominating the forces of nature (civilization) and the disinterested, idealist task of realizing values (culture). This distinction, which might have meaning from a viewpoint which differs from that of psychoanalysis, has none as soon as we decide to treat culture from the viewpoint of a balance sheet of libidinal cathexes and anticathexes.

This economic interpretation is what dominates all of Freud's reflections on culture.

The first phenomenon we should consider from this point of view is that of coercion, because of the *instinctual renunciation* which it implies. This is the phenomenon which opens *The Future of an Illusion*. Culture, as Freud points out, began with the prohibition of man's most ancient desires—incest, cannibalism, and murder. And yet coercion does not constitute all of culture. The *illusion* whose future Freud calculates is involved in a wider task, of which prohibition is merely the rough outer shell. Freud gets to the kernel of this problem by posing three questions: To what extent can the burden of the instinctual sacrifices imposed on men be *lessened*? How can men be *reconciled* with those sacrifices which must necessarily remain? Moreover, how can satisfying *compensations* be offered to individuals for these sacrifices? These questions are not, as one might at first believe, interrogations formulated by the author about culture; rather, they constitute culture itself. What is in question in the conflict between prohibition and instinct is the triple problematic of lessening the burden of instinctual renunciation, reconciliation with the inescapable, and compensation for sacrifice.

What, then, are these interrogations if they do not belong to an economic interpretation? With this question we come to an understanding of the single viewpoint which not only binds together all of Freud's essays on art, morality, and religion but also connects "individual" and "group" psychology and anchors them both in "metapsychology."

This economic interpretation of culture is itself elaborated in two steps, and *Civilization and Its Discontents* shows clearly how these two moments interact: first comes all that can be said without resorting to the death instinct and then what cannot be said without its intervention. The essay had developed with a calculated mildness prior to this inflection, which turns it toward the culturally tragic. The economics of culture seemed to coincide with what might be called a general "erotics": the ends pursued by the individual and those which animate culture appear as sometimes convergent and sometimes divergent forms of the same Eros:

> [The] process of civilization is a modification which the vital process experiences under the influence of a task that is set it by Eros

and instigated by Ananke—by the exigencies of reality; and . . . this task is one of uniting separate individuals into a community bound together by libidinal ties.[1]

It is the same "erotics," therefore, which is responsible for the internal bonds within groups and which makes the individual seek pleasure and flee suffering—the threefold suffering inflicted by the world, his body, and other men. The development of culture is, like the growth of the individual from childhood to adulthood, the fruit of Eros and Ananke, love and work. We should even say: more of love than of work, for the necessity of uniting in work for the exploitation of nature is a poor second to the libidinal bonds which unite individuals into a single social body. It seems, therefore, that the same Eros which animates the search for individual happiness also seeks to unite men in ever larger groups. But then the paradox appears: as an organized struggle against nature, culture gives to man the power previously conferred upon the gods, and yet his resemblance to the gods leaves him unsatisfied—the discontent of civilization. Why? We can, of course, solely on the basis of this general "erotics," account for certain tensions between the individual and society, but not for the serious conflict which creates the tragedy of culture. For example, we can easily explain that family ties resist extension to wider groups. For each adolescent the passage from one group to another necessarily appears as a rupture of his oldest and most intimate bond. We also understand that something peculiar to feminine sexuality resists the transfer from private sexuality to the libidinal energies of social bonds. We can go much further in the direction of situations of conflict without, however, encountering radical contradictions. Culture, we know, imposes sacrifices on all sexual enjoyment— the prohibition of incest, the censorship of infantile sexuality, the strict regulation of sexuality into the narrow pathways of legitimacy and monogamy, the imposition of the imperative of procreation, etc. But however painful these sacrifices may be, and however unavoidable these conflicts, they do not reach the point of constituting a genuine antagonism. The most we can say is, first, that the libido resists with all the strength of its inertia the task, imposed on it by culture, of abandoning its earliest positions, and, second, that society's libidinal ties feed on the energy drained off from sexuality to the point of threatening

1. *Civilization and Its Discontents, SE,* XXI, 134. [Subsequent page numbers in parentheses refer to this work.]

it with atrophy. All of this is so "untragic," however, that we can even imagine a sort of armistice or compromise between the individual libido and the social bond.

And so the question reappears: why does man fail to be happy, and why he is unsatisfied as a cultural being?

This is the turning point of Freud's analysis. It is here that man is faced with an absurd commandment (Love thy neighbor as thyself)—an impossible requirement (Love your enemies) and a dangerous order, which squanders love, aids and abets the wicked, and betrays the imprudent one who tries to apply it. But the truth which is hidden behind the *folly of the imperative* is the folly of an instinct which escapes the limits of any erotic explanation:

> The element of truth behind all this, which people are so ready to disavow, is that men are not gentle creatures who want to be loved, and who at the most can defend themselves if they are attacked; they are, on the contrary, creatures among whose instinctual endowments is to be reckoned a powerful share of aggressiveness. As a result, their neighbour is for them not only a potential helper or sexual object, but also someone who tempts them to satisfy their aggressiveness on him, to exploit his capacity for work without compensation, to use him sexually without his consent, to seize his possessions, to humiliate him, to cause him pain, to torture and kill him. *Homo homini lupus* (p. 111).

The instinct which thus disrupts interhuman relationships and forces society to set itself up as the implacable agent of justice is, as we know, the *death instinct*—man's primordial hostility toward man.

The entire economy of Freud's essay is altered by the introduction of the death instinct. Although "social erotics" might, strictly speaking, appear as an *extension* of sexual erotics, as a displacement of its object or a sublimation of its goal, the division between Eros and death on the cultural level can no longer appear as the extension of a conflict which has already been analyzed on the individual level. On the contrary, the tragic in culture is privileged to reveal an antagonism which on the level of life and the individual psychism remains silent and ambiguous. Freud had, of course, already forged his doctrine of the death instinct by 1920 (*Beyond the Pleasure Principle*), but he did so within an apparently *biological* framework and without emphasizing the *social* aspect of aggressiveness. However, in spite of experimental support for his theory (repetition neurosis, infantile play, the tendency to relive painful episodes, etc.), it retained a quality of adventurous speculation. By 1930 Freud saw more clearly that the death instinct remains a silent instinct "within" the living organism and that it becomes manifest only in its social expression as aggressiveness and destruction. This is the sense of our earlier statement that the interpretation of culture possesses the unique privilege of revealing the antagonism of the instincts.

Thus, in the second part of Freud's essay we witness a sort of rereading of the theory of instincts in terms of their cultural expression. We can better understand why, on the psychological level, the death instinct is both an inescapable inference and an experience difficult to locate. It is never grasped except in the shadow of Eros, for Eros is what uses it by diverting it upon something other than the living organism. In this way the death instinct becomes blended with Eros when it takes the form of sadism, and we find it at work against the living organism itself through masochistic satisfaction. In short, the death instinct reveals itself only in conjunction with Eros, either by doubling the object libido or by overloading the narcissistic libido. It is unmasked and unveiled only as *anticulture*. A progressive revelation of the death instinct takes place across the three levels of the biological, the psychological, and the cultural. Its antagonism grows louder and louder as Eros progressively registers its effects of uniting first the living organism with itself, then the ego with its object, and finally individuals in ever larger groups. In repeating itself from level to level, the struggle between Eros and Death becomes more and more manifest and attains its full meaning only on the level of culture:

> This aggressive instinct is the derivation and the main representative of the death instinct which we have found alongside of Eros and which shares world dominion with it. And now, I think, the meaning of the evolution of civilization is no longer obscure to us. It must present the struggle between Eros and Death, between the instinct of life and the instinct of destruction, as it works itself out in the human species. This struggle is what all life essentially consists of, and the evolution of civilization may therefore be simply described as the struggle for the life of the human species. And it is this battle of the giants that our nurse-maids try to appease with their lullaby about Heaven: *Eiapopeia vom Himmel!* (p. 122).

But this is not the end. In the final chapters of *Civilization and Its Discontents* the relationships between psychology and the theory of culture are completely reversed. At the beginning of this essay it was the economy of the libido, a term borrowed from the metapsychology, which served as a guide in the elucidation of the phenomenon of culture. Then, with the introduction of the death instinct, the interpretation of culture and the dialectic of the instincts begin to rebound upon each other in a circular movement. With the introduction of the feeling of guilt the theory of culture takes over as that which by rebound supports psychology. The feeling of guilt is in fact introduced as a "means" used by civilization to tame aggressiveness. The cultural interpretation is pushed so far that Freud can assert that the express intent of his essay is "to represent the sense of guilt as the most important problem in the development of civilization" (p. 134) and to explain why the progress of civilization should exact a loss of happiness due to the reinforcement of this sense. He quotes Hamlet's famous line in support of this conception: "Thus conscience does make cowards of us all."

If, therefore, the feeling of guilt is the specific means used by civilization to tame aggressiveness, it is not surprising that *Civilization and Its Discontents* contains the most developed interpretation of this feeling. Although its fabric is fundamentally psychological, the psychology of this feeling is possible only as the result of an "economic" interpretation of culture. From the viewpoint of individual psychology, in fact, the feeling of guilt appears to be no more than the effect of the internalized and introjected aggressiveness which the supergo takes over in the name of moral consciousness and then returns against the ego. Its entire "economy," however, appears only when the need for punishment is relocated within a cultural perspective: "Civilization, therefore, obtains mastery over the individual's dangerous desire for aggression by weakening and disarming it and by setting up an agency within him to watch over it, like a garrison in a conquered city" (pp. 123–24).

Hence the economic and, one might say, structural interpretation of guilt feelings can be constructed only from within a cultural perspective. It is only within the framework of this structural interpretation that the various partial genetic interpretations concerning the murder of the primitive father and the institution of remorse which Freud elaborated at different stages of his thought can be understood and put into place. Considered alone, this explanation remains problematic because of the contingency it introduces into the history of a feeling which is otherwise represented with features of "fatal inevitability"

(p. 132). The contingent character of the process reconstructed by genetic explanation is attenuated as soon as genetic explanation itself is subordinated to a structural-economic one:

> Whether one has killed one's father or has abstained from doing so is not really the decisive thing. One is bound to feel guilty in either case, for the sense of guilt is an expression of the conflict due to ambivalence, of the eternal struggle between Eros and the instinct of destruction and death. This conflict is set going as soon as men are faced with the task of living together. So long as the community assumes no other form than that of the family, the conflict is bound to express itself in the Oedipus complex, to establish the conscience, and to create the first sense of guilt. When an attempt is made to widen the community, the same conflict is continued in forms which are dependent on the past; and it is strengthened and results in a further intensification of the sense of guilt. Since civilization obeys an internal erotic impulsion which causes human beings to unite in a closely knit group, it can only achieve this aim through an ever-increasing reinforcement of the sense of guilt. What began in relation to the father is completed in relation to the group. If civilization is a necessary course of development from the family to humanity as a whole, then—as a result of the inborn conflict arising from ambivalence, of the eternal struggle between the trends of love and death—there is inextricably bound up with it an increase of the sense of guilt, which will perhaps reach heights that the individual finds hard to tolerate (pp. 132–33).

By the end of these various analyses we come to believe that the economic viewpoint is what reveals the meaning of culture. But conversely, we must say that the supremacy of the economic viewpoint over all others, including the genetic viewpoint, will be complete only when psychoanalysis takes the risk of placing its instinctual dynamic in the much larger framework of a theory of culture.

2. Illusion and the Turn to the "Genetic" Model

It is within the cultural sphere, defined in terms of the topographic-economic model borrowed from the *Papers on Metapsychology*, that Freud can relocate art, morality, and religion. But he takes up these topics by way of their "economic" function instead of their presumed object. This is the price for assuring a unity of interpretation.

Religion's role in such an economic model is that of "illusion." We must not protest. Even if Freud the rationalist recognizes only the observable and verifiable as real, it is not as a sort of "rationalism" or "unbelief" that this theory of "illusion" is important. Both Epicurus and Lucretius had said, long before, that it is primarily fear which produces gods. What is new in Freud's theory is an *economic* theory of illusion. The question Freud poses is not that of God as such but that of the god of men and his economic function in the balance sheet of the instinctual renunciations, substitutive satisfactions, and compensations by which men try to make life tolerable.

The key to illusion is the harshness of life, which is barely tolerable for man, since he not only understands and feels pain but yearns for consolation as a result of his innate narcissism. As we have seen, culture's task is not only to reduce human desire but also to defend man against the crushing superiority of nature. Illusion is the reserve method used by culture when the effective struggle against the evils of existence either has not begun or has not yet succeeded, or has failed, whether temporarily or definitively. It creates gods to exorcise fear, to reconcile man to the cruelty of his lot, and to compensate for the suffering of culture.

What new element does illusion introduce into the economy of the instincts? Essentially an ideational or representational core—the gods—about which it makes assertions—dogma— and these assertions are supposed to grasp a reality. It is this stage of belief in some reality which is responsible for the specificity of illusion in the balance of satisfactions and discontents. The religion forged by man satisfies him only through the medium of assertions that are unverifiable by proofs or rational observations. The question arises, therefore, of the source of this representational core of illusion.

Here is where global interpretation along the lines of the economic model takes in all partial interpretations in terms of some "genetic" model. The rivet which holds together explanations by origin with explanations by function is *illusion,* i.e., the enigma proposed by a representation without an object. Freud concludes that this can make sense only by means of a genesis of the irrational. Such a genesis, however, remains homogeneous with economic explanation. The essential characteristic of "illusion," he repeats, is that it arises from human desire. Where does a doctrine without object get its efficacy if not from the force of the most tenacious desire of humanity, the desire for security, which among all others is the desire most foreign to reality?

Totem and Taboo and *Moses and Monotheism* provide the genetic schema which is indispensable for an economic explanation. They reconstitute the historical memories which form not only the true content, which is at the source of ideational distortion, but also (as we shall see when the quasi-neurotic aspect of religion is introduced) the "latent" content, which gives rise to the return of the repressed.

Let us provisionally distinguish the following two aspects: true content, which is dissimulated in distortion, and repressed memories, which later come back in disguised form in religious consciousness.

The first aspect merits attention, first because it conditions the second, but also because it gives us the opportunity to emphasize a curious feature of Freudianism. As opposed to the schools of "demythologization" and even more strongly against those which treat religion as a "myth" disguised as history, Freud insists on the *historical core* which constitutes the phylogenetic origin of religion. This is not surprising, for Freud's genetic explanation requires a *realism* of origins. Hence the depth and care of his research into the beginnings of civilization, as well as those of Jewish monotheism. A series of real fathers who are really massacred by real sons is needed to nourish the return of the repressed. "After this discussion I have no hesitation in declaring that men have always known (in this special way) that they once possessed a primal father and killed him." [2]

The four chapters of *Totem and Taboo* constitute in their author's eyes "the first attempt . . . at applying the point of view and the findings of psychoanalysis to some unsolved problems of social psychology." [3] The genetic viewpoint prevails over the economic viewpoint, which has not yet been clearly elaborated as a model. Freud wants to understand moral constraint, including Kant's categorical imperative (*ibid.*, p. xiv), as a survival of old totemic taboos. On a suggestion by Charles Darwin, he argues that in former times men lived in small hordes, each of which was governed by a vigorous male who had unlimited and brutal power at his disposal, kept all the women to himself, and castrated or massacred any rebellious sons. Then, according to a hypothesis borrowed from Atkinson, he speculates that the sons banded together against the father, killed him, and de-

2. *Moses and Monotheism, SE,* XXIII, 101.
3. Preface to *Totem and Taboo, SE,* Vol. XIII.

voured him, not only to take vengeance upon him but to identify with him. Finally, following the theory of Robertson Smith, Freud argues that the totemic clan of brothers succeeded the father's horde. So that they would not destroy one another in useless struggles, the brothers arrived at a sort of social contract and instituted the taboo of incest and the rule of exogamy. At the same time, they remained under the influence of filial devotion and restored the image of the father in the substitutive form of the animal taboo. The totemic meal thus had the meaning of a solemn repetition of the murder of the father. Religion was born, and the figure of the father, long ago killed, was made its center. It is this same figure who will reemerge in the form of gods, or rather in one omnipotent god. The circle will be complete in the death of Christ and the eucharistic communion.

Here is the common ground between *Moses and Monotheism* and *Totem and Taboo*, the point where they share a mutual project as well as a mutual content. Freud writes at the beginning of the two essays published in *Imago* (Vol. XXIII, nos. 1 and 3) that "we shall even be led on to important considerations regarding the origin of monotheist religions in general." [4] For this purpose he must reconstruct with some claim to authenticity the event of the murder of the father which will be to monotheism what the murder of the primitive father had been to totemism. Hence his attempt to give credence to the hypothesis of an "Egyptian Moses," votary of the cult of Aten, the ethical, universal, and tolerant god, who is himself constructed on the model of a peaceful prince, such as the Pharaoh Akhenaten could have been and such as Moses could have imposed on the Semitic tribes. It is this "hero"—in the sense of Otto Rank, whose influence on this theory is considerable—who was killed by the people. Then the cult of the god of Moses was founded on that of Yahweh, the god of volcanoes, in which it dissimulated its true origin and attempted to forget the murder of the hero. It is thus that the prophets would have been the artisans of a return of the god of Moses and the traumatic-event return in the form of an ethical god. The return *to* the god of Moses would at the same time be the return *of* the repressed trauma. Thus we are faced with the explanation of a resurgence on the level of representation and a return of the repressed on the emotional level as well. The Jewish people furnished Western culture with

4. *Moses and Monotheism*, p. 4. [Subsequent page numbers in parentheses refer to this work.]

the model of self-accusation with which we are familiar because its sense of guilt is nourished on the memory of a murder which it nevertheless spared no effort to dissimulate.

Freud has no intention of minimizing the historical reality of this chain of traumatic events. He points out that "in the group too an impression of the past is retained in unconscious memory-traces" (p. 94). He considers the universality of linguistic symbolism much more as a proof of memory traces of the great traumas of humanity, in terms of the genetic model, than as an incitement to explore other dimensions of language, the imaginary, and myth. The distortion of this memory is the only function of the imaginary to be explored. The hereditary transmission itself, which is irreducible to any direct communication, is of course an embarrassment to Freud, but it must be postulated if we want to cross "the abyss which separates individual and group psychology" and "deal with peoples as we do with an individual neurotic. . . . If this is not so, we shall not advance a step further along the path we entered on, either in analysis or in group psychology. The audacity cannot be avoided" (p. 100). Thus we cannot call this an accessory hypothesis. Freud sees in it one of the principles of the cohesion of his system. "A tradition that was based only on communication could not lead to the compulsive character that attaches to religious phenomena" (p. 101). There can be a return of the repressed only if a traumatic *event* actually took place.

At this point we would be tempted to say that Freud's hypotheses concerning origins are mere subordinate interpretations and have no bearing on the "economic" interpretation, the only fundamental interpretation of "illusion." Quite the contrary is true, however, for in reality it is the genetic interpretation that perfects and completes the economic theory of "illusion." The economic theory integrates the results of these investigations concerning origins, and these investigations in turn emphasize a characteristic which had not before been brought to light, namely, the role played by the *return of the repressed* in the genesis of illusion. It is this characteristic which makes religion the "universal obsessional neurosis of humanity." But this characteristic could not appear before genetic explanation had suggested the existence of an analogy between the religious problematic and the childhood situation. The child, as Freud recalls, reaches maturity only through a more or less distinct phase of obsessional neurosis which usually is spontaneously liquidated but which sometimes requires the intervention of analysis. In the same way, mankind is forced during its own adolescence—a stage which we have not yet left behind—into an instinctual renunciation by way of a neurosis which arises from the same ambivalent position of the instincts with respect to the father. A number of texts written by Freud and also Theodore Reik develop this analogy between religion and obsessional neurosis. *Totem and Taboo*, for example, had already seen the neurotic character of taboos, in that an analogous delirium of touching can be discerned in both taboo and neurosis, having the same mixture of desire and horror. Customs, taboos, and symptoms of obsessional neurosis have in common the same absence of motivation, the same laws of fixation, displacement, and contagiousness, and the same ceremonial procedures which spring from prohibitions.[5] In both cases the fact that the repressed has been forgotten confers on the prohibition the same character of strangeness and unintelligibility, feeds the same desires for transgression, provokes the same symbolic satisfactions, the same phenomena of substitution and compromise and expiatory renunciations, and, finally, nourishes the same ambivalent attitudes with respect to prohibition (pp. 100 ff.). During the period when Freud had not yet elaborated his theory of the superego, and especially his theory of the death instinct, "moral" consciousness or conscience (which he still interpreted as the internal perception of the repudiation of certain desires) was treated as a derivative of the taboo sense of guilt (p. 68). "In fact, one may venture to say that if we cannot trace the origin of the sense of guilt in obsessional neurotics, there can be no hope of *ever* tracing it" (pp. 68–69). The ambivalence of this attraction and repulsion is at the center of all his comparisons during this period.

Freud, of course, was struck by certain differences between taboos and neuroses. "Taboos are not neuroses but social formations," he says (p. 85). But he sought to reduce the gap by explaining the social aspect of the taboo by means of the organization of punishment and this organization by fear of the contagion of the taboo (p. 86). He added that social tendencies themselves contain a mixture of egotistical and erotic elements (p. 88). This theme is also developed in *Group Psychology and the Analysis of the Ego* (and particularly in chapter V, "The Church and the Army"). In this essay, which dates from 1921, Freud proposed

5. *Totem and Taboo*, p. 72. [Subsequent page numbers in parentheses refer to this work.]

an entirely "libidinal" or "erotic" interpretation of the attachment to the leader and the cohesion of groups on an authoritarian base and hierarchical structure.

Moses and Monotheism emphasizes as much as possible the neurotic nature of religion, and its principal occasion for doing so lies in the "phenomenon of latency" in the history of Judaism —that delay in the resurgence of the religion of Moses which had been repressed in the cult of Yahweh. Here we come across the intersection between the genetic and the economic models. Between "traumatic neurosis and Jewish monotheism there is one point of agreement: namely, in the characteristic that might be described as 'latency.'" [6] "This analogy is so close that one can almost speak of an identity" (p. 72). Once the schema of the evolution of neurosis is admitted (early trauma—defense—latency—outbreak of neurotic illness—partial return of the repressed) the rapprochement of the history of the human race with that of the individual does the rest:

> Something occurred in the life of the human species similar to what occurs in the life of individuals: of supposing, that is, that there too events occurred of a sexually aggressive nature, which left behind them permanent consequences but were for the most part fended off and forgotten, and which after a long latency came into effect and created phenomena similar to systems in their structure and purpose (p. 80).

Jewish monotheism thus takes over from totemism in Freud's history of the return of the repressed. The Jewish people renewed the primitive contract in the personage of Moses, an eminent substitute for the father. The murder of Christ is another reinforcement of the memory of origins, while Passover and Easter are the resurrection of Moses. Finally, the religion of Saint Paul completes the return of the repressed by leading it back to its prehistoric source, which is named original sin. A crime had been committed against God, according to this theory, and only death can redeem it. Freud passes quickly over the "phantasm" of expiation, which is at the center of the Christian kerygma (p. 86), and suggests that the Redeemer had to be the most guilty one, the chief of the fraternal clan, the parallel to the rebellious tragic hero in Greek tragedy (pp. 87 ff.): "behind him [is hidden] the returned primal father of the primitive

---

6. *Moses and Monotheism,* p. 68. [Subsequent page numbers refer to this work.]

horde, transfigured, and, as the son, put in the place of the father" (p. 90).

This analogy with traumatic neurosis confirms our interpretation of the reciprocal action in Freud's work between the etiology of neuroses and the hermeneutics of culture. Religion presents an occasion for a rereading of neurosis, just as the analogous sense of guilt plunges it back into the dialectic of death and life instincts. The "topographic" model (in which the id, the ego, and the superego are differentiated), the "genetic" model (the role of childhood and phylogenesis), and the "economic" model (cathexis and anticathexis) converge in the ultimate interpretation of the return of the repressed (p. 97).

3. Religious "Illusion" and Aesthetic "Seduction"

Freud's economic interpretation of illusion finally allows us to locate aesthetic seduction with respect to religious illusion. As is well known, Freud's severity toward religion is in sharp contrast to his sympathy for the arts. This difference of tone is not fortuitous. The reason can be found in the general economy of cultural phenomena. For Freud, art is the nonobsessional, nonneurotic form of substitutive satisfaction. The *charm* of aesthetic creation does not arise from the return of the repressed.

At the beginning of this study we alluded to the article in the review *Imago* which, as early as 1908, Freud devoted to "Creative Writers and Daydreaming" and to the analogical method which he set into operation. A general theory of fantasy already underlay his method here, and an opening can be glimpsed leading toward the later theory of culture. Freud poses the question of whether, if poetry is so close to daydreaming, the artist's *technique* aims at hiding the fantasy as much as communicating it. Does he not seek to overcome by the seduction of purely formal pleasure the repulsion that would arise from an overly direct evocation of what has been prohibited? The *ars poetica* thus evoked[7] now appears as the other pole of illusion. The artist seduces us, Freud writes, by a "yield of pleasure which he offers us in the presentation of his fantasies." The whole interpretation of culture from the years 1929–39 is contained *in nuce* in the following lines:

7. "Creative Writers and Daydreaming," *SE*, IX, 153. [Subsequent page numbers refer to this work.]

We give the name of an *incentive bonus,* or a *fore-pleasure,* to a yield of pleasure such as this, which is offered to us so as to make possible the release of still greater pleasure arising from deeper psychical sources. In my opinion, all the aesthetic pleasure which a creative writer affords us has the character of a fore-pleasure of this kind, and our actual enjoyment of an imaginative work proceeds from a liberation of tension in our minds. It may even be that not a little of this effect is due to the writer's enabling us thenceforward to enjoy our own daydreams without self-reproach or shame (p. 153).

Freud's eventual articulation of aesthetics into a general theory of culture can perhaps best be seen in "The Moses of Michelangelo." Nowhere else can we better understand how many apparently immovable obstacles this interpretation will upset. This essay is the fruit of a long familiarity with the masterpiece and of many drawings by which Freud attempted to reconstitute the successive positions which are condensed in Moses' actual gesture; and Freud's interpretation indeed proceeds, just as in the interpretation of dreams, from the details. This appropriately analytical method allows Freud to superimpose dream work on creative work and an interpretation of dreams on interpretation of the work of art. Therefore, rather than seeking to interpret the nature of the satisfaction which is generated by works of art on the level of the widest generalities (a task in which too many psychoanalysts have gone astray), the psychoanalyst attempts to resolve the general enigma of aesthetics by turning first to a single work and the meanings created by that work. We are acquainted with the patience and detail of this interpretation. Here, as in a dream analysis, it is the precise and apparently minor fact which counts and not the impression of the whole: the position of the prophet's right index finger (the only finger which touches his beard, while the rest of the hand holds back), the unstable position of the Tablets, about to escape from the pressure of his arms. Freud's interpretation reconstitutes, in the filigree of this momentary posture, which is in a sense frozen in the stone, the series of opposing movements which found a sort of unstable compromise in this arrested movement. Moses must first of all have brought his hand to his beard in a gesture of anger—at the risk of allowing the Tablets to fall —while his eyes were violently attracted to one side by the spectacle of his idolatrous people. An opposing movement, however, checks the first and, arising from the strong consciousness of his religious mission, brings his hand back. What is before our eyes is the residue of a movement which had taken place and which Freud took upon himself to reconstruct in the same way that he reconstructs the opposing representations which generate compromise formations in dreams, neuroses, errors, and jokes. Freud digs beneath this compromise formation and discovers in the depths of apparent meaning, in addition to the exemplary expression of a triumph over inner conflict which is worthy of guarding a pope's tomb, a secret reproach to the violence of the dead pope and, in a sense, a warning to itself.

The exegesis of "The Moses of Michelangelo" is thus not a mere sidelight. It is situated on a single trajectory, which begins with *The Interpretation of Dreams* and passes through *The Psychopathology of Everyday Life* and *Jokes and Their Relation to the Unconscious.*

This unity of purpose allows us to question Freud's right to submit the work of art to the same treatment. For the art work is, as they say, a lasting and, in the widest sense of the term, a memorable creation of the day, while the dream is, as we know, a fugitive and sterile production of the night. Does not the work of art last and remain for the simple reason that it possesses undying meanings which enrich our patrimony of cultural values? This objection cannot be ignored, for it gives us the occasion to grasp the range of what we have hesitantly called a hermeneutics of culture. The psychoanalysis of culture is valuable not *in spite of* the fact that it is unaware of the value difference between dream productions and works of art but *because* it knows this difference and attempts to take account of it from an economic viewpoint. The whole problem of sublimation comes from this decision to place a fully recognized value opposition within the unitary viewpoint of a genesis and economics of the libido.

The value contrast between the "creative" and the "sterile"— an opposition which a descriptive phenomenology would hold as an originary given—poses a *problem* for an "economics." Freud so little ignores this value contrast that he feels compelled to carry the unitary dynamics further (or backwards, if you will) and to understand what allocation of cathexes and anticathexes is capable of generating the contrasting production of symptoms, on the level of dreams and neuroses, and of expression, on the level of the arts and of culture in general. This is why the analyst must take into account all the arguments that might be brought against a naïve assimilation of phenomena of cultural *expressivity* to a hastily plagiarized *symptomatology*, which really belongs to the theory of dreams and neuroses. He must recapitulate all the themes which emphasize the contrast between the two orders of production, themes which he can find in the aesthetics of Kant, Schelling, Hegel, or Alain. On this condition alone does his interpretation not suppress but retain and contain the duality of symptom and expression. Even after his interpretation, it remains true that the dream is a private expression, lost in the solitude of sleep, an expression which lacks the mediation of work, the incorporation of a meaning into an unyielding substance, and the communication of this meaning to a public—in short, the power of advancing consciousness toward a new comprehension of itself. The force of psychoanalytic explanation is precisely that of relating the contrasting cultural values of the creation of a work and neurosis to a single scale of creativity and a unified economics. By the same token it unites Plato's views on the fundamental unity of poetics and erotics, those of Aristotle on the continuity between purgation and purification, and those of Goethe on demonism.

Perhaps we must go even further. What analysis claims to overcome is not only the phenomenological contrast between dreams and culture but also a contrast internal to the economic model itself. A second objection will help us to formulate this theme.

One might object to the interpretation of Michelangelo's *Moses,* and even more to that of Sophocles' *Oedipus Rex* and Shakespeare's *Hamlet,* by pointing out that, if these works are creations, it is because they are not simple projections of the artists' conflicts but are outlines of their solutions. The argument will be that the dream looks backward toward childhood and the past, while the art work is an advance on the artist himself. It is a prospective symbol of personal synthesis and of the future of man rather than a regressive symbol of his unresolved conflicts. This is why the art lover's understanding is not a simple reliving of his personal conflicts, a fictive realization of the desires awakened in him by the drama, but a participation in the work of truth which is realized in the soul of the tragic hero. Thus Sophocles' creation of the character of Oedipus is not the simple manifestation of the childhood drama which bears his name but the invention of a new symbol of the pain of self-consciousness. This symbol does not repeat our childhood; it explores our adult life.

At first sight this objection comes directly into conflict with certain of Freud's own declarations, in "On Dreams," about

Sophocles' *Oedipus Rex* or Shakespeare's *Hamlet*. But the objection is decisive, perhaps, only against a still naïve formulation of the hermeneutics that results from analysis, and perhaps it arises from a conception, itself naïve, of creation as a promotion of meanings for a supposedly pure consciousness. Thus, like the preceding objection, this one is less to be refuted than surpassed and integrated, at the same time as the thesis to which it is opposed, in a larger and more penetrating view of the dynamics which commands the two processes. "Regression" and "progression" would be not so much two diametrically opposed processes as two aspects of the same creativity. Kris, Loewenstein, and Hartmann proposed an all-encompassing and synthetic expression in their formula "regressive progression" (*Organization and Pathology of Thought*)[8] for designating the complex process by which the psychism elaborates new conscious meanings and revivifies surpassed unconscious formations. Regression and progression would designate abstract terms deduced from a single concrete process whose two extreme limits they designate (pure regression and pure progression) instead of two processes which are actually opposed to each other. Is there, indeed, a single dream which does not have an exploratory function and does not "prophetically" outline a conclusion to our conflicts? Conversely, is there a single great symbol, created by art and literature, which does not plunge over and over again into the archaism of the conflicts and dramas of individual or collective childhood? Is not the genuine meaning of sublimation the promotion of new meanings by mobilizing old energies which had first been cathected into archaic figures? Do not the most innovative forms an artist, writer, or thinker can generate not have the twofold power of concealing and revealing, of dissimulating the old, in the same way as dream symptoms or neuroses, and of revealing the most incomplete and unrealized possibilities as symbols of the man of the future?

This is the direction in which psychoanalysis can realize its wish to rejoin an integral hermeneutics of culture. To reach this end it must surpass the necessary but abstract opposition between an interpretation which would do no more than extrapolate the symptomatology of dreams and neuroses and an interpretation which would claim to find the domain of creativity in consciousness. Further, it must first reach the level of this opposition and bring it to maturity before it can attain to a concrete

8. Ed. David Rapaport (New York: Columbia University Press, 1951).

dialectic, in which the provisional and finally deceptive alternative between regression and progression will be surpassed.

II. THE PLACE OF FREUDIAN HERMENEUTICS

WE SAID AT THE BEGINNING that psychoanalysis becomes part of culture by *interpreting* it. How will our culture come to understand itself by means of the representation given to it by psychoanalysis?

We should understand from the start that this interpretation is biased and incomplete and even systematically unjust toward other approaches to the phenomenon of culture. But this criticism is not very important, because Freudian interpretation touches on the essential precisely as a result of its narrowness. The only reason that we must first outline the limits of this hermeneutics of culture, therefore, is so that we may eventually better locate ourselves in the center of what it circumscribes and there adopt its position of force. However legitimate criticisms may be, they must yield to a willingness to be taught and to submit such criticism itself to the interrogation to which psychoanalysis subjects all rationalizations and justifications. For this reason, as opposed to the usual procedure, we will base ourselves on the criticism (Part II) in order to allow to reverberate in us, in the mode of free reflection (Part III), the deliberately didactic account that we have been developing up till now (Part I).

1. *Limits of Principle in the Freudian Interpretation of Culture*

Every comparison of Freudianism with other theories of culture is made difficult by the fact that its creator himself never proposed a reflection on the limits of his interpretation. He admits that there are other instincts than the one he studies, but he never proposes a complete list. He speaks of work, of social bonds, of necessity, and of reality, but he is never clear as to how psychoanalysis might be coordinated with sciences or interpretations other than its own. This is fortunate. Freud's robust partiality leaves us usefully perplexed. Everyone bears the responsibility of *situating* psychoanalysis in his own vision of things.

Yet how can we orient ourselves at the outset? One of our initial remarks can serve as a guide, namely, that Freud grasps the whole of the phenomenon of culture—and even of human reality—but grasps it only from a single point of view. We must therefore seek the limits of the principles of the Freudian interpretation of culture in terms of the "models"—topographic-economic and genetic—instead of in terms of the interpreted content.

What do these models *not* allow to be grasped?

The explanation of culture by its affective cost in pleasure and pain and its phylogenetic and ontogenetic origins is certainly quite illuminating. We will point out later the considerable importance of such an effort (essentially related to that of Marx and Nietzsche) for the unmasking of "false" consciousness. We should not, however, expect from this enterprise anything more than a critique of authenticity. Above all, we must not ask of it what could be called a critique of foundations. That is the task of another method, which is not so much the hermeneutics of psychic expressions—dreams, art works, symptoms, and even religious dogmas—as a reflective method applied to human activity as a whole, i.e., to the effort to exist, to the desire to be, and to the various mediations by which man strives to appropriate for himself the most originary assertion which inhabits his efforts and desires. The interweaving of a reflective philosophy and a hermeneutics of meaning is currently the most urgent task of a philosophical anthropology. But almost the entirety of the "structure of assimilation" in which Freudian metapsychology might be articulated, along with other types of hermeneutics which are foreign to psychoanalysis, is waiting to be constructed. This is not the place to attempt such a construction, but it is at least possible to point out certain border zones within that vast field, and we can take as our touchstone the theory of illusion, whose central meaning in Freud we have seen.

The interest of Freud's concept of illusion is that it demonstrates how representations which "console" us and make suffering tolerable are built not only *on* instinctual renunciation but also *from* this renunciation. The desires and their dynamism of cathexis and anticathexis are what constitute the entire substance of illusion. In this sense we were able to say that the theory of illusion is itself thoroughly economic. But to recognize it as such means that we must also give up seeking in it an exhaustive interpretation of the phenomenon of *value*, for this can be understood only by a more fundamental reflection on the dynamics of action.

Just as we do not resolve the enigma of political power by saying that the bonds to the chief mobilize an entire libidinal cathexis of a homosexual nature, we do not resolve the enigma of the "authority of values" by discerning in the filigree of the moral and social phenomenon the figure of the father and the partly real, partly fantasied, identification with this figure. The *foundation* of a phenomenon such as power or value is one thing, and the affective cost of our experience of it, the balance sheet of human lived experience in pleasure and pain, is another.

Such a distinction between problems of foundation and problems of instinctual economy is surely one of principle. At least it marks the limit of an interpretation in terms of an economic model. Can it be argued that this distinction remains too theoretical and at no point affects the concepts of psychoanalysis, much less the work of the psychoanalyst? I do not believe so. It seems to me that this limit actually appears very concretely in the Freudian notion of *sublimation*, which is in reality an impure, mixed notion which combines an economic and an axiological point of view without formulating principles. In sublimation an instinct works at a "higher" level, although it can be said that the energy cathected in new objects is the *same* as that which before had been cathected in a sexual object. The economic point of view takes account only of that relationship of energy and not of the novelty of value promoted by this renunciation and transfer. The difficulty is modestly hidden by speaking of socially acceptable ends and objects. But social utility is a cloak of ignorance which is thrown over the problem of value introduced by sublimation.

The very meaning of religious "illusion" is thus once again at issue. As we pointed out above, Freud does not speak of God but of the god of men. Psychoanalysis has no means of radically resolving the problem of what Leibniz called "the radical origin of things." It is quite prepared, however, to unmask the infantile and archaic representations through which we live this problem. This distinction is not simply one of principle, for it also concerns the work of the psychoanalyst, who is neither a theologian nor an antitheologian. *As* an analyst he is an agnostic, i.e., incompetent. *As* a psychoanalyst he cannot say whether God is *merely* a phantasm of god, but he can help his patient surpass the infantile and neurotic forms of religious belief and decide, or recognize, whether or not his religion is *only* an infantile and neurotic belief whose true mainspring the psychoanalyst has discovered. If the patient's belief does not survive this critical process, the only reason can be that it was not worthy to survive. But in that case nothing has been said either for or against faith in God. In another language I might say that, if faith must differ from religion, then religion must die in order that faith may be born.

The fact that Freud personally objects to this sort of distinction is of little importance. Freud is an *Aufklärer*, a man of the Enlightenment. His rationalism and, as he says himself, his lack of belief are not the fruit but the presupposition of his interpretation of religious illusion, and he considers his interpretation to be exhaustive. It is unquestionable that the discovery of religion as illusion profoundly changes the conditions of every process of becoming conscious, and we shall argue strongly for that in what follows. But psychoanalysis has no access to problems of radical origin *because* its point of view is economic and only economic.

I will attempt to make a bit more specific what I consider to be wrong with the Freudian interpretation of the cultural phenomenon as a whole and of illusion in particular. For Freud an illusion is a representation to which no reality corresponds. His definition is positivist. Is there not, however, a function of the imagination which escapes the positivist alternative of the real and the illusory? A lesson that we have learned, which is parallel to Freudianism but independent of it, is that myths and symbols are carriers of a meaning which escapes this alternative. A different hermeneutics, distinct from psychoanalysis and closer to the phenomenology of religion, teaches us that myths are not fables, i.e., "false" and "unreal" stories. As opposed to all positivism, this hermeneutics presupposes that the "true" and the "real" cannot be reduced to what can be verified by mathematical and experimental methods but has to do with our relationship to the world, to other beings, and to being as well. It is this relationship which in an imaginative mode the myth begins to explore. Freud is both very close to and very far from recognizing this function of the imagination, with which, in different ways, Spinoza, Schelling, and Hegel were all acquainted. What brings him close to it is his *practice* of "interpretation," but what separates him from it is his "metapsychological" *theorizing*, i.e., the implicit philosophy of the economic model itself. In one sense

Freud indeed constructed his whole theory of interpretation, by the time of the *The Interpretation of Dreams*, against the physicalism and biologism reigning in psychology. Interpretation means going from a manifest to a latent meaning. It moves entirely in relations of meaning and includes relations of force (repression, return of the repressed) only as relations of meaning (censorship, disguise, condensation, displacement). No one since has contributed as much as Freud to breaking the charm of *facts* and opening up the empire of *meaning*. Yet Freud continues to include all of his discoveries in the same positivistic framework which they destroy. In this respect the "economic" model plays an extremely ambiguous role. It is heuristic in its exploration of the depths it reveals but conservative in the tendency which it encourages to transcribe all relationships of "meaning" into the language of a mental *hydraulics*. By the first aspect, that of discovery, Freud breaks through the positivist framework of explanation; by the second, that of theorizing, he strengthens this framework and authorizes the naïve doctrine of "mental dynamics" which too often rages in the school.

It will be the task of a philosophical anthropology to undo these equivocations at the very heart of Freudian metapsychology and coordinate the diverse styles of contemporary hermeneutics, in particular that of Freud with the phenomenology of myths and symbols. But these diverse styles cannot be coordinated unless they are subordinated to that fundamental reflection which we alluded to above.

This limit of the principles of the "economic" model governs the genetic model as well. As we have seen, Freud explains genetically whatever does not possess positive truth. The "historical" origin (in the phylogenetic and ontogenetic sense) takes the place of an axiological or radical origin. This blindness to all functions of illusion which are not mere distortions of positive reality explains Freud's utter lack of interest for whatever is not a simple repetition of an archaic or infantile form and, in the end, a simple "return of the repressed." This is striking in the case of religion. All that could have been added to primitive consolation, conferred by gods conceived in the image of the father, is without importance. Who can settle the question, then, of whether religion lies in the *return* of memories bound to the murder of the father of the horde rather than in the innovations by which religion moves away from its primitive model? Is meaning in genesis or in epigenesis? In the return of the repressed or in the rectification of the old by the new?[9] A genetic explanation cannot decide this question, for it requires a radical explanation, such as, for example, Hegel's in *The Philosophy of Religion*. It requires a reflection which turns to the progress of religious representation and not to its repetition.

Our doubts concerning the legitimacy of the genetic model are directly linked to our previous question of the limits of the economic model. It could indeed be the case that in its function of ontological exploration the mythopoetic imagination is the instrument of this innovative correction, which moves in a direction opposite to archaizing repetition. There is a progressive history of the symbolic function, of imagination, which does not coincide with the regressive history of illusion in the form of a simple "return of the repressed." But are we in a position to distinguish between these two histories, this movement forward and this regression, this creation and this repetition?

Our self-assurance fails us at this point, we know that however well-founded and legitimate our discernment of limits may be, it is indistinguishable from the justifications and rationalizations unmasked by psychoanalysis. This is why we must leave our critique in suspense and turn without defense to the interrogation of self-consciousness by psychoanalysis.

It may even appear at the end of this survey that the "place" of psychoanalysis at the heart of contemporary culture remains and should remain indeterminate as long as what it has to teach has not yet been assimilated. This is so in spite of and perhaps

9. Freud ran into the limits of his theory on a number of occasions. Where, he asks in *Moses and Monotheism,* is the origin of the later advancement of the idea of God which begins with the prohibition to adore Him in visible form? Belief in thought as all-powerful (*ibid.,* p. 170), which accompanies man's estimation of the development of language, seems to operate on a different level from that ordered by the genetic and topographic-economic models. Freud, however, does not develop this theme any further. In the same way, the shift of emphasis away from motherhood (which is *perceived*) to fatherhood (which is *conjectured*) suggests that not everything is said when the ambivalence of love and fear is discussed. Furthermore, is the happiness of renunciation fully explained by turning first to the idea of a surplus of love, by which the superego, the heir of the father, responds to renunciation of instinctual satisfaction, and second to the idea of an increasing narcissism which accompanies the consciousness of a worthy act (pp. 174–78)? And why must the meaning of religion be sought only in "instinctual renunciation"? Why does it not support the pact of the brothers as well and the recognition of the equality of rights for all the members of the fraternal clan? Not everything here is the perpetuation of the will of the father or the return of the repressed. There is also the emergence of a new order.

because of its limits. Comparing it with other interpretations of culture, no longer opposed but concurrent, will help us take this new step.

2. Marx, Nietzsche, Freud

Freud's work is clearly as important for the heightened consciousness of modern man as the work of Marx or Nietzsche. The relatedness of these three critiques of "false" consciousness is striking. But we are still far from assimilating these three interrogations of self-consciousness and integrating these three exercises in *suspicion* within ourselves. We still pay too much attention to their differences, i.e., to the limitations which the prejudices of their time imposed on these three thinkers; and we are, above all, still victims of the scholasticism in which their epigones have enclosed them. Marx is thus relegated to Marxist economism and to the absurd theory of consciousness as reflex, while Nietzsche is associated with biologism if not with an apology for violence, and Freud is confined within psychiatry and dressed up in a simplistic pansexualism.

I hold that the meaning for our time of these three exegetes of modern man can be rectified only if they are considered jointly.

First of all, they all attack the same illusion, that illusion which bears the hallowed name of self-consciousness. This illusion is the fruit of a preceding victory, which conquered the previous illusion of the *thing*. The philosopher trained in the school of Descartes knows that things are doubtful, that they are not what they appear to be. But he never doubts that consciousness is at it appears to itself. In consciousness, meaning and the consciousness of meaning coincide. Since Marx, Nietzsche, and Freud, however, we doubt even this. After doubting the thing, we have begun to doubt consciousness.

These three masters of suspicion, however, are not three masters of skepticism. They are surely three great "destroyers," but even that should not distract us. Destruction, as Heidegger says in *Being and Time*, is a moment in *every new foundation. The "destruction" of hidden worlds is a positive task,* and this includes the destruction of religion insofar as it is, as Nietzsche says, "a Platonism for the people." Only after such a "destruction" is the question posed of knowing what thought, reason, and even faith still mean.

All three free our horizon for a more authentic speaking, a new reign of truth, not only by means of a "destructive" critique but by the invention of an art of *interpreting.* Descartes triumphs over his doubts about things through the evidence of consciousness, while Marx, Nietzsche, and Freud triumph over their doubt about consciousness through an exegesis of meanings. For the first time comprehension is hermeneutics. Henceforth, seeking meaning no longer means spelling out the consciousness of meaning but, rather, *deciphering its expressions.* We are therefore faced not with three types of suspicion but with three types of deception. If consciousness is not what it believes itself to be, a new relationship must be established between the apparent and the latent. It would correspond to the relationship which consciousness had previously instituted between the thing's appearance and its reality. The fundamental category of consciousness for all three thinkers is the relationship "concealed-revealed"—or, if you will, the relationship "counterfeit-manifest." That Marxists stubbornly insist on their theory of the "reflex," that Nietzsche contradicts himself by dogmatizing over the "perspectivism" of the will to power, or that Freud mythologizes with his "censor," "doorkeeper," and "disguises"—these obstacles and dead ends are not what is essential. What is essential is that all three create with the means they possess—i.e., with and against the prejudices of their epoch—a mediating *science of meaning* which is irreducible to the immediate *consciousness of meaning.* What all three attempted in different ways was to make their "conscious" methods of decoding coincide with the "unconscious" *work* of establishing a code which they attributed to the will to power, to the social being, or to the unconscious psyche. They do it through guile—and guile and a half. In Freud's case it is the admirable discovery of "On Dreams." The analyst deliberately takes in the opposite direction the path that the dreamer took, without willing it or knowing it, in his "dream work." Consequently, what distinguishes Marx, Freud, and Nietzsche is both their method of decoding and their representations of the process of coding which they attribute to unconscious being. It could not be otherwise, since method and representation are coextensive and verify each other. Thus for Freud the meaning of the dream—more generally, the meaning of symptoms and compromise formations and, even more generally, the meaning of psychic expressions as a whole—is inseparable from "analysis" as a tactic of decoding. One can even say, in a nonskeptical sense, that this meaning is proposed and even created by analysis and is therefore relative to the procedures which instituted it. This can be said, but only on the condition of saying the opposite: that the method is verified by the coherence of the *discovered* meaning and, moreover, that the method is justified by the fact that the discovered meaning not only satisfies the understanding through an intelligibility greater than the disorder of apparent consciousness but that it *liberates* the dreamer or the patient when he comes to recognize it and make it his own—in short, when the carrier of meaning *consciously becomes this meaning*, which up till now existed only outside him, "in" his unconscious and afterwards "in" the consciousness of his analyst.

That this meaning which had been only for *another* should become conscious for itself, that is precisely what the analyst wants for his patient. By the same token, an even deeper relationship is discovered between Marx, Freud, and Nietzsche. All three, as we said, begin with suspicions about the illusions of consciousness and operate by the guile of decipherment. All three, finally, far from being detractors of "consciousness," aim at extending it. What Marx wants is to liberate *praxis* by the awareness of necessity. This liberation, however, is inseparable from a "becoming conscious" which victoriously opposes the mystifications of false consciousness. What Nietzsche wants is to augment man's *power* and restore his *force*, but what the will to power means must be regained by the mediation of the code of the "overman," the "eternal return," and "Dionysus," without which this power would be no more than the violence of the immanent. What Freud wants is for the patient to make the meaning which was foreign to him his own and thus enlarge his field of consciousness, live better, and, finally, be a bit freer and, if possible, a bit happier. One of the most important homages rendered to psychoanalysis speaks of the "cure through consciousness." Correct—as long as we realize that analysis wants to substitute a mediating consciousness under the tutelage of the reality principle for immediate and deceptive consciousness. Thus the same *doubter* who depicts the ego as a "poor wretch" dominated by three masters (the id, the superego, and reality or necessity) is also the exegete who rediscovers the logic of the illogical kingdom and dares, with a modesty and discretion without parallel, to end his essay on *The Future of an Illusion* by invoking the god Logos, whose voice is weak but indefatigable, a God who is not all-powerful but simply efficacious in the long run.

III. The Repercussions of Freudian Hermeneutics in Culture

This, then, is what these three exegetes wanted to do for modern man. But we are far from having assimilated their discoveries and from understanding ourselves fully through the means of interpretation of ourselves which they offer us. We must admit that their interpretations still float at a distance from us and that they have not yet found their proper place. The gap between their interpretation and our comprehension remains immense. Moreover, we are not faced with a unified interpretation to be assimilated as a whole but with three distinct interpretations, whose discordances are more manifest than their similarities. There as yet exists no structure of assimilation, no coherent discourse, no philosophical anthropology which is capable of integrating our hermeneutic consciousness of Marx, Nietzsche, and Freud into a whole. Their traumatizing effects accumulate and their powers of destruction add up, but their exegeses have not been coordinated in the unity of a new consciousness. This is why we must admit that the meaning of psychoanalysis as an event within modern culture remains in suspense and its place undetermined.

1. *Resistance to the Truth*

It is remarkable that psychoanalysis itself takes account of this delay and suspension in becoming conscious of the event which it represents for culture, and it does so through its own interpretative schemata. Consciousness "resists" self-comprehension, just as Oedipus "resisted" the truth known by everyone else. He refused to recognize himself in the man he had condemned. Self-recognition is the true tragedy, a tragedy on a second level. What is tragic in consciousness—the tragic quality of refusal and anger—doubles the primary tragedy, the tragedy of such a being, of incest and parricide. Freud spoke magnificently of this "resistance" to the truth in a famous and often quoted text, "A Difficulty in the Path of Psychoanalysis" (1917).[10]

10. *SE*, Vol. XVII.

Psychoanalysis, he says, is chronologically the most recent of the "severe blows" which "the universal narcissism of men, their self-love, has up to the present suffered . . . from the researches of science" (p. 139). First there was the cosmological humiliation inflicted upon man by Copernicus, who destroyed the narcissistic illusion by which the home of man remained at rest in the center of the universe. Then there came biological humiliation, when Darwin put an end to man's claim to be unconnected with the animal kingdom. Finally came psychological humiliation. Man, who already knew that he was lord of neither the cosmos nor all living things, discovers that he is not even lord of his own psyche. Psychoanalysis thus addresses itself to the ego:

> You feel sure that you are informed of all that goes on in your mind if it is of any importance at all, because in that case, you believe, your consciousness gives you news of it. And if you have had no information of something in your mind you confidently assume that it does not exist there. Indeed, you go so far as to regard what is "mental" as identical with what is "conscious"— that is, with what is known to you—in spite of the most obvious evidence that a great deal more must constantly be going on in your mind than can be known to your consciousness. Come, let yourself be taught something on this point! . . . You behave like an absolute ruler who is content with the information supplied him by his highest officials and never goes among the people to hear their voice. Turn your eyes inward, look into your own depths, learn first to know yourself! Then you will understand why you were bound to fall ill; and perhaps you will avoid falling ill in the future (pp. 142–43).

"Come, let yourself be taught something on this point! . . . Turn your eyes inward, look into your own depths, learn first to know yourself!" It is in this way that psychoanalysis understands its own insertion into community consciousness by way of instruction and clarity. Such instruction, however, encounters the *resistance* of a primitive and persistent narcissism, that is, of a libido which is never cathected completely in objects but is retained by the ego for itself. This is why the instruction of the ego is necessarily lived as a humiliation, a wound in the libido of the ego.

The theme of narcissistic humiliation greatly clarifies all that we have just said about suspicion, guile, and the extension of the field of consciousness. We now know that it is not consciousness which is humiliated but the pretension of consciousness, the libido of the ego. We also know that what does the humiliating is precisely a higher consciousness, a "clarity," scientific knowledge, as Freud the good rationalist says. In a larger sense we can say that it is a consciousness which is decentered from itself, unpreoccupied, and "displaced" toward the immensity of the cosmos by Copernicus, toward the mobile genius of life by Darwin, and toward the shadowy depths of the psyche by Freud. Consciousness nourishes itself by recentering itself around its Other: cosmos, bios, or psyche. It finds itself by losing itself. It finds itself instructed and clarified after losing itself and its narcissism.

2. The "Immediate" Reactions of Community Consciousness

The gap between the *interpretation* of culture introduced by psychoanalysis and its *comprehension* by community consciousness explains, if not totally at least partially, the perplexity of community consciousness. As we said above, psychoanalysis finds its place in culture only with difficulty. We now know that we become conscious of its meaning only across the truncated representations which arise from the resistance of our narcissism.

These truncated *representations* are what we encounter on the level of short-term influences and immediate reactions. The level of "short-term" influences is one of *vulgarization,* and that of "immediate" reactions is one of *small talk.* Still, it is not without interest to pause a moment on this level. Psychoanalysis has taken the risk of being judged, praised, and condemned on such an everyday level. From the moment that Freud began giving lectures and publishing books he addressed himself to nonanalysts and nonanalysands and brought psychoanalysis into the public domain. In any case, his words fell outside the precise intersubjective relation between the doctor and his patient from the very beginning. This diffusion of psychoanalysis out of the therapeutic context is a considerable cultural event, which social psychology has in its turn made into a subject of scientific inquiry, measure, and explanation.

It is first of all as a global phenomenon of *demystification* that psychoanalysis has penetrated the public. A hidden and silent part of man became public. "They" speak of sexuality, "they" speak of perversions, repression, the superego, and censorship. In this respect psychoanalysis is an event of the "they," a theme for "small talk." But the conspiracy of silence is also an event of the "they," and hypocrisy is no less small talk than the public exhibition and ridicule of every individual's secret.

No one knows what to do with this demystification, for it is the starting point of the most complete misunderstanding. On the level of "short-term" influences, "they" want to draw an *immediate* ethics from psychoanalysis. Thus "they" use psychoanalysis as a system of *justification* for moral positions whose profundity has not itself undergone psychoanalytic interrogation. Yet psychoanalysis was supposed to have been a tactic for unmasking all justifications. Hence, some ask psychoanalysis to ratify permissive education—since neurosis comes from repression—and find in Freud the discreet and unavowed apologist for a new Epicureanism. Others, placing their emphasis on the theory of stages of maturation and integration and the theory of perversions and regressions, mobilize psychoanalysis in the service of traditional morality. Did Freud not define culture by instinctual sacrifice?

It is true that on a first approximation one might hesitate as to what Freud really wanted. The temptation is to a "wild" psychoanalysis of psychoanalysis. Did Freud not make a public and bourgeois defense of the institution of monogamy while making a secret and revolutionary defense of the orgasm? But the consciousness which poses this question and attempts to enclose Freud within this *ethical* alternative is one which has not experienced the psychoanalytical critique.

The Freudian revolution is that of diagnosis, lucid coldness, and hard-won truths. In an immediate sense, Freud preaches no morality. "I bring no consolation," he says at the end of *The Future of an Illusion.* But men want to convert his science into dogma. When he speaks of perversion and regression, they wonder whether or not it is the scientist who describes and explains or the Viennese bourgeois justifying himself. When he says that man is led by the pleasure principle, they suspect him —for praise or for blame—of slipping approval of an unannounced Epicureanism into his diagnosis, although he looks at the crafty behavior of the moral individual with the unemotional eye of science. This is the misunderstanding: Freud is hearkened to as a prophet, while he speaks as an unprophetic thinker. He does not herald a new ethic but rather changes the consciousness of those for whom the question of ethics remains open. He changes consciousness by changing our knowledge of consciousness and by giving it the key to some of its deceptions. Freud can change our ethic in the long run because he is not a moralist for the immediate future.

3. Is Freud a Tragic Thinker?

Only by rectifying these superficial reactions will community consciousness feel in depth the influence of psychoanalysis. As we have seen, the short term leads only to misunderstandings and contradictions, which result from attempting to draw an immediate ethic from psychoanalysis. The long-term way will be by way of a transformation of self-consciousness through the mediate comprehension of human signs. But where will the long road lead us? We do not know *yet*. Psychoanalysis is an indirect revolution. It will change our customs only by changing the quality of our outlook and the tenor of man's way of speaking about himself. It is first of all the work of truth and enters into the ethical sphere only through the *task of truth* which it proposes.

We can already recognize some lines of force along which can be discerned the influence on the consciousness of modern men of what I just now called the mediate comprehension of human signs.

By placing ourselves once more in the attempt to carry forward the general effort of demystification exercised by psychoanalysis on the most elementary, unsophisticated level, we can say that psychoanalysis focuses attention on what Freud himself calls the *harshness of life*. We can say that it is difficult to be a man. If psychoanalysis appears to plead both for the *diminution* of instinctual sacrifice by means of a relaxation of social prohibitions and for an *acceptance* of this sacrifice as a result of the submission of the pleasure principle to the reality principle, it is not because it believes in an immediate "diplomatic" action between opposing agencies [*instances*]. Rather, it puts all its emphasis on the change in consciousness which will come out of a wider and subtler comprehension of the tragic in humanity, without rushing too quickly to draw the ethical conclusions.

Unlike Nietzsche, Freud does not say that man is a "sick animal." Rather, he makes it clear that conflict is inescapable in human interaction. Why? First, man is the only being who possesses so long a childhood and who, as a result, remains for an incomparably long time in a condition of dependence. He is "historical," as has been said in many ways. Freud says, however, that as a result of his childhood fate, man is first pre-historical and remains so for a long time. The great figures—whether real or fantasied—of the father, the mother, brothers and sisters, the Oedipal crisis, the fear of castration—none of this would be meaningful for a being who was not fundamentally subject to his childhood and marked by the difficulty of becoming adult. Are we acquainted with what would be an adult feeling of guilt?

The tragedy of childhood fate, and also the tragedy of "repetition": It is this tragedy of repetition which is behind all the genetic explanations the limits of whose principles we spoke of above. It is not by methodological caprice but by respect for the truth that Freud leads us ceaselessly back to the *beginning*. Childhood would not be a fate if something did not constantly pull man backwards. No one has been more sensitive than Freud to the tragedy of this backward drift and its various forms, such as the return of the repressed, the libido's tendency to return to surpassed positions, the difficulty of the work of mourning, and in general the decathexis of censored energy and the absence of libidinal mobility. We should not forget that his reflections on the death instinct are for a large part born from this reflection on the tendency to repetition, which Freud did not hesitate to compare to the tendency in the organic world to return to an inorganic state. Thanatos forms a conspiracy with the archaizing spirit in Psyche.

The tragedy of libidinal contradictions: From the *Three Essays on the Theory of Sexuality* we know that the energy of the libido is not simple, that it has neither a single object nor a single end, and that it can always disintegrate and take the path of perversions and regressions. The growing complexity of the Freudian schema of instincts—the distinction between the libido of the ego and the object libido, the reinterpretation of sadism and masochism after the introduction of the death instinct—cannot but reinforce this feeling of a *wandering* nature of human desire. The difficulty of living is thus also—and perhaps above all—the difficulty of loving and of succeeding in a life of love.

This is not all. All these motivations presuppose that psychoanalysis did no more than demystify the sexual. If, over and above exploring the instinctual basis of man, however, it proposes to recognize the "resistance" of consciousness to this demystification and to unmask the justifications and rationalizations by which this "resistance" is expressed, and if it is true that this "resistance" belongs to the same network as the prohibitions and identifications which are the themes of the superego, then we would not be exaggerating to say that the tragedy has two foci, the id and the superego, and not just one. This is why, in addition to the difficulty of becoming adult and the difficulty of loving, there is the difficulty of self-knowledge and of honestly judging oneself. Thus the task of truthfulness is posed for us at the central point of the difficulty of living. In the Oedipus story the true tragedy is not in his having unwittingly killed his father and married his mother. *That* took place long ago. It is a destiny behind him. The tragedy taking place now is that the man he has condemned for this crime is *himself* and that such a fact must be recognized. Wisdom would be in recognizing oneself and in refraining from self-condemnation: but when the aged Sophocles wrote *Oedipus at Colonus,* he knew that Oedipus, even in his old age, had not come to the end of his "rage" against himself.

We can thus understand why it is useless to demand an immediate ethic from psychoanalysis without first having changed human consciousness. Man is an unjustly accused being.

It is perhaps here that Freud is closest to Nietzsche. Accusation is what must be accused. Hegel as well, in criticizing the "moral world view" in the *Phenomenology of Spirit,* had said long before Nietzsche that the judging consciousness is disparaging and hypocritical. Its own finitude and *equality* with the consciousness being judged must be recognized in order that the "remission of sins" can be possible as a reconciling self-knowledge. But Freud does not accuse accusation. He understands it and thus renders *public* its structure and stratagems. The possibility of an authentic ethic, where the cruelty of the superego would yield to the severity of love, lies in this direction. But we must first spend time in learning that the catharsis of desire is nothing without the catharsis of the judging consciousness.

This is not all we must learn *before* coming to an ethic. We have not yet exhausted the instruction which precedes an ethic.

It is indeed possible to reinterpret all that we have said above about culture in the light of these remarks on the twofold tragedy of the id and the superego.

We have seen the place of the notions of "illusion," "substitutive satisfaction," and "seduction" in culture. These notions also belong to the tragic cycle whose foci of proliferation we have just pointed out. Culture is indeed made up of all the procedures by which man escapes in the imaginary mode from the unresolvable situation where desires can be neither suppressed nor satisfied. Between satisfaction and suppression the way of *sublimation* opens up, but this way is also difficult. Yet it is because man can no longer be an animal and is not divine that he enters into this situation from which he cannot extricate himself. Hence he *creates* "delusions and dreams," as does the hero of Jensen's *Gradiva*. He also creates works of art and gods. The great storytelling function which Bergson found in closed societies Freud attributes to the tactic of evasion and illusion elaborated by man not simply *above* his renunciations but with their very flesh. This is an idea with an extraordinary profundity. Since the reality principle bars the way of the pleasure principle, it remains the case that man must "cultivate" the art of *substitutive enjoyment*. Man, as we hear again and again, is a being who can *sublimate*. But sublimation brings back the tragic instead of resolving it. Consolation in its turn, i.e., the reconciliation with inevitable sacrifices and the art of supporting the suffering inflicted upon us by our body, the world, and other men, is never harmless. The relationship between religious "illusion" and obsessional neurosis is there to provide evidence that man leaves the sphere of instincts and "rises"—sublimates—only to rediscover in a more insidious form and more twisted disguises the very tragedy of childhood, where we recognized the first tragedy. Only art seems to be without danger, or at least Freud would lead us to believe so. Clearly, all he was acquainted with in art was its idealizing form, its ability to *muffle* the forces of darkness through sweet incantation. Freud seems to have had no suspicion of its vehemence, power of opposition, exploration, excavation, and scandalous explosion. This is why art seems to be the only power which Freud spared from his suspicion. In reality, "sublimation" opens up a new cycle of contradictions and dangers, but is it not the fundamental ambiguity of the imagination to serve two masters at once, Lie and Reality? It serves the lie because it deceives Eros with its fantasies (as we say that hunger is deceived) and reality because it accustoms the eye to Necessity.

Finally, it is the *lucid awareness* of the necessary character of conflicts which is, if not the last word, at least the first of a wisdom which would incorporate psychoanalytic instruction. In this way Freud renewed not only the sources of the tragic but "tragic knowledge" itself, insofar as it is the reconciliation with the inevitable. It is not by chance that Freud—the naturalist, determinist, scientist, heir to the Enlightenment—always turned to the language of tragic myth to say the essential: Oedipus,

Narcissus, Eros, Ananke, and Thanatos. It is this tragic knowledge which must be assimilated in order to reach the threshold of a new ethic which we must no longer attempt to extract from Freud's work by immediate inference. It will be slowly prepared by the fundamentally nonethical teachings of psychoanalysis. The conscious emergence offered by psychoanalysis to modern man is difficult and painful because of the narcissistic humiliation it inflicts. But at this price it is related to the reconciliation whose law was stated by Aeschylus: τῷ πάθει μάθος, "Understanding comes through suffering" (*Agamemnon,* l. 177).

Before such a reconciliation, the critique first outlined and the internal repetition which we spoke of above must be conducted jointly and on a single front. A reflection on the limits of Freudian interpretation remains *in suspense,* as does the profound meaning of that great subversion of self-consciousness inaugurated by Marx, Nietzsche, and Freud.

A Philosophical Interpretation of Freud

Exposition

It is important to distinguish two attitudes a philosopher may adopt toward Freud's written work. These are a "reading" or a "philosophical interpretation." The reading of Freud is the work of a historian of philosophy. It does not pose problems which differ from those we would encounter in a reading of Plato, Descartes, or Kant, and it makes a claim to the same sort of objectivity. A philosophical interpretation is the work of a philosopher. It presupposes the sort of reading which makes a claim to objectivity but goes on to take a position toward the work. It adds a relocation in a different discourse to the architectonic reconstitution of the work. The new discourse is that of the philosopher who thinks from Freud—that is, after, with, and against him. I propose "one" philosophical interpretation of Freud.

1. The reading I presuppose considers Freudian discourse to be a mixed discourse. It intermingles questions of meaning (the meaning of dreams, symptoms, culture, etc.) and questions of force (cathexis, economic accounting, conflict, repression, etc.). I allow here that this mixed discourse is not equivocal but is appropriate to the reality which it wishes to take into account, namely, the binding of force and meaning in a semantics of desire. This reading does justice to the most realistic and naturalistic aspects of Freudian theory, while it never neglects to

Translated by Willis Domingo.

treat "instincts," the "unconscious," and the "id" as significations to be deciphered in their effects of meaning.

2. The question which gives birth to the present interpretation is the following: Can a reflective philosophy make sense of analytical experience and theory? I will assume here that the *Ego cogito* and the *Ego sum* are the foundation of all legitimate propositions about man. If that is true, one can understand Freud by formulating the concept of the archaeology of the subject. This concept defines the philosophical position of analytical discourse. It is not Freud's concept. I formulate it in order to understand myself in my understanding of Freud. It is in and for reflection that psychoanalysis is an archaeology.

But of what subject?

The reading of Freud is also the crisis of the philosophy of the subject. It imposes the dispossession of the subject such as it appears primarily to itself in the form of consciousness. It makes consciousness not a given but a problem and a task. The genuine *cogito* must be gained through the false *cogito*s which mask it.

It is thus that the reading of Freud becomes an adventure of reflection.

3. The question which follows is: Can a subject have an archaeology without having a teleology? This question does not exist without the preceding one. It is not posed by Freud but by reflective thought, which says that only a subject with a *telos* can have an *archē*. The appropriation of a meaning constituted in the past presupposes the movement of a subject drawn ahead of itself by a succession of "figures" (such as in Hegel's *Phenomenology of Spirit*) each of which finds its meaning in those to follow.

This dialectic of archaeology and teleology allows us to reinterpret some Freudian concepts, such as sublimation and identification, which do not, in my opinion, have a satisfactory status in Freud's own systematics.

Finally, this dialectic is the philosophical ground on which the complementarity of rival hermeneutics of art, morality, and religion can be established. Outside it, these interpretations either confront one another without any possible arbitration or else are thrown together in idle eclecticisms which are the caricature of thought.

DEVELOPMENT

I WILL NOT ACT AS COUNSEL for a book in this lecture but will rather devote myself to a free reflection on its difficulties.

Two questions immediately come to mind:

1. Can we, as I have just done, distinguish between *the* reading and *a* philosophical interpretation of Freud?

2. Do we have the right to construct a philosophical interpretation which consists, as I said in my exposition, in relocating the work in a different discourse, especially if this discourse is reflective philosophy?

I will answer the first question both generally and specifically. I can answer generally that philosophy (or, as is awkwardly said, general philosophy) and the history of philosophy are two distinct philosophical activities. A tacit and distinct consensus among historians of philosophy concerning the objectivity that can be attained in their discipline has, I believe, been established. It is possible to understand an author in himself without necessarily deforming or repeating him. I used a term devised by Guéroult in speaking of the "architectonic reconstitution" of a work. But I believe that all other historians—even if they speak in a more Bergsonian sense of philosophical intuition—admit that it is impossible to duplicate a work. The most one can do is grasp it anew from a constellation of themes which have been produced by intuition and especially from a network of articulations which in a sense constitute its substructure and underlying framework. This is why one does not repeat but reconstructs. From a different viewpoint, however, the historian does not falsify the work he studies if he manages to produce, if not a copy of the work (which would be useless), its homologue in the strict sense of a vicarious *object* which presents the same arrangement as the work. This is how I understand objectivity, because —in a negative sense, of nonsubjectivity—the philosopher brackets his own convictions, positions, and above all his manner of beginning, attacking, and strategically handling his thought, and because—in a positive sense—he submits his reading to what the work itself—which remains the *quid* which guides his reading—wants and means.

And so I say that Freud can be read just as our colleagues and teachers read Plato, Descartes, and Kant. This is what I claim; it is my first wager and has not yet necessarily been won.

The reference of doctrine to an experience which requires apprenticeship and competence, which is a craft and even a technique—does this reference not completely separate Freud from the thinkers and philosophers cited above? I still think that such an objection is not invincible and that the reading of Freud poses no different problem from the reading of Plato, Descartes, and Kant and can claim the same type of objectivity. Why? First, because Freud wrote works which were not addressed simply to his students, colleagues, and patients but to all of us. By giving lectures and publishing books, he agreed to occupy in the minds of his readers and listeners the same field of discourse as do philosophers. He is the one who took the risk, not me. But my argument is still too contingent and too bound to the hazards of communication. I claim that what appears in the analytical relationship is not radically different from what someone who has not been analyzed can understand. I say "understand" and not "live," for no comprehension gained from books will ever be a substitute for the factual experience of psychoanalysis. However, the meaning of what is thus lived is essentially communicable. Because it is communicable, the analytical experience can be transposed through doctrine to the level of theory with the aid of descriptive concepts which result from a second level of conceptuality. Just as in the theater I can understand situations, feelings, and conduct which I have not experienced myself, so I can understand in a mode of reflective empathy the meaning of an analytical experience I have not undergone. This is why, in spite of serious misunderstandings which I do not underestimate, a philosopher, as a philosopher, is capable of understanding psychoanalytic theory and even in part the psychoanalytic experience. Should I add an even more decisive argument? It is Freud who came onto our territory. How? Because the object of his investigation is not, as is too hastily assumed, human desire, the wish, libido, instincts, Eros (all of these words having a precise sexual context), but rather desire in a more or less conflicting relationship with a world of culture, a father and mother, authorities, imperatives, prohibitions, works of art, social ends, and idols. This is why Freud does not, when he writes about art, morality, and religion, transpose to cultural reality a science and practice which found their definite place in human biology or psychophysiology. From the beginning his science and practice are held at the point of interaction between desire and culture. Take *The Interpretation of Dreams* or *Three Essays on the Theory of Sexuality,* just to consider two of the major works, where the instinctual level is taken in its relationship with "censorship," "repression," "prohibitions," and "ideals." The nuclear figure of the father in the Oedipal episode is merely this system's center of gravity. This is why in the first and then in the second topography we are faced from the beginning with a plurality of "places" and "roles" in which the unconscious is diametrically opposed to consciousness and preconsciousness and where the id is at once in a dialectical relationship with the ego and the superego. This dialectic is that of the very situation explored by psychoanalysis, namely, the interlacing of desire and culture. This is why I said that Freud came onto our ground; for, even when he speaks to us of instincts, he speaks of them in and from the level of expression, that is, in and from certain effects of meaning which give themselves to be deciphered and can be treated as texts: dream texts or symptomatic texts—yes, texts which occur in the network of communications, of exchanges of signs. It is precisely in this milieu of signs that the analytical experience (as the work of speech, an encounter between speaking and listening, a complicity between speech and silence) takes place. The fact that the analytical experience belongs, as much as Freudian doctrine, to the order of signs is what fundamentally justifies not only the communicability of analytical experience but also its fundamentally homogeneous character with the totality of human experience which philosophy undertakes to reflect upon and understand.

These, then, are the presuppositions which guided my decision to read Freud as I read other philosophers.

I will say very little about this reading here because I have chosen to speak, before the Société de Philosophie, about the philosophical interpretation which I propose. I will simply comment upon what I called architectonic reconstitution and will intentionally give my development a more systematic presentation than I did in my book.[1]

Freud's work seems to me to be divided into three great masses, each of which has its own architecture and can be considered as a conceptual level. These three levels find their fullest expression in different states of system, which can be charted diachronically. The first network is constituted with the interpretation of dreams and neurotic symptoms and ends up, in the writings of *The Papers on Metapsychology*, in a state of system

1. Paul Ricoeur, *Freud and Philosophy: An Essay on Interpretation*, trans. Denis Savage (New Haven: Yale University Press, 1970).

which is known by the name of the first topography (the series ego, id, superego constituting rather, in Lagache's terms, a "personology"). The next great mass of facts and notions, which constitutes the second theoretical network, contains the interpretation of culture: works of art, ideals, and idols. This second network comes out of the former one, in that the first already contained the dialectic of desire and culture. But, by applying the dream model of wish-fulfillment to all the meaning effects which we may encounter in the life of culture, we are led to profoundly alter the equilibrium attained in *The Papers on Metapsychology*. The result of this alteration is a second state of system which is expressed in the sequence ego, id, superego. It does not replace the first system but is superimposed on it. The final great mass of facts and notions, which constitutes the third theoretical network, arises from the alteration imposed by the introduction of the death instinct into the preceding edifice. This alteration reaches the very foundations of existence, for it involves a redistribution of forces in terms of the polarity Eros-Thanatos. As the relation between instinct and culture remains the principal leading thread, however, this basic alteration also affects every aspect of culture. Indeed, the entry of the death instinct implies the most important reinterpretation of culture, that which is expressed in *Civilization and Its Discontents*. It is in guilt, in the discontent of the civilized individual, and in the clamor of war that the mute instinct begins to cry out.

This, in broad terms, is the architecture of Freudianism.

As we can see, there is a development, but it is comprehensible only if we move from one state of system to another. We can thus pick out a sensible continuum which goes from a mechanistic representation of the psychic mechanism to a romantic dramaturgy of life and death. But this development is not incoherent. It proceeds by successive alterations of structures. This parade of alterations is produced within a homogeneous milieu, namely, the desire's effects on meaning. It is the homogeneous milieu of all the restructuring of Freudian doctrine which I called the *semantics of desire*.

Let us return to the principal object of this lecture, however, which is *a* philosophical interpretation of Freud. We might begin to consider it by the second objection that could be brought against such an undertaking. Can one not legitimately challenge all attempts to relocate a work like Freud's in a *different* discourse? It will be argued that Freud's work is a totality sufficient unto itself and that we are falsifying it if we place it in another field of thought from that which it generates. This argument has considerable force. It would work for any other thinker, but it has a particular force in Freud's case. It is always possible to consider the philosophical enterprise which would claim to integrate it as the supreme denial and the craftiest of resistances. That is probably true. Still, my opinion is that, even though victorious, the objection does not affect the problem of a philosophical interpretation of Freud.

Two arguments can be brought against the fanatic exclusivity of certain Freudians. The first is that it is false that Freud and psychoanalysis furnish us with a totality. Need we recall all the texts where Freud declares, without any ambiguity whatsoever, that he has clarified only a single group of instincts, those which were accessible to his practice, and that the realm of the ego, in particular, is only partly explored by the specific ego instincts which belong to the same cycle as the object libido? Psychoanalysis is only one beam among others projected upon human experience. But above all—and this argument is drawn from analytical practice itself—we must consider the doctrine as an ordering of a very specific experience by the use of concepts which have been constructed and coherently linked together. This is the analytical experience, and we must hold strictly to the point that, in the end, Freudian concepts come into play (that is, mimic and confirm one another) within its circumference. There are more things in heaven and on earth than in all our psychoanalysis. I just said that this experience can be understood and is homogeneous with human experience as a totality, but it is so precisely as one part in a whole. The vocation of philosophy is to arbitrate between not only the plurality of interpretations but, as I will try to say in conclusion, the plurality of experiences as well.

That is not all. Not only are analytical doctrine and experience partial; both also involve a dissonance and a breach which calls for philosophical interpretation. I am thinking here of the shift which occurs between Freud's discovery and the concepts at work in his system. This is, of course, true of all works. Eugen Fink recently pointed it out about Husserl. The concepts with which a theory operates are not all objectivized in the field which that theory thematizes. Thus a new philosophy expresses itself partly in the language of preceding philosophies, which is the source of doubtless inevitable misunderstandings. In Freud's case the shift is manifest. His discovery operates on the level of effects of meaning, but he continues to express it in the language and through the concepts of energetics of his masters in Vienna and Berlin. It could be argued that this dissonance calls, not for a philosophical reconsideration, but for a clarification of the grammar of our language—as the English say, a recognition of the rules of this language game. But this anomaly on the part of Freudian discourse requires a more radical treatment. It is not simply a matter of a shift between the discovery and the available vocabulary, for this anomaly in Freudian discourse goes to the very nature of things. If it is true that psychoanalysis applies to the inflection between desire and culture, we can expect that it operates with notions which belong to two different levels of coherence and two universes of discourse, that of force and that of meaning. The language of force is all the vocabulary which designates the conflictual dynamics whose result, repression, is the best known and most studied of these mechanisms, but it is also the entire economic vocabulary, such as cathexis, decathexis, overcathexis, etc.

Thus, all the vocabulary about the absurdity or significance of symptoms and dream thoughts, about their overdetermination and the word plays which take place there, is the language of meaning. It is this sort of relation between meanings which is disentangled in interpretation. Between the apparent and the hidden meaning there is the relation between an intelligible and an unintelligible text. These meaning relations are thus entangled with force relations. Everything in "dream work" is stated in this mixed discourse. Force relations are enunciated and dissimulated in meaning relations at the same time that meaning relations express and represent force relations. This mixed discourse is not, in my opinion, equivocal in the sense of simply lacking clarity. It is not a "category mistake." It comes close to the very reality which our reading of Freud revealed and which we called the semantics of desire. All the philosophers who have reflected on the relations between desire and meaning have come across this problem. Plato, for example, balances the hierarchy of ideas by a hierarchy of love, and Spinoza binds the degrees of clarity of the idea to those of the assertion and action of the *conatus*, while Leibniz relates the monad's degrees of appetition and perception. "The action of the internal principle which brings about the change or passage from one perception to another may be called *appetition* . . ." (*Monadology*, § 15). Freud can thus be relocated on a well-known trajectory. By the same token, however, an interpretation is imposed. The reading leads us to a critical point, "where one sees that the energetics implies a hermeneutics and the hermeneutics discloses an energetics. That point is where the positing or emergence of desire manifests itself in and through a process of symbolization." [2]

That is, moreover, what distinguishes the psychological concept of drive (*Trieb*) from the psychophysiological concept of instinct. Drives are accessible only in their psychic derivatives, their effects of meaning, and, more precisely, their distortions of meaning. Because drives occur in language in its psychic representing, one can interpret desire, although it may remain unspeakable as such. But if this mixed discourse prevents psychoanalysis from swinging toward the natural sciences, it prevents it from swinging toward semiology as well. The laws of meaning in psychoanalysis cannot be reduced to those of linguistics as inherited from Ferdinand de Saussure, Hjelmslev, or Jakobson. The ambiguity of the relation sustained by desire with language is irreducible to such an extent that, as Emile Benveniste has clearly shown, the symbolism of the unconscious is not a linguistic phenomenon *stricto sensu*. It is common to many cultures without a common language. It presents phenomena, such as displacement and condensation, which operate on the level of the image and not that of phonematic or semantic articulation. In Benveniste's terminology, dream mechanisms will appear sometimes as infra- and sometimes as supralinguistic. For our purposes, they manifest the confusion of the infra- and the supralinguistic. They are on an infralinguistic level in the sense that they mark the distortion of the distinctive function of language. They are on a supralinguistic level if we consider the dream, as Freud himself says, as finding its true relations in the great unities of discourse such as proverbs, maxims, folklore, and myths. From this point of view it is rather on the level of rhetoric, with its metaphors, metonymy, synecdoche, euphemisms, allusions, antiphrases, and litotes that a comparison should be made. Rhetoric concerns not the phenomena of language but the procedures of subjectivity as manifested in discourse.[3] Furthermore, Freud always used the word *Vorstellung*—"representation"—to designate the effect of meaning to which drives are assigned. For him it is *Dingvorstellungen*—"thing representations"—which serve as models for *Wortvorstellungen* or "word representations." It is words that are treated as things and

2. *Ibid.*, p. 65.
3. *Ibid.*, p. 395.

not the opposite. I included in *Freud and Philosophy*[4] Freud's important texts in this respect.

The representing of instincts (*Trieben*) is thus at the center of our problem. It is neither biological nor semantic. It is delegated by the instincts and promised to language and reveals instincts only in their derivatives while gaining access to language only by the twisted combinations of object cathexes which precede verbal representation. We must invoke an irreducible type of relationship between signifiers and signifieds. These signs and meaning effects have a linguistic vocation but are not, in their specific texture, of the order of language. This is what Freud indicates by the word *Vorstellung* or representation, and it is what keeps the level of fantasy distinct from that of speech. Leibniz said as much in the text from which I just quoted a short passage: "The action of the internal principle which brings about the change or passage from one perception to another may be called *appetition*. It is true that appetite may not always entirely attain the whole perception toward which it tends, but it always obtains something of it and arrives at new perceptions" (*Monadology*, § 15).

And so, there we are—with Leibniz' transposition of the Freudian problem of libido and symbol—at the threshold of the philosophical problem.

I am not saying that a single philosophy is capable of furnishing the vehicle in which relations between force and meaning can be explained. I believe that *the* correct reading of Freud is possible, while only *a* correct philosophical interpretation is possible. The one I propose is connected with reflective philosophy and is related to the work of Jean Nabert, to whom I long ago dedicated my *Symbolism of Evil*. It is in Nabert that I found the best formulation of the close relationship between the desire to be and the signs in which desire is expressed, projected, and explained. I stand fast with Nabert in saying that understanding is inseparable from self-understanding and that the symbolic universe is the milieu of self-explanation. This means that there is no longer a problem of meaning unless signs are the means, the milieu, and the medium thanks to which a human existent seeks to situate, project, and understand himself. In contrast, however, there is no direct apprehension of the self by the self, no internal apperception or appropriation of the self's desire

4. Footnote 69, p. 398.

to exist through the short cut of consciousness but only by the long road of the interpretation of signs. In short, my philosophical working hypothesis is concrete reflection, i.e., the *cogito* as mediated by the whole universe of signs.

I do not deny that this working hypothesis does not come from the reading of Freud. The reading of Freud encounters it only as something problematic. It encounters it exactly at the point where Freud also poses the question of the subject. Indeed, how can the sequence Unc., Pcs., Cs. and the sequence ego, id, superego even be stated without posing the question of the subject? And how can the question of desire and meaning be posed without at the same time asking "Whose desire?" and "Whose meaning?" But if the question of the subject is implied problematically by psychoanalysis, it is not posed thematically. Even less is the subject posed apodictically. The act by which the subject is posited can be generated only out of itself. It is Fichte's thetic judgment. In this judgment, existence is posited as thought and thought as existence. I think, I am. With respect to this position and this apodictic proposition, all the "places" of the first topography and the "roles" of the second Freudian sequence are objectivizations. The entire question will be one of justifying and legitimizing these objectivizations as the privileged path toward a less abstract *cogito* and as the necessary way of concrete reflection.

I would like to emphasize, therefore, that there is a *gap* between the problematic implications of the question of the subject in psychoanalysis and its apodictic position in reflective philosophy. It is this gap which is responsible for the distance between *the* reading and *a* philosophical interpretation of Freud.

It was necessary to clearly recognize this gap in order to clear away two types of misunderstanding, both of which arise from a confusion between reading and philosophical interpretation.

I cannot be accused of confusing Freud with reflective philosophy, because I am developing the reading of psychoanalysis without presupposing the *cogito*. The reading of Freud rests on a Platonic *hypotheton* which we have called the relation between desire and meaning, the semantics of desire. For psychoanalysts, it is a *ti hikanon*, "something sufficient," in the sense of sufficient for an understanding of all that takes place in the field of experience and theory. In constituting the question of the subject from the position "I think, I am," philosophy asks for the condition of the condition and turns toward the *anhypotheton* of this *hypotheton*. We must not, therefore, confuse the objections that can be made to the reading of Freud and those that can be brought against my philosophical interpretation.

A second misunderstanding occurs if we leap over this philosophical moment, omit the initial philosophical act, and bring ourselves directly to the furthest consequences of such a philosophical choice. This is what happens when one grabs hold of reflective conclusions on faith and religion and short-circuits them into the Freudian critique of religion. There is a necessary progression in the succession of steps which I posit: *the positing of the subject, the renewal of psychoanalysis as an archaeology of the subject, the dialectical positioning of archaeology and teleology, and the vertical irruption of the Wholly Other,* as the alpha and the omega in the twofold question of archaeology and teleology. We can, of course, separate these theses, which have indeed appeared in different orders and different places in other philosophies. But philosophy is not a puzzle of ideas or a heap of scattered themes which can be arranged in just any order. The way that philosophy proceeds and makes connections is all that is pertinent. Its architecture commands its theses. This is why my "ideas" on religion and faith are less important philosophically than the way in which they interact with the dialectic of archaeology and teleology. This dialectic in turn is of value only insofar as it articulates concrete reflection internally. And, finally, this concrete reflection makes sense only insofar as it succeeds in asking anew the Freudian question of the unconscious, the id, of instincts and meaning, in the promotion of the subject of reflection.

We must hold onto this, for it is the bolt which keeps everything together and by which this interpretation stands or falls.

I WOULD LIKE TO EXPLAIN now this reflective renewal of Freudian concepts. My question is the following: What happens to a philosophy of reflection when it allows itself to be instructed by Freud?

This question has two sides. First, it means, how can Freud's mixed discourse on desire and meaning be taken into reflective philosophy? But it also means, what happens to the subject of reflection when the guile of consciousness is taken seriously and consciousness is discovered as false consciousness, which says something other than it says or believes it says? These two sides of the question are as inseparable as those of a coin or a cloth. For at the same time that I say that the philosophical location of analytical discourse is defined by the concept of the archaeology of the subject, I also followed Freud to say that one can no longer establish the philosophy of the subject as a philosophy of consciousness. Reflection and consciousness no longer coincide. Consciousness must be lost in order that the subject may be found. The subject is not what we think it is. There can be evidence for the apodicticity of the *cogito* only if the inadequation of consciousness is recognized at the same time. Like the meaning of the thing, the meaning of my own existence is itself either presumed or presumptive, although the reasons for this are different. It is thus possible to repeat Freudianism, make a reflective repetition of it, which will also be an adventure of reflection. I called dispossession or disappropriation this movement to which I am constrained by Freudian systematics. It is the necessity of this dispossession which justifies Freudian naturalism. I would adopt what is more shocking, more philosophically insupportable in the Freudian realism of psychic "places." I would adopt its decided antiphenomenology and its dynamics and economics as the instruments of a suit which is filed against the illusory *cogito* which first occupies the place of the founding act of the *I think, I am.* In short, I make use of psychoanalysis just as Descartes made use of skeptical arguments against the dogmatism of the thing; but this time it is against the *cogito* itself— or rather at the heart of the *cogito*—that psychoanalysis splits the ego's claims to apodicticity and the illusions of consciousness. In an essay written in 1917 Freud speaks of psychoanalysis as a wound and humiliation to narcissism analogous to the discoveries of Copernicus and Darwin when in their own way they decentered the world and life with respect to the claims of consciousness. Psychoanalysis decenters in the same way the constitution of the world of fantasy with respect to consciousness. At the end of this dispossession, consciousness has switched philosophical signs. It is no longer a given. There are no longer "immediate givens of consciousness." There is, rather, a task, the task of becoming-consciousness. Where there had been *Bewusstsein,* or being-consciousness, there is now *Bewusstwerden,* or becoming-consciousness. Thus the dynamic and economic side of Freudianism was asserted twice. First, in the reading of Freud, against all semiological reduction and in order to rescue the very specificity of psychoanalysis and hold it at the junction between force and meaning, and second, in the philosophical interpretation, in order to guarantee the authenticity of the ascesis and deprivation through which reflection must pass in order to remain authentic. At the same time, what is the enigma of Freudian discourse—an enigma at least for a pure epistemological consideration—becomes a paradox of reflection. As you will remember, the enigma of Freudian discourse was the intertwining of dynamic and hermeneutic language. Transcribed into reflective language, that gives the reality of the id and the ideality of meaning: reality of the id in the act of disappropria-tion and the regression of effects of meaning, appearing on the conscious level, to the point of instinct on the level of the uncon-scious; ideality of meaning in reappropriating and in the move-ment of interpretation which initiates the movement of becom-ing-conscious. It is thus that our reading of Freud itself becomes an adventure of reflection. What emerges from this reflection is a wounded *cogito*, which posits but does not possess itself, which understands its originary truth only in and by the confession of the inadequation, the illusion, and the lie of existing conscious-ness.

THE SECOND STAGE of the philosophical interpretation which I propose is characterized by the dialectic between archae-ology and teleology. This advance in reflection indeed represents something new, a polarity between the reflective *archē* and *telos*. I reach this stage by a reappropriation of the temporal aspects of Freudianism which are precisely bound to the Freudian realism of the unconscious and the id. Furthermore, they pertain to Freudian economics rather than Freudian topography. There is indeed in the positing of desire an *anteriority* which is both phy-logenetic and ontogenetic, historical and symbolic. Desire is in every respect prior; it is anticipatory. The theme of anteriority pervades Freudianism. I would defend it against all the cultural-isms which have tried to extract its fangs and pull its claws by reducing to defects of our current relationship to the environ-ment the savage side of our instinctual existence, this prior de-sire, which pulls us backwards and insinuates the whole back-ward drift of affectivity on the level of family relationships, fantasies and works of art, ethics and guilt, religion and the fear of punishment and the infantile wish for consolation. Freud is on secure ground when he speaks of the unconscious as *timeless*, i.e., as rebellious to the temporalization which is linked to becoming-conscious. This is what I call archaeology, the re-strained archaeology of instincts and narcissism, the generalized archaeology of the superego and idols, the hyperbolic archaeology of the war of the giants Eros and Thanatos. But we must see that the concept of archaeology is itself a reflective concept.

Archaeology is the archaeology of the subject. This is what Merleau-Ponty saw and said clearly in his introduction to the work of Dr. Hesnard, *L'Oeuvre de Freud.*

Because the concept of archaeology is a philosophical concept—a concept of reflective philosophy—the articulation between archaeology and teleology is also an articulation of and in reflection. It is reflective thought which says that only a subject which has an *archē* has a *telos;* for the appropriation of a meaning constituted prior to me presupposes the movement of a subject drawn ahead of itself by a succession of "figures," each of which finds its meaning in the ones which follow it.

This new advance on the part of thought surely constitutes a problem; this is why I propose to comment upon it by a few remarks of a more problematic nature. First, it is quite true that psychoanalysis is analysis, i.e., in Freud's own rigorous terms, a regressive decomposition. According to Freud, there is no psychosynthesis, or, at least, psychoanalysis as such need not propose any synthesis. This is why the teleology of the subject is not a Freudian idea but rather a philosophical notion which the reader of Freud forms at his own risk. Still, this notion of the teleology of the subject is not without support in Freud himself, who hinted at its equivalent or its beginning in a certain number of experiences and theoretical concepts set into motion by the practice of analysis. But these experiences and concepts do not find their place in the Freudian schema of the psychic apparatus. This is why they remain in the air, as I tried to show for the concepts of *identification* and *sublimation,* for which Freud said expressly that he had found no satisfactory explanation.

Second remark: I attached the idea of a teleology of the subject to Hegel's *Phenomenology of Spirit.* This example is not restrictive, only illuminating, in that teleology—or, to cite Jean Hyppolite exactly, "dialectical teleology"—is the only law for the construction of the figures of the spirit. It is illuminating also in that the dialectic of the figures gives philosophical sense to all psychological maturation and to man's growth out of childhood. Psychology asks how man leaves his childhood. Indeed, he does so by becoming capable of a certain meaningful itinerary which has been illustrated by a certain number of cultural configurations which themselves draw their sense from their prospective arrangement. The example of Hegel is again illuminating in the sense that it allows us to dissociate teleology and finality, at least in the sense of final causes criticized by Spinoza and Bergson. Teleology is not finality. The figures in a dialectical teleology are not final causes but meanings which draw their sense from the movement of totalization which carries them along and pushes them ahead of themselves. The Hegelian example is illuminating, last of all, in that it allows us to give content to the empty idea of an existential project which would continually remain its own project and determine itself only in contingency, despair, or simply the flattest conformism.

If the Hegelian example is indeed exemplary, however, it is not restrictive. For my part I tried to outline the sequence of cultural spheres, from economic possession (*avoir*) to political power (*pouvoir*) and personal values (*valoir*), all of whose contents are quite different, even though their general orientation is the same. In all of this our problem is the passage, not to consciousness, but from consciousness to self-consciousness. What is at stake is the Self or Spirit.

It is not unimportant to discover that consciousness' pretensions are no less humiliated in the ascending dialectic of figures of the spirit than they are in the regressive decomposition of fantasies of desire. Concrete reflection consists in this twofold self-dispossession and decentering of meaning. But reflection is still what holds together regression and progression. It is in reflection that the relationship between what Freud calls the unconscious and Hegel Spirit, between the primordial and the terminal, fate and history, functions.

You will allow me to stop here and not delve into the final circle of concrete reflection. I say in my synopsis, "This dialectic is the philosophical ground on which the complementarity of rival hermeneutics of art, morality, and religion can be established." I intentionally did not consecrate a special paragraph to this question of rival hermeneutics. The dialectical solution which I attempt to apply to this problem has no autonomy whatsoever with respect to what I called the dialectic of progression and regression, teleology and archaeology. I wish to apply a determinate philosophical method to a determinate problem, that of the constitution of the symbol, which I described as an expression with a double meaning. I had already applied this method to the symbols of art and the ethics of religion. But the reason behind it is neither in the domains considered nor in the objects which are proper to them. It resides in the overdetermination of the symbol, which cannot be understood outside the dialecticity of the reflection which I propose. This is why all discussion which treats my double interpretation of religious symbols as an isolated theme necessarily retrogresses to a philosophy of compromise from which the incentive for struggle has been withdrawn. In this terrible battle for meaning, nothing and no one comes out unscathed. The "timid" hope must cross the desert of the path of mourning. This is why I will stop on the threshold of the struggle of interpretations and do so by giving myself this warning: outside the dialectic of archaeology and teleology, these interpretations confront one another without possible arbitration or are juxtaposed in lazy eclecticisms which are the caricature of thought.

Technique and Nontechnique in Interpretation

MYTHS POSSESS A TECHNIQUE,[1] as Professor Castelli has pointed out,[2] and this technique is the ultimate aspect of the process of demythization. I have wondered to what degree such a judgment can be applied to psychoanalysis, for Professor Castelli seems to include psychoanalysis in the "iconoclasm of the intimate" (in his remarks on daytime and nighttime technique).

I will answer the following two questions: (1) In what sense is psychoanalysis a technique of the night? (2) To what degree is it an iconoclasm of the intimate?

I. PSYCHOANALYSIS AS A TECHNIQUE OF THE NIGHT

OUR QUESTION IS PERFECTLY LEGITIMATE. Psychoanalysis is indeed a technique, one of many in the modern world. We do not yet know its exact place, which it is undoubtedly still in

Translated by Willis Domingo.

1. [While English distinguishes between "technique" and "technology," the German word *Technik* means both; and, although *technologie* does exist in French, *technique* can also be used in this sense by French writers. Thus the present essay follows Heidegger's lead (cf. "Die Frage nach dem Technik" in *Vorträge und Aufsätze*) by playing on this ambiguity. Since this is an analysis of Freud's *Papers on Technique,* our translation will be generally "technique," except where the context dictates "technology."—TRANS.]

2. In his opening remarks to the International Colloquium on "Technique and Casuistry," Professor Castelli connected the central theme of the Colloquium to the question which had occupied former annual meetings in Rome, namely, demythization as an aspect of modernity.

search of. But one thing is certain: it is a technique. It arises from a therapeutical maneuver which is constituted as a profession. It is a profession which is studied and taught, which requires a didactics and a deontology. The philosopher learns this at his own cost if he attempts to reconstruct the entire structure of psychoanalysis from another experience, such as Husserlian phenomenology. He can, of course, approach the mountain range of psychoanalysis and climb its foothills with concepts such as the phenomenological reduction, sense and nonsense, temporality, and intersubjectivity; but there is a point at which this approximation of psychoanalysis through phenomenology fails, and this point is, precisely, all that is discovered in the analytical situation itself. It is within the specific field of the analytical relationship that psychoanalysis operates as a technique.

In what sense is it a technique? Let us begin with the word itself. In a text of methodological importance,[3] Freud distinguishes three terms in order to bind them inseparably together: *method* of investigation, *technique* of treatment, and the elaboration of a body of *theory*. Technique is understood here in the strict sense of a therapeutics leading to a cure. The word is thus distinguished from the art of interpretation, or hermeneutics, and from the explanation of mechanisms, or metapsychology. But for our purposes it is important to show how psychoanalysis is praxis through and through and contains within itself both the art of interpretation and a speculative theory. In order to pose Professor Castelli's question in all its force, I will therefore understand technique, not as one of the three aspects which I have just listed, but as the benchmark and point of reference of the analytic maneuver as a whole.

So that this will be understood, I will introduce an intermediary concept—the fundamental concept of *work*. Indeed, the analytic maneuver is a form of work, to which another form of work corresponds on the part of the patient, the work of becoming conscious. In turn, these two forms of work, that of analysis and that of the patient, reveal the psychism as a whole as a form of work: dream work, mourning work, and, we might say, the work of neurosis. Metapsychology as a whole—its topography and its economics—is destined to take account of this function of work by means of dynamic metaphors.

With this schema we are in a position to show how the

---

3. "'Psychoanalysis' and 'Libido Theory,'" *SE*, XVIII, 235.

method of investigation and the metapsychological theory are aspects of psychoanalysis considered as praxis.

Let us begin with the work of the analyst. Why is analysis work? Freud's unvarying answer is the following: because it is a struggle against resistances. The key idea, therefore, is that the resistances which block analysis are the same as those which lie at the origin of the neurosis. The idea that analysis is a struggle against resistances is so important that in retrospect Freud will cite it as the reason for his break with Breuer. He rejected all forms of cathartic method which continued to use hypnosis because that procedure claims to obtain anamnesis without work. Moreover, it was his growing comprehension of the role of analytic strategy which led to the later adjustments of analytic practice, during the period from 1905 to 1907. Thus Freud writes that the goal of analytic exploration is less to restore the instinctual base and bring about the resurgence of the abolished than to circumscribe and liquidate resistances.

What is the result for the relation between technique and hermeneutics? Two things. First, the art of interpretation should itself be considered as part of the art of handling resistances. This art of interpretation—which Freud compares, with somewhat less than total satisfaction, to an art of translation and which, in any event, is a sort of comprehension, understanding, or production of intelligibility—is, considered from the point of view of the analytic maneuver, only the intellectual side of a handling, of a praxis. In this respect the important article from 1912 entitled "The Handling of Dream-Interpretation in Psycho-Analysis" should be consulted. It shows how the concern for realizing an exhaustive interpretation of the dream can be used by resistance as a sort of trap into which the analyst is attracted for the sake of delaying the progress of the cure. This is why Freud continually repeats that the struggle against resistance is arduous and costs the patient sincerity, time, and money, while it demands from the doctor ability and a command over his own affects if he wants to be able to enter into the transference as the opponent of the patient's demands, as someone who does not respond but rather leads his adversary into the dead-ends of frustration.

But this subordination of interpretation, in the precise sense of an intellectual comprehension, to *technē* or the analytic maneuver bears a second aspect, which leads us from the work of the analyst to the work of the person being analyzed. To cure the patient, it is not enough to communicate to him the content of an exact interpretation because, from the side of the analyst, comprehension is only a part of his own work. Freud writes, in " 'Wild' Psychoanalysis" (1910):

> Informing the patient of what he does not know because he has repressed it is only one of the necessary preliminaries to the treatment. If knowledge about the unconscious were as important for the patient as people inexperienced in psychoanalysis imagine, listening to lectures or reading books would be enough to cure him. Such measures, however, have as much influence on the symptoms of nervous illness as distribution of menu-cards in a time of famine has upon hunger. The analogy goes even further than its immediate application, for informing the patient of his unconscious regularly results in an intensification of the conflict in him and an exacerbation of his troubles.[4]

Thus analysis does not consist in replacing ignorance by knowledge but in provoking a work of consciousness by means of work on resistances. In 1913 Freud came back to the same problem in an article "On Beginning the Treatment," in which he takes exception to the excessive importance attached to the fact of knowing at the beginning of psychoanalysis:

> After this there was no choice but to cease attributing to the fact of knowing, in itself, the importance that had previously been given to it and to place the emphasis on the resistances which had in the past brought about the state of not knowing and which were still ready to defend that state. Conscious knowledge, even if it was not subsequently driven out again, was powerless against those resistances.[5]

Moreover, it often happens that the early communication of a purely intellectual interpretation reinforces resistances. Hence the art of psychoanalysis consists in relocating knowledge and the communication of the knowledge in this strategy of resistance.

What, then, does the work of analysis consist in? It begins with the application of the fundamental rule that one must communicate in analysis all that comes to mind, whatever the cost. This is work and not observation; it is a work of face-to-face encounter. In "Remembering, Repeating, and Working-Through" Freud writes:

4. *SE*, XI, 225.
5. *SE*, XII, 142.

The patient must find the courage to direct his attention to the phenomena of his illness. His illness must no longer seem to him contemptible, but must become an enemy worthy of his mettle, a piece of his personality which has solid ground for its existence and out of which things of value for his future life have to be derived.[6]

It is face-to-face work. Freud often states, ". . . it is impossible to destroy anyone *in absentia* or *in effigy.*"[7]

Thus we arrive at the following idea: there is an economic problem in becoming conscious, or *Bewusstwerden,* which completely distinguishes psychoanalysis from any phenomenology of becoming conscious, of dialogue, or of intersubjectivity. It is this economics of becoming conscious which Freud calls *Durcharbeiten,* or working-through:

> This working-through of the resistances may in practice turn out to be an arduous task for the subject of the analysis and a trial of patience for the analyst. Nevertheless it is a part of the work which effects the greatest changes in the patient and which distinguishes analytic treatment from any kind of treatment by suggestion.[8]

We can hardly go further in this direction without incorporating into our analysis Freud's reflections on transference. We will speak of transference here only in its relationship to the concept of work. It is indeed the heart of the analytic maneuver and the domain of its autonomy. In "On Beginning the Treatment," cited above, Freud shows how the handling of transference is involved with "the play of forces which is set in motion by the treatment" (p. 143). "The primary motive force in the therapy is the patient's suffering and the wish to be cured which arises from it." But these are powerful forces:

> It supplies the amounts of energy that are needed for overcoming the resistances by making mobile the energies which lie ready for the transference; and, by giving the patient information at the right time, it shows him the paths along which he should direct those energies (*ibid.*).

It is thus that transference rallies the excessively weak forces of suffering and of the wish to be cured. This involvement is so im-

6. *SE,* XII, 152.
7. "The Dynamics of Transference," *SE,* XII, 108.
8. "Remembering, Repeating, and Working-Through," *SE,* XII, 155–56.

portant that Freud writes, a little further on, "It only deserves the name of psychoanalysis if the intensity of the transference has been utilized for the overcoming of resistances." The "handling" of transference gives the most convincing evidence of the technical character of psychoanalysis. In "Remembering, Repeating, and Working-Through" Freud analyzes in detail this major constellation of every analytical maneuver: the struggle against resistances, the handling of transference, and the patient's tendency to substitute repetition for remembering. This is why, in his address to beginning analysts ("Observations on Transference-Love" [1915]), he will say:

> Every beginner in psycho-analysis probably feels alarmed at first at the difficulties in store for him when he comes to interpret the patient's associations and to deal with the reproduction of the repressed. When the time comes, however, he soon learns to look upon these difficulties as insignificant, and instead becomes convinced that the only really serious difficulties he has to meet lie in the management of the transference.[9]

The critical moment thus seems to me to be this: the discipline of analysis is essentially a discipline of satisfaction; *the entire maneuver consists in using transference love without satisfying it.* Freud even came to the point of writing ("Lines of Advance in Psycho-Analytic Therapy" [1918]) that this "fundamental principle" is obviously called upon to govern the entire domain of the new technique. He propounds this fundamental principle in the following way: "Analytic treatment should be carried through as far as possible under privation—in a state of abstinence." [10] This rule relates essentially to "the dynamics of falling ill and recovering" (*ibid.*). How? We must return to the economic meaning of symptoms as substitutive satisfaction. To leave the patient's demand without response is to prevent the premature spending of "the instinctual force impelling the patient towards recovery" (*ibid.*, p. 163). Freud adds:

> Cruel though it may sound, we must see to it that the patient's suffering, to a degree that is in some way or other effective, does not come to an end prematurely. If, owing to the symptoms having been taken apart and having lost their value, his suffering becomes mitigated, we must re-instate it elsewhere in the form of some appreciable privation; otherwise we run the danger of never achieving any improvements except quite insignificant and transi-

9. "Observations on Transference-Love," *SE*, XII, 159.
10. "Lines of Advance in Psycho-Analytic Therapy," *SE*, XVII, 162.

tory ones . . . ; activity on the part of the physician must take the form of energetic opposition to premature substitutive satisfactions . . . . As far as his relations with the physician are concerned, the patient must be left with unfulfilled wishes in abundance (*ibid.,* pp. 163–64).

I consider these texts to be of an exemplary clarity. They suffice to open an abyss between everything that reflection can draw out of itself and that which only a craft can teach. I would willingly see in Freud's observations on the handling of transference the ultimate and irreducible difference between phenomenology— even the most existential sort—and psychoanalysis. It is a work-to-work relation—the work of the analyst and that of the analysand—which is responsible for the specificity of psychoanalysis and constitutes it as technique.

Allow me to finish this reflection on the work of analysis with the quotation from *Hamlet* which Freud uses: " 'Sblood, do you think I am easier to be played on than a pipe? Call me what instrument you will, though you can fret me, you cannot play upon me." [11]

"Play upon the psychic instrument . . .": It seems to me that this expression leads us to a fundamental aspect of analytic technique, namely, that the theory which corresponds to it, and which Freud calls its metapsychology, is itself a function of praxis.

Let us again take the concept of work for our guide, this time in the metapsychological apparatus of psychoanalysis. As we know, this concept of work is at the center of *The Interpretation of Dreams.* If dreams can be considered as wish fulfillments (*Wunscherfüllungen*), it is because unconscious thoughts are "distorted" in dreams. Such distortion (*Einstellung*) is interpreted by Freud as work. Dream work (*Traumarbeit*) and all the procedures which go along with it—such as condensation work (*Verdichtungsarbeit*) or displacement work (*Verschiebungsarbeit*)—are *ways* of working. Thus the work which makes up analysis (in the double form of the analyst's and the analysand's work) reveals psychic functioning itself as work. Freudian dynamics is, of course, metaphorical, but it is a metaphor which protects the specificity of metapsychology with respect to any sort of phenomenology of intentionality, meaning, or motivation. This is why, in his important preface to Hesnard's *L'Oeuvre de Freud,* Merleau-Ponty, after noting his reservations as to the

11. "On Psychotherapy," *SE,* VII, 225.

place of psychoanalysis' conceptual apparatus, admits, "At least the dynamic and mechanistic metaphors guard, against any idealization, the threshold of an intuition which is one of the most precious in Freudianism" (p. 9). Vergote says, in a similar fashion, "The Freudian unconscious cannot but be haunted by praxis." It is precisely the psychism as work which pervades psychoanalytic work. Up to a certain point we can use this remark to justify Freud's topography in its most naïve form, that of the double inscription (*Niederschrift*) of the same representations in two distinct "psychic localities" (as when one becomes conscious in a purely intellectual way of a memory without uprooting it from its archaic soil). This topography is the discourse—philosophically barely comprehensible—which is proper to the concept of the psychism as work. The areas of the topography expressly account for the "remoteness" (*Entfernung*) and the distortion (*Entstellung*) which separate (*Ent-*) and make unrecognizable that other discourse which comes to light in the discourse of analysis. The remoteness and distortion of the "derivatives" of the unconscious are at the origin of those resistances which require self-recognition itself to become work. I will say that metapsychology attempts to account for a sort of bad workmanship, a work of misunderstanding, which makes recognition a kind of work. There is a problem of interpretation because wishes are fulfilled in a disguised and substitutive mode. The work in question in *dream work* is the maneuver by which the psychism realizes the *Ent-stellung*, the distortion of meaning, by which wishes are rendered unrecognizable to themselves. Metapsychology as a whole is thus the theoretical construction, the conceptual elaboration, which makes it possible to comprehend the psychism as work of mis-understanding, as technique of distortion.

We can now complete our description of psychoanalysis as technique. Its technical object (to use Simondon's term as a designation for the respondent and opponent of the analytic maneuver) is man insofar as he is himself a process of deformation, trans-position and dis-tortion applied to all the presentations (whether affective or ideational) of his oldest wishes, those which *The Interpretation of Dreams* calls "indestructible" or "atemporal" and which the article on "The Unconscious" declares to be *zeitlos* or timeless. Psychoanalysis is constituted as technique because, in the process of *Entstellung*, man himself behaves as a mechanism, submits to an external law, and "condenses" or "displaces" his thoughts. Man behaves like a mechanism in order to accomplish by deception the aims of wish-fulfillment. In this way the psyche is itself a technique practiced on itself, a technique of disguise and misunderstanding. The soul of this technique is the pursuit of the lost archaic object which is constantly displaced and replaced by substitute, fantastic, illusory, delirious, and idealized objects. In short, what of the psychic *work* is revealed in dreams and neuroses? It is the *technique* by which wishes become unrecognizable. In turn, this technique, which is immanent in the wish itself, gives rise to the maneuver which we have placed under the heading of analytic technique. Freud's "naturalism" and "mechanism" are partially justified by the network constituted by the three forms of work (the work of analysis, the work of becoming conscious, and dream work).

II. Psychoanalysis as Iconoclasm of the Intimate

Now I will take up the questions raised by Professor Castelli concerning technique understood as demythologization carried to its extreme point. According to him, all technique excludes the classically casuistical, by eliminating choice and by the unique determination of intentionalities. If this is the case, the only conceivable casuistry would be one of ultimates and extremes, i.e., an eschatological casuistry.

In what sense, then, is psychoanalysis a contribution to technique understood as a total way of acting toward the world and the sacred? I would like to emphasize two points. I will argue first with as much force as I have that in its profound finality psychoanalysis does not belong in *this* technical world, inasmuch as this world involves techniques for the domination of nature or "technology." In this sense, psychoanalysis is more an antitechnique. That is what I meant by the title of this essay.

When I say that psychoanalysis is not a technique of domination, I wish to emphasize its important feature of being a technique of veracity. What is at stake in psychoanalysis is self-recognition, and its itinerary goes from lack of recognition to self-recognition. In this respect its model is the Greek tragedy *Oedipus Rex*. Oedipus' fate is to have already killed his father and married his mother. But the drama of recognition begins beyond this point and consists in this man's recognition that he had begun by pronouncing a curse. I was that man; and in a

sense I have always known it, but in another sense I was unaware of the fact. Now I know who I am. What is the meaning
of the expression "technique of veracity" at such a moment?
First, it takes place entirely in the field of speech. It is this initial
situation which is completely unknown by all those, either psy-
chologists or psychoanalysts, who have tried to integrate psychoanalysis into a general, behavioral type of psychology. Thus they
prepared for the integration of the analytic maneuver into techniques of adaptation which are themselves branches of the technique of the domination of nature. In reality psychoanalysis is
not a science of the observation of behavior, and this is why it is
not a technique of adaptation. And since it is not, it is, by fate
and vocation, in an overhanging relationship with all technological ambitions for the domination of nature. An entire school of
American psychoanalysts, such as Hartmann and Rapaport,
work toward this reintegration of psychoanalysis into academic
psychology and do not realize that all the corrections and refor-
mulations which they propose constitute surrender pure and
simple. Yes, it takes courage to say that psychoanalysis is not a
branch of the natural sciences and that this is why its technique
is not an applied natural science or a branch of technology understood as domination of nature. The price to pay for this
avowal is indeed heavy: psychoanalysis does not satisfy the
standards of the sciences of observation, and the "facts" it deals
with are not verifiable by multiple independent observers. The
"laws" it formulates cannot be converted into relationships of
variables ("independent variables" of place, "dependent variables" of behavior, and "intermediate variables"). Its unconsciousness is not one extra variable inserted between stimulus and
response. Properly speaking, there are no "facts" in psychoanalysis in the sense that experimental science understands "facts."
This is why its theory is not a theory in the same way that the
theory of gases in physics and the theory of genes in biology
are.

Why? Because the "work" we spoke of in the first part of this
essay is entirely work within language. The psychic work de-
tected by analysis is a work of distortion on the level of meaning, on the level of a text which may be recounted in a narration.
For psychoanalysis, to proceed technically is to proceed like a
detective. Its economics is inseparable from a semantics. This is
why there are no "facts" nor any observation of "facts" in psychoanalysis but rather the interpretation of a narrated history. Even
facts observed from the outside and related in the course of

analysis are valued not as facts but as expressions of changes in meaning which occur in this history. Changes in conduct are not valued because they are "observable" but because they are "meaningful" for the history of desire. Hence the real object of psychoanalysis is always effects of meaning—symptoms, delirium, dreams, illusions—which empirical psychology can consider only as segments of conduct. For the analyst, it is conduct which is a segment of meaning. The result is that its method is much closer to that of the historical sciences than to that of the natural sciences. The problem of a technique of interpretation has more kinship with the question asked by Schleiermacher, Dilthey, Max Weber, and Bultmann than with the problems of even the tamest behaviorism. Agreement is the only rejoinder one can bring against the attacks of logicians, semanticists, and methodologists who argue against the scientific character of psychoanalysis. We must grant them all their points and transform this admission into a counterstroke. We must agree that its dissent with behaviorism is original and complete. Original, because the break is complete from the beginning: analysis does not begin with observable conduct but rather with meaninglessness that must be interpreted. All attempts to assimilate psychoanalysis to a science of observation and to a technique which issues from a science of observation ignores the essential point: that it is in the field of speech that the analytic experience takes place and that, within this field, what comes to light is, as Lacan says, another language, which is dissociated from common language and which gives itself to be deciphered by means of these effects of meaning.

We are thus faced with a strange technique. It is a technique, by its character as work and its commerce with energies and mechanisms which are attached to the economy of desire. But it is an utterly unique technique in that it encounters and handles energies only through effects of meaning—what Freud calls the "derivatives" of instinctual representatives. The analyst never handles forces directly but always indirectly in the play of meaning, double meaning, and substituted, displaced, or transposed meanings. An economy of desire, yes—but across a semantics of desire. A dynamics, yes—but across a hermeneutics. It is in, and by, meaning effects that the psychism works.

Perhaps we can begin to understand the sense in which psychoanalysis is a nontechnique if we measure it against techniques which manipulate forces and energies directly, for the purpose of guiding and directing them. All the techniques which come out of the psychology of the observation of behavior are, in the last resort, aimed toward adaptation for the sake of domination. What is at stake in analysis is access to true discourse, and that is quite different from adaptation, the tactic by which the scandal of psychoanalysis has been hastily undermined and rendered socially acceptable. For who knows where a single true discourse may lead with respect to the established order, i.e., with respect to the idealized discourse of established disorder? Psychoanalysis seems to me to be linked, rather, to the express will to bracket the question of adaptation, which is the question inevitably posed by the others, that is, by existing society on the basis and foundation of its reified ideals and the mendacious relationship between the idealized profession of its beliefs and the effective reality of its practical relationships.

Although one may argue that psychoanalysis conceives of itself as the transition from the pleasure principle to the reality principle, it seems to me that the major divorce between what is called "the adaptational point of view" and psychoanalysis concerns precisely the reality principle. The reality in question for analysis is radically distinguished from homologous concepts such as stimuli or environment. This reality is fundamentally the truth of a personal history in a concrete situation; it is not, as in psychology, the order of stimuli as they are known by the experimenter but rather the true meaning which the patient must arrive at through the obscure labyrinth of the fantasy. Reality consists in a conversion of the meaning of the fantasy. This relation to the fantasy, as it is given to be understood in the closed field of analytic speech, brings about the specificity of the Freudian concept of reality. Reality must always be interpreted by the aim of the instinctual object; it must be interpreted as that which is alternately shown and disguised by this instinctual aim. We need only recall the epistemological application which Freud made of narcissism in 1917 in a brilliant little essay entitled "A Difficulty in the Path of Psychoanalysis," where he elevates narcissism to the rank of a fundamental methodological obstacle. In the end, narcissism is what is responsible for our resistance to the sort of truth which makes us appear wandering and lost in a nature deprived of this center in love with itself. Narcissism is what resisted Copernicus' discovery, since it resulted in the fact that we would no longer be the physical center of the universe; and narcissism was also responsible for the resistance to Darwin's discovery, which stripped us of the title of masters of life; finally, narcissism was what resisted psychoanalysis itself, when it taught us that we were not even masters of our own domain. Indeed, this is why the "reality test" characteristic of the secondary process cannot be simply superimposed on an adjustment procedure. It must be relocated within the framework of the analytical situation. In this context, the reality test is correlative with the *Durcharbeiten,* or working-through, toward a true meaning, whose only equivalent is in the struggle for self-recognition in *Oedipus Rex.*

My second point will be strictly corollary to the preceding thesis. If the analytic technique is a nontechnique with respect to the ambition to dominate nature and other men, then it does not take part in the process of demythization in the same way as techniques of domination. As Castelli has quite adequately pointed out, the demythization which is linked to technique as such is disenchantment. This *Entzauberung* and *Entgötterung* are essentially linked to the reign of the manipulable and usable. This is utterly different from the path of psychoanalysis, which is that of "disillusion." These are not at all the same. Disillusion has nothing to do with progress in the usable and manipulable, i.e., progress in mastery. The demythization which belongs to psychoanalysis is expressly connected to the semantics of desire by which it is constituted. The "gods" it dethrones are those in whom the pleasure principle has found a refuge, in the most twisted figures of substitutive satisfaction. When Freud attributes godhead to the father complex, he smashes an idol in which he recognizes, not simply prohibition, but, just as much, and even more, the magnified image of infantile consolation. I will not reiterate my discussion of the interpretation of religion proposed by Freud in *Totem and Taboo, The Future of an Illusion,* and *Moses and Monotheism,* which I presented in a previous colloquium under the title "A Hermeneutics of Reflection." [12] At that time I proposed to show how a reductive hermeneutics was compatible with one which would restore meaning. Today my concerns are entirely different and much more specific. I would ask what is the place of this demythization—which is true in its own terms—with respect to what arises out of the progress of the technical as such? I would say that this demythization is as distinct from all others as analytic technique itself is from techniques of domination. It remains within the dimension of veracity and not that of mastery. It does not belong to the enterprise

12. See below, "The Hermeneutics of Symbols and Philosophical Reflection: II," pp. 315 ff.

of using oneself, nature, and other men but to that of knowing oneself better through the detours of desire. Doubtless you will agree with me when I say that such demythization is good and necessary. It concerns the death of religion as superstition, which may or may not be the counterpart to an authentic faith. Yet this final meaning of demythization can no longer be determined by psychoanalysis itself.

I have no intention of denying that the iconoclasm which belongs to psychoanalysis rejoins in a certain way the iconoclasm which belongs to techniques of domination. It is in its social effects that psychoanalysis rejoins the general mentality of technological civilization. Indeed, psychoanalysis is not only a well-determined experience, which unfolds in a dual relationship. It is also a cultural event. It fell, by itself, into the *public* domain. This fall put into motion a kind of *publicity*, in the strong sense of the word. The crimes of desire are put in the pillory and offered for everyone to see, and iconoclasm thus becomes a *public* iconoclasm. This is where Castelli's formulation seems to be justified: a technique of the night is an iconoclasm of the intimate. Yet even this situation is not completely lacking in positive signification. Freud foresaw this quite clearly in an interesting essay from 1910, entitled "The Future Prospects of Psycho-Analytic Therapy":

> You know, of course, that the psychoneuroses are substitutive satisfactions of some instinct the presence of which one is obliged to deny to oneself and to others. Their capacity to exist depends on this distortion and lack of recognition. When the riddle they present is solved and the solution is accepted by the patients, these diseases cease to be able to exist. There is hardly anything like this in medicine, though in fairy tales you hear of evil spirits whose power is broken as soon as you can tell them their name, the name which they have kept secret.[13]

Transposing these remarks from the individual to the group, Freud does not hesitate to predict a time when the social effect of indiscretion will be at the same time the impossibility of dissimulation:

> Sick people will not be able to let their various neuroses become known . . . if they themselves know that in the manifestations of their illness they are producing nothing that other people cannot

13. "The Future Prospects of Psycho-Analytic Therapy," *SE*, XI, 148.

instantly interpret. The effect, however, will not be limited to the concealment of the symptoms—which, incidentally, it is often impossible to carry out; for this necessity for concealment destroys the use of being ill. Disclosure of the secret will have attacked, at its most sensitive point, the "aetiological equation" from which neuroses arise—it will have made the gain from illness illusory, and consequently the final outcome of the changed situation brought about by the physician's indiscretion can only be that the production of illness will be brought to a stop. . . . A certain number of people, faced in their lives by conflicts which they have found difficult to solve, have taken flight into neurosis and in this way have won an unmistakeable, although in the long run costly, gain from illness. What will these people have to do if their flight into illness is barred by the indiscreet revelations of psycho-analysis? They will have to be honest, confess to the instincts that are at work in them, face the conflict, fight for what they want, or go without it; and the tolerance of society, which is bound to ensue as a result of psycho-analytic enlightenment, will help them in their task (pp. 149–50).

I am not unaware of the fact that this text expresses a sort of Freudian *Aufklärung*. This type of salvation through psycho-analysis, this social repugnance for neurosis, this "more realistic and creditable attitude on the part of society" (p. 150) could easily be turned into an object of derision as a new form of illusion. I would nevertheless like to draw out the better part of this text and reflect along with you on the phenomenon of *disocc-cultation* which is its theme. It is not possible that a repugnance for insincerity and hypocrisy should remain meaningless in the dimension of truth. What then could be the authentic meaning of disoccultation?

Just as I strongly feel that the vulgarization of psychoanalysis accompanies everything which makes man banal, profane, and insignificant, so am I also strongly convinced that a prolonged meditation on psychoanalysis can have the same sort of healthy effect as the understanding of Spinoza, which begins by the reduction of free will and of ideas of good and evil—or ideals, as we would say with Freud and Nietzsche. Like Spinoza, Freud begins by denying the apparent freedom of consciousness, to the extent that this freedom is a misunderstanding of hidden motivations. This is why, as opposed to Descartes and Husserl, who begin with an act of suspension and express thereby the subject's free disposition of itself, psychoanalysis proceeds in the image of Spinoza's *Ethics*, by suspending the control of consciousness and thus rendering the subject equal to its real slavery. It is precisely by beginning with the level of this slavery, by delivering oneself without restraint to the imperious flux of deep motivations, that the true situation of consciousness is discovered. The fiction of the absence of motivation, by which consciousness supported its illusion of self-control, is recognized as such. The fullness of motivation is located at the same place as the emptiness of the freedom of consciousness. It is this process of illusion which opens, as does Spinoza, a new problematic of liberty, no longer bound to the arbitrariness of free will but to determination which has been understood. It seems to me, therefore, that meditation on Freud's work, if not on analytic practice and experience themselves, can restore to us a new concept of liberty very close to that of Spinoza. *No longer free will, but liberation.* This is the most radical possibility opened up to us by psychoanalysis. What then are the relationships between this enterprise of liberation and the human world of technique and technology? It seems to me that we can legitimately say that psychoanalysis, when it is well understood and thought through, frees man for projects other than that of domination.

What projects? I wish to put this liberation into two categories, *the ability to speak* and *the ability to love;* but it should be understood that they form one single project.

The ability to speak: Let us begin at the level of thought we just reached, the disclosure of what is secret as an enterprise of disoccultation. In an inauthentic sense this disclosure can be understood as a reduction pure and simple. Thus, after transposing without precaution or nuance the schema of neuroses to the domain of ideals, myths, and religions, we shall say, "Now we know that these representations are *nothing* other than . . . ." This "nothing other than" could surely be the last word of psychoanalysis and the expression of disillusioned consciousness. I will not argue with the fact that a part, perhaps the most important part, of Freud's work tends in this direction; and yet another possibility seems to me to be open, or at least this appears to be the case in the short writings on art, "The Moses of Michelangelo" and *Leonardo da Vinci and a Memory of His Childhood.* Here interpretation definitely does not consist in exhausting meaning. Let me here contrast "secret" and "enigma" and say that the disclosure of the former does not dissipate the latter. The secret is the absurd product of the work of distortion; the enigma is what is rendered manifest by interpretation. The secret is the function of false consciousness; the enigma is the result which has been restored by interpretation.

Recall the famous interpretation of the vulture fantasy in *Leonardo*. Freud uses it, together with a few other biographical traits, like a detector to penetrate to the layer of the young Leonardo's childhood memories, when the artist was taken from his natural mother and transplanted to the unfamiliar household of his legal father. At the end of *Leonardo* we would be tempted to say, "Well, now we know what is hidden behind the enigmatic smile of *La Gioconda*. It is nothing more than the reproduction in fantasy of the smile of Leonardo's lost mother." But what have we learned, what do we know, at the end of such an analysis (which is, moreover, purely analogical, since it does not enter into a dialogue with Leonardo)? This mother's love and kisses are, strictly speaking, lost—lost for everyone: for us, for Leonardo, and for the mother; and Mona Lisa's smile is precisely the artistic creation by which, as Freud says, Leonardo both "surpassed" and "created" the lost archaic object. The mother's smile does not exist, no longer exists. All that exists now before our eyes is the work of art. Thus analysis has not presented us with any reality which we might use. It has instead opened up beneath the work of art this play of references which, on every layer, denotes the wounding of a desire and an absence which is itself no more than the reference of the fantasy's impotence to the symbol's power.

The ability to speak: To rediscover in the semantics of desire the impulse to speak without end and the ability to express and communicate—is this project not essentially and fundamentally opposed to the dream of domination? Does it not point us toward what can be better called a nontechnique, which is discourse?

I am well aware that one could object to this (an objection which will take me to the second panel of the diptych). One could say that Freud explains himself in terms of power. Does he not say in one of the last of the *New Introductory Lectures on Psychoanalysis* that psychoanalysis can be compared to the project of filling in the Zuider Zee? Does he not add, answering in this way his former characterization of the ego as a poor creature enslaved to three masters, that our task is to reinforce the ego, make it more independent of the superego and the id, and so furnish it with domination over the shreds which have been taken from the id and restored to its control? More generally, do we not regress to the usable and manipulable when we speak of psychoanalysis in terms of control and mastery of energies? Is Freud not in the end closer to Feuerbach and Nietzsche than to

Spinoza when he speaks of giving man back his power? Are we not ourselves saying: the *ability* to speak and the *ability* to love?

Here is where we must understand that the only power offered to man by psychoanalysis is a new orientation for his desire, a new power to love. Lest this idea be banalized and extenuated as soon as it is proposed, I would write deliberately: a new capacity for enjoyment. Men are not masters of their power to love and enjoy when it is destroyed by prohibition and libidinal conflicts. Finally, the great problem introduced by psychoanalysis is the problem of *satisfaction*. Psychoanalysis is completely opposed to the pleasure principle as a curtailing of enjoyment. All the symptoms which it unmasks are figures of substitutive satisfaction, derivatives of the pleasure principle. Thus psychoanalysis would like to be, like Spinoza's *Ethics*, a reeducation of desire. It is this reeducation which it posits as the prior condition for all human reform, whether intellectual, political, or social.

We can now understand why psychoanalysis has no prescriptive or normative answers, nor does it even enter the field of the question we have posed concerning casuistry in either its old or new forms. Its problem is, if I dare say so, much more primary: with what desires do we approach moral problems? And in what state of distortion is our desire when we pose such questions?

I would wager that the psychoanalyst would put the frenetic lover of technology and its disenchanted detractor in the same category. He would ask whether it is not the same distortion of language and enjoyment which animates both and delivers the first over to infantile projects of domination and the second to the fear of things he cannot control. *Totem and Taboo* taught us to situate—psychogenetically and ontogenetically—omnipotence among the most archaic dreams of desire. This is why the reality principle is the answer to our power only when desire is stripped of its omnipotence. Only desire which has accepted its own death can freely dispose of things. But the illusion of its own immortality is the last refuge of the omnipotence of desire. Only desire that has passed through what Freud calls resignation, i.e., the ability to endure the harshness of life (*die Schwere des Daseins zu ertragen*), as the poet says, is capable of freely using things, people, and the benefits of civilization and culture.

As regards the casuistry of extreme situations, which we would be tempted to contrast with a technological demiurgy, perhaps it belongs to the same circle of disenchantment as technological frenzy. Who says that the proposed casuistry does not remain a technique of domination and prevention? Prevention of guilt by the ritualization of the everyday; domination of the strange and extraordinary by the imaginary resolution of extreme cases.

This is why I think psychoanalysis has nothing specific to say for or against casuistry, just as it has nothing to say for or against prescriptive or normative thought. I know that it is willing to remain silent on this point. Its function is to pose prior questions: Are our wishes free or constrained? Regain the ability to speak and to enjoy, and all the rest will be given to you as a bonus. Is this not to say, along with Augustine, "Love, and do what you want"? For if your love has rediscovered its place [*sa justesse*], your will will also find its justice—but by grace rather than by law.

Art and Freudian Systematics

THE TITLE OF THIS STUDY refers to Freudian systematics. How can we understand this term? Freud understands it in the strict sense as denoting the application to aesthetic phenomena of what he calls the "systematic point of view," which is clearly opposed to the descriptive or even to the simply dynamic point of view. What makes up the systematic point of view?

It consists, we are told in the *Papers on Metapsychology*, in submitting all analyses to two requirements. The first requirement is to plot all explanations, however partial they may be, on the psychic topography (the unconscious, preconsciousness, consciousness; ego, id, superego). The representation of the psychic apparatus as a series of nonanatomical points distinguishes the systematic point of view from any descriptive phenomenology. This is not the place to justify such a maneuver. I will take it as a working hypothesis and a discipline of thought. The second requirement is to establish the economic balance sheet of the phenomenon, i.e., the investments or cathexes of energy which can be discovered in a system of forces and its dynamics, its conflicts and compromises. Thus the problem of pleasure, which concerns us here, is an economic problem to the extent that its quality or value does not come into play so much as its function as real, deferred, substitutive, fictive, etc., satisfaction.

We shall see how this recourse establishes order and constitutes a discipline at the same time that it marks the limits of explanatory validity.

Translated by Willis Domingo.

I. The Economy of "Forepleasure"

FREUD'S APPLICATION of the topographic-economic viewpoint to works of art serves more than one purpose. It was a way of relaxing for the doctor of medicine who was also a great traveler, a passionate collector and bibliophile, and was widely read in classical literature, from Sophocles, Shakespeare, and Goethe to contemporary poetry. Freud was an amateur ethnographer and historian of religions as well. This application also meant for the apologist for his own doctrine—above all during the period of isolation which preceded the First World War—a defense and an illustration of psychoanalysis which was accessible to the general and nonscientific public; for the metapsychological theoretician it was a proof and test of the truth of his theories; finally, it was a signpost toward the great philosophical design which had never left his mind, although it was as much hidden as manifested in the theory of psychoneuroses.

The exact place of aesthetics in this grand design does not appear immediately, for the very reason of the fragmentary quality which we will deal with and even emphasize in order to defend Freud's various exercises in psychoanalytic aesthetics. But if we realize that Freud's sympathy for art is equaled only by his harshness toward religious "illusion" and that, moreover, aesthetic "seduction" does not completely satisfy the ideal of veracity and truth which is served by science alone without compromise, we can expect to discover, under even the apparently most gratuitous analyses, great tensions, which will not be clarified until the very end, when aesthetic seduction itself finds its place among Love, Death, and Necessity. Art is for Freud the nonobsessional, nonneurotic form of substitutive satisfaction. The "charm" of aesthetic creation does not indeed arise from the return of the repressed. But where, then, is its place between the pleasure principle and the reality principle? This is the great question which remains in suspense behind the short essays on "applied psychoanalysis."

What we must understand from the very beginning is that Freud's aesthetic essays are both systematic and fragmentary in character. It is precisely the systematic point of view which imposes and reinforces the fragmentary quality. The analytical explanation of works of art could hardly be compared to a therapeutic or didactic psychoanalysis for the simple reason that it does not make use of the method of free association and cannot place its interpretation in the field of the relation between doctor and patient. In this respect the biographical documents to which interpretation can turn are no more meaningful than third-person information in actual analytical therapy. Psychoanalytic interpretation is fragmentary because it remains analogical.

This is how Freud himself conceived his essays. They resemble some archaeological reconstruction in which an entire monument is sketched out from a single architectural detail and its probable context. The systematic unity of Freud's point of view responds by holding these fragments together while waiting for the universal interpretation of the works of culture, which will come later. Thus is explained the unique character of these essays, as well as the surprising minuteness of detail and the rigor, even the inflexibility, of the theory which coordinates these fragmentary studies with the great fresco of dreams and neuroses. Considered as isolated works, each of these studies is quite circumscribed. *Jokes and Their Relation to the Unconscious* is a brilliant but prudent generalization of the laws of dream work and fictional substitution to humor and the comical. The interpretation of Jensen's *Gradiva* does not claim to present a general theory of the novel but simply to cross-check the theory of dreams and neuroses by the fictional dreams which a novelist ignorant of psychoanalysis lends to his hero and by the quasi-psychoanalytic cure toward which the hero is led. The statue in "The Moses of Michelangelo" is treated as a single work, without proposing a general theory of genius or creation. *Leonardo da Vinci and a Memory of His Childhood* does not go beyond its modest title, in spite of appearances. All that is clarified are certain peculiarities of Leonardo's artistic destiny, like streaks of light in a group painting which remains in shadows. Streaks of light, shafts of light, which, as we shall see, may be only talking shadows.

The process in all of this is the structural analogy from one type of work to another, from dream work to art work, and, I dare say, from fate to fate, from instinctual to artistic fate.

It is this oblique understanding that we are going to try to explain by following some of Freud's analyses fairly closely. Without holding myself to a rigorous historical order, I will begin with the short essay from 1908 entitled "Creative Writers and Daydreaming." [1] Two reasons justify our placing it at the start of

1. *SE*, IX, 143–53.

our considerations. First, this little essay, which seems extremely unpretentious, illustrates perfectly the indirect approach to the aesthetic phenomenon by way of a skillful step-by-step approximation. The poet resembles the child at play. "He creates a world of fantasy which he takes very seriously—that is, which he invests with large amounts of emotion—while separating it sharply from reality" (p. 144). From play we pass to "fantasying," not through vague resemblances but through the presupposition of a necessary link to the effect that man does not give up anything but simply exchanges one thing for another by creating substitutes. It is thus that, instead of playing, the adult turns to fantasying, which, in its role as play substitute, is the daydream. We are now on the threshold of poetry, and the intermediate link is furnished by the novel, i.e., by works of art in narrative form. Freud discerns in the fictional story of the hero the figure of "His Majesty the Ego" (p. 150); the other forms of literary creation are considered to be linked, by a series of continuous transitions, to this prototype.

Thus the contours of what could be called the oneiric in general are outlined. Through a striking foreshortening, Freud brings together the two extremes of the fantasy chain, dreams and poetry. Both testify to the same fate, the fate of discontented and unsatisfied man. "The motive forces of fantasies are unsatisfied wishes, and every single fantasy is the fulfillment of a wish, a correction of unsatisfactory reality" (p. 146).

Are we saying that Freud now has to reiterate *The Interpretation of Dreams*? Two hints warn us that this is not the case. First, he is not indifferent to the fact that the chain of analogies passes through play. *Beyond the Pleasure Principle* will inform us that a mastery of absence can already be discerned in play. This mastery is of a different nature from the simple hallucinatory fulfillment of desires. Second, the stage of the daydream is also not lacking in meaning; here the fantasy is presented with a "date mark" (*Zeitmarke*), something which the pure unconscious representations which we have contrastingly described as "outside of time" do not have. Fantasying, as opposed to pure unconscious fantasy, is able to integrate the present of the current impression, the past of childhood, and the future of the projected realization. These two hints remain isolated, as if in expectation.

Moreover, this brief study contains an important suggestion *in fine* which leads us from its fragmentary to its systematic side. Although unable to penetrate creation in its profound dynamism, we could perhaps say something about the relationship between the pleasure it inspires and the technique it employs. If the dream is a type of work, psychoanalysis only naturally takes the work of art in more or less craftsmanly terms in order to unveil, with the help of the structural analogy, a functional analogy which is much more important. Thus research must be oriented toward breaking down resistances. Enjoying our own fantasies with neither scruples nor shame—that would be the widest aim of the work of art. This intention would thus be served by two procedures, that of masking the egotism of the daydream by appropriate alterations and veils and that of seducing by means of a yield of purely formal pleasure which is attached to the representations of the poet's fantasies. "We give the name of an *incentive bonus,* or a *fore-pleasure,* to a yield of pleasure such as this, which is offered to us so as to make possible the release of still greater pleasure arising from deeper psychical sources" ("Creative Writers and Daydreaming," p. 153).

This general conception of aesthetic pleasure as the detonator of profound discharges constitutes the most audacious intuition of the entire psychoanalytic aesthetics. This connection between technical means and hedonistic effect can serve as a guiding thread in the most penetrating investigations of Freud and his school. It satisfies both the modesty and the coherence required of an analytical interpretation. Instead of posing the immense question of creativity, one explores the limited problem of the relations between the effects of pleasure and the technique involved in producing the work. This reasonable question remains within the competence of an economics of desire.

II. INTERPRETATIONS OF THE WORK OF ART

FREUD FIRST SET OUT a few precise indications of this economic theory of forepleasure in *Jokes and Their Relation to the Unconscious* (1905). What this brilliant and meticulous essay proposes is not a general theory of art but the study of a specific phenomenon: an effect of pleasure sanctioned by discharge of laughter. Within these strict limits, however, the analysis unfolds in depth.

Freud first studies the verbal techniques of *Witz* [wit], where he finds the essentials of dream work, such as condensation, displacement, representation through opposites, etc., and thus verifies the reciprocity which is continually posited between work, which arises from an economics, and rhetoric, which allows for interpretation. At the same time that *Witz* verifies the linguistic interpretation of dream work, however, the dream responds by furnishing the elements for an economic theory of humor and the comic. Here is where Freud continues and surpasses the work of Theodor Lipps (*Komik und Humor,* 1898), and here especially we rediscover the enigma of forepleasure. *Witz,* in fact, lends itself to an analysis in the strict sense, i.e., to a decomposition which isolates the surface pleasure which is stimulated by the verbal mechanism of the joke from the profound pleasure which it then unleashes and which obscene, aggressive, or cynical word plays bring to the forefront. This connection between technical pleasure and instinctual pleasure is what constitutes the heart of Freudian aesthetics and binds it to the economics of instinct and pleasure. If we agree that pleasure is linked to a reduction of tension, we will also say that pleasure deriving from technique is minimal and is linked to savings of psychic work realized by condensation, displacement, etc. Thus the pleasure of nonsense frees us from the restrictions which logic imposes on our thought and eases the burden of all intellectual disciplines. But if this pleasure is minimal, like the savings it expresses, it has the remarkable power of acting as interest or even as part of the capital of erotic, aggressive, and skeptical tendencies. Here Freud uses one of Fechner's theories on the "conjunction"—or accumulation—of pleasure and integrates it into a schema of functional liberation which is more Jacksonian than Fechnerian.[2]

This liaison between the technical aspect of the work of art and the production of an effect of pleasure constitutes the guiding thread and the thread of rigor, so to speak, of psychoanalytic aesthetics. We can even distinguish between Freud's aesthetic essays by whether they are more or less faithful to the interpretative model of *Jokes and Their Relation to the Unconscious.* "The Moses of Michelangelo" would be the foremost example of the first group, *Leonardo da Vinci and a Memory of His Childhood* of the second group. (We will see that what first leads us astray in *Leonardo* may also be what eventually leads us furthest in our considerations about the true analytical explanation in art and in other domains as well.)

What is striking in "The Moses of Michelangelo" is that the

2. *Jokes and Their Relation to the Unconscious, SE,* VIII, 136–38.

interpretation of this masterpiece is performed, like an interpretation of a dream, by beginning with the details. This genuinely analytical method allows us to superimpose dream work and creative work, interpretation of dreams and interpretation of works of art. Instead of seeking to explain the nature of the satisfaction generated by the work of art on the level of the widest generalities—a task on which too many psychoanalysts have wasted their time—analysis attempts to resolve the general enigma of aesthetics by the detour of a particular work and the meanings it creates. We are acquainted with the patience and precision of this interpretation, which we have summarized in "Psychoanalysis and the Movement of Contemporary Culture" (see above).

"The Moses of Michelangelo" does go beyond the limits of a mere applied psychoanalysis. It does not limit itself to verifying the analytical method but points toward a type of overdetermination which will be better seen in *Leonardo,* in spite of or because of the contempt that that essay seems to encourage. This overdetermination of the symbol embodied in the statue of Moses allows us to understand that analysis does not close the door on explanation but opens the way toward a broadening of meaning. The essay on Michelangelo already says more than it says. Its overdetermination concerns Moses, the dead pope, Michelangelo —and perhaps Freud himself in his ambiguous relation to Moses. An endless commentary opens up, which multiplies the enigma instead of reducing it. Does this not already indicate that the psychoanalysis of art is essentially interminable?

Now WE COME TO *Leonardo.* Why did I call it an occasion or a source of contempt? Simply because this ample and brilliant essay seems to encourage a bad psychoanalysis of art— biographical psychoanalysis. Did Freud not intend to discover the very mechanism of aesthetic creation in general in its relation, first, to inhibitions (especially sexual perversions) and then to sublimations of the libido into curiosity, as expressed in scientific investigaton? Did he not reconstruct on the fragile basis of the vulture fantasy (which does not even involve a vulture!) the enigma of Mona Lisa's smile?

Did he not say that the memory of the lost mother and her excessive kisses is transposed not only into the fantasy of the vulture's tail in the child's mouth or into the artist's homosexual tendencies but also into the enigmatic smile of the Mona Lisa? "[It] was his mother who possessed the mysterious smile—the smile that he had lost and that had fascinated him so much when he found it again in the Florentine Lady." [3] This is the same smile which is reiterated in the double image of the mother in *The Virgin and Saint Anne.* "For if the Gioconda's smile called up in his mind the memory of his mother, it is easy to understand how it drove him at once to create a glorification of motherhood, and to give back to his mother the smile he had found in the noble lady" (pp. 111–12). And he adds, "The picture contains the synthesis of the history of his childhood: its details are to be explained by reference to the most personal impressions in Leonardo's life" (p. 112).

> The maternal figure that is further away from the boy—the grandmother—corresponds to the earlier and true mother, Caterina, in its appearance and in its spatial relation to the boy. The artist seems to have used the blissful smile of St. Anne to disavow and to cloak the envy which the unfortunate woman felt when she was forced to give up her son to her better-born rival, as she had once given up his father as well (pp. 113–14).

What makes this analysis suspect—according to the criteria we found in *Jokes and Their Relation to the Unconscious*—is that Freud seems to go far beyond the structural analogies which only an analysis of the technique of composition would authorize and goes all the way to the instinctual thematic which the work veils and obscures. It is not this very pretension which nourishes bad psychoanalysis—the analysis of the dead and that of writers and artists?

Let us take a closer look. Is it first of all remarkable that Freud does not really speak of Leonardo's creativity but of its inhibition by the spirit of investigation: "The aim of our work has been to explain the inhibitions in Leonardo's sexual life and in his artistic activity" (p. 131). It is these deficits in creativity which constitute the true object of the first chapter of *Leonardo* and give rise to Freud's most remarkable observations on the relationships between knowledge and desire. Moreover, right within this restricted framework, the transposition of instinct into curiosity appears as a particular fate for repression which is irreducible to any other. Repression, says Freud, can lead either to the inhibition of curiosity itself, which thus shares the situation of sexuality (this is the type of neurotic inhibition), or

---

3. *Leonardo da Vinci and a Memory of His Childhood, SE,* XI, 111.

to obsessions with sexual overtones, where thought itself is sexualized (this is the obsessional type). But,

> in virtue of a special disposition, the third type, which is the rarest and most perfect, escapes both inhibition of thought and neurotic compulsive thinking. It is true that here, too, sexual repression comes about, but it does not succeed in relegating a component instinct of sexual desire to the unconscious. Instead, the libido evades the fate of repression by being sublimated from the very beginning into curiosity and by becoming attached to the powerful instinct for research as a reinforcement. Here, too, the research becomes to some extent compulsive and a substitute for sexual activity; but owing to the complete difference in the underlying psychical processes (sublimation instead of an irruption from the unconscious) the quality of neurosis is absent; there is no attachment to the original complexes of infantile sexual research, and the instinct can operate freely in the service of intellectual interest. Sexual repression, which has made the instinct so strong through the addition to it of sublimated libido, is still taken into account by the instinct, in that it avoids any concern with sexual themes (p. 80).

It is quite clear that in this case we are only describing and classifying and thus actually reinforcing the enigma by calling it sublimation. Freud willingly grants this in his conclusion. We are indeed saying that creative work is a diversion of sexual desires (p. 133) and that it is this instinctual base which had been liberated by regression to childhood memories stimulated by the encounter with the Florentine lady. "With the help of the oldest of all his erotic impulses he enjoyed the triumph of once more conquering the inhibition in his art" (p. 134). But here we are only touching the outlines of a problem. "Since artistic talent and capacity are intimately connected with sublimation, we must admit that the nature of the artistic function is inaccessible to us along psycho-analytic lines" (p. 136). And, a little later, "Even if psycho-analysis does not throw light on the fact of Leonardo's artistic power, it at least renders its manifestations and its limitations intelligible to us" (p. 136).

Freud remains within this limited framework and thus does not perform an exhaustive inventory so much as a restricted foraging "beneath" four or five enigmatic features which are treated as archaeological debris. This is where the interpretation of the vulture fantasy—specifically treated as debris—plays a pivotal role. Because a genuine psychoanalysis is impossible, this interpretation is purely analogical. It is obtained by a convergence of indices borrowed from diverse sources, such as the psychoanalysis of homosexuals (erotic relationship with the mother, repression and identification with the mother, narcissistic object choice, projection of the narcissistic object onto an object of the same sex, etc.), the sexual theory of children about the mother's penis, and mythological parallels (the phallus of the vulture goddess attested to by archaeology). It is in a purely analogical style that Freud writes, "The child's assumption that his mother has a penis is thus the common source from which are derived the androgynously-formed mother goddesses such as the Egyptian Mut and the vulture's *coda in* Leonardo's childhood fantasy" (p. 97).

What understanding of the work of art is communicated to us in this way? Here is where contempt for the meaning of Freud's *Leonardo* can lead us further than the interpretation of "The Moses of Michelangelo."

On a first reading we think we have unmasked Mona Lisa's smile and shown what is hidden behind it. We have been able to see the kisses which the rejected mother showered on Leonardo. But let us listen with a more critical ear to a sentence like the following: "It is possible that in these figures Leonardo has denied the unhappiness of his erotic life and has triumphed over it in his art, by representing the wishes of the boy, infatuated with his mother, as fulfilled in this blissful union of the male and female natures" (pp. 117–18). This sentence sounds like the one we quoted earlier from the analysis of "Moses." What do "denied" and "triumphed over" mean? Is the representation which fulfilled the child's wish anything more than a copy of the fantasy, an exhibition of desire, or a simple revelation of something hidden? Would not interpreting La Gioconda's smile be "showing" in our turn, in the master's paintings, the fantasy which has been uncovered by the analysis of the childhood memory? These questions lead us from overconfident explanation to a second level of doubt. Analysis did not lead us from the less to the better known. The kisses with which Leonardo's mother smothered her child are neither a reality which I could take as a starting point for analysis nor a solid ground on which I could construct an understanding of the work of art. The mother and father and the child's relations with them, the conflicts, the first woundings of love, all this no longer exists except in the mode of the absent signified. If the painter's brush recreates the mother's smile in Mona Lisa's, we must say that the memory exists nowhere else than in the smile (itself unreal) of

La Gioconda, who is signified only by the presence of color and drawing. *Leonardo da Vinci and a Memory of His Childhood*, as the title runs, is exactly what La Gioconda's smile refers to, but it itself exists only as the symbolizable absence whose void lurks beneath the Mona Lisa's smile. Lost like a memory, the mother's smile is an empty spot in reality. It is the point where all real traces get lost and the abolished memory borders on fantasy. Thus it is not something better known which would explain the enigma of the work of art. It is an envisioned absence which, far from dissipating it, redoubles the initial enigma.

III. THE VALUE AND LIMIT OF ANALYTICAL INTERPRETATION

HERE IS WHERE THE DOCTRINE—I mean the metapsychology—protects us against the excesses of its own "applications." We never gain access to instincts as such but only to their psychic expressions, their representatives in ideas and affects. Hence the economics becomes dependent on textual decipherment, and the balance sheet of instinctual cathexes is read only across the grid of an exegesis of the play of signifieds and signifiers. The work of art is a remarkable form of what Freud himself calls "psychic derivatives" of instinctual representatives. Properly speaking, these are created derivatives. In other words, the fantasy, which is merely a signified given as lost (the analysis of the childhood memory points precisely toward this absence), is presented as a work which exists as a cultural treasure. The mother and her kisses exist for the first time in works offered to human contemplation. Leonardo's brush *creates* the memory of his mother as a work of art; it does not recreate it. It is in this sense that Freud could say ". . . in these figures Leonardo has denied the unhappiness of his erotic life and has triumphed over it in his art" (p. 118). The work of art is thus both the symptom and the cure.

These last observations allow us to pose a few questions of principle:

1. To what extent is psychoanalysis justified in submitting works of art and dreams to the single point of view of an economics of instincts? Does not the work of art endure for the very reason that it enriches our patrimony of cultural values with new meanings? Psychoanalysis does not ignore this value

difference, for this is precisely what it approaches indirectly in terms of sublimation. Sublimation, however, is as much the title of a problem as the name of a solution.[4]

2. This common frontier between psychoanalysis and a philosophy of creation can be discovered in another point. The work of art is not only socially valuable, but, as the examples of "The Moses of Michelangelo," *Leonardo,* and, most strikingly, Freud's discussion of Sophocles' *Oedipus Rex* have shown us, these works are creations insofar as they are not simple projections of the artist's conflicts but the outline of their solution. The dream looks backward, toward childhood and the past. The work of art surges forward beyond the artist himself. It is a prospective symbol of personal synthesis and the future of man rather than a regressive symbol of his unresolved conflicts. But perhaps this opposition between regression and progression is true only as a first approximation. Perhaps we need to surpass it in spite of its apparent force. The work of art puts us precisely on the road toward new discoveries about the symbolic function and about sublimation itself. Would not the true meaning of sublimation be to propose new meanings by mobilizing old energies which have already been cathected in archaic figures? Is it not here that Freud himself invites us to seek when he distinguishes, in *Leonardo,* sublimation from inhibition and obsession and when he contrasts even more strongly, in "On Narcissism: An Introduction," sublimation with repression itself?

But in order to surpass this opposition between regression and progression, we must first elaborate it and lead it to the point where it destroys itself.

3. This invitation to investigate psychoanalysis itself by confronting it with other points of view which seem to be diametrically opposed allows us to glimpse the real meaning of its limits. These limits are in no way fixed but are mobile and indefinitely surpassable. They are not, properly speaking, boundaries, like a closed door which bears the inscription "Thus far, but no further." As Kant has taught us, a limit is not an external boundary but rather a function of the internal validity of a theory. Psychoanalysis is limited by the very thing which justifies it, namely, its decision to know, in cultural phenomena, only that which falls under an economics of desire and resistances. I must say that it is this firmness and rigor which makes me prefer Freud to

4. See, above, "Psychoanalysis and the Movement of Contemporary Culture," p. 144.

Jung. With Freud, I know where I am and where I am going; with Jung, everything (the psyche, the soul, the archetypes, the sacred) is in danger of becoming confused. It is precisely this limitation within the Freudian problematic which invites us first to contrast it with another explanatory point of view which seems to be more appropriate to the constitution of cultural objects as such and then to rediscover within psychoanalysis itself the reason why it has been surpassed. Our discussion of Freud's *Leonardo* allows us to glimpse something of this movement: explanation by means of the libido has led us to a threshold instead of a terminus. Interpretation does not reveal something real or even something psychic. The wish to which it refers is itself a reference to its trail of "derivatives" and an indefinite self-symbolizing. It is this proliferation of symbols which lends itself to investigation by other methods: phenomenological, Hegelian, or even theological. We must discover in the semantic structure of the symbol itself the *raison d'être* for these other approaches and for their relationship to psychoanalysis. The psychoanalyst himself, we should mention, has to be prepared by his own culture for this confrontation, certainly not to learn to limit his own discipline externally but to rediscover within it the reasons for constantly pushing forward the boundaries already attained. It is thus that psychoanalysis itself passes from a first purely reductionist reading to a second interpretation of cultural phenomena. The task of this second reading would no longer be to unmask the repressed and the repressive, in order to make us see what lies beneath the masks, but to enter into the movement of the signifier, which constantly points away from the absent signifieds of desire to works which presentify fantasies in a world of culture and thus create them as a reality on the level of the aesthetic.

PART III

Hermeneutics
and Phenomenology

Nabert on
Act and Sign

THIS ESSAY EXPLORES at greater length and in a more leisurely way a difficulty in Nabert's philosophy which I touched on too quickly in my preface to his *Elements for an Ethic*.[1] The difficulty appears for the first time in Nabert's *The Inner Experience of Freedom*,[2] where the problem of motives and values is raised. Then, in *Elements for an Ethic*, the difficulty is fully formulated and a more radical solution is reached. In its broadest generality, this difficulty concerns the relationships between the act whereby consciousness posits and produces itself and the signs wherein consciousness represents to itself the meaning of its action. This problem is not restricted to Nabert's thought. It is common to every philosophy which tries to subordinate the objectivity of idea, representation, understanding, or whatever to the founding act of consciousness, regardless of whether this act is called will, appetite, or action. When Spinoza moves from the idea of existence to the effort each being makes to exist, when Leibniz articulates perception with appetite, when Schopenhauer links representation to will, when Nietzsche subordinates perspective and value to the will to power, and when Freud subordinates representation to libido—each of these thinkers

Translated by Peter McCormick.
  1. Jean Nabert, *Eléments pour une éthique* (Paris: Presses Universitaires de France, 1943; 2d ed., Aubier, 1960), pp. 10–13. English translation by William J. Petrek, *Elements for an Ethic* (Evanston, Ill.: Northwestern University Press, 1969), pp. xvii–xxviii. [Translations of passages quoted from this book are Petrek's.—TRANS.]
  2. Jean Nabert, *L'Expérience intérieure de la liberté* (Paris: Presses Universitaires de France, 1924). [Translations of passages quoted from this book are mine.—TRANS.]

makes an important decision about the fate of representation. Representation is no longer the primary fact, the primary function, or what is best known for psychological consciousness or for philosophical reflection. Representation becomes a secondary function of effort and of desire. Representation is no longer what brings about understanding but what must be understood.

Nabert poses the problem in such abstract and general terms only in his article in the *Encyclopédie française,* where he sketches the genealogical tree of the reflective method.[3] There we discover the extent of the problem. In claiming descent from Maine de Biran rather than from Kant, Nabert formulates the problem we are going to analyze later, and he does so in precise and limited terms. In the tradition stemming from Maine de Biran, the operations of active consciousness are not reducible to those which control knowledge and science, and reflective analysis applied to action must be liberated from the hegemony of epistemology. In these terms *The Inner Experience of Freedom* distinguishes between inquiry about the *cogito*'s "function of objectivity and of truth" (p. x) and reflection on "that productivity of consciousness which the categories at the basis of the truth of knowledge cannot account for" (p. xi). Nabert also credits Maine de Biran in the following way:

> We believe it is fitting to return to the inspiration of Maine de Biran, provided that he is interpreted more in terms of the idea of philosophy that he was trying to create than on some kind of faith in his literal formulas. For what Maine de Biran wanted to express is the idea that only an act produces consciousness and that the *cogito,* which is essentially the positing of the self in active consciousness, is not to be confused (at least where there is question of the volitional life) either with an act of understanding or with a method for grounding the objectivity of knowledge (p. 157).

> Never before has it been so well understood that consciousness could be liberated from the models borrowed from representation and knowledge of the external world (p. 169).

This emancipation is what creates the problem we are concerned with here. For if the constitutive operations of true knowledge cannot yield the key to this "productivity," then the question now is: What becomes of representation in the reflective method?

3. "La Philosophie réflexive," *Encyclopédie française,* XIX, 19.04-14–19.06-3.

The provisional solution that distinguishes and juxtaposes multiple "openings to reflection," an opening to truth and an opening to freedom, is inadequate. It is true that Nabert has several texts to this effect. But these texts are not meant to account for the radical constitution of consciousness and existence, but only to describe the historical ramifications of reflective philosophy. More important is his suggestion that an "interdependence" and a "complementarity" must be established between the regulative norms of true knowledge and the constitutive operations of free action. This precept does not invite an eclecticism that would put Kant and Maine de Biran side by side; rather, it introduces a philosophy of the act that would account *within itself* for the function of objectivity and truth. Nabert expects the final balance of reflective philosophy from this reintegration of the objective *cogito* with and within active and productive consciousness. "Without this counterweight," the 1924 preface continues, "inquiry that is immediately oriented toward the discovery of concrete forms of inner experience, irreducible to the categories we use for the construction of nature, would incline philosophy toward a sterile irrationalism" (p. x). It is notable that the 1957 article in the *Encyclopédie française* repeats the same warning:

> It was necessary that a critical theory of knowledge situate the function of objectivity and truth on the first level of the *cogito*. The reason was to avoid a situation where the inquiry that was immediately concerned with the concrete forms of inner experience would be an accomplice of a sterile irrationalism (p. 19.06-1).

But this declaration, made in identical terms at the two limits of Nabert's work, outlines the contour of a problem more than it sketches a solution. The first solution arises in the context of a much more limited and, at first glance, different problem. This problem is very much the classic and almost academic one where the immense question of *act* and *sign* is at issue, the problem of the role of motives in a psychology of the will. *The Inner Experience of Freedom* is an attempt to give an account of freedom in terms of the problem of psychological causality. "What is more difficult than sorting out determinism and indeterminism is showing how freedom participates, without losing itself, in the life of a consciousness and in the system of psychological facts deployed there" (p. 63).

But the author immediately warns us that "when the coincidence of freedom and psychological causality is affirmed, no solution is forthcoming; rather, a problem is raised" (p. 64). Actually, we run the risk of merely consecrating the duality of the *cogito*'s two functions, the function of truth, which is at work in determinism, and the function of freedom, which is at work in active and productive consciousness. This is what happens in the Kantian doctrines which push the chain of motivation back to the phenomenal level and concentrate everything which accrues to the subject in the action of a thinking aimed at objectivity. Everything is saved but nothing is gained; for the subject who is given shelter in this way is neither myself nor anyone at all. Nothing is gained either if we seek to find in the quality of certain representations and certain ideas the capacity to set action moving. We know nothing about this motive power of ideas. And the question remains whether representation is the basic reality we must start from.

Nabert thinks that we must start resolutely with the act in order to find again in decision-making the reason why this act afterward appears to the understanding as an empirical series of facts (pp. 123–55). This reason is what we will later on be calling "the law of representation."

But this law appears only if we move from act to representation and not the other way round. If we are faithful to this reading, we must grasp again, even in the motives which are supposed to precede the fulfilled act of decision, the sketches, rough drafts, and initial stirrings of the act. These are the sketches which, after the event, seem to me like some kind of tracing of the act in the representation. And it is in this way that we come to treat motives as antecedent representations capable of producing the act. But what precedes the fulfilled act are inchoate, incomplete, and unfulfilled acts. And these unfulfilled acts, grasped with the help of retrospection, appear in the guise of a progression and a connection in the representations. This fall of the unfulfilled act into representation is what we call motive. Objectified in this way, deliberation appears to us like a body of necessity in which we no longer know where to fit a spirit which is free. But these motives are only the effect, or rather the consequence, of the causality of consciousness. In each of them "the incomplete acts where our consciousness tries to act are transposed." But this transposition proceeds from a retreat, a withdrawal of our responsibility, which, in concentrating itself in the ultimate act, abandons the previous course to the law of representation.

So the entire difficulty is contracted in the double nature of motive, which on the one hand "participates in the act" and on the other "lends itself to becoming very quickly an element of a psychological determinism" (p. 127). It is this double nature of motive that allows an escape not only from the Kantian antinomy between noumenal freedom and empirical causality but also from the Bergsonian opposition between the *durée* and the superficial self.

But have we, in turn, done anything more than name the problem? What is this expressive power whose strange virtue consists in "deploying the act in representation" (p. 129)? We understand, of course, that in becoming a spectacle the act is made recognizable for us. By our motives we know what we have willed. But why is this knowledge presented, not in its signs as the knowledge of an actual willing, but as the knowledge of a willing which is abolished in an inert given? Must one go so far as to say that this function of revelation, of manifestation, in itself invites the abandonment and the forgetfulness of the causality by which these signs become what they are? Here is a strange evil spell. By making itself a "commentary" (p. 130) on itself, a text to be deciphered, the act is unrecognized at the same time that it is recognized. And it is always by a painful uprooting that consciousness must recover itself in its own expression. And yet nothing is further from Nabert's thinking than to take this passage, from the act to its sign and from the sign to representation, for a downfall. The possibility of reading the text of consciousness under the law of determinism exactly coincides with the effort of clarity and sincerity we need in order to know what we want. Moreover, if they were not enclosed in an uninterrupted narrative, our acts would be only momentary flashes and would not make a history or even a duration. Hence, the moment the act is grasped again in its own verbalization, the tendency is strongest to forget the act in its sign and to exhaust the meaning of psychological causality in determinism.

Therefore, the genesis of representation and the problem of motivation both arise in the passage from the act to its expression. This is why one must never cease to make the opposite move, what Nabert calls "recovery"—the move from the representation to the act. Just as more is in the act, even when it is only a tentative act, than what is in its representation as motive, this movement of recovery always seems to get the maximum from the minimum. This is how tendencies and other forces which conspire in the volitional act are embodied in representations. These representations in turn are presented to us as models of movements to be made. Then, to account for the gratuity of the "I want," these representations must be assigned different values; that is, what is actually no more than a sign of the causality of consciousness must be incorporated in them. In brief, to account for the movement from representation to act, the psychological fact must seem "to surpass itself by becoming the element of an act (which in some way it is only the material for) and hence by referring back to a causality which it does not contain" (p. 149). This move, from the psychological fact, displayed on the level of representation, back to the act of consciousness is actually the model of this genesis of representation in the act:

> Everything takes place as if empirical consciousness did not continue, did not maintain itself, did not progress except by the renewed act of a nonempirical consciousness which creates in the phenomenon something that enables it to render and to prolong the spiritual life (p. 149).

In these two moves which reflection makes, psychological determinism is grasped again as "the mold of another kind of causality" (p. 149). Because of a failure to understand this bond between the act and the sign, philosophy hesitates between the profession of an exiled freedom and that of an empirical explication, faithful only to the law of representation.

SUCH WAS NABERT'S 1924 effort to bring together the nonempirical act of consciousness and the empirical consequence of its conditions. At stake in this effort was something clearly beyond the precise problem of the relations between the philosophy of freedom and the psychology of volition. In basing the law of representation on the double nature of motive, Nabert tried to introduce an interdependence and complementarity into the two functions of the *cogito* that the tradition had separated. But what does this solution mean? Clearly, it is necessary to go beyond this structure of motives. The conversion of motive into representation, spread out under the regard of the understanding, points up the unfulfilled character of the act whose motive is expression. But the true act, the fulfilled act, the accomplished act, where the causality of consciousness would be identical with itself, is an act which we will never accomplish. All of our decisions are in reality unsuccessful attempts at this complete and concrete act. The effort itself testifies to this lack of fulfillment. In fact, effort is not the surplus of an act but the lack of one. The fulfilled act is to be a tireless one, an act without difficulty, without effort. The lack of identity with our own selves is therefore our lasting condition. Into this gap between empirical consciousness and "the *cogito,* which is essentially the positing of self by active consciousness" (p. 157), slips the law of representation and, with it, the conviction that our whole existence can be understood under the sign of determinism. At the same time, the free act is exiled into the ideal of itself and is projected before and above us in the idea of the timeless choice in Plato and Kant. This idea of absolute choice is the counterpart of the dissimulation of the act which is unfulfilled in a determinist stream of representations. It is thus not by accident that reflective consciousness and psychological explication are split, but by necessity.

Reflective philosophy therefore has only pushed the duality between operative consciousness and the objective function of the understanding further back. It is no longer the classic duality between acting and knowing. There is a more subtle division, at the very heart of active consciousness, between its pure power of positing itself and its laborious production by "the mediation of psychological elements" (p. 155). It is this division which makes possible "the slipping of the act of consciousness toward nature and its insertion into the determinism of psychological life" (p. 269). And this forgetfulness, this relaxation, seems to have resulted from the unfulfillment of the human act and its lack of conformity to the pure positing of consciousness.

The final pages of *The Inner Experience of Freedom* show that we are touching here on a much greater enigma than the initial problem we started from. The problem of psychological causality is not the only place where this enigma crops up. The understanding itself, where we have recognized the rule of determinism and, more generally, the norm of truth, is only an aspect of reason understood as a "set of norms" (p. 304). "The understanding expresses reason only to the degree that reason helps bring about objectivity. But, as Malebranche said, besides the relations of greatness, there are the relations of perfection" (p. 304). The understanding is therefore only the specification of a more general function of order, an order from which the norms of beauty and morality also derive.

The solution sketched at the level of the "law of representation," that is, of the understanding, is therefore only a partial one. The question must be raised about the entire breadth of the relation between freedom and reason. *The Inner Experience of Freedom* tries to do this quickly. The solution glimpsed there introduces the pages of *Elements for an Ethic* which we will comment on below. In effect, the last chapter of the 1924 thesis limits itself to establishing the "complementarity" of freedom and norms. And it is in the idea of value that the "convertibility" of freedom and reason appears. So, the idea of value displays at the end of the work the same *mixed* character that the idea of motive displayed earlier. Value belongs at the same time on the side of the "objective" norm and on the side of the contingent adherence of consciousness. "Reason can furnish norms only. It is the synthesis between these norms and freedom which produces values. Values require a contingent adherence of consciousness to the norms of a thinking stamped with impersonality" (p. 310). The objectivity of values expresses the resistance of norms to our desire; their subjectivity expresses the consent without which value would be a force only. This double aspect of value, similar to the double aspect of motive, occasions the same split or division. The forgetfulness of the initiative which sustains value produces the same effacement of consciousness before the truth of order. It is the same "transfer" (p. 314) of the subject of action toward the pole of understanding or of reason which gives to the *ideal* its apparent exteriority. This "transfer" is not a forfeiture. Thanks to it, I am able to judge myself. Nevertheless, it is a slope which must constantly be reclimbed in order to rescue the first spontaneity, which occasions the acts, of the contemplation of order and of the fascination with order.

This ultimate duality between act and norm shows the incompleteness of the theory of the sign in Nabert's first work. The expressions "collaboration" and "equilibrium" (pp. 318 and 332) show that an invincible duality is reborn between freedom and reason. The theory of motivation had "reconciled" [*rapproché*] the spontaneity of consciousness and the objectivity of understanding. By enlarging the problem to the dimensions of reason, understood as the level of norms, the final chapter reopens the debate which the theory of motive had seemed to close. *The Inner Experience of Freedom* has at least strongly indicated the direction of the solution.

This direction is a general theory of signs. The *Encyclopédie française* article puts this forcefully:

> It is therefore true that in all of the domains where spirit reveals itself as creative, reflection is called on to retrieve the acts which works conceal, because, living their own life, these works are almost detached from the operations that have produced them. It is a question of bringing to light the intimate relationship between

an act and the significations in which it is objectified. Reflective analysis does not overlook the fact that in every order the spirit must first of all be operative and be produced in history and in an experience comprehensive enough to grasp its most profound possibilities. Rather, reflective analysis reveals all its richness in surprising the moment when the act of the spirit is invested in a sign which may immediately be turned against it (p. 19.06-1).

The Inner Experience of Freedom sketches this general theory of signs twice: at the level of motive and at the level of value. These two levels correspond to two points of view which at that time remained exclusive, the viewpoint of psychological explanation and the viewpoint of normative ethics. And these two viewpoints are, finally, those of the understanding and of reason.

CHAPTER 5 OF *Elements for an Ethic*, "Promotion of Values," aims at surpassing both points of view and, at the same time, overcoming their mutual exclusiveness. Psychological causality and ethical normativity are no longer points of view constituted outside reflection. Moreover, the epistemological question of the diversity of reflective levels is transcended in the interests of a more radical problematic, that of existence. If a difference always remains between the consciousness that moves itself and the consciousness that regards itself, it is because existence itself is constituted by a double relation: between an affirmation which institutes it and surpasses its consciousness, and a lack of being, which is attested to by the feelings of fault, failure, and solitude. "The inadequation of existence to itself" (p. 57) is primary in relation to the plurality of reflective levels. It is this inadequation, this lack of identity, which puts at the center of philosophy the task of appropriating to itself the originary affirmation through the signs of its activity in the world or in history. It is this lack of identity that makes of this philosophy an ethics, in the strong and vast sense that Spinoza gave this word, that is, an exemplary history of the desire to be.

But in this kind of ethics, what becomes of the theory of signs which we saw sketched, in the 1924 thesis, against the double background of the theory of motive and of values? The second theme now envelops the first. The theory of value can now play this role because it is itself separated from an antecedent theory of norms. Now it presupposes one thing only—the relationship that freedom establishes with the world at the heart of *the work*.

In fact, what immediately follows from the lack, in existence, of identity with itself is an "alternation" between two movements, between "a concentration of the self at its source" and "its expansion in the world" (p. 57). Resituated in the field of this alternation, the problem of value takes on new meaning:

> What reflection grasps and affirms as pure consciousness of self the self appropriates as value to the extent that it creates itself and becomes really for itself. This means that value appears in view of existence and for existence when pure consciousness of self has turned toward the world to become the principle or rule of action and, at the same time, the measure of satisfaction in a concrete consciousness (p. 58).

It is in this movement that we again find the forgetfulness of the act in the sign:

> Value is always linked to a certain obfuscation of the principle on which it is based and which sustains it. . . . In this respect, the obfuscation of the generative principle of value is the expression of a law which affects all manifestations of the human spirit. What Maine de Biran says about signs, that is, about acts which reveal its constitutive power to consciousness, must also be said about values (p. 58).

And nevertheless, this obfuscation is "not an abatement or weakening of this principle" (p. 58), as in Neoplatonic philosophies of the intelligible. The risk of treachery is on the very path of trial or proof without which there is no self-appropriation at all.

Can we go beyond this law of the sign? Nabert suggests that the shift from value predicates like "courageous" and "generous" to the essence of courage or generosity follows from forgetfulness of the fact that "it is characteristic of the human spirit to be affected by its own creations" (p. 66). This activity of the self on itself, which Kant already invoked in the second edition of the *Critique*, makes possible the division between the generative movement and the interior law of this movement: an essence is born when the creative act withdraws itself from its creations, from its rhythms of intimate existence, which are henceforth offered to contemplation. The activity of the self on itself seems to be a kind of inertia of the productive imagination:

> It is patent that the ideality of value-essences is nothing more than the ideality of creations, of permanent directions born of productive imagination which have become rules for action and evaluation for the individual consciousness. They are clothed, certainly, in an authority which transcends the contingent movements of an

individual consciousness. However, only the twofold character of the human spirit, capable at once of creating and of affecting itself by its own creations, gives a specious character to the transcendence of essences (p. 67).

Perhaps what must be found here is the law of every symbol, the symbol which, as psychoanalysis has shown, both conceals and reveals, both expresses and diguises. Nabert himself outlines a similar generalization when he explores the opposite path of desire in the direction of value, by a movement similar to that of the previous work, going back from psychological tendency toward motive and act. Starting, then, from desire, we will say that all meaning and every value claim is "obtaining from the real and from life an expression [of creative intention which] transcends all expression and all realization" (p. 60). But this heightening of desire by value is the passage to the symbol:

> Conditions of increased rigor, rules, forms, signs, and languages, substitute perceptions and new actions for actions and perceptions rooted in instinct. . . . Each of the systems of symbols produced according to this effort of rigor is first of all a method of dissolution of the real as it is offered to immediate consciousness (p. 75).

By this double access to value—objectification of pure act and symbolization of natural desire—we arrive at the level we have sought so long. As in Kant, "the imagination is . . . a mediator" (p. 76). It is the imagination that conceals the double power of expression because it "symbolizes" the principle (p. 58) in verifying it and because it elevates desire to symbol by the will for rigor. This imagination "creates the instrument, the matter of value, as much as the value itself" (p. 77). In this imagination and in the law of the self's effect on itself, which belongs to it—*and which is time itself*—must be sought the key to the division we have been concerned with in this essay, the division between the pure production of acts and their concealment in signs. Creation springs up like a stream of time, a *durée;* but it is as time itself that works are deposited behind the stream of time and remain inert, offered to the eye as objects for contemplation or as essences for imitation.

If there must be a summary of this play between manifestation and concealment in motive and in value, then "phenomenon" must be the preferred expression.

The *phenomenon* is the manifestation, in a "graspable expression," "of an inner operation, which can assure itself as to what it is only by forcing itself toward this expression" (p. 77).

The phenomenon is the correlate of this assurance of the self in its difference from itself. Because we do not enjoy immediate self-possession and always lack perfect self-identity, because, according to *The Inner Experience of Freedom,* we never produce the total act that we gather up and project in the ideal of an absolute choice, we must endlessly appropriate what we are through the mediation of the multiple expressions of our desire to be. The detour by way of the phenomenon, then, is based on the very structure of originary affirmation as both difference and relation between pure consciousness and real consciousness. The law of the phenomenon is indivisibly a law of expression and a law of concealment.

Thus we can understand that "the entire sensible world and all the beings with which we have dealings sometimes appear to us as a text to be deciphered" (p. 77). Or, to use other words, which are not Nabert's but which his work encourages: reflection, because it is not an intuition of the self by the self, can be, and must be, a hermeneutics.

Heidegger and the Question
of the Subject

MY INTENTION HERE is to understand the scope of the well-known critique of the subject-object relation which underlies the denial of the priority of the *cogito*. I stress the word "scope" because I want to show that this denial implies more than a mere rejection of a notion of the ego or of the self—as if they lacked any meaning or were necessarily infected by the basic misconception that governs the philosophies generated by the Cartesian *cogito*. On the contrary, the kind of ontology developed by Heidegger gives ground to what I shall call *a hermeneutics of the "I am,"* which is a refutation of the *cogito* conceived of as a simple epistemological principle and at the same time is an indication of a foundation of Being which is necessarily spoken of as grounding the *cogito*. In setting out to comprehend this complex relation between the *cogito* and this hermeneutics of the "I am," I shall relate this problem to the destruction of the history of philosophy on the one hand and, on the other, to the restatement or retrieval of the ontological purpose which was in the *cogito* and which has been forgotten in the formulation of Descartes.

This general thesis suggests the following order of discussion.

Originally published in English under the title "The Critique of Subjectivity and Cogito in the Philosophy of Heidegger," in *Heidegger and the Quest for Truth*, edited by Manfred S. Frings. Copyright © 1968 by Quadrangle Books, Chicago. Reproduced by permission of Quadrangle/The New York Times Book Co. The English text which appears in the Quadrangle book was derived from a tape of a paper delivered by Professor Ricoeur during the Heidegger Symposium held at De Paul University in Chicago, November 11 and 12, 1966. Discrepancies between that text and the one in the present volume derive from editorial changes made by Ricoeur in the French text of the essay when he was preparing this volume of collected essays for his French publisher.

[223]

First, taking as a guide Heidegger's introduction to *Being and Time,* I shall point to the primordial link between the question of Being and the emergence of Dasein in the very interrogation of the inquirer. This primordial link makes possible both a destruction of the *cogito* as first truth and its restatement on the ontological level as the "I am."

Second, shifting to the *Holzwege,* and principally to the essay "The Age of the World as View," I shall develop the main critique of the *cogito* with the intention of showing that it is less a critique of the *cogito* as such than of the metaphysics which underlies it. That is to say, the critique focuses upon the conception of the existent as *Vorstellung,* as "representation."

Third, after this excursion into matters which are destructive in a Heideggerian sense, I want to explore the positive hermeneutics of the "I am" which replaces the *cogito,* in both senses of the word "to replace." This third analysis will take as its basis §§ 9, 12, and 25 of *Being and Time* and what is said in them about the self.

At this point it could be objected that such an analysis could be justified only as long as we rely on Heidegger I,[1] and that we could not proceed to the *Kehre,* to the turning or reversal. Therefore, it could also be objected that this *Kehre* puts an end to this complex relation with the *cogito.* This is why I shall try, in my fourth point, to show that the kind of circular implication between *Sein* and *Dasein,* between the question of Being and the self, of which we read in the introduction of *Being and Time,* keeps ruling the philosophy of the later Heidegger. This time, however, it does so on the level of the philosophy of language and no longer on the level of an Analytic of Dasein. To put Being into words repeats the same problematics, the rise of the being which "I am" in and through the disclosure of Being as such. This kind of second proof or countertest, which I should have liked to develop at length, will be only a short sketch. The whole problem overflows into the area of Heidegger's philosophy of language. This is to say that the rise of Dasein as self and the rise of language as speech or discourse [*parole*] are *one and the same problem.*

---

1. [Ricoeur, in this essay, is taking for granted the familiar designation of the early Heidegger as "Heidegger I" and the later Heidegger as "Heidegger II," a distinction originated by William Richardson's interpretation of Heidegger. Ricoeur is, in fact, disputing this too strong distinction and is arguing for a unitary interpretation of Heidegger.—Ed.]

I

I SHALL TAKE AS MY STARTING POINT and as a guide what I call the primordial link between the question of Being and the emergence of Dasein as the inquirer.

Everybody knows how *Being and Time* starts: "This question [of Being] has today been forgotten." [2] Heidegger's first sentence clearly implies the shift of emphasis from a philosophy which starts with the *cogito* as the first truth to a philosophy which starts with the question of Being as a question which is forgotten, and which is forgotten in the *cogito*. Now the important thing is that the problem of Being occurs as a question precisely in the treatment of the concept of "question" in which we shall discover this reference to a self. What does it mean that the problem of Being occurs as a question and that what has been forgotten is not only Being but the question of Being? Forgottenness bears on the question, but there is not merely a pedagogical precaution here. In the question as question there is a structure which has definite implications for our problem. These implications are of two kinds.

First, the structure is the denial of the priority of the self-positing or of the self-asserting of the *cogito*. This is not to be taken in the sense that the question as question would imply a degree of uncertainty and of doubt lacking in the *cogito*. This opposition is still an epistemological one. An objection against the Cartesian *cogito* will be precisely that it starts with a previous model of certitude and places itself on the epistemological basis which has been raised as a mirror of certitude. Thus, the structure of the question is not defined by its epistemological degree, so to speak, or by the fact that if we raise a question it is because we are not certain. No. What is important in the question is that it is ruled by the questioned—by the thing about which the question is asked. "Every inquiry is a seeking. Every seeking gets guided beforehand by what is sought. . . . Any inquiry, as inquiry about something, has that which is asked about [*hat sein Befragtes*]" (p. 24). This is the first implication which will be developed as the negative aspect in the critique of the *cogito*.

2. Martin Heidegger, *Sein und Zeit* (Halle: Max Niemeyer, 1928), p. 5. English translation by John Macquarrie and Edward Robinson, *Being and Time* (New York: Harper & Row, 1962), p. 21. [Page numbers cited throughout refer to the English translation.]

But at the same time we discover the possibility of a new philosophy of the ego in the sense that the genuine ego is constituted by the question itself. By "genuine ego" we do not need to understand an epistemological subjectivity of some kind but simply the one who inquires. This ego would no longer be the center, since the question of Being and the meaning of Being are the forgotten center which has to be retrieved by philosophy. Thus, in the position of the ego, there is both the forgottenness of the question as question but also the birth of the ego as the inquirer. It is this twofold relation which is the real object of this study.

This ego, as implied in the question, is not posited as certain of itself. That is to say, it is posited as being itself a being, the being for which there is the question of Being. Let us consider the first reference to Dasein in *Being and Time:*

> Looking at something, understanding and conceiving it, choosing, access to it—all these ways of behaving are constitutive for our inquiry, and therefore are modes of Being of such a particular being (*Seiendes*), viz., that which we the inquirers are ourselves [—are constitutive, are modes of Being, for those particular entities which we, the inquirers ourselves are] (pp. 26–27, modified).

Thus, it is immediately as an "I am" and not as an "I think" that I am implied in the inquiry; and so, to work out the question of Being adequately, we must assume an entity, *ein Seiendes:*

> The very asking of this question is an entity's mode of *Being;* and as such it gets its essential character from what is inquired about —namely, Being. This entity which each of us is himself and which includes inquiring as one of the possibilities of its Being, we shall denote by the term *Dasein* (p. 27).

Thus, the opposition to the *cogito* becomes more subtle, since the question of Dasein has a certain priority in the question of Being. But this priority, which has led to so many misunderstandings, and, above all, to anthropological interpretations of *Being and Time,* is only, and remains, an ontic priority, mixed or involved in the ontological priority of the question of Being. And this relation is the origin of a new philosophy of the ego. Everyone knows the famous formula according to which Dasein is "ontically distinctive in that it *is* ontological" (p. 32), or, in less cryptic terms: "Understanding of Being is itself a definitive characteristic of Dasein's being" (*ibid.*). We are thus led to a kind of circular relation which is not a vicious circle. Heidegger tries to master this extraordinary situation in these terms: "In the question of the meaning of Being there is no 'circular reasoning' but rather a remarkable 'relatedness backward or forward' [*Rück- oder Vorbezogenheit*] which what we are asking about (Being) bears to the inquiry itself as a mode of Being of an entity" (p. 28). Here is the birth of the subject. The question of the meaning of Being oscillates backward and forward in the inquiry itself as the mode of being of a possible ego. I propose to take this relation as the guiding line for the rest of this discussion. In it are contained not only a contesting of the philosophy of the *cogito* but its restatement on its own ontological level, precisely because the problem for Descartes was ultimately "I am" and not "I think." This is evidenced by the series of propositions which proceeds from the *existence* of the ego to the *existence* of God and to the *existence* of the world.

II

THE CONTESTATION of the *cogito* is a part of the destruction of the history of ontology (to use an expression of Heidegger himself) such as he sought in the introduction of *Being and Time*. In the famous section on Descartes (§ 6) we read that the assertion of the "*Cogito sum*" proceeds from an essential omission: the omission of an ontology of Dasein. Heidegger says: "what [Descartes] left undetermined when he began in this 'radical' way [with '*cogito sum*'] was the kind of Being which belongs to the *res cogitans*, or—more precisely—the *meaning of the Being of the 'sum'*" (p. 46). This means the Being of the "I am." What is the omission? Or rather, what positive decision kept Descartes from raising the question of the meaning of the Being which this entity possesses? *Being and Time* makes only a partial response: it is "the absolute certainty of the *cogito*" which has foreclosed the problem of the meaning of the Being of this entity. Thus the question now becomes: in what sense does the quest for certainty belong to the forgottenness of Being?

The question is elaborated in a text from 1938: "Die Zeit des Weltbildes" (The Age of the World as View).[3] Here we learn that the *cogito* is not an innocent assertion; it belongs to an age

3. Martin Heidegger, *Holzwege* (Frankfort a.M.: Vittorio Klostermann, 1953), pp. 69–105. English translation by Marjorie Grene, *Measure*, II (1951), 269–84.

of metaphysics for which truth is the truth of existents and as such constitutes the forgottenness of Being. How and in what sense does the *cogito* belong to the age of metaphysics? The argumentation is very dense and must be followed scrupulously. The philosophical ground on which the *cogito* emerged is the ground of science in particular, but, more generally, it is a mode of understanding in which the existent (*das Seiende*) is put at the disposal of an "explanatory representation." The first pre-supposition is that we raise the problem of science in terms of research (*suchen*), which implies the objectification of an existent and which places that existent before us (*vor-Stellung*). Thus calculating man perhaps becomes sure (*sicher*), gains certainty (*Gewissheit*), of the existent. It is at the point where the problem of certitude and the problem of representation coincide that the *cogito* emerges. In the metaphysics of Descartes, the existent was defined for the first time as the objectivity of representation and truth as certainty of representation.[4] With objectivity comes subjectivity, in the sense that this being-certain of the object is the counterpart of the positing of a subject. So we have both the *positing* of the subject and the *proposition* of the representation. This is the age of the world as view or picture (*Bild*).

Let us try to understand this new move more precisely; we have introduced the "subject," but it is not the "subject" in the sense of the "I" but in the sense of the substratum. *Subjectum* does not first mean "ego," but, according to the Greek *hypokeimenon* and the Latin *substratum*, it is that which gathers everything to itself to become a basis. This *subjectum* is not yet man and not at all the "I." What happens with Descartes is that man becomes the first and real *subjectum*, the first and real ground. There is a kind of complicity and identification between the two notions of the *subjectum* as ground and *subjectum* as "I." The subject, as myself, becomes the center to which the existent, *das Seiende*, is related. But this is possible only because the world has become a *Bild* (picture). It stands before us. "Where the world becomes a 'view' [*Bild*], the existent as a whole is posited as that with respect to which a man orients himself, which, therefore, he wishes to bring and have before himself, and thus, in a decisive sense, re-presents to himself." [5] The representational character of the existent is the correlate of the emergence of man as subject.

4. *Holzwege*, p. 220.
5. *Ibid.*, p. 82; Eng. trans., p. 279.

Now, the existent is brought before man as what is objective or what may be determined. According to this analysis, the *cogito* is not an atemporal truth, but it belongs to an age, and not only to an age, but to the first age for which the world is made into a view [*Bild*]. That is why there was no *cogito* for the Greeks, since man did not "face" the world. For the Greeks it is rather man who is faced *by* the existent and "who is gathered into its presence by self-disclosing." [6] Heidegger does not say that there was not yet man for the Greeks. On the contrary, this man had an essence and the task to "collect (*legein*) the self-disclosing in its disclosure and to save (*sōzein*) it, to catch it up and preserve it, and to remain exposed to all sundering confusion (*alētheuein*)." [7]

Let us preserve this theme, since we shall return to it. It will give us a key for a link between Heidegger I and II in terms of the continuity of the philosophy of the self. Let us say simply that the *cogito* is not an absolute; it belongs to an age, the age of "world" as representation and as picture. Henceforth, man puts himself into this setting, he posits himself as the setting in which the existent must from now on represent itself, present itself—that is, be a view of the picture. "Man becomes the representative of the existent in the sense of the objective." [8] The claim to master the existent as a whole, in technology, is only a consequence, and a formidable consequence, of this emergence of man on the *stage* of his own representation. The strength of this analysis is that it does not stay on the level of the *cogito* as an argument. We are not discussing the *"ergo"* of the *"cogito ergo sum."* This analysis digs underneath; what it discloses is the underlying event of our culture and, more than that, the event (*Ereignis*) which affects the existent as a whole. Now humanism is born, if by humanism we designate "that philosophical interpretation of man which explains and evaluates the existent as a whole from the viewpoint of an inner relation to man." [9]

We understand now in what sense the *cogito* belongs to the metaphysical tradition. The subject-object relationship interpreted as *Bild*, as picture, as view, obliterates, dissimulates, the belonging of *Dasein* to *Sein*. It dissimulates the process of truth as nonconcealment of this ontological implication. But does this critique exhaust all possible relations between the Analytic of

6. *Ibid.*, p. 83; ET, p. 280.
7. *Ibid.*, p. 84; ET, p. 280.
8. *Ibid.*; ET, p. 281.
9. *Ibid.*, p. 86.

Dasein and the tradition of the *cogito*? I want to show now, at least briefly, that this destruction of the *cogito*, with the destruction of the age to which it belongs, is the condition for a justified repetition of the question of the ego.

III

THAT THE QUESTION OF THE EGO—of the self—is not ruled out by the foregoing critique may be ascertained by returning to our point of departure. Dasein has reference to itself. Dasein has the characteristic of the self. Of course, Dasein is not defined as this self-reference, but rather by its relation to the question of Being. It is the question as question, however, which gives self-reference to Dasein. "This entity which each of us is himself, and which includes inquiring as one of the possibilities of its Being, we shall denote by the term *Dasein*" (*Being and Time*, p. 27). And further: "That kind of being towards which Dasein can comport itself in one way or another, and always does comport itself somehow, we call *existence* [*Existenz*]" (p. 32).

A problem now arises from the coincidence between the two definitions of Dasein: as the one who inquires and as the one who has to be its own being and has it as its own. I think that the identity of the two definitions of Dasein is nothing else but the *Rückbezogenheit*, the "relatedness backward," from which we started. In §§ 9, 12, and 25 of *Being and Time* Heidegger explains in what sense Dasein implies existentiality. Dasein always understands itself in terms of its existence and in terms of its own possibilities: to be itself or not itself. Here we must not object that this is the *existenziell*, and that Heidegger is not interested in the *existenziell*, but only in the existential; for existentiality is nothing other than the totality of the structures of an existent who exists only in the fulfillment or the lack of fulfillment of his own possibilities. If a *given* decision can be called *existenziell*, the fact *that* we have to decide is an "existential" of existence itself. Thus the circle of Dasein and the existent, mentioned above, now takes the shape of a circle between existentiality and Being.

Yet, this circle is nothing else than the circle of the inquirer and the thing inquired about. This is implied in any questioning. The great difference with the Cartesian *cogito* is that the ontic priority of which we have spoken does not imply any immediateness. "Ontically, of course, Dasein is not only close to us—even that which is closest: we *are* it, each of us, we ourselves. In spite of this, or rather for just this reason, it is ontologically that which is farthest" (p. 36). At this point, the retrieval of the "I am" must be not only of phenomenological concern—that is to say, in the sense of an intuitive description—but concerned with interpretation, precisely because the "I am" is forgotten. It has to be recovered by an interpretation which brings it from concealment. Dasein is ontically the closest to itself, but ontologically farthest. And it is in this distance that the "I am" becomes the theme of a hermeneutics and not simply of intuitive description. Therefore, a retrieval of the *cogito* is possible only as a regressive movement beginning with the whole phenomenon of "being-in-the-world" and turned toward the question of the *who* of that being-in-the-world.

But the meaning of the question in itself is hidden. We read in § 25—which, by the way, it would be very interesting to compare in detail with Freud's psychoanalysis—that the question of the *who* remains and must remain a question. It has the same structure of a question as the question of Being. It is not a given—it is not something on which we can rely—but something into which we must inquire. It is not a posit—a proposition; the who remains a question for itself, because the question of the self as self is first hidden; it is not by chance that the problem of the self appears interwoven with that of the "one," of [the German] *"man,"* or, better, of the "they" [as in "they say . . ."]. It appears in the problematic of "everydayness," of the everyday being where "Everyone is the other, and no one is himself" (p. 165). This intricate situation makes of the ego a question, not a given. "It could be that the 'who' of everyday Dasein just is *not* the 'I myself'" (p. 150).

Nowhere is it more true than in this point that phenomenology is a hermeneutics, because nowhere is the kind of closeness belonging to the ontic more deceptive (pp. 61–62). I think that this is the moment to repeat, but with more emphasis, that "*Proximally* the 'who' of Dasein is not only a problem *ontologically;* even *ontically* it remains concealed" (p. 152). This concealment does not imply a skepticism as to the question of the self. On the contrary, the "I" remains an essential characteristic of Dasein, and for that reason it must be interpreted existentially. It is well known that this part of *Being and Time* starts with an inquiry on the encountering of others and everyday being-with (§ 26). We shall not pursue this analysis, but I wanted to show its philosophical locus. We cannot proceed in the question of the who without introducing the problem of everyday life, self-knowledge, the problem of the relation to the other—and, ultimately, the relation to death. For Heidegger, at least in *Being and Time* (and we shall see that perhaps this constitutes the major difference with Heidegger II), the authenticity of the who is reached only when we have gone to the end of this process and have reached the theme of freedom for death. Only then is there a who. There was not yet a who in ordinary life; there was only a kind of anonymous self: "one," [the German] *"man."* This means that the question of the self remains formal as long as we have not developed the whole dialectic of inauthentic and authentic existence. In this way the question of the who of Dasein emerged in that of the potentiality of being one's self as a whole. The recapitulation of existence in the face of death is the response to the question of the who of Dasein. And then we have a hermeneutics of the "I am" which culminates in a hermeneutics of the finite totalization in the face of death.

IV

AT THIS POINT I wish to reintroduce the objection which was mentioned in the introduction. One could say that this hermeneutics of the "I am" is the topic of *Being and Time* only and that the reversal from Heidegger I to Heidegger II implies a fading and perhaps even a disappearance of the hermeneutics of the "I am." Indeed, the objection could be extended to the problematic of the self, of inauthentic and authentic existence, and of resoluteness in the face of death. One could also say that all these themes were still too *existenziell* rather than existential, that they would have to recede, and that the exegesis of Dasein must be replaced by an exegesis of the speech or discourse, the word, of the poet and the thinker. It is my conviction, however, that the continuity between Heidegger I and Heidegger II lies mainly in the persistence of the circle which I described above: the "backward relatedness" between Being, about which we are asking in the inquiry, and the inquirer himself, as a mode of being. Because the question is no longer an Analytic of Dasein, this circle does not occur in the same way and is not expressed in the same terms. But it can be recognized as the center of the *philosophy of language* which, to a certain extent, replaces the Analytic of Dasein.

The same problems which have been linked to the self of Dasein now occur in the problem of language; they are linked to the problem of the *word*, of *speech*. This is the problem of bringing Being into language. The word represents in the later Heidegger exactly the same problem as the *Da* of *Dasein*, since the word is the *Da*. In the *Introduction to Metaphysics* Heidegger speaks in these terms of the function of the word; more precisely, of *Nennen*, the forming of a name. He says: "A word, the forming of a name [establishes] in its Being a being that is opening itself up and preserves it in this open-ness, constriction, and constance." [10] Thus the word, in the *Nennen*, maintains, preserves (*bewahrt*), what has been opened up as such; it expresses the *noein*, the *Denken*, in which are mingled the recollective acceptance and the violence of delimitation. Thus naming [*dénomination*] designates the place and role of man in language. Here, Being is brought into language, and a finite, speaking existent is born. In forming a name, we have both disclosure of Being and enclosure in the finitude of language, which Heidegger implies in the terms "to preserve" and "to maintain." By preserving, man contains, does violence, and also begins to conceal. We are here at a point where man's domination of Being by reasoning—in the science of logic, for example—is made possible. This possibility may be traced back to the birth of language in words and the process of naming. The act of gathering, which is *logos*, implies this kind of delimitation, according to which Being is forced into disclosure. In this respect there is a violence of the word. This containment belongs to the concealment of Being which is part of its disclosure. This concealment makes possible our illusion that as men we "have" language "at our disposal." Henceforth, Dasein takes itself as the creator of language.

Such is the kind of restatement, not only of the *cogito*, but also of Heidegger I's Analytic of Dasein. And here Heidegger I

10. Translation by W. J. Richardson, in *Heidegger: Through Phenomenology to Thought* (The Hague: Martinus Nijhoff, 1963), p. 292. See also Martin Heidegger, *Einführung in die Metaphysik* (Tübingen: Niemeyer Verlag, 1953), p. 131. English translation by Ralph Manheim, *Introduction to Metaphysics* (New Haven: Yale University Press, 1959), p. 172: ". . . and maintains it in its openness, delimitation and permanence."

is himself retrieved, restated, in the philosophy of language of Heidegger II. As Richardson says:

> Language takes it origin, then, along with the irruption of "There-being," for in this irruption language is simply Being itself formed into word. It follows that in the rise of language, as in the emergence of the "There" itself, Being retains its primacy. Language as the Over-powering itself, is a might within which the "There" finds itself, that dominates the "There" through and through and must be subdued by it.[11]

This emergence of the "word" under the primacy of Being repeats exactly the emergence of the "There," in *Being and Time*, as the one who inquires into Being.

The parallelism is even more complete than we would have expected. The notion of the self in *Being and Time* (chap. IV) required a hermeneutics of the "I am," and it culminated in the sense of "resolve" implied in freedom in the face of death. In the same way, the position of man in language may result in his pretension to rule language by logic and to make judgment the tribunal before which Being must stand. Thus, to the emergence of Dasein is linked the necessity to claim language as our work. The life which was called "freedom for death" in *Being and Time* has, as its correspondence in Heidegger II, the obedience of the poet and the thinker, bound by the word which creates them. In *Urdichtung*, primordial poetizing, the poet testifies to a kind of language in which the Over-powering of Being founds the power of man and his language. I should say here that *Urdichtung* replaces freedom for death as the answer to the problem of the who and to the problem of the authenticity of the who. Authentic Dasein is born from the response to Being and, in responding, preserves the strength of Being by the strength of the word. Such is the ultimate repetition of the *sum*, of the "I am," beyond the destruction of the history of philosophy and beyond the destruction of the *cogito* as a mere epistemological principle.

My conclusion is, then, first, that the destruction of the *cogito* as self-positing being, the destruction of the *cogito* as an absolute subject, is the reverse side of a hermeneutics of the "I am" as constituted by its relation to Being. Second, this hermeneutics of the "I am" is not fundamentally changed from *Being and Time* to the last essays of Heidegger. It remains

11. Richardson, *Heidegger: Through Phenomenology to Thought*, p. 293.

faithful to the same pattern of a "backward relatedness" from Being to man. Third, a similar dialectic between authentic and inauthentic life gives a concrete form to this hermeneutics. The basic difference, perhaps, between the later Heidegger and Heidegger I would be that the self no longer finds its authenticity in freedom for death but in *Gelassenheit*, which is the gift of a poetic life.

The Question of the Subject:
The Challenge of Semiology

THE PHILOSOPHY OF THE SUBJECT, it is said, is in danger of disappearing. So be it; but this philosophy has always been challenged. *The* philosophy of the subject has never existed; rather, there have been a series of reflective styles, arising out of the work of redefinition which the challenge itself has imposed.

Thus, Descartes's *cogito* is not isolated, like an immutable proposition, like an eternal truth suspended above history. For Descartes himself the *cogito* is only a moment of thought; it concludes an operation and opens a new series; it is contemporaneous with a vision of the world in which the whole of objectivity is spread out like a spectacle on which the *cogito* casts its sovereign gaze.[1] In particular, Descartes's *cogito* is only one of the summits—even if the highest—of a chain of *cogito*s which constitute the reflective tradition. In this chain, in this tradition, each expression of the *cogito* reinterprets the preceding one. Thus one can speak of a Socratic *cogito* ("Look after your soul"), an Augustinian *cogito* (the "inner" man distinct from the flux of "external" things and "higher" truths), a Cartesian *cogito* —of course, a Kantian *cogito* ("the *I think* must be able to accompany all my representations"). The Fichtean "Self" is, without any doubt, the most significant instance of modern reflective philosophy; as Jean Nabert remarked, there is no contemporary reflective philosophy which does not reinterpret Descartes through Kant and Fichte. And the "egology" that Husserl attempted to graft onto phenomenology belongs to this line.

Translated by Kathleen McLaughlin.
1. See, above, "Heidegger and the Question of the Subject."

All of these, in imitation of the Socratic *cogito*, respond to a challenge, whether from Sophism, empiricism, or, in the opposite sense, dogmatism of ideas; for all these represent the allegation of a truth without a subject. By this challenge, reflective philosophy is invited, not to remain intact by warding off enemy assaults, but rather to take support from its adversary, to ally itself with that which most challenges it.

We are going to examine two challenges, one coming from psychoanalysis and the other from structuralism, which together can be called the challenge of semiology. They indeed have in common a consideration of *signs* which questions any intention or any claim that the subject's reflecting *on* himself or the positing of the subject *by* himself is an original, fundamental, and founding act.

I. THE CHALLENGE OF PSYCHOANALYSIS

PSYCHOANALYSIS MERITS being called upon first, for it carries its challenge to the precise point where Descartes thought he had found the firm ground of certainty. Freud undermines the effects of meaning which constitute the field of consciousness and starkly reveals the play of phantasies and illusions in which our desire is masked.

The challenge to the primacy of consciousness does, in truth, go much further; for the psychoanalytic explanation, known as topography, consists in establishing a field, a place, or rather a series of places, without considering the internal perception of the subject. These "places"—unconscious, preconscious, and conscious—are in no way defined by descriptive, phenomenological properties but as *systems,* that is, as sets of representations and affects governed by specific laws which enter into mutual relationships which, in turn, are irreducible to any quality of consciousness, to any determination of the "lived."

Thus, the explanation begins with a general suspension of the properties of consciousness. It is an antiphenomenology which requires, not the reduction *to* consciousness, but the reduction *of* consciousness. This preliminary abandonment is the prerequisite for the separation that exists between the field of all Freudian analyses and the descriptions of "lived" consciousness.

Why is this exacting approach necessary? Because the

intelligibility of the effects of meaning yielded by immediate consciousness—dreams, symptoms, phantasies, folklore, myths, and idols—cannot be grasped at the same level of discourse as these effects of meaning. And this intelligibility is inaccessible to consciousness because the latter is itself cut off from the level of the constitution of meaning by the *bar* of repression. The idea that consciousness is cut off from its own sense by an impediment it can neither direct nor know is the key to Freudian topography: the dynamism of repression, in placing the unconscious system beyond our reach, requires an interpretive technique adapted to the distortions and displacements which are best illustrated by dream work and the work of neurosis.

The result of this is that consciousness itself becomes a symptom and thus only one system among others, namely, the perceptual system which regulates our access to reality. Certainly, consciousness is not nothing (we will come back to this point later); it is at least the place of all the effects of meaning, the data to which the analysis is applied. But consciousness is not the principle, not the judge, not the measure of all things; and this is the challenge that counts for a philosophy of the *cogito*. Later we will speak about the revision, from top to bottom, which such a philosophy must undergo.

Before considering the implications of this painful revision, let us consider a second series of notions which further accentuate the divorce between psychoanalysis and the philosophies of the subject. As we know, Freud was led to superimpose a second topography—the ego, the id, and the superego—on the first: unconscious, preconscious, and conscious. In truth, it is not really a topography in the precise sense of a series of "places" where representations and affects are inscribed according to their position relative to repression. It is rather a question of a series of "roles" constituting a personology. Certain roles form a primary sequence: the neutral or the anonymous, the personal, and the superpersonal. Freud was led to this new division of agencies [*Instanzen*] by the following consideration: it is not only the "deepest" part of the ego but also the "highest" part that is unconscious. In other words, the unconscious is not only characteristic of the repressed; it is also characteristic of the complex operations by which we internalize the imperatives and the rules which come from agencies of society and, first of all, from the parental agency, the primary source of restrictions during infancy and childhood.

Freud had the intuition of this mechanism while studying the pathological exaggeration of it which appears in obsessional neurosis and, in particular, in melancholia. The latter ailment shows clearly how a lost object can be internalized: the object cathexis is replaced by an identification, that is, by a restoration of the object inside the ego. Whence the idea of an alteration of the ego by means of an identification with lost objects. This operation—and the desexualization which accompanies it—is the key to all "sublimation." Freud thinks he has found its equivalent (and finally the general pattern) in the episode of the dissolution of the Oedipus complex. The play of forces which oppose three persons and two sexes is resolved, in the normal case, by an identification with the father, which takes the place of the wish to supplant him; the erotic object passes through the ordeal of mourning. The parental figures are abandoned as erotic objects and are internalized and sublimated: thus arises the identification with the father and mother as ideals.

Freud then undertakes a real *genealogy of morality*—in the quasi-Nietzschean sense. It is a genealogy in the sense that the superego is called "the heir of the Oedipus complex," "the expression of the most important libidinal vicissitudes (*Schicksale*) of the id";[2] it is a genealogy of morality in the sense that this operation, which remains instinctual from the standpoint of the forces engaged in a work comparable to the work of mourning, nevertheless engenders "ideals," since the libidinal goal is replaced by a socially acceptable goal. This replacement of the libidinal goal by the ideal is the key to the sublimation initiated as a consequence of the Oedipus complex. By means of this work—of this introjection and this identification—the level of the "ego ideals" is integrated with the structure of the personality and becomes the internal agency called the "superego," which judges and condemns. Around this primitive core of the superego and the ego ideal are arranged, like precipitates, all subsequent identifications with sources of authority, with models, with cultural figures—the same ones that Hegel lists under the heading of objective spirit. Thus, by means of sedimentation, moral "consciousness" and the "cultural" agency of the personality in general are constituted.

As we see, this unconscious "from above" is no less irreducible to the autoconstitution of the Cartesian-style *ego cogito* than the unconscious "from below," which is henceforth called "the

2. Sigmund Freud, *The Ego and the Id and Other Works*, Vol. XIX of *The Standard Edition of the Complete Works of Sigmund Freud*, ed. and trans. James Strachey (London, 1961), p. 36.

id," in order to emphasize its strength and its estrangement from the agency of the ego.

At the same time Freud adds, to the notion of consciousness conceived as one of the *places* of his topography, the notion of the ego as a *force* in the hands of masters who dominate it. Thus the question of the subject is split: consciousness is related to the task of vigilance, of active perception, of the ordered and regulated apprehension of reality; the ego is dedicated to the task of mastering and dominating forces which at first crush it. The essay on "The Ego and the Id" [3] ends with the pessimistic portrayal of the multiple allegiances of the ego, which is compared to a servant claimed by several masters: the superego, the id, and reality. Its task is likened to the compromises of a politician charged with reconciling demands by reducing the pressure they bring to bear. Thus, the becoming-subject takes on the double aspect of becoming-conscious and becoming-self, that is, of *becoming vigilant* at the boundary between the pleasure principle and reality and of *becoming master* at the crossroads of a complex of forces. The conquest of the reality principle and the conquest of the force of the ego are, moreover, one and the same thing, in spite of the fact that analysis distinguishes two problematics corresponding to two different sequences, that of the three "places" and that of the three "roles." Freud has explained the superimposition of the two triads in his *New Introductory Lectures*.[4] He compares them to three populations separated into three districts, where the distribution of the population does not completely correspond to the geographical divisions of the districts. The noncoincidence of the two divisions allows the two problematics to appear, one which corresponds to the resolution of a problem of *perception* and *reality*, the other which corresponds to the resolution of a problem of *allegiance* and *dominance*. The first is a Kantian problem, the critical problem of objectivity; the second is a Hegelian problem, the dialectic of the master and the slave. As in Hegel, the conquest of objectivity remains an abstract moment, that of the judgment decision (*Ur-teil*), of the understanding which separates (*teilen*) the illusion from the real. The concrete moment is the moment

3. *Ibid.*
4. Freud, *New Introductory Lectures on Psycho-Analysis and Other Works*, Vol. XXII of *The Standard Edition of the Complete Works of Sigmund Freud*, ed. and trans. James Strachey (London, 1964), pp. 72–73.

of mutual recognition at the end of a struggle which has taught the master—himself the vehicle of thought, leisure, and enjoyment—how to understand himself through the work of the slave. It is finally through this exchange of roles, by which each passes into the other, that the consciousnesses are equalized. It is of this quasi-Hegelian operation that Freud speaks in the celebrated saying: *Wo es war, soll ich werden*—"Where id was, there ego shall be." [5]

This brief recall of the principal points of the Freudian doctrine of the subject discloses that psychoanalysis has in no way eliminated consciousness and the ego; it has not replaced the subject, it has displaced it. As we have seen, consciousness and the ego still figure among the places and the roles which, taken together, constitute the human subject. The displacement of the problematic consists in the following: neither consciousness nor the ego is any longer in the position of principle or origin. How, then, must the problem be reformulated as a result of this displacement?

Let us start from the final point reached in the preceding analysis: "ego" shall be where "id" was. This conclusion joins an earlier remark concerning consciousness: Freud, we said, substitutes, for conscious being (*Bewusst-sein*), becoming-conscious (*Bewusstwerden*). What was origin becomes task or goal. This can be understood on a very concrete level: pschoanalysis can have no therapeutic ambition other than enlarging the field of consciousness and giving back to the ego some of the strength ceded to its three powerful masters. This positing of consciousness and the ego as task and as mastery continues to link psychoanalysis to the positing of the *cogito*. Only, the *cogito* which has passed through the critical test of psychoanalysis is no longer the one claimed by philosophy in its pre-Freudian naïveté. Before Freud, two moments were confused: the moment of apodicticity and the moment of adequation. In the moment of apodicticity, the *I think–I am* is *truly* implied even in doubt, even in error, even in illusion; even if the evil genius deceives me in all my assertions, it is necessary *that* I, who think, be. But this impregnable moment of apodicticity tends to be confused with the moment of adequation, in which I am *such as* I perceive myself. Thetic judgment, to use Fichte's expression—the absolute positing of existence—is identified with a judgment of

5. *Ibid.*, p. 80.

perception, with the apperception of my *being-such*. Psychoanalysis drives a wedge between the apodicticity of the absolute
positing of existence and the adequation of the judgment bearing on the *being-such*. I am, but what am I who am? That is
what I no longer know. In other words, reflection has lost the
assurance of consciousness. *What* I am is just as problematical
as *that* I am is apodictic.

This consequence could have been foreseen by the Kantian
or Husserlian type of transcendental philosophy. The *empirical*
character of consciousness gives license to the same errors and
the same illusions as worldly perception. In Husserl's *Cartesian
Meditations*, §§ 7 and 9, one finds the theoretical recognition of
this dissociation between the certain character of the *cogito* and
the dubious character of consciousness. The sense of what I am
is not given, but hidden; it can even remain problematical indefinitely, like a question without an answer. But the philosopher
knows it only abstractly. Now, psychoanalysis teaches that to
know something theoretically is nothing so long as the economy
of underlying desires has not been altered. This is why the reflecting philosopher cannot go beyond abstract and negative
statements like: Apodicticity is not immediacy; Reflection is not
introspection; The philosophy of the subject is not the psychology of consciousness. All these propositions are true, but lifeless.

In the absence of an actual passage through analysis, a mere
meditation on psychoanalysis allows us to go beyond these abstractions and arrive at a concrete critique of the *cogito*. I will
say that the aim of this concrete critique is to deconstruct the
false *cogito*, to undertake the ruin of the idols of the *cogito* and
thus to inaugurate an operation similar to the mourning for the
libidinal object. The subject is first of all heir to a love of self
which in its profound structure is analogous to the object libido.
There is a libido of the ego which is homogeneous with the *libido*
of the object. Narcissism fills the entirely formal truth of the
I think–I am—fills it with an illusory concreteness. Narcissism
induces the identification of the reflective *cogito* with immediate
consciousness and makes me believe that I am such as I think
I am. But if the subject is not who I think he is, then consciousness must be lost if the subject is to be found.

Thus, I can understand reflectively the necessity for this
abandonment of consciousness and can combine with a philosophy of the subject even Freudian antiphenomenology. It is indeed the necessity for this release of all immediate consciousness

which justifies the most realist, naturalist, "thinglike" concepts of Freudian theory. The likening of the psyche to an apparatus, to a primitive functioning, ruled by the pleasure principle, the topographical conception of psychic "locations," the economic conception of cathexis and withdrawal of cathexis, etc.—all these theoretical procedures arise from a single strategy and are directed against an illusory *cogito,* which at first takes the place of a founding act: *I think–I am.* Reading Freud in this way becomes itself an adventure of the reflection. What results from this adventure is a wounded *cogito,* a *cogito* which posits but does not possess itself, a *cogito* which understands its primordial truth only in and through the avowal of the inadequation, the illusion, the fakery of immediate consciousness.

Does the philosophy of the subject receive any other lesson from psychoanalysis besides this critical rectification? Rooting subjective existence in desire permits a *positive* implication of psychoanalysis to appear, one which goes beyond the *negative* task of deconstructing the false *cogito.* Merleau-Ponty suggested calling this incarnation of instinctual drives the "archaeology of the subject."

This aspect of Freudian thought is no less important than the preceding one: the dissolution of the illusions and the idols of the conscious system is only the inverse of a discovery, the discovery of "an economy," which Freud said was as fundamental as the "topography." It is in terms of this "economy" that the *temporal* aspects of wishes are discerned, or rather what stands out is the absence of a relation of wishes to the ordered time of the real. The "atemporal," "timeless" character of unconscious wishes is, as we know, one of the traits which distinguishes the Ucs. system from the Cs. system. It is this character which governs the primitive side of our instinctual life. In particular, it is what inflicts the affective regression that analysis tracks down at the center of neuroses and at all levels of phantasies, from dreams to idols and illusions. It is this archaic character of desire which is glimpsed in guilt on the ethical plane and in the fear of punishment and the infantile wish to be consoled on the religious plane.

This thesis of the anteriority, the archaism, of desire is fundamental to a reformulation of the *cogito:* like Aristotle, like Spinoza and Leibniz, like Hegel, Freud places desire at the center of the act of existing. Before the subject consciously and willingly posits himself, he has already been placed in being at the instinctual level. The anteriority of instinct in relation to aware-ness and volition signifies the anteriority of the ontic plane to the reflective plane, the priority of *I am* to *I think*. From this there results a less idealist, more ontological interpretation of the *cogito;* the pure act of the *cogito,* insofar as it posits itself absolutely, is only an abstract and empty truth, as vain as it is invincible. This positing of the *cogito* remains to be mediated by the totality of the world of signs and by the interpretation of these signs. This long detour is, precisely, suspicion. Thus, both the apodicticity of the *cogito* and its indefinitely dubious char-acter must be assumed together. The *cogito* is at once the in-dubitable certainty *that* I am and an open question as to *what* I am.

I will thus say that the philosophical function of Freudian thought is to introduce a gap between the apodicticity of the abstract *cogito* and the reconquest of the truth of the concrete subject. Into this gap slips the critique of the false *cogito,* the deconstruction of the ego ideals which form a screen between the ego and myself. This deconstruction is a sort of work of mourning, transferred from the object relation to the reflective relation. As part of this discipline of renunciation, the entire methodological apparatus which Freud called "metapsychology" belongs to this deconstruction: the realism of psychic "location," the naturalism of the concepts of energy and economy, the genetic and evolutionist derivation of cultural dimensions based on the first instinctual objects, etc. This apparent loss, of the *cogito* itself and of the understanding belonging to it, is required by the strategy of the work of mourning applied to the false *cogito.* It resembles the determinist explanation which Spinoza in the first books of the *Ethics* applies to the false evidence of free will before reaching the true freedom (Book IV) and the beatitude (Book V) which follow from the rational understand-ing of the state of slavery itself. Consequently, as in Spinoza, the loss of the illusions of consciousness is the condition for any reappropriation of the true subject.

It is this reappropriation, in and through the work of mourn-ing which we traced out above, which to my mind constitutes the future task of a reflective philosophy. For my part, I see this task in the following terms: if one can call psychoanalysis an *archaeology of the subject,* the task of a reflective philosophy following Freud will be to dialectically relate a teleology to this archaeology. This polarity of the *archē* and the *telos,* of the origin and the end, of the instinctual ground and the cultural aim, can alone tear the philosophy of the *cogito* from abstraction, idealism, solipsism, in short, from all the pathological forms of subjectivism which infect the positing of the subject.

How can we envisage a teleology of subjectivity which would have been subjected to the critical examination of a Freudian archaeology? It would be a progressive construction of the forms of the spirit, after the manner of Hegel's *Phenomenology of the Spirit,* but one which, to a greater extent than in Hegel, would unfold on the very terrain of the *regressive* analysis of the forms of desire.

I allude here to a Hegelian rather than a Husserlian model for two reasons. First of all, Hegel uses a dialectical instrument to conceive a *sublation* on the naturalist level of subjective existence which *preserves* the initial instinctual impulse. In this sense, I would say that the Hegelian *Aufhebung,* insofar as it is the preservation of the sublated, is the philosophical truth of Freudian "sublimation" and "identification." Besides, Hegel himself conceived the dialectic of the figures of the *Phenomenology* as a dialectic of desire. The problem of satisfaction (*Befriedigung*) is the affective motivation for the passage from consciousness to self-consciousness: the infinite nature of desire, its splitting into the desire of another desire, which at the same time would be the desire of another, arriving at the equality of consciousnesses by means of struggle—all these well-known vicissitudes of the Hegelian *Phenomenology* constitute an example which is enlightening but not constraining for a teleological dialectic of the spirit grounded in the life of desire. Of course, the Hegelian *Phenomenology* cannot be repeated today; new figures of the self and the spirit have appeared since Hegel, and new abysses have been hollowed out beneath our feet. But the problem remains the same: how can a prospective arrangement of the figures of the spirit and a progressive linking of the spheres of culture be made to appear which would, in truth, be the sublimation of substantial desire, the reasonable effectuation of this energy which has been unmasked by psychoanalysis through the archaisms and the regressions of the human world of phantasies?

The task of a philosophical anthropology after Freud is to pose this problem in ever more rigorous terms and to resolve it in a synthesis which satisfies both the Freudian *economics* of desire and the Hegelian *teleology* of spirit.

II. THE CHALLENGE OF "STRUCTURALISM"

WITHOUT MAKING another detailed analysis of the *semiological model* which today presides over the various structuralisms,[6] I would like to show the convergence of the attacks mounted against the philosophy of the subject on the bases of psychoanalysis and linguistics.

The attack is carried on principally against Husserlian and post-Husserlian phenomenology. One can understand why: phenomenology joins the philosophy of the subject to a theory of meaning which falls within the same epistemological field as that delineated by the semiological model. More precisely, phenomenology unites three theses: (1) meaning is the most comprehensive category of phenomenological description; (2) the subject is the bearer of meaning; (3) reduction is the philosophical act which permits the birth of a being for meaning. These three theses are inseparable and can be ordered in two senses. The way we have listed them characterizes the order of their discovery, from the *Logical Investigations* to *Ideas I:* in this order one sees logical meaning lodged at the center of gravity of linguistic meaning, and the latter inscribed within the vaster perimeter of the intentionality of consciousness. Because of this expansion of the investigation from the logical to the perceptive plane, linguistic expression and, so much the more, logical expression appear to constitute merely the reflective form of a signifying activity rooted deeper than judgment and characteristic of *Erlebnis* in general. It is in this sense that meaning becomes the most comprehensive category of phenomenology. And the notion of the *ego* receives a proportional extension to the extent to which the *ego* is what lives in the aiming [*visée*] at meaning and is constituted as the identical pole of all these rays of meaning.

But the third thesis listed in the order of their discovery is the first in the order of their founding. If meaning, for the creator of phenomenology, covers the entire field of phenomenological descriptions, it is because this field is founded in its entirety by the transcendental reduction, which transmutes every question about being into a question about the *sense* of being. This function of reduction is independent of idealist inter-

6. See, above, "Structure, Word, Event."

pretations of the *ego cogito* and, first of all, of the interpretation Husserl himself gives from *Ideas I* to the *Cartesian Meditations*. Our relation to the world becomes apparent as a result of reduction; in and through reduction every being comes to be described as a phenomenon, as appearance, thus as a meaning to be made explicit.

One can thus descend, following the order of their founding, from reduction toward the subject as *ego cogito cogitatum*, and from the subject of the theory toward meaning as the universal mediation between the subject and the world. All is meaning when every being is seen [*visée*] as the meaning of the lived by means of which a subject opens toward transcendencies.

In this way, one can present phenomenology as a generalized theory of language. Language ceases to be an activity, a function, an operation among others: it is identified with the entire signifying milieu, with the complex of signs thrown like a net over our field of perception, our action, our life. Thus, Merleau-Ponty was able to say that Husserl "moves (language) into a central position." [7] Phenomenology can even claim that it alone opens the space of meaning, and thus of language, by thematizing for the first time the intentional and signifying activity of the incarnate, perceiving, acting, speaking subject.

And yet, phenomenology has radicalized the question of language in a way which excludes dialogue with modern linguistics and with the semiologic disciplines which are built on a linguistic model. The partial failure of Merleau-Ponty's philosophy of language is instructive in this respect.

The "return to the speaking subject" which Merleau-Ponty foresaw and began, following the later Husserl, is conceived in such a way that it rushes past the objective science of signs and moves too quickly to speech. Why? Because, from the beginning,

7. In a paper delivered in 1951 before the first International Conference on Phenomenology, Merleau-Ponty wrote: "In the philosophical tradition, the problem of language does not pertain to 'first philosophy,' and that is just why Husserl approaches it more freely than the problems of perception or knowledge. He moves it into a central position, and what he says about it is both original and enigmatic. Consequently, this problem provides us with our best basis for questioning phenomenology and recommencing Husserl's efforts instead of simply repeating what he said. It allows us to resume, instead of his theses, the very movement of his thought" (*Signs*, trans. Richard C. McCleary [Evanston, Ill.: Northwestern University Press, 1964], p. 84). I like to cite this passage because our relation to the greatest of French phenomenologists has perhaps already become what his was to Husserl: not a repetition but a renewal of the very movement of his reflection.

the phenomenological attitude and the objective attitude have been placed in opposition:

> Taking language as a *fait accompli*—as the residue of past acts of signification and the record of already acquired meanings—the scientist inevitably misses the peculiar clarity of speaking, the fecundity of expression. From the phenomenological point of view (that is, for the speaking subject who makes use of his language as a means of communicating with a living community), a language regains its unity. It is no longer the result of a chaotic past of independent linguistic facts but a system all of whose elements cooperate in a single attempt to express which is turned toward the present of the future and thus governed by a present logic.[8]

As we see, the dialogue with the scientist is poorly begun; in fact, it is not even begun at all. It is not language taken as an object of science that forms the system; contrary to Saussure and his initial definitions, it is stated that linguistics sees "language in the past." [9] On the contrary, it would be in the present moment of speech that a system would be established. Having placed synchrony on the side of the speaking subject and diachrony on the side of objective science, the phenomenologist tries to incorporate the objective viewpoint in the subjective viewpoint, to show that a synchrony of speech envelops the diachrony of language.

Formulated in this way, the problem seems easier to resolve than it will prove to be for the next generation. The problem consists in showing how past language lives in present language: it is the task of a phenomenology of speech to show this insertion of the past of language into the present of speech. When I speak, the signifying intention is, in me, only a certain void to be filled by words; this intention must then become full by realizing

> a certain arrangement of already signifying instruments or already speaking significations (morphological, syntactical, and lexical instruments, literary *genres*, types of narrative, modes of presenting events, etc.) which arouses in the hearer the presentiment of a new and different signification, and which inversely (in the speaker or writer) manages to anchor this original signification in the already available ones.[10]

8. *Signs*, p. 85.
9. *Ibid.*
10. *Ibid.*, p. 90.

In this way, speech is itself the reanimation of a certain linguistic knowledge which comes from the previous words of other men, words which are deposited, "sedimented," "instituted," so as to become this available *credit* by which I can now endow with verbal flesh this oriented void in me (which is signifying intention) when I want to speak.

The analysis of *Signs* is in the line of the great chapters of *The Phenomenology of Perception,* where language was likened to a "gesture" which puts in operation a know-how, an acquired power. Is language as it is considered by linguists taken seriously? The fact that the notion of language as an autonomous system is not taken into consideration weighs heavily on this phenomenology of speech. Its recourse to the process of "sedimentation" carries it back to the old psychological notion of *habitus,* of acquired powers, and the structural fact as such is missed.

In truth, what matters to Merleau-Ponty is not the dialogue with the linguist but the philosophical result: if I can express myself only by reactivating sedimented and available significations, then speech is never transparent to itself, and consciousness is never constituting; consciousness is always dependent on the "instructive spontaneity" [11] of my body, with its acquired powers and its available verbal tools. It is an entire philosophy of truth which is at issue here: truth as the process of recovering available meanings in new meanings, in the absence of any ultimate statement given in a pure, absolute, total meaning.

> Truth is another name for sedimentation, which is itself the presence of all presents in our own. That is to say that even and especially for the ultimate philosophical subject, there is no objectivity which accounts for our super-objective relationship to all times, no light that shines more brightly than the living present's light.[12]

Of course, this phenomenology of speech and of the speaking subject holds in reserve questions that structuralism avoids and does not resolve: How does an autonomous system of signs, postulated without a speaking subject, enter into operations, evolve toward new states, or lend itself to usage and to history? Can a system exist anywhere but in the act of speech? Is it anything other than a cross-section of a living operation? Is language anything more than a system, that is potential but never

11. *Ibid.,* p. 97.
12. *Ibid.,* p. 96.

completely actual, burdened by latent changes, apt for a sub-jective and intersubjective history?

These questions are doubtless legitimate. But they are pre-mature. We can recover them today only at the end of a long detour by way of linguistics and in general by way of the science of signs. Now, this detour includes, at least provisionally, bracketing the question of the subject with the intention of constituting a science of signs worthy of the name.

Before proposing a detour, structural linguistics thrusts a challenge at the philosophy of the subject: the challenge consists in the fact that the notion of signification is placed in a different field from that of the intentional aimings of a subject. The displacement is quite comparable to the one that psychoanalysis imposes on the effects of meaning of immediate consciousness. But it results from a system of assumptions different from that of Freudian topography. We presented these postulates earlier,[13] and we will only recall the series here. First postulate: the dichotomy of language and speech (in language, we retain the established convention, with its institutional character and its concept of social constraint; in speech, we fall back on execution, with its character of individual innovation and unlimited com-binations). Second postulate: the subordination of the dia-chronic point of view to the synchronic point of view (the comprehension of system states precedes that of changes, which are conceived only as the crossing from one system state to another). Third postulate: the reduction of the substantial as-pects of language—phonemic substance and semantic substance —to formal aspects. Language, thus relieved of its fixed con-tents, becomes a system of signs defined by their differences alone; in such a system there is no longer any signification—if by that we mean the content proper to an idea considered in itself—but only values, that is, relative, negative, and opposi-tional dimensions. What is at stake in any structural hypothesis is now clear—and this is what the fourth postulate expresses: "it is scientifically legitimate to describe language as being essentially an autonomous entity composed of internal de-pendencies, in a word, a structure." [14]

In other words, the system of signs no longer has any out-side, it has only an inside; the last postulate, which can be termed the postulate of the closed system of signs, summarizes

13. See, above, "Structure, Word, Event."
14. L. Hjelmslev, *Essais linguistiques* (Copenhagen, 1959), p. 21.

and commands all the others. It constitutes the major challenge for phenomenology. For the latter, language is not an object but a mediation through which and by means of which we are directed toward reality (whatever it may be); language consists in saying something about something; by this it loses itself as it moves toward what it says, going beyond itself and establishing itself in an intentional movement of reference. For structural linguists, language is self-sufficient: all its differences are immanent in it, and it is a system which precedes the speaking subject. In this way, the subject postulated by structuralism requires a *different* unconscious, a *different* "location" from the instinctual unconscious, yet it is a similar unconscious, a homologous location. This is why the displacement in the direction of this other unconscious, this other "location" of meaning, imposes on reflecting consciousness the same renunciation as the displacement in the direction of the Freudian unconscious; this is also why one can speak in both cases of one and the same *semiological* challenge.

What kind of philosophy of the subject will be capable of taking up this challenge in the form given to it by structuralism? Let us look once more at the three theses of phenomenology: its theory of meaning, its theory of the subject, its theory of reduction—whose solidarity we have shown. The theory of the subject is certainly our major preoccupation in the present essay; but, as we have said, its meaning arises from the theory of signification to which it is joined on the descriptive level and from the theory of reduction which founds it on the transcendental level. This is why we can arrive at the subject of phenomenological philosophy from the theory of signification and from the theory of reduction.

How is the phenomenological concept of meaning affected by the challenge of semiology? A renewed phenomenology of meaning cannot be content with repeating descriptions of speech which do not acknowledge the theoretical status of linguistics and the primacy of structure over process which serves as an axiom for linguistics. Nor can it be content to juxtapose what it would call the *openness* of language to the lived world of experience to the *closed* state of the universe of signs in structural linguistics: it is through and by means of a linguistics of language that a phenomenology of speech is possible today. Only through a hand-to-hand combat with the presuppositions of semiology will phenomenology reconquer the sign's relation of transcendence or its reference.

Now language, considered according to the hierarchy of its levels, contains a kind of unit other than those which figure in inventories of elements, whether these are phonemic units, lexical units, or syntactical units. The new linguistic unit on which the phenomenology of meaning can lay its foundation is not language but speech or discourse; and this unit is the *sentence* or *utterance*. It must be termed a semantic and not a semiological unit because it is what properly *signifies*. The problem of signification has thus not been eliminated by substituting for it the difference between signs; the two problems are of different levels. Nor does one have to choose between a philosophy of sign and a philosophy of representation: the first articulates the sign at the level of potential systems available for the performance of discourse; the second is contemporaneous with the accomplishment of the discourse. The semantic problem differs from the semiological problem precisely in that the sign, constituted by difference, is transferred to the universe by means of reference; and this counterpart that reference constitutes in relation to difference can legitimately be called representation in accordance with the whole mediaeval, Cartesian, Kantian, and Hegelian tradition. A linguist like Benveniste evinces an extreme tact and an acute sense of tradition when he compares "saying something," "signifying," and "representing." [15] Opposing sign to sign is the *semiological* function; representing the real by signs is the *semantic* function, and the first is subordinate to the second. The first function serves the second; or, if one prefers, language is articulated for the purpose of the signifying or representative function.

It is on the basis of this fundamental distinction between the semiological and the semantic that it is possible to realize a convergence of the linguistics of the sentence (considered as an occurrence of discourse), the logic of meaning and of reference (after the manner of Frege and Husserl), and the phenomenology of speech (after the manner of Merleau-Ponty); but one can

---

15. Cf. Emile Benveniste, *Problèmes de linguistique générale* (Paris, 1966); English translation by Mary E. Meek, *Problems in General Linguistics*, Miami Linguistics Series, no. 8 (Coral Gables: University of Miami Press, 1971). [Page numbers refer to English edition.] "For the naïve speaker as for the linguist, the function of language is 'to say something.' What exactly is this 'something' in regard to which language is articulated, and how is it defined with respect to language itself? The problem of meaning is raised" (p. 7). Now, this function is nothing other than the "faculty of *representing* the real by a 'sign' and of understanding the 'sign' as representing the real" (p. 23).

no longer, like the latter, leap directly to the phenomenology of speech. One must patiently disentangle semantics from semiology and, consequently, must first take the detour of the structural analysis of taxonomic systems, then build the level of the utterance on the phonological, lexical, and syntactical levels. The theory of utterances, in turn, requires that the level of meaning be constructed, moment by moment, as ideal or nonreal, and then the level of reference—with its requirement of truth, of apprehending the real, or, as Husserl says, of fulfillment. Then, and only then, will it be possible to recover in a nonpsychological sense the notions of intentionality, outward directedness, and expression in the sense of Merleau-Ponty. The passage through language restores to the analysis of speech its properly linguistic character, which can be preserved only if one seeks it in the direct extension of the "gesture." It is, on the contrary, as the semantic realization of the semiological order that speech, by an inverse reaction, causes human gesture to appear as signifying, at least inchoately. A philosophy of expression and signification which has not passed through these semiological and logical mediations is condemned to stop short of the properly semantic level.

In return, it is legitimate to affirm that, outside the semantic function in which they are actualized, semiological systems lose all intelligibility; one can even wonder whether the distinction between the signifier and the signified would retain a sense outside the referential function. Now this distinction appears as a requirement of the linguistic sign, to such an extent that Hjelmslev makes it the criterion for distinguishing the latter from nonlinguistic signs, which do not present the duality of the expressive level and the level of content. Is it not then the aim [*visée*] of significance—which the sentence confers by degrees on each of its elements and first of all on the words[16]—which assures, through its movement of transcendence, the internal unity of the sign? Would the signifier and the signified remain connected if the aim of signification did not pass through them like an arrow directed toward a possible referent, which exists or does not exist?

Thus, the semiological order, considered alone, is only the set of conditions of *articulation* without which language could

16. On the notion of the word as a lexical sign in relation to the sentence, cf. "Structure, Word, Event," above. The word, we stated in that essay, is the point of articulation of the semiological and the semantic, of form and meaning, in every instance of discourse.

not exist. But, the *articulated* as such is not yet language in its power of signifying. It is only the system of systems, which could be called language in general, whose existence, which is only potential, makes something like discourse possible; but discourse exists in each instance only in the occurrence of discourse. Here are knotted the potential and the actual, articulation and operation, structure and function, or, as we said elsewhere, system and event.[17]

Such is the theory of signification which would be capable of leading, by a descriptive route, to a theory of the subject which, following the initial intention of this article, would take support from its obstacle and embrace its adversary.

It is indeed on this level of organization and realization that language has a reference and a subject: since the system is anonymous or, rather, has no subject—not even "one"—because the question "Who is speaking?" has no sense at the level of language, it is with the sentence that the question of the subject of language arises. This subject might not be me or who I think I am; in any case, the question "Who is speaking?" has a sense at this level, even if it must remain a question without an answer.

Here again it would be useless to repeat the classical analyses of Husserlian and post-Husserlian phenomenology. They must be incorporated into the linguistic domain in the manner suggested above: just as the passage from the semiological to the semantic must be shown, so, too, it must be shown how the speaking subject arrives at his own discourse.

Now the phenomenology of the speaking subject finds solid support in the investigations of certain linguists concerning the personal pronoun and the related verbal forms, the proper noun, the verb and verb tenses, affirmation and negation, and, in general, locutionary forms inherent in every occurrence of discourse. The very expression "occurrence of discourse" indicates rather plainly that it is not enough to juxtapose a vague phenomenology of the act of speech to a rigorous linguistics of the system of language; it is, rather, a matter of *tying* language to speech in the work of discourse.

I will limit myself here to a single example, that of the personal pronoun and the relation of persons in the verb, which was the object of a conclusive study by Benveniste.[18] The per-

17. See, above, "Structure, Word, Event."
18. Benveniste, *Problems in General Linguistics*, pp. 195–204, 217–30.

sonal pronouns (I-you-he) are, of course, first of all facts of language: a structural study of the relations of person in the verb must precede any interpretation of the incidence of the pronoun in each occurrence of discourse. Thus, *I* and *you* together oppose *he* as the person to the nonperson and are themselves opposed as "he who speaks" and "he whom one addresses." But this structural study is unable to exhaust the comprehension of these relations; it constitutes only a preface to this endeavor. The signification of *I* is formed only in the instant when he who speaks appropriates its meaning in order to designate himself; the signification *I* is singular in each instance; it refers to the occurrence of discourse which contains it and refers solely to it. "*I* signifies 'the person who is uttering the present instance of the discourse containing *I*.'" [19] Outside this reference to a particular individual who designates himself in saying *I*, the personal pronoun is an empty sign that anyone can seize: the pronoun is waiting there, in my language, like an instrument available for converting this language into discourse through my appropriation of this empty sign.

In this way, we overtake the language-speech articulation: it rests in part on particular signs—or "indicators"—of which the personal pronouns form only one group alongside demonstrative pronouns and adverbs of time and place. These signs do not connote a class of objects but designate the present occurrence of discourse; they do not name but indicate the *I*, the *here*, the *now*, the *this*, in short, the relation of a speaking subject to an audience and a situation. What is admirable is that "language is organized in such a way that it allows each speaker to appropriate the entire language by designating himself as the *I*." [20]

The problem of the verb would have to be reconsidered in the same way. On the one hand, there is a structure of temporal relations characteristic of a given language; on the other hand, there is the utterance of time in an occurrence of language, in a sentence which, as such, temporalizes the whole of its utterance. It is this utterance which designates itself by the present tense and, by this, puts all the other tenses into perspective. This reference to the present is entirely comparable to the ostensive (or deictic) role of the demonstrative pronouns and of adverbial locutions ("here," "now," etc.): "this 'present' . . . has only a linguistic fact as its temporal reference: the coincidence of the

19. *Ibid.*, p. 218.
20. *Ibid.*, p. 226.

event described with the instance of discourse that describes it." [21]

Is this to say that the *I* is a creation of language? The linguist is tempted to say so ("language alone," writes Benveniste, "establishes the concept of 'ego' in reality, in *its* reality, which is that of the being").[22] The phenomenologist will object that the ability of the speaker to posit himself as subject and to oppose to himself another as listener is the extralinguistic presupposition of the personal pronoun. He will remain faithful to the distinction between the semiological and the semantic, according to which it is only in language that signs are reduced to *internal* differences; as such, *I* and *you* as empty signs are creations of language; but the *hic et nunc* use of this empty sign through which the vocable *I* becomes a signification and acquires a semantic value supposes the appropriation of this empty sign by a subject who posits himself in expressing himself. Of course, the postulate *I* and the expression *I* are contemporaneous; but the expression *I* as little creates the postulate *I* as the demonstrative pronoun *this* creates the spectacle of this world toward which the deictic indicator points. The subject posits itself, just as the world shows itself. Pronouns and demonstratives are in the service of this positing and this showing; they designate as clearly as possible the absolute character of this positing and this showing, which are the within and the without of language: the world toward which it is directed, insofar as it says something about something; the nonworldly within of the ego which radiates in its acts. Language is no more a foundation than it is an object; it is mediation; it is the *medium*, the "milieu," in which and through which the subject posits himself and the world shows itself.

Phenomenology's task becomes more precise: this positing of the subject, which the entire tradition of the *cogito* invokes, must henceforth be performed in language and not alongside it, under pain of never transcending the antinomy of semiology and phenomenology. This positing must be made to appear in the occurrence of discourse, that is, in the act by which the potential system of language becomes the actual event of speech.

The phenomenological notion of the subject has still to be related to the transcendental reduction. We have explained our position in regard to this double relation of the subject, its rela-

21. *Ibid.*, p. 227.
22. *Ibid.*, p. 224.

tion to signification and its relation to reduction. The first relation remains on the descriptive level, as the preceding discussion confirmed: the subject, in fact, is what refers to itself in referring to the real; retroreference and reference to the real are symmetrically constituted. The second relation adds nothing to the first on the level of description; it concerns the necessary conditions of self-reference in the reference to something: in this sense it is like the "transcendental" in relation to the "empirical."

What happens, then, to reduction after structuralism?

As we know, Husserl saw in the reduction the primordial philosophical act by which consciousness cuts itself off from the world and constitutes itself as an absolute; after reduction, every being is a meaning for consciousness and, as such, is relative to consciousness. The reduction thus places the Husserlian *cogito* at the heart of the idealist tradition by extending the Cartesian *cogito*, the Kantian *cogito*, the Fichtean *cogito*. The *Cartesian Meditations* go much further in the direction of the self-sufficiency of consciousness and move as far as a radical subjectivism which no longer allows any outcome other than conquering solipsism by its own excesses and deriving the other from the originary constitution of the *ego cogito*.

The privilege thus conferred on consciousness in an idealist conception of reduction is radically incompatible with the primacy that structural linguistics accords to language over speech, system over process, structure over function. In the eyes of structuralism, this absolute privilege is the absolute prejudice of phenomenology. With this antinomy the crisis of the philosophy of the subject reaches its extreme point.

Must phenomenological reduction be sacrificed at the same time as the prejudice of consciousness conceived as absolute? Or is another interpretation of reduction possible? I should like to explore another path and to propose an interpretation of reduction which would more closely connect it to the theory of *signification*, whose central position in phenomenology we have acknowledged. Thus, forgoing the identification of reduction with the direct passage which, at once and in one step, would make the phenomenological attitude spring from the natural attitude and would snatch consciousness from being, we will take the long detour of signs; and we will look for the reduction among the necessary conditions of signifying relations, of symbolic function as such. Thus carried to the level of a philosophy of language, reduction ceases to appear as a fantastic operation at the end of which consciousness would be a remainder, a residue left by the abstraction of being. Reduction appears rather as the "transcendental" of language, the possibility for man to be something other than a nature among natures, the possibility for him to relate to the real by designating it through signs. This reinterpretation of reduction, in connection with a philosophy of language, is perfectly homogeneous with the conception of phenomenology as the general theory of meaning, as the theory of generalized language.

Let us follow this path: we are encouraged to do so by a penetrating remark made by Lévi-Strauss in his celebrated "Introduction to the Work of Marcel Mauss":

> Whatever the moment or circumstance of its appearance in some stage of animal life, language could only have come into being instantaneously. Things could not have come to be meaningful little by little . . . ; this radical change has no counterpart within the domain of knowledge, which is developed slowly and progressively. In other words, at the moment when the entire universe, at once, became meaningful, it was not known any better for this, even if it is true that the appearance of language must have precipitated the rhythm of the development of knowledge. Thus there is a fundamental opposition in the history of the human mind between symbolism, which offers a character of discontinuity, and knowledge, which is characterized by continuity . . . .[23]

The symbolic function is thus not on the same level as the various classes of signs that can be discerned and articulated by a general science of signs, by a semiology; it is not any kind of class or genus but a condition of possibility. What is at issue here is the very birth of man to the order of signs.

Posed in these terms, the question of the origin of the symbolic function seems to me to give rise to a completely new interpretation of the phenomenological reduction: the reduction, we said, marks the beginning of a signifying life, and this beginning is nonchronological, nonhistorical; it is a transcendental beginning, in the way that the contract is the beginning of life in society. The two beginnings, thus understood in their radicalness, are one and the same beginning if, following Lévi-Strauss's remark, the symbolic function is the origin and not the result of

23. Claude Lévi-Strauss, "Introduction à l'*Oeuvre de Marcel Mauss*," in Marcel Mauss, *Sociologie et anthropologie* (Paris, 1950), p. 42.

social life: "Mauss still believes it possible to develop a sociological theory of symbolism, while obviously what must be sought is a symbolic origin of society." [24]

But an objection arises: the ideal genesis of the sign, you will say, requires only a separation, a difference, but not necessarily a subject. So that the same Lévi-Strauss who just alluded to the sudden emergence of symbolism vehemently rejects any philosophy which would place the subject at the origin of language and is more willing to speak in terms of "unconscious categories of thought." [25] Henceforth, is one not obliged to include difference among these unconscious categories of thought, and is this subjectless difference not the necessary condition of all the differences that appear in the linguistic field: difference between signs, difference, within the sign, between the signifier and the signified? If this is so, Husserl's fundamental error would be to have postulated a transcendental subject for this difference, which, strictly speaking, is only the transcendental condition which allows for all the empirical differences between signs and within signs. The difference must then be "desubjectivized" if it is to be the transcendental of the sign.

If the objection were valid, we would have gained nothing for a philosophy of the subject by identifying the reduction with the origin of the symbolic function, since the transcendental order to which the difference belongs would require no transcendental subject.

But the objection is not valid. It results from a confusion between the semiological and the semantic levels. Now, as we have said, discourse is something other than language, and signification is something other than the sign. After acknowledging this, any reflection which would limit itself to making explicit the necessary conditions of the semiological order would quite simply miss the problem of the necessary conditions of the semantic order as such, which is what is living, concrete, and actual in language.

It is not surprising that an investigation applied to the transcendental of language, but which misses the passage from language to discourse, discovers only a negative and not a subjective condition of language: difference. This is not nothing, of course, but it is not yet the primary dimension of reduction, namely, the transcendental production of difference. Husserl,

24. *Ibid.*, p. 23.
25. Claude Lévi-Strauss, *Anthropologie structurale* (Paris, 1959), p. 82.

too, recognized this negative side of the signifying relation; he called it "suspension," "placing in brackets," "placing out of bounds," and he applied it directly to the natural attitude in order to cause the phenomenological attitude to spring from it through difference. If he called the being, born of this difference, consciousness, this difference was only the nonnaturalness, the nonworldliness required by the sign as such. But this consciousness offers no egological character; it is only a "field," the field of *cogitationes*. Absolutely speaking, a *consciousness without an ego* is perfectly conceivable, and Sartre's well-known essay "The Transcendence of the Ego" has demonstrated this perfectly. As a result, the birth of consciousness as the difference of nature, or, to speak like Lévi-Strauss, the appearance of language through which "the entire universe, at once, became meaningful," does not require a subject, even if it does require a consciousness, that is, a field of *cogitationes*. This philosophical conclusion contains nothing that should surprise us: the semiological order is by definition that of a system without a subject.

But the semiological order does not constitute the whole of language. One must still pass from language to discourse: it is only on this level that one can speak of signification.

What, then, becomes of reduction in this crossing-over from sign to signification, from the semiological to the semantic? One can no longer remain within its negative dimension of variation, of distance, of difference; one must reach its positive dimension, namely, the possibility for a being who is torn away from intranatural relationships by difference to turn toward the world, to direct his attention toward it, to apprehend it, to grasp it, to understand it. And this movement is entirely positive; it is the movement in which, according to the statement of Gustave Guillaume mentioned above, signs are directed back to the universe; it is the moment of the sentence, which says something about something. Henceforth, the "suspension" of the natural relation to things is only the negative condition of the establishment of signifying relation. The differential principle is only the other side of the referential principle.

One must then take reduction not merely in its negative sense but in its positive sense and must challenge all the pretenses of negativity, all the hypostases of difference, which follow from a truncated model of language in which the semiological has taken the place of the semantic.

But if reduction must be taken in its positive sense, as the necessary condition of reference, it must also be taken in its subjective sense, as the possibility for an *ego* to designate itself in the occurrence of discourse. Positing and subjectivity go hand in hand to the degree to which the reference to the world and self-reference—or, as we said above, the showing of a world and the positing of an *ego*—are symmetrical and reciprocal. In the same way, there could be no aiming at the real, thus no claim to truth, without the auto-assertion of a subject who is both determined by and involved in his speaking.

If, then, I can conceive a nonsubjective origin of difference which establishes the sign as sign, the same cannot be said of the origin of reference. In this respect, I would be willing to say that the symbolic function, that is, the possibility of designating the real by means of signs, is complete only when it is thought in terms of the double principle of difference and reference, thus in terms of an "unconscious" category and an "egological" category. The *symbolic function* is, of course, the ability to place every exchange (and, among these, exchanges of signs) under a law, under a rule, thus under an anonymous principle which transcends subjects. But, even more, it is the ability to actualize this rule in an event, in an occurrence of exchange, of which the occurrence of discourse is the prototype. The latter involves me as subject and places me in the reciprocity of the question and the answer. A sense of symbol too often forgotten reminds us of this: under its social form, and not its purely mathematical form, symbolism implies a rule of recognition between subjects. In his fine book, which owes much to Lévi-Strauss but differs from him in this particular point, Edmond Ortigues writes: this law "compels every consciousness to return to itself by way of its other . . . ; society exists only through this process, which is internal to each subject." [26] Reduction, in its full sense, is this *return to the self by way of its other* which makes the transcendental no longer a kind of sign but a kind of signification.

After meeting the semiological challenge, such is the true "return to the subject." It is no longer separable from a meditation on language; it is a meditation which does not stop short, a meditation which crosses the threshold separating the semiological from the semantic. For this way of thinking, the subject founded by reduction is nothing other than the beginning of signifying life, the simultaneous birth of the spoken being of the world and the speaking being of man.

26. Edmond Ortigues, *Le Discours et le symbole* (Paris, 1962), p. 199.

III. TOWARD A HERMENEUTICS OF THE "I AM"

THE TIME HAS COME to compare the two series of analyses which make up this study. The reader will undoubtedly have been struck by the discordant character of these critiques and even more so by that of the responses. For one thing, it is difficult to superimpose the two kinds of "realism" which follow from the two critiques: the realism of the id, the realism of the structures of language. What do the topographic, economic, and genetic concepts of psychoanalysis have in common with the semiological notions of structure and system, the instinctual unconscious of the former with the categorial unconscious of the latter?

Now, if these two critiques are independent in their most fundamental presuppositions, it is not surprising that the renewals to which they give rise in the philosophy of the subject are of a different nature as well. This is why the philosophy of the subject that holds a future is not merely one which will have undergone the test of psychoanalytic criticism and linguistic criticism; it is the philosophy which will be able to project a new receptive structure for including in its thought both the lessons of psychoanalysis and those of semiology. The last part of this paper aims at staking out this direction, and this explains its rather exploratory and tentative character.

1. First of all, it seems to me that reflection on the speaking subject allows us to return to the conclusions reached at the close of the discussion involving psychoanalysis and to place them in a new light. Consciousness, we said then, is always presupposed by topography, as is the ego by Freudian personology, and we added that psychoanalytic criticism was unable to touch the core of apodicticity of the "I think" but attacks only the belief that I am such as I perceive myself. This split between the apodicticity of the "I think" and the adequation of consciousness takes on a less abstract meaning if it is connected to the notion of the speaking subject. The apodictic core of the "I think" is also the transcendental of the symbolic function; in other words: what is beyond all doubt is the act of retreat and distance which creates the separation through which the sign is possible, and its possibility is the possibility of being related in a signifying—and not just a causal—manner to all things.

What is the benefit of this comparison between apodicticity

and symbolic function? It is the following: that all philosophical reflection on psychoanalysis must henceforth unfold in the milieu of sense, of meaning. If the subject is the speaking subject par excellence, the whole adventure of reflection, when it passes through the interrogation of psychoanalysis, is an adventure on the level of the signifier and the signified. This rereading of psychoanalysis in the light of semiology is the first task imposed on a philosophical anthropology that wants to reassemble the scattered results of the human sciences. It is notable that, even when Freud speaks of instinct, it is always in and based on an expressive level, in and based on certain effects of meaning which lend themselves to deciphering and which can be treated like texts: oneiric texts or symptomatic texts. It is in this milieu of signs that the analytic experience itself unfolds, insofar as it is the work of speech, the duel of speaking and listening, the complicity of speech and silence. Belonging to the order of signs justifies in a fundamental manner not only the communicability of analytic experience but also its ultimate homogeneity with the totality of human experience which philosophy attempts to reflect and to understand.

The specificity of psychoanalytic discourse comes from the effects of meaning that it deciphers which express relations of force. From this results the apparent ambiguity of Freudian discourse: it appears to operate with notions belonging to two different levels of coherence, to two universes of discourse, that of force and that of meaning. It is a language of force, whence the entire vocabulary designating the dynamism of conflicts and the economic play of cathexes, withdrawal of cathexes, and countercathexes. It is a language of meaning, whence the entire vocabulary concerning the absurdity or the meaning of symptoms, dream thoughts, their overdetermination, and word plays—all of which converge in it. These are relations among meanings, which are disentangled in interpretation: between the apparent meaning and the hidden meaning there is the relation of an unintelligible text to an intelligible text. These relations of meaning are thus found entangled in the relations of force; the entire dream work is expressed in this mixed discourse: relations of force are exhibited and disguised in relations of meaning at the same time that the relations of meaning express and represent relations of force. This mixed discourse is not an equivocal discourse for want of clarification: it grips firmly the very reality we discover when we read Freud and which we can call *the semantics of desire*. All the philosophers who have reflected on the relations between desire and meaning have encountered this problem, from Plato, who duplicates the hierarchy of ideas in the hierarchy of love, to Spinoza, who relates the degrees of the clarity of the idea to the degrees of affirmation and action of the *conatus;* in Leibniz, as well, the degrees of appetition of the monad and those of his perception are correlatives: "the action of the internal principle which causes the change or the movement from one perception to another can be called appetition; it is true that the appetite cannot always completely reach the perception toward which it tends, but it always obtains something from it and attains new perceptions" (*Monadology,* § 15).

Thus reinterpreted in the light of semiology, psychoanalysis has as its theme the relationship between the libido and the symbol. It can then be included in a more general discipline which we can call hermeneutics. Here, I am defining as hermeneutics any discipline which proceeds by interpretation, and I give to the word "interpretation" its strong sense: the discerning of a hidden meaning in an apparent meaning. The semantics of desire stands out against the much vaster field of the *effects of double meaning:* the very ones that a linguistic semantics encounters under another name, which it calls transfer of meaning, metaphor, allegory. The task of a hermeneutics is to bring face to face the various functions of interpretation by disciplines as different as the semantics of linguists, psychoanalysis, the phenomenology and the comparative history of religions, literary criticism, etc. One then sees how, through this general hermeneutics, psychoanalysis can be related to a reflective philosophy: by passing through a hermeneutics, reflective philosophy emerges from abstraction; the affirmation of being, the desire and the effort of existing which constitute me, find in the interpretation of signs the long road of awareness. The desire to be and the sign are in the same relation as libido and symbol. This means two things: on the one hand, understanding the world of signs is the means of understanding onself; the symbolic universe is the milieu of self-explanation; in fact, there would no longer be any problem of meaning if signs were not the means, the milieu, the medium by grace of which a human being seeks to situate himself, to project himself, to understand himself. On the other hand, in the opposite direction, this relation between desire to be and symbolism means that the short path of the intuition of the self by the self is closed. The appropriation of my desire to exist is impossible by the short path of consciousness; only the long path of interpretation of signs is open. Such is my working hypothesis in philosophy. I call it *concrete reflection,* that is, *the* cogito *mediated by the entire universe of signs.*

2. It is no less important to subject a final reflection on semiology to the knowledge of psychoanalysis. Nothing could be more dangerous, in fact, than to extrapolate the conclusions of a semiology and to say: everything is sign, everything is language. The reinterpretation of the *cogito* as the act of the speaking subject can tend in this direction, and, to an even greater extent, so can the interpretation of the phenomenological reduction as this separation which opens the chasm between the sign and the thing: man then seems to be no more than language, and language seems to be absence from the world. In relating the symbol to instinct, psychoanalysis forces us to move in the opposite direction and to immerse the signifier in the existent once more. In a sense, language is primary, because it is always starting from what man says that the network of signifying in which presences are grasped can be unfolded. But, in another sense, language is secondary; the distance of the sign and the absence of language from the world are only the negative counterpart of a positive relation: language *speaks,* that is, *shows,* makes present, brings into being. The absence of the sign from the thing is only the negative condition for the sign to reach the thing, touch it, and die in this contact. This sense of language as belonging to being requires, then, that one reverse the relation once more and that language appear itself as a mode of being in being.

Now, psychoanalysis prepares this reversal in its own fashion: the anteriority, the archaism of desire, which justifies our speaking of an archaeology of the subject, forces us to subordinate consciousness, symbolic function, language, to the primary position of desire. As we said above, Freud, like Aristotle, like Spinoza and Leibniz, like Hegel, places the act of existing on the axis of desire. Before the subject consciously and willingly posits himself, he has already been posited in being at the instinctual level. That instinct is anterior to awareness and volition signifies the anteriority of the ontic level to the reflective level, *the priority of the* I am *to the* I think. What we said earlier in regard to the relation of instinct to awareness must now be said of the relation of instinct to language. The *I am* is more fundamental than the *I speak.* Philosophy must then get under way toward the *I speak* by starting from the positing of the *I am;* from the very heart of language, philosophy must begin "the road toward language," as

Heidegger demands. The task of a philosophical anthropology is to show in what ontic structures language occurs.

I just mentioned Heidegger; a philosophical anthropology today, with the resources of linguistics, semiology, and psychoanalysis, must retrace the route outlined by *Being and Time*, the route which starts from the structure of being-in-the-world, crosses through a consideration of situation, the projection of concrete possibilities, and understanding, and moves toward the problem of interpretation and language.

In this way, a hermeneutic philosophy must show how interpretation itself arrives at being-in-the-world. First there is being-in-the-world, then understanding, then interpreting, then saying. The circular character of this itinerary must not stop us. It is indeed true that it is from the heart of language that we say all this; but language is so made that it is able to designate the ground of existence from which it proceeds and to recognize itself as a mode of the being of which it speaks. The circularity between *I speak* and *I am* gives the initiative by turns to the symbolic function and to its instinctual and existential root. But this circle is not a vicious circle; it is the living circle of expression and of the being-expressed.

If this is so, the hermeneutics which reflective philosophy must include must not be limited to effects of meaning and double meaning: it must boldly be a hermeneutics of the *I am*. Only in this way can the illusion and the pretensions of the idealist, subjective, solipsistic *cogito* be conquered. This hermeneutics of the *I am* can alone include both the apodictic certainty of the Cartesian *I think* and the uncertainties, even the lies and illusions, of the self, of immediate consciousness. It alone can yoke, side by side, the serene assertion *I am* and the poignant doubt *Who am I?*

Such is my answer to the initial question: what in reflective philosophy holds a future? I answer: a reflective philosophy which, having completely incorporated the corrections and the lessons of psychoanalysis and semiology, takes the long and roundabout route of an interpretation of private and public, psychic and cultural signs, where the desire to be and the effort to be which constitute us are expressed and made explicit.

PART IV

The Symbolism
of Evil Interpreted

"Original Sin":
A Study in Meaning

WE READ in one of the Confessions of Faith of the Re-
formed Churches that the will of man is "totally captive to sin"
(the *La Rochelle Confession of Faith*, art. 9). It is easy to find
in this word "captivity" the entire prophetic and apostolic preaching. But the *Confession of Faith* immediately adds: "We believe
that the entire descent of Adam is infected with this contagion.
The contagion is original sin and a hereditary vice. It is not just
an imitation, as the Pelagians, whose errors we deplore, have
held" (art. 10). Original sin, hereditary vice: these words indicate that a change in level has occurred. We have passed from
the field of preaching to that of theology, from the domain of
the pastor to that of the doctor. And at the same time a change
is produced in the domain of expression. Captivity was an image,
a parable; hereditary sin tries to be a concept. The following
text suggests even more. "We also believe that this vice is truly
sin and that it suffices to condemn the entire human race, even
infants in the wombs of their mothers, and that it is taken as a
sin before God (etc.)" (art. 11). We have the impression not
only of entering the discipline of theology, which is the concern
of doctors, but also of entering into controversy, the disputes
of the schools. The interpretation of original sin as an original
guilt of little children in the wombs of their mothers is no longer
on the level of preaching. It has reached a point where the
theologian's work veers toward abstract speculation, toward
scholasticism.

I do not intend to oppose one formulation to another on this

Translated by Peter McCormick.

abstract level. I am not a dogmatic theologian. Rather, I intend to reflect on the *meaning* of the theological work crystallized in a concept like original sin. I am posing, then, a methodological problem. This concept as such is not a biblical one. And yet, by means of a rational apparatus which we will have to reflect upon, it tries to account for the very content of the religious confession and the ordinary preaching of the church. Hence, to reflect on its *meaning* is to retrieve the intentions of the concept, its power to refer back to what is an announcement and not a concept. This announcement both denounces evil and pronounces absolution. In short, to reflect on its meaning is in a certain way *to deconstruct the concept,* to break down its motivations, and by a kind of intentional analysis to retrieve the arrows of meaning which aim at the *kerygma itself.*

I have just used a disquieting expression, "to deconstruct the concept." I think that the concept must be destroyed as a concept in order to understand the meaning intention. The concept of original sin is false knowledge, and it must be broken as knowledge. It involves the quasi-juridical knowledge of the guilt of the newborn and the quasi-biological knowledge of the transmission of a hereditary taint. This false knowledge compresses in an inconsistent notion a juridical category of debt and a biological category of inheritance.

The point of this apparently destructive criticism, however, is to show that false knowledge is at the same time true symbol, a symbol of something which it alone is capable of transmitting. So the criticism is not just a negative one. *The defeat of knowledge* is the other side of working toward the recovery of meaning. This recovery is a retrieval of the "orthodox" *intention,* the strict sense, and the ecclesiastical meaning of original sin. And this meaning, as we shall see, is no longer juridical knowledge, biological knowledge, or, worse yet, juridical-biological knowledge concerning some kind of monstrous hereditary guilt; it is rather a *rational symbol* of what we declare most profoundly in the confession of sins.

What impulse brought Christian theology to this conceptual elaboration? Two answers can be given to this question. First, an external one, the impulse of Gnosticism. In *The Extracts of Theodotus* we read the questions which Clement of Alexandria took as a definition of Gnosticism. "Who were we? What have we become? Where were we previously? From what world have we been ejected? Toward what goal are we hastening? From what have we been delivered? What is birth ($\gamma\acute{\epsilon}\nu\nu\eta\sigma\iota\varsigma$)? What is rebirth (ἀναγέννησις)?" The Gnostics were the ones, a Christian author says further, who posed the question πόθεν τὰ κακά — "Whence comes evil?" Let us understand that it was the Gnostics who tried to make this question a speculative one and to formulate an answer to it that would be knowledge, γνῶσις, Gnosticism.

Our first working hypothesis, therefore, will be this: that it was for apologetic reasons—to combat Gnosticism—that Christian theology came to orient itself along the lines of Gnostic thought. Although clearly anti-Gnostic, the theology of evil let itself become engaged on the very ground of Gnosticism and hence elaborated a similar conceptual structure.

Anti-Gnosticism became quasi-Gnosticism. I will try to show that the concept of original sin is anti-Gnostic in its basic purpose but quasi-Gnostic in its articulation.

This first answer, however, requires a second one. The apologetic concern cannot by itself explain why Christian theology let itself become engaged on alien ground. We shall need to search out the reasons for its elaboration in the very meaning this quasi-Gnosticism carried. In the experience of evil and in the avowal of sin there is perhaps something terrible and impenetrable that makes Gnosticism the permanent temptation of thinking, a mystery of iniquity whose pseudo-concept of original sin is like an enciphered language.

Before plunging into our meditation I want to note that the majority of our examples and quotations will be taken from Saint Augustine. This is inevitable. Saint Augustine witnesses to the great historical moment when this concept is formed. Augustine first led the battle against the Manichaeans and then against the Pelagians. And in this battle on two fronts the polemical and apologetic concept of original sin was developed. But my work is not the work of a historian. It is not the history of the anti-Manichaean polemic and then the anti-Pelagian polemic which interests me. I am interested rather in Augustine's own motivations, to the degree that we are able to recover them when we try to *think* what we believe and profess.

I am, then, neither a dogmatic theologian nor a historian; I would like, very precisely, to contribute to what I will call a hermeneutics of the so-called dogma of original sin. This interpretation, which is reductive on the epistemological level but recuperative on the symbolic level, is a development of what I have elsewhere attempted under the title *The Symbolism of Evil*. It moves the criticism of theological language from the level of *images and mythical symbols* like "captivity," "fall," "error," "perdition," "rebellion," etc., to that of *rational symbols,* like those in Neoplatonism, Gnosticism, and the Church Fathers.

I

AS A POLEMICAL AND APOLOGETIC CONCEPT, "original sin" first of all means one thing: that evil is not something that exists, that evil has no being, no nature, because it comes from us, because it is the work of freedom. This first thesis, we will see, is insufficient, for it accounts only for the clearest aspect of evil, what we may call actual evil in the double sense of the exercise or act of evil and of the presence of evil, of evil in the process of being realized. This second sense is the one Kierkegaard would say is posited in the instant. In any case, this first thesis must be well established. For when we speak later on of *peccatum originale* or *naturale,* the reintroduction of a quasi-nature for evil must not budge us from refusing evil a nature or a substance. This is what will make trouble for the pseudo-concept of *peccatum naturale.*

In order to comprehend how faithful this concept is, at least in its first aspect, to the biblical tradition, we must keep in mind the enormous countervailing pressure which Gnosticism exercised on the Church's confession of faith for several centuries. If Gnosticism is *gnōsis,* that is, understanding and knowing and knowledge, then the reason is, as Jonas, Quispel, Puech, and others have shown, that evil for Gnosticism is an almost physical reality that infects man from outside. Evil is external. It is body, thing, and world. And the soul has fallen into it. This exteriority of evil immediately furnishes the schema of some thing, of a substance that infects by contagion. The soul comes from "elsewhere," falls "here," and must return "there." The existential anguish which is at the root of Gnosticism is immediately situated in oriented space and time. The cosmos is a machine for damnation and salvation. Soteriology is cosmology. At the same time, everything which is image, symbol, and parable—such as error, fall, captivity, etc.—congeals into a so-called knowing which sticks to the letter of the image. In this way, as Puech says, a dogmatic mythology is born which is inseparable from a spatial cosmic configuration. The cosmos which the psalmist heard singing the glory of God and whose beauty and divinity the Stoic philosopher spoke of, is not only divinized but counterdivinized. The cosmos, one might say, is satanized and hence provides the human experience of evil with the support of an absolute exteriority, an absolute inhumanity, an absolute materiality. Evil is the very worldliness of the world. Far from proceeding *from* human freedom *toward* the vanity of the world, evil proceeds from the powers of the world toward man.

Moreover, the evil which man confesses is less the act of doing evil, malfeasance, than the *state* of being in the world, the *misfortune* of existing. Sin is destiny interiorized. This is also why salvation comes to man from elsewhere, from out there, by a pure magic of deliverance, without any connection with human responsibility or even personality. In Gnosticism, false knowledge, which is the mimicry of rationality, derives from the very interpretation of evil. Because evil is thing and world, myth is "knowledge." The gnosis of evil is a realism of the image, a making worldly the symbol. In this way the most fantastic dogmatic theology in Western thought is born and the most fantastic imposture of reason has the name "gnosis."

It is against this gnosis of evil that the Greek and Latin Fathers, with a striking unanimity, repeatedly argued that evil has no nature; evil is not something; evil is not matter; evil is not substance; evil is not world. Evil does not exist in itself. Evil comes *from us*. What has to be rejected is not only the answer to the question but the question itself. I cannot answer *malum esse* (evil is) because I cannot ask *quid malum?* (what is evil?); I can only ask *unde malum faciamus?* (whence comes the fact that we do evil?). Evil is not *being* but *doing*.

With this doctrine the Fathers held firmly to the uninterrupted tradition of Israel and of the Church, which I will call the *penitential* tradition, which found in the story of the Fall its plastic form, its exemplary symbolic expression. What the symbol of Adam transmits is first of all and essentially the affirmation that man is, if not the absolute origin, at least the point where evil emerges in the world. Sin has entered the world through one man. Sin is not world; it comes into the world. Well before Gnosticism, the Yahwist—or his school—had had to fight against the Babylonian representations of evil which made of evil a power contemporary with the origin of things. Evil was a power that God had combatted and vanquished before the foundation of the world and in order to found the world. The idea of a catastrophe befalling an innocent creation through an exemplary man already animated the great myth of Primordial

Man. The very name of the historic artisan of evil summarized what is essential in this symbol. Adam is the earthly one, the man created from a sod and destined for dust.

This existential bearing of the Adamic account is what Augustine found again in his struggles against Mani and the Manichaeans. In the dramatic two-day controversy with Fortunatus, Augustine denounced the basis of the Gnostic myth. The soul hurled into evil could say to its God: "You have thrown me into unhappiness. Are you not cruel to have wanted me to suffer for your kingdom, against which this nation of dark ones can do nothing?" (end of the first day). In this way Augustine elaborated a purely *ethical* vision of evil, where man is integrally responsible. He distinguishes this vision from a *tragic* vision, where man is no longer the actor but the victim of a God who himself suffers even if he is not cruel. Perhaps in the *Contra Felicem* Augustine pushed this first conceptualization of original sin farthest when he opposed the evil will to evil nature. In commenting on Matthew 12:33 ("either make the tree good and its fruit good, or make the tree bad and its fruit bad"), he writes: this "either . . . or" designates a power and not a nature (*potestatem indicat, non naturam*). Then he summarizes the essence of the Christian theology of evil as opposed to Gnosticism: "If there is repentance, there is guilt; if there is guilt, there is will; if there is will in sin, it is not a nature that constrains us" (*Contra Felicem*, § 8).

Having come to this point, we might think that the conceptualization of sin had to be oriented toward the idea of a *contingency* of evil, toward the idea of an evil that arises as a purely irrational event or, as Kierkegaard would say, as a qualitative "leap." But a mind which was contemporary with Neoplatonism had no way of thematizing such concepts. To approach such an idea, it had no other course than to reshape certain Neoplatonic concepts which were fixed in the spectrum of the degrees of being. Hence Augustine can say in the *Contra Secundinum* that evil is "the inclination of what has more being toward what has less being" (*inclinat ab . . . ad*, § 12); or,

to be deficient (*deficere*) is not yet nothing, but it tends toward the nothing. Because, when things which have more being deviate (*declinant*) toward those which have less being, the deficient things are not the latter but are rather those which are deviating and which from that moment have less being than before, not by becoming the things toward which they have deviated but by each one in its proper species becoming less (§ 11).

In this way the concept of *defectus* is painfully developed as the concept of a negatively oriented consent. "Nothing" designates here not an ontological counterpole to being but an existential direction, the opposite of conversion. It is an *aversio a Deo* which is the negative moment of the *conversio ad creaturam* (*De libero arbitrio* I. 16. 35; II. 19. 53–54).

So Augustine saw at this moment that the confession of evil had to reach toward impossible concepts. The answer to the question *unde malum faciamus?* must be: *Sciri non potest quod nihil est* (It is impossible to know the nothing) (*De lib. arb.* II. 19. 54). "The movement of turning away (*aversio*) which, we realize, constitutes sin is a deficient movement (*defectivus motus*), and every deficiency comes from nonbeing (*omnis autem defectus ex nihilo est*). This is why we come to confess without hesitation that this movement cannot be from God" (*ibid.*). So, too, in the *Contra Fortunatum:* "If it is true that cupidity is the root of all evils, it is useless for us to look beyond cupidity for any other kind of evil." Later on Augustine will say to Julian of Eclanum: "You want to know whence comes bad will? You will find man" (*Contra Julianum,* chap. 41).

Doubtless this impossible concept was too negative—*defectus, declinatio, corruptio* (the last term designating for Augustine a *defectus* in a *natura*). Moreover, the advance toward nothingness—the *ad non esse* of evil—is difficult to distinguish from the *ex nihilo* of the creature (an expression which designates only the creature's imperfect being, its dependence as creature). Augustine did not have the means to conceptualize the *positing* of evil. Hence, to combat the idea of an evil *matter,* he had to take over the *ex nihilo* of the creation doctrine which had served to combat the idea of an uncreated matter and to make of it an *ad non esse,* a movement toward nothingness. But this nothingness of inclination would always remain poorly distinguished, in a theology which employed Neoplatonic terms, from the nothingness of origin, which designates only the total character of creation.

Nonetheless, it was not the equivocation between the two nothings—the nothing of creation and the nothing of deficiency —which exploded this first conceptualization, which was perpetuated in our Confessions of Faith as "corruption" and "nature totally corrupted."

This *negativity* does not account for a certain number of traits in the Hebrew and Christian experience which the Adamic myth had transmitted and which do not pass into the idea of a *defectus,* of a *corruptio naturae.* But these are the traits which the anti-Pelagian controversy will accentuate. These are the ones which will compel the elaboration of a much more positive concept—our concept of original sin, of hereditary vice—and will bring thinking back to Gnostic modes of expression by making thought construct a concept as consistent as the Valentinians' precosmic Fall or the Manichaeans' aggression of the Prince of Darkness—in short, a dogmatic myth parallel to the Gnostic myths.

II

AND SO THE ADJECTIVE "original" is what we now have to explicate. We have seen that Saint Augustine also employs the expression *naturale peccatum.* In addition, he says *per generationem* or *generatim* to indicate that it is not a question of sins we commit, of actual sin, but of the state of sin in which we find ourselves existing by reason of our birth.

If we try to reconstitute the filiation or line of descent of meaning, what I will call the strata of meaning which are sedimented in the concept, we find at the beginning an interpretive schema which is absolutely irreducible to any philosophy of the will, the schema of *inheritance* (the Germans say *Erbsünde*). This is the inverse schema of the one we have been commenting on up to now, the inverse of individual inclination. Contrary to every individual initiation of evil, inheritance is a question of a continuation, of a perpetuation, which is like a hereditary taint transmitted to the entire human race by a first man who is the ancestor of all men.

As can be seen, this schema of inheritance is linked to the representation of the first man as the initiator and propagator of evil. In this way, speculation on original sin finds itself bound to the Adamic speculation of late Judaism. Saint Paul introduced this speculation into the Christian deposit of faith by making a parallel between Christ, the perfect man, second Adam, and initiator of salvation, and the first man, the first Adam, the initiator of perdition.

The notion of the first Adam, who in Paul was only an antitype, "the figure of someone who was to come" ($\tau\acute{v}\pi\sigma s$ $\tauο\hat{v}$ $\mu\acute{\epsilon}\lambda\lambda\sigmaν\tau\sigmas$), was to become itself a nexus of speculation. The Fall of Adam cuts history in two, *just as* the coming of Christ cuts history in two. The two schemata are more and more super-imposed like inverse images. A perfect and fabulous humanity precedes the Fall in the same way as humanity at the end of time succeeds to the manifestation of the archetypal Man.

On the basis of this core of meaning, the concept of original sin as Augustine himself willed it to the Church will be constituted.

It is useful to stress the rigidity that Augustine introduced into Paul's text, the text dealing with the parallel between the two Adams, Romans 5:12 and following.

To begin with, for Augustine the individuality of Adam, a historical personage and the first ancestor of man, who appeared only a few millennia before us, is not questionable. But this was not a question for Pelagius and the Pelagians either. The δι' ἑνὸς ἀνθρώπου of Romans 5:12 and 19 literally means *per unum*, "by a single man." Moreover, Augustine understood the ἐφ' ᾧ πάντες ἥμαρτον of verse 12 as *in quo omnes peccaverunt*, "in whom we have sinned"—*in quo* referring to Adam. The Augustinian exegesis is, as we see, already a theological interpretation. For if ἐφ' ᾧ means "all have sinned *in Adam*," then it is tempting to find all men already contained in some fashion in the loins of Adam, as was frequently said; by contrast, if ἐφ' ᾧ means "by means of which," "concerning which," or even "because of the fact that" all have sinned, then the role of individual responsibility in this chain of hereditary sin is preserved.

In addition, the Augustinian exegesis minimizes everything which in the Pauline speculation about Adam comes to limit the literal interpretation of the role of the first man. First, the fact that this figure is an antitype of the Christ figure—"in the same way as . . . so too." Next comes the progression which is added to the parallel of the two figures—"if by the fault of a single man . . . how much more those who receive grace." "Where sin abounded, grace did much more abound." Finally, for Saint Paul, sin was not invented by the first man; sin is a mythic magnitude which goes beyond the figure of Adam. Certainly this magnitude is transmitted by the first man—δι' ἑνὸς ἀνθρώπου, *per unum*, by a single man. But this *unus* is not so much a first agent, a first author, as a first vehicle. It is sin as a supraindividual magnitude that gathers all men together, from the first man even to us, that "constitutes" each sinner, that "abounds" and "reigns." So much for traits which can slow down a purely juridical and biological interpretation of inheritance. What I have just called the mythic magnitude of sin in Saint

Paul, in order to designate the suprapersonal character of entities like law, sin, death, and flesh, resists the juridicizing that makes its way through other Pauline concepts like that of imputation (ἐλλογεῖσθαι): Romans 5:13 says that no sin is imputed when no law exists. We can expect that the loss of the mythic dimension, still present in Saint Paul, ends by dissolving the suprapersonal magnitude of sin in a juridical interpretation of individual guilt corrected by a biologism of hereditary transmission.

Augustine is responsible for the classic elaboration of the concept of original sin and for its introduction into the dogmatic deposit of the Church on an equal footing with Christology as a chapter in the doctrine of grace.

Here is where we must assign its true weight to the role of the anti-Pelagian quarrel. It is certain that the polemic against the Pelagians had been crucial, even though, as we shall see, this does not free us from looking for the deep motive of the dogma of original sin in the internal growth of Augustine's thought.

Indeed, Pelagius is in the line of the voluntarism of the anti-Manichaean writings. In his commentary on the *Thirteen Epistles of Saint Paul,* Pelagius can be seen to draw all of the consequences of a coherent voluntarism. Each man sins for himself. God is just and can want nothing unreasonable. Hence, God could not punish a man for someone else's sin. Moreover, the "in Adam" which everyone, or almost everyone, used to read in Romans 5 can only mean a relation of imitation. *In* Adam means *like* Adam. More radically, the austere and demanding Pelagius does not doubt at all that man invokes his own powerlessness and the power of sin only to excuse and to dispense himself from wanting not to sin. This is why it must be said that man always has the power not to sin, *posse non peccare.* Hence Pelagius was in the narrow line of what we might call the *contingency* of evil, which we have seen both is and remains an authentically biblical theme. "I propose to you life or death, blessing or curse. Choose, then, life"—which Pelagius translates as the *libertas ad peccandum et ad non peccandum.* For a voluntarism of this kind, which has been pushed to the point of a coherent theory of contingency, the *naturale peccatum* interpreted as an inherited guilt can only mean a fall back into Manichaeism. "You will never cleanse yourself of the mysteries of Manes," Julius Eclanus will later say to Augustine.

It was to combat the interpretation of Pelagius, which does away with the dark side of sin as a power that encompasses all men, that Saint Augustine went to the bitter end of the concept of original sin by more and more giving it the meaning, on the one hand, of a guilt of a personal character which juridically merits death and, on the other, of a taint inherited by birth.

But if the doctrinal stiffness and the false logic of this concept can be attributed to the anti-Pelagian polemic, its profound motivation cannot. While he was pursuing the voluntaristic line against the Gnostics, the very experience of his conversion and his vivid experience of the resistance of desire and habit to good will brings Augustine to refuse with all his power the Pelagian idea of freedom. For the Pelagians, freedom is without any acquired nature, without habit, without history and encumbrances. It is a freedom that in each one of us would be a unique and isolated instance of the absolute indetermination of creation. The end of Book VIII of the *Confessions* testifies to this experience, an experience which recalls Saint Paul and anticipates Luther. It is the experience of a will that escapes from itself and obeys another law than itself.

The decisive proof that the controversy with Pelagius does not explain everything is that we find in the *Treatise to Simplicianus* of 397—and so more than 15 years before the first anti-Pelagian treatise (the *De peccatorum meritis et remissione* against Celestius dates from 414/5)—the almost definitive formulation of original sin. For the first time Augustine no longer speaks only of an "inherited *punishment*" or of a "bad *habit*," as he does in the previous treatises, but speaks rather of inherited guilt and hence of a fault deserving punishment, a fault anterior to every personal fault, and linked to the very fact of birth itself.

This step is taken by the meditation on Romans 9:10–29, which shifts the exegetical center of the debate, so that it is no longer, as in Romans 5, in the antithesis of two men, Adam and Christ, but in the duality of God's two choices: "I loved Jacob and I hated Esau." "He grants mercy to those he wishes, and he hardens his heart against those he wills." Hence the problem of evil is again the problem of an *antitype*, no longer the antitype of the man Christ but the antitype of an absolute act of God— *election*. This antitype is *reprobation*. To shore up the justice of this reprobation, symmetrical with election, Augustine states that Esau was guilty even from before his birth. Here is the famous text which links predestination and guilt from birth:

All men form, as it were, a mass of sin requiring a debt of expiation toward the divine and sovereign justice. This debt God can demand or remit without committing injustice (*supplicium debens divinae summaeque justiciae quod sive exigatur, sive donetur, nulla est iniquitias*). It is the debtors' act of pride which decides from whom one must demand payment and to whom one will remit the debt (1. 2. 16).

Here the beautiful image of earthenware and the potter is mobilized for designating the infection of all men by the first man.

I will not follow the accumulation of argument in the course of the difficult battle, first from 412 against Celestius, then from 415 against Pelagius, and, finally, against Julius Eclanus, who was more of a Pelagian than the sober Pelagius himself. On the one hand, the juridical argument is ceaselessly tightened and hardened. The indictment of humanity as a whole is the exoneration of God. The concern for coherence leads to the statement that because sin is always voluntary—if it were not, Mani would be right—then, even before its exercise, our will must already be implicated in the bad will of Adam—*reatu ejus implicatos.* It will be necessary, then, to speak of a natural will in order to establish the guilt of infants in the wombs of their mothers. On the other hand, to combat the Pelagian thesis of a simple *imitation* of Adam by the entire human succession, it will be necessary to look for the vehicle of this infection in "generation" (*per generationem*), at the risk of reviving the ancient associations in archaic consciousness between stain and sexuality. In this way the concept of inherited guilt is crystallized, a concept that unites in an inconsistent notion a juridical category (voluntary punishable crime) and a biological category (the unity of the human species by generation). I do not hesitate to say that, from the epistemological point of view, this concept does not have a rational structure different from the Gnostic concepts—Valentine's fall prior to the empire, the empire of darkness according to Mani, and so on.

Anti-Gnostic in origin and intention, because evil remains integrally human, the concept of original sin becomes quasi-Gnostic to the degree that it is rationalized. Henceforth it constitutes the cornerstone of a dogmatic mythology that is comparable, from the epistemological viewpoint, to that of Gnosticism. In order to *rationalize* divine reprobation, which in Saint Paul was only the antitype of election, Saint Augustine constructed what I have been daring to call a quasi-Gnosticism. Certainly, for Augustine the divine mystery remains total. But this mystery is that of election: no one knows why God gives grace to one person and no grace at all to another. In return, there is no mystery of reprobation: election is by grace, perdition is by law [*droit*], and it is in order to justify this perdition by law that Augustine has constructed the idea of a natural guilt, inherited from the first man, effective as an act and, as a crime, punishable.

I ask then: does this train of thought differ essentially from that of Job's friends, who explain to the suffering just man the justice of his sufferings? Does not the old law of retribution, which Ezekiel and Jeremiah vanquished on the level of the collective guilt of Israel, take its revenge on the level of humanity as a whole? Must not the eternal theodicy and its mad project of justifying God, although it is God who justifies *us*, be denounced? Is it not the absurd rationalizing of the advocates of God which now inhabits the great Saint Augustine?

But then someone will ask, how is it that the concept of original sin is part of the most orthodox tradition of Christianity? I do not hesitate to say that Pelagius can be right a thousand times against the pseudo-concept of original sin. Nevertheless, Saint Augustine transmits with this dogmatic mythology something essential that Pelagius completely misunderstood. Perhaps Pelagius is correct in his quarrel with the mythology of original sin, and principally with the Adamic mythology. But it is Augustine who remains right, through and in spite of this Adamic mythology.

This is what I want to try to show in the last section of this paper. The moment has come to apply the rule of thought I proposed at the beginning. The concept, I said, must be deconstructed. One has to go by way of knowledge's failure to retrieve the orthodox intention, the narrow meaning, the ecclesiastical meaning. And I would suggest that this narrow meaning can no longer be a concept but a symbol—a rational symbol, a symbol for reason—of what we *declare* most profoundly and most essentially in the confession of sins.

III

WHAT DID I WANT TO INDICATE by the expression "rational symbol"? This: that concepts do not have their own consistency but refer back to expressions which are *analogous*, not because of a lack of rigor but because of an excess of meaning. What we have to fathom, then, in the concept of original sin is not its false clarity but its dark analogical riches. So, we must retrace our steps. Instead of moving even further into speculation, we must come back to the enormous burden of meaning contained in prerational "symbols," like those contained in the Bible, prior to any elaboration of an abstract language—symbols like wandering, revolt, the missed target, the curved and tortuous path, and especially *captivity* (the captivity of Egypt, then the captivity of Babylon), which becomes the cipher of the human condition under the reign of evil.

With these symbols, which are more descriptive than explanatory, the biblical writers were aiming at certain obscure and obsessive traits of the human experience of evil which cannot be transformed into the purely negative concept of fault. What, then, are these traits of the confession of sin which resist every transcription into the voluntaristic language of the anti-Manichaean writings, every interpretation in terms of a conscious waning of individual will?

In this penitential experience I would underline three remarkable traits. The first is what I would call the *realism* of sin. The consciousness of sin is not its measure. Sin is my true situation before God. The "before God" and not my consciousness of it is the measure of sin. That is why there must be an other, a prophet, to denounce sin. No becoming aware of myself on my part is sufficient, all the more so because consciousness is itself included in the situation and is guilty of both lies and bad faith. This realism of sin cannot be retrieved in the too brief and too clear representation of a *conscious* veering of the will. It is rather a wandering course of being, a more radical *mode of being* than any individual act. Thus Jeremiah compares the evil tendency of the hardened heart to the black skin of the Ethiopian and to the spots of the leopard (Jer. 13:23). Ezekiel calls this hardening of a life become inaccessible to the divine call the "heart of stone."

The second trait is the following. For the prophets this sinful condition is not reducible to a notion of individual guilt like the one the juridical Greco-Roman mind developed to give a just basis for the administration of sentence by the tribunals. The sinful condition has from the outset a communal dimension. Men are included in it in a body. It is the sin of Tyre, of Edom, of Gilead, the sin of Judah. A "we"—the "we other poor sinners" of the liturgy—is uttered in the confession of sins. This transbiological and transhistorical solidarity of sin constitutes the metaphysical unity of the human race. It, too, is unanalyzable in terms of *multiple* veerings of individual human wills.

The third trait is this. The penitential experience of Israel had already underlined a darker aspect of sin. Sin is not only a state, a situation in which man is sunk; sin is a power which binds man and holds him captive. In this respect, sin is not so much a veering as a fundamental impotence. It is the distance between "I want" and "I can." It is sin as "misery."

Now in his conversion experience, Saint Paul had already stressed this aspect of impotence, of slavery and passivity, to the point of apparently conceding to the Gnostic vocabulary. Thus he speaks of "the law of sin which is in our members." Sin is for Paul a demonic power, a mythical magnitude, like Law and Death. Sin "inhabits" man more than man commits sin. Sin "enters" into the world; it "intervenes"; it "abounds"; sin "reigns."

As can be seen, this experience more than any other differs on all counts from that proud voluntarism of the first writings of Augustine. It suffices simply to recall the formula in the *De libero arbitrio*—*nusquam nisi in voluntate esse peccatus*—which the *Retractationes* (I. 13. 2; I. 15. 2) will have such difficulty in saving from Pelagian raillery. In a word, this experience is oriented toward the idea of a quasi-natural evil, an idea that dangerously is taken from the existential anguish which is at the origin of Gnosticism. The experience of possession, of bondage, of captivity, tends toward the idea of being infected from without, of a contagion by a bad substance, which is the source of the tragic myth of Gnosticism.

Perhaps we begin to glimpse the *symbolic function* of original sin. I would say two things. First, that this function is the same as that of the story of the Fall, which is situated not at the level of concepts but at that of mythical images. This story has an extraordinary symbolic power because it condenses in an *archetype* of man everything which the believer experiences in a fugitive fashion and confesses in an allusive way. Far from explaining anything at all (and thereby being nothing more than an etiological myth, comparable to all the popular fables), this story expresses, by means of a plastic creation, the unexpressed basis of human experience—which is inexpressible in direct and clear language. It can be said that the story of the Fall is mythical. But if one remains there, the story's meaning is lost. It is not sufficient to exclude the myth from history. The truth which is not historical must be disengaged from this myth. The

Cambridge theologian, C. H. Dodd, in his admirable little book *The Bible Today,* is very much to the point when he assigns a primary function to the Adamic myth, that of *universalizing* to the human race the tragic experience of exile. "It is the tragic fate of Israel projected upon mankind as a whole. The Word of God that drove man out of Paradise is the word of judgment that sent Israel into exile, now given a universal application."[1] Hence, it is not the myth as such which is the word of God, for its primary meaning could be completely different. It is its *revealing* power concerning the human condition as a whole which constitutes its *revealed* meaning. Something is discovered, unconcealed, which, without myth, would have remained covered, concealed.

But this function of universalizing to the human race the experience of Israel is not all. The Adamic myth reveals at the same time this mysterious aspect of evil, namely, that if any one of us initiates evil, inaugurates it—something Pelagius saw very well—each of us also *discovers evil,* finds it already there, in himself, outside himself, and before himself. For every consciousness which awakens when responsibility is taken, evil is *already there.* In tracing back the origin of evil to a distant ancestor, the myth discovers the situation of every man: evil has already taken place. I do not begin evil; I continue it. I am implicated in evil. Evil has a past; it is its past; it is its own tradition. Hence, myth unites in the figure of an ancestor of the human race all these traits we have just enumerated—the reality of sin anterior to every awakening of conscience, the communal dimension of sin, which is irreducible to individual responsibility, the impotence of will that surrounds every actual fault. This triple description, which modern man can articulate, crystallizes in the symbol of a "before" which the myth of the first man gathers up.

We are here at the source of the schema of *inheritance* which we have found at the basis of the Adamic speculation from Saint Paul to Saint Augustine. But the meaning of this schema appears only if we completely renounce projecting the Adamic figure into history, only if we interpret it as a "type," "the type of the old man." We must not make the transition from myth to mythology. It will never be said enough just what evil has been done to Christianity by the literal interpretation, the "his-

---

1. C. H. Dodd, *The Bible Today* (Cambridge, Eng.: At the University Press, 1968), p. 113.

toricist" interpretation, of the Adamic myth. This interpretation has plunged Christianity into the profession of an absurd history and into pseudo-rational speculations on the quasi-biological transmission of a quasi-juridical guilt for the fault of an *other* man, back into the night of time, somewhere between Pithecanthropus and Neanderthal man. At the same time, the treasure hidden in the Adamic symbol has been squandered. The strong mind, the reasonable man, from Pelagius to Kant, Feuerbach, Marx, or Nietzsche, will always be right against mythology, although beyond every reductive critique the symbol will always invite thought. Between the naïve historicism of fundamentalism and the bloodless moralism of rationalism the way of the hermeneutics of symbols opens up.

Someone will object here that I have accounted for symbols only on the mythical level, for example, the Yahwist story of the Fall, but not at all for symbols on the rational level, and hence not for the concept of original sin which was the object of this lesson. Did I not say, in fact, that this concept had the same symbolic function as the story of the Fall in Genesis? This is true, but it is still only half the meaning. On the one hand, it must be said that the concept refers back to the myth, and the myth refers back to the penitential experience of ancient Israel and of the Church. Intentional analysis goes from pseudo-rationality to pseudo-history, and from pseudo-history to ecclesiastical *lived experience*. But the path that must be taken is the opposite one: myth is not only pseudo-history, it is a revealing. As such, it unearths a dimension of experience which otherwise would have remained without expression and which would have aborted precisely as lived experience. We have suggested some of the revelations proper to myth. Must we say that the process of rationalization inaugurated by Paul's Adamic speculation, which resulted in the Augustinian concept of original sin, is denuded of its *proper* meaning, that it is only a pseudo-knowledge grafted onto myth, interpreted literally, and dressed up in pseudo-history?

I see the essential function of the concept—or pseudo-concept—of original sin in the effort to preserve what was gained in the first conceptualization, namely, that sin is not nature but will, and to incorporate in this will a quasi-nature of evil. Augustine pursues the rational phantom of this quasi-nature that affects not nature but will. This can be seen in the article in the *Retractationes* where Augustine takes up again the anti-Manichaean affirmation of his youth: "Sin is not to be sought elsewhere than in the will." This affirmation is the one which the Pelagians now throw back at him and to which he responds: the original sin of infants is "spoken of without voluntary absurdity, because it was contracted as a consequence of the evil will of the first man and hence is in some way hereditary" (I. 13. 5). And, further on, he writes that the sin by which we are "implicated in his guilt" is "the work of the will" (I. 15. 2). There is something desperate here from the viewpoint of conceptual representation and something very profound from the metaphysical viewpoint. It is in the will itself that there is something of a quasi-nature. Evil is a kind of involuntariness at the very heart of the voluntary, no longer facing the voluntary but within the voluntary; and it is this which is the servile will. And this is why there must be a monstrous combination of a juridical concept of imputation in order for evil to be voluntary and a biological concept of inheritance in order for it to be involuntary, acquired, contracted. At the same time, conversion is brought to the same profound level. If evil is in a symbolic and not in a real sense at the radical level of "generation," conversion itself is "regeneration." I would say that, with original sin, there is constituted, by means of an absurd concept, the antitype of regeneration, the antitype of the new birth. Thanks to this antitype, the will here appears as charged with a passive constitution implied in an actual power of deliberation and of choice.

I will conclude with these three warnings. (1) We never have the right to speculate about the concept of original sin— which, taken in itself, is only a rationalized myth—as if it had a proper consistency. It makes explicit the Adamic myth, just as this myth makes explicit the penitential experience of Israel. One must always come back to the Church's confession of sins. (2) We never have the right to speculate on *the evil already there,* outside the evil that we do. Here, doubtless, is the ultimate mystery of sin. We *inaugurate* evil. It is through us that evil comes into the world. But we inaugurate evil only on the basis of an evil already there, of which our birth is the impenetrable symbol. (3) We never have the right to speculate on either the evil that we inaugurate, or on the evil that we find, without reference to the history of salvation. Original sin is only an antitype. But type and antitype are not only parallel ("just as . . . so too"), but there is a movement from one to the other, a "how much more," an "all the more": "where sin abounded, grace did much more abound" (Romans 5:20).

The Hermeneutics of Symbols
and Philosophical Reflection: I

THE AIM OF THIS ESSAY is to sketch out a general theory of symbol by investigating one precise symbol, or rather a determined complex of symbols: the symbolism of evil.

The essay is organized about the following preoccupation: How can thought that has once entered into the immense problematic of symbolism and into the *revealing* power of symbol develop along the line of rationality and rigor that has been proper to philosophy from its origins? In brief, how can philosophical reflection be *articulated* upon the hermeneutics of symbols?

I shall first say a few words about the question itself. A meditation on symbols occurs at a certain moment of reflection; it answers to a certain situation of philosophy and perhaps even of modern culture. This recourse to the archaic, the nocturnal, and the oneiric, which is also an approach to the birthplace of language, represents an attempt to avoid the difficulties in the problem of a starting point in philosophy. We are all too familiar with the harassing backward flight of thought in search of the "first truth" and, still more radically, of inquiry after a radical starting point that might not be a first truth at all.

Perhaps one must have experienced the deception that accompanies the idea of a presuppositionless philosophy to enter sympathetically into the problematic we are going to evoke. In contrast to philosophies concerned with starting points, a meditation on symbols starts from the fullness of language and of

Translated by Denis Savage. This translation first appeared in the *International Philosophical Quarterly*, Volume II, no. 2 (May, 1962), pages 191–218, and is reproduced here by permission of the publisher.

meaning already there; it begins from within language which has already taken place and in which everything in a certain sense has already been said; it wants to be thought, not pre-suppositionless, but in and with all its presuppositions. Its first problem is not how to get started but, from the midst of speech, to recollect itself.

However, to oppose the problematic of symbol to the Cartesian and Husserlian search for a starting point is to tie this meditation too narrowly to a precise stage of philosophical discourse. Perhaps we should take a larger view: if we raise the problem of symbol *now*, at *this* period of history, we do so in connection with certain traits of our "modernity" and as a rejoinder to this modernity. The historical moment of the philosophy of symbol is both the moment of forgetting and the moment of restoring: forgetting hierophanies, forgetting the signs of the Sacred, losing hold of man himself as belonging to the Sacred. This forgetting is the counterpart of the imposing task of nourishing men and satisfying their needs through a technical control of nature. The dim recognition of this forgetting is what bestirs us to restore the integrity of language. In the very age in which our language is becoming more precise, more univocal, more technical, better suited to those integral formalizations that are called precisely "symbolic" logic (we shall return to this surprisingly equivocal use of the word "symbol")—it is in this age of discourse that we wish to recharge language, start again from the *fullness* of language. But this too is a gift from "modernity." For we moderns are men of philology, of exegesis, of phenomenology, of psychoanalysis, of the analysis of language. The same age develops the possibility of emptying language and the possibility of filling it anew. It is therefore no yearning for a sunken Atlantis that urges us on but the hope of a re-creation of language. Beyond the wastelands of critical thought, we seek to be challenged anew.

"Symbol gives rise to thought." This maxim that I find so appealing says two things. The symbol gives: I do not posit the meaning, the symbol gives it; but what it gives is something for thought, something to think about. First the giving, then the positing; the phrase suggests, therefore, both that all has already been said in enigma and yet that it is necessary ever to begin again and rebegin everything in the dimension of thought. It is this articulation of thought left to itself in the realm of symbols and of thought positing and thinking that I would like to intercept and understand.

I. The Order of Symbol

OF WHAT VALUE is the example of the symbolism of evil for an investigation of such a wide range? It is an excellent touchstone in several respects.

1. It is quite noteworthy that before all theology and all speculation, even before any mythical elaboration, we should still encounter symbols. These elementary symbols are the insubstitutable language of the domain of experience that we shall, to be brief, call the experience of "avowal" or self-confession [*l'aveu*]. In fact there is no direct, nonsymbolic language of evil undergone, suffered, or committed; whether man admits his responsibility or claims to be the prey of an evil which takes hold of him, he does so first and foremost in a symbolism whose articulations can be traced out thanks to various rituals of "confession" that the history of religion has interpreted for us.

Whether we are dealing with the stain image in the magical conception of evil as pollution, or with deviation images of the crooked path, of transgression, of wandering or error, in the more ethical conception of sin, or with the weight image of a burden in the more interiorized experience of guilt—in all these cases the symbol of evil is constituted by starting from something which has a first-level meaning and is borrowed from the experience of nature—of contact, of man's orientation in space. I have used the term "primary symbols" for this elementary language to distinguish it from mythical symbols. Mythical symbols are more articulated; they leave room for the dimension of narrative, with its fabled characters, places, and times, and tell the Beginning and End of the experience of which the primary symbols are the avowal.

The primary symbols clearly point out the intentional structure of symbol. Symbol is a sign in this, that like every sign it intends something beyond and stands for this something. But not every sign is a symbol. Symbol conceals in its intention a double intentionality. There is, first, the primary or literal intentionality, which, like any meaningful intentionality, implies the triumph of the conventional sign over the natural sign: this is the stain, the deviation, the weight—words which do not resemble the thing signified. But upon this first intentionality is built a second intentionality, which, through the material stain, the deviation in space, the experience of burden, points to a certain situation of man in the Sacred; this situation, aimed at through the first meaning, is precisely stained, sinful, guilty being. The literal and obvious meaning, therefore, points beyond itself to something which is *like* a stain, *like* a deviation, *like* a burden. Thus, in distinction to technical signs, which are perfectly transparent and say only what they mean by positing the signified, symbolic signs are opaque: the first, literal, patent meaning analogically intends *a second meaning which is not given otherwise than in the first.* This opaqueness is the symbol's very profundity, an inexhaustible depth.

But let us rightly understand this analogical bond between the literal and the symbolic meanings. Analogy is a nonconclusive reasoning that proceeds through a fourth proportional term (A is to B as C is to D). But in symbol I cannot objectivize the analogical relation that binds the second meaning to the first. By living in the first meaning I am drawn by it beyond itself: *the symbolic meaning is constituted in and through the literal meaning, which brings about the analogy by giving the analogue.* Unlike a comparison that we *look at* from the outside, symbol is the very movement of the primary meaning that makes us share in the latent meaning and thereby assimilates us to the symbolized, without our being able intellectually to dominate the similarity. This is the sense in which symbol "gives"; it gives because it is a primary intentionality that gives the second meaning.

2. The second advantage of this investigation of the primary symbols of avowal is that it brings directly to light a dynamics, a life of symbols. Semantics opens to us the fact that there are veritable linguistic revolutions, oriented in a definite direction; a certain experience blazes its own trail by means of these verbal stages. The trajectory of the experience of fault or guilt is thus marked off by a succession of symbolic sketches. Hence we are not delivered over to a doubtful introspection on the sense of guilt; in place of the short and, to my mind, suspect way of introspective psychology, there must be substituted the long and more sure way of reflection upon the dynamics of the great cultural symbols.[1]

1. The long way seems to me all the more necessary when I confront my interpretation with that of psychoanalysis. An introspective psychology does not hold up in face of the Freudian or Jungian hermeneutics; whereas a reflective approach, by the detour of a hermeneutics of cultural symbols, not only holds up but opens a true debate of one hermeneutics with another. The regressive movement to the archaic, the infantile, the instinctual, must be confronted with the progressive movement of an ascending synthesis.

The dynamics of the primary symbols, marked off by the three constellations of stain, sin, and guilt, has a double meaning, and this very equivocation is most revealing of the dynamics of symbol in general. From one of these symbols to the next, there is on the one hand a movement of incontestable interiorization; on the other, there is a movement of impoverishment of symbolic richness; that is why, let it be said in passing, one must not let oneself be misled by a "historicist" and "progressivist" interpretation of the evolution of consciousness in these symbols. What is gain from one point of view is loss from the other. In this progression, each "step" maintains itself only by taking up the symbolic charge of the preceding; so we shall not be surprised that stain, the most archaic symbol, survives as the essential in the third step. Though submerged in fear, the experience of the impure already achieves speech, thanks to the extraordinary richness of the stain theme.

From the beginning, in fact, stain is more than a spot; it points to an affection of the person as a whole as regards his situation in relation to the Sacred. Whatever it is that affects the penitent cannot be removed by any physical washing. Through interchangeable acts (covering with earth, spitting, throwing at a distance, etc.) the rituals of purification intend an integrity that can be spoken of in none but a symbolic language. This is why it is the magic conception of pollution or stain, however archaic and obsolete it be, that has transmitted to us the symbolism of the pure and the impure with all its richness of harmonics. At the center of this symbolism stands the schema of "exteriority," of investiture or infection by evil, which is perhaps the inscrutable depths of the "mystery of iniquity." Evil is evil only insofar as I posit it, but at the very heart of freedom's positing of evil is revealed a power of seduction by "evil already there" which the ancient "stain" had from the start already affirmed in the symbolic mode.

But an archaic symbol survives only through the revolutions of experience and of language which submerge it. The iconoclast movement does not proceed first from reflection but from symbolism itself; a symbol is first of all a destroyer of a prior symbol. Thus we see the symbolism of sin take shape about images which are the inverse of stain images; in place of exterior contact, it is now deviation (from the target, the straight path, the limit not to be crossed, and so on) which serves as guiding schema. This switch in themes is the expression of an overturning of fundamental motifs. A new category of religious experience is born: that of "before God," of which the Jewish *berit*, the Covenant, is the witness. An infinite exigency of perfection comes to light, which keeps remodeling the terse, limited commandments of the old codes. To this infinite exigency is coupled an infinite menace that revolutionizes the old fear of the taboos and makes one dread the encounter of God in his wrath.

What becomes, then, of the initial symbol? On the one hand, evil is no longer a thing but a broken relationship, hence a nothing; this nothing is expressed in the images of the breathiness, the emptiness, the vaporousness and vanity of the idol. The very wrath of God is like the nothingness of his absence. But at the same time a new positivity of evil arises, no longer an exterior "something" but a real enslaving power. The symbol of captivity, which transforms a historical event (the Egyptian captivity, then the Babylonian captivity) into a schema of existence, represents the highest expression achieved by the penitential experience of Israel. Because of this new positivity of evil, the first symbolism, that of stain, was able to be taken up again: the schema of exteriority is recovered, but at an ethical and no longer at a magical level.

The same movement of breaking with and taking up again can be observed in the transition from sin symbols to guilt symbols. On the one hand, the purely subjective experience of fault tends to be substituted for the realist and, if we may so express it, ontological affirmation of sin. Whereas sin is real even when it is not known, guilt is measured by man's awareness of it in becoming the author of his own fault. In this way the weight and burden image is substituted for the image of separation, deviation, wandering; in the depths of consciousness, "before God" is being replaced by "before myself"; man is guilty when he feels guilty. To this new revolution we incontestably owe a finer and more measured sense of responsibility which, from being collective, becomes individual, gradual instead of total. We have entered the world of reasonable indictment, the indictment by the judge and the scrupulous conscience. But the ancient stain symbol is not, for all that, lost, for hell is displaced from the exterior toward the interior. Crushed by the law which it shall never satisfy, consciousness recognizes itself captive in its own injustice and, even worse, in the lie of its pretension to justice proper. At this extreme point of involution the stain symbol has become that of servile liberty, servile will, of which Luther and Spinoza speak in terms so different, but borrowed from the same symbolism.

3. I have deliberately carried to this point the exegesis of the primary symbols of fault, as well as the general theory of symbol which depends on this exegesis, without relying on the mythical structure that usually surcharges these symbols. It was necessary to bracket the second-degree symbols both to make clear the structure of the first-degree symbols and to bring out the specificity of myth itself. These great narratives, which, as was said, put into play space, time, and characters woven into story form, have in fact an irreducible function. It is a threefold one. First, they place the whole of mankind and its drama under the sign of an exemplary man, an Anthropos, an Adam, who symbolically stands for the concrete universal of human experience. Second, they give to this history an *élan,* a direction, an orientation, by unfolding it between a beginning and an end; they thus introduce a historical tension into human experience, a tension produced by the double horizon of a genesis and an apocalypse. Finally, and more fundamentally, they explore the cleavage in human reality represented by the passage or leap from innocence to guilt; they recount how man, originally good, has become what he is in the present. That is why myth can exercise its symbolic function only through the specific means of narrative; what it wants to say is already drama.

But at the same time myth can take root only in a multiplicity of narratives and leaves us before an endless diversity of symbolic systems, similar to the multiple tongues of an unfixable Sacred. In the particular case of the symbolism of evil, the difficulty of an exegesis of myths appears from the start under a double form. On the one hand, the infinite multiplicity of the myths must be overcome by imposing upon them a typology that permits thought to become oriented within their endless variety, while not doing violence to the specificity of the mythical figures brought to the light of language by diverse civilizations; on the other hand, the difficulty is to move from a static classification of myths to a dynamics of them. For it is the understanding of the oppositions and secret affinities among diverse myths that prepares the way for the philosophical assimilation of myth. The world of myths, even more than that of the primary symbols, is not a serene and amicable world; myths have never stopped battling one another; every myth is iconoclastic toward others, in the same way that every symbol left to itself tends to thicken, to solidify into an idolatry. It is necessary, therefore, to share in this battle, in this dynamics, by which symbolism is subject to being itself surpassed.

This dynamics is animated by a deep-seated opposition: on one side are the myths that take the origin of evil back to a catastrophe or primordial conflict prior to man; on the other are the myths that take the origin back to man.

To the first group belongs the drama of creation, illustrated by the Babylonian poem of creation, *Enuma elish*, which tells of the primordial combat whence proceed the birth of the most recent gods, the foundation of the cosmos, and the creation of man. To this same group belong the tragic myths which show the hero subject to a fatal destiny. According to the tragic schema, man falls into fault as he falls into existence; and the god who tempts and misleads him stands for the primordial lack of distinction between good and evil. With the Zeus of *Prometheus Bound*, this god has attained the terrifying stature that no thought can sustain. The Orphic myth of the soul in exile in an evil body should also be placed in this first group; for this exile is necessarily prior to every positing of evil by a free and responsible man. The Orphic myth is a situational myth which clearly seems to have been later projected into an origin myth; the roots of the latter reach back to the theomachy which is close to the cosmogonic and tragic myths.

Over against this triple myth stands the biblical narrative of Adam's Fall. This alone is the anthropological myth proper. In it can be seen the mythical expression of the whole penitential experience of Israel. It is man who is accused by the prophet; it is man who, in the confession of sins, discovers himself to be the author of evil and who discerns, beyond his evil acts told off in time, an evil constitution more original than any individual decision. The myth recounts the arising of this evil constitution in an irrational event that unexpectedly takes place in a good creation. It compresses the origin of evil into a symbolic instant that is the end of innocence and the beginning of malediction. Through the chronicle of the first man is unveiled the meaning of the history of every man.

The world of myths is thus polarized between two tendencies: one takes evil back beyond the human; the other concentrates it in an evil choice from which stems the pain of being man. So again we come across, at a higher level of elaboration, the polarity of the primary symbols, stretched between a schema of exteriority, which is dominant in the magical conception of evil as stain, and a schema of interiority, which only fully triumphs with the painful experience of the guilty and scrupulous conscience.

But that is not yet what is most remarkable. The conflict is not only between two groups of myths, it is repeated within the Adam myth itself. This myth has in fact two faces. It is the narrative of the instant of the Fall, such as we have just presented it. But at the same time it is the narrative of the temptation, which is spread out over a duration, a lapse of time, and puts into action a number of characters: the God who interdicts, the object of the temptation, the woman who is seduced, and finally and above all the serpent who seduces. The same myth that concentrates the event of the Fall in one man, one act, one instant, likewise disperses it over several characters and several episodes. The qualitative leap from innocence to fault is, in this second aspect, a gradual and indiscernible passage. The myth of the caesura is thus at the same time the myth of the transition; the myth of evil choice is the myth of temptation, of intoxication, of imperceptible slipping into evil. The woman, figure of fragility, is the polar counterpart of the man, figure of evil decision.

The conflict of the myths is thus included in a single myth. That is why the Adam myth, which at first reading might be looked upon as the net result of an energetic demythologizing of all the other myths concerned with the origin of evil, introduces into the narrative the highly mythical figure of the serpent. The serpent, at the very heart of the Adam myth, stands for evil's other face, which the other myths tried to recount: evil already there, pregiven evil, evil that attracts and seduces man. The serpent signifies that man does not begin evil. He finds it. For him, to begin is to continue. Beyond the projection of our own covetousness, the serpent stands for the tradition of an evil more ancient than man himself. The serpent is the *Other* of human evil.

From this can be understood why there is a dynamics of myths. The schema of exteriority which finds projection in the body-tomb of the Orphics, the wicked god of Prometheus, the primordial combat of the drama of creation—this schema, doubtless, is invincible. That is why, dispelled by the anthropological myth, it rises again within it and takes refuge in the figure of the serpent. The figure of Adam is much more than the paradigm of all present evil. Adam, as primordial man, is prior to every man; in his own fashion he is once again the figure of evil prior to every actual evil. Adam is older than every man, and the serpent older than Adam. Thus the tragic myth is at the same time reaffirmed and destroyed by the Adam myth. This is undoubtedly why tragedy lives on after its double destruction by Greek philosophy and Christianity; if its theology cannot be thought, if it is, in the proper sense of the term, unavowable, still, what it wants to say—and cannot say—continues to be *shown* in the basic spectacle of the tragic hero, innocent and guilty.

It is this war of the myths that invites us to attempt the passage from a simple exegesis of myths to a philosophy through symbols.

II. FROM SYMBOLISM TO REFLECTIVE THOUGHT

ACCORDINGLY, THE TASK IS NOW to think starting from the symbolic and according to the genius of the symbolic. And it *is* a matter of thinking. For my part, I do not in the least abandon the tradition of rationality that has animated philosophy since the Greeks. It is not at all a question of giving in to some kind of imaginative intuition, but rather of thinking, that is to say, of elaborating concepts that comprehend, and make one comprehend, concepts woven together, if not in a closed system, at least in a *systematic* order. But at the same time it is a question of transmitting, by means of this rational elaboration, a richness of meaning or signification that was already there, that has already preceded rational elaboration. For such is the situation: on the one hand, all has been said *before* philosophy, by sign and by enigma. That is one of the meanings of the phrase of Heraclitus: "The master whose oracle is at Delphi does not speak, does not dissimulate: he signifies (ἀλλὰ σημαίνει)." On the other hand, we have the task of speaking clearly, by taking perhaps also the risk of dissimulating, by interpreting the oracle. Philosophy begins with itself; it *is* a kind of beginning. Hence the coherent discourse of philosophies is at once hermeneutic recovery of the enigmas which precede, envelop, and nourish this discourse and also inquiry into the beginning, search for order, desire for system. Happy and rare would be the conjunction within one and the same philosophy of both the abundance of signs and retained enigmas and the rigor of a discourse without complacency.

The key, or at least the crux, of the difficulty lies in the relationship between hermeneutics and reflection. For every symbol gives birth to understanding by means of an interpretation. How can this understanding be both *in* the symbol and *beyond* the symbol?

I see three stages of this *understanding,* three stages that stake out the movement which advances from *living in* symbols toward thought that *thinks from* symbols.

The first stage, that of a simple phenomenology, remains an understanding of symbol by symbol, by the totality of symbols. This is already a kind of understanding, since it runs through and interconnects the domain of symbols and gives it the consistency of a world. But it is still a life abandoned to symbol, delivered up to symbol. The phenomenology of religion rarely goes beyond this level; for it, to understand a symbol is to place it within a larger homogeneous totality which, remaining on the level of symbol, forms a system. Sometimes this phenomenology lays out the multiple values of one and the same symbol to show its inexhaustible character. In this first sense, to understand is to repeat within oneself this multiple unity, this permutation of all the values within the same theme. Sometimes phenomenology devotes itself to understanding one symbol by another; understanding is then gradually extended, according to a remote intentional analogy, to all the other symbols that have some affinity with the symbol under study. In another way, phenomenology will understand a symbol by a ritual and a myth, i.e., by other manifestations of the Sacred. It will further be shown, and this shall be the fourth way of understanding, how the same symbol unifies several levels of experience or representation: the exterior and the interior, the vital and the speculative. Thus, in multiple ways, the phenomenology of symbol brings to light an internal coherence, something like a symbolic system. On this level, to interpret is to bring out a coherence.

This is the first stage, the first level of thought that starts from symbols. But one cannot rest here; for the question of *truth* has not yet been posed. If a phenomenologist should give the name truth to internal coherence, to the systematization of the world of symbols, it is a truth without belief, truth at a distance, a reduced truth. From such truth this question has been eliminated: *Do I myself believe that? What do I personally make of these symbolic meanings?* Now this question cannot be raised as long as one remains at the level of comparativism, passing from one symbol to another without taking a stand. This stage can only be a stage, the stage of an understanding that is horizontal and panoramic, curious but not concerned. We now have to enter into a relationship with symbols that is emotionally intense and at the same time critical. To do so I must leave the comparativist point of view aside; I must follow the exegete and become implicated in the life of one symbol, one myth.

Beyond the horizontal understanding of the phenomenology of the comparativist, there opens up the field of hermeneutics proper: interpretation applied in each case to an individual text. It is in modern hermeneutics that the symbol's giving of meaning and the intelligent initiative of deciphering are bound together. Hermeneutics makes us share in the battle, the dynamics, by which symbolism is subject to being itself surpassed. Only by sharing in this dynamics does understanding enter the properly critical dimension of exegesis and become a hermeneutics.

But then I must quit the position, or better, the exile, of the remote and disinterested spectator in order to appropriate in each case an individual symbolism. Then is discovered what may be called the circle of hermeneutics, which the simple amateur of myths unfailingly misses. The circle can be stated bluntly: "You must understand in order to believe, but you must believe in order to understand."

This circle is not vicious; still less is it deadly. It is quite alive and stimulating. You must believe in order to understand. No interpreter in fact will ever come close to what his text says if he does not live in the aura of the meaning that is sought. And yet it is only by understanding that we can believe. The second immediacy, the second naïveté that we are after, is accessible only in hermeneutics; we can believe only by interpreting. This is the "modern" modality of belief in symbols; expression of modernity's distress and cure for this distress. Such is the circle: hermeneutics proceeds from the preunderstanding of the very matter which through interpretation it is trying to understand. But thanks to this hermeneutic circle, I can today still communicate with the Sacred by explicating the preunderstanding which animates the interpretation. Hermeneutics, child of "modernity," is one of the ways in which this "modernity" overcomes its own forgetfulness of the Sacred. I believe that being can still speak to me, no longer indeed in the precritical form of immediate belief but as the second immediacy that hermeneutics aims at. It may be that this second naïveté is the postcritical equivalent of the precritical hierophany.

But hermeneutics is not yet reflection; it is bound up with individual texts whose exegesis it governs. The third stage of the understanding of symbols, the properly philosophical stage, is that of *thought starting from symbol*.

However, the hermeneutic relation between philosophic discourse and the symbols that nourish it is threatened by two spurious substitutes. On the one hand, it can be reduced to a simple allegorical tie. This is what the Stoics did with the fables of Homer and Hesiod. The philosophical meaning rises victorious from its imaginative shell; it was there all armed like Athena in the head of Zeus. The fable was but an outer wrapping; stripped off, it is rendered vain. Allegory implies that the true meaning, the philosophical meaning, preceded the fable, which was only a second disguise, a veil deliberately thrown over the truth to mislead the simple. I am convinced that we must think, not *behind* the symbols, but starting from symbols, *according* to symbols, that their substance is indestructible, that they constitute the *revealing* substrate of speech which lives among men. In short, the symbol *gives rise to* thought. On the other hand, a further peril lies in wait for us: that of repeating the symbol in a mime of rationality, of rationalizing symbols as such, and thereby fixing them on the imaginative plane where they are born and take shape. This temptation of a "dogmatic mythology" is the temptation of gnosis. It is impossible to exaggerate the historical importance of this movement of thought, which has covered three continents, held sway over numerous centuries, and animated the speculation of so many minds eager for knowledge and salvation through knowledge. Between gnosis and the problem of evil there is a disquieting and in fact deceptive alliance. It was the Gnostics who posed in all its pathetic bluntness the question: πόθεν τὰ κακά—whence comes evil?

In what does this power of misleading, inherent in gnosis, consist? First of all in this, that by its content it is structured exclusively upon the tragic theme of fall or disgrace, which is characterized by its schema of exteriority. For the Gnostic, evil is outside. It is a quasi-physical reality that invests man from the exterior. By the same token—and this is the second characteristic we wish to emphasize—all the images of evil, inspired by this schema of exteriority, "gell" in this represented materiality. Thus is born a dogmatic mythology, as Puech says, inseparable from its spatial and cosmic figuration.[2]

My problem, then, is this: How can thought be elaborated in starting from symbol, without going back to the old allegorizing interpretation or falling into the trap of gnosis? How can a

---

2. On all this, cf. " 'Original Sin': A Study in Meaning," above.

meaning be disengaged from symbol that will put thought into motion, without presupposing a meaning already there, hidden, dissimulated, covered over, or without getting involved in the pseudo-knowing of a dogmatic mythology? I would like to try another way, the way of a creative interpretation, an interpretation that would respect the original enigma of symbols, let itself be taught by this enigma, but, with that as a start, bring out the meaning, give it form, in the full responsibility of an autonomous systematized thought. But how can thought be at once *bound* and *free*? How can one maintain both the immediacy of symbol and the mediation of thought?

It is this battle between thought and the symbolic that I wish now to explore, with the help of the problem of evil taken as a paradigm case. In it, in effect, thought manifests itself alternately as *reflection* and as *speculation*.

Thought as reflection is essentially "demythologizing." Its transposition of myth is at the same time an elimination not only of its etiological function but of its power to open and uncover; it interprets myth only by reducing it to allegory. The problem of evil is in this regard an exemplar: *reflection upon the symbolism of evil reaches its peak in what we shall henceforth call the ethical vision of evil.* This philosophizing interpretation of evil feeds on the richness of primary symbols and of myths, but it continues the movement of their demythologization that we have sketched out above. On the one hand, it prolongs the progressive reduction of stain and sin to personal and inner guilt; on the other, it prolongs the movement of demythologization of all the myths except the Adam myth and reduces this latter to a simple allegory of servile will.

Reflective thought, in its turn, is at battle with speculative thought. Speculative thought wants to save what an ethical vision of evil tends to eliminate. It not only wants to save it but to show its *necessity*. And its specific peril is *gnosis*.

We shall turn first to the ethical vision of evil. This level must be attained and traversed all the way to the end. It is a level on which we will not be able to stay for long, but it is from within it that we shall have to go beyond it. To do that, it is necessary to have completely thought out a purely ethical interpretation of evil.

By "ethical interpretation of evil" I understand an interpretation in which evil as far as possible is reset within the context of freedom; in which, therefore, evil is an invention of freedom.

Reciprocally, an ethical vision of evil is a vision in which freedom is revealed in its depths as power to act and power to be; the freedom that evil supposes is a freedom capable of digression, deviation, subversion, wandering. This mutual "explanation" of evil by freedom and of freedom by evil is the essence of the moral vision of the world and of evil.

How does the moral vision of the world and of evil relate to the symbolic and mythical universe? In two ways: first, it is a radical demythologization of the dualist myths, the tragic and the Orphic; second, it is the assimilation of the Adam narrative into an intelligible philosophical theme. The moral vision of the world is thought that goes *counter to* evil as substance and *in accordance with* the fall of primordial man.

Historically the ethical vision of evil carries the stamp of two great names who are not customarily associated but whose intimate relationship I would like to make felt: Augustine and Kant. When I say Augustine, I mean at least Augustine in his fight against Manichaeism; for we shall see further on that "Augustinianism," in the precise and narrow sense that Rottmayer gives it, stands—in opposition now not to Mani but to Pelagius—for the surpassing of the moral vision of the world and, in certain respects, for its liquidation. We shall return to this point later.

From its demythologizing side, the Augustinian interpretation of evil, prior to the struggle against Pelagius, is dominated by the following affirmation: evil has no nature; evil is not a something; it is not matter, substance, world. The reabsorption of the schema of exteriority is pushed to its furthest limits: not only does evil not have being, but one must suppress the question: *quid est malum?* (what is evil?) and put in its place the question: *unde malum faciamus?* (whence do we do evil?). Hence it will be necessary to say that evil, as regards substance and nature, is a "nothing."

This "nothing," inherited from the Platonic nonbeing and the Plotinian nothing, but desubstantialized, has now to be coupled with concepts inherited from another tradition of Greek philosophy, the *Nicomachean Ethics*. It was here, in fact, that was first elaborated the philosophy of the voluntary and the involuntary (*Nic. Eth.*, Book III), but Aristotle does not go all the way to a radical philosophy of *freedom*. He elaborates the concepts of "preference" ($\pi\rho o\alpha\iota\rho\epsilon\sigma\iota\varsigma$), of deliberate choice, of rational desire, but not of freedom. It can be affirmed that it was Saint Augustine who made evil's power of *nothing* meet head on with freedom at work in the will and thereby so radicalized reflection upon freedom as to make it into the originary power of saying "No" to being, the power of "defaulting" (*deficere*), of "declining" (*declinare*), of tending toward nothingness (*ad non esse*).

But Augustine, as I have said elsewhere,[3] does not have the conceptual tools to give integral expression to his discovery. Thus we see him, in the *Contra Felicem*, oppose evil will and evil nature. But the Neoplatonic framework of his thought does not allow him to lay out and stabilize the opposition nature/will in a coherent conception; that would take a philosophy of action and a philosophy of contingence, in which evil would be said to surge up as an event, as a qualitative leap.

Nor is it certain that the overly negative concept of *defectus*, of *declinatio*, accounts for the positive power of evil. He would have had to go further and conceive of the *positing* of evil as a qualitative "leap," as an event, an instant. But then Augustine would no longer be Augustine but Kierkegaard.

What is, now, the significance of Kant, and especially of his "Essay on Radical Evil" (found in his *Religion within the Limits of Reason Alone*), as regards the anti-Manichaean treatises of Augustine? I propose that we try to understand them through each other. To start with, Kant elaborates the conceptual framework that is wanting to Augustine by pushing to the extreme the specificity of the "practical" concepts: *Wille, Willkür, Maxim,* will, freedom (free will or free choice), maxim of the will. This conceptualization is achieved in the Introduction to the *Metaphysics of Morals* and in the *Critique of Practical Reason*. By it, Kant brings to full explicitness the opposition will/nature sketched out by Augustine in the *Contra Felicem*.

But above all Kant elaborated the principal condition of a conceptualization of evil as radical evil, namely, formalism in morality. This relationship does not appear on a reading of the "Essay on Radical Evil" apart from its ties with the *Critique of Practical Reason*. But by his formalism Kant brings to achievement a movement already started in Plato: if "injustice" can be the figure of radical evil, it is because "justice" is not just one virtue out of many but the very form of virtue, the unifying principle which makes the soul, from being several, into one (*Republic*, Book IV).

3. On the *aversio a Deo*, the opposition *potestas/natura* in the *Contra Felicem*, and the fragile distinction between the two "nothings" (the *ex nihilo* of creation and the *ad non esse* of evil), see above, pp. 274–75.

Aristotle, in the *Nicomachean Ethics,* is also on the road to a formalization of good and evil: virtues are defined both by their object and by their formal character of "mean" ($\mu\epsilon\sigma\acute{o}\tau\eta s$); evil therefore is absence of "mean," deviation, extremity in deviation. The Platonic ἀδικία, the Aristotelian ἀκρασία, foreshadow, therefore, *qua* imperfect formalisms, the entire formalization of the principle of morality. I am not unaware that one cannot remain in a formalism in ethics; but it is without doubt necessary to have reached it in order to surpass it.

Now, the advantage of this formalism is to construct the concept of evil maxim as a rule that the free will forges itself. Evil no longer resides in sensibility. An end is put to the confusion between evil and the affective, the passional. It is worth noting that it was the reputedly most pessimistic of ethics that accomplished the feat of disjoining evil from sensibility; this separation is the result of formalism and its bracketing of desire in the definition of the good will. Kant can say: "Natural inclinations that result from sensibility do not even have a direct relationship with evil." But neither can evil reside in the subversion of reason: a completely lawless being would no longer be bad but diabolic. It remains that evil resides in a relationship, or the subversion of a relationship. It is what happens, says Kant, when man subordinates the pure motive of respect to sensible motives, when "he reverses the moral order of motives by accepting them in his maxims."

Thus the biblical schema of deviation, opposed to the Orphic schema of affecting exteriority, receives its rational equivalent in the Kantian idea of the subversion of the maxim. More precisely still, I see in Kant the complete philosophical manifestation that the supreme evil is not the gross infraction of a duty but the malice that makes pass for virtue what is virtue's betrayal. The evil of evil is the fraudulent justification of the maxim by apparent conformity with law—it is the semblance of morality. Kant was the first, as I see it, to orient the problem of evil in the direction of imposture or bad faith.

Here we have the extreme point of clarity attained by the ethical vision of evil: freedom is the power of deviation, of disrupting order. Evil is not a something but the subversion of a relation. But who does not see that, at the very moment we say this, we triumph, in a way, in emptiness? The price of clarity is the loss of depth.

III. DIMMING OF REFLECTION AND RETURN TO THE TRAGIC

WHAT IS LACKING in the ethical vision of evil? What is lacking, what is lost, is the darksome experience of evil which surfaces in different ways in the symbolism of evil and which constitutes properly speaking the "tragic" aspect of evil.

At the lowest level of the symbolic, the level of primary symbols, we have seen the confession of sins acknowledge evil as evil *already* there, evil in which I am born, evil which I find in myself before the awakening of my conscience, evil which cannot be analyzed into individual guilt and actual faults. I have shown that the symbol of "captivity," of slavery, is the specific symbol of this dimension of evil as power that binds, of evil as reign.

It is this same experience of evil already there, powerful in my powerlessness, that gives rise to the whole cycle of myths other than the Adam myth, all of which start out from the schema of exteriority. But this mythic cycle is not simply excluded by the Adam myth; it is in a certain way *incorporated* in it, at a subordinate level, surely, but not a negligible one. Adam is for all men the prior man and not only the exemplary man: he is the very priority of evil as regards every man; and he himself has his other, his prior, in the figure of the serpent, already there and already sly. Thus the ethical vision of evil thematizes only the symbol of actual evil, the "swerving," the "contingent deviation." Adam is the archetype, the model of this present, actual evil that we repeat and imitate each time that we begin evil; and in this sense each one begins evil each time.

But by starting evil we continue it, and that is what we have to try to express now: evil as tradition, as historical concatenation, as reign of the already there. But here we also take great risks, for by introducing the schema of "heritage" and by trying to coordinate it with that of "deviation" in a coherent concept, we again run up against gnosis, taken in the largest sense, namely: (1) dogmatic mythology; (2) reification of evil in a "nature." The concept of *nature* is put forth here in order to counterbalance that of *contingence*, which ruled the first movement of thought. We are going to try to think something like a *nature of evil*, but a nature which would not be a nature of things but an originary nature of man, a nature of liberty, hence a contracted *habitus,* freedom's manner of having come to be.

Here again we come across Augustine and Kant, Augustine when he moves from actual evil to original sin, Kant when he goes from the wrong maxim of free will back to the *ground* of all wrong maxims. (Let me digress here for a moment to remark that I reject the usual disjunction of spheres of competence to which people are so ready to submit the work of Augustine, as if the philosophy of actual evil were the philosopher's province and that of original sin the theologian's. I, for one, do not divide philosophy and theology in this way. As *revealing*—and not as revealed—the Adam symbol belongs to a philosophical anthropology just as much as all the other symbols. Its belonging to theology is determined, not by its own structure, but by its relation in Christology with the "event" and "coming" of the Man par excellence, Jesus the Christ. For my part, I hold that no symbol *qua* opening and uncovering a truth of man is foreign to philosophical reflection. Hence I do not take the concept of original sin to be a theme extraneous to philosophy but, on the contrary, to be a theme subject to an intentional analysis, to a hermeneutics of rational symbols whose task is to reconstruct the layers of meaning which have become sedimented in the concept.)

Now what does this intentional analysis bring to the surface? It brings this: as a so-called intelligible concept, the concept of original sin is a false knowledge and should be likened, as for epistemological structure, to the concepts of gnosis: a meta-empirical fall according to Valentinus, an aggression of the realm of darkness according to Mani. Anti-Gnostic in its intention, original sin is a quasi-Gnostic concept in its form. The task of reflection here is to break it as false knowledge in order to get hold of its intention as rational symbol—for which there is no substitute—of evil already there.

Let us make this double movement of reflection.

We must, we said, break the concept as false knowing; in effect "Augustinianism," in the narrow sense that we used before, combines in an inconsistent notion both a juridical concept, that of imputation, of imputable guilt, and a biological concept, that of heredity. On the one hand, for there to be sin, fault must be a transgression of will: such was the fault of man understood as an individual having really existed at the origin of history. On the other hand, this imputable guilt must be carried *per generationem* so that, each and all, we may be made guilty "in Adam." Throughout the polemic with Pelagius and the Pelagians we see take shape the idea of a personal guilt juridically meriting death and inherited by birth in the manner of a blemish. Augustine's motivation[4] merits a pause: he aims essentially at *rationalizing* the most mysterious of Pauline themes, that of reprobation: "I loved Jacob and I hated Esau." Because God is just, the reprobation of little infants in the womb of their mother must be just; perdition must be by right and salvation by grace. From this derives the idea of a guilt of nature, effective as an act and punishable as a crime, though inherited as a sickness.

This is an intellectually inconsistent idea, we maintained, inasmuch as it mixes two universes of discourse—that of ethics or of right, and that of biology. It is an intellectually scandalous idea, inasmuch as it returns prior to Ezekiel and Jeremiah to the old idea of retribution and *en masse* inculpation of men. It is an intellectually derisory idea, inasmuch as it throws up again the eternal theodicy and its project of justifying God.

What must be scrutinized in the concept of original sin is not its false clarity but its obscure analogical richness. Its force lies in intentionally referring back to what is most radical in the confession of sins, namely, the fact that evil precedes my awareness, that it cannot be analyzed into individual faults, that it is my pregiven impotence. It is to my freedom what my *birth* is to my actual consciousness, namely, always already there; birth and nature here are analogous concepts. Hence the intention of the pseudo-concept of original sin is this: to incorporate in the description of the bad will, such as the will was elaborated against Mani and Gnosis, the theme of a quasi-nature of evil. *The concept's irreplaceable function is therefore to integrate the schema of inheritance with that of contingence.*

There is here something of hopelessness from the point of view of conceptual representation, and of irreplaceability from the metaphysical point of view. The quasi-nature is in the will itself; evil is a kind of involuntariness at the very heart of the voluntary, no longer over against it but in it—and there you have the servile will. In a stroke, confession is shifted to a deeper level than that of simple repentance for acts; if evil is at the radical level of "generation"—in a symbolic, not a factual, sense—conversion itself is "regeneration." Thus is constituted, by means of an absurd concept, an *anti-type of regeneration;* because of this

---

4. The *Treatise to Simplicianus* of the year 397 is interesting in this regard, for it precedes the first anti-Pelagian treatise by fourteen years; it already contains the essence of the Augustinian argumentation.

anti-type, will is shown to be affected by a passive constitution implied in its actual power of deliberation and of choice.

IT IS THIS ANTI-TYPE of regeneration that Kant tried to elaborate as an *a priori* of the moral life. The philosophical interest of the "Essay on Radical Evil," which we left hanging in mid-air, lies in its having achieved what I a moment ago called the critique of original sin as false knowing and in having attempted its "deduction"—in the sense in which the transcendental deduction of the categories is a justification of rules by their power to constitute a domain of objectivity. The evil of nature is thus understood as the condition of possibility of evil maxims, as their *ground*.

As such, the propensity to evil is "intelligible." Kant says: "Even if the *Dasein* of this propensity can be demonstrated (*dargetan*) by empirical proofs of conflict in time, the nature (*Beschaffenheit*) and ground (*Grund*) of this propensity must be apprehended *a priori*, for it is a relation of freedom to law, the concept of which is always nonempirical." [5] Experience "confirms our judgments about radical evil, but it "can never reveal the root of evil in the supreme maxim of the free will relating to the law, a maxim which, as *intelligible act*, precedes all experience." [6] Thus is swept away all *naturalism* in the conception of a "natural," "innate" tendency toward evil. It can be said to be given "at birth," but birth is not its cause. It is rather a "manner of being of freedom which comes to it from freedom." The idea of a "contracted" habit of free will thus furnishes the symbol of the reconciliation of the contingence and antecedence of evil. [7]

---

5. [The translation in the text is based on the French translation of Kant, *La Religion dans les limites de la simple raison* (Vrin, 1952), p. 56. In the English translation by Theodore M. Greene and Hoyt H. Hudson, *Religion within the Limits of Reason Alone* (New York: Harper Torchbooks, 1960), pp. 30–31, the passage reads: "But even if the existence of this propensity to evil in human nature can be demonstrated by experiential proofs of the real opposition, in time, of man's will to the law, such proofs do not teach us the essential character of that propensity or the ground of this opposition. Rather, because this character concerns a relation of the will, which is free (and the concept of which is therefore not empirical), to the moral law as an incentive (the concept of which, likewise, is purely intellectual), it must be apprehended *a priori* through the concept of evil, so far as evil is possible under the laws of freedom (of obligation and accountability)."—ED.]

6. *Ibid.*, English translation, p. 34, asterisked note.

7. "By propensity (*propensio*) I understand the subjective ground of the possibility of an inclination (habitual appetite, *concupiscentia*) so far as mankind in general is liable to it"(Eng. trans., pp. 23–24).

But then, in distinction to every "gnosis" which pretends to *know* the origin, the philosopher recognized here that he was entering upon the inscrutable and the unfathomable: "The rational origin of this . . . propensity to evil remains inscrutable to us, because this propensity itself must be set down to our account, and because, as a result, that ultimate ground of all maxims would in turn involve the adoption of an evil maxim [as its basis]." [8] More strongly still: "There is then for us no conceivable ground from which the moral evil in us could originally have come." [9] As I see it, the inconceivability consists precisely in this, that evil, which always begins *by* freedom, is always already there *for* freedom: it is act *and* habit, arising *and* antecedence. That is why Kant expressly relates this enigma of evil for philosophy to the mythical figure of the serpent. The serpent, I think, represents the "always already there" of evil, of this evil that is nevertheless beginning, act, determination of freedom by itself.

THUS KANT COMPLETES AUGUSTINE: first by definitively destroying the Gnostic wrappings of the concept of original sin, next by attempting a transcendental deduction of the ground of evil maxims, finally by replunging into nonknowing the search for a ground of the ground. Thought has here a kind of movement of emergence, then of replunging: emergence into the clarity of the transcendental, replunging into the darkness of nonknowing. But perhaps philosophy is responsible not only for the circumscription of its knowing but also for the *limits* by which it restricts to nonknowing; limit is no longer here a confine but an active and sober self-limitation. Let us say again with Kant: "the origin of this propensity to evil remains impenetrable to us *because it must be imputed to us.*"

Having arrived at this point, we may legitimately ask ourselves why reflection reduces the symbolic richness that yet keeps nourishing it. Perhaps in order to answer this we must return to the initial situation. A symbolism that would be only a symbolism of the soul, of the subject, of the "I," is from the start iconoclastic; for it represents a split between the "psychic" function and the other functions of symbol: cosmic, nocturnal, oneiric, poetic. A symbolism of subjectivity already marks the breaking-up of the symbolic totality. A symbol starts to be de-

8. *Ibid.*, p. 38.
9. *Ibid.*

stroyed when it stops playing on several registers: cosmic and existential. The separation of the "human," of the "psychic," is the beginning of forgetfulness. That is why a purely anthropological symbolism is already on the way to allegory and foreshadows an ethical vision of evil and of the world.

Hence we understand that the resistance of symbol to the allegorizing reduction proceeds from the nonethical facet of evil. The Adam symbol is protected against all moralizing reduction by the mass of the other myths; and it is the tragic figure of the serpent at the heart of the Adam symbol that protects it against all moralizing reduction. That is why the myths of evil have to be taken all together; it is their very dialectic that is instructive. Therefore, just as the figure of the serpent, at the center of the Adam myth, counters the demythologization of the Babylonian myths, so, too, original sin marks, within the ethical vision of the world, the resistance of the tragic to the ethical. But is it really the tragic that resists? We should rather say that it is an aspect irreducible to the ethical, and complementary to every ethics, which has found a privileged expression in the tragic. For a tragic anthropology is inseparable, as we have seen, from a tragic theology; and this latter is at bottom unutterable.

Nor can philosophy reaffirm the tragic as such without committing suicide. The function of the tragic is to question self-assurance, self-certitude, one's critical pretensions, we might even say the presumption of the moral conscience that is laden with the entire weight of evil. Much pride is concealed, perhaps, in this humility. It is then that the tragic symbols speak in the silence of the humiliated ethical. They speak of a "mystery of iniquity" that man cannot entirely handle, that freedom cannot give reasons for, seeing that it already finds it within itself. Of this symbol there is no allegorical reduction. But, it will be objected, the tragic symbols speak of a *divine* mystery of evil. Perhaps it is necessary also to envelop in darkness the divine which the ethical vision has reduced to the moralizing function of judge. Against the juridicalism of accusation and justification, the God of Job speaks "out of the whirlwind."

At its base the symbolism of evil is never purely and simply the symbolism of subjectivity, of the separated human subject, of interiorized self-awareness, of man severed from being, but symbol of the union of man with being. One must, then, come to the point where one sees evil as the adventure of being, as part of the history of being.

IV. SPECULATIVE THOUGHT AND ITS FAILURE

IS EVERY POSSIBILITY OF THOUGHT, therefore, extinguished with the nonknowing of the origin of the ground of evil maxims? Does the battle between reflective rigor and symbolic richness cease with the return of the impenetrable symbol of the Fall? I do not think so. For there remains a hiatus between the understanding that we can have of man's essential nature and the avowal of evil's unfathomable contingence. Can one leave side by side the necessity of fallibility and the contingency of evil?

But it seems that we have neglected a whole dimension of the world of mythical symbols, namely, that symbols of the "beginning" receive their complete meaning only from their relations to symbols of the "end": purification of stain, remission of sins, justification of the guilty. The great myths are at once myths of the beginning *and* of the end—thus the victory of Marduk in the Babylonian myth, reconciliation in the tragic and through the tragic, salvation through knowledge of the exiled soul, finally the biblical redemption characterized by the figures of the end: the king of the last times, the suffering servant, the Son of Man, the second Adam, type of the man to come. What is noteworthy in these symbolic representations is that the meaning proceeds from the end to the beginning, from the future to the past. So the question becomes: What does this chain of symbols, this retrograde movement of meaning, *give us to think about?*

Does it not invite us to move from the contingency of evil to a certain "necessity" of evil? This is the greatest task but also the most perilous one for a philosophy nourished by symbols. It is the most perilous task: as we have said above, thought advances between the two chasms of allegory and gnosis. Reflective thought skirts the first chasm, speculative thought the second. Yet it is the greatest task, for the movement which in symbolic thought goes from the beginning of evil to its end seems indeed to suppose the idea that all this finally has a meaning, that a meaningful figure imperiously takes form through the contingency of evil—in short, that evil belongs to a certain totality of the real. A certain necessity . . . a certain totality . . . . But not just any necessity, not just any totality. The schemata of necessity that we can test have to satisfy a very strange demand; the necessity appears only afterwards, viewed from the end, and "in spite of" the contingency of evil.

Saint Paul, it seems, invites such an inquiry when he confronts the two figures, that of the first Adam and that of the second Adam, the type of the old man and the type of the man to come. He does not limit himself to comparing and contrasting them: "Therefore, as by the offense of one *judgment came* upon all men to condemnation; even so by the righteousness of one *the free gift came* upon all men unto justification of life" (Rom. 5:18). In addition to the parallel, there is, from one figure to the other, a movement, a progress, a rise in value: "If through the offense of one many be dead, how much more (πολλῷ μᾶλλον) the grace of God, and the gift by grace, which is by one man, Jesus Christ, hath abounded unto many" (verse 15); "where sin abounded, grace did much more abound" (20). This "how much more," this "superabundance," outlines a great task for thought.

But it must be admitted that no great philosophy of the *totality* is capable of giving an account of this inclusion of the contingency of evil in a meaningful schema. For *either* the thought of necessity leaves contingency aside, *or* it so includes it that it entirely eliminates the "leap" of evil which posits itself and the "tragic" of evil which always precedes itself.

The first case is that of the great nondialectical systems, those of Plotinus and Spinoza, for example. Both knew something of this problem but were unable to account for it within the system. Thus did Plotinus in his last treatises try to account for the "declination" of souls fascinated by their own image in their bodies and make it fit with the necessity of the procession. In *Ennead* IV. 3. 12–18 he tries to reduce the narcissistic seduction that stems from the reflection of the soul in its own body to an impulse by which the soul yields to a universal law: "one would think that it is moved and carried by a magic power of irresistible attraction" (§ 12). Thus evil does not come from us; it exists before us and possesses man in spite of himself (κατέχει οὐχ ἑκόντας). Finally, in the last treatises (III. 2–3) on Providence (πρόνοια), Plotinus reanimates the old theme of λόγος, descended from Heraclitus through the Stoics and Philo, and proclaims that order is born of dissonance and even that order is the reason of disorder (ὅτι τάξις ἀταξία). Thus Providence makes use of evils that it does not produce; in spite of obstacles, harmony is born *nevertheless* (ὅμως). In spite of evil, good prevails.

But who does not see that theodicy never goes beyond the

level of an argumentative and persuasive rhetoric? It is no accident that it has recourse to so many arguments, all the more abundant in proportion to their weakness. For how could thought raise itself to the point of view of the whole and be able to say: "Because there is order, there is disorder"? And if it could, would it not reduce the sorrow of history to a farce, to the sinister farce of a play of light and shadows, or even to an esthetic of discord ("Discord has its beauty"; "Every town must have its tyrant; it is good he is there; he has his place")! Such is the bad faith of theodicy: it does not triumph over real evil but only over its esthetic phantom.

Spinoza will completely disavow this suspect argumentation of theodicy. In a nondialectical philosophy of necessity like his, there is place for finite modes, surely, but not for evil which is an illusion, which stems from the ignorance of the whole. However, even in Spinoza there remains an enigma, which finds its expression in the astonishing axiom of Book IV: "No single thing is given in nature than which there is not given another more powerful. But if anything whatsoever is given, another more powerful, by which the first can be destroyed, is given." As in the last treatises of Plotinus, a law of internal *contrariety* is included in the movement of the expansion or expression of being. But this contrariety is necessary like the movement itself. The contingency of evil, held to in an ethical vision of evil, is not there retained, but dissipated like an illusion.

Will a philosophical *dialectic* of necessity do better justice, so to speak, to the tragic of evil? There is no doubt that it will. That is why a philosophy like Hegel's represents both the greatest *attempt* to account for the *tragic* aspect of history and the greatest *temptation*. The abstraction in which every moral vision of the world takes refuge is done away with. Evil is given its place at the same time that the history of the figures of Spirit starts to unfold. Evil is truly retained and surpassed; conflict is enlisted as instrument of the recognition of consciousnesses; everything takes on meaning; it is necessary to pass through conflict and through the unhappy consciousness, and through the noble soul, and through the Kantian morality, and through the split between the guilty conscience and the judging conscience.[10]

But if evil is acknowledged and integrated in *The Phenomenology of Spirit*, it is so not as evil but as contradiction;

10. G. W. F. Hegel, *The Phenomenology of Mind*, trans. J. B. Baillie (New York: Humanities Press, 1964), in the chaper "Evil and the Forgiveness of It."

its specificity is submerged in a universal function, of which Kierkegaard said that it is the jack-of-all-trades of Hegelianism: *negativity*. Negativity likewise means the inversion of the singular in the universal, the opposition of interior and exterior in force, death, conflict, fault. All negativities are drowned in *the* negativity.

The chapter of the *Phenomenology* entitled "Evil and Forgiveness" leaves no doubt about this. Remission is already reconciliation in absolute knowledge by the passage of one contrary into the other, of singularity into universality, of the judged conscience into the judging conscience and reciprocally. "Pardon" is the destruction of "judgment" as being itself a category of evil and not of salvation. This is indeed very Pauline. The law itself is judged; but at the same time the symbol of the remission of sins is lost, for evil is less "pardoned" than "surpassed"; it disappears in this reconciliation. By the same stroke, the tragic accent is displaced from moral evil to the movement of exteriorization, of alienation (*Entfremdung, Entäusserung*) of Spirit itself. Since human history is a revelation of God, the infinite takes to itself the evil of finitude. As Hyppolite puts it: "The whole long history of errors that human development presents and that the *Phenomenology* retraces is indeed a fall, but we must learn that this fall is part of the absolute itself, that it is a moment of total truth." [11] The all-tragic is the reply of the dissolution of the ethical vision of the world; it comes to achievement in absolute knowledge with the transposition of the remission of sins into philosophical reconciliation. There remains nothing of the injustice of evil nor of the gratuity of reconciliation.

If, then, the nondialectical necessity of Plotinus and Spinoza and the dialectical necessity of Hegel both fail, must we not seek the answer to our quest for intelligibility in *a meaningful history* rather than in a *logic of being*? Does not the movement from the Fall to the Redemption, a movement so full of meaning, exclude a "logic," whether it be nondialectical or dialectical? Is it then possible to conceive of a meaningful history, wherein the contingency of evil and the initiative of conversion would be retained and encompassed? Is it possible to conceive of a

---

11. Jean Hyppolite, *Genèse et structure de la "Phénoménologie de l'Esprit"* (Paris: Aubier, 1946), p. 509. The translation used in the text is taken from the English translation, *Genesis and Structure of "The Phenomenology of the Spirit,"* by John Heckman and Samuel Cherniak (forthcoming from Northwestern University Press).

becoming of being in which the tragic of evil—of this evil always already there—would be both recognized and surmounted?

I am not in a position to answer the question; I glimpse only a possible direction for meditation. I shall say, in closing, what I do perceive. Three formulas present themselves to my mind, which express three connections between the experience of evil and the experience of a reconciliation. First, reconciliation is looked for *in spite of* evil. This "in spite of" constitutes a veritable category of hope, the category which contradicts evil. However, of this there is no proof but only signs; the milieu, the locus, of this category is a history, not a logic; an eschatology, not a system. Next, this "in spite of" is a "thanks to"; out of evil, the Principle of things brings good. The final contradiction of evil is at the same time hidden instruction: *etiam peccata*, says Saint Augustine, as an inscription, as it were, to the *Satin Slipper;* "The worst is never sure," replies Claudel in a litotes; but there is no absolute knowledge of the "in spite of" or of the "thanks to." The third category of this meaningful history is the "how much more," the πολλῷ μᾶλλον. This law of superabundance englobes in its turn the "thanks to" and the "in spite of." That is the miracle of the Logos; from Him proceeds the retrograde movement of the true; from wonder is born the necessity that retroactively places evil in the light of being. What in the old theodicy was only the expedient of false knowledge becomes the understanding of hope. The necessity that we are seeking is the highest rational symbol that this understanding of hope can engender.

The Hermeneutics of Symbols and Philosophical Reflection: II

THE POINT OF DEPARTURE for this second essay arises out of my previous investigation concerning the symbols of evil that are elaborated in the ritual literature, the myths and wisdom, of the ancient Middle East, Israel, and Greece.

Let us remember that that investigation, though it was deliberately confined to a specific problem—the problem of evil —and to a particular region of cultures—those which lie at the root of our Greco-Judaic heritage—actually encompassed a much more general problem: what is the function of the interpretation of symbols in the economy of philosophical reflection? I call this problem, considered in its greatest generality, the hermeneutic problem, if, by hermeneutics, we mean the science of interpretation.

Let us take up the methodological problem more precisely by beginning with those aspects that are peculiar to the symbolism of evil and by showing how such an example can be generalized to all types of religious symbolism.

We saw that if we take the problem of the symbols of evil on the semantic level, i.e., the interpretation of linguistic expressions such as stain, sin, and guilt, our first surprise is to discover that whether evil be passively endured or actively committed, whether it be a question of ethical evil or suffering, the only access to the experience of evil itself is through symbolic expressions. Such expressions emerge from some literal meaning (such as stain or pollution, deviation or wandering in space, and weight or burden, bondage, slavery, fall), and they aim at

Translated by Charles Freilich.

[315]

another meaning which we can call existential, i.e., precisely being impure, sinful, guilty, etc. Although these concepts have a somewhat abstract appearance in our modern languages, they have a symbolic structure in the languages and cultures in which the recognition, or rather the avowal, of evil was first elaborated. The existential signification is here given indirectly, analogically, by means of the primary, literal signification. For this reason, to undergo the experience of evil is also to express it in a language; but furthermore, to express it is already to interpret its symbolic expressions.

Now the semantic level must not be separated from the mythological level of symbols (nor from the dogmatic level of rationalized symbols, which I will not discuss at this time); as we can see in the Babylonian, tragic, and Orphic myths and in the biblical account of the Fall, new aspects of our experience of evil are here manifested and, so to speak, revealed to us. These myths relate our experience to the deeds of paradigmatic figures such as Prometheus, Anthropos, and Adam. Moreover, because they take the form of a story that happened "long ago," *in illo tempore,* they give our experience a certain temporal orientation. They direct it from a beginning toward an end, from memory toward hope. Finally, these myths tell us the story, in the form of a transhistorical event, of the irrational rupture and absurd leap which permit us to relate the confession of our sinful existence to the affirmation of the innocence of our created being. At this level, symbols not only have an expressive value, as on the semantic level, but also an exploratory value, because they confer a universality, a temporality, and an ontological significance on the expressions of evil, such as stain, sin, and guilt.

It is here that the problem arises as to whether there is a necessary connection between the interpretation of symbols and reflection. This question becomes exceedingly acute when we consider that the symbolism of evil is a particular part of religious symbolism in general. One can suppose that the symbolism of evil is always the contrary of a symbolism of the good or salvation or that a symbolism of salvation is the counterpart of a symbolism of evil: the pure corresponds to the impure, forgiveness to sin, freedom to guilt and bondage. In the same manner one must say that there is a correspondence between the imagery of the beginning and the imagery of the end: the king enthroned by Marduk, Apollo and his purification, the new Anthropos, the Messiah, the Just Sufferer, the Son of Man, the Lord

(Kyrios), the Logos, etc. The philosopher, as philosopher, can have nothing to say with regard to the claims of the Gospel, according to which these figures are "fulfilled" with the coming of Christ; but, as philosopher, he can and must reflect on the meaning of these symbols insofar as they stand as representations of the End of Evil. We thus reach the general level of our question. The hermeneutics of evil appears as a particular domain that lies at the heart of a general interpretation of religious symbolism. For the moment we shall consider the symbolism of evil only as the inverse of a religious symbolism. We shall ultimately see, however, that the hermeneutics of evil is not an indifferent domain but the most significant domain, perhaps the very source of the hermeneutic problem itself.

Why, then, is there a problem for the philosopher? The reason is that there is something astonishing and even scandalous about the use of symbols.

1. The symbol remains opaque, not transparent, since it is given by means of an analogy based on a literal signification. The symbol is thus endowed with concrete roots and a certain material density and opacity.

2. The symbol is a prisoner of the diversity of languages and cultures and, for this reason, remains contingent: Why *these* symbols rather than any others?

3. The symbol is given to thought only by way of an interpretation which remains inherently problematical. There is no myth without exegesis, no exegesis without contestation. The deciphering of mysteries is not a science in either the Platonic or Hegelian sense or in the modern meaning of the word science. Opacity, cultural contingency, and dependency on a problematical interpretation—such are the three deficiencies of the symbol as measured by the ideal of clarity, necessity, and scientific order in reflection.

In addition, there does not exist a general hermeneutics, that is, a general theory of interpretation, a general canon for exegesis; there are only various separate and contrasting hermeneutic theories. Thus, our initial problem continues to become more and more complicated. It is no longer simple but double; we must ask not only why reflection requires interpretation but also why it requires conflicting interpretations.

The first part of this essay will be devoted to the most extreme opposition in the field of hermeneutics, the opposition between the phenomenology of religion and the psychoanalytical interpretation of religion. In the process, our task will be to show the necessity of such an opposition within a philosophy of reflection.

I. The Conflict between Interpretations

I PROPOSE TO EMPHASIZE three themes that represent, in my opinion, the principal presuppositions of the phenomenology of religion. I shall contrast these three themes with the three working hypotheses of psychoanalysis with regard to the religious phenomenon.

The first characteristic of the phenomenology of religion is that its aim is descriptive, not explanatory. To explain the religious phenomenon means to relate it to its causes, its origin, or its function, whether this be a psychological, sociological, or any other type of function. To describe the religious phenomenon means to relate it to its object as this object is intended and given in cult and faith, in ritual and myth. What are the implications of this initial distinction with regard to the problem of symbols? We could say that the theme of the phenomenology of religion is the "something" that is intended in ritual action, mythical speech, and mystical feeling. Our task is to extract this "object" from the multiple intentionalities of behavior, discourse, and emotion. Let us call this intended object the "sacred" without making any claims as to its precise nature. In this general sense, we shall say that every phenomenology of religion is a phenomenology of the "sacred," and in this way we emphasize its concern for the intentional object.

To this first characteristic we shall presently oppose the corresponding characteristic of Freudian hermeneutics, the definition of the religious phenomenon in terms of its economic function, not in terms of its intentional object.

The second characteristic of the phenomenology of religion is that there is a "truth" of symbols, a truth in the sense which Husserl gives to this word in the *Logical Investigations*, a truth which signifies the fulfillment—*die Erfüllung*—of the signifying intention.

What does this mean in relation to the symbols of the sacred? In the same manner in which we have opposed understanding in terms of the object to explanation in terms of the cause, we shall now make use of the distinction between symbol and sign in order to suggest the essential fullness or plenitude of symbols. For the first characteristic of the function of the sign (the semiotic function) is the arbitrary nature of the convention which links the signifier to the signified, but an essential characteristic of the symbol is the fact that it is never completely arbitrary. It is not empty; rather, there always remains the trace of a natural relationship between the signifier and the signified, as in the analogy that we have suggested between the existential experience of impurity and the actual physical stain or blemish. In the same manner, to take an example from the work of Mircea Eliade, the force of cosmic symbolism lies in the non-arbitrary relationship between the visible sky and the invisible order which it manifests: the sky *speaks* of wisdom and justice, of immensity and order, by virtue of the analogical power of its primary signification. Such is the fullness of the symbol as opposed to the essential emptiness of the sign.

To this second characteristic we shall later oppose that characteristic of psychoanalytical interpretation which Freud calls "illusion," as in his famous title *The Future of an Illusion.*

This leads to a third aspect of hermeneutics, which has to do with the ontological significance of the symbols of the sacred. The concern for the object, which was our first point, and the concern for the fullness of symbols, which was our second point, already suggest a certain type of ontological understanding. This understanding achieves its culminating expression in Heidegger's philosophy of language, according to which symbols are like a voice of Being. Ultimately, it is this philosophy of language that is implicit in the phenomenology of religion. It reveals that language is less spoken *by* men than spoken *to* men, that men are born at the heart of language within the light of the Logos "which illuminates each man who enters the world." In this sense, the implicit philosophy of the phenomenology of religion is a renewal of the [Platonic] theory of recollection. The modern concern for symbols implies a new contact with the sacred, a movement beyond the forgetfulness of Being which is today manifested in the manipulation of empty signs and formalized languages.

To this third and final characteristic we shall oppose the Freudian thesis of the "return of the repressed."

LET US NOW LEAP OVER the apparently unbridgeable gap which divides the hermeneutic field into a psychoanalytical and a phenomenological conception of symbolism. I shall not attempt to conceal or gloss over this conflict. In the same way in which I have radicalized the implicit philosophy of the first system of interpretation, I would now like to confront the interpretation which stands directly opposed to this ontology of the sacred. Dismissing those more reassuring and conciliatory interpretations of religion that have been proposed by certain schools of psychoanalysis, I would prefer to deal with the most decisive and radical interpretation of them all, that of Freud himself. Ultimately, he remains the master, and it is with him that we must "explain" ourselves.

We shall first oppose the functional interpretation of religion in psychoanalysis to the object-oriented interpretation of religion in phenomenology; then we shall oppose the idea of "illusion" to that of "truth" (in the sense of the "fullness" of symbols); and finally, we shall oppose the theme of the "return of the repressed" to the "recollection of the sacred."

What do we mean by a *functional* approach as opposed to an object-oriented approach? First of all, the interpretation of religion takes place within the general framework of a theory of culture. When Freud undertakes to interpret civilization as a whole, he does not go outside the limits of psychoanalysis; on the contrary, he is manifesting its ultimate intention to be a general hermeneutics of culture, not only a branch of psychiatry. This is the reason why psychoanalysis covers the same domain as the other hermeneutics. There is no way to distinguish the various hermeneutic perspectives with regard to their domain, for each one of them embraces the whole of man and each claims to interpret and understand the totality of man's being. If there is a limit to psychoanalytical interpretation, we must look for it not in its object but in its point of view. The psychoanalytical point of view is that of an "economy" of instincts or drives [*pulsions*], a balance of renunciations and satisfactions—satisfactions that may be real, deferred, substituted, or purely fictional.

Thus, it is necessary to begin with the most comprehensive phenomenon, that of "civilization," and then inscribe within it the religious phenomenon in the form of illusion. When Freud undertakes in *The Future of an Illusion* to grasp the phenomenon of civilization in its entirety, he approaches the problem in terms of three questions. To what extent is it possible to reduce the burden of instinctual sacrifices that are imposed upon men? How is it possible to reconcile men to those renunciations that are both unavoidable and necessary? How can satisfactory compensations be offered for these sacrifices? We must understand that these questions that we are asking and that Freud himself asked are not questions *about* civilization but that, in effect, they constitute civilization itself, both in its intentions and its expectations. Thus, the problem of civilization is immediately taken up within the context of an economic point of view. Religion has to deal with these three questions. First of all, it can be said that religion reduces the neurotic burden of the individual by relieving him of his individual guilt with the idea of a substitutive sacrifice (we shall later see how the individual is protected from individual neurosis only at the price of collective neurosis). In addition, religion functions as a consolation, as an aid in reconciling the individual to the necessity of sacrifice. And finally, religion provides the individual with a multitude of pleasures that can be considered as sublimations of the instincts, of fundamental eros.

At this point it is necessary to oppose the psychoanalytical theory of *illusion* to the phenomenological theory of "truth," i.e., truth in the sense of "fulfillment" or "plenitude." In Freud this notion of illusion has a functional metapsychological meaning and must be taken seriously as such. We cannot avoid the problem by saying that the statement that religion is an illusion is nonanalytical or preanalytical and that it merely reflects the prejudices of a modern scientism, heir to Epicurean "skepticism" and eighteenth-century rationalism. What is important here, what is novel about the Freudian point of view, is precisely its "economic" interpretation of "illusion." The question is not that of the "truth" in the phenomenological sense but that of the function of religious representations in the balance of renunciations and satisfactions by means of which man tries to sustain his life. The key to "illusion" is the harshness of life: life is difficult to bear for a being who not only understands and suffers but is eager for some form of consolation by virtue of his innate narcissism. Now civilization, as we have seen, has the task not only of restraining the instincts but also of protecting man against the overwhelming forces of nature. "Illusion" is this other method which civilization employs when the struggle against nature fails; it invents gods in order to exorcise fear, to reconcile man to the cruelty of fate, and to compensate him for the feeling of "malaise" which the death instinct renders incurable.

We are now reaching the most extreme point of conflict between psychoanalysis and phenomenology. We have projected onto the latter the light of an ontological understanding, according to which all understanding ultimately implies a pre-comprehension of Being; the interpretation of the symbolism of the sacred has appeared in this context as the renewal of the ancient doctrine of recollection. There is also a concept of "recollection" in psychoanalysis, but it emerges along the lines of a genesis of the religious illusion, having its source in those symbols and images in which the initial conflicts of primitive men and children first come to be expressed. From a methodological point of view, this part of our analysis is important, for it is at this point that the genetic explanation is incorporated in the topical and economic explanation. If religious representations in fact have no truth and are merely illusions, then they can only be understood in terms of their origin. Accordingly, *Totem and Taboo* and *Moses and Monotheism* reconstruct the historical memories which constitute the "truth in religion" (according to a subhead in *Moses and Monotheism*); this truth consists in those originary representations which lie at the root of the ideational distortion. I will not refer here to the well-known account of this genesis: the murder of the father, the institution of the laws of incest and exogamy by the community of brothers, the restoration of the image of the father in the substituted form of the totemic animal, the ritual repetition of the murder of the father during the totemic feast, the reappearance of the father figure in the figures of the gods, etc. I will merely emphasize one fundamental aspect of this genetic explanation. Religion as we know it today is a reappearance, in the form of fantasy, of forgotten images of the human past and the individual past. This return of the forgotten, in the form of religious fantasy, can be compared to the return of the repressed in the obsessional neurotic. Such a comparison between the regeneration of religious symbolism and the return of the repressed provides the opportunity to consider once again that rupture in the hermeneutic field which we have previously discussed. Recollection of the sacred, in the sense of an ontology of the symbol, and the return of the repressed, in the sense of an etiology of fantasies, together constitute the two poles of a dynamic tension.

II. THE HERMENEUTIC POLARITY

MY PROBLEM IS NOW THE FOLLOWING: How can these two hermeneutics, opposed as they are, coexist? My hypothesis is that each is legitimate within its own context. We cannot, of course, content ourselves with a simple juxtaposition of these two styles of interpretation; it is necessary to set up a dialogue between them and demonstrate their complementary functions. We shall look for a provisional answer to our problem in the relationship between consciousness and the unconscious. It might be objected that this manner of approaching the problem is itself derivative of one of the two systems of interpretation, that of psychoanalysis, and I would certainly agree. I believe, nevertheless, that after Freud's work it is no longer possible to speak of consciousness in the same way that we did before. Moreover, if a new concept of consciousness must be found, perhaps we can at the same time discover a new connection between this consciousness and what we have called the manifestation or even the recollection of the sacred. Consciousness is not the first reality which we can know but the last. We must arrive at it, not begin with it. And since consciousness is the place where the two interpretations of the symbol come together, a double approach to the notion of consciousness should be a good way of also gaining access to the polarity of symbols.

The principal motive which animates the analytical attempt to demystify is the desire to contest the privileged status of consciousness.[1] It is on the basis of this critique of what could be called "the illusion of consciousness" that we can understand the methodological decision to move away from a description of consciousness to a topography of psychic structure. The philosopher must admit that the recourse to these naturalistic models takes on its true meaning from the tactic of decentering and dispossession directed against the illusion of consciousness, which is itself rooted in narcissism.

At the same time, however, we can readily understand that the source of meaning can be displaced or decentered in another manner. The topographical and economic point of view has not suppressed all other forms of interrogation but has rather renewed them. The very concept of the "unconscious" itself reminds us of its intimate connection to consciousness: consciousness has not been abolished, either theoretically or practically.

Thus, an interpretation which began by abandoning the point of view of consciousness does not serve to eliminate conscious-

---

1. I have commented elsewhere on Freud's famous text which situates the psychoanalytic movement in the continuing progress of both the Copernican and Darwinian revolutions; cf. above, pp. 151–52.

ness but in fact radically renews its meaning. What is definitely denied is not consciousness but its pretension to know itself completely from the very beginning, its narcissism. We must reach that point of confusion where we no longer know what consciousness means in order to recover the sense of consciousness as that mode of existence which has the unconscious as its other. This shift in our analysis is decisive, for it is this dialectical relation between the unconscious and consciousness which governs the articulation of a relation between the two hermeneutics.

Let us now consider this new approach to consciousness. Everything that we can say about consciousness after Freud seems to be included in the formula: "Consciousness is not immediate, but mediate; it is not a source, but a task, the task of becoming more conscious." We come to understand this formula when we oppose the function of consciousness to the tendency toward repetition and regression which is implicit in the Freudian interpretation of illusion. The later works of Freud, in particular, emphasize the theme of the return of the repressed and the endless reenactment of the primal murder of the father; the interpretation of religion becomes more and more an occasion for emphasizing the regressive tendency in the history of humanity.

Consequently, the problem of consciousness seems to me to be related to this question: How does a man emerge from his childhood, how does he become an adult? At first sight this seems to be a purely psychological question, since it is the theme of every genetic psychology and every theory of the personality. But in fact it takes on its true meaning when we begin to examine which figures, which images and symbols, guide this growth, this maturation of the individual. I believe that this indirect manner of approaching the problem is more revealing than a direct psychology of growth. Growth itself here appears as the intersection of two systems of interpretation.

At this point another type of hermeneutics is required, one whose way of decentering the nucleus of meaning is different from that of psychoanalysis. It is not within consciousness itself that the key to understanding resides; we must discover new figures, new symbols, which are irreducible to those that are rooted in the libidinal ground. These figures and symbols draw consciousness forward out of its own infancy. After Freud, the only possible philosophy of consciousness would be one that is related to the Hegelian phenomenology of Spirit.[2] In this phenomenology immediate consciousness does not know itself. To employ once again our previous mode of expression, I will say that man becomes adult, becomes "conscious," if and when he becomes capable of these new figures, the succession of which constitutes "Spirit" in the Hegelian sense of the word. An exegesis of consciousness would involve an inventory and a step-by-step constitution of the spheres of meaning which consciousness must encounter and appropriate for itself so as to reflect upon itself as a self, as an adult, human, ethical self. Such a process is by no means a type of introspection or immediate consciousness; it is by no means a figure of narcissism, for the nucleus of the self is not a psychological *ego* but Spirit, that is, the dialectic of the figures themselves. "Consciousness" is only the interiorization of this movement, a movement which must be rediscovered in the objective structure of institutions, monuments, works of art, and culture.

LET US PAUSE FOR A MOMENT to consider the results of this analysis. We have reached the provisional conclusion that the meaning of consciousness is never given within a psychology of consciousness but only by means of a detour through several metapsychologies which displace the center of reference, either toward the concept of the "unconscious" in Freudian metapsychology or toward the concept of "Spirit" in Hegelian metapsychology.

The two types of hermeneutics which we have described in the first part of this essay rest on this polarity of "metapsychologies." The opposition between *the unconscious* and *Spirit* is expressed in the very duality of these interpretations. The two sciences of interpretation represent two contrary movements: an analytical and regressive movement toward the unconscious and a synthetic and progressive movement toward Spirit. On the one hand, in Hegelian phenomenology, every figure receives its meaning from the one that follows it: Stoicism is the truth of the mutual recognition of master and slave, but skepticism, which destroys the distinction between master and slave, is the truth of the Stoic position, etc. The truth of one moment resides in the subsequent moment; intelligibility always

2. [The English translation of Hegel's *Geist* as "mind" already too thoroughly subjectifies Ricoeur's interpretation. Thus "Spirit" will be used here.—TRANS.]

proceeds from the end to the beginning. This is the reason why we can say that consciousness is a task, that it is ultimately complete and secure only when it comes to an end. On the other hand, the concept of the unconscious signifies that understanding always proceeds from figures that are prior to it; man is the only being who remains the victim of his childhood for such a long period of time; man is that being who is always drawn back toward his own infancy. The unconscious is thus the principle of all regressions and all stagnation. As a result, we could say in very general terms that Spirit is the order of the ultimate, whereas the unconscious is the order of the primordial. This is the reason why the same play of symbols can support two types of interpretation; the one is oriented toward the emergence of figures that are always "behind" us, while the second is oriented toward the emergence of figures that are always "ahead" of us. The exact same symbols are endowed with these two dimensions and offer themselves to these two opposing interpretations.

III. REFLECTION AND INTERPRETATION

IT IS NOW TIME TO POSE the basic question which we left in suspense. If philosophy is reflection, as we said at the beginning, why must reflection have recourse to a symbolic language? Why must reflection become interpretation? Apparently we must go back and try to elaborate a concept of reflection, which until now has remained a simple presupposition.

When we say that philosophy is reflection, we mean this in the sense of reflection on *itself*. But what do we mean by the self? I will admit here that the positing of the self is the first truth for philosophy, at least for that vast tradition of modern philosophy which begins with Descartes and develops with Kant, Fichte, and the whole reflective current of Continental philosophy. For this tradition (which we are here considering as a whole before distinguishing among its principal representatives) the positing of the self is a truth which posits itself. Incapable of being either verified or deduced, it is simultaneously the positing of a being and an act, a form of existence and an operation of thought: I am, I think; to exist for myself is to think; I exist insofar as I think. Since this truth can be neither verified as a fact nor deduced as a conclusion, it must be posited in reflection; its own self-positing is reflection. Fichte termed this first truth the thetic judgment. Such is our philosophical point of departure.

But the first reference to the positing of the Self as existing and thinking is not sufficient to characterize reflection. In particular, we do not yet understand why reflection requires the work of deciphering, an exegesis and a science of exegesis or hermeneutics. Even less do we understand why this interpretation must be either a psychoanalysis or a phenomenology of the sacred. This point cannot be understood so long as reflection appears as a return to the so-called evidence of immediate consciousness. We must introduce a second characteristic of reflection, which may be stated in this way: *reflection is not intuition;* or, in positive terms: reflection is the effort to recomprehend the *ego* of the *ego cogito* in the mirror of its objects, it works, and ultimately its acts. Now, why must the positing of the *ego* be recomprehended through its acts? Precisely because the *ego* is not given in psychological evidence or in intellectual intuition or in mystical vision. A reflective philosophy is precisely the opposite of a philosophy of the immediate. The first truth—*I think, I am*—remains as abstract and empty as it is unassailable. It must be "mediated" by representations, actions, works, institutions, and monuments which objectify it; it is in these objects, in the largest sense of the word, that the *ego* must both lose itself and find itself. We can say that a philosophy of reflection is not a philosophy of consciousness if, by consciousness, we mean immediate self-consciousness. Consciousness is a task, we said before, but it is a task precisely because it is not a given. There is no doubt that I have an apperception of myself and my acts and that this apperception is a type of evidence. Descartes cannot be dislodged from this incontestable proposition. I cannot doubt myself without observing that I am doubting. But what is the meaning of this apperception? It is an undeniable certitude, but a certitude without any truth value. As Malebranche well understood, as opposed to Descartes, this immediate grasp of myself is only a feeling and not an idea. If the idea is understood essentially in terms of light and vision, there is neither a vision of the *ego* nor a light of apperception; I merely *feel* that I exist and that I think. The mere feeling that I am awake is the essence of apperception. In Kantian terms, an apperception of the *ego* can accompany all of my representations, but this apperception is not self-knowledge. It cannot be transformed into an intuition concerning a substantial soul. Finally, reflection is completely separated from all knowledge of the self by the decisive Kantian criticism directed at every "rational psychology."

This second proposition, that reflection is not intuition, permits us to adumbrate the role of *interpretation* in knowledge of the self; this role is reciprocally designated precisely by the difference between *reflection* and *intuition*.

A new step will bring us closer to our goal: having opposed reflection to intuition (following Kant as opposed to Descartes), I would now like to distinguish the task of reflection from a simple critique of knowledge. This new approach will move us away from Kant in the direction of Fichte. The fundamental limitation of a critical philosophy lies in its exclusive concern for epistemology; reflection is thereby reduced to a single dimension. The only canonical operations of thought are those which found the "objectivity" of our representations. This priority given to epistemology explains why, in Kant's philosophy, in spite of all appearances, practical philosophy remains subordinate to theoretical philosophy. Kant's second *Critique*, in fact, borrows all of its structures from the first. The single dominating question of all critical philosophy is: what is *a priori* and what is empirical in knowledge? This distinction, the key to the theory of objectivity, is purely and simply transposed in the second *Critique*. The objectivity of the maxims of the will rests on the distinction between the validity of duty, which is *a priori,* and the content of empirical desires.

It is against this reduction of reflection to a simple critique that I maintain, along with Fichte and his French successor, Jean Nabert, that reflection is less a justification of science and duty than it is a reappropriation of our effort to exist. Epistemology is only a part of this much broader task. We must recover the sense of existential activity, the positing of the self within all the density of its works. Now, why is it necessary to characterize this recovery as an appropriation and even as a reappropriation? I must recover something which has first been lost. I "appropriate" that which is "proper" to me, that which has ceased to be mine. I make "mine" that from which I am separated by space or time, by distraction or "diversion," or by virtue of some guilty act of forgetting. The concept of appropriation signifies that the original situation from which reflection proceeds is "forgetfulness"; I am lost, "astray" among the objects of the world, separated from the center of my own existence, just as I am separated from others and the enemy of all. Whatever may be the secret of this separation, this *diaspora,* it signifies that

I do not originally possess that which I am. The truth which Fichte called "thetic judgment" is situated in the emptiness of an absence from myself. This is why reflection is a task—an *Aufgabe*—the task of equating my concrete experience with the affirmation: *I am.* Such is the final elaboration of our initial proposition that reflection is not intuition. We can now say: the positing of the self is not a given, it is a *task;* it is not *gegeben* but *aufgegeben.*

One might ask whether we have not overemphasized the practical and ethical side of reflection. Is this not a new limitation, comparable to the epistemological emphasis of Kantian philosophy? Moreover, are we not now more distant than ever from the problem of interpretation? I do not think so. The emphasis placed on the ethical side of reflection is not a limitation if we understand the notion of ethics in its broadest sense, much in the manner of Spinoza, who referred to "ethics" as the total project of philosophy.

Philosophy is ethical insofar as it transforms alienation into freedom and beauty; for Spinoza, this conversion is attained when knowledge of the self becomes equivalent to knowledge of the unique substance; but this speculative process has an ethical meaning insofar as the alienated individual is transformed by this knowledge of the whole. Philosophy is ethics; but ethics is not purely concerned with morals. If we follow this Spinozistic usage of the word "ethics," we must say that reflection is ethical before it becomes a critique of morality. Its goal is to grasp the *ego* in its effort to exist, in its desire to be. It is here that a reflective philosophy rediscovers and perhaps preserves both the Platonic idea that the source of knowledge is itself *eros*, desire, or love, and the Spinozistic idea that it is *conatus*, effort. This effort is a desire because it is never satisfied; but conversely, this desire is an effort because it is the affirmation of a unique being, not simply a lack of being. Effort and desire are the two aspects of this positing of the self in the first truth: I am.

We are now ready to complete our negative proposition—reflection is not intuition—with a positive proposition—*reflection is the appropriation of our effort to exist and our desire to be by means of works which testify to this effort and this desire.* This is why reflection is more than a simple critique of moral judgment; prior to any critique of judgment, it reflects on this activity of existence which we manifest in both our effort and in our desire.

This third approach has led us to the threshold of our

problem of interpretation. We suspect now that effort and desire are not only deprived of all intuitive knowledge but are affirmed only by works whose meaning remains uncertain and revocable. Reflection here appeals to interpretation and seeks to transform itself into hermeneutics. Such is the ultimate root of our problem; it resides in this primitive connection between our activity of existence and the signs which we manifest in our works; reflection must become interpretation, for I can grasp the activity of existence only through those signs that are scattered through the world. This is why a reflective philosophy must include the results of the methods and presuppositions of all the sciences that attempt to decipher and interpret the signs of man.

IV. JUSTIFICATION OF THE HERMENEUTIC CONFLICT

ONE ENORMOUS DIFFICULTY REMAINS; we understand that reflection must find its way among symbols which constitute an opaque language, symbols that belong to the uniqueness and contingency of different cultures and which give rise to equivocal interpretations. But why must these signs be interpreted as symbols *of* the sacred or manifestations *of* the unconscious? Moreover, neither the realism of the unconscious in psychoanalysis nor the transcendence of the sacred in the phenomenology of religion seems to be well suited to reflective method. Is not reflection a method of immanence? Must it not resist a transcendence from above as much as a transcendence from below? How can it include this double transcendence?

The two interpretations that we have tried to set in a kind of confrontation or dialogue have at least one trait in common: both of them reduce the status of consciousness and displace the source of meaning. A philosophy of reflection not only understands this decentering but requires it. The problem would be resolved if we understood *why reflection implies both an archaeology and an eschatology of consciousness.*

Let us consider in succession the two sides of the question. Reflection requires a reductive and destructive interpretation because consciousness is originally false consciousness, "the pretension to self-knowledge." A connection is immediately apparent between the task of becoming conscious and the type of demystification of false consciousness that psychoanalysis elucidates. The importance of this demystification appears in its full significance when we place Freud himself among the great masters of "suspicion," from de la Rochefoucauld to Nietzsche and Marx. The closeness of the relationship between Freud and Nietzsche is perhaps the most illuminating: for both of them, it is not consciousness which is the original given, but false consciousness, prejudice, illusion, and for this reason consciousness must be interpreted. Nietzsche was the first to make a connection between suspicion and interpretation. From German philology he borrowed the concept of *Deutung*, exegesis or interpretation, and he extended it to the dimensions of the philosophical knowledge of the "will to power." It is not by accident that the same concept of *Deutung* reappears in Freud's work in the title and in the content of his great work *Die Traumdeutung—The Interpretation of Dreams*. In both cases, the problem is to oppose to the ruse of the will to power, or the *libido,* the ruse of deciphering enigmas and the great art of suspicion. "Consciousness" of the self must become "knowledge" of the self, i.e., indirect, mediate, and suspicious knowledge of the self. In this manner, reflection is disassociated from all immediate consciousness. Such immediate consciousness offers itself to be explicated as a pure symptom and to be interpreted by an external observer. If consciousness is primarily false consciousness, reflection must accept this decentering of consciousness. It must, in the words of the Bible, first lose itself in order to find itself.

Let us now consider the other interpretation, that of the phenomenology of religion. We understand now why it must take the form of a restoration of the sacred. We have previously characterized the order of Spirit in opposition to the order of the unconscious. We have said that Spirit, according to the profound insight of Hegel, is a progressive and synthetic movement through various figures or stages, in which the truth of one moment resides in the truth of the following moment. For this reason, we noted, consciousness is a task and is never complete and fulfilled until it comes to an end, whatever this end may be. Spirit is the order of the ultimate, the unconscious is the order of the primordial. Thus, the meaning of consciousness is not in itself but in Spirit, that is, in the succession of figures that draw consciousness forward away from itself.

An ambiguity now appears in our meditation. We have felt that the progressive unfolding of figures that we have called "Spirit" does not attain the level of a phenomenology of religion. Between the figures of Spirit and the symbols of the sacred there is a serious ambiguity. I shall not deny this. I myself, however, see the articulation between the phenomenology of religion, with its symbols of the sacred, and the phenomenology of Spirit, with its figures of historical cultures, as the point where Hegel failed. For Hegel, as we know, an end is given to this progression of figures, and this end is absolute knowledge. Would it not be possible to say, however, that the end is not absolute knowledge, that is, the completion of all reflections in a whole, in an all-inclusive totality, but rather that the end is only a *promise*, promised through the symbols of the sacred. For me, the sacred thus takes the place of absolute knowledge, though it is not merely its substitute. The meaning of the sacred remains eschatological and can never be transformed into knowledge or gnosis. I would like to show that this impossibility is not arbitrary.

One of the reasons why I do not think that absolute knowledge is possible is precisely because of the problem of evil, the problem which was our original point of departure and which then appeared to us to be merely an occasion for posing the problem of symbolism and hermeneutics. At the end of this discussion, we discovered that the great symbols concerning the nature, the beginning, and the end of evil are not ordinary symbols but are endowed with a certain privileged status. If we are concerned with extending the scope of the problem of symbols, it does not suffice to say, as we have shown, that evil is merely the inverse of good or that all symbolism of evil is the counterpart of a symbolism of the good. These symbols teach us something decisive with regard to the transition from a phenomenology of Spirit to a phenomenology of the sacred. These symbols, in fact, are resistant to any reduction to rational knowledge. The failure of all theodicies, of all systems that attempt to deal with the problem of evil, is testimony to the failure of absolute knowledge in the Hegelian sense. All symbols invite thought, but the symbols of evil demonstrate in an exemplary manner that there is always something more in myths and symbols than in all of our philosophy and that, hence, a philosophical interpretation of symbols will never become absolute knowledge. The symbols of evil, in which we can read the limits of our own existence, announce at the very same time the limits of all systems of thought which would try to incorporate these symbols in an *absolute knowledge*. This is one of the reasons, perhaps the most striking, why no absolute knowledge but only the *symbols of the sacred* lie beyond the figures of Spirit. I will say that these figures are summoned by the sacred through the medium of signs. The signs of the summons are just as much given in the context of history, but the summons itself designates the other, that which is other than all history. We might say that these symbols are the prophecy of consciousness. They manifest the dependence of the self on an absolute source of existence and meanings, on an *eschaton,* an ultimate end toward which all the figures of Spirit point.

We can now conclude our discussion. We could fully understand the problem of hermeneutics if we could grasp the double dependence of the self on the unconscious and on the sacred, since this double dependence is manifested only in a symbolic mode. In order to elucidate this double dependence, reflection must reduce the status of consciousness and interpret it in terms of the symbolic meanings that approach it from behind and ahead, from above and below. In short, reflection must embrace both an archaeology and an eschatology.

Within this philosophical foundation, the two opposing interpretations of religion with which we began no longer appear to us to be a mere accident of modern cultural history but a necessary opposition which reflection comprehends. As Bergson and others have said, there are two sources of morality and religion. On the one hand, religion is idolatry, falsity, fabulation, illusion; ancient poetry tells us that it is fear which originally created the gods. We understand, in the full sense of the word, that religion depends on an "archaeology" of consciousness to the extent to which it is a projection of an ancient destiny, both ancestral and infantile. This is why the interpretation of religion first takes the form of a demystification. It has been observed that Freud never speaks of God but only of the gods of men. And, in truth, we have never wholly rid ourselves of these gods.

But I understand this demystification to be the inverse of a renewal of the signs of the sacred, those signs which are the prophecy of consciousness. This prophecy of consciousness, however, always remains ambiguous and equivocal; we are never certain that a given symbol of the sacred is not also a "return of the repressed"; or rather, it is certain that every symbol of the Sacred is also simultaneously a return of the repressed, the reemergence of both an ancient and an infantile symbol. The two symbolisms are intermingled. There is always some trace of archaic myth which is grafted to and operates within the most prophetic meanings of the sacred. The progressive order of symbols is not exterior to the regressive order of fantasies; the plunge into the archaic mythologies of the unconscious brings to the surface new signs of the sacred. The eschatology of consciousness is always a creative repetition of its own archaeology.

Was it not Freud who said: *Wo es war, soll ich werden*— Where id was, there ego shall be?

The Demythization of Accusation

I WANT TO TAKE UP today, from the standpoint of *accusation*, that is, from the standpoint of consciousness[1] when *judging*, the question of evil which I have elsewhere discussed from the standpoint of avowal, that is, from the standpoint of consciousness as *judged*.

This new approach will allow me to return to the question of guilt, where I left it at the end of my book, *The Symbolism of Evil*. It will allow me to introduce new points which my more recent reading of Freud has helped me discover.

It seems to me that the question of accusation—more precisely, the question of the accusatory agency—helps bring out the double function of demythization.[2] On the one hand, demythization recognizes myth as myth but with the purpose of renouncing it. In this sense we must speak of demystification. The result of this renunciation is the gaining of a thought and a will which are no longer alienated. The positive side of this destruction is the manifestation of man as maker of his own human existence. It is an anthropogenesis. On the other hand, demythization is recognizing myth as myth but with the purpose of freeing its symbolic basis. In this sense we must speak of demythologization. What is deconstructed here is not so much

Translated by Peter McCormick.

1. [Although *conscience*, in the expressions *conscience jugée* and *conscience jugéante*, carries the senses of both "conscience" and "consciousness," we have used the latter term, to retain the sense of an analysis of the subject in keeping with Ricoeur's broader problematic.—ED.]

2. ["Agency" is the translation used in the Standard Edition of Freud's works for *Instanz*, French *instance*.—ED.]

myth as the secondary rationalization that holds it captive, the pseudo-logos of myth. The result of this discovery is the gaining of the revealing power that myth conceals under the mask of objectification. The positive side of this destruction is the establishing of human existence on the basis of an origin which it does not have at its command but which is announced to it symbolically in a word which founds it.

I propose to apply this hypothesis of a *double demythization* to the agency of accusation.

But the philosopher cannot be content with a superficial eclectic juxtaposition of the two modalities of demythization. He must construct the relationship between them. He must, therefore, determine what problematic will provide a basis for systematically articulating demystification and demythologization, the renunciation of myth and the reconquest of myth on its symbolic base.

What is this properly philosophical problematic which must regulate our working hypothesis here? It is not, I think, what the entire Kantian tradition calls moral obligation in its double aspect of formalism and constraint. This double elimination of desire, as both foreign to the pure form of duty and rebellious to commandment, seems to me the major illusion of Kantian ethics. I would like to associate and incorporate the double movement of demythization—the renunciation of the fable and the reconquest of the symbol—into a reflective work aimed at disengaging the *originary question of ethics*. It is this reflective work which will enable us to hold the two movements of demythization together.

In part I, I will look for the properly philosophical bearing of a destructive hermeneutics applied to the theme of accusation, and I will show that what can and must be demystified is the false transcendence of the imperative. Thus the horizon will be freed for a more primordial interrogation, a more fundamental one, which will discover the essence of ethics in our desire to be, in our effort to exist.

In part II, I will look for the properly philosophical bearing of a positive hermeneutics, and I will show that what the philosopher can understand of a kerygma of salvation is less concerned with the commandment that oppresses us than with the desire that constitutes us. The ethics of desire thus gains an articulation, a focus, and a philosophical basis for the double process of demythization.

Only then, and this will be part III, will we be able to ask ourselves what becomes of the avowal of evil when accusation has been subjected to demystification and when the ethical problem has been placed again in the light of a kerygma which does not condemn but which calls to life.

I. The Demystification of Accusation

As a result of the Hegelian critique of the ethical view of the world, there is constituted what can be called an accusation of accusation. This critique is developed through Feuerbach, Marx, Nietzsche, and Freud.

Because of my previous studies, I will limit myself here to the Freudian critique. My purpose, however, is not to remain there but to use it to initiate a critique of Kant's views on obligation. What I want to retain from the enormous Freudian corpus which runs from *Totem and Taboo* to *Civilization and Its Discontents* is the responding encounter between the psychoanalysis of the superego and the critique of obligation. I will begin with the methodological divorce between Freud and Kant.

The basic gain of psychoanalysis is, I think, its inauguration of what seems impossible, that is, of a genealogy of the so-called principle of morality. Where the Kantian method discerns a primitive and irreducible structure, another method discerns a derived and acquired agency. What is primary—and this is what "principle" means—for a regressive analysis of the formal conditions of the good will is no longer primary for another type of analysis. But this other method, which is also called analysis, is no longer a reflection on conditions of possibility but an interpretation, a hermeneutics of the figures in which the agency of the judging consciousness invests itself.

Let us understand this point well. If I say that accusation is what is unspoken in obligation, that accusation is what is understood in obligation, then this "unspoken" and this "understood" are not accessible to any kind of direct analysis. This proposition, rather, is an interpretation, a hermeneutic proposition. It presupposes that a method of deciphering drawn from philology and exegesis is substituted for the formal method borrowed from the axiomatization of the knowledge of nature. Kantianism proceeds from a categorial analysis, Freudianism from a philological one. This is why what is primary for one can be something derived for the other, why what is principle for one can be genealogy for the other. One cannot, therefore, separate the Freudian genealogy—or its model in the Nietzschean genealogy—from the hermeneutic method, which erects a structure of double meaning where a simple axiomatics of voluntary intention discerns only a simple form, the form of morality in general.

This opposition between genealogical and formal method can be pursued further. The recourse to philology is at the same time the mobilizing of a suspicion which displaces the apparent meaning toward another text, which the first conceals. The introduction of concealment into the sphere of the good conscience marks a decisive turn. Consciousness judging becomes consciousness judged. The tribunal is submitted to a critique of a second order, which puts the judging consciousness back into the field of desire, from which Kant's formal analysis had tried to remove it. Obligation, interpreted as accusation, becomes a function of desire and fear.

What are the consequences of this methodological opposition for the interpretation of accusation? In what follows I will take for this analysis four characteristics, which I will treat in ascending order, from the most superficial to the most profound.

The demystification of accusation is obtained initially by the convergence of several *clinical* analogies between ethical fear and taboo fear, between scrupulosity and obsessional neurosis, between moral vigilance and observed madness, between remorse and melancholy, between moral strictness and masochism. This network of analogies sketches what can be called a pathology of duty precisely where Kant spoke only of a pathology of desire. According to this new pathology, man is a being sick with the sublime.

If the exemplary history of the individual or the species is considered, this descriptive relation becomes a *genetic* filiation. But what distinguishes Freudian geneticism from every other kind is the fact that it is elaborated on the level of the phantasm, by the play of figurative substitutions. Hence Freud's geneticism rediscovers a bond between the imperative and the figurative which places the agency of obligation in the signifying structures of discourse. At the center of this symbolic system the father figure of the Oedipus complex dominates. Freud often calls it the "paternal complex." The institution of the law is thus found coupled to a system of figures, let us even say, to a "primitive scene"—the murder of the father—which in Kant's eyes could appear only as the empirical constitution of man. It is precisely this contingent constitution which is revealed to be, for an exegetical method, the founding structure and, finally, the irreducible destiny, as the connection with Sophoclean tragedy attests.

Therefore, where Kant says law, Freud says father. What stands out here is the difference between formalism and exegesis. For the hermeneutics of accusation, the formal law is a secondary rationalization and, finally, an abstract substitute, in which the concrete drama is hidden yet underlined by several key, numerically limited, meanings—birth, father, mother, phallus, death.

Third characteristic: from the descriptive relation, by way of the genetic filiation, we must move to the *economic* derivation of the agency of accusation, which we shall now call the superego in order to treat it as a differentiation of the inner world. The superego, Freud says, is much closer to the obscure world of drives than is the ego, whose function of consciousness—an essentially superficial function—represents the exterior world. The analysis of the ego and the id is well known. The hypothesis of an economic redistribution of libidinal energy between the id and the superego has a profound meaning. It is from the stuff of our desires that our renunciations are made. The analogy between moral consciousness and the structure of melancholy is in this respect very illuminating. It makes it possible to approach again from the economic viewpoint the moral agency of the archaic object which was lost and installed in the interiority of the ego.

Final characteristic: in the overdetermined and ambivalent figure of the father two functions intersect—the function of repression and the function of *consolation*. It is the same figure who threatens and protects. In the same figure the fear of punishment and the desire for consolation are tied together. Hence, by a sequence of substitutions and equivalencies, the cosmic figure of God can be derived as the dispenser of consolation for man, who remains a child and is delivered over to the harshness of life. This is why the "renunciation of the father" will also be the renunciation of consolation. This renunciation is no small thing, for we prefer moral condemnation to the anguish of an existence that is both unprotected and unconsoled.

All of these traits—and especially the last one—make the demystification of accusation resemble a work of *mourning*.

The point now is to disengage the *philosophical significance* of the Freudian critique of accusation. I will sum it up in this formula: it is to move from the morality of obligation back to an ethics of the desire to be or of the effort to exist.

But this philosophical meaning could not come from the Freudian critique. On the contrary, it is the ethics of desire which determines the meaning of the critique. Actually, nothing is resolved here, everything remains to be done. What is the significance of the analogy between moral consciousness and the various pathological structures which are its clinical equivalent? What does the genetic filiation signify if the source of morality, like the father of the Oedipus phantasm, remains foreign to desire? What does identification with this father mean if it is true that there are two identifications—a cannibal desire to have and to possess, and a desire to be like, to resemble? It must be granted that the genealogy is sufficient to dethrone the pretended absolute of obligation, but the origin it designates is not a primordial one.

The philosopher's task is to conjoin the demystification of accusation with the problematic of a *fundamental ethics,* but one whose horizon has been cleared by the destruction of false transcendencies.

For my part, I would look for this fundamental ethics along the lines of a reflective philosophy like that of Jean Nabert. To be sure, a reflective philosophy is a philosophy of the subject but not necessarily a philosophy of consciousness, that is, a philosophy where the central question is the question of the subject, a philosophy where the question "Who is the one who speaks?" is the origin we are returning to. My working hypothesis, therefore, is that only a reflective philosophy can assume, together, the two modes of demythization—the destruction of myth as the false transcendence of obligation and the liberation of the symbolic potential of the kerygma.

Fundamental or originary ethics, therefore, is the hinge between these two movements of our thought: the movement of mythical destruction and the movement of symbolic instruction.

The possibility that obligation is not the primary structure of ethics can be seen by a simple reference to the title of Spinoza's *Ethics. Ethics* is the appropriation of our endeavor to exist, in its total process from slavery to beatitude. But this is what a reflection on obligation initially hides. It conceals the actual dimensions of human activity under formal categories derived from the structures of objectivity in a critique of knowledge. The unjustified parallel between the two Kantian *Critiques* imposes a division between *a priori* and *a posteriori* which is contrary to the intimate structure of action. Hence, the principle of morality is severed from the faculty of desire. When the faculty of desire, considered in its entirety, is set aside, then happiness is denied, because it is denounced as the "material" principle of the determination of willing, and a "formal" principle of obligation is isolated abstractly. The demystification of accusation has the philosophical consequence of again putting into question this privilege of formalism as the *first* step of an ethics. I have already said that formalism appears to us as a secondary rationalization, obtained on the practical level by a simple transposition of the critique of knowledge and the distinction between the transcendental and the empirical. This transposition completely misconstrues the specific quality of *acting* in relation to knowing. So it is necessary to renounce every kind of opposition of form and matter, which insists on the constitutive operations of truth, and instead arrive at a dialectic of action, whose central theme is the relation between operation and work, between the desire to be and the effectuation of this desire.

I say effort and also desire in order to place at the origin of ethical reflection an identity between effort, in Spinoza's sense of *conatus*, and eros, in both its Platonic and Freudian senses. I take "effort" the way Spinoza does in the *Ethics*, that is, as the positing of existence—*ponit sed non tollit*—an affirmation of being to the degree that this affirmation involves an indefinite time, a duration which is nothing other than the continuation of existence itself. It is this positive aspect of existence which is at the basis of the most primordial or originary affirmation, the "I am" that Fichte called thetic judgment. It is this affirmation that constitutes us, and it is this affirmation of which we are dispossessed in multiple ways. It is this affirmation which must be attained and reattained indefinitely, even though basically this affirmation is not subject to loss, is inalienable, primordial.

But while it is affirmation, this effort is at the same time self-dividedness, lack, desire for the other. What has to be understood here is that *conatus* is at the same time eros. Love, Plato says in the *Symposium*, is love of something, of something that is not possessed, of something one is deprived of, of something one lacks. *The affirmation of being in the lack of being:* in its most primordial structure, this is what effort is.

What does this primordial affirmation found an ethics on?

On this: that the "I am" is for itself its own need. It has to be what it primordially is. Duty is only the peripeteia between need and aspiration. As Nabert says:

Consciousness owes its possibility to be to the relationship which its desire sustains with a primary certitude of which the law is only a symbol. The order of duty contributes to revealing to the self a desire to be whose deepening is identified with ethic itself.[3]

II. THE KERYGMATIC CORE OF ETHICS

REORIENTING THE PROBLEM OF ETHICS on the basis of the desire to be instead of on the basis of pure obligation enables us to pose the question of the religious core of ethics in new terms.

Is the threshold between ethics and religion genuinely crossed when moral commandment is linked with the historical manifestation of a divine will? Does morality become religion when the universality which is duty becomes the uniqueness of the *semel jussit semper paret*, the *hapax legomenon* of a commencement, which is commandment? This is what I would seriously like to dispute here. The demystification of accusation brings suspicion to bear precisely at the point where interdiction is sacralized.

But restoring an ethical basis to our desire to be authorizes us to pose the problem in completely different terms. It allows us to entertain a new kind of connection between the event of the Gospel and our morality. Let us follow Saint Paul when he organizes his entire moral theology around the conflict between law and grace, or the author of the Epistle to the Hebrews when he reorganizes the major significations of the Old Testament around faith rather than law: "By faith Abraham when he was called to go out into a place which he should after receive for an inheritance, obeyed. . . . By faith Abraham, when he was tried, offered up Isaac" (Hebrews 11:8, 17).

The attempt to think the religious core of ethics as a commandment which has its beginning or commencement in a divine event—perhaps this is the myth of moral religion, the myth which must be demystified. And perhaps it is on the basis of this demystification that the *event* can be recovered, the pure event of kerygma and its relation to the origin of our desire to be.

For my part, I woud leave ethics in its anthropological ele-

---

3. Jean Nabert, *Elements for an Ethic,* trans. William J. Petrek (Evanston, Ill.: Northwestern University Press, 1969), p. 117.

ment; I would reunite the notion of value with the dialectic between a principle of unlimitation, linked to the desire to be, and a principle of limitation, linked to the works, institutions, and structures of economic, political, and cultural life. I would not project value into the heavens, where it becomes an idol. If value is an *event,* if it is a *commencement* or *beginning,* if it is a *historical mystery* which is announced and attested to only in the element of *witness,* then value is the event of a kerygma which relocates man—man and his law, man and his ethics—in a history of salvation, that is, in a history where everything can be lost and where everything can be saved or, rather, in a history where everything is already lost on the basis of an event which endlessly occurs, the Fall, and in a history where everything is already saved on the basis of an event endlessly remembered and signified, the death of the Just One. It is this contextualization of man and his human ethics in relation to the evangelical summons that constitutes the kerygmatic moment of ethics.

The task of a moral theology, it seems to me, is to think as far as possible the relation, not so much between the kerygma and obligation, but between the kerygma and that desire of which obligation is a secondary function. I am not saying that we will find nothing like "obedience"—Abraham twice obeyed: the call to depart and the call to offer Isaac—but it is a question of something completely different from the sacralization of moral obligation. As Kierkegaard realized, it is a matter of an obedience beyond the suspension of the ethical, of an "absurd" obedience, one related to the singularity of a call and to a need which renders the believer a stranger and a sojourner on earth and which consequently opens the chasm of his desire. This is what the author of the Epistle to the Hebrews calls, in almost Gnostic language, "the desire [for] a better country" (Heb. 11:16). It is in the origin, in the emptiness, in the tension of desire that the kerygmatic moment of ethics must be recovered. The kerygma—because it is related to the singularity of the "departure" and the "offering," as the story of Abraham recalls, and is not at all related to the generality of law, because it is the singular relation of a singular event to the historicity of our desire—is accessible only as *witness.*

If this is how things are, then what can a philosophy of religion and faith say? As I see it, the cleavage between philosophy and theology takes place in the following way. Theology deals with relations of intelligibility in the domain of witness. It is a logic of the Christological interpretation of salvation events. In saying this, I am remaining basically Anselmian and Barthian. Theology is an *intellectus fidei*. The philosophy of faith and religion is something else. What philosophy organizes in terms of the Christological basis of witness, the philosophy of religion organizes in terms of man's desire to be. And here I do not hesitate to say that I return to the Kantian analyses in *Religion within the Limits of Reason Alone*, to the degree that they diverge from a formalism.

I would follow Kant in two places, first in his definition of the ethical *function* of religion, and second in his definition of the *representative* content of religion.

For Kant, religion has an ethical function irreducible to *The Critique of Practical Reason*, irreducible but not at all foreign. It has as its theme "the whole object of the will." This theme is distinct from the "principle of morality," which is the object of a simple *analytic*. It is in terms of the *dialectic* that the problematic of religion is articulated, because the *dialectic* concerns the necessity of reason in the practical order, that is, "the unconditioned totality of the object of pure practical reason." Religion must be situated where evil will have to be resituated, that is, on the level where the demand of practical reason is contradicted. The fact that Kant conceived this whole object of the will as a synthesis of virtue and happiness is less important to us than the demand for a totality which situates us on the level of an irreducible question. In Kant's own language, the question "What can I hope for?" is completely different from the question "What must I do?" To the degree that religion is where this question arises, religion is not simply the double of morality, as it would be were religion to limit itself to enunciating duty as a divine command. In this respect religion would be only an "as if" pedagogy: obey as if God himself commanded you. But the commandment is resituated in a new problematic when it becomes a moment of hope, that of participating in the kingdom of God, of entering into the kingdom of reconciliation.

With Kant himself the inclusion of duty (the theme of the Analytic) in the movement of hope (the province of the Dialectic) marks the transition from morality to religion. The specificity of the religious object is thus outlined at the very core of Kant's *Critique of Practical Reason*. It belongs to the mediating character of the synthesis that it effects between virtue and happiness. It is a new object in relation to the *Faktum* of the moral law, and it maintains a specific exteriority with relation to the synthesis that it effects.

This is why there is a specificity in religious alienation and why, in Kant, the doctrine of radical evil is completed only with the doctrine of religion, with the theory of the church and of cult in Books III and IV of *Religion within the Limits of Reason Alone*. If, in fact, hope is added to duty, just as the question "What may I hope?" is distinct from the question "What must I do?", then the fulfillment which is the object of the promise has the character of a given which permeates both man's actions and his morality. Hence, religious alienation is an alienation which is proper to the dimension of the promise. What Kant denounces as *Schwärmerei* and *Pfaffentum*—mysticism and priestly fanaticism—is part of the problematic of totalization and fulfillment which is specific to religion. A point which has not been sufficiently emphasized is that the problem of evil in Kant is related not only to the Analytic, that is, to the regressive demonstration of the formal principle of morality, but to the Dialectic, that is, to the agreement and reconciliation between reason and nature. Truly human evil concerns premature syntheses, violent syntheses, short circuits in the totality. It culminates in the sublime, with the "presumption" of the theodicies and their numerous successors in modern politics. But this is possible precisely because the aim of the totality is an irreducible aim and because it opens the space of a Dialectic of *total* will which cannot be reduced to the simple Analytic of the *good* will. There are indeed perverse syntheses because there is an authentic question of the synthesis, of the totality, in what Kant calls the total object of the will.

I would also follow Kant in his definition of the *representative* content of religion. Up to now we have defined only the most general possibility of religion with the question "What can I hope?" The "postulate" itself of God does not yet make a real religion. Religion is born with the "representation" of the "good principle" in an "archetype." Here is where the Christology which the theologian takes as his space of intelligibility is related to the will in the philosophy of religion. The central question of the philosophy of religion is this: How is the will affected in its most intimate desire by the representation of this model, this archetype of a humanity agreeable to God, which the believer calls the Son of God? The question of religion—and here Kant prefigures Hegel—is deployed at the level of a schematism of the desire for totality. This question is essentially the problem of the relation of *representation* to the dialectic of *practical reason*. It concerns the schematization of the good principle in an archetype.

Kant's Christology, of course, is not without relation to Spinoza. In this respect Kant's Christology satisfies, I think, the requirements for a *philosophy* of religion. Like Spinoza, Kant does not think that man can himself produce the idea of a suffering just man who offers his life for all men. Certainly the theologian would hardly admit the reduction of what can only be an event to an *idea*. And we can easily say that this reduction is in line with the formalism and the entire abstract mentality of Kantianism, a philosophy which misunderstands the dimension of witness to the degree that it misunderstands, more generally, the dimension of historicity. Moreover, it is only as a quasi-event that the philosopher can represent to himself this coming of the idea of the Son of God into the human will. But if a theology cannot partake of this Kantian infirmity, the philosophy of religion can be satisfied with it. Its problem is how the human will is *affected* by this archetype in which the good principle is schematized. But in this respect Kantianism is quite precise. "This idea," Kant says, "has taken root in man without our understanding how human nature has been able to welcome it." Hence Kant's Christ concerns our meditation to the precise degree that Christ is not the hero of duty but the symbol of fulfillment. He is not the example of duty but the exemplar of the sovereign good. In my terms I would say that, for the philosopher, Christ is the schema of hope. He comes from a mythicopoetic imagination, which concerns the *completion* of the desire to be.

This does not suffice for the theologian, who asks how the schema is rooted in the historical witness of Israel and how the apostolic generation was able to recognize it in 'the Word made flesh." But this is sufficient for the philosopher, who now has what he needs for elaborating a kerygmatic conception of an ethics which is no longer in principle a sacralization of interdiction. Religion—or rather what in religion is faith—is not in its essence condemnation but "good news." In witnessing to the Christ event, it offers to reflection and to philosophic speculation an *analogon* of the sovereign good, a schema of totality. In short, faith gives to philosophical thinking an object other than duty; it offers it the representation of a *promise*. At the same time, it engenders an original problematic, that of the relation between the imagination that produces such schemata and the *élan* itself of our desire. The abstract problem of formalism yields to the concrete problem of the genesis of desire. This genesis of desire, this poetics of the will, is what faith yields for understanding in the symbol of the new man and in all the symbols of the second birth and regeneration, which we must now reappropriate, beyond every moralizing allegorism, in their primordial power.

III. Evil as a Kerygmatic Problem

WE WILL HAVE SUCCEEDED in our attempt to demystify accusation, and we will have fully recovered the kerygmatic dimension, of ethics, when we will have resituated the object of accusation—guilt—in the field of kerygma, in the light of the promise.

So long as religion is linked to accusation, so long as it is limited to sacralizing interdiction, evil remains itself transgression, remains disobedience to the divine commandment. The demystification of accusation must go all the way, to the demystification of transgression. The religious dimension of evil is not there. Here again Saint Paul has said what is essential: sin is not transgression; it is the link between law and covetousness, on the basis of which there is transgression; sin is remaining within the narrow economy of the law, where the commandment excites covetousness. The contrary of sin is not morality but faith.

Hence, the problem must be reversed in its entirety. Evil is not the first thing that we understand but the last; it is the last article of the creed and not the first. A prior reflection on the origin of evil is not religious because it seeks out a radical evil behind evil maxims. Nor is it religious because it discerns something inscrutable which can be expressed only mythically. What qualifies this meditation as religious is a complete reinterpretation, on the basis of the kerygma, of our notions of evil and of guilt. This is why I am speaking of a kerygmatic interpretation of evil.

Let us attempt this reinterpretation of evil, I would say this recurrent reinterpretation of evil, on the basis of the evangelical kerygma. If this movement of eschatology back toward genesis is not to constitute a shameful reverse, it must satisfy three basic conditions: (1) the pressure of demystification, when applied to accusation, must be constantly maintained; (2) this demystification of accusation must remain linked to the demystification of consolation; and (3) demystification must proceed from the kerygmatic core of faith, that is, from the good news that God is love. Let us take up these three points in turn.

1. What does the feeling of evil mean, once accusation has been demystified? This first question deals with what might be called the epigenesis of the feeling of guilt. The question is far from being a simple one. It cannot be dealt with simply by means of the resources of a psychology. It would be childish to believe that someone could add to the psychology or to the psychoanalysis of the superego. It is not a question of completing Freud. This epigenesis of the feeling of guilt can be obtained only indirectly, by means of an exegesis in the Diltheyan sense of the word, of an exegesis of the text of penitential literature, where an exemplary history of guilt is constituted. A man arrives at adult guilt when he understands himself according to the figures of this exemplary history. An epigenesis of the feeling of guilt, therefore, cannot be obtained directly. It has to pass by way of an epigenesis of representation, which would be a conversion of the imaginary into symbols or, in another language, a conversion of the vestigial phantasm of a primitive scene into a poem of origins. The primordial crime, in which Freud sees the primitive scene of the collective Oedipus complex, can become a founding representation if it is permeated with authentic *creation of meaning*.

The question the demythizing of evil poses, then, is this: besides the demystification of accusation, can the phantasm of the "primitive scene" be *reinterpreted* as a symbol of origins? In more technical terms: can such a phantasm furnish the first level of meaning for an imagination of origins that is more and more detached from its function of infantile and quasi-neurotic repetition and more and more available for an investigation of the fundamental meanings of human destiny?

This cultural creation on the basis of a phantasm constitutes what I call the symbolic function. I see here the reappropriation of a phantasm of the primitive scene converted into an instrument of discovery and into an exploration of origins.

Thanks to these "detecting" representations, man *says* the inauguration of his humanity. Hence the stories of struggle in Babylonian and Hesiodic literature, the story of the fall in Orphic literature, and the stories of the primitive fault and of exile in Hebraic literature can be treated the way Otto Rank treated them, as a kind of collective oneirism. But this oneirism is not a relic of prehistory. Rather, across its vestigial function the symbol shows an imagination of origins at work. This imagination can be called *geschichtlich*, because it says an advent, a coming to being; but it cannot be called *historisch*, because it has no chronological signification. Making use of Husserlian terminology, I would say that the phantasms Freud explored constitute the hyletic data of the mythicopoetic imagination. This new intentionality, by which the phantasm is symbolically interpreted, is suggested by the very character of the phantasm, since it speaks of a lost origin, of lost archaic objects, of the lack inscribed in desire. What stimulates the endless movement of interpretation is not the fullness of remembering but its emptiness, its openness. Ethnology, comparative mythology, and biblical exegesis confirm that each myth is the reinterpretation of an earlier story. Hence, the interpretations of interpretations can very well be operative on phantasms which are assignable to different ages and to different stages of the libido. But what is important is not so much this "suggestive material" as the movement of interpretation which is included in the promotion of meaning and which constitutes its intentional innovation. Myth can thus receive a theological signification, as is seen in the biblical stories of origins, by means of this endless correction, which becomes concentrated and then becomes systematic.

It seems to me, therefore, that two methods must converge, one, closer to psychoanalysis, which shows the conditions for the reinterpretation of the phantasm as a symbol, and the other, closer to textual exegesis, which shows this promotion of meaning at work in the great mythical texts. Taken separately, these two methods are powerless. For the movement from phantasm to symbol can be recognized only by the mediation of the documents of culture, more precisely of texts, which are, as Dilthey taught, the direct objects of hermeneutics. This is really Freud's error in *Moses and Monotheism:* he thought he could economize on biblical exegesis, that is, on the texts in which biblical man formed his faith, and proceed directly to the psychological genesis of religious representations while contenting himself with several analogies furnished by clinical experience. Because he did not link the psychoanalysis of the symbol with the exegesis of the great texts in which the thematic of faith is constituted, he found, at the end of his analysis, only what he knew before undertaking it—a personal God, who, according to Leonardo da Vinci's phrase, is only a transfigured father.

On the other hand, a *textual* exegesis is abstract and remains meaningless for us so long as the "figuratives" it comments on are not inserted into the affective and representative dynamism. The task here is to show how cultural products preserve lost archaic objects and yet go beyond the function of the simple return of the repressed. The prophecy of consciousness is not exterior to its archaeology. The symbol is a phantasm disavowed and overcome but not at all abolished. It is always *on* some trace of archaic myth that the symbolic meanings appropriate to reflective interpretation are grafted.

Finally, it is in the element of the word [*parole*] that this promotion of meaning is deployed. The conversion of the phantasm and that of the affect are only the shadow cast on the imaginary level and the level of drives by the conversion of meaning. If an epigenesis of affect and of image is possible, then it is because the word is the instrument of this *hermēneia*, this interpretation, which is itself the symbol in relation to the phantasm.

The result of this indirect exegesis, which cannot be reduced to any kind of direct introspection, is that guilt progresses by passing over two thresholds. The first is that of injustice—in the sense of the Platonic *adikia*—and of the "justice" of the Jewish prophets. The fear of being unjust, the remorse for having been unjust, are no longer taboo fear, taboo remorse. The breaking of the interpersonal bond, the wrong done to the person of another, are more important than the threat of castration. The consciousness of injustice constitutes the first creation of meaning in relation to the fear of vengeance, to the fear of being punished. The second threshold is that of the sin of the just man, of the evil of justice itself. In this presumption of the honest man the delicate conscience discovers radical evil. To this second cycle are attached the most subtle evils, those which Kant links to the pretension of empirical consciousness to say the totality, to impose its own vision of it on others.

It appears that the sexual is not at the center of this exegesis of true guilt. Sexual guilt must itself be reinterpreted. Everything which maintains the trace of a condemnation of life must be eliminated from an interpretation which is to proceed entirely from the consideration of the relation with others.

And if the sexual is no longer at the center, this is because the place whence judgment proceeds is no longer the parental agency or any agency derived from the father figure. It is the figure of the prophet, the figure outside the family, outside politics, outside culture, the eschatological figure par excellence.

2. But guilt is rectified only if consolation also goes through a radical ascesis. The moral God, in fact, is also the providential God, as the old law of retribution, discussed as early as the

Babylonian sages, attests. It is God who regulates the physical order of things according to the moral interests of humanity. It is necessary to reach the point where the ascesis of consolation takes precedence over the ascesis of guilt, guiding the mourning of punishment and of recompense.

Again, it is literature which stakes out this ascesis: the "wisdom" literature. In its archaic forms, "wisdom" is a long meditation on the prosperity of the wicked and the unhappiness of the just. This wisdom literature, taken up again and transposed into the register of reflective thought, is essential to the rectification of accusation. It, too, bears a mourning, the mourning of recrimination. It is on the basis of this renunciation of recrimination that the critique of accusation can itself be carried to its furthest point. Actually, it is this critique which makes *judging consciousness* appear as impure consciousness. Under the recrimination of judging consciousness the power of resentment is unmasked, a power which is simultaneously a very hidden hatred and a very shrewd hedonism.

This critique of judging consciousnesss in its turn grants access to a new form of inner conflict between faith and religion. This is the faith of Job confronted by the religion of his friends. Faith, instead of undergoing an iconoclasm, now effects one. In making itself critical of the judging consciousness, faith gives its own account of the critique of accusation. It is faith itself that fulfills the task that Freud called "renunciation of the father." Job in fact receives no explanation of the meaning of his suffering. His faith is simply removed from every moral vision of the world. In return, the only thing shown to him is the grandeur of the whole, without the finite viewpoint of his own desire receiving a meaning directly from it. A path is thus opened: that of a nonnarcissistic reconciliation. I renounce my viewpoint; I love the whole as it *is*.

3. The third condition for a kerygmatic reinterpretation of evil is that the symbolic figure of God should preserve from the theology of anger only what can be assumed into the theology of love.

With this, I hardly think that all severity is abolished. The "good Lord" is more derisory than the God hidden in anger. There is also an epigenesis of God's anger. What is the anger of love? It is perhaps what Saint Paul calls grieving the Spirit. The sadness of love is more difficult to endure than the anger of a magnified father. It is no longer the fear of punishment—in

Freudian language, the fear of castration—which inhabits it but the fear of not loving enough, of not loving correctly. Here is the final level of fear, of the fear of God. At the same time, Nietzsche's phrase is fulfilled: "The only God that is refuted is the God of morality."

I do not conceal the problematic character of this third theme; it is the weakest, though it should be the strongest. It is weak because it is at the point of convergence of two sublimations—that of accusation and that of consolation. But these two sublimations effect the suspension of the ethical in apparently irreconcilable senses. The first sublimation, that of accusation, puts one on Kierkegaard's path; the second, that of consolation, on the path of Spinoza. The task of a theology of love would be to show their identity. That is why I am saying that the theme of the God of love ought to be the strong point of this whole dialectic. Far from being lost in effusiveness or drowned in sentimentality, the task of such a theology would be to witness to the profound unity between the two modalities of the suspension of ethics, the profound identity between the supreme Thou and the *Deus sive natura*. It is perhaps here that the figure of the father, disavowed, overcome as phantasm and lost as idol, re-awakens as symbol. But it is then nothing more than the surplus of meaning aimed at by this theorem of Book V of Spinoza's *Ethics:* "The intellectual love of the mind toward God is the very love with which he loves "himself"—*quo Deus seipsum amat.*[4]

The last stage of the father figure is the *seipsum* of Spinoza. The symbol of the father is no longer at all that of a father I am able to have. In this regard the father is not a father. But it is the likeness of the father, in conformity to which the renunciation of desire is not death but love, again in the sense of the corollary of Spinoza's theorem: ". . . the love of God toward men and the intellectual love of the mind toward God are one and the same thing."[5]

How are the two modalities of the suspension of the ethical—that of accusation and that of consolation—the same? To understand this is the task of intellectual love. My thesis here is that this comprehension remains intelligible to faith in the endless correction of its symbols: intelligible, because understanding must struggle, without a truce, with the antinomy; and faith—

---

4. Benedict Spinoza, *Ethics,* trans. James Gutmann (New York: Hafner, 1949), p. 274.
    5. *Ibid.,* p. 275.

and, even more, love—because what actuates this understanding is the ceaseless work of purification applied to desire and to fear.

It is only in the light of the intellectual love of God that man can be rightly accused and consoled in truth.

Interpretation of the
Myth of Punishment

BECAUSE OF THE CONFUSION of its themes, the myth of punishment calls for a deliberately analytical treatment. That is why I am inclined, first of all, to enumerate the difficulties and paradoxes which adhere to the notion in order to determine the rational nucleus of the law of punishment. I shall then inquire if there is not a *stronger* law than the law of punishment by which the myth might be shattered.

I. DIFFICULTIES AND PARADOXES

THE MAJOR PARADOX is doubtless placing the notion of punishment in the category of myth. But we will understand what, so to speak, produces myth in the notion of punishment only by examining a preliminary paradox, which would appear to lead in another direction than that of myth.

I shall call this first aporia the aporia of the rationality of punishment. Nothing, indeed, is more rational, or at least nothing puts in more of a claim to rationality, than the notion of punishment. Crime merits chastisement, says the collective consciousness; and the Apostle confirms this: the wages of sin is death. The paradox is that this presumed rationality, which we shall call the logic of punishment, is an undiscoverable rationality. It posits a necessary connection between the manifestly heterogeneous moments that we shall find gathered to-

Translated by Robert Sweeney.

gether in the following definition, which I have taken from the Littré dictionary: "Punishment: what one is forced to submit to for something judged reprehensible or blameworthy." Let us subject to scrutiny the elements of this definition.

First, punishment implies from the beginning a suffering (the painful element of punishment), which is found in the affective order and consequently belongs to the sphere of the body; this first element makes of punishment a physical evil which is added to a moral evil. But, second, this passivity, this affection, this affliction, does not occur in the manner of the contingencies of life and history; it is ordained by a will, which thus affects another will; it is the "forced submission" at the origin of the "submission." We say: "order" punishment, "inflict" punishment. This second element establishes the punishing at the source of the painful. Third, the meaning of punishment, insofar as it is a conjunction of submission and forcing submission, resides in the presumed equivalence between, on the one hand, evil suffered and inflicted, and, on the other hand, evil committed, at least as it has been so judged in a judicial suit. This equivalence constitutes the rationale of punishment, around which will revolve our whole discussion; it goes without saying that, for penal reasoning, a penalty can be of equal value to a crime. This is what our definition says: "What one is forced to submit to *for* something"; this "for" is a "for" of value, which we sometimes express in the language of price. We say: "Make him pay the penalty"; "Punishment is the price of crime." Fourth, the culprit is the subject of the will in which the equivalence of crime and punishment is posited; he is presumed to be one and the same in the committed evil of the wrongdoing and in the suffered evil of punishment; it is in him that punishment suppresses, effaces, annuls the wrongdoing or fault.

Such are the elements into which punishment is analyzed.

The whole enigma rests in the rationale that we have called price or value; this rationale of punishment is not indeed an identity for the understanding. This is for two reasons. What is there in common, first of all, between the suffering of punishment and the commission of wrongdoing? How can a physical evil equal, compensate for, and cancel out a moral evil? Crime and punishment are inscribed in two different frames, that of enduring and that of acting; but we must think them as united in the same will, that of the culprit. Moreover, submission and forcing submission are in two different wills, that of the accused and that of the judge, assuming that the commission and the submission are in the same subject—but we have seen that, even then, they are not in the same frame—forcing submission and submission are in two different subjects: the judging consciousness and the judged consciousness; yet we must think of judge and culprit as only one will.

Thus, the rationale of punishment would appear split apart between acting and suffering in the same will, between submission and forcing submission in two distinct wills. It overcomes this double fracture by the thought of an equivalence, the equivalence of crime and punishment. This equivalence is presumed to reside in the culprit himself, so that what has been done by the crime may be undone by punishment. Such is the reasoning behind punishment; it appears only in a duality for understanding: duality of the committed crime and the punishment submitted to, duality of the judging consciousness and of the consciousness judged. In short, an identity of reason is hidden behind this duality of understanding.

It is here that the second aporia presents itself and, with it, the question of the myth. What the understanding divides, the myth thinks as one in the Sacred.

Let us consider, indeed, the relation of stain or pollution to purification in the sacral universe. Stain is a certain attack on an order, itself defined by a network of prohibitions. Purification comes as a process of cancellation; it consists in a group of acts, themselves codified in a ritual, which are reputed to act on the process of stain to destroy it as stain. Punishment is a moment in this process of cancellation; we call "expiation" this quality of punishment in virtue of which it can cancel stain and its effects in the order of the sacred. Expiation thus occupies in the sacral universe the place of the rationale that an initial analysis looked for in vain on the level of understanding.

In what way does expiation create an aporia? In the fact that the myth and reason occur in it together. A curious aporia in truth. The myth, indeed, does not occur in the form of a narrative but in the form of a law. To be sure, we always find origin narratives which tell how the law was first given to men, how a certain ritual was first established, why such a punishment erases stain, why a certain sacrifice equals punishment and purification. By these origin narratives the myth of punishment is rendered homogeneous, from a literary point of view— I mean by the very form of the narrative—to other myths: myths of the origin of the cosmos, the enthronement of the king, the founding of the city, the institution of the cult, etc. But the form of the narrative is here only the exterior form of an internal form, which is the law. Yet, the myth of punishment is a strange myth, since the myth is reason. Among all myths, that of punishment has the privilege of revealing that law that lies at the heart of every origin narrative, the law which anchors historical time in primordial time. But, in return, it is a strange reason which establishes a divisive understanding within a law which does not relate to a logic of ideas but to a logic of powers; by punishment, a power of stain or pollution is canceled by a power of purification.

Such is the second aporia: the identity of reason which we have sought for at the root of the duality of crime and punishment, for the understanding, occurs first as myth of the law, of the Way, the *Hodos*, the Tao. It is this mythic reason which creates the power of expiation. Thus punishment puts us face to face with a mytho-logy, with an indivisible unit of mythology and rationality.

I shall now develop this aporia in two directions: that of the right to punish and that of religion, since these are the cultural spheres in which the question of punishment is posed. But it is this very association which expresses the preceding aporia: the identity of myth and reason in the logic of punishment has its most extraordinary cultural expression in the kinship between the sacred and the juridical. Without cessation, indeed, the sacred sacralizes the juridical: this will be our third aporia. Without cessation, on the other hand, the juridical juridicizes the sacred: this will be our fourth aporia.

That the sacred sacralizes the juridical is easily seen in the kind of religious respect which surrounds judicial action even in the most secularized societies. This should not fail to astonish us; indeed, the sphere of the right to punish is the one where the greatest effort of rationality has been expended. To measure punishment, to proportion it to the misdeed, to equalize, by increasing approximation, the balance between the two scales of guilt and punishment is clearly the work of understanding—the understanding of measures; and measures by means of a reasoning of proportionality of the following type: punishment *A* is to punishment *B* what crime *A'* is to crime *B'*. Ceaselessly to refine this reasoning of proportionality is the whole work of juridical experience in its penal form. Its brightest jewel is to think of punishment in terms of the rights of the guilty: the guilty one has a right to a punishment proportioned to his crime. But, and this is our third aporia, to the degree that this rationality progresses—this rationality of the understanding that proportions the punishment to the crime—there is also discovered the mythic rationality which undergirds the whole edifice. If it is reasonable to proportion the punishment to the crime, it is under the condition of an "interior identity which, within exterior existence, is reflected in the understanding as equality" (this citation of Hegel, which I here present in an enigmatic form, will find its justification below, in the second part). We are therefore referred, by the understanding's very work of approximation to the law of punishment which intends that chastisement be the price of crime, to the action of suppressing a committed evil by an evil that is submitted to: "If we do not understand the virtual internal connection between a crime and the act which abolishes it . . . , we succeed in seeing in a punishment properly so-called only the arbitrary connection between an inflicted evil and a forbidden action." Thus the very progress of understanding in penal justice reveals the problematic character of the principle of punishment. The unthought element of the crime is the violation of the right; what is not thought of in the punishment is the suppression of the violation. It is on this aporia that all theories of punishment stumble. What good is it to proportion the magnitude of the penalty to that of the crime if we do not comprehend the function assigned to punishment? It is well, indeed necessary, that the defense of society prevail over vengeance, intimidation over chastisement, menace over execution, rehabilitation over liquidation. But if one excludes every intention to suppress the violation of the right in the subject of the violation, the very idea of punishment vanishes. Crime and the criminal are then simply noxious, and "one can perhaps judge it senseless to will an evil because an evil already exists" (Hegel). Such is the aporia of the right to punish: to rationalize punishment in accordance with understanding, by eliminating the myth of expiation, is at the same time to deprive it of its principle. Or, to express this aporia in terms of a paradox: What is most rational in punishment, namely, that it fits the crime, is at the same time most irrational, namely, that it erases it.

If now—fourth aporia—we turn toward the properly religious sphere, the aporia of punishment becomes particularly insupportable. What is at stake is no longer the sacralization of right but the juridicization of the sacred. The same proximity of the sacred and the juridical, whose effects in the penal order we have just considered, is present in the opposite sense on the theological level, where it rules what I shall call penal theology. If today we can speak of the myth of punishment in terms of an aporia, it is because of this penal theology. More precisely, it is because of the death of this penal theology in Christian preaching and in the whole of our culture. Modern man no longer understands what one is talking about when one defines original sin as a juridically imputable crime in which humanity is implicated collectively. To belong to a *massa perdita*, guilty and punishable according to the juridical terms of the crime, to be condemned to death according to the juridical law of punishment—that is what we no longer understand. But this penal theology would appear to be indissociable from Christianity, at least at first glance. The whole of Christology is situated within the framework of penal theology by the double channel of expiation and justification. These two theological "grounds" are traditionally tied to punishment by the most solid of rational ties. The death of the Just One has been understood as the sacrifice of a substitute victim who satisfies the law of punishment. "He has suffered for us" signifies that He has paid for us the price of the ancient crime. I shall say, further on, that this purely penal interpretation does not totally cover the mystery of the Cross and that the theory of satisfaction is only a second-degree rationalization of a mystery whose center is not punishment but the gift. It remains to be said that the reinterpretation of this mystery in terms that are different from those of penal theology is rendered very difficult by reason of the support that this latter seems to receive from the Pauline theme of "justification." As we know, Saint Paul has expressed the mystery of the new economy in a language impregnated with judicial references. Justification (*dikaiosunē*) refers to a process in which man figures as the accused (*katakrinein*) and is subject to condemnation (*katakrima*). In this judicial context, grace is expressed in terms of an acquittal; to be justified is to be exempted from punishment, whereas chastisement was due. The justified man is the one whose faith is counted (*logizesthai*) as justice. We know the place these texts have held in the great debate between Protestants and Catholics. But what was the object of this debate, namely, the role of man in justification, is not what causes me to be interested in them here. They interest me for the much more fundamental reason that they seem, indeed, to confirm the law of punishment at the very moment when that law is split apart; they seem to say that we cannot think of grace, pardon, and mercy except in relation to the law of punishment, which is found thus to be retained as well as suspended. Doesn't acquittal still make reference to the law of punishment? Doesn't grace itself remain a judicial grace, against the background of judicial retribution? Doesn't discovery remain judicial discovery, to the degree that it remains a verdict, even if it be a verdict of non-imputation, of acquittal? Such is the ultimate aporia: what seems most contrary to the logic of punishment, namely, the gratuitousness of grace, would appear to be the most radical confirmation of it.

II. DECONSTRUCTION OF THE MYTH

BY THIS LAST APORIA we are brought to the heart of the matter. The myth of punishment is of such a special character that it is necessary to apply a specific treatment to it and to take up once again the whole program of demythologization.

What is it to demythologize punishment?

It is, first of all, as everywhere, to deconstruct the myth. But what is it to deconstruct a myth of logical appearance? It seems to me that it is, essentially, to reconnect the logic of punishment with its sphere of validity and thus deprive it of its onto-theological bearing. Now I find this first step fully accomplished by Hegel in his *Philosophy of Right*.[1] What Hegel has pointed out, and, in my opinion, definitively demonstrated, is that the law of punishment is valid, but only in a limited sphere which he calls "abstract right." To justify punishment within this sphere and to reject it outside this sphere is one and the same enterprise, which, taken *en bloc*, constitutes the deconstruction of the myth of punishment.

Hegel, then, has thought through punishment. It is from him that I have just borrowed the strongest formulas of my analysis of punishment. It is a matter now of thinking through, in accordance with the concept, this interior identity between crime and punishment, which the understanding attains only in exteriority, as a synthetic connection between an acting and a suffering, between a judge and a guilty party. What, asks Hegel, is this "inner identity whose reflection in the external world appears to the Understanding as 'equality'"? (p. 72). Answer:

1. G. W. F. Hegel, *The Philosophy of Right*, trans. T. M. Knox (New York: Oxford University Press, 1942), pp. 68–73. [All quotations will be from this translation.]

Let us conceive first the idea of a "philosophical science of right," and let us define its domain as being that of "the free will" or of "realized freedom" (Hegel says again: "the world of spirit brought forth out of itself like a second nature" [*Introduction*, § 4]). It is therefore on a certain course, one which turns its back on "the freedom of the void" (§ 5), that a logic like this can be encountered. It is when freedom returns to an order, renounces being for itself only an abstract representation and realizing itself only as a "fury of destruction" (§ 5), in brief, it is when it is bound to determinations, wills itself as a reflected particularization, that it can enter into the dialectic of crime and punishment. This dialectic achieves the first stage, the most immediate one, which the idea of free will, in and for itself, runs through in its development; this stage is that of abstract and formal right. Why abstract and formal? Because the real is not yet included in the definition of free will, and because only the conscious relation of self without content posits the will as subject, as person. Only a subject of right is posited: the imperative of right which corresponds to it says only: "Be a person and respect others as persons" (§ 36).

How is the dialectic of crime and punishment going to be set within this formal framework? Under two conditions. It is necessary, first, that, by appropriation, the juridical person place his will in a thing; the I henceforth has something under its exterior power; in return, the I exists in exteriority. Under this first condition, it becomes comprehensible that the law of punishment can itself be unfolded in exteriority. It is necessary, next, that, by means of a contract, a relation be established among several wills when there are things to appropriate. The exclusion of the other, correlative to the appropriation of things by one particular will only, prepares the way for a law of exchange and, in general, a relation of reciprocity among independent immediate persons. Under this double condition—existence of freedom in an exterior thing, contractual relation between wills external one to the other—something like an injustice is possible: the violation of right, at this abstract and formal level, will be nothing else than "a force against the existence of my freedom in an external thing" (§ 94).

It then becomes possible to conceive of punishment on the basis of injustice itself. Indeed, force exercised against the will is a force and a constraint which is "in its very conception directly self-destructive because it is an expression of a will which annuls the expression or determinate existence of a will"

(§ 92). Now this contradicts itself, the will being idea or real freedom only to the degree that it occurs in exteriority. Everything turns henceforth around this internal contradiction of injustice. The right of coercion is secondary with respect to this internal contradiction which gnaws at the unjust act. Hence § 97 of the *Philosophy of Right,* in which the whole logic of punishment is summed up. I quote § 97:

> The infringement of right as right is something that happens and has positive existence in the external world, though inherently it is nothing at all. The manifestation of its nullity is the appearance, also in the external world, of the annihilation of the infringement. This is the right actualized, the necessity of the right mediating itself with itself by annulling what has infringed it.

We grasp finally the *concept* of punishment; it results from the very negativity of crime. The concept of punishment is nothing else than

> that necessary connection between crime and punishment already mentioned; crime, as the will which is implicitly null, *eo ipso* contains its negation in itself, and this negation is manifested as punishment. It is this inner identity whose reflection in the external world appears to the Understanding as "equality" (§ 101).

What is more, we understand why it is the guilty person himself who must pay: his will is the existence which contains the crime and which should be suppressed. "It is this existence which is the real evil to be removed, and the essential point is the question of where it lies" (§ 99). It is necessary to go even further: "The injury [the penalty] which falls on the criminal is not merely *implicitly* just . . . ; it is also a right *established* within the criminal himself, i.e., in his objectively embodied will, in his action" (§ 100). Indeed, in punishing the criminal I recognize him as a rational being who posits the law in violating it; I subject him to his own right. Hegel goes so far as to say: "Since that is so, punishment is regarded as containing the criminal's right, and hence by being punished he is honoured as a rational being" (§ 100).

Thus is resolved the enigma of punishment. But it is resolved only if the logic of punishment remains enclosed within the problematic wherein it is developed, namely, within the limits of the philosophy of right. Let us group together these conditions

of validity: (1) a philosophy of the will, that is, of the realization of freedom; (2) the level of abstract right, that is, of the
will not yet reflected in its subjectivity; (3) the idea of a determination that the will takes from things, specifically from things
appropriated and possessed; (4) the reference to a contractual
right which binds wills that are external to one another. If
such are the conditions of the possibility of punishment, we
must understand the right to punish as contemporaneous with
this right of things and contracts. Like it, it is anterior—logically,
if not chronologically—to *subjective morality* (Part II of the
Philosophy of Right) and, a fortiori, anterior to the objective
morality which rules the family, civil society, and finally the
state (Part III of the *Philosophy of Right*).

On this foundation, demythization can be rationally understood; it signifies nothing else, at least in its negative phase, than
the return of punishment to abstract right. This return is itself
simply the critical counterpart of the thought of abstract right
in accordance with its concept.

What does this mean? It means that one can neither
moralize nor *divinize* punishment.

We cannot moralize it, because the first appearance of the
subjective self-conscious will in the exercise of punishment is
revenge. From the moment I consider the inflicting of punishment as the action of a subjective will, the particularity and the
contingency of this will become very obvious. Revenge is the
very contingency of justice in the punisher. In the punisher,
punishment is, from the first, impure; punishment is from the
first only a manner of perpetuating violence in an infinite chain
of crimes; the "bad infinity" returns to the scene and contaminates justice; it was undoubtedly of Aeschylus and the *Oresteia*
that Hegel was thinking when he wrote: "Hence revenge, because it is a positive action of a particular will, becomes a new
transgression; as thus contradictory in character, it falls into an
infinite progression and descends from one generation to another
ad infinitum" (§ 102).

The abolition of wrongdoing thus opens up a new contradiction—that between justice and the punisher, between law and
the contingency of force. In order for punishment not to be
vengeance, it would be necessary that the will "as particular and
subjective, will the universal as such" (§ 103). It is the task of
subjective morality to reflect this contingency onto itself in
such a way that this infinity is not only in itself but for itself.

With this new task, Hegel notes, we leave antiquity for Christianity and the modern age:

> The right of the subject's particularity, his right to be satisfied, or in other words the right of subjective freedom, is the pivot and centre of the difference between antiquity and modern times. This right in its infinity is given expression in Christianity, and it has become the universal effective principle of a new form of civilization (§ 124).

And yet this enterprise of moralizing punishment, of vanquishing the spirit of revenge within the framework of subjective morality, must run aground and lead to the point of view of objective morality, that is, of concrete historical communities (family, civil society, state). Why this failure and this impossibility of remaining within the point of view of subjective morality? Because, says the *Philosophy of Right*, "abstract reflection fixes [the] moment [of particularity] in its distinction from and opposition to the universal and so produces a view of morality as nothing but a bitter, unending, struggle against self-satisfaction . . ." (§ 124).

We see, then, that the philosophy of right cannot incorporate the concept of moral certitude—of *Gewissen*—into the doctrine of subjective morality without taking with it the whole cortege of antinomies that the *Phenomenology of Spirit* developed in Chapter VI.[2] Now the *Phenomenology of Spirit* had shown that we cannot transfer the logic of punishment outside the sphere of abstract right and introduce it into a morality of intention without entering into a hopeless problematic. To will to extirpate evil, no longer as a violation of right but as impure intention, is to be delivered over to the mortal conflict between the *judging consciousness* and the *judged consciousness*. Now this conflict, we remember, finds its result in a theory, not of punishment, but of the *reconciliation* that is called "pardon." *Gewissen* cannot therefore lead from crime to punishment, according to a logic of identity, but to an interior laceration. It is then the judging consciousness which must take the initiative to break out of the hell of punishment. It will have to discover itself as hypocritical and hard; hypocritical, because it

---

2. G. W. F. Hegel, *The Phenomenology of Mind*, trans. J. B. Baillie (New York: Harper Torchbooks, 1967), pp. 644–62. [All quotations will be from this translation. As noted elsewhere, we are referring to this book as *The Phenomenology of Spirit*, since this translation of *esprit* (*Geist*) is more in keeping with Ricoeur's terminology.—TRANS.]

has withdrawn from action and all effectiveness; hard, because it has rejected equality with the acting consciousness. There remains for it only one outcome: not punishment, which remains the point of view of the judging consciousness, but pardon, by which the judging consciousness renounces the particularity and the unilateralness of its judgment:

> The forgiveness it extends to the first is the renunciation of self, of its *unreal* essence, since it identifies with this essence that other which was real action, and recognizes what was called bad—a determination assigned to action by thought—to be good; or rather it lets go and gives up this distinction of determinate thought with its self-existent determining judgment, just as the other forgoes determining the act in isolation and for its own private behoof. The word of reconciliation is the objectively existent spirit, which immediately apprehends the pure knowledge of itself *qua* universal essence in its opposite, in the pure knowledge of itself *qua* absolutely self-confined single individual—a reciprocal recognition which is Absolute Spirit (*ibid.*, p. 677).

The moment of reconciliation, which the *Phenomenology* placed at the juncture of the theory of culture and the theory of religion, is full of meaning of us. If we compare this development with what corresponds to it in the *Philosophy of Right,*[3] we understand that the problem of punishment no longer finds any place in the sphere of subjective morality.[4] The logic of crime and punishment retains a meaning that is only juridical and not at all moral; from the moment one speaks of evil and no longer of crime, of moral evil and no longer of the violation of

3. *The Philosophy of Right* refers expressly to the *Phenomenology of Spirit* at the end of §§ 135 and 140.

4. Hegel speaks once of crime, but in order to say that it is not necessary to have the psychology of the criminal enter into the imputation of crime: "The claim is made that the criminal in the moment of his action must have had a 'clear idea' of the wrong and its culpability before it can be imputed to him as a crime. At first sight, this claim seems to preserve the right of his subjectivity, but the truth is that it deprives him of his indwelling nature as intelligent . . ." (*Philosophy of Right,* § 132). Thus subjectivity must not be retrospectively projected into the sphere of abstract right. Hegel adds: "The sphere in which these extenuating circumstances come into consideration as grounds for the mitigation of punishment is a sphere other than that of rights, the sphere of pardon" (*ibid.*). Is it not legitimate to connect this remark with the dialectic of evil and forgiveness in the *Phenomenology of Spirit*? The only possible projection of subjective morality onto abstract right is not the moralization of punishment but pardon itself; but, by the same token, we are beyond pure right.

right, one enters into the antinomies of infinite subjectivity: the consciousness of evil, when it no longer has support from abstract right, without yet having that of objective morality, that is, of the concrete community, is too "subjective" to develop an objective logic. In this respect, § 139 of the *Philosophy of Right*, dedicated to moral evil, is not inferior to the *Phenomenology of Spirit*: the logic of injustice and punishment, which has served us as a guiding thread through the schema of abstract right, cannot any longer be extrapolated to the schema of subjective consciousness, because reflection and evil have the same origin, namely, the separation between subjectivity and the universal; that is why, says Hegel, moral certitude is itself "on the verge of slipping into evil" (*ibid.*). Strange paradox, in truth: reflection is condemned to vacillate on that point where consciousness *of* evil and consciousness *as* evil become indiscernible; this point of indecision rests precisely "in independent self-certainty, with its independence of knowledge and decision" (*ibid.*). We could certainly conclude from this, with Saint Paul, Luther, and Kant, that evil is necessary, that is, "Man is therefore evil by a conjunction between his natural or undeveloped character and his reflection unto himself" (*ibid.*). But no logic of punishment can proceed from an evil which no longer has any objective measure in right. Here the contradiction is sterile. This is why the consciousness of evil is no longer resolved in a punishment equal to the wrongdoing but in the decision not to be held to this "stage of diremption"; the overcoming is not in punishment but in abandoning the point of view of subjectivity.

Whereas the *Phenomenology of Spirit* opens out into the problematic of forgiveness, through the dialectic of the judging consciousness and consciousness judged, the *Philosophy of Right* emerges from the swamp of subjective conviction by the path of objective morality, that is, of a theory of the state. But the fundamental meaning is the same: punishment sanctions the distance between the judging consciousness and consciousness judged; the transcending of punishment is the equalization of the two consciousnesses, the reconciliation, which we call "forgiveness" in the language of religion or "community" in the language of objective morality, that is, finally, in the language of politics.[5]

5. It is on the basis of this comparison that the *Philosophy of Right* integrates the analyses of the *Phenomenology of Spirit*: "In my *Phenomenology of Spirit*, I have shown how this absolute self-complacency fails to rest in a solitary worship of itself but builds up a sort of com-

At the end of this second part of our essay, where Hegel has served as our guide, the task of demythologizing punishment would appear to be simple and clear. To the degree that the myth of punishment is a mytho-logic of crime and punishment, to demythologize punishment is to restore the logic of punishment to its original place, where it is a logic without myth. This original place is abstract right, of which the right to punish is an aspect. Here, the reason of punishment is without myth because it rests on the concept of rational will. We shall say, then, that the logic of punishment is a logic without myth to the degree that it can be restored to a logic of the will, that is, to a logic of the historical determinations of freedom.

Myth begins whenever the moral consciousness attempts to transpose into the sphere of interiority a logic of punishment which has only a juridical meaning and which rests on the double presupposition of the exteriorization of freedom in a thing and of the external connection between wills in a contract. Such is the rationale of punishment. But the counterpart of it is no less strict: any attempt to moralize punishment is lost in the antinomies between the judging consciousness and the judged consciousness. Even more, one cannot *divinize* it without returning to the "unhappy consciousness" which consecrates separation, distance: that is, the world of religion as terror, the world of Kafka's *Trial* and of the *unpaid debt*.

Thus the logic, without the myth, of punishment, in reverting to abstract right, uncovers the vast expanse of the myth of expiation. Is this a myth without reason, the converse of a reason without myth? Put differently, is the demythologizing of punishment exhausted in the deconstruction of the myth? For my own part, I do not believe so. The whole matter remains thinkable in the idea of a punishment that is nonjuridical, hyperjuridical. But then it is necessary to give a new meaning to demythologizing, to join reinterpretation to deconstruction. This will be the object of the third part.

---

munity whose bond and substance is, e.g., the 'mutual asseveration of conscientiousness and good intentions, the enjoyment of this mutual purity,' but is above all the 'refreshment derived from the glory of this self-knowledge and self-expression, from the glory of fostering and cherishing this experience.' I have shown also how what has been called a 'beautiful soul'—that still nobler type of subjectivism which empties the objective of all content and so fades away until it loses all actuality—is a variation of subjectivism like other forms of the same phenomenon akin to the series of them here considered" (§ 140, at end).

III. From the Judicial "Figurative"
to the "Memorial" of Punishment

WHAT IS IT TO REINTERPRET PUNISHMENT? In posing this final question, we are confronted with the most extreme difficulties, the same ones we considered in the fourth aporia under the heading of the "juridicizing of the sacred." Now, we will be bringing to this aporia an incomplete response if we limit ourselves to passing from the literal meaning of punishment in the right to punish to its analogous or symbolic meaning in the dimension of the sacred. To be sure, this should be done. But the myth of punishment, by reason of its rational structure, demands a special treatment, as much in the order of reinterpretation as in that of deconstruction. We would remain within the framework of image or representation if we claimed to overcome the logic of law and punishment by a symbol which would be left unthought. Only a new logic can overcome an outmoded logic. It is therefore the whole economy of thought, of which punishment is only a moment, which must be surpassed in a new economy, following an intelligible progression. That is why the analogical treatment of punishment will be only a first moment in looking toward another logic. This other logic—other than the logic of *equivalence*—I will try to disengage from the Pauline doctrine of justification; this new reading will correspond to the nondialectical reading which undergirded our fourth aporia. This new logic, this "absurd" logic, to speak like Kierkegaard, will be expressed in the law of *superabundance,* which alone renders null and void the economy of punishment and the logic of *equivalence*. Only then will it be possible to propose a good usage of the myth of punishment; the only conceivable status of the myth of punishment is indeed that of a stricken myth, of a ruined myth, of which we always have to make a memorial. It is toward this idea of a memorial of punishment that our meditation will henceforth be oriented. "Figurative" of punishment, "logic" of superabundance, "memorial" of punishment: such will be the three moments of our progression.

Here is what I understand by the "figurative" of punishment.

Punishment belongs to a constellation of representations, along with terms like "tribunal," "judgment," "condemnation," "acquittal"; this constellation, taken together, constitutes a schema of representations in which relations of another order come to be projected.

What judicial language *codifies*, in the strict sense of the word, are essentially ontological relations susceptible of being represented by analogy with person-to-person relations. Hegel has shown precisely that, in a *logic* of the will, punishment is contemporary with the constitution of the right of persons. It is this same person-to-person relation that we shall find again, in an analogous sense, in what would be a *poetics* of the will and not solely a *logic* of the will. With this person-to-person relation come all the other relations of the same level: debt, ransom, redemption.

That this poetics of the will is not exhausted in the analogy of the relation of right is attested to by other analogies, which balance and rectify it. I shall mention only two, which are opposed to each other but which together are opposed to the juridical metaphor. The first, the "conjugal" metaphor, is of the lyrical order; the second, the metaphor of the "wrath of God," is of the tragic order. Taken together, they permit a dejuridicizing of the personal relation itself that ancient Israel expressed in a notion that is more fundamental than any right, the notion of the Covenant.

Certainly, this theme of the Covenant lends itself to a juridical transcription. The clothing in the judicial "figurative" is made possible by the eminently ethical character of the religion of Yahweh; more specifically, the transition between the hyper-juridical pact of the Covenant and its juridical *analogon* was assured by the notion of *Torah*, which signifies, very broadly, instruction for life but whose Latin equivalent—*lex*—by way of the *Nomos* of the Septuagint, was charged with connotations of Roman law in Latin Christianity. In this respect, the jurisprudence of rabbinical law and the whole conceptual system attached to it greatly facilitated the juridicizing of the group of relations concentrated in the theme of the Covenant.

But the juridical conceptual system has never exhausted the meaning of the Covenant. This latter has never ceased to designate a living pact, a community of destiny, a bond with creation, which infinitely surpasses the relation of right. This is why the meaning of the Covenant has been able to be clothed in other "figuratives," such as the conjugal metaphor in Hosea and Isaiah; it is there that there comes to be expressed the surplus of meaning which does not come under the figure of right. The conjugal metaphor grasps more closely than any juridical figure the relation of concrete fidelity, the bond of creation, the pact of love—in short, the dimension of gift, which no code can succeed in capturing and institutionalizing. We venture to say that this order of the gift is, to that of law, what the order of charity is to that of the spirits in the famous Pascalian doctrine of the Three Orders.

It is into this dimension of the gift—proper to a poetics of the will—that the myth of punishment ought to be transposed. In such a poetics, what can sin and punishment signify? Sin dejuridicized does not fundamentally signify violation of a right, transgression of a law, but separation, uprooting.

That, in this experience of separation, the juridical aspect is secondary and derivative is attested to by the other symbolism we mentioned above, that of the "wrath of God." This symbolism, with its tragic accent, would at first appear to be incompatible with the conjugal symbolism, with its lyric accent; by reason of its nocturnal side, it would appear to lean toward terror and to be enlisted on the same side as the logic of punishment. But it differs profoundly from this by its character of *theophany*. As distinct from the *anonymous* law of punishment, of the impersonal demand for a restoration of order, the symbol of the "wrath of God" brings in the presence of the living God; this is what places it in the same cycle as the conjugal symbol, at the heart of a poetics of the will. The order of the gift, contrary to all appearances, does not lead to sweet effusions; one enters there by the doorway of the "terrible." The tragic in the "wrath," the lyricism of the "conjugal" bond, are, as it were, the nocturnal and diurnal sides of the encounter with the living God. The tragic and the lyric transcend, each in its own way, the ethical framework of law, commandment, transgression, and punishment.

I am quite aware that in ancient Israel this theme of God's wrath was heavily moralized by contact with the law and the commandments. But its irrational side surged up again when the "wisdom" of Babylon and Israel was confronted with another problem than transgression, namely, the problem of the failure of theodicy. If the course of history and of individual destinies escapes the law of retribution, then the moral vision of the world collapses; it is necessary to accept, in resignation, confidence, and reverence, an order which is in no way transcribable into ethical terms. The tragic God arises again from the ruins of retribution, in the same measure that the ethical God has been juridicized on the path of the law and innumerable ordinances.

This is why the return to the theme of God's wrath forms part of the dejuridicization of the sacred which we are pursuing along several paths at the same time. The symbolism of "wrath" and that of the "conjugal" bond are here concurrent: if indeed the Covenant is more than a contract, if it is the sign of a creative relation, and if sin is more than a transgression, if it is the expression of an ontological separation, then the wrath of God can be another symbol of this same separation, experienced as threat and as active destruction.

If such is sin in its hyperjuridical sense, it must be said that punishment is nothing else than sin itself; it is not an evil which is added to evil; it is not what a punitive will makes someone undergo as the price of a rebel will. This juridical relation of willing to willing is only the image of a more fundamental situation, in which the punishment for sin is sin itself as punishment, namely, the separation itself. In this sense I shall venture to say that it is necessary to dejuridicize punishment as much as it is necessary to desacralize the juridical. We must rediscover this radical dimension where sin and punishment are one, and together signify a break within a creative community. The two operations are conjoined: we must restore punishment to the sphere of abstract right and at the same time deepen it in its nonjuridical sense, to the point where it is identified with the fundamental evil of separation.

Such is the "figurative" of punishment. We now understand its derivative character and, at the same time, its efficacy and attraction. It is a myth of second degree, a rationalization, which replaces more primitive symbols of a lyric or tragic character; as such, the whole symbolism of law is placed on the same level as mythologies of a cosmological character. But it has a preeminence over artificialist and animist myths which is easily explained: first of all, the myth of law, which includes that of punishment, represents the personalizing intention of the bond of creation, by virtue of the "personalist" aspects of abstract right, whereas the artificialist or animist myth represents the nonpersonal, cosmic aspects of this bond. In addition, as distinct from other metaphors of Judaeo-Christian creationism, the juridical metaphor articulates highly rationalizable traits of human experience, nothing having more clarity, rigor, or historical continuity than the juridical experience, under its double form of contract and punishment; the juridical mythology has this advantage over all others of being a "mytho-logic." Finally, just as, in the myth, the rationality of right rejoins the sources of terror at that point where the sacred signifies absolute menace, the conjunction of reason and danger makes of this "mytho-logic" the most deceiving, the most fallacious of mythologies, the most difficult, consequently, to deconstruct, but, above all, the one which resists reinterpretation most strenuously.

Now, HAVE WE SATISFIED THE REQUIREMENTS of a re-interpretation, worthy of this "mytho-logic," by treating punish-ment as a simple "figurative"? Ought we to be content with a procedure that is limited to breaking the shell of one metaphor by striking it against that of opposed metaphors? It is clear that this game remains a prisoner of representation and does not overcome the law of punishment on the level of the concept. This is why *analogy* ought only to give access to a new logic, one which is first enunciated in the traits of antilogic or "absurd" logic. This is the way of the Pauline paradox, in the famous texts on justification which we have already mentioned once, but in accordance with the logic of punishment. It is a matter now of making the myth of punishment "self-destruct" by a kind of *"reversal of the pro and the con,"* performed in the very schema of the law and with the resources of judicial language itself. I will therefore attempt a second reading of Pauline justi-fication, which will correspond point by point with the literal reading at the beginning.

From the first words of the great text of the Epistle to the Romans (1:16–17, 5:21), it is clear that what Paul calls the justice of God—*dikaiosunē Theou*—is hyperjuridical in its con-ception; here is the opening statement of this famous develop-ment: "For I am not ashamed of the Gospel: it is the power of God saving all who have faith—Jews first, but Greeks as well—since this is what reveals the justice of God to us: it shows how faith leads to faith, or as scripture says: The just man finds life through faith" (Rom. 1:16–17).[6] It is noteworthy that all the commentators have had to confront this complex theme, which condemns them to lay out and juxtapose heterogeneous ele-ments: judicial justice *and* grace; punishment *and* fidelity to promises; expiation *and* mercy. But can the properly juridical moment subsist simply alongside the moment of mercy, without undergoing a transformation which destroys it as juridical? How

6. [The Jerusalem version of the Bible is used for these citations.—TRANS.]

could the living justice which is life-giving remain judicial in one self-enclosed part?

Let us follow the movement of the Epistle.

As we said in our first reading, Paul enters the problematic of justification by the gateway of anger: "The anger of God is being revealed from heaven against all the impiety and injustice of men who keep truth imprisoned in injustice" (Rom. 1:18). Here it is the case, then, that the justice which vivifies reiterates the justice which condemns; the so-called logic of punishment is even inserted like a block in the development: "on that day of Wrath . . . when the just judgment of God will be made known. He will repay each one as his works deserve. For those who sought renown and honor and immortality by always doing good there will be eternal life; for the unsubmissive who refused to take truth for their guide and took injustice instead, there will be anger and fury" (Rom. 2:5–8). How can this *closed* economy of judgment, which separates the good from the wicked outside any Gospel, be complementary with anything other than itself within a broader economy, whose principle we shall speak of below? How can a fragment of judicial justice subsist within life-giving justice? Will this "pre-gospel" remain unassimilated, an island within the Gospel of grace?

It seems to me that the logic of Paul is much more paradoxical than we are able to understand within a juridical mentality, which, Hegel has shown, remains a logic of identity.

Paul is truly the creator of this *reversal of the pro and the con* which Luther, Pascal, and Kierkegaard have raised to the rank of a logic of faith.

For Paul, it is first necessary to go to the *extreme* of condemnation in order then to go to the *extreme* of mercy: "For the wages of sin is death; the present given by God is eternal life in Christ Jesus our Lord" (Rom. 6:23). This absurd logic, as Kierkegaard calls it, makes the logic of law shatter upon an internal contradiction: the law pretends to give life but gives only death. An absurd logic, which produces only its contrary. What would appear to us as a logic of identity—"the wages of sin is death"—becomes the lived contradiction which makes the economy of the law break apart. By this absurd logic, the concept of law destroys itself and, with the concept of law, the whole cycle of notions which are governed by it: judgment, condemnation, punishment. This economy is now placed *en bloc* under the sign of death.

The logic of punishment serves thus as contrast, as counterpart, as counterpoint for the annunciation and proclamation which is the Gospel itself: "But now, without the law, the justice of God is manifested . . ." (Rom. 3:21). It is still justice, but the justice which vivifies: "This justification by faith without the deeds of the law" (Rom. 3:28) poses an unprecedented problem for thought: is it the justification which falls within the logic of punishment by reason of the expiation of Christ, as we were saying at the beginning? We can certainly maintain justification within the juridical framework where it is expressed and claim that the tribunal is confirmed by acquittal, which, strictly speaking, is still a judicial act. But does not one then remain a prisoner of words, of images, and, if I dare say it, of the stage setting? The judicial apparatus plays the role, in the doctrine of justification, of an awesome and grandiose staging, comparable to the primitive "scenes" that the archaeology of the unconscious discovers. One could speak, by way of symmetry, of the "eschatological scene": one drags the accused before the tribunal; the public prosecutor convicts him of crime; he deserves death; and then, here is the surprise: he is declared just! Another has paid; the justice of this other one is imputed to him. But how could one take this imagery literally? What kind of tribunal is it where the accused, convicted of crime, is acquitted? Isn't this a nontribunal? Isn't the verdict of acquittal a non-verdict? The imputation a nonimputation?

We cannot, therefore, treat the logic of punishment as an autonomous logic: it is eliminated in the absurd demonstration of its contrary; it has no internal consistency; and about anger, condemnation, and death we know only one thing, namely, that in Jesus Christ we have been delivered from them. It is only when we have crossed the border, into grace, that we can look back on what we have been exempted from.

It is toward this interpretation that the argument of Paul points when, in its second moment, the absurd logic is surpassed by what one can call the logic of "superabundance." We know the parallel often cited between Adam and Jesus Christ in Chapter 5 of the Epistle to the Romans: "As the fault of one brought condemnation upon all men, so also the justice of one procures for all a justification that gives life. For as by one man's disobedience, the whole race was rendered sinful, so by the obedience of one, the whole race will be rendered just." This parallel is only the rhetorical framework in which is inserted another logic: with a feigned negligence, Paul begins the parallel, then suspends it and suddenly breaks it: "Just as by one man sin entered the world and through sin death and thus death has passed through the whole human race because everyone has sinned"—then follows a succession of incidents: "When law came . . . ," "Nevertheless death . . ."—and then, suddenly, the break in the construction and the reversal: "But the gift considerably outweighed the fall," "But not as the fault, so also the gift" (Rom. 5:12–15). It is another economy that is expressed rhetorically by this syntactical rupture:

> For if by the fault of one many died, *how much more* (πολλῷ μᾶλλον) the grace of God and the gift conferred by the grace of one man, Jesus Christ, have abounded unto many. And again, the gift is not to be compared in its effect with that one man's sin. The results of the gift also outweigh the results of one man's sin: for after one single fall came judgment with a verdict of condemnation, now after many falls comes grace with its verdict of justification. For if the reign of death was established by the one man through the sin of him alone, *how much more* (πολλῷ μᾶλλον) shall the reign of life be established in those who receive with profusion the grace and gift of justice by the one man Jesus Christ (Rom. 5:15–17).

"How much more . . . ," "How much more . . . ." Will one still dare to call logic this *reversal of the pro and the con* which makes the grammar of comparison break into pieces? "Moreover the law entered, that fault might abound. But where sin abounded, grace did much more abound" (Rom. 5:20–21). The logic of punishment was a logic of equivalence (the wages of sin is death); the logic of grace is a logic of surplus and excess. It is nothing else than the folly of the Cross.

The consequences are considerable. Is not the representation of a judgment which would separate the just from the unjust by a kind of method of division which would send some to hell and others to heaven itself surpassed, as nondialectical, as foreign to this logic of superabundance? The ultimate paradox seems to be that of a double destination, each overlapping the other: the justification of all men is superimposed in some way on the condemnation of all, by means of a kind of outbidding at the heart of the same history. The economy of superabundance is there intermixed with the work of death in the midst of the same "multitude" of men. Whoever could understand the "how much more" of the justice of God and the "superabundance" of his grace would thereby be finished with the myth of punishment and its logical appearance.

BUT WHAT IS IT to be finished with the myth of punishment? Is it to relegate it to the bin of lost illusions? I would suggest one solution to all our aporias, a solution which would satisfy both the Hegelian demythologization and the absurd logic of Paul: the logic of punishment would appear to me to subsist in the manner of a shattered myth, a ruin, at the heart of this new logic, that is at the same time foolishness, the folly of the Cross. The status of the myth is then that of the *memorial*. By "memorial" I understand this paradoxical status of an economy which can be preached only as a ruined epoch. For Paul, punishment forms part of an entire economy which he calls *nomos*, law, and which has its own internal logic: law leads to covetousness, which evokes transgression, which entails condemnation and death. This whole economy oscillates within the past under the thrust of the "but now": "But now, without the law, the justice of God is made manifest . . ." (Rom. 3:21).

Thus the memorial is a transcended past, on which one can confer neither the status of illusion, from which one would be delivered, without relapse, by a simple movement of demythologization at the service of our thought, nor that of an eternal law of truth, which would find in the atonement of the Just One its supreme confirmation. Punishment is more than an idol to break and less than a law to idolize. It is an economy which "marks an epoch" and which preaching retains in its memory of the Gospel. If the wrath of God no longer had any meaning for me, I would no longer understand what pardon and grace signify; but if the logic of punishment had its own meaning, if it were sufficient unto itself, it would be forever invincible as a law of being; the atonement of Christ would have to be inscribed within this logic, and this would be the greatest victory, because it occurs in the theologies of "vicarious satisfaction," which remain theologies of punishment and not of gift and grace.

Can we now *think* this memorial of punishment? This is perhaps the last aporia we have to consider here; this aporia concerns the *epochal* character of a ruined economy, which is something more than a human representation or than an illusion to be dissolved, and something less than an eternal law. Can we *think* the passage from one economy to the other as an event in the divine, as an accession to the sacred? Philosophers perhaps do not yet have a logic that conforms to this thinking; poets, at least, have always had a language for expressing these epochs of being. Aeschylus asks, in the *Oresteia:* "Third is for the savior.

He came. Shall I call it that, or death? Where is the end? Where shall the fury of fate be stilled to sleep, be done with?" (*The Libation-Bearers*, ll. 1073–75). Amos answers Aeschylus: "The wrath of God is for a moment; his *hesed*, his fidelity, is for the whole of life."

PART V

Religion and Faith

Preface to Bultmann

TO PRESENT TO A FRENCH PUBLIC today two works of Rudolf Bultmann as significant as the *Jesus* of 1926 and the book which resulted from the 1951 conferences, *Jesus Christ and Mythology*,[1] does not require summarizing a text that speaks clearly for itself. More urgent, perhaps, is first of all inviting the reader to adopt an interrogatory point of view so that the question which motivates this text can be posed. This is the hermeneutic question in Christianity. It might next be useful to clear up several false conceptions, principally about myth and demythologizing, which obscure the work for the reader and prevent him from reading Bultmann correctly. Finally, it might be illuminating to confront these essays with other kinds of contemporary work in hermeneutics which can highlight Bultmann's work and help the reader to better comprehend his enterprise. An introduction will have fulfilled its task if it permits the reader to better question, read, and think the book he is about to take up.

I. THE HERMENEUTIC QUESTION

ALTHOUGH THERE HAS ALWAYS BEEN a hermeneutic problem in Christianity, the hermeneutic question today seems to

Translated by Peter McCormick.
1. Rudolf Bultmann, *Jesus and the Word*, trans. Louise P. Smith and Erminie Huntress (New York: Scribner's, 1934), and *Jesus Christ and Mythology*, ed. Paul Schubert (New York: Scribner's, 1958).

us a new one. What does this situation mean, and why does it seem marked with this initial paradox?

There has always been a hermeneutic problem in Christianity because Christianity proceeds from a proclamation. It begins with a fundamental preaching that maintains that in Jesus Christ the kingdom has approached us in decisive fashion. But this fundamental preaching, this word, comes to us through writings, through the Scriptures, and these must constantly be restored as the living word if the primitive word that witnessed to the fundamental and founding event is to remain contemporary. If hermeneutics in general is, in Dilthey's phrase, the interpretation of expressions of life fixed in written texts, then Christian hermeneutics deals with the unique relation between the Scriptures and what they refer to, the "kerygma" (the proclamation).

This relation between writing and the word and between the word and the event and its meaning is the crux of the hermeneutic problem. But this relation itself appears only through a series of interpretations. These interpretations constitute the history of the hermeneutic problem and even the history of Christianity itself, to the degree that Christianity is dependent upon its successive readings of Scripture and on its capacity to reconvert this Scripture into the living word. Certain characteristics of what can be called the hermeneutic situation of Christianity have not even been perceived until our time. These traits are what makes the hermeneutic problem a modern problem.

Let us try to chart this hermeneutic situation, in a more systematic than historical way. Three moments can be distinguished here which have developed successively, even though implicitly they are contemporaneous.

The hermeneutic problem first arose from a question which occupied the first Christian generations and which held the fore even to the time of the Reformation. This question is: what is the relation between the two Testaments or between the two Covenants? Here the problem of allegory in the Christian sense was constituted. Indeed, the Christ-event is hermeneutically related to all of Judaic Scripture in the sense that it interprets this Scripture. Hence, before it can be interpreted itself—and there is our hermeneutic problem—the Christ-event is already an interpretation of a preexisting Scripture.

Let us understand this situation well. Originally, there were not, properly speaking, two Testaments, two Scriptures; there was one Scripture and one event. And it is this event that makes the entire Jewish economy appear ancient, like an old letter. But there is a hermeneutic problem because this novelty is not purely and simply substituted for the ancient letter; rather, it remains ambiguously related to it. The novelty abolishes the Scripture and fulfills it. It changes its letter into spirit like water into wine. Hence the Christian fact is itself understood by effecting a mutation of meaning inside the ancient Scripture. The first Christian hermeneutics is this mutation itself. It is entirely contained in the relation between the letter, the history (these words are synonyms), of the old Covenant and the spiritual meaning which the Gospel reveals after the event. Hence this relation can be expressed quite well in allegorical terms. It can resemble the allegorizing of the Stoics or that of Philo, or it can adopt the quasi-Platonic language of the opposition between flesh and spirit, between shadow and true reality. But what is issue here is basically something else. It is a question of the typological value of the events, things, persons, and institutions of the old economy in relation to those of the new. Saint Paul creates this Christian allegory. Everyone knows the interpretation of Hagar and Sarah, the two wives of Abraham, and of their lineage. In their regard the Epistle to the Galatians says: "These things are said allegorically." The word "allegory" here has only a literary resemblance to the allegory of the grammarians, which, Cicero tells us, "consists in saying one thing to make something else understood." Pagan allegory served to reconcile myths with philosophy and consequently to reduce them as myths. But Pauline allegory, together with that of Tertullian and Origen, which depend on it, is inseparable from the mystery of Christ. Stoicism and Platonism will furnish only a language, indeed a compromising and misleading surplus.

Hence there is hermeneutics in the Christian order because the kerygma is the rereading of an ancient Scripture. It is noteworthy that orthodoxy has resisted with all its force the currents, from Marcion to Gnosticism, which wanted to cut the Gospel from its hermeneutic bond to the Old Testament. Why? Would it not have been simpler to proclaim the event in its unity and thus to deliver it from the ambiguities of the Old Testament interpretation? Why has Christian preaching chosen to be hermeneutic by binding itself to the rereading of the Old Testament? Essentially to make the event itself appear, not as an irrational irruption, but as the fulfillment of an antecedent meaning which remained in suspense. The event itself receives a temporal density by being inscribed in a signifying relation of "promise" to "fulfillment." By entering in this way into a historical connection, the event enters also into an intelligible liaison. A contrast is set up between the two Testaments, a contrast which at the same time is a harmony by means of a transfer. This signifying relation attests that the kerygma, by this detour through the reinterpretation of an ancient Scripture, enters into a network of intelligibility. The event becomes advent. In taking on time, it takes on meaning. By understanding itself indirectly, in terms of the transfer from the old to the new, the event presents itself as an understanding of relations. Jesus Christ himself, exegesis and exegete of Scripture, is manifested as logos in opening the understanding of the Scriptures.

Such is the fundamental hermeneutics of Christianity. It coincides with the spiritual understanding of the Old Testament. Of course, the spiritual meaning is the New Testament itself; but because of this detour through a deciphering of the Old Testament, "faith is not a cry" but an understanding.

The second root of the hermeneutic problem is also Pauline. This is so even though it did not reach its full growth until very recently and, in certain respects, only with the moderns, specifically with Bultmann. This idea is that the interpretation of the Book and the interpretation of life correspond and are mutually adjusted. Saint Paul creates this second modality of Christian hermeneutics when he invites the hearer of the word to decipher the movement of his own existence in the light of the Passion and Resurrection of Christ. Hence, the death of the old man and the birth of the new creature are understood under the sign of the Cross and the Paschal victory. But their hermeneutic relation has a double meaning. Death and resurrection receive a new interpretation through the detour of this exegesis of human existence. The "hermeneutic circle" is already there, between the meaning of Christ and the meaning of existence which mutually decipher each other.

Thanks to the admirable work of de Lubac on the "four meanings" of Scripture—historical, allegorical, moral, anagogical—the breadth of this mutual interpretation of Scripture and existence is known. Beyond this simple reinterpretation of the old Covenant and the typological correlation between the two Testaments, medieval hermeneutics pursued the coincidence between the understanding of the faith in the *lectio divina* and the understanding of reality as a whole, divine and human, historical and physical. The hermeneutic task, then, is to broaden the comprehension of the text on the side of doctrine, of practice, of meditation on the mysteries. And consequently it is to equate the understanding of meaning with a total interpretation of existence and of reality in the system of Christianity. In short, hermeneutics understood this way is coextensive with the entire economy of Christian existence. Scripture appears here as an inexhaustible treasure which stimulates thought about everything, which conceals a total interpretation of the world. It is hermeneutics because the letter serves as foundation, because exegesis is its instrument, and also because the other meanings are related to the first in the way that the hidden is related to the manifest. In this way the understanding of Scripture somehow enrolls all the instruments of culture—literary and rhetorical, philosophical and mystical. To interpret Scripture is at the same time to amplify its meaning as sacred meaning and to incorporate the remains of secular culture in this understanding. It is at this price that Scripture ceases to be a limited cultural object: explication of texts and exploration of mysteries coincide. This is the aim of hermeneutics in this second sense: to make the global sense of mystery coincide with a differentiated and articulated discipline of meaning. It is to equate the *multiplex intellectus* with the *intellectus de mysterio Christi*.

Now, among the "four meanings" of Scripture, the Middle Ages made a place for the "moral meaning," which marks the application of the allegorical meaning to ourselves and our morals. The "moral meaning" shows that hermeneutics is much more than exegesis in the narrow sense. Hermeneutics is the very deciphering of life in the mirror of the text. Although the function of allegory is to manifest the newness of the Gospel in the oldness of the letter, this newness vanishes if it is not a daily newness, if it is not new *hic et nunc*. Actually, the function of the moral sense is not to draw morals from Scripture at all, to moralize history, but to assure the correspondence between the Christ-event and the inner man. It is a matter of interiorizing the spiritual meaning, of actualizing it, as Saint Bernard says, of showing that it extends *hodie usque ad nos*, "even to us today." That is why the true role of moral meaning comes after allegory. This correspondence between allegorical meaning and our existence is well expressed by the metaphor of the mirror. It is a matter of deciphering our existence according to its conformity with Christ. We can still speak of interpretation because, on the one hand, the mystery contained in the book is made explicit in our experience and its actuality is confirmed here, and because, on the other hand, we understand ourselves in the mirror of the word. The relation between the text and the mirror—*liber et speculum*—is basic to hermeneutics.

This is the second dimension of Christian hermeneutics.

The third root of the hermeneutic problem in Christianity was not fully recognized and understood until the moderns—until the critical methods borrowed from the secular sciences of history and philology had been applied to the Bible as a whole. Here we return to our initial question: how is it that the hermeneutic problem is so old and so modern? Actually this third root of our problem relates to what can be called the hermeneutic situation itself of Christianity, that is, it is related to the primitive constitution of the Christian kerygma. We must return, in fact, to the witness character of the Gospel. The kerygma is not first of all the interpretation of a text; it is the announcement of a person. In this sense, the word of God is, not the Bible, but Jesus Christ. But a problem arises continually from the fact that this kerygma is itself expressed in a witness, in the stories, and soon after in the texts that contain the very first confession of faith of the community. These texts conceal a first level of interpretation. We ourselves are no longer those witnesses who have seen. We are the hearers who listen to the witnesses: *fides ex auditu*. Hence, we can believe only by listening and by interpreting a text which is itself already an interpretation. In short, our relation, not only to the Old Testament, but also to the New Testament itself, is a hermeneutic relation.

This hermeneutic situation is as primitive as the two others because the Gospel is presented from the time of the second generation as a writing, as a new letter, a new Scripture, added to the old in the form of a collection of writings which will one day be gathered up and enclosed in a canon, the "Canon of Scriptures." The source of our modern hermeneutic problem, then, is this: the kerygma is also a Testament. To be sure, it is new, as we said above; but it is a Testament, that is, a new Scripture. Hence the New Testament must also be interpreted. It is not simply an interpreting with regard to the Old Testament, and an interpreting for life and for reality as a whole; it is itself a text to be interpreted.

But this third root of the hermeneutic problem, the hermeneutic situation itself, has somehow been masked by the two other functions of hermeneutics in Christianity. So long as the New Testament served to decipher the Old, it was taken as an absolute norm. And it remains an absolute norm as long as its literal meaning serves as an indisputable basis on which all the other levels of meaning—the allegorical, moral, and anagogical—are constructed. But the fact is that the literal meaning is itself a text to be understood, a letter to be interpreted.

Let us reflect on this discovery. At first glance it may seem to be a product of our modernity, that is, something which could have been discovered only recently. This is true, for reasons which will be mentioned later. But these reasons themselves refer us back to a fundamental structure which, despite its having been recently discovered, nonetheless was present from the beginning. This discovery is a product of our modernity in the sense that it expresses the backlash of the critical disciplines— philology and history—on the sacred texts. As soon as the whole Bible is treated like the *Iliad* or the Presocratics, the letter is desacralized and the Bible is made to appear as the word of humans. In the same way, the relation "human word/word of God" is placed, no longer between the New Testament and the rest of the Bible, no longer even between the New Testament and the rest of culture, but at the very heart of the New Testament. For the believer, the New Testament itself conceals a relation that needs deciphering. This relation is between what can be understood and received as word of God and what is heard as human speaking.

This insight is the fruit of the scientific spirit, and in this sense it is a recent acquisition. But reflection brings us to discover in the first hermeneutic situation of the Gospel the ancient reason for this later discovery. This situation, we have said, is that the Gospel itself has become a text, a letter. As a text, it expresses a difference and a distance, however minimal, from the event that it proclaims. This distance, always increasing with time, is what separates the first witness from the entire line of those who hear the witness. Our modernity means only that the distance is now considerable between the place I myself occupy at the center of a culture and the original site of the first witness. This distance, of course, is not only spatial; it is above all a temporal one. But the distance is given at the beginning. It is the very first distance between the hearer and the witness of the event.

Thus the somehow accidental distance of a twentieth-century man, situated in another, a scientific and historical culture, reveals an original distance which remained concealed because it was so short; yet it was already constitutive of primitive faith itself. This distance has only become more manifest, particularly since the work of the *Formgeschichte* school. This school has made us conscious of the fact that the witnesses gathered in the New Testament are not only individual witnesses—free witnesses, one might say; they are already situated in a believing community, in its cult, its preaching, and the expression of its faith. To decipher Scripture is to decipher the witness of the apostolic community. We are related to the object of its faith through the confession of its faith. Hence, by understanding its witness, I receive equally, in its witness, what is summons, kerygma, "the good news."

I hope this reflection has shown that hermeneutics has for us moderns a sense that it did not have for the Greek or Latin Fathers, for the Middle Ages, or even for the Reformers, that the very development of the word "hermeneutics" indicates a "modern" sense of hermeneutics. This modern meaning of hermeneutics is only the discovery, the manifestation, of the hermeneutic situation which was present from the beginning of the Gospel but hidden. It is not paradoxical to defend the thesis that the two ancient forms of hermeneutics we have described have contributed to concealing what was radical in the Christian hermeneutic situation. The meaning and function of our modernity is to unveil, by means of the distance which today separates our culture from ancient culture, what has been unique and extraordinary in this hermeneutic situation since the beginning.

II. Demythologization

IT SEEMS TO ME that the hermeneutic question in its third form contains the principle of what Bultmann calls demythologization or demythization. But if the hermeneutic question has been correctly understood, it is important not to separate two problems which are related for Bultmann. It would be wrong to treat them in isolation since in a sense they constitute inverse sides of the same thing. The first problem is demythologization; the second is what is called the hermeneutic circle.

At first glance demythologization is a purely negative enterprise. It consists in becoming conscious of the mythic clothing around the proclamation that "the kingdom of God has drawn near in a decisive fashion in Jesus Christ." In this way we become attentive to the fact that this "coming" is expressed in a mythological representation of the universe, with a top and a bottom, a heaven and an earth, and celestial beings coming from up there to down here and returning from down here to up there. To abandon this mythic wrapping is quite simply to discover the distance that separates our culture and its conceptual apparatus from the culture in which the good news is expressed. In this sense, demythologization cuts to the letter itself. It consists in a new use of hermeneutics, which is no longer *edification,* the construction of a spiritual meaning on the literal meaning, but a boring under the literal meaning, a *de-struction,* that is to say, a de-construction, of the letter itself. This enterprise has something in common with demystification, which I will be speaking about later on. It too is a modern accomplishment, in the sense that it belongs to a postcritical age of faith.

But demythologization is distinguished from demystification by the fact that it is moved by the will to better comprehend the text, that is, to realize the intention of the text which speaks not of itself but of the event. In this sense, demythologization, far from being opposed to kerygmatic interpretation, is its very first application. It marks the return to the original situation, namely, that the Gospel is not a new Scripture to be commented on but is effaced before something else because it speaks of someone who is the true word of God. Demythologization then is only the inverse side of the grasp of the kerygma. Or, one might say, it is the will to shatter the false scandal constituted by the absurdity of the mythological representation of the world by a modern man and to make apparent the true scandal, the folly of God in Jesus Christ, which is a scandal for all men in all times.

Here the question of demythologization refers back to the other question, which I have called the hermeneutic circle. The hermeneutic circle can be stated roughly as follows. To understand, it is necessary to believe; to believe, it is necessary to understand. This formulation is still too psychological. For behind believing there is the primacy of the object of faith over faith; and behind understanding there is the primacy of exegesis and its method over the naïve reading of the text. This means that the genuine hermeneutic circle is not psychological but methodological. It is the circle constituted by the object that regulates faith and the method that regulates understanding. There is a circle because the exegete is not his own master. What he wants to understand is what the text says; the task of understanding is therefore governed by what is at issue in the text itself. Christian hermeneutics is moved by the announcement which is at issue in the text. To understand is to submit oneself to what the object means. Here Bultmann rejects Dilthey's view that understanding the text means grasping in the text an expression of life. This means that the exegete must be able to understand the author of the text better than the author has understood himself. Bultmann says no. It is not the life of the author that governs understanding, but the essence of the meaning that finds expression in the text. Here Bultmann agrees perfectly with Karl Barth, who says in his commentary on the Epistle to the Romans, that understanding is under the command of the object of faith. But what distinguishes Bultmann from Barth is that Bultmann has perfectly understood that this primacy of the object, this primacy of meaning over understanding, is performed only through the understanding, through the exegetical work itself. It is necessary therefore to enter the hermeneutic circle. Only in the understanding of the text do I in fact know the object. Faith in what the text is concerned with must be deciphered in the text that speaks of it and in the confession of faith of the primitive church which is expressed in the text. This is why there is a circle: to understand the text, it is necessary to believe in what the text announces to me; but what the text announces to me is given nowhere but in the text. This is why it is necessary to understand the text in order to believe.

These two series of remarks, one about demythologization and the other about the hermeneutic circle, are inseparable. Indeed, by cutting into the letter, by taking off the mythological wrappings, I discover the summons which is the primary meaning of the text. To separate kerygma from myth is the positive function of demythologization. But this kerygma becomes the positive side of demythologization only in the movement of interpretation itself. That is why it cannot be fixed in any objective statement that would remove it from the process of interpretation.

WE ARE NOW IN A POSITION to confront the errors and mistakes which Bultmann's demythologization has occasioned. In my opinion all of these come from the fact that attention has not been paid to the fact that demythologization is operative on several strategically different levels.

In what follows I want to distinguish the levels of demythologization in Bultmann as well as the successive definitions of myth which correspond to these levels.

At a first level, the most extrinsic and superficial one and hence the most obvious, it is modern man who demythologizes.

What he demythologizes is the cosmological form in primitive preaching. In fact, the conception of a world composed of three stories—heaven, earth, and hell—and peopled with supernatural powers which descend down here from up there is purely and simply eliminated, as out of date, by modern science and modern technology as well as by how man represents ethical and political responsibility. Everything that partakes of this vision of the world in the fundamental representation of the events of salvation is from now on void. And at this level Bultmann is right in saying that demythologization must be pursued without reserve or exception, for it is without a remainder. The definition of myth which corresponds to this level of demythologization is that of a prescientific explanation of the cosmological and eschatological order, an explanation which for modern man is unbelievable. It is in this sense that myth is an additional scandal, added to the true scandal, which is the "folly of the Cross."

But myth is something else than an explanation of the world, of history, and of destiny. Myth expresses in terms of the world —that is, of the other world or the second world—the understanding that man has of himself in relation to the foundation and the limit of his existence. Hence to demythologize is to interpret myth, that is, to relate the objective representations of the myth to the self-understanding which is both shown and concealed in it. Again, we are the ones who are demythologizing, but according to the intention of the myth, which aims at something other than what it says. Myth, then, can no longer be defined in opposition to science. Myth consists in giving worldly form to what is beyond known and tangible reality. It expresses in an objective language the sense that man has of his dependence on that which stands at the limit and at the origin of his world. This definition sets Bultmann in complete opposition to Feuerbach. Myth does not express the projection of human power into a fictitious beyond but rather man's grasp on his origin and end, which he effects by means of this objectification, this putting in worldly form. If myth is really a projection on the level of representation, then it is first of all the reduction of what is beyond to what is on this side. Imaginative projection is only one means and one stage of the giving of a worldly form to the beyond, in terms of the here and now.

At the second level, demythologization is no longer the exclusive work of the modern spirit. The restoration of the myth's intention, counter to its objectifying movement, requires an existential interpretation, such as Heidegger's in *Sein und Zeit*. Far from expressing a necessity of the scientific spirit, this existential interpretation challenges the philosophic and in itself unscientific pretension to exhaust the meaning of reality by science and technology. Heidegger's philosophy furnishes only the philosophical preliminary of a criticism of myth which has its center of gravity in the process of objectification.

But this second level is not the final one. For a Christian hermeneutics, it is not even the most decisive one. Existential interpretation is rightfully applicable to all myths, as Hans Jonas's work indicates. Jonas first applied it, not to the Gospels, but to Gnosticism, in his *Gnosis und spätantiker Geist,* a work published as early as 1930, with an important preface by Rudolf Bultmann. At the first level this myth had no specifically Christian aspects. This is still true at the second level. Thus, Bultmann's entire undertaking is pursued on the assumption that the kerygma itself wants to be demythologized. It is no longer modern man, educated by science, who calls the shots. It is no longer the philosopher and his existential interpretation applied to the universe of myths. It is the kerygmatic core of the original preaching which not only requires but initiates and sets in motion the process of demythologization. Already in the Old Testament the creation stories effect a vigorous demythologization of the sacred cosmology of the Babylonians. More fundamentally still, the preaching of the "name of Yahweh" exercises a corrosive action on all the representations of the divine, on the Baals and their idols.

The New Testament, despite a new recourse to mythological representations, principally to those of Jewish eschatology and the mystery cults, begins the reduction of the images which serve it as a vehicle. The description of man outside of faith puts into play what can already be called an anthropological interpretation of concepts like "world," "flesh," and "sin" which are borrowed from cosmic mythology. Here, it is Saint Paul who begins the movement of demythologization. As to eschatological representations in the proper sense, it is John who goes farthest in the direction of demythologization. The future has already begun in Jesus Christ. The new age has its root in the Christic now. From now on, demythologization proceeds from the very nature of Christian hope and from the relation that the *future of God* maintains with the present.

I think that this hierarchy of levels, in demythologization and in myth itself, is the key to reading Bultmann correctly. If these different levels are not distinguished, Bultmann will be accused either of being inconsistent or of doing violence to the texts. On the one hand, he will be accused of wanting to save a remnant, the kerygma, after having said that demythologization must be brought to its conclusion, without reservation or attenuation. On the other hand, he will be reproached with imposing alien preoccupations on the texts—those of modern man, the heir of science, and those of existential philosophy, borrowed from Heidegger. But Bultmann speaks in turn as a man of science, an existential philosopher, and a hearer of the word. When he occupies this last circle, he preaches. Yes, he preaches; he makes the Gospel heard. Hence it is as a disciple of Paul and Luther that Bultmann opposes justification by faith to salvation by works. By works man is justified and is glorified, that is, man sovereignly determines the meaning of his own existence. In faith he divests himself of his pretension of being self-determined. So it is the preacher who gives the definition of myth as a work wherein man determines God instead of receiving from God his justification. The preacher here turns against the mythmaker, against the man of science, and against the philosopher himself. If the philosopher claims to find something else, in his description of authentic existence, than a formal and empty definition, a possibility for which the New Testament announces the realization, then the philosopher himself falls under the blow of condemnation. Because he declares that he knows how authentic existence becomes realized, he too claims to determine himself. Here is the limit of existential interpretation and, in general, of the recourse to philosophy. This limit is perfectly clear. It coincides with the passage from the second interpretation of myth to the third, that is, to the interpretation which begins from the kerygma itself. More precisely, it begins from the theological core of justification by faith, according to the Pauline and Lutheran tradition.

If, therefore, Bultmann thinks he can still speak in nonmythological terms of the Christ-event and of the acts of God, it is because, as a man of faith, he makes himself dependent on an act which determines him. This decision of faith is thus the center from which the previous definitions of myth and demythologization can begin to be taken up again. Consequently a circulation is set up among all the forms of demythologization— demythologization as work of science, as work of philosophy, and as proceeding from faith. By turns, it is modern man, then the existential philosopher, and finally the believer who calls the shots. The entire exegetical and theological work of Rudolf

Bultmann consists in setting up this great circle in which exegetical science, existential interpretation, and preaching in the style of Paul and Luther exchange roles.

III. THE TASK OF INTERPRETATION

WE NEED TO THINK THROUGH Bultmann's work still more fully. Sometimes we must think with him and sometimes against him. What is not yet sufficiently thought through in Bultmann is the specifically nonmythological core of biblical and theological statements and hence, by contrast, the mythological statements themselves.

Bultmann holds that the "signification" of "mythological statements" is itself no longer mythological. It is possible, he says, to speak in nonmythological terms of the finitude of the world and of man before the transcendent power of God, even of the signification of eschatological myths. The notion of an "act of God" and of "God as act" is, according to him, not mythological. This even includes the notions of "the word of God" and also that of the "call of the word of God." The word of God, he says, calls man and draws him back from self-idolatry. It calls man to his true self. In short, the activity of God, more precisely his acting for us, in the event of the summons and of decision, is the nonmythological element, the nonmythological signification of mythology.

Do we *think* this signification?

It would be tempting to say first off, in Kantian language, that the transcendent, the completely other, is what we "think" preeminently but which we "represent" to ourselves in objective and worldly terms. The second definition of myth goes in this direction: putting the beyond into worldly terms consists in an objectification of what must remain limit and foundation. In general, everything that opposes Bultmann to Feuerbach—and I insist strongly on the total character of the opposition—draws Bultmann close to Kant. "Myth" holds in the first thinker the same place that "transcendental illusion" holds in the second. This interpretation is confirmed by the constant use of the word *Vorstellung*—"representation"—to designate the "images of the world" with which we illusorily fill the thoughts of the transcendent. Does not Bultmann also say that the incomprehensibility of God does not reside on the level of theoretical thought but only on the level of personal existence, that is, on the level of our idolatrous and rebellious will?

But this interpretation of nonmythological elements in the meaning of the limit-idea is contradicted by much more important dimensions of Bultmann's work. Thus it seems that the notions "act of God," "word of God," and "future of God" are statements of pure faith and derive their entire meaning from the surrender of our will when it renounces self-determination. Only in this event do I experience what "act of God" signifies, that is, at the same time *order* and *gift,* birth of the imperative and of the indicative (because you *are* conducted by the spirit, you *walk* according to the spirit). Just as for his teacher, Wilhelm Hermann, so too for Bultmann the object of faith and its foundation are one and the same thing: what I believe is that whereby I believe, that which gives me something to believe. Finally, the nonmythological core is constituted by the statement of the justification of faith which appears consequently as the Gospel in the Gospel. In this Rudolf Bultmann is thoroughly Lutheran, Kierkegaardian, and Barthian. But, with the same stroke, the very question of the meaning of such expressions as wholly other, transcendent, and beyond, as well as act, word, and event, is avoided. It is striking that Bultmann makes hardly any demands on this language of faith, whereas he was so suspicious about the language of myth. From the moment language ceases to "objectify," when it escapes from worldly "representations," every interrogation seems superfluous concerning the meaning of this *Dass*— of this event of encounter—which follows on the *Was*—on general statements and on objectifying representations.

If this is the case, then there is no reflection in Bultmann on language in general but only on "objectification." Hence Bultmann does not seem to be very much preoccupied with the fact that another language replaces the language of myth and hence calls for a new kind of interpretation. For example, he grants without difficulty that the language of faith can take up myth again in the form of symbol or image. He grants also that the language of faith, besides symbols or images, has recourse to analogies. This is the case for all the "personalist" expressions of "encounter." God summons me as a person, encounters me as a friend, commands me as a father. These expressions, Bultmann says, are neither symbols nor images but a way of speaking analogically. Protestant theology believed that it could rely on the "personalist" relation of the I-Thou kind and develop on this basis a theocentric personalism that would escape the difficulties of a natural theology in the Catholic vein, a natural theology considered as a hypostasis of cosmology. But is it possible to avoid critical reflection on the use of analogy in this transposition of the human you to the divine Thou? What relation does analogy have with the symbolic use of myth and with the limit concept of the wholly other? Bultmann seems to believe that a language which is no longer "objectifying" is innocent. But in what sense is it still a language? And what does it signify?

Is the question no longer raised, is the question still under the sway of an objectifying thinking, which looks for the security of the *Was* in "general statements" and puts off surrendering to the insecurity of the *Dass*, of the decision of faith? But in this case, what must be renounced is the very question which has set the entire inquiry in motion, the question of the "signification" of mythological representations. It must be said, then, that the nonmythological signification of myth is no longer of the order of signification at all, that, with faith, there is no longer anything to think, anything to say. The *sacrificium intellectus* we refused to employ for myth is now employed for faith. Moreover, kerygma can no longer be the origin of demythologization if it does not initiate thought, if it develops no understanding of faith. How could it do so if it were not both event and meaning together and therefore "objective" in another acceptation of the word than the one eliminated with mythological representations?

This question is at the center of post-Bultmannian hermeneutics. The opposition between explanation and understanding that came from Dilthey and the opposition between the objective and the existential that came from an overly anthropological reading of Heidegger were very useful in a first phase of the problem. But, once the intention is to grasp in its entirety the problem of the understanding of faith and the language appropriate to it, these oppositions prove to be ruinous. Doubtless it is necessary today to award less importance to *Verstehen* ("understanding"), which is too exclusively centered on existential decision, and to consider the problem of language and of interpretation in all its breadth.

I am not formulating these questions against Bultmann but with the aim of thinking more adequately what remains unthought in Bultmann. And I am doing this for two reasons.

First of all, his work as a New Testament exegete has an inadequate basis in his hermeneutic philosophy. Yet Bultmann— who is too little known in France—is above all the author of the ample and solid *Theology of the New Testament* and the admirable *Commentary on the Gospel of John.* (Here a task remains, that of confronting Bultmann's actual exegesis with the representation he gives of it in his theoretical writings.) His exegesis, it seems to me, is more opposed to Dilthey than his hermeneutics. His exegesis breaks with Dilthey on the essential point. The task of interpretation, when applied to a specific text, is not "to understand its author better than he understood himself," according to a phrase which goes back to Schleiermacher. Rather, the task is to submit oneself to what the text says, to what it intends, and to what it means. But this independence, this sufficiency, this objectivity of the text presupposes a conception of meaning which borrows more from Husserl than from Dilthey. Even if it is true, finally, that the text accomplishes its meaning only in personal appropriation, in the "historical" decision (and this I believe strongly with Bultmann against all the current philosophies of a discourse without the subject), this appropriation is only the final stage, the last threshold of an understanding which has first been uprooted and moved into another meaning. The moment of exegesis is not that of existential decision but that of "meaning," which, as Frege and Husserl have said, is an objective and even an "ideal" moment (ideal in that meaning has no place in reality, not even in psychic reality). Two thresholds of understanding then must be distinguished, the threshold of "meaning," which is what I just described, and that of "signification," which is the moment when the reader grasps the meaning, the moment when the meaning is actualized in existence. The entire route of comprehension goes from the ideality of meaning to existential signification. A theory of interpretation which at the outset runs straight to the moment of decision moves too fast. It leaps over the moment of meaning, which is the objective stage, in the nonworldly sense of "objective." There is no exegesis without a "bearer [*teneur*] of meaning," which belongs to the text and not to the author of the text.

Therefore, far from the objective and the existential being contraries—as happens when there is too exclusive an attachment to the opposition between myth and kerygma—it must be said that the meaning of the text holds these two moments closely together. It is the objectivity of the text, understood as content—bearer of meaning and demand for meaning—that begins the existential movement of appropriation. Without such a conception of meaning, of its objectivity and even of its ideality, no textual criticism is possible. Therefore, the semantic moment, the moment of objective meaning, must precede the existential moment, the moment of personal decision, in a hermeneutics concerned with doing justice to both the objectivity of meaning and the historicity of personal decision. In this respect the problem Bultmann posed is the exact inverse of the problem which contemporary structuralist theories pose. The structuralist theories have taken the "language" side, whereas Bultmann has taken the "speaking" side. But we now need an instrument of thought for apprehending the connection between language and speaking, the conversion of system into event. More than any other discipline that deals with "signs," exegesis requires such an instrument of thought. If there is no objective meaning, then the text no longer says anything at all; without existential appropriation, what the text does say is no longer living speech. The task of a theory of interpretation is to combine in a single process these two moments of comprehension.

This first theme brings us to a second. It is not only the exegete in Bultmann but the theologian in him who demands that the relation between the meaning of the text and existential decision be more adequately conceived and stated. In effect only the "ideal meaning" of the text, its nonphysical and nonpsychological meaning, can be the vehicle of the coming of the word toward us, or, in Bultmann's own language, of "the decisive act of God in Jesus Christ." I do not say that this act of God, this word of God, find their sufficient condition in the objectivity of meaning; but they find their necessary condition there. The act of God has its first transcendence in the objectivity of meaning which it announces for us. The idea itself of announcement, of proclamation, of kerygma, presupposes, if I may say so, an initiative on the part of meaning, a coming to us of meaning, which makes speech a partner or correlate of existential decision. If the meaning of the text does not already confront the reader, how shall the act it announces not be reduced to a simple symbol of inner conversion, of the passage from the old man to the new? To be sure, there is no authorization for saying that God for Bultmann is only another name for authentic existence. Nothing in Bultmann seems to authorize any kind of a "Christian atheism," in which Christ would be the symbol of an existence devoted to others. For Bultmann as for Luther, justification by faith comes from an other than the self, from an other who grants me what he commands of me. Otherwise, authenticity would again become a "work" whereby I would be determining my own existence.

What "lays claim to me" comes to man and does not proceed from him.

But if Bultmann's intention is not dubious, is it provided with the means to think this other origin? Does not his entire enterprise threaten to veer toward fideism since it lacks the support of a meaning that could announce its other origin by confronting me? Here a Husserlian theory of meaning is insufficient. The claim (*Anspruch*) which God's word addresses to our existence, if it is to be thought, presupposes not only that the meaning of the text is constituted as an ideal correlate of my existence. It presupposes also that the word itself belongs to the being who addresses himself to my existence. A complete meditation on the word, on the claim of the word by being, and hence a complete ontology of language is essential here if the expression "word of God" is to be meaningful or, in Bultmann's terms, if this statement is to have a nonmythological signification. But, in Bultmann's work, this remains to be thought. In this regard the help he has looked for from Heidegger is not completely satisfying. What Bultmann asks of Heidegger is essentially a philosophical anthropology capable of furnishing the "proper conceptuality," at the moment of entering upon a biblical anthropology and of interpreting the cosmological and mythological statements of the Bible in terms of human existence. The recourse to Heidegger and to the "preunderstanding" that he offers does not seem condemnable in principle. What Bultmann says about the impossibility of an interpretation without presuppositions seems convincing to me. But I would reproach Bultmann with not having sufficiently followed the Heideggerian "path." In order to avail himself of Heidegger's "existentials" he has taken a short cut, without having made the long detour of the question of being without which these existentials—being-in-the-world, fallenness, care, being-toward-death, and so on—are nothing more than abstractions of lived experience, of a formalized *existenziell*. It must not be forgotten that in Heidegger the existential description does not concern man but the place—the *Da-sein*—of the question of being. This aim is not preeminently anthropological, humanistic, or personalist. Consequently, meaningful statements about man and the person and, *a fortiori*, the analogies concerning God as a person can be thought and grounded only ulteriorly. This inquiry about being, which is part of the being that we are and which makes of us the "there" of being, the Da of Dasein, is in some sense short-circuited in Bultmann. At the same time, the labor of thought connected with this inquiry is also lacking.

But two important things—important even to Bultmann's enterprise—are bound to this labor of thought which he has economized on.

First is the examination of a kind of death of metaphysics as the site of the forgetfulness of the question of being. This examination, which extends also to the metaphysics of the I-Thou relation, belongs today in an organic way to the entire "return to the foundation of metaphysics" itself. Everything that we have said above about *limit* and *foundation,* even with respect to myth, has something in common with this return and with the crisis of metaphysics connected with it. The second implication of the labor of thought proposed by Heidegger concerns language and consequently our effort to think the expression "word of God." If one runs too quickly to the fundamental anthropology of Heidegger, and if one lacks the questioning of being to which this anthropology is attached, then one also lacks the radical revision of the question of language which it allows. The theologian is directly concerned by the attempt to "bring language into language." Let us understand this as bringing the language we speak to the language which is the saying of being, the coming of being into language.

I do not say that theology *must* go by way of Heidegger. I say that, *if* it goes by way of Heidegger, then it is by this path and to this point that it must follow him. This path is longer. It is the path of patience and not of haste and precipitation. On this path the theologian must not be in a hurry to know whether being for Heidegger is the God of the Bible. It is by postponing this question that the theologian may later on think again what the expressions "act of God" and "action of God in his word" denote. To think the expression "word of God" is to agree to be engaged on paths which may become lost. In Heidegger's own words, "It is only by beginning from the truth of being that the essence of the Sacred lets itself be thought. It is only by beginning from the essence of the Sacred that the essence of divinity is to be thought. And it is only in the light of the essence of divinity that whatever the word God names can be thought" (*Letter on Humanism*).

All of this remains to be thought. There is no shorter path for joining a neutral existential anthropology, according to philosophy, with the existential decision before God, according to the Bible. But there is the long path of the question of being and of the belonging of saying to being. It is on this longer path that this can be understood: that the ideality of the meaning of the text, in the spirit of Husserl, is still a "metaphysical" abstraction, a necessary abstraction, to be sure, when faced with the psychological and existential reductions of the meaning of the text, but an abstraction nonetheless in relation to being's primordial claim to *say*.

Yes, all of this remains to be thought, not at all as a rejection of Bultmann or even as a mere supplement to his work, but as somehow a foundation supporting it.

Freedom in the Light of Hope

THE CONCEPT OF RELIGIOUS FREEDOM can be approached in several ways and on several levels. For my part, I discern three. First, one can raise questions about the freedom of the act of faith; one then situates the problem in the field of an essentially psychological or anthropological discussion. But faith is not thereby recognized in its theological specificity; it is treated like a species of belief, and the freedom of the act of faith appears as a particular case of the general power of choosing, or, as we say, of forming an opinion.

On a second level, questions of political science can be raised about the right to profess a specific religion; it is not only a matter of subjective conviction but of public expression of opinion. Religious freedom is then a particular case of the general right to profess opinions without being intimidated by public power. This right forms part of the political pact (contract) which renders the right of one person reciprocal to the right of another. In the last analysis, the basis of this freedom consists not in the psychological power to choose but in the mutual recognition of free wills within the framework of a politically organized community. In this politics of freedom, religion figures as a cultural power, a recognized public force; and the freedom that one claims for it is the more legitimate as religion is not its exclusive beneficiary.

On a third level, the one on which I will try to situate myself, religious freedom signifies the quality of freedom that pertains to the religious phenomenon as such. There is a hermeneutics

Translated by Robert Sweeney.

[402]

of this freedom to the degree that the religious phenomenon itself exists only in the historical process of interpretation and
reinterpretation of the word that engenders it. Therefore I understand the hermeneutics of religious freedom as the explication of
the meanings of freedom which accompany the explication of the
founding word or, as we say, the proclamation of the kerygma.

This third way of posing the problem does not exclude the
preceding ways; I hope to show that this quality of freedom, developed by proclamation and interpretation, recapitulates the
anterior degrees of freedom inasmuch as it concerns what I shall
henceforth call the completion of the discourse of freedom. This
power of recapitulation will even be my constant preoccupation.
In fact, the task of the philosopher appears to me here to be
distinguished from that of the theologian, in the following manner: biblical theology has the function of developing the kerygma
according to its own conceptual system; it has the duty of criticizing preaching, both by confronting it with its origin and by
reorganizing it in a meaningful framework, in a discourse of its
own kind, corresponding to the internal coherence of the
kerygma itself. The philosopher, even the Christian one, has a
distinct task; I am not inclined to say that he brackets what he
has heard and what he believes, for how could he philosophize
in such a state of abstraction with respect to what is essential?
But neither am I of the opinion that he should subordinate his
philosophy to theology, in an ancillary relation. Between absten-
tion and capitulation, there is the autonomous way which I have
located under the heading "the philosophical approach."

I take "approach" in its strong sense of "approximation." I
understand by this the incessant work of philosophical discourse
to put itself into a relation of proximity with kerygmatic and
theological discourse. This work of thought is a work that begins
with listening, and yet within the autonomy of responsible
thought. It is an incessant reform of thinking, but within the
limits of reason alone. The "conversion" of the philosopher is a
conversion within philosophy and to philosophy according to its
internal exigencies. If there is only one *logos*, the *logos* of Christ
requires of me as a philosopher nothing else than a more complete and more perfect activation of reason; not more than reason, but *whole* reason. Let us repeat this phrase, whole reason;
for it is this problem of the integrality of thinking which will
prove to be the core of the whole problematic.

Here, then, is how we shall proceed. I will first of all sketch
out what I, as a hearer of the Word, consider to be the kerygma

of freedom. Then I shall attempt to say—and this is the principal point of my paper—what kind of discourse on freedom philosophy can articulate, beyond psychological and political discourse, that will still merit the name of "discourse" on religious freedom. This homologous discourse is that of religion within the limits of reason alone.

I. The Kerygma of Freedom

It is not initially of freedom that the Gospel speaks to me; it is because it speaks to me of something else that it speaks to me also of freedom: "The truth shall make you free," says John.

Where shall we begin then, if not with freedom? For my part I have been very much taken with—I should say, won over by— the eschatologocal interpretation that Jürgen Moltmann gives to the Christian kerygma in his work *The Theology of Hope*.[1] As we know, Johannes Weiss and Albert Schweitzer are at the origin of the reinterpretation of the whole of the New Testament, starting with the preaching of the Kingdom of God and of the last things and breaking with the moralizing Christ of the liberal exegetes. But then, if the preaching of Jesus and of the primitive church proceeds from the eschatological source, it is necessary to readjust all theology in accordance with the norm of eschatology and cease to make of discourse on the last things a sort of more or less optional appendix to a theology of revelation centered on a notion of *logos* and of manifestation which would itself owe nothing to the hope of things to come.

This revision of theological concepts beginning with an exegesis of the New Testament centered on the preaching of the Kingdom to come finds support in the parallel revision of the theology of the Old Testament inspired by Martin Buber, which insists on the massive opposition between the God of the promise —the God of the desert, of the wandering—and the gods of the "epiphanic" religions. This systematized opposition goes very far. The religion of the "name" is opposed to that of the "idol," as the religion of the God who is coming is opposed to the religion of the God of present manifestation. The first engenders a history, while the second consecrates a nature full of gods. As to

1. Jürgen Moltmann, *The Theology of Hope*, trans. J. W. Leitch (New York: Harper & Row, 1967).

this history, it is less the experience of the change of everything than the tension created by the expectation of a fulfillment; history is itself hope of history, for each fulfillment is perceived as confirmation, pledge, and repetition of the promise. This last designates an increase, a surplus, a "not yet," which maintains the tension of history.[2]

It is this temporal constitution of the "promise" that must now guide us in the interpretation of the New Testament. At first glance, one might think that the Resurrection, the heart of the Christian kerygma, has exhausted the category of promise by fulfilling it.

What has appeared to me precisely as most interesting in the Christology of Moltmann is his effort to resituate the central preaching of the Resurrection in an eschatological perspective. This is crucial for our being able to speak shortly concerning freedom in the light of hope. One might be tempted to say that the Resurrection is the past event par excellence. One thinks of the Hegelian interpretation of the empty tomb as a memorial to nostalgia. All the more might one prefer to locate it within the category of the present by applying it to ourselves, to the new man, as in the existential interpretation of Rudolf Bultmann.

How can we interpret the Resurrection in terms of hope, of

2. I have retained from the exegetical studies of the Old Testament only the core of the promise insofar as it engenders a historical vision. It would be necessary to distinguish, at the interior of this general schema of the promise, prophecy and its intrahistorical hope of later eschatologies, and, among them, the Apocalypses, properly so called, which carry beyond history the final term of all threat and all expectation. But if these distinctions and even these oppositions—particularly those between worldly and transcendent eschatologies—are essential for a theology of the Old Testament, they are less so for the implicit philosophical meaning, namely, the horizon structure of history itself. The horizon is both that which delimits expectation and that which moves along with us. For the imagination, the distinction between a hope in history and a hope outside history is fundamental. Furthermore, in his "The Theology of Israel's Historical Traditions," Gerhard von Rad invites us to redraw the dividing line between prophecy and eschatology: the message of the prophets must be considered eschatological in every case where it considers the old historical bases of salvation null and void. We will therefore call eschatological not just any expression of faith in the future, even if this future is that of sacred institutions; prophetic teaching deserves to be called eschatological only when the prophets dislodge Israel from the security of earlier saving actions and abruptly move the basis of salvation in the direction of a future action of God (von Rad, *Old Testament Theology*, trans. D. M. G. Stalker [New York: Harper & Row, 1962], p. 126). Yet the opposition is never complete, inasmuch as acts of deliverance, announced as new, are represented by analogy to saving acts of the past: New Earth, New David, New Zion, New Exodus, New Covenant.

promise, of the future? Moltmann attempts it by resituating the Resurrection entirely within the framework of the Jewish theology of the promise and by removing it from the Hellenistic schemas of epiphanies of eternity. The Resurrection, interpreted within a theology of promise, is not an event which closes, by fulfilling the promise, but an event which opens, because it adds to the promise by confirming it. The Resurrection is the sign that the promise is henceforth for all; the meaning of the Resurrection is in its future, the death of death, the resurrection of all from the dead. The God who is witnessed to is not, therefore, the God who is but the God who is coming. The "already" of his Resurrection orients the "not yet" of the final recapitulation. But this meaning reaches us disguised by the Greek Christologies, which have made the Incarnation the temporal manifestation of eternal being and the eternal present, thus hiding the principal meaning, namely, that the God of the promise, the God of Abraham, Isaac, and Jacob, has approached, has been revealed as He who is coming for all. Thus disguised by epiphanic religion, the Resurrection has become the pledge of all divine presence in the present world: cultic presence, mystic presence. The task of a hermeneutics of the Resurrection is to reinstitute the potential of hope, to tell the future of the Resurrection. The meaning of the "Resurrection" is in suspense insofar as it is not fulfilled in a new creation, in a new totality of being. To recognize the Resurrection of Jesus Christ is to enter into the movement of hope in resurrection from the dead, to attain the new creation *ex nihilo*, that is, beyond death.

If such is the meaning of hope on its own level of discourse, that of a hermeneutics of the Resurrection, what is the meaning of freedom if it also must be converted to hope? What is freedom *in the light of* hope? I will answer in one word: it is the meaning of my existence in the light of the Resurrection, that is, as reinstated in the movement which we have called the future of the Resurrection of the Christ. In this sense, *a hermeneutics of religious freedom is an interpretation of freedom in conformity with the Resurrection interpreted in terms of promise and hope.*

What does this mean?

The above formula attests that the psychological, ethical, and even political aspects are not absent; but they are not basic because they are not original. Hermeneutics consists in deciphering these original traits in their psychological, ethical, and political expressions, then in reascending, from these expressions, to the nucleus—which I shall call kerygmatic—of freedom in the light of hope.

Indeed, we can speak in psychological terms of a choice for or against life, of a radical alternative; we find texts in this sense which make us think of a philosophical conception of freedom of choice, for example in Deuteronomy: "I call heaven and earth to witness against you today: I set before you life or death, blessing or curse. Choose life, then, so that you and your descendants might live, in the love of Yahweh your God, obeying his voice, clinging to him" (Deut. 30:19–20).[3] The preaching of John the Baptist, and, even more, that of Jesus, is an appeal which incites a *decision*, and this decision can be transcribed into the alternative: either/or. We know the use that has been made, from Kierkegaard to Bultmann, of the theme of the existential decision. But the existential interpretation of the Bible has not been sufficiently attentive to the specificity of this choice; perhaps it even marks a subtle emptying of the eschatological dimension and a return to the philosophy of the eternal present. In any case, there is a great risk of reducing the rich content of eschatology to a kind of instantaneousness of the present decision at the expense of the temporal, historical, communitarian, and cosmic aspects contained in the hope of the Resurrection. If we wish to express freedom in the light of hope in appropriate psychological terms, it will be necessary to speak, with Kierkegaard again, of the *passion for the possible*, which retains in its formulation the mark of the future which the promise puts on freedom. Indeed, it is necessary to draw all the consequences for a meditation on freedom of Moltmann's *antithesis* between religion of promise and religion of presence, to extend the debate with the theophanic religions of the Orient to a debate with the whole of Hellenism, to the degree that this latter proceeds from the Parmenidean celebration of the "It is." It is then not only the Name that must be opposed to the idol, but the "He is coming" of Scripture must be opposed to the "It is" of the *Proem* of Parmenides. This dividing line is henceforth going to separate two conceptions of time and, through them, two conceptions of freedom. The Parmenidean "It is" in effect calls for an ethics of the eternal present; this is sustained only by a continual contradiction between, on the one hand, a detachment, an uprooting from passing things, a

3. [The Jerusalem version of the Bible is used in all biblical quotations in this essay.—Trans.]

distancing and an exile in the eternal, and, on the other hand, consent without reservation to the order of the whole. Stoicism is doubtless the most developed expression of this ethics of the present; the present, for Stoicism, is the unique time of salvation; the past and the future are equally discredited; in one stroke, hope is rejected for the same reason as fear, as a disturbance, an agitation, which proceeds from a revocable opinion concerning imminent evils or coming goods. *Nec spe—nec metu* (Do not hope—do not fear) Spinozist wisdom will say with equal emphasis. And perhaps today what there is of Spinozism in contemporary philosophy returns us to this same wisdom of the present, by means of suspicion, demystification, and disillusionment. Nietzsche speaks of love of fate and pronounces the eternal yes to existence; and Freud reintroduces the tragic *anakē* into the principle of reality. But hope is diametrically opposed, as passion for the possible, to this primacy of necessity. It is allied with the imagination insofar as the latter is the power of the possible and the disposition for being in a radical renewal. Freedom in the light of hope, expressed in psychological terms, is nothing else than this creative imagination of the possible.

But we can also speak in ethical terms and emphasize its character of obedience, of listening. Freedom is a "following" (*Folgen*). For ancient Israel, the Law is the way that leads from promise to fulfillment. Covenant, Law, Freedom, as power to obey or disobey, are derivative aspects of the promise. The Law imposes (*gebietet*) what the promise proposes (*bietet*). The commandment is thus the ethical face of the promise. Of course, with Saint Paul this obedience is no longer transcribed in terms of law; obedience to the Law is no longer the sign of the efficacy of the promise; rather, the Resurrection is the sign.

Nevertheless, a new ethics marks the linkage of freedom to hope—what Moltmann calls the ethics of the *mission* (*Sendung*); the *promissio* involves a *missio;* in the mission, the obligation which engages the present proceeds from the promise, opens the future. But more precisely, the mission signifies something other than an ethics of duty, just as the passion for the possible signifies something other than what is arbitrary. The practical awareness of a "mission" is inseparable from the deciphering of the signs of the new creation, of the *tendential* character of the Resurrection, to quote Moltmann once more.

The mission would thus be the ethical equivalent of hope,

just as the passion for the possible was its psychological equivalent.

This second trait of freedom in the light of hope removes us further than the first trait did from the existential interpretation, which is too much centered on present decision; for the ethics of the mission has communitarian, political, and even cosmic implications, which the existential decision, centered on personal interiority, tends to hide. A freedom open to new creation is in fact less centered on subjectivity, on personal authenticity, than on social and political justice; it calls for a reconciliation which itself demands to be inscribed in the recapitulation of all things.

But these two aspects, psychological and ethicopolitical, of freedom according to hope are the second expressions of a core of meaning which is properly the *kerygmatic center* of freedom, of which we will soon undertake a philosophical approximation.

I shall say this: "Christian freedom"—to take a phrase from Luther—is to belong existentially to the order of the Resurrection. There is its specific element. It can be expressed in two categories, on which I have reflected and worked several times, which explicitly tie freedom to hope: the category of "in spite of" and that of "how much more." They are the obverse and reverse of each other, just as are, with Luther, "freedom from" and "freedom for."

For the "in spite of" is a "free from," but in the light of hope; and the "how much more" is a "free for," equally in the light of hope.

In spite of what? If the Resurrection is resurrection from the dead, all hope and freedom are in spite of death. This is the hiatus which makes of the new creation a *creatio ex nihilo*—a hiatus so profound that the identity of the risen Christ with Jesus crucified is the great question of the New Testament. That identity is not certain; the apparitions do not teach it, but only the word of the Risen One: "It is I, the same." The kerygma announces it as the good news: "the living Lord of the church is the same as Jesus on the Cross." The same question of identity has its equivalent in the Synoptics: how tell the story of the Resurrection? Well, properly speaking, one does not tell it; the discontinuity in the account is the same as in the preaching; for the account also, there is a hiatus between the Cross and the apparitions of the Resurrected. The empty tomb is the expression of this hiatus.

What follows from this for freedom? Henceforth all hope

will carry the same sign of discontinuity, between what is heading toward death and what denies death. This is why it contradicts actual reality. Hope, insofar as it is hope of resurrection, is the living contradiction of what it proceeds from and what is placed under the sign of the Cross and death. According to an admirable phrase of the Reformers, *the Kingdom of God is hidden under its contrary,* the Cross. If the connection between the Cross and the Resurrection is of the order of paradox and not of logical mediation, freedom in the light of hope is not only freedom for the possible but, more fundamentally still, freedom for the denial of death, freedom to decipher the signs of the Resurrection under the contrary appearance of death.

But defiance of death is in its turn the counterpart or inverse of a life-force, of a perspective of growth, which the "how much more" of Saint Paul comes to express. Here I link up with my earlier reflection on the "Interpretation of the Myth of Punishment";[4] there I was opposing to the logic of equivalence, which is the logic of punishment par excellence, the logic of superabundance:

> but the gift itself considerably outweighed the fall. If it is certain that through one man's fall so many died, it is even more certain that divine grace, coming through the one man, Jesus Christ, came to so many as an abundant free gift. . . . If it is certain that death reigned over everyone as the consequence of one man's fall, it is even more certain that one man, Jesus Christ, will cause everyone to reign in life who receives the free gift. . . . When law came, it was to multiply the opportunities of falling, but however great the number of sins committed, grace was even greater (Rom. 5:12–20).

This logic of surplus and excess is as much the folly of the Cross as it is the wisdom of the Resurrection. This wisdom is expressed in an *economy of superabundance,* which we must decipher in daily life, in work and in leisure, in politics and in universal history. To be free is to sense and to know that one belongs to this economy, to be "at home" in this economy. The "in spite of," which holds us ready for disappointment, is only the reverse, the dark side, of the joyous "how much more" by which freedom feels itself, knows itself, wills to conspire with the aspiration of the whole of creation for redemption.

With this third trait the distance is further widened between an eschatological interpretation of freedom and an existential

4. See, above, pp. 374–76.

interpretation which contracts it within the experience of present, interior, subjective decision. Freedom in the light of hope of resurrection has a personal expression, certainly, but, even more, a communitarian, historical, and political expression in the dimension of the expectation of universal resurrection.

It is by starting from this kerygmatic core of hope and freedom that we should now search out a philosophical approximation.

II. A PHILOSOPHICAL APPROXIMATION OF FREEDOM IN THE LIGHT OF HOPE

IN BEGINNING THE TASK that is proper to the philosopher, I wish to recall what I said in the introduction concerning the approximation in philosophical discourse to the kerygma of hope. This setting in proximity, I said, is both a work of listening and an autonomous enterprise, a thinking "in the light of . . ." and a free thinking.

How is this possible?

There is, it seems to me, in the kerygma of hope, both an innovation of meaning and a demand for intelligibility, which simultaneously create the measure and the task of approximation.

An innovation of meaning is what Moltmann emphasizes by opposing the promise to the Greek *logos;* hope begins as "a-logical." It effects an irruption into a closed order; it opens up a career for existence and history. Passion for the possible, mission and exodus, denial of the reality of death, response of super-abundance of meaning to the abundance of non-sense—these are so many signs of the *new* creation whose *novelty* catches us, in the strict sense, unawares. Hope, in its springing forth, is "aporetic," not by reason of lack of meaning but by excess of meaning. Resurrection surprises by being in excess in comparison to the reality forsaken by God.

But if this novelty did not make us think, then hope, like faith, would be a cry, a flash without a sequel; there would be no eschatology, no doctrine of last things, if the novelty of the new were not made explicit by an indefinite repetition of signs, were not verified in the "seriousness" of an interpretation which incessantly separates hope from utopia. Likewise, the exegesis of hope by means of freedom, as we have just outlined it, is already a way of *thinking* according to hope. The passion for the possible must graft itself onto real tendencies, the mission onto a sensed history, the superabundance onto signs of the Resurrection, wherever they can be deciphered. It is necessary, therefore, that the Resurrection deploy its own logic, which obviates the logic of repetition.

We cannot restrict ourselves to the nondialectical opposition between the promise and the Greek *logos;* we cannot remain there, under pain of not being able to say, with the theologian himself, *spero ut intelligam*—I hope in order to understand.

But what understanding?

At the end of the introduction I was suggesting a possible direction of research by saying that the discourse of the philosopher on freedom which stays close to the kerygma, which makes itself homologous with it, is the discourse of religion within the limits of reason alone.

The phrase sounds Kantian, to be sure; it "shows its colors." But the Kantianism that I wish to develop now is, paradoxically, more to be constructed than repeated; it would be something like a post-Hegelian Kantianism, to borrow an expression from Eric Weil, which, it appears, he applied to himself. For my own part I accept the paradox, for reasons that are both philosophical and theological.

First, for reasons that are philosophical: chronologically, Hegel comes after Kant, but we later readers go from one to the other. In us, something of Hegel has vanquished something of Kant; but something of Kant has vanquished something of Hegel, because we are as radically post-Hegelian as we are post-Kantian. In my opinion, it is this exchange and this permutation which still structure philosophical discourse today. This is why the task is to think them always better by thinking them together —one against the other, and one by means of the other. Even if we begin by thinking something else, this "thinking Kant and Hegel better" pertains, in one way or the other, to this "thinking differently from Kant or Hegel," "something other than Kant or Hegel."

Such "epochal" considerations, internal to philosophy, join up with another order of reflection, which concerns what I have called "approximation," "putting into proximity." This closeness to a kerygmatic thought provokes, it seems to me, "effects of meaning," on the level of philosophical discourse itself, which often take the form of dislocation and recasting of systems. The theme of hope has precisely a *fissuring* power with regard to closed systems and a power of *reorganizing* meaning; it is inclined by this very fact to the exchanges and permutations I was just now suggesting.

I therefore see as converging toward the idea of a post-Hegelian Kantianism the spontaneous restructurings of our philosophical memory and those which proceed from the shock effect of the kerygma of hope on the philosophical problematic and on the structures of its discourse.

The route I propose to explore is opened up by the important distinction instituted by Kantian philosophy between understanding and reason. This split contains a potential of meaning whose suitability to an *intellectus fidei et spei* I would like to demonstrate. How? Essentially by the function of horizon that reason assumes in the constitution of knowledge and will. That is, I address myself directly to the dialectical part of the two Kantian *Critiques*: Dialectic of theoretical reason and Dialectic of practical reason. A philosophy of limits which is at the same time a practical demand for totalization—this, to my mind, is the philosophical response to the kerygma of hope, the closest philosophical approximation to freedom in the light of hope. Dialectic in the Kantian sense is to my mind the part of Kantianism which not only survives the Hegelian critique but which triumphs over the whole of Hegelianism.

For my own part, I abandon the ethics of duty to the Hegelian critique with no regrets; it would appear to me, indeed, to have been correctly characterized by Hegel as an abstract thought, as a thought of understanding. With the *Encyclopaedia* and the *Philosophy of Right,* I willingly concede that formal "morality" is simply a segment in a larger trajectory, that of the realization of freedom (Preface to *Philosophy of Right,* § 4). Defined in these terms, terms that are more Hegelian than Kantian, the philosophy of the will neither begins nor ends with the form of duty; it begins with a confrontation of will with will, with respect to things that can be appropriated; its first conquest is not duty but the contract, in a word, abstract right. The moment of morality is only the infinite reflective moment, the moment of interiority, which makes ethical subjectivity appear. But the meaning of this subjectivity is not in the abstraction of a separated form; it is in the further constitution of concrete communities: family, economic collectivity, political community. We recognize there the movement of the *Encyclopaedia* and the *Philosophy of Right:* movement from the sphere of abstract right to the sphere of subjective and abstract morality, then to the sphere of objective and concrete morality. This philosophy of the will which traverses all the levels of objectification, universalization, and realization is to my eyes *the* philosophy of the will, with much more justification than the meager determination of the *Wille* by the form of the imperative in the Kantian philosophy. Its greatness derives from the diversity of problems that it traverses and resolves: union of desire and culture, of psychology and politics, of the subjective and the universal. All the philosophies of the will, from Aristotle to Kant, are there assumed and subsumed. This great philosophy of the will is, for me, an inexhaustible reservoir of descriptions and mediations. We have not yet exhausted it. A theology of hope cannot but be in dialogue with it, so close to it is the problem of the *actuation* of freedom.

And yet, Kant remains. What is more, he surpasses Hegel from a certain point of view—a point of view which is precisely essential for our present dialogue between a theology of hope and a philosophy of reason. The Hegel I reject is the philosopher of retrospection, the one who not only accompanies the dialectic of the Spirit but reabsorbs all rationality in the already happened meaning. The point of discordance between the *intellectus fidei et spei* and Hegel becomes clear to me when I reread the famous text which terminates the Preface of the *Philosophy of Right:*

> To say one more word about preaching what the world ought to be like, philosophy arrives always too late for that. As *thought* of the world it appears at a time when actuality has completed its developmental process and is finished. What the conception teaches, history also shows as necessary, namely, that only in a maturing actuality the ideal appears and confronts the real. It is then that the ideal rebuilds for itself this same world in the shape of an intellectual realm, comprehending this world in its substance. When philosophy paints its gray in gray, a form of life has become old, and this gray in gray cannot rejuvenate it, only understand it. The owl of Minerva begins its flight only when dusk is falling.[5]

"Philosophy always comes too late." Philosophy, without a doubt. But what about reason?

It is this question which sends me from Hegel to Kant, to a Kant who does not founder in the ethic of the imperative, to a Kant who, in his turn, understands Hegel. As I have said, this is the Kant of the dialectic, the Kant of the two Dialectics.

5. G. W. F. Hegel, *The Philosophy of Right,* trans. T. M. Knox (New York: Oxford University Press, 1942), Preface, *ad fin.*

For both Dialectics accomplish the same movement, examine the same division, by instituting the tension which makes of Kantianism a philosophy of limits and not a philosophy of system. That division is discerned from the first and decisive distinction between *Denken*, or thought of the unconditioned, and *Erkennen*, or thought by way of objects, proceeding from the conditioned to the conditioned. The two Dialectics result from this initial division between *Denken* and *Erkennen;* and, with the two Dialectics, is thus born the question which sets in motion the philosophy of religion: What can I hope for? It is that sequence, Dialectic of pure reason—Dialectic of practical reason—philosophy of religion, which we must now scrutinize.

The first is necessary to the second and the third because it introduces, at the very heart of the thought of the unconditioned, the critique of transcendental illusion, a critique that is indispensable to an *intellectus spei*. The domain of hope is quite precisely coextensive with the region of transcendental illusion.

I hope, there where I necessarily deceive myself, by forming absolute objects: self, freedom, God. In this respect we have not sufficiently stressed the idea that the critique of the paralogism of subjectivity is as important as the critique of the antinomy of freedom and, of course, as important as the critique of the proofs for the existence of God. The sophisms of the substantiality of the "I" even today retain a particular luster, along with the Nietzschean and Freudian critiques of the subject; it is not without importance to find the root and philosophical meaning of them in the Kantian dialectic; this latter has condemned in advance any claim to dogmatize on personal existence and knowledge of the person; the person is manifested only in the practical act of treating it as an end and not merely as a means. The Kantian concept of the transcendental illusion, applied to the religious object par excellence, is one of inexhaustible philosophical fecundity; it grounds a critique that is radically different from that of Feuerbach or Nietzsche. It is because there is a legitimate thought of the unconditioned that the transcendental illusion is possible; this latter does not proceed from the projection of the human into the divine but, on the contrary, from the filling-in of the thought of the unconditioned according to the mode of the empirical object. That is why Kant can say: it is not experience that limits reason but reason that limits the claim of sensibility to extend our empirical, phenomenal, spatiotemporal knowledge to the noumenal order.

This entire movement—thought of the unconditioned,

transcendental illusion, critique of absolute objects—is essential to an understanding of hope. It constitutes a receptive structure within the framework of which the descriptions and denunciations of the post-Hegelian era will be able to be reassumed. Kantian philosophy comes out of this enriched; but, in return, atheism, whenever it is recharged by the Kantian philosophy of the transcendental illusion, is stripped of another illusion—its own: the anthropological illusion.

What does the Dialectic of practical reason add that is new? Essentially a transposition to the will of what we might call the completion structure of pure reason. This second step is concerned very closely with our meditation on the understanding of hope. Indeed, the Dialectic of practical reason adds nothing to the principle of morality, assumed to be defined by the formal imperative; nor does it add anything more to our knowledge of our duty than the Dialectic of pure reason adds to our knowledge of the world. What it does give to our will is essentially a *goal—die Absicht aufs höchste Gut.* That goal is the expression, on the level of duty, of the demand, the claim—the *Verlangen*—which constitutes pure reason in its speculative and practical use; reason "demands the absolute totality of conditions for a given conditioned thing" (beginning of the Dialectic of the *Critique of Practical Reason*). By the same stroke, the philosophy of the will takes on its true meaning: it is not exhausted in the relation between the maxim and the law, between the arbitrary and the willed; a third dimension appears: arbitrary—law—aim of totality. What the will thus requires, Kant calls "the entire object of pure practical reason." He says again: "the unconditioned totality of the object of pure practical reason, that is, of a pure will." That he applies to it the old name of "highest good" should not hide the novelty of his move: the concept of the highest good is both purified of all speculation by the critique of the transcendental illusion and entirely measured by the problematic of practical reason, that is, of the will. It is the concept by which the *completion of the will* is thought. It thus takes the place of Hegelian absolute knowledge exactly. More precisely, it does not permit any knowledge, but only a demand which, we will see further on, has something to do with hope. But we already have some presentiment of it in the role played by the idea of totality; "highest" signifies not solely "supreme" (nonsubordinated) but "whole" and "complete" (*ganz und vollendete*). Now this totality is not given but demanded; it cannot be given, not only because the critique of the transcendental illusion accompanies it without fail, but because practical reason, in its dialectic, institutes a new antinomy; what it demands, in fact, is that happiness be added to morality; it thus requires to be added to the object of its aim, that this object may be whole, what it excluded from its principles, that they might be pure.

This is why a new kind of illusion accompanies it, no longer a theoretical illusion but a practical one, that of a subtle hedonism, which would reintroduce an interest into morality under the pretext of happiness. In this idea of an antinomy of practical reason I see a second receptive structure for a critique of religion, applied more properly to its instinctual aspects, as in Freud. Kant gives us the means of thinking that critique of "hedonism" in religion—reward, consolation, etc.—by means of the very close-knit dialectic where pleasure, enjoyment, satisfaction, contentment, beatitude, are confronted. Henceforth, the connection—the *Zusammenhang*—between morality and happiness must remain a transcendent synthesis, the union of different things, "specifically distinct." Thus the meaning of the Beatitudes is approached philosophically only by the idea of a nonanalytic liaison between the work of man and the contentment susceptible of satisfying the desire which constitutes his existence. But for the philosopher this liaison is not meaningless, even if it cannot be produced by his will; he can even say boldly: "It is *a priori* (morally) necessary to bring forth the highest good through the freedom of the will; the condition of its possibility therefore must rest solely on *a priori* grounds of knowledge." [6]

Such is the second rational approximation of hope: it resides in this *Zusammenhang*, in this connection that is necessary yet not given, but simply demanded, expected, between morality and happiness. No one as much as Kant has had a sense for the transcendent character of this connection, and this against the whole of Greek philosophy to which he is directly opposed, rejecting Epicurean and Stoic equally: happiness is not our accomplishment: it is achieved by superaddition, by surplus.

A third rational approach to hope is that of religion itself, but of religion within the limits of reason alone. Kant explicitly brings religion to the question "What can I hope for?" I do not know any other philosopher who has defined religion exclusively

6. Immanuel Kant, *Critique of Practical Reason*, trans. L. W. Beck (New York: Liberal Arts Press, 1956), "Dialectic," p. 117. [All page numbers in parentheses in text in the remainder of this essay refer to this volume.]

with that question. Now, that question is born both *within* and *outside* the critique: within the critique, by means of the famous "postulates"; outside the critique, by the detour of a reflection on radical evil. Let us try to understand this new linkage. So little is it arbitrary that it alone contains the final implication of freedom within hope—an implication on which the first part of our meditation rested.

First, the postulates. These are, as we know, beliefs of a theoretical character—bearing on existents—but necessarily dependent on practical reason. This status would be scandalous if one had not previously established the status of practical reason itself in its dialectical part. Theoretical reason, as such, is postulation, the postulation of a fulfillment, of a complete achievement. The postulates therefore participate in the process of totalization initiated by the will in its terminal directedness; they designate an order of things to come to which we know we belong; each one designates a moment of the institution, or better, of the installation, of that totality which, as such, is to be effected. One does not, therefore, understand the true nature of it if one sees there the surreptitious restoration of transcendent objects whose illusory character had been denounced by the *Critique of Pure Reason;* the postulates are theoretical determinations, to be sure; but they correspond to the practical postulation which constitutes pure reason as a demand for totality. The very expression "postulate" should not mislead us; it expresses, on the properly epistemological level and in the language of modality, the "hypothetical" character of the existential belief involved in the demand for completion, for totality, which constitutes practical reason in its essential purity. The corresponding postulates will be forever restrained from veering toward "fanaticism" and "religious folly" (*Schwärmerei*) by the critique of the transcendental illusion; this latter plays in their regard the role of a speculative "death of God." The postulates speak in their own way of a God "resurrected from the dead." But their way is that of religion within the limits of reason alone; they express the minimal existential implication of a practical aim, of an *Absicht,* which cannot be converted into an intellectual intuition. The "extension"—*Erweiterung*—the "accession"—*Zuwachs*—they express is not an extension of knowledge and awareness but a "disclosure," an *Eröffnung* (*Critique of Practical Reason,* p. 140); this "disclosure" is the philosophical equivalent of hope.

The specific character of the "postulates" appears clearly if we enumerate them beginning with freedom and not with immortality or the existence of God. Freedom is the true pivot of the doctrine of the postulates; the other two are in some sort its complement or explication. One might be surprised that freedom is postulated by the dialectic when it is already implied by duty and has been formulated as autonomy in the framework of the Analytic of the *Critique of Practical Reason*. But freedom thus postulated is not the same as the freedom analytically entailed by duty. Postulated freedom is what we are looking for here; it has a direct relation with hope, as we shall see. What does Kant say about freedom as the object of the postulate of practical reason? He calls it "freedom affirmatively regarded (as causality of a being so far as he belongs to the intelligible world)" (p. 137). Two traits characterize this postulated freedom. First of all, it is an effective freedom, a freedom which *can*, which is suitable to "this perfect willing of a rational being who at the same time would have omnipotence." A freedom which can be willed good. It is therefore a freedom which has "objective reality"; whereas theoretical reason has only the idea of it, practical reason postulates its existence, as being that of a real causality. We shall see shortly how the problem of evil is articulated exactly at this point of real efficacy. Moreover, it is a freedom which belongs *to*, which is member *of*, which participates. We will not fail to relate this second aspect of postulated freedom to the third formulation which the *Fundamental Principles of the Metaphysics of Morals* gives to the categorical imperative; speaking of the "possible kingdom of ends," Kant remarks that this formulation, which comes in the third part, crowns a progression of thought which runs from the unity of the principle—namely, the single rule of universalization—to the plurality of its objects—namely, persons taken as an end— "and from there, to the totality or integrality of the system" (p. 159). It is indeed this capacity to exist, by belonging to a system of freedoms, which is postulated here; thereby is concretized "that perspective" (*Aussicht*), evoked from the beginning of the Dialectic, that view "into a higher immutable order of things, in which we already are, and in which, to continue our existence in accordance with the supreme decree of reason, we may now, after this discovery, be directed by definite precepts" (p. 112).

That is what we will supremely; but that our capacity be equal to our will, that we exist according to this supreme vow, that is what can only be postulated. Postulated freedom is this manner of existing free among freedoms.

That this postulated freedom is indeed freedom according to hope is, to my mind, what the other two postulates which frame it signify (following the order of the three parts of the Dialectic of the *Critique of Pure Reason,* which runs from rational psychology to rational cosmology and to rational theology). The other two postulates, I shall say, serve only to make explicit the potential of hope of the postulate of existential freedom. Postulated immortality implies no substantialist or dualist thesis about the soul or its separated existence; this postulate develops the temporal implications of freedom suggested by the text cited above, which speaks of the order in which we are capable of "continuing our existence . . . ." Kantian immortality is therefore an aspect of our need to effectuate the highest good in reality; now, this temporality, this "progress toward the infinite," is not in our power; we cannot give it to ourselves; we can only "encounter" it (*antreffen*). It is in this sense that the postulate of immortality expresses the face of hope of the postulate of freedom: a theoretical proposition concerning the continuation and indefinite persistence of existence is the philosophical equivalent of the hope for resurrection. It is not by chance that Kant uses the term "expectation"—*Erwartung*—for this belief. Insofar as it is practical, reason demands completeness; but it believes in the mode of expectation, of hope, in the existence of an order where the completeness can be actual. Kerygmatic hope is thus approximated by the movement which proceeds from practical requirement to theoretical postulate, from demand to expectation. This movement is the same as that which enables us to pass from ethics to religion.

Now, this postulate is nothing else than the preceding one: for "hope of participating in the highest good" is freedom itself, concrete freedom, that which finds itself in itself. The second postulate only succeeds in deploying the temporal-existential aspect of the postulate of freedom; I shall say: it is the dimension of hope of freedom itself. This latter belongs to the order of ends, participates in the highest good, only to the extent that one may "hope for uninterrupted continuance of this progress, however long his existence may last, even beyond this life" (p. 128). In this respect, it is worth noting that Kant recognized this practical temporal dimension, for his philosophy hardly leaves any room for a conception of time beyond the time of representation according to the Transcendental Aesthetic, that is, the time of the world.

As to the third postulate, that of the existence of God, we

respect its character as postulate, that is, as a theoretical proposition dependent on a practical exigency, if we tie it very directly
to the first through the second: if the postulate of immortality
deploys the temporal-existential dimension of freedom, the
postulate of the existence of God manifests existential freedom
as the philosophical equivalent of the gift. Kant has no place for
a concept of gift, which is a category of the Sacred. But he has
a concept for the origin of a synthesis which is not in our power;
God is "the adequate cause of this effect which is manifested
to our will as its entire object, namely, the highest good." What
is postulated is the *Zusammenhang*, the connection, in a being
who encompasses the principle of accord between the two
constituents of the highest good. But the postulate holds only
insofar as we will, from the depths of our will, that the highest
good be realized. The expectation, here again, is grafted onto
the exigency. The "theoretical" expectation is articulated on
the "practical" exigency. This nexus is that between the practical
and the religious, between obligation and belief, between moral
necessity and existential hypothesis. And, here again, Kant is
not Greek but Christian; the Greek schools, he says, did not
resolve the problem of the practical possibility of the highest
good: they believed that the wisdom of the sage enclosed in its
analytic unity the just life and the happy life. The transcendent
synthesis of the highest good is, on the contrary, the closest
philosophical approximation of the Kingdom of God according
to the Gospels. Kant even has a word which is consonant with
what Moltmann says of hope when he calls it "totally new":

> Ethics, because it formulated its precept as pure and uncompro-
> mising (as befits a moral precept), destroyed man's confidence of
> being wholly adequate to it, at least in this life; but it reestab-
> lished it by enabling us to hope that, if we act as well as lies in
> our power, what is not in our power will come to our aid from an-
> other source, whether we know in what way or not. Aristotle and
> Plato differed only as to the origin of our moral concepts (p. 132,
> note 2).

Such, therefore, is the first origin of the question "What can
I hope for?" It is situated again at the heart of moral philosophy,
itself engendered by the question "What should I do?" Moral
philosophy engenders the philosophy of religion when the hope
of fulfillment is added to the consciousness of obligation:

> The moral law commands us to make the highest possible good in
> a world the final object of all our conduct. This I cannot hope to
> effect except through the agreement of my will with that of a holy

and beneficent Author of the world. . . . Therefore, morals is not really the doctrine of how to make ourselves happy but of how we are to be *worthy* of happiness. Only if religion is added to it can the hope arise of someday participating in happiness in proportion as we endeavored not to be unworthy of it (p. 134).

Why should the philosophical meaning of religion be constituted a second time at the exterior of ethics? The reply to that question will make us take a new step—the last—in what we have called the philosophical approximation of hope and of freedom in the light of hope.

In fact, it is the consideration of evil which constrains us to make this new move; now, with the consideration of evil, it is the very question of freedom, of the real freedom evoked by the postulates of the *Critique of Practical Reason,* which returns; the problematic of evil requires us to tie, more directly than we have so far been able to do, the actual reality of freedom to the regeneration which is the very content of hope.

What the *Essay on Radical Evil* teaches about freedom, indeed, is that this same power that duty imputes to us is in reality a nonpower; the "propensity for evil" has become "corrupt nature," although evil is still only a manner of being of the freedom which comes to it from freedom. Freedom has from the beginning always chosen badly. Radical evil signifies that the contingency of the evil maxim is the expression of a necessarily corrupt nature of freedom. This subjective necessity of evil is at the same time the reason for hope. To correct our maxims—that we can do, since we should do it; to regenerate our nature, the nature of our freedom—that we cannot do. This descent into the abyss, as Karl Jaspers has seen very well, expresses the most advanced point of a thought of limits, which henceforth extends from our knowledge to our power. The nonpower signified by radical evil is discovered in the very place whence our power proceeds. Thus is posed in radical terms the question of the real causality of our freedom, the very same freedom which the *Practical Reason* postulated at the end of its Dialectic. The "postulate" of freedom must henceforth cross through, not only the night of knowing, with its crisis of the transcendental illusion, but also the night of power, with its crisis of radical evil. *Real* freedom can spring up only as hope beyond this speculative and practical Good Friday. Nowhere are we closer to the Christian kerygma: hope is hope of resurrection, resurrection from the dead.

I am not unaware of the hostility of philosophers, since

Goethe and Hegel, toward the Kantian philosophy of radical evil. But have we understood it in its true connection with the ethical? I mean, not only in regard to the Analytic, to the doctrine of duty, but, even more, to the Dialectic, to the doctrine of the highest good. One has seen there the projection of the unhappy consciousness, of rigorism, of puritanism. There is something true in this. And a post-Hegelian interpretation of Kant must proceed by way of this radical contestation. But there is something else in the theory of radical evil, which only our prior reading of the Dialectic permits us to discern; radical evil concerns freedom in its process of totalization as much as in its initial determination. That is why the critique of Kantian moralism does not liquidate his philosophy of evil but, perhaps, reveals it in its true meaning.

That meaning ultimately appears in *Religion within the Limits of Reason Alone.* Indeed, it has not been sufficiently noted that the doctrine of evil is not completed in the *Essay on Radical Evil,* which initiates the philosophy of religion, but that it accompanies the latter through and through. True evil, the evil of evil, is not the violation of an interdict, the subversion of the law, disobedience, but fraudulency in the work of totalization. In this sense, true evil appears only in the very field where religion is produced, namely, in the field of contradictions and conflicts determined, on the one hand, by the demand for totalization which constitutes reason, both theoretical and practical, and, on the other hand, by the illusion which misleads thought, the subtle hedonism which vitiates moral motivation, and finally by the malice which corrupts the great human enterprises of totalization. The demand for a complete object of the will is basically antinomic. The evil of evil is born in the area of this antinomy.

By the same token, evil and hope are more closely connected than we will ever think them; if the evil of evil is born on the way of totalization, it would appear only in a pathology of hope, as the inherent perversion in the problematic of fulfillment and of totalization. To put it in a few words, the true malice of man appears only in the state and in the church, as institutions of gathering together, of recapitulation, of totalization.

Thus understood, the doctrine of radical evil can furnish a receptive structure for new figures of alienation besides the speculative illusion or even the desire for consolation—of alienation in the cultural powers, such as the church and the state; it is indeed at the heart of these powers that a falsified expression of the synthesis can take place; when Kant speaks of "servile faith," of "false cult," of a "false Church," he completes at the same time his theory of radical evil. This culminates, we might say, not with transgression, but with flawed syntheses in the political and religious spheres. That is why true religion is always in a debate with false religion, that is, for Kant, statutory religion.

Henceforth, the regeneration of freedom is inseparable from the movement by which the figures of hope[7] are liberated from the idols of the market place, as Bacon put it.

This whole process constitutes the philosophy of religion within the limits of reason alone; it is this process which constitutes the philosophical *analogon* of the kerygma of the Resurrection. It is also this process which constitutes the whole adventure of freedom and which permits us to give a comprehensible meaning to the expression "religious freedom."

7. A historical study of *Religion within the Limits of Reason Alone* should be dedicated to showing just how far the philosopher can go in the representation of the origin of regeneration. The Kantian schematism offers us an ultimate resource here. What we can conceive abstractly as the "good principle," which struggles within us with the "evil principle," we can also represent concretely as the man, pleasing to God, who suffers for sake of the promotion of the universal good. To be sure, Kant is in no way interested in the historicity of Christ: "this man, the only one pleasing to God," is an Idea. However, this archetype is not at all an idea that I can give myself arbitrarily. Although it is reducible as an event of salvation, this archetype is irreducible as an Idea to a moral intention: "we are not authors of it" (p. 54). It "has established itself in man without our comprehending how human nature could have been capable of receiving it" (*ibid.*). That is the irreducible element: "the incomprehensibility of a union between [the good principle] and man's sensible nature" in the moral constitution of man (p. 77). Now this Idea corresponds completely with the synthesis demanded by pure reason or, more exactly, with the transcendent object which causes that synthesis. This is not only an example of duty, in which case it would not exceed the Analytic, but an ideal exemplar of the highest good, in that this Idea illustrates the resolution of the Dialectic. Christ is an archetype and not a simple example of duty because he symbolizes this fulfillment. He is the figure of the End. As such, this "representation" of the good principle does not have for its effect "to extend our knowledge beyond the world of sense but only to make clear *for practical use* the conception of what is for us unfathomable" (p. 52). "Such is the *schematism of analogy*, with which (as a means of explanation)," says Kant, "we cannot dispense" (p. 58, note). It is within the strict limits of a theory of the schema and analogy, hence, of a theory of transcendental imagination, that the philosopher approaches not only the meanings of hope but the figure of Christ in which these meanings are concentrated. [Page numbers in parentheses refer to the English translation of Kant's *Religion within the Limits of Reason Alone*, by T. M. Greene and H. H. Hudson (New York: Harper Torchbooks, 1960).]

Guilt, Ethics, and Religion

My principal task will be to determine the distinction between ethical discourse and religious discourse on the question of guilt. These will be the two main divisions of my analysis.

But, before treating these two respective discourses with a view to distinguishing them and understanding their relationship, I suggest that first we come to an agreement about the meaning of the terms in question. Allow me, then, by way of preface, to develop a semantic analysis of the very term "guilt."

I. Guilt: Semantic Analysis

I propose, first, to consider this term, not in its psychological, psychiatric, or psychoanalytic usage, but in the *texts* where its meaning has been constituted and fixed. These texts are those of penitential literature wherein the believing communities have expressed their avowal of evil; the language of these texts is a specific language, which can be designated, in a very general way, as "confession of sins," although no particular confessional connotation is attached to this expression, not even a specifically Jewish or Christian meaning. Some decades ago, Professor Pettazzoni of Rome wrote a collection of works

This English version of this essay first appeared in *Talk of God*, edited by G. N. A. Vesey for the Royal Institute of Philosophy Lectures, Volume II, 1967–1968. Copyright © 1969 by Macmillan and Co. Ltd., London and Basingstoke, and by St. Martin's Press, New York. Reproduced by permission of the publishers.

[425]

covering the entire field of comparative religions. He called this precisely *Confession of Sins*. But it is not from the comparative point of view that I take up the problem. My point of departure is in a *phenomenology of confession or avowal*. Here I understand by phenomenology the description of meanings implied in experience in general, whether that experience be one of things, of values, of persons, etc. A phenomenology of confession is therefore a description of meanings, and of signified intentions, present *in a certain activity of language,* namely, *confession.* Our task, in the framework of such a phenomenology, is to re-enact in ourselves the confession of evil, in order to uncover its aims. By sympathy and through imagination, the philosopher adopts the motivations and intentions of the confessing consciousness; he does not "feel" but "experiences" in a neutral manner, in the manner of "as if," that which has been lived in the confessing consciousness.

But with which expressions shall we start? Not with expressions of confessions that are the most developed, the most rationalized, for example the concept or quasi-concept of "original sin," which has so often guided philosophical thought. On the contrary, philosophical reasoning should consult expressions of the confession of evil which are the least elaborated, the least articulated.

We should not be embarrassed by the fact that behind these rationalized expressions, behind these speculations, we encounter myths, that is, traditional narratives which tell of events which happened at the origin of time and which furnish the support of language to ritual actions. Today, for us, myths are no longer explanations of reality, but, precisely because they have lost their explanatory pretension, they reveal an exploratory signification; they manifest a symbolic function, that is, a way of expressing indirectly the bond between man and what he considers sacred. Paradoxical as it may seem, myth thus demythologized in its contact with physics, cosmology, and scientific history becomes a dimension of modern thought. In its turn, myth refers us to a level of expressions more fundamental than any narration and any speculation. Thus, the narrative of the Fall in the Bible draws its signification from an experience of sin rooted in the life of the community; it is the cultic activity and the prophetic call to "justice" and to "mercy" which provide myth with its substructure of significations.

Therefore, it is to this experience and to its language that we must have recourse; or rather, to this experience *in* its language.

For it is the language of confession which elevates to the light of discourse an experience charged with emotion, fear, and anguish. Penitential literature manifests a linguistic inventiveness which marks the way for existential outbursts of the consciousness of fault.

Let us, therefore, interrogate this language.

The most remarkable characteristic of this language is that it does not involve expressions which are more primitive than the symbolic expressions to which myth refers. The language of confession is symbolic. Here I understand by "symbol" a language which designates one thing in an indirect way by designating another thing directly. It is in this way that I speak symbolically of "elevated" thought, "low" sentiments, "clear" ideas, the "light" of understanding, the "kingdom" of heaven, etc. Therefore, the work of repetition as applied to the expressions of evil is, in essence, the explicitation, the development, of different levels of direct and indirect significations which are intermingled in the same symbol.[1] The most archaic symbolism from which we can start is that of evil conceived as defilement or stain, that is, as a spot which contaminates from the outside. In more elaborated literatures, such as that of the Babylonians and especially of the Hebrews, sin is expressed in different symbolisms, such as to miss the target, to follow a tortuous path, to rebel, to have a stiff neck, to be unfaithful as in adultery, to be deaf, to be lost, to wander, to be empty and hollow, to be inconstant as dust.

This linguistic situation is astonishing; the consciousness of self, so intense in the sentiment of evil, does not, at first, have at its disposal an abstract language but a very concrete language, on which a spontaneous work of interpretation is performed.

The second remarkable characteristic of this language is that it knows itself as symbolic and that, before any philosophy and theology, it is *en route* toward explicitation; as I have said elsewhere, the symbol "invites" thought; the *mythos* is on the way toward *logos*. This is true even of the archaic idea of defilement or stain: the idea of a quasi-material something which contaminates from the outside, which harms by means of invisible properties. This idea possesses a symbolic richness, a potential of symbolization, which is precisely attested to by the survival of this symbol in more and more allegorical forms. We speak

---

1. Cf. above, "The Hermeneutics of Symbols and Philosophical Reflection: I," pp. 289–96.

even today, in a nonmedical sense, of contamination by the spirit of monetary profit ("filthy lucre"), by racism, etc.; we have not completely abandoned the symbolism of the pure and the impure. And this, precisely because the quasi-material representation of stain is already symbolic of something else. From the beginning it has symbolic power. Stain has never literally signified a spot, impurity has never literally signified filth; it is located in the chiaroscuro of a quasi-physical infection and a quasi-moral unworthiness. We see this clearly in rites of purification, which are never just a simple washing; ablution and lustration are already partial and fictive actions which signify, on the level of body, a total action which addresses itself to the person considered as an undivided whole.

The symbolism of sin, such as is found in Babylonian and Hebraic literature, in Greek tragedies, or in Orphic writings, is certainly richer than that of stain, from which it is sharply distinguished. To the image of impure contact it opposes that of a wounded relationship, between God and man, between man and man, between man and himself; but this relation, which will be thought of as a relation only by a philosopher, is symbolically signified by all the means of dramatization offered in daily experience. So too the idea of sin is not reduced to the barren idea of the rupture of a relation; it adds to this the idea of a power which dominates man. Thus it maintains a certain affinity and continuity with the symbolism of stain. But this power is also the sign of the emptiness, of the vanity of man, represented by breath and by dust. So the symbol of sin is at one and the same time the symbol of something negative (rupture, estrangement, absence, vanity) and the symbol of something positive (power, possession, captivity, alienation). It is on this symbolic foundation, in this network of images and nascent interpretations, that the word *guilt* should be resituated.

If we want to respect the proper intention of words, the expression "guilt" does not cover the whole semantic field of "confession." The idea of guilt represents the extreme form of interiorization which we have seen sketched in the passage from stain to sin. Stain was still external contagion, sin already the rupture of a relation. But this rupture exists even if I do not know it. Sin is a real condition, an objective situation; I would venture to say, an ontological dimension of existence.

Guilt, on the contrary, has a distinctly subjective accent: its symbolism is much more interior. It describes the consciousness of being overwhelmed by a burden which crushes. It indicates, further, the bite of a remorse which gnaws from within, in the completely interior brooding on fault. These two metaphors of burden and of biting express well the arrival at the level of existence. The most significant symbolism of guilt is that which is attached to the theme of tribunal. The tribunal is a public institution; but metaphorically transposed into the internal forum, it becomes what we call the "moral consciousness." [2] Thus guilt becomes a way of putting oneself before a sort of invisible tribunal which measures the offense, pronounces the condemnation, and inflicts the punishment; at the extreme point of interiorization, moral consciousness is a look which watches, judges, and condemns; the sentiment of guilt is therefore the consciousness of being inculpated and incriminated by this interior tribunal; it is mingled with the anticipation of the punishment. In short, the *coulpe*—in Latin, *culpa*—is self-observation, self-accusation, and self-condemnation by a *consciousness doubled back on itself*.

This interiorization of guilt gives rise to two series of results: on the one hand, the consciousness of guilt marks a definite progress in relation to what we have described as "sin"; while sin is still a collective reality, in which a whole community is implicated, guilt tends to individualize itself. (In Israel, the prophets of the Exile are the artisans of this progress [Ezek. 31:34]; this preaching is a liberating action; at a time when a collective return from exile, comparable to the ancient Exodus from Egypt, appeared impossible, a personal path of conversion opened itself to each one. In ancient Greece, it was the tragic poets who assured the passage from hereditary crime to the guilt of the individual hero, placed alone before his own destiny.) Moreover, in becoming individualized, guilt acquires degrees; to the *egalitarian* experience of sin is opposed the *graduated* experience of guilt. Man is entirely and radically sinner, but he is more, or less, guilty. It is the progress of penal law itself, principally in Greece and Rome, which has an effect here on moral consciousness: the whole of penal law is actually an effort to limit and to gauge the penalty in proportion to the fault. The idea of a parallel scale of crimes and sins is interiorized, in its own turn, in favor of the metaphor of the tribunal; moral consciousness becomes itself a graduated consciousness of guilt.

2. [On the double meaning of French *conscience* ("conscience" and "consciousness"), see note 1, p. 335.—ED.]

This individualization and this gradation of guilt surely indicate a progress, compared to the collective and unqualified character of sin. We cannot say as much for the other series of results. With guilt there arises indeed a sort of demand which can be called *scrupulosity* and whose ambiguous character is extremely interesting. A scrupulous consciousness is a delicate consciousness, a precise consciousness, enamored of increasing perfection; it is a consciousness anxious to observe all the commandments, to satisfy the law in all things, without making an exception of any sector of existence, without taking into account exterior obstacles, for example the persecution of a prince, and which gives as much importance to little things as to great. But at the same time scrupulosity marks the entrance of moral consciousness into its own pathology; a scrupulous person encloses himself in the inextricable labyrinth of commandments; obligation takes on an enumerative and cumulative character, which contrasts with the simplicity and sobriety of the commandment to love God and man. The scrupulous consciousness never stops adding new commandments. This atomization of the law into a multitude of commandments entails an endless "juridization" of action and a quasi-obsessional ritualization of daily life. The scrupulous person never arrives at satisfying all the commandments or even any one. At the same time, even the notion of obedience is perverted; obedience to a commandment, because it is commanded, becomes more important than love of neighbor and even love of God; this exactitude in observance is what we call legalism. With it we enter into the hell of guilt, such as Saint Paul described it: the law itself becomes a source of sin. In giving a knowledge of evil, it excites the desire of transgression and incites the endless movement of condemnation and punishment. The commandment, says Saint Paul, "has given life to sin" and thus "hands me over to death" (Rom. 7). Law and sin give birth to each other mutually in a terrible vicious circle, which becomes a mortal circle.

Thus, guilt reveals the malediction of a life under the law. At the limit, when the confidence and tenderness, which are still expressed in the conjugal metaphors of Hosea, disappear, guilt leads to an accusation without accuser, a tribunal without judge, a verdict without author. Guilt has then become that irreversible misfortune described by Kafka: condemnation has become damnation.

A conclusion of this semantic analysis is that guilt does not cover the whole field of the human experience of evil; the study of these symbolic expressions has permitted us to distinguish in them a particular moment of this experience, the most ambiguous moment. On the one hand, guilt expresses the interiorization of the experience of evil and, consequently, the promotion of a morally responsible subject—but, on the other hand, it marks the beginning of a specific pathology, wherein scrupulosity marks the point of inversion.

Now the problem is posed: what do ethics and the philosophy of religion make of this ambiguous experience of guilt and of the symbolic language in which it is expressed?

II. The Ethical Dimension

In what sense is the problem of evil an ethical problem? In a twofold sense, it seems to me. Or rather, by reason of a double relationship, on the one hand with the question of freedom and, on the other hand, with the question of obligation. Evil, freedom, and obligation constitute a very complex network, which we shall try to unravel and to order in several stages of reflection. I shall begin and end with freedom, for it is the essential point.

In a first stage of reflection, I say: to affirm freedom is to take upon oneself the origin of evil. By this proposition, I affirm a link between evil and freedom which is so close that the two terms imply one another mutually. Evil has the meaning of evil because it is the work of freedom; I am the author of evil. By that fact, I reject as an alibi the claim that evil exists after the manner of a substance or of a nature, that it has the same status as things which can be observed by an outside spectator. This claim is to be found not only in the metaphysical fantasies, such as those against which Augustine fought—Manichaeism and all sorts of ontologies which conceive of evil as a being. This claim can take on a positive appearance, or even a scientific appearance, under the form of psychological or sociological determinism. To take upon oneself the origin of evil is to lay aside as a weakness the claim that evil is something, that it is an effect in a world of observable things, whether these things be physical, psychic, or social realities. I say: it is I who have acted —*Ego sum qui feci.* There is no evil-being; there is only the evil-done-by-me. To take evil upon oneself is an act of language comparable to the performative, in this sense, that it is a language which does something, that is to say, that it *imputes* the act to me.

I said that the relationship is reciprocal; indeed, if freedom qualifies evil as a "doing," evil is that which reveals freedom. By this I mean to say: evil is a privileged occasion for becoming aware of freedom. What does it actually mean to *impute* my own acts to myself? It is, first of all, to assume the consequences of these acts for the future; that is, he who has acted is also he who will admit the fault, who will repair the damages, who will bear the blame. In other words, I offer myself as the bearer of the sanction. I agree to enter into the dialectic of praise and blame. But in placing myself *before* the consequences of my act, I refer myself *back* to the moment prior to my act, as one who not only acted but who could have acted otherwise. This conviction of having done something freely is not a matter of observation. It is once again a performative: I declare myself, *after the fact*, as being he who *could* have done otherwise; this "after the fact" is the backlash of taking upon oneself the consequences. He who takes the consequences upon himself declares himself free and discerns this freedom as already at work in the incriminated act. At that point I can say that I have *committed* the act. This movement from in front of to behind the responsibility is essential. It constitutes the identity of the moral subject through past, present, and future. He who *will bear* the blame is the same as he who *now* takes the act upon himself and he who *has* acted. I posit the identity of him who accepts the future responsibilities of his act and him who has acted. And the two dimensions, future and past, are linked in the present. The future of sanction and the past of action committed are tied together in the present of confession.

Such is the first stage of reflection in the experience of evil: the reciprocal constitution of the signification of *free* and the signification of *evil* is a specific performative: *confession* or *avowal*. The second stage of reflection concerns the link between evil and *obligation*. I do not at all want to discuss the meaning of expressions such as "You ought" or their relation with the predicates "good" and "evil." This problem is well known to English philosophy. I will limit myself to the contribution that a reflection on evil can bring to this problem.

Let us take as our point of departure the expression and the experience "I could have done otherwise." This is, as we have seen, an implication of the act by which I impute to myself the responsibility for a past act. But the awareness that one could have done otherwise is closely linked to the awareness that one *should* have done otherwise. It is because I recognize my "ought" that I recognize my "could." A being who is obligated is a being who presumes that he can do what he should do. We are well aware of the usage to which Kant put this affirmation: you must, therefore you can. It is certainly not an argument, in the sense that I could deduce the possibility from the obligation. I would rather say that the "ought" serves here as a detector: if I feel, or believe, or know that I am obligated, it is because I am a being that can act, not only under the impulsion or constraint of desire and fear, but under the condition of a law which I represent to myself. In this sense Kant is right: to act according to the representation of a law is something other than to act according to laws. This power of acting according to the representation of a law is the will.

But this discovery has long-range consequences: for in discovering the power to follow the law (or that which I consider as the law for myself) I discover also the *terrible* power of acting *against*. (Indeed, the experience of remorse, which is the experience of the relation between freedom and obligation, is a twofold experience: I recognize an obligation, and therefore a power corresponding to this obligation; but I admit to having acted against the law which continues to appear to me as obligatory. This is commonly called a transgression.) Freedom is the power to act according to the representation of a law *and* not to meet the obligation. ("Here is what I should have done, therefore what I could have done, and look at what I did." The imputation of the past act is thus morally qualified by its relation to the "ought" and "can.")

By the same fact, a new determination of evil and a new determination of freedom appear together, in addition to the forms of reciprocity which are described above. The new determination of evil can be expressed in Kantian terms: it is the reversal of the relation between motive and law, interior to the maxim of my action. This definition is to be understood as follows: if I call a maxim the practical enunciation of what I propose to do, evil is nothing in itself; it has neither physical nor psychical reality; it is only an inverted relationship; it is relation, not a thing, a relation inverted with regard to the order of preference and subordination indicated by obligation. In this way, we have achieved a "de-realization" of evil: not only does evil exist only in the act of taking it upon oneself, of assuming it, of claiming it, but what characterizes it from a moral point of view is the order in which an agent disposes of his maxims; it is a preference which *ought* not to have been (an inverted relation within the maxim of action).

But a new determination of freedom appears at the same time. I spoke a moment ago of the *terrible* power of acting against. It is, indeed, in the confession of evil that I discover the power of subversion of the will. Let us call it the "arbitrary," to translate the German *Willkür*, which is at the same time free choice, i.e., the power of contraries, that which we recognized in the consciousness that one could have done otherwise, and in the power not to follow an obligation which one simultaneously recognizes as just.

Have we exhausted the meaning of evil for ethics? I do not think so. In the "Essay on Radical Evil" which begins *Religion within the Limits of Reason Alone,* Kant poses the problem of a common origin of all evil maxims; indeed, we have not gone far in a reflection on evil as long as we consider separately one bad intention, and then another, and again another. Kant says:

> In order, then, to call a man evil, it would have to be possible *a priori* to infer from several evil acts done with consciousness of their evil, or from one such act, an underlying evil maxim; and further, from this maxim to infer the presence in the agent of an underlying common ground, itself a maxim, of all particular morally-evil maxims.[3]

This movement toward greater depth, which goes from evil maxims to their evil foundation, is the philosophical transposition of the movement from sins to *sin* (in the singular), of which we spoke in part I, on the level of symbolic expressions, and in particular of myth. Among other things, the myth of Adam signifies that all sins are referred to a unique root, which is, in some way or other, anterior to each of the particular expressions of evil; yet the myth could be told because the confessing community raised itself to the level of a confession of evil as involving all men. It is because the community *confesses* a fundamental guilt that the myth can describe the unique coming-to-be of evil as an event which happens only once. The Kantian doctrine of radical evil is an attempt to recapture philosophically this experience and this myth.

What qualifies this reexamination as philosophical? Es-

---

3. Immanuel Kant, *Religion within the Limits of Reason Alone,* trans. T. M. Greene and H. H. Hudson (New York: Harper Torchbooks, 1960), p. 16.

sentially the treatment of radical evil as the foundation of multiple evil maxims. It is therefore upon this notion of foundation that we should bring to bear our critical effort.

Now, what do we mean by a foundation of evil maxims? We might well call it an *a priori* condition in order to emphasize that it is not a fact to be observed or a temporal origin to be retraced. It is not an empirical fact but a first disposition of freedom that must be supposed so that the universal spectacle of human evil can be offered to experience. Neither is it a temporal origin, for this theory would lead back to a natural causality. Evil would cease to be evil if it ceased to be "a manner of being of freedom, which itself comes from freedom." Therefore, evil does not have an origin in the sense of an antecedent cause. "In the search for the rational origin of evil actions, every such action must be regarded as though the individual had fallen into it directly from a state of innocence." [4] Everything is in this "as if." It is the philosophical equivalent of the myth of the Fall; it is the rational myth of the coming-to-be of evil, of the instantaneous passage from innocence to sin; as Adam—rather than *in* Adam—we originate evil.

But what is this *unique* coming-to-be which contains within itself all evil maxims? It must be admitted that we have no further concept for thinking of an evil will.

For this coming-to-be is not at all an act of my arbitrary will, an act which I could do or not do. For the enigma of this foundation is that reflection discovers, as a fact, that freedom has already chosen in an evil way. This evil is *already there*. It is in this sense that it is radical, that is anterior (in a nontemporal way) to every evil intention, to every evil action.

But this failure of reflection is not in vain; it succeeds in giving a proper character to a *philosophy* of limit and in distinguishing it from a philosophy of system, such as that of Hegel.

The limit is twofold: limit of my knowledge, limit of my power. On the one hand, *I do not know* the origin of my evil freedom; this nonknowledge of the origin is essential to the very act of my confession of my radically evil freedom. The nonknowledge is a part of the performative of confession or, in other words, of my self-recognition and self-appropriation. On the other hand, I discover the *nonpower* of my freedom. (Curious nonpower, for I declare that I am responsible for this nonpower. This nonpower is completely different from the claim of an

4. *Ibid.*, p. 36.

outside constraint.) I claim that my freedom has already made itself not-free. This admission is the greatest paradox of ethics. It seems to contradict our point of departure. We began by saying: evil is what I *could have* not done; and this remains true. But at the same time I claim: evil is this prior captivity, which makes it so that I *must do* evil. This contradiction is interior to my freedom; it marks the nonpower of power, the nonfreedom of freedom.

Is this a lesson in despair? Not at all: this admission is, on the contrary, the access to a point where everything can begin again. The return to the origin is a return to that place where freedom discovers itself as something to be delivered—in brief, to that place where it can *hope* to be delivered.

III. THE RELIGIOUS DIMENSION

I HAVE JUST ATTEMPTED, with the aid of the philosophy of Kant, to characterize the problem of evil as an ethical problem. It is the twofold relation of evil to obligation and to freedom which has seemed to me to characterize the problem of evil as an ethical problem.

Now, if I ask what is the specifically religious way of speaking about evil, I would not hesitate for a moment to answer: the language is that of *hope*. This thesis requires an explanation. Leaving aside for a moment the question of evil, to which I shall return later, I would like to justify the central role of hope in Christian theology.[5] Hope has rarely been the central concept in theology. And yet the preaching of Jesus was concerned essentially with the Kingdom of God: the Kingdom is at hand; the Kingdom has drawn near to you; the Kingdom is in your midst. If the preaching of Jesus and of the primitive church thus proceeds from an eschatological perspective, we should rethink all of theology from this eschatological viewpoint. The God who comes is a *name;* the god who shows himself is an idol. The God of the promise opens up a history; the god of natural epiphanies animates a nature.

What follows from this for freedom and for evil, which ethical consciousness has grasped in their unity? I shall begin by

5. See "Freedom in the Light of Hope," above, where we reveal the exegetical foundations, in the Old and New Testaments, of the eschatological interpretation of biblical theology.

a discussion of freedom, for a reason which will become clear in a moment. It seems to me that religion is distinguished from ethics, in the fact that it requires that we think of freedom under the sign of hope.

In the language of the Gospel, I would say: to consider freedom in the light of hope is to resituate my existence in the movement which might be called, with Jürgen Moltmann, the "future of the Resurrection of Christ." This "kerygmatic" formula can be translated in several ways in contemporary language.[6] First of all, with Kierkegaard, we could call freedom in the light of hope the "passion for the *possible*"; this formula, in contrast to all wisdom of the present, to all submission to necessity, underscores the imprint of the promise on freedom. Freedom, entrusted to the "God who comes," is open to the radically new; it is the creative imagination of the possible.

But, in a deeper dimension, freedom *in the light of* hope is a freedom which affirms itself *in spite of* death and is willing, in spite of all the signs of death, to deny death.

Likewise, the category of "in spite of" is the opposite or reverse side of a vital thrust, of a perspective of belief which finds its expression in the famous "how much more" of Saint Paul. This category, more fundamental than the "in spite of," expresses what might be called the logic of superabundance, which is the logic of hope.

This logic of surplus and excess is to be uncovered in daily life, in work and in leisure, in politics and in universal history. The "in spite of" which keeps us in readiness for the denial is only the inverse, the shadow side, of this joyous "how much more" by which freedom feels itself, knows itself, and wills itself to belong to this economy of superabundance.

This notion of an economy of superabundance permits us to return to the problem of evil. It is from this point of departure, and in it, that a religious or theological discourse on evil can be held. Ethics has said all it can about evil in calling it (1) a work of freedom, (2) a subversion of the relation of the maxim to the law, and (3) an unfathomable disposition of freedom which makes it unavailable to itself.

Religion uses another language about evil. And this language keeps itself entirely within the limits of the perimeter of the promise and under the sign of hope. First of all, this discourse

---

6. See "Freedom in the Light of Hope," pp. 407–10, above, on the "passion for the possible," the "in spite of," and the "how much more."

places evil *before* God. "Against you, against you alone have I sinned, I have done evil in your sight." This invocation, which transforms the moral confession into a confession of sin, appears, at first glance, to be an intensification in the consciousness of evil. But that is an illusion, the moralizing illusion of Christianity. Situated before God, evil is installed again in the movement of the promise; the invocation is already the beginning of the restoration of a bond, the initiation of a new creation. The "passion for the possible" has already taken possession of the confession of evil; repentance, essentially directed toward the future, has already cut itself off from remorse, which is a brooding reflection on the past.

Next, religious language profoundly changes the very content of the consciousness of evil. Evil in moral consciousness is essentially transgression, that is, subversion of a law; it is in this way that the majority of pious men continue to consider sin. And yet, situated before God, evil is qualitatively changed; it consists less in a transgression of a law than in a *pretension* of man to be master of his life. The will to live according to the law is, therefore, also an expression of evil—and even the most deadly, because the most dissimulated: worse than injustice is one's own justice. Ethical consciousness does not know this, but religious consciousness does. But this second discovery can also be expressed in terms of promise and hope.

Indeed, the will is not constituted, as we have seemed to believe in the context of the ethical analysis, merely by the relation between the arbitrary and the law (in Kantian terms, between the *Willkür*, or arbitrary will, and the *Wille*, or determination by the law of reason). The will is more fundamentally constituted by a desire of fulfillment or achievement.[7] Kant himself, in the Dialectic of the *Critique of Practical Reason* recognized this intended goal of totalization. It is this precisely which animates the Dialectic, as the relation to the law animates the Analytic. Now this tendency toward totalization, according to Kant, requires the reconciliation of two moments which rigorism has separated: "virtue," that is, obedience to pure duty, and "happiness," that is, satisfaction of desire. This reconciliation is the Kantian equivalent of hope.

This rebound of the philosophy of will entails a rebound of the philosophy of evil. If the tendency toward totalization is thus the soul of the will, we have not yet reached the founda-

---

7. Cf. "Freedom in the Light of Hope," p. 416, above.

tion of the problem of evil so long as we have kept it within the limits of a reflection on the relations of the arbitrary and the law. The true evil, the evil of evil, shows itself in false syntheses, i.e., in the contemporary falsifications of the great undertakings of totalization of cultural experience, that is, in political and ecclesiastical institutions. In this way, evil shows its true face—the evil of evil is the lie of premature syntheses, of violent totalizations.

But this greater deepening of our understanding of evil is, once again, a conquest of hope: it is because man is a goal of totality, a will of total fulfillment, that he plunges himself into totalitarianisms, which really constitute the pathology of hope. As the old proverb says, demons haunt only the courts of the gods. But, at the same time, we sense that evil itself is a part of the economy of superabundance. Paraphrasing Saint Paul, I dare to say: Wherever evil "abounds," there hope "superabounds." We must therefore have the courage to incorporate evil into the epic of hope. In a way that we know not, evil itself cooperates, works toward, the advancement of the Kingdom of God. This is the viewpoint of faith on evil.

This view is not that of the moralist. The moralist contrasts the *predicate* evil with the *predicate* good; he condemns evil; he imputes it to freedom; and finally, he stops at the limit of the inscrutable; for we do not know how it is possible that freedom could be enslaved. Faith does not look in this direction; the origin of evil is not its problem; the *end* of evil is its problem. With the prophets, faith incorporates this end into the economy of the promise; with Jesus, into the preaching of the God who comes; with Saint Paul, into the law of superabundance. This is why the view of faith on events and on men is essentially *benevolent*. Faith justifies the man of the *Aufklärung,* for whom, in the great romance of culture, evil is a factor in the education of the human race, rather than the puritan, who never succeeds in taking the step from condemnation to mercy and who thus remains within the ethical dimension and never enters into the perspective of the Kingdom to come.

Religion, Atheism, and Faith

INTRODUCTION

THE SUBJECT OF THIS ESSAY compels me to take up a radical challenge. I would like to state to what extent I am willing to accept the critique of religion which has emerged from an atheism like that of Nietzsche and Freud, and to what extent I consider myself a Christian in spite of and beyond such a critique. If the title "The Religious Meaning of Atheism" is not nonsensical, it implies that atheism is not limited in meaning to the mere negation and destruction of religion but that, rather, it opens up the horizon for something else, for a type of faith that might be called, in a way that we shall further elucidate, a postreligious faith or a faith for a postreligious age. This is the hypothesis that I propose to examine and eventually defend.

The title that I actually chose for this essay—"Religion, Atheism, and Faith"—clearly expresses my own intention in this regard. The word "atheism" has here been placed in an intermediate position, both as a division and as a link between religion and faith; it looks back toward what it denies and forward toward what it makes possible. I am not unaware of the difficulties of such a formulation. In a sense, it is both too simple and too difficult. It is too simple if one accepts the distinction between religion and faith as a given fact, or if one permits oneself to use atheism as an indiscreet means of apologetics, a means of "preserving faith," or, worse, if one uses it as a clever and hypocritical method of taking back with one hand what

Translated by Charles Freilich.

[440]

one was forced to relinquish with the other. Such an opposition must itself be elaborated in a responsible manner; it is not something that is purely given but a difficult task that presents itself to thought. I, however, prefer to run the opposite risk, that of failing to reach the goal by attempting to break a path which, as it were, goes astray en route. In a sense, this is what will occur in the two parts of this essay. They both begin something that is never completed; they point toward something that is never revealed; moreover, they suggest from a distance something that is never made fully manifest. It is in this sense that my project is too difficult. I believe, however, that such is the unavoidable situation of the philosopher when he is confronted by the dialectic, such as it exists, between religion, atheism, and faith. The philosopher is not a preacher. He may listen to preaching, as I do; but insofar as he is a professional and responsible thinker, he remains a beginner, and his discourse always remains a preparatory discourse. Perhaps this is not something to be regretted. This period of confusion, in which the true consequences of the death of religion perhaps still remain concealed, is also the time of long, slow, and indirect preparation.

Since I cannot expect to cover the entire field of questions that suggest themselves, I have chosen two themes, those of *accusation* and *consolation*. I have chosen them because they represent the two main aspects of religion: taboo and refuge. And these two fundamental significations in turn determine the two poles of religious feeling, at least in its simplest and most archaic form: the fear of punishment and the desire for protection. We might add that it is the same god who both threatens and consoles. I thus understand religion as a primitive structure of life which must always be overcome by faith and which is grounded in the fear of punishment and the desire for protection. Accusation and protection are, so to speak, "the corrupt parts of religion," in the same sense in which Marx referred to religion itself as the corrupt part of philosophy. It is here that atheism discovers its true justification and perhaps reveals its double signification as both destructive and liberating. It is also here that atheism opens up the way to a faith situated beyond accusation and protection. This is the kind of dialectic that I would like to explore in the two parts of this essay, the first of which will deal with accusation, the second with consolation.

I. ON ACCUSATION

1. THE TYPE OF ATHEISM I have in mind is that of Nietzsche and Freud. The reason for this choice is not merely the fact that they are the most outstanding representatives of the critique of religion insofar as it exists in the form of prohibition, accusation, punishment, and condemnation. What is more significant is to know exactly why they have been able to attack religion on this ground. For Nietzsche and Freud have created a kind of hermeneutics which is completely different from the critique of religion that is rooted in the tradition of British empiricism and French positivism. The problem for them is not that of the so-called proofs of the existence of God, nor do they criticize the concept of God as something devoid of meaning. They have created a new kind of criticism, a critique of cultural representations considered as disguised symptoms of desire and fear.

For both of them, the cultural dimension of human existence, to which ethics and religion belong, has a hidden meaning which requires a specific mode of interpretation, a stripping-away of masks. Religion has a meaning that remains unknown to the believer by virtue of a specific act of dissimulation which conceals its true origin from the investigation of consciousness. For this reason, religion demands a type of interpretation that is adapted to its own peculiar mode of dissimulation, i.e., an interpretation of illusion as distinct from simple "error," in the epistemological sense of the word, or as distinct from "lying," in the ordinary ethical sense of the word. Illusion is itself a cultural function. Such a fact presupposes that the public meanings of our consciousness conceal true meanings, which can be brought to light only by adopting the attitude of suspicion and cautious critical scrutiny.

Nietzsche and Freud have developed in a parallel manner a type of reductive hermeneutics which is at the same time a kind of philology and a kind of genealogy. It is a philology, an exegesis, an interpretation insofar as the text of our consciousness can be compared to a palimpsest, under the surface of which another text has been written. The task of this special exegesis is to decipher this text. But this hermeneutics is at the same time a genealogy, since the distortion of the text emerges from a conflict of forces, of drives [*pulsions*] and counterdrives, whose origin must be brought to light. It is evident that this is not a genealogy in the ordinary chronological sense of the word. For even when it refers to historical stages, this genesis does not lead back to a temporal origin but rather to a possible source or, better, an empty place from which ethical and religious values emerge. The genealogical task is to reveal the emptiness of this source.

The fact that Nietzsche calls this true origin the "will to power" while Freud calls it the "libido" is not essential to the present argument. On the contrary, in spite of differences with regard to background, focus, major interests, and even intentions, their respective analyses of religion, considered as the source of prohibition, mutually reinforce each other. It might even be said that we can better understand each of them individually when we have first considered them both together.

On the one hand, Nietzsche reveals so-called ideal being as a "realm" that is exterior and superior to human volition. Prohibition and condemnation come down to man from this realm of the outside and up-above. But this "realm" is, after all, "nothing." It emerges only from the weakness of the slave morality, which projects itself into the heavens. The task of the philological and genealogical method is to reveal this ideal source as a nothingness. The God of prohibition is this ideal realm which does not exist and which is yet the source of all prohibitions. This nonexistent realm is what traditional metaphysics has described as the intelligible, as the absolute good, as the transcendent and invisible source of all values; but since this realm is essentially empty, insofar as it is ideal, the destruction of metaphysics in our own era must take the form of nihilism. Nietzsche did not create nihilism, nor did nihilism create nothingness. Nihilism is a historical process to which Nietzsche bears witness, and nihilism in itself is only the historical manifestation of the nothingness that pertains to the illusory origin. Thus, nothingness does not emerge from nihilism; even less does nihilism emerge from Nietzsche. Nihilism is the soul of metaphysics, insofar as metaphysics posits an ideal and supernatural origin. Such a conception expresses nothing other than scorn for life, calumny of the earth, hatred of the vitality of the instincts, resentment of the weak against the strong. Christianity must also be included in this reductive hermeneutics to the extent that it serves as "a Platonism for the people," a kind of ethical supernaturalism. Finally, the famous *Umwertung*, the "transvaluation," the overthrowing, of traditional values is only the reversal of a prior reversal and, hence, the restoration of the true origin of values, which is the will to power.

This well-known critique of religion, which can be found in *Beyond Good and Evil* and in *The Genealogy of Morals*, is a good introduction to what Freud called the superego. The superego is also an ideal construction that serves as a source of prohibition and condemnation. Thus, psychoanalysis is, in its own way, an exegesis that allows us to read the drama of Oedipus behind the official text of moral consciousness, and it is, at the same time, a genealogy that links the energies invested in repression to forces derived from the id, i.e., from the profundity of life. In this way, although the superego takes up a position above the ego and functions as a tribunal, an agency [*instance*] that observes, judges, and condemns, it is stripped of its absolute appearance; it rather appears to be a structure that is derivative and acquired. There is, of course, an element in Freud that is not to be found in Nietzsche. The reduction of ethical consciousness to the superego arises out of the convergence between, on the one hand, the clinical experience of the obsessional neurotic, his melancholy and moral masochism, and, on the other hand, a sociology of culture. It is in this manner that Freud was able to elucidate what we might call a pathology of duty or conscience. In addition, the genesis of neurosis provided Freud with a key to the genetic interpretation of the phenomena of totem and taboo within the field of ethnology. These phenomena, in which Freud thought he could discern the source of our ethical and religious consciousness, emerge as the result of a process of substitution that refers back to the hidden role of the father figure within the Oedipus complex. Oedipus as an individual in turn serves as a model for a sort of collective Oedipus who belongs to the archaeology of humanity. The institution of law is thus related to a primitive drama, the famous murder of the father. It is difficult to say, however, whether this is really only the psychoanalytic myth, the "Freudian myth," or whether Freud actually succeeded in uncovering the profound origin of the gods. In any case, even if all we have here is Freud's own personal mythology, it still does express an intuition that is very close to Nietzsche's in *The Genealogy of Morals*, namely, the idea that the concepts of good and evil are created by means of projection within a situation of weakness and dependency. But Freud had something of his own to say; the *Umwertung*, the transvaluation that we have called the reversal of a prior reversal, not only involves the agonizing challenge to culture that

Nietzsche called nihilism but also involves a personal renunciation that Freud referred to in his book on Leonardo as "the renunciation of the father." This renunciation can be compared to the process of mourning, or the mourning work, which Freud mentions elsewhere. Nihilism and mourning are thus the two parallel ways in which the origin of values is restored to itself, i.e., to the will to power, to Eros in its eternal battle with Thanatos.

If we are now to investigate the theological meaning of this atheism, we must first say what sort of atheism is here in question. Everyone is familiar with the famous expression of the madman in *The Gay Science:* "God is dead." But the true question is to know, first of all, which god is dead; then, who has killed him (if it is true that this death is a murder); and finally, what sort of authority belongs to the announcement of this death. These three questions qualify the atheism of Nietzsche and Freud as opposed to that of British empiricism or French positivism, whose methods are neither exegetical nor genealogical in the sense we have specified.

Which god is dead? We can now reply: the god of metaphysics and also the god of theology, insofar as theology rests on the metaphysics of the first cause, necessary being, and the prime mover, conceived as the source of values and as the absolute good. Let us say that it is the god of onto-theology, to use the expression that was coined by Heidegger, following Kant.

This onto-theology has found its highest philosophical expression, at least with respect to ethical philosophy, in Kantian philosophy. As we know, Kant makes a very close connection between religion and ethics: the first function of religion is to consider the commandments of consciousness as the commandments of God. Religion, of course, has other functions as well, according to Kant, specifically in relation to the problem of evil, the realization of freedom, and the totalization of the will and nature within an ethical world. But because of the initial link that is established between God, conceived as the supreme lawgiver, and the law of reason, Kant still belongs to the age of metaphysics and still remains faithful to its fundamental dichotomy between an intelligible world and a sensible world.

The function of Nietzschean and Freudian criticism is to submit the principle of obligation, onto which has been grafted the ethical god of Kantian philosophy, to a regressive analysis that strips this principle of its *a priori* character. This reductive hermeneutics opens the way to a genealogy of the so-called *a priori*. At the same time, what seemed to be a strict necessity, the formal principle of obligation, now appears as the result of a hidden process, a process that refers back to an original act of accusation rooted in the will. Concrete accusation thus appears as the truth of formal obligation. Accusation cannot be grasped within the kind of reflective philosophy that separates the *a priori* from the empirical. Only the hermeneutic method is capable of uncovering accusation at the root of duty. In replacing a simple abstractive methodology, such as the Kantian categorial analysis, with a philological and genealogical methodology, reductive hermeneutics discovers behind practical reason the functioning of instincts, the expression of fear and desire. Behind the so-called autonomy of the will is hidden the resentment of a particular will, the will of the weak. Because of this exegesis and this genealogy, the god of morality, to speak in the manner of Nietzsche, reveals himself as the god of accusation and condemnation. Such is the nature of the god who has perished.

We are thus led to the second question: Who is the murderer? It is not the atheist but rather the specific nothingness that lies at the heart of the ideal, the superego's lack of absolute authority. The murderer of the god of morality is nothing other than that which Nietzsche described as a cultural process, the process of nihilism, or what Freud referred to in psychological terms as the mourning work that is carried out in relation to the image of the father.

But when we turn to the third question—What sort of authority is invested in the words that proclaim this death of the god of morality?—everything suddenly becomes problematical once again. We believe that we know which god is dead; we have said it is the god of morality. We also believe that we know the cause of this death: the self-destruction of metaphysics through nihilism. But everything becomes doubtful again when we ask: Who is saying this? The madman? Zarathustra? The madman as Zarathustra? Perhaps. At least we can say in negative terms that this type of thinking does not prove anything conclusively, one way or the other. "The man with the hammer" has only the authority of the message that he proclaims, namely, the sovereignty of the will to power. Nothing is capable of proving it, unless it be the new form of life that this message makes possible, or the affirmation of Dionysus, or the *amor fati*, the surrender to the "eternal return of the same." This positive

Nietzschean philosophy, which alone is capable of conferring authority on his negative hermeneutics, remains buried under the ruins that Nietzsche has accumulated around him. It is doubtful whether anyone can live on the level of Zarathustra. Nietzsche himself, the man with the hammer, is not the superman that he proclaims. His aggression against Christianity remains caught up in the attitude of resentment; the rebel is not, and cannot be, at the same level as the prophet. Nietzsche's major work remains an accusation of accusation and hence falls short of a pure affirmation of life.

For this reason, I do not think that anything has been definitely decided; everything still remains open after Nietzsche. It seems to me that only one path has been decisively closed off, that of an onto-theology which culminates in the idea of a moral god, conceived as the origin and foundation of an ethics of prohibition and condemnation. I believe that we are henceforth incapable of returning to an order of moral life which would take the form of a simple submission to commandments or to an alien or supreme will, even if this will were represented as divine. We must accept as a positive good the critique of ethics and religion that has been undertaken by the school of suspicion. From it we have learned to understand that the commandment that gives death, not life, is a product and projection of our own weakness.

2. The way in which the question is now posed is more urgent and more disconcerting than ever. Can we recognize any religious meaning at all in atheism? Certainly not, if we understand the word "religion" in the narrow sense of the primitive relationship of man to the dangerous power of the sacred. But, if it is true that "only the god of morality has been refuted," then a way still remains open—though filled with uncertainty and danger—which we shall now attempt to explore.

How shall we begin along this path? We might be tempted to go directly to the goal and give a name—both an old name and a new name—to this last stage of our itinerary: we might simply call it "faith." I have, in fact, already dared to do so in my introduction, in which I spoke of a dialectic between religion and faith, a dialectic mediated by atheism; but I have also said that the philosopher cannot go so far, so quickly. Only a preacher, or, I should say, a prophetic preacher, with the power and the freedom of Nietzsche's Zarathustra would be able to make a radical return to the origins of Jewish and Christian faith and, at the same time, make of this return an event which speaks to our own time. Such preaching would be both originary and post-religious. The philosopher, however, is not this prophetic preacher; at the most, he is what Kierkegaard called himself, "the poet of the religious." He dreams of a prophet who would realize today the message of Exodus that exists prior to all law: "I am the Lord thy God who brought thee out of the land of Egypt, out of the house of bondage." He dreams of the prophet who would speak only of freedom but would never utter a word of prohibition or condemnation, who would preach the Cross and the Resurrection of Christ as the beginning of a creative life, and who would elaborate the contemporary significance of the Pauline antinomy between the Gospel and the Law. In terms of this antinomy, sin itself would appear less as the transgression of a prohibition than as the opposite of a life ruled by grace. Sin, then, would mean life ruled by law, i.e., the mode of being of human existence which remains caught in the infernal circle of law, transgression, guilt, and rebellion.

There are several reasons why the philosopher is not this prophetic preacher. First of all, because the philosopher belongs to a time of dryness and thirst in which Christianity, insofar as it is a cultural institution, still remains "a Platonism for the people," a kind of law in Saint Paul's sense of the word. Second, the process of nihilism has not achieved its end, perhaps not even its culminating point. The period of mourning for the gods who have died is not yet over, and it is in this intermediate time that the philosopher does his thinking. Third, the philosopher, as a responsible thinker, remains suspended between atheism and faith. For he cannot content himself with the simple juxta-position of a reductive hermeneutics, which would dethrone the idols of the gods who have died, and a positive hermeneutics, which would be a recollection, a repetition—beyond the death of the god of morality—of the Biblical kerygma (the preachings of the prophets and the primitive Christian community). The philosopher's responsibility is to think, that is, to dig beneath the surface of the present antinomy until he has discovered the level of questioning that makes possible a mediation between religion and faith by way of atheism. This mediation must take the form of a long detour; it might even appear as a path that has gone astray. Heidegger refers to some of his essays as *Holzwege*, pathways in the forest that do not lead anywhere, except perhaps to the forest itself and the work of the woodsmen.

I suggest that we take two steps along this winding path which is thus, perhaps, a *Holzweg* in the Heideggerian sense.

First of all, I would like to consider my relationship to word [*la parole*][1]—to the word of the poet or thinker and, in fact, to all forms of word that say something, that reveal something about beings and about Being. In this relationship to word, to every meaningful word, there is implied a kind of total obedience that is entirely devoid of any ethical implications. It is this non-ethical obedience that can lead us out of the labyrinth of the theory of values, which is perhaps the sore spot of philosophy itself.

We must recognize the fact that philosophy at the present time is entirely at an impasse concerning the problem of the origin of values. We are condemned to vacillate between an impossible creation of values and an impossible intuition of values. This theoretical failure is reflected in the practical antinomy between submission and rebellion that infects the daily concerns of education, politics, and ethics. If no decision can be made at this level, we must retrace our steps, extricate ourselves from the impasse, and try to gain access, by means of a nonethical approach, to the problem of autonomy and obedience.

The only way to think ethically is first to think nonethically. In order to attain this goal, we must discover that place where the autonomy of our will is rooted in a dependence and an obedience that is no longer infected with accusation, prohibition, and condemnation. This preethical situation is that of "hearkening" [*l'écoute*]. In hearkening there is revealed a mode of being which is not yet a mode of doing and which thus avoids the alternative of subjection and revolt. Heraclitus said: "Do not attach importance to my words, but heed the logos." When word says something, when it reveals not only something about the meaning of beings but something about Being itself, as is the case with the poet, we are then confronted by what could be called the occurrence of word: something is said of which I am neither the source nor the master. Word is not at my disposition, as are the instruments of work and production or the goods of

1. [In the theological and Heideggerian context of this essay, *parole* has been translated as "word." In this sense, "word" is often used by Ricoeur as a "third term" between language and the "speaking" of the subject. "Word" is not at our disposal; it comes to us. "Speech" or "discourse" would occasionally have made for a smoother translation, but we have used "word" throughout for the sake of consistency. It should be noted that *parole* here has quite a different sense from the one it has in Ricoeur's essays on linguistics, where the Saussurean distinction between *langue* and *parole* is in question.—ED.]

consumption. In the occurrence of word I do not have anything at my command; I do not impose myself; I am no longer the master; I am led beyond the feelings of anxiety and concern. This situation or nonmastery is the origin of both obedience and freedom. Heidegger says, in *Being and Time:*

> We can make clear the connection of discourse with understanding and intelligibility by considering an existenial possibility which belongs to talking itself—hearing. If we have not heard "aright," it is not by accident that we say we have not "understood." Hearing is constitutive for discourse. . . . Dasein hears, because it understands. As a Being-in-the-world with Others, a Being which understands, Dasein is "in thrall" to Dasein-with and to itself; and in this thraldom it "belongs" to these.[2]

It is not by accident that in most languages the word for "obedience" is etymologically related to the word for "hearing." Hearing (*horchen* in German) is the possibility of obeying (*gehorchen*). Meaningful connections are thus established between word, listening, and obedience:

> It is on the basis of this potentiality for hearing, which is existentially primary, that anything like *hearkening* [*Horchen*] becomes possible. Hearkening is phenomenally still more primordial than what is defined "in the first instance" as "hearing" in psychology —the sensing of tones and the perception of sounds. Hearkening too has the kind of Being of the hearing which understands (p. 207).

This hearing which understands is the crux of our problem.

Nothing, of course, has been said concerning word as the word of God; and this is altogether fitting and proper. At this point, the philosopher is far from being in a position to designate a kind of word that would truly qualify to be called the word of God. He is capable, however, of designating the type of being that would make something like the word of God existentially possible. "Being-with develops in listening to one another [*Aufeinander-hören*], which can be done in several possible ways: following, going along with, and the privative modes of not-hearing, resisting, defying, and turning away" (pp. 206–7). Thus, for the first time and prior to all moral instruction and all moralism, we perceive in the act of "hearkening" the founda-

2. Martin Heidegger, *Being and Time,* trans. John Macquarrie and Edward Robinson (New York: Harper & Row, 1962), p. 206. [Subsequent page numbers in parentheses refer to this volume.]

tion of other modes of "listening": following and not-following. This hearkening (*hören*) implies a "belonging-to" (*zugehören*) which constitutes preethical obedience. This is the concept toward which I am now trying to direct myself.

This is not all. Not only is *hearkening* existentially prior to obeying, but *keeping silent* is existentially prior to speaking. Should we say silence? Yes, if silence does not mean muteness. Silence opens up a space for hearkening:

> *Keeping silent* is another essential possibility of discourse, and it has the same existential foundation. In talking with one another, the person who keeps silent can "make one understand" (that is, he can develop an understanding), and he can do so more authentically than the person who is never short of words. Speaking at length [*Viel-sprechen*] about something does not offer the slightest guarantee that thereby understanding is advanced. On the contrary, talking extensively about something, covers it up and brings what is understood to a sham clarity—the unintelligibility of the trivial. . . . Keeping silent authentically is possible only in genuine discoursing. To be able to keep silent, Dasein must have something to say—that is, it must have at its disposal an authentic and rich disclosedness of itself. In that case one's reticence [*Verschwiegenheit*] makes something manifest, and does away with "idle talk" [*"Gerede"*]. As a mode of discoursing, reticence Articulates the intelligibility of Dasein in so primordial a manner that it gives rise to a potentiality-for-hearing which is genuine, and to a Being-with-one-another which is transparent (p. 208).

We are at the point where silence is the origin of hearkening and obedience.

This analysis, and "the fundamental analysis of Dasein" to which it pertains, reveals the horizon and opens up the way to approximations, yet to be established, to a relation to God as the word which precedes all prohibition and accusation. I am prepared to recognize the fact that I shall not encounter the occurrence of word that is known as the Gospel by means of a simple extension of the categories of practical reason. The God for whom we are searching will not exist as the source of moral obligation, the author of commandments, the one who places the seal of the absolute on man's ethical experience. On the contrary, this type of meditation would seem to suggest that we not let the kerygma become trapped in the labyrinth of obligation and duty.

Let us now take the second step. What sort of ethics is possible on the basis of this existential relationship to word? If we attend to the spirit of the mourning work developed by atheism, and if we attend to the mode of nonethical understanding that is implicit in hearkening and in silence, we are now ready to pose the problem of ethics in terms that do not imply, at least in the beginning, a relationship to prohibition. Such terms are still neutral with regard to accusation and condemnation. Let us try to elaborate the original ethical problem that is suggested both by the *destruction* of the god of morality and by nonethical *instruction* through word.

I shall call this ethics that exists prior to the morality of obligation *an ethics of the desire to be or the effort to exist.* The history of philosophy provides us with a valuable precedent in this connection, that of Spinoza. It was Spinoza who referred to ethics as the total process through which man passes from slavery to happiness and freedom. This process is not governed by a formal principle of obligation, nor by an intuition of ends and values, but by the unfolding of effort, *conatus*, which is determinate of our existence as a finite mode of being. We are speaking here of effort; but we must also mention desire, so as to establish at the source of the ethical problem the identity between effort, in the Spinozistic sense of *conatus*, and desire in the Platonic and Freudian sense of *eros* (Freud does not hesitate to mention that what he calls libido and eros is related to the concept of eros in Plato's *Symposium*). By effort, I mean one's situation in existence, the affirmative power to exist. Effort thus implies an indefinite time span, a duration which is merely the continuing process of existence. This situation within existence is the foundation of the most fundamental affirmation: "I am," "je suis," "ich bin." This affirmation, however, must be recovered and restored, because (and here the problem of evil emerges) it has been alienated in many ways. This is why it must be regrasped and reinstated. The task of ethics is thus the reappropriation of our effort to exist. Since our power to be has been alienated, however, this effort remains a desire, the desire to be. Desire, here as always, signifies lack, need, or demand. This nothingness at the heart of our existence transforms our effort into a desire and establishes an equivalence between Spinoza's *conatus* and the *eros* of Plato and Freud. The affirmation of being within the lack of being is the most fundamental structure in the foundation of ethics.

Ethics, in this radical sense of the word, is the progressive appropriation of our effort to be.

This radical dimension of the problem of ethics is, as it were, concealed by the consideration of obligation as the governing principle of practical reason. Formalism in ethics conceals the dialectic of human action or, to use a stronger expression, the dialectic of human existence. The latter is recovered by means of a problematic that is not original but derivative, the problematic of the *a priori* foundation of practical reason. I refer to this as a derivative problematic because it seems to me that it is immediately derived from the *Critique of Pure Reason*. It is here fully elaborated within the framework of a regressive analysis which leads back to the categorial structures that make all knowledge possible. Can the same dichotomy between the empirical and the *a priori*, however, be extended to the internal structure of human action, to what I have called the dialectic of existence? I am doubtful. This transference to the realm of practical reason of a distinction that was fully elaborated in the first *Critique* is responsible for the opposition that Kant sets up between obligation, considered as the *a priori* of the will, and desire, as the empirical element in human action. The exclusion of desire from the sphere of ethics has had disastrous consequences. The effort to achieve happiness is excluded from the moralist's field of consideration insofar as it is a material principle of will. The formal principle of obligation is thus isolated from the process of action; ethical rigor is substituted for the Spinozistic problem of happiness and freedom. The hermeneutics of Freud and Nietzsche criticize this privileged status of formalism as the foundation of ethics. Formalism, for them, appears as a second-order rationalization, resulting from the introduction into the field of practical reason of a distinction that is valid within the realm of theoretical reason.

Must we then say that the problem of duty has no ethical meaning? I do not think so; even prohibition has its place, but its place is not originary or fundamental. At the most, it is a criterion of the objective character of the goodness of our will. The same thing could be said with regard to the concept of value: it also has its place, though it is in no sense primordial. The concept of value emerges at a certain stage of ethical reflection, when it becomes necessary for us to establish a harmony between our powers and our existential situation, i.e., the institutions and structures of economic, political, and cultural life. Value appears at the intersection between our unlimited desire to be and the finite conditions of its actualization. This function of value does not authorize us to hypostasize *the* Value or to worship the idol of value. It is sufficient to relate the process of

evaluation and value to the dialectic of action and to the historical conditions of human ethical experience.

It is not only the hermeneutics of Nietzsche and Freud that
encourages us to relate formalism in ethics and the creation of
values to the existential foundation of our effort and desire. The
kind of philosophy of word that we have just developed invites
us to take the very same step. When we speak of word as a
positive, vital reality, we are suggesting an underlying connection between word and the active core of our existence. Word
has the power to change our understanding of ourselves. This
power does not originally take the form of an imperative. Before
addressing itself to the will as an order that must be obeyed,
word addresses itself to what I have called our existence as effort and desire. We are changed, not because a will is imposed on
our own will; we are changed by the "listening that understands." Word reaches us on the level of the symbolic structures
of our existence, the dynamic schemes that express the way in
which we understand our situation and the way in which we
project ourselves into this situation. Consequently, there is
something that precedes the will and the principle of obligation,
which, according to Kant, is the *a priori* structure of this will.
This something else is our existence itself insofar as it is capable
of being modified by word. This intimate connection between
our desire to be and the power of word is a consequence of what
we have referred to above as the act of hearkening, of paying
attention, of obeying. This articulation, in turn, makes possible
what we describe in ordinary terms as will, evaluation, decision,
and choice. This psychology of the will is only the superficial
projection of a more profound articulation between the meaning
of our existential situation, understanding, and discourse—to
take up the principal notions of the Heideggerian analysis of
Dasein.

Such is the second step along the long detour from atheism
to faith. I shall not go any farther in the present essay. I readily
admit that it falls far short of the goal. The discussion that
follows, concerning consolation and resignation, will perhaps
permit us, nevertheless, to take several new steps in the same
direction. Even after this new progression, however, a gap will
still remain between the philosopher's interminable exploration
of new beginnings and the powerful words of the preacher. In
spite of this gap, a certain correspondence may appear between
a theology which would remain faithful to its own origins and
a philosophical investigation which would have adopted athe-

ism's critique of religion. I shall explain this correspondence in the following section.

II. On Consolation

I. The connection between accusation and consolation is perhaps the most striking characteristic of religion. God threatens and protects. He is the ultimate danger and the ultimate protection. In the most primitive theologies, traces of which we find in the Old Testament, these two aspects of divinity have been coordinated in a rational scheme in the form of the law of retribution. The god who gives protection is the god of morality; he corrects the apparent inequality in the distribution of individual destinies by establishing the relationship between suffering and wickedness as well as the relationship between happiness and justice. By means of this law of retribution, the god who threatens and the god who protects becomes one and the same god, the god of morality. This primitive rationalization establishes religion not only as the absolute foundation of morality but also as a *Weltanschauung*—the moral vision of the world framed within a speculative cosmology. As Providence (in Greek, *pronoia;* in Latin, *providentia*), the god of morality is the organizing power in a world that operates in terms of the law of retribution. Such is perhaps the most primitive and the most comprehensive structure of religion. This religious vision of the world, however, has never exhausted the field of possible relationships between man and God, and, in fact, there have always been men of faith who have rejected it as entirely blasphemous. Even in the Babylonian and biblical literature known as wisdom literature (especially in the Book of Job), true faith in God is violently contrasted with this law of retribution. Such a faith might rather be described as an essentially tragic faith, beyond all assurance and protection.

Hence, my working hypothesis: atheism means, at the very least, the destruction of the god of morality, not only as the ultimate source of accusation but also as the ultimate source of protection, i.e., Providence.

If atheism is to have some *religious* meaning, however, then the death of the god of Providence should point toward a new kind of faith, a tragic faith, which would stand in the same relationship to classical metaphysics to Job's faith stood in relation to the primitive law of retribution, professed by his pious friends. By "metaphysics" I mean the closely woven tissue of philosophy and theology that has taken the form of theodicy in order to defend and justify the goodness and omnipotence of God in face of the existence of evil. In this regard, the theodicy of Leibniz is the paradigm for all attempts to understand the order of this world as a providential order, i.e., as expressing the subordination of physical laws to ethical laws under the sign of the justice of God.

I do not intend to criticize theodicies on the level of their own argumentation, that is, on epistemological grounds, as Kant has done in his famous essays against theodicies, both Leibnizian and post-Leibnizian. This critique, as we know, is principally concerned with teleological concepts in general and with the notion of the final cause in particular; it deserves to be considered in itself with the greatest of care. I prefer to consider, in accordance with the preceding section, the atheism of Freud and Nietzsche—and this for two reasons. First of all, because the critique of the god of morality finds its completion in a critique of religion as refuge and protection; second, because the critique developed by Freud and Nietzsche goes much further than any epistemological critique. It digs beneath the surface of the argument so as to lay bare the underlying level of motivations on which theodicy is based. This substitution of hermeneutics for epistemology relates not only to theodicies of the Leibnizian genre but to all philosophies that pretend to go beyond theodicy and still attempt to establish a rational reconciliation between the laws of nature and human destiny. Thus Kant, after criticizing Leibniz, attempts in turn, with his famous Postulates of Practical Reason, to reconcile freedom and nature under the rule of a moral God. In the same manner, Hegel criticizes Kant and his moral vision of the world but proceeds to construct a rational system in which all contradictions are reconciled: the ideal is no longer opposed to the real; it has become the latter's immanent law. For Nietzsche, Hegel's philosophy realizes the essence of all moral philosophy. Of course, this violent reduction, to the realm of morality, of philosophies as diverse as those of Leibniz, Kant, and Hegel is unacceptable to the historian of philosophy. The historian of philosophy must preserve the unique rational structure of each one of these philosophies against a vulgar confusion of all philosophies of the classical age under the title of "morality." But by means of this violence, which reduces and denies the most obvious differences, Nietzsche opens up the way to a hermeneutics that perceives the common motif behind the most diverse styles of philosophizing. What is significant in this hermeneutics is the type of will that expresses itself as a search for a rational reconciliation, whether this be in the Leibnizian theodicy, in the Kantian Postulates of Practical Reason, or in the absolute knowledge of Hegel. For Nietzsche, the will that is hidden behind these rationalizations is always a weak will. Its weakness consists precisely in the recourse to a vision of the world in which the ethical principle that Nietzsche calls the "ideal" comes to dominate the process of reality. The interest and value of this procedure lies in the fact that every epistemological critique of teleology is transposed into a hermeneutics of the will to power. The doctrines of the past are in this way related to the degree of weakness or power of the will, to its negative or positive tendencies, to its reactive or active impulses.

In the first part of this essay we interrupted our discussion of the Nietzschean hermeneutics at the point where it remained an "accusation of accusation." It was legitimate to remain at this point in a discussion that was devoted to the concept of prohibition. Nietzsche's style of philosophizing, moreover, encourages us to emphasize this critical side of his work. In an essential way, Nietzsche's style takes the form of an accusation of accusation and to this extent remains tied to the kind of resentment for which he reproaches the moralists.

We must now go further. Our critique of metaphysics and its search for rational reconciliation must give way to a positive ontology, beyond resentment and accusation. Such a positive ontology consists in an entirely nonethical vision, or what Nietzsche described as "the innocence of becoming" (*die Unschuld des Werdens*). The latter is merely another name for "beyond good and evil." Of course, this kind of ontology can never become dogmatic, or it will risk falling under its own criticisms. It must remain an interpretation, inseparable from the interpretation of all interpretations. There is no certainty that such a philosophy can escape its own self-destruction. In addition, such an ontology remains unavoidably caught up in the network of mythology—whether a mythology in the Greek sense of the word, such as the mythology of Dionysus, a mythology in the language of modern cosmology, such as the myth of the eternal return of the Same and its relation with *amor fati*, a mythology in the language of the philosophy of history, such as the myth of the superman, or, finally, a mythology that exists beyond the oppositions among these three other mythologies, such as the myth of the world as game. All of these myths say the same thing: they all proclaim the absence of guilt, i.e., the absence of the ethical character of all being.

Confronted with this hard doctrine, I by no means intend to prove or refute it, nor do I intend to put it in the service of some clever apologetics and thereby convert it into Christian faith. I must rather leave it where it is, in a place where it remains alone and perhaps out of reach, inaccessible to any form of repetition. It maintains itself in this place as my most formidable adversary, as the measure of radicality against which I must measure myself. Whatever I think and whatever I believe must be worthy of it.

But before taking up again the path that leads from atheism to faith, in the manner in which we have attempted this above, I would like to elucidate some of the implications of the Nietzschean critique of religion with respect to Freud. The kind of mythology that is represented by the Nietzschean conception of the innocence of becoming finds it more prosaic counterpart in what Freud called the reality principle. It is not by accident that Freud sometimes refers to this principle by another name, one that recalls the Nietzschean *amor fati*: the name of Ananke, i.e., the concept of necessity, drawn from the tradition of Greek tragedy. As we know, Freud always contrasted the reality principle with the pleasure principle and with all types of thinking that are influenced by the pleasure principle, i.e., all the forms of illusion.

It is at this point that a certain critique of religion appears in Freud's work. I have insisted several times on the fact that religion for Freud is not essentially the source of absolute authority in regard to the requirements of moral consciousness; it is rather a compensation for the harshness of life. Religion, in this sense, is the highest function of culture; its task is to protect man against the superior force of nature and to compensate him for the sacrifice of the instincts that is demanded by social existence. The new aspect that religion turns toward the individual is no longer that of prohibition but that of protection. At the same time, religion addresses itself less to fear than to desire.

This regressive-reductive analysis leads back a second time to the notion of a collective image of the father, though the father figure has now become more ambiguous, more ambivalent. Now he is not only the figure who accuses; he is also the figure who protects. Now he responds not only to our fear of punishment but also to our desire for protection and consolation, and the name for this desire is nostalgia for the father. Religion thus appears as one of the most cunning and most concealed forms of the pleasure principle. As a result, the reality principle involves a renunciation of this nostalgia for the father, not only on the level of our fears, but also on the level of our desires. A vision of the world that no longer contains the image of the father is the price that must be paid for this ascesis of desire.

It is at this point that Freud comes together with Nietzsche once again. The Freudian reversal, the move from the pleasure principle to the reality principle, has the same meaning as the Nietzschean reversal, the move from the moral view of the world to the innocence of becoming and the notion of the world as "game." Freud's tone is less lyrical than Nietzsche's; his attitude is also closer to resignation than to jubilation. Freud remains too well aware of the anguish of the human condition to go beyond a simple acceptance of the immutable order of nature, and he remains too attached to a coldly scientific view of the world to give free reign to an uncontrolled lyricism. In his last works, however, the theme of Ananke is deemphasized and balanced by another theme, which is much closer in spirit to Nietzsche. I am referring here to the theme of Eros, a theme that leads back to the Faustian motif of Freud's youth. This motif was later suppressed, due to his scientific preoccupations. In fact, Freud's philosophical temperament is perhaps determined by the obscure struggle between a positivist conception of reality and a romantic conception of life. When he is under the sway of the latter, we listen to a voice that could be that of Nietzsche: "And now we can expect that the other of those two celestial powers, eternal Eros, will affirm itself in the struggle against its equally immortal adversary"—this adversary being death. This great drama of Eros and Thanatos, underlying the inexorable order of nature, is the echo of Nietzsche in Freud. The scholarly discretion that prevails in Freud's mythology prevents it from attaining the lyrical and philosophical power of Nietzsche's writings; but it brings Nietzsche somewhat closer to us. Through Freud's work, some of the dangerous teachings descend to us from the heights of Sils-Maria.

2. What sort of faith is possible after the Freudian and Nietzschean critiques?

I suggested in the first part of this essay a prophetic preaching that would return to the roots of Judeo-Christian faith and would also be a new beginning for our time. With regard to the problem of accusation, this preaching would speak only in terms of freedom and would elaborate the contemporary meaning of the Pauline antinomy between the Gospel and the Law. With respect to the problem of consolation, this prophetic preaching would be heir to the tragic faith of Job. It would adopt the same attitude in regard to the teleological metaphysics of Western philosophy that Job adopted in regard to the pious words of his friends concerning the god of retribution. It would be a faith that moves forward through the shadows, in a new "night of the soul"—to adopt the language of the mystics—before a God who would not have the attributes of "Providence," a God who would not protect me but would surrender me to the dangers of a life worthy of being called human. Is not this God the Crucified One, the God who, as Bonhoeffer says, only through his weakness is capable of helping me? The night of the soul means above all the overcoming of desire as well as fear, the overcoming of nostalgia for the protecting father figure. Beyond this night, and only beyond it, can we recover the true meaning of the God of consolation, the God of the Resurrection, the Byzantine and Roman Pantocrator.

I can imagine such a prophetic preacher; at times, I hear his voice. But again, it is not the voice of the philosopher. The philosopher thinks in the intermediate time between nihilism and purified faith. Above all, his task is not to reconcile, within a feeble eclecticism, the hermeneutics that destroys the idols of the past and the hermeneutics that restores the kerygma. To think is to dig deeper until one reaches the level of questioning that makes possible a mediation between religion and faith by means of atheism. This mediation appears as a long detour, or even as a road that has gone astray. Perhaps we shall go farther in the same direction, since the overcoming of the fear of punishment and the desire for protection constitute one and the same process, a process that goes beyond what Nietzsche called the "spirit of vengeance."

The first step: Let us recall that we have discovered in our relationship to word—whether it be the word of the poet or that of the thinker or any sort of word that reveals something about our situation within the totality of being—the point of departure, the origin and the model for an "obedience to being" beyond all fear of punishment, beyond all prohibition and condemnation. Perhaps we shall even be able to discover in this obedience the source of a kind of *consolation* that would be just as far removed from the infantile desire for protection as obedience is from all fear of punishment. My initial relationship to word, when I receive it in the fullness of its signification, not only neutralizes all accusation and thereby all fear; it also serves to effectively bracket my desire for protection. It puts out of play, so to speak, the narcissism of my desire. I return to a realm of meaning in which there is no longer a question of myself but only of being as such. The totality of being is manifested in the forgetting of my own desires and interests.

It is this impersonal unfolding of being, in the absence of personal concerns and through the fullness of word, that was already operative in the revelation that comes at the end of the Book of Job: "Then the Lord answered Job out of the whirlwind, and said . . . ." But what did he say? Nothing that could be considered as a response to the problem of suffering and death; nothing that could be used as a justification for God in a theodicy. On the contrary, he spoke of an order that was alien to man, of that which is beyond the limits of human finitude: "Where wast thou when I laid the foundations of the earth? declare, if thou hast understanding." The path of theodicy has here been closed off; even the vision of the Behemoth and the Leviathan, which is the culmination of the revelation, has no relationship to Job's personal situation. No teleology emerges from the whirlwind; no intelligible connection is established between physical order and the ethical order; what remains is the unfolding of being within the fullness of word; what remains is only the possibility of an act of acceptance which would be the first step in the direction of consolation, the first step beyond the desire for protection.

I call this first step *resignation*.

In what sense does this resignation to a nonethical order constitute the first step toward consolation? In the sense that this nonethical order is not alien to word and in spite of the fact that it is alien to my own narcissistic interests. Being can be brought to word.

For Job, the revelation of the whole is not originally a spectacle but a voice. The fact that the Lord speaks is what is essential. He does not speak of Job; he speaks to Job; and that alone is sufficient. The occurrence of word as such creates a link; dialogue is in itself a mode of consolation. The occurrence of word is being become word; the hearkening to word makes possible the view of the world as an ordered whole. "I have heard

of thee by the hearing of the ear; but now mine eye seeth thee."
But even so, Job's question concerning himself receives no resolution; it suffers dissolution due to the displacement of the center
that word performs.

At this point, we are led back from Job to the pre-Socratics.
The pre-Socratic thinkers also perceived the displacement of the
center that word effects: "To be and to be thought are one and
the same thing." Such is the fundamental possibility of consolation. The unity of being and logos makes it possible for man to
belong to being insofar as he is a speaking being. Because my
own speech belongs to word, because the speaking of my own
language belongs to the saying of being, I no longer demand that
my desire be reconciled with the order of nature. In this sort
of belonging resides the origin, not only of obedience beyond
fear, but of consent beyond desire.

Let us elaborate this concept of *consent*. This will be our
second step. We shall not do this in psychological terms; the
philosopher is not a therapist; he cures desires by changing
ideas. As a result, to move from the desire for protection to the
act of consent, it is necessary to take the difficult path of a critique applied to the type of metaphysics that is implicit in the
desire for protection.

The type of metaphysics that is involved here is that which
tries to relate value and fact within a system that we would
like to call the meaning of the universe or the meaning of life.
In such a system the natural order and the ethical order are
unified in a higher totality. The question is to know whether this
attempt does not itself proceed from the forgetfulness of the
kind of unity that the pre-Socratics recognized when they spoke
of the identity of being and logos. As we know, this is the question that Heidegger poses to metaphysics. Even the concepts of
value and fact, which we employ as a fundamental division of
reality, already imply the loss of the primordial unity in which
value, fact, ethics, and physics do not yet exist. If this is so,
we must not be surprised if we are unable to join together again
the broken fragments of the lost unity. I myself take Heidegger's
question seriously. It may be that all the constructions of classical metaphysics, concerning the subordination of causal laws
to final laws, represent a desperate attempt to recreate a unity
at a level which is itself the result of a fundamental forgetting of
the question of being. In the essay called "Die Zeit des Weltbildes" Heidegger characterizes the age of metaphysics as the
age in which "being is placed at the disposal of an explicit

representation": "[in Descartes's metaphysics] being is determined for the first time as the objectivity of the representation, and truth, as the certainty of the representation." [3] At the same time, the world becomes a spectacle:

> When the world becomes conceived as an image, the totality of Being is understood and fixed as that in relation to which man can orient himself, as that which man thus wishes to present and have in front of him, hoping thereby to decisively arrest Being in the form of a representation (*ibid.*, p. 82).

The representative character of Being is thus correlated with the emergence of man as subject. Man pushes himself to the center of the picture; hence, Being is placed in front of man as something objective, at his disposal. Later, with Kant, with Fichte, and finally with Nietzsche himself, man as subject becomes man as will. The will appears as the origin of values, while the world retires into the background as simple fact, deprived of all value. Nihilism is not far distant. The gap can no longer be bridged, the gap which exists between a subject who posits himself as the origin of values and a world which unfolds itself as a collection of appearances stripped of all value. As long as we continue to regard the world as an object for representation and the human will as the locus of value, reconciliation and integration will be impossible. Nihilism is the historical verification of this impossibility. In particular, nihilism reveals the failure of the God of metaphysics to effect this reconciliation, the failure of all attempts to fulfill causality within a teleological scheme. Insofar as the problem of God is posed in these terms and at this level, even the question of God emerges from that forgetfulness which has given rise to the conception of the world as an object of representation and the conception of man as a subject who posits values.

For this reason, we must now return to a point that is situated prior to the dichotomy between subject and object if we wish to overcome the antinomies that proceed from it: the antinomy of value and fact, the antinomy of teleology and causality, the antinomy of man and the world. This regression will not take us back to the dark night of a philosophy of identity; it will rather lead us to the manifestation of Being as the logos that gathers all things.

3. Martin Heidegger, *Holzwege* (Frankfurt a.M.: Klostermann, 1957), p. 80.

If this is truly the case, then the foundation of any response to Nietzsche must lie in a meditation on the gathering force of the logos rather than in the emergence of the will to power. For the will to power perhaps still belongs to the age of metaphysics, in which man was precisely defined as will. For Heidegger, the logos is that aspect or dimension of our language which is linked to the question of Being. By means of the logos, the question of Being is brought to language; thanks to the logos, man emerges, not only as a will to power, but as a being who interrogates Being.

This is the radical path of thought which opens up the horizon onto a new understanding of consolation and which would make of atheism a real mediation between religion and faith. If man is fundamentally posited as man only when he is "gathered" by the logos which itself "gathers all things," then a kind of consolation is possible which is nothing less than the happiness of belonging to the logos and to Being as logos. This happiness first emerges in primordial poetry (*Urdichtung*) and then in thought. Heidegger says somewhere that the poet sees the sacred while the philosopher sees Being, that they reside on the tops of different mountains, whence their voices echo and respond.

Let us take one more step toward this function of the logos as consolation.

Heidegger employs other expressions which suggest such a functioning; he says that the *logos* of the pre-Socratics is the same as *physis*. Physis is not nature as opposed to convention, history, or mind. It is something which, in its gathering, predominates over all; it is that which "surpasses" (*das Überwältigende*). Once again we are brought back to the connection between Job and the pre-Socratics. Already in the revelation of the Book of Job we find an expression of that which surpasses and the experience of being joined to that which surpasses. This experience is not the result of a physical, spiritual, or mystical process; it is something that occurs only within the clarity of "saying" (*Sagen*).

The logos signifies not only the power which makes things manifest and gathers them together; it is also that which links the poet to this gathering power under the sign of that which surpasses. The power to gather things together by means of language does not originally belong to man as a speaking subject. Gathering and revealing belong first of all to that which surpasses and predominates, that which was symbolized by the original Greek notion of physis. Language is less and less the work of man. The power of saying is not something that we appropriate but that which appropriates us; and it is because we are not the masters of our own language that we can be "gathered," that is, joined to that which gathers. As a result, our language becomes something more than a simple, practical means of communicating with others and a means of controlling nature. When speaking becomes saying or, rather, when saying resides within the speaking of our language, we experience language as a gift, and we experience thought as a recognition of this gift. Thought gives thanks for the gift of language; in this manner, language once again gives birth to a form of consolation. Man finds consolation when, through language, he lets things be, lets them be revealed. Because Job understands word as that which gathers, he sees the world as gathered.

Kierkegaard calls this sort of consolation "repetition." In the Book of Job he sees this repetition expressed in the mythical form of an act of restitution: "and Yahweh restored Job to his former situation because he had interceded in behalf of his friends: and Yahweh increased Job's possessions twice over." If "repetition," according to Kierkegaard, is not simply another name for the law of retribution (which Job had rejected, and which would have been an ultimate justification of his pious friends, whom the Lord had condemned), then it can mean only one thing: the fulfillment of hearkening in seeing. Such a concept of repetition can thus appear as the counterpart of a pre-Socratic theme; it is itself essentially similar to the pre-Socratic understanding of both *logos,* as that which gathers, and *physis,* as that which surpasses and prevails. Once again we find that the Book of Job and the Fragments of Heraclitus say one and the same thing.

To more fully understand this point, let us go back one last time to Nietzsche. Nietzsche also gave the name "consolation" (*Trost*) to the great desire, "the greatest hope": that man might overcome himself. Why did he refer to this hope as consolation? Perhaps because consolation bears in itself the notion of deliverance from feelings of revenge (*Rache*). "For *that man be delivered from revenge* is for me the bridge to the highest hope, and a rainbow after long storms." [4] Deliverance from vengeance is at the heart of our meditation on consolation, for vengeance means: "Where once was suffering, punishment must appear."

4. *Thus Spake Zarathustra,* Pt. II, "The Tarantulas."

Heidegger comments in the following manner: vengeance is an activity which opposes itself and is degrading—though not primarily and fundamentally in a moral sense. The critique of vengeance is not itself a moral critique. The spirit of vengeance is directed against time, against that which passes. Zarathustra says: "This, yes, this alone is vengeance itself, resentment of the will against time and its *this was*."[5] Vengeance is the will in self-opposition (*des Willens Widerwillens*), and hence, resentment against time. The fact that time passes is the catastrophe which causes the will to suffer and on which the will takes revenge by denouncing that which passes because it passes. To overcome vengeance is to overcome the negation within the affirmation.

Is not Zarathustra's "recapitulation" very similar to the act of "repetition" which Kierkegaard finds in the Book of Job and to the "gathering" which Heidegger finds in the pre-Socratic writings? Though the relationship cannot be denied, the resemblance would be even greater were it not for the fact that Nietzsche's work itself is infected with the spirit of vengeance to the very extent that it remains an accusation of accusation. We read in the last lines of *Ecce Homo*: "Have I been misunderstood? Dionysus versus the Crucified." Herein lies the limitation of Nietzsche's work. Why is he incapable of answering Zarathustra's call to overcome vengeance? Is it not because, for Nietzsche, the creation of the superman capable of overcoming vengeance is dependent on the will and not on word? For this reason, does not Nietzsche's will to power remain both an act of acceptance and an act of vengeance? Only the kind of *Gelassenheit* which marks the submission of individual language to discourse is beyond vengeance. Consent must be joined to poetry.

Heidegger comments on Hölderlin's poem which contains the line "*dichterisch wohnt der Mensch*" ("poetically . . . dwells Man on this earth"): to the extent to which the poetic act is not a pure extravagance but the beginning of the end of a wandering by means of an act of creation, poetry makes it possible for man to dwell on earth. This occurs when my normal relationship to language is reversed, when language speaks. Thus, man responds to language by listening to what it says to him. At the same time, dwelling becomes for us mortals a "poetic" dwelling. "Dwelling" is another name for Kierkegaard's "repetition"; it is the opposite of fleeing. In fact, Hölderlin says: "Full of merit,

5. *Ibid.*, Pt. III, "The Great Nostalgia."

and yet poetically, dwells man on this earth." The poem suggests that man dwells on earth insofar as a tension is maintained between his concern for the heavens, for the divine, and for the rootedness of his own existence in the earth. This tension confers a certain dimensionality and assigns a locus to the act of dwelling. In terms of its total extension and radical comprehension, poetry is what locates the act of dwelling between heaven and earth, under the sky, but on the earth, within the domain of word.

Poetry is more than the art of making poems. It is *poiēsis*, or creation in the largest sense of the word. It is in this sense that poetry is equivalent to primordial dwelling; man dwells only when poets exist in the world.

This philosophical investigation into the religious meaning of atheism has led us from resignation to consent and from consent to a mode of dwelling on earth that is governed by poetry and thought. This mode of being is no longer "the love of fate" but a love of creation. Such a fact suggests a movement from atheism toward faith. The love of creation is a form of consolation which depends on no external compensation and which is equally remote from any form of vengeance. Love finds within itself its own compensation; it is itself consolation.

We have thus indicated a certain correspondence between this philosophical analysis and an interpretation of the kerygma which is faithful to the origins of the Judeo-Christian faith and at the same time bears a contemporary significance. Biblical faith represents God, the God of the prophets and the God of the Christian Trinity, as a father; atheism teaches us to renounce the image of the father. Once overcome as idol, the image of the father can be recovered as symbol. This symbol is a parable of the foundation of love; it is the counterpart, within a theology of love, of the progression that leads us from simple resignation to poetic life. I believe that such is the religious meaning of atheism. An idol must die so that a symbol of being may begin to speak.

Fatherhood: From Phantasm to Symbol

First I shall present in abbreviated form the working hypothesis which I propose to test. It can be stated in three parts:

1. The father figure is not a well-known figure whose meaning is invariable and which we can pursue in its avatars, its disappearance and return under diverse masks; it is a problematic figure, incomplete and in suspense. It is a *designation* that is susceptible of traversing a diversity of semantic levels, from the phantasm of the father as castrater, who must be killed, to the symbol of the father who dies of compassion.

2. In order to understand this symbolic mutation, we must resituate the paternal image within the milieu of the other paradigms of the interhuman relation. According to my hypothesis, the internal evolution of the paternal symbol results from the attraction, of an external kind, exercised by the other figures, which rescue it from its primitive character. The father figure owes to its insertion in the rule-governed game of kinship an initial limitation, an inertia, indeed a resistance to symbolization, which is surmounted only by action of a lateral kind, exerted by other figures which do not belong to the kinship relation. These are the nonparental figures, which, by their action of breaking in, crack the shell of literalness of the father figure and liberate the symbols of fatherhood and sonship.

3. But if the symbolism of fatherhood must undergo a certain reduction of the initial image, which might even appear as a certain renunciation, indeed a mourning, the terminal expres-

Translated by Robert Sweeney.

sions of this symbolism do not lose their connection with the
initial forms, of which they are, in a way, a repetition on a higher
level. This return of the primitive figure after its own death
constitutes in my opinion the central problem of the process of
symbolization which is at work in the father figure. For this return, to the degree that it is susceptible of several actualizations,
opens the field to several interpretations which belong in their
turn to the designation of the father.

Such is, in its schematic articulation, my working hypothesis.
It designates fatherhood as a *process* rather than a *structure,*
and it proposes a dynamic and dialectical constitution of it.

I propose submitting this thesis to the test by successively
considering three registers, three "fields," which can provide an
analogical constitution of the process of fatherhood. The first
field is delineated by *psychoanalysis,* which articulates an "economy of desire." In the second, a *phenomenology of spirit* sketches
out a felt or reasoned history of basic cultural figures. The third
relates to the *philosophy of religion,* which develops here an interpretation of the "divine names" and the designations of God.

I shall not make a pronouncement here on the respective
status of these three fields; I shall limit myself to stating that
they have been delimited by different methodologies and that
they imply in each case a conceptual framework and specific
procedures. Instead of radically justifying the right to existence
of several problematics and several readings of reality, I shall
rather take advantage of the diversity of approaches to justify
the soundness of my working hypothesis. If something like an
identical constitution of fatherhood, an identical structural
rhythm, an identical return of the initial figure throughout the
network of other figures, can be discerned in three different registers, then there will be some chance that the analogy, or better,
the homology of constitution, will reveal a single schema of
fatherhood.

I. The Father Figure in an Economy of Desire

I DEFINE THE FIRST FIELD by the fate of the instincts, to
use Freud's expression, thus giving the lead to *economic* explanation over all others. I cannot justify this here. I think it is the
most fundamental intention, and in addition the most explicit,
in Freudianism; it is also the most interesting explanation for

the philosopher by reason of the shift it imposes with respect to the field of consciousness. I am therefore assuming that the sphere of competence of psychoanalysis is defined by the presence and the interplay of life and death instincts, along with the figures that are dependent upon their vicissitudes.

It seems possible to me to retain from Freud's work concerning the father figure three themes which correspond to the three moments of my working hypothesis; these are the very ones that will permit us to construct the schema of fatherhood further along, when we shall have traversed the three other schemas of articulation of the father figure. I am calling these three themes (1) the *formation* of the Oedipus complex, (2) the *destruction* of the Oedipus complex, and (3) the *permanence* of the Oedipus complex.

First, there is the formation of the Oedipus complex as the obligatory landmark. As Freud has said on many occasions: with the Oedipus complex, psychoanalysis stands or falls. It is a matter of taking it or leaving it. The Oedipus complex is in a certain sense the crucial question posed by psychoanalysis to its public. I assume here, as well known, the essentials of the theory of the Oedipus complex. What I shall retain from it for what follows is this: the critical point of the Oedipus complex is to be sought for in the initial constitution of desire, namely, its megalomania, its infantile omnipotence. From this proceeds the phantasm of a father who would retain the privileges which the son must seize if he is to be himself.

This phantasm of a being who retains power and withholds it in order to deprive his son of it is, as we know, the basis of the castration complex, on which is articulated the desire to murder. It is no less important to know that it is from this same megalomania that the glorification of the killed father, the search for reconciliation and propitiation with the interiorized image, and finally the building-up of guilt proceed. Death of the father and punishment of the son are thus placed at the origin of a single history, which is quite real in respect to instinct, although quite unreal in respect to representation. Formation of the Oedipus complex; then destruction of the Oedipus complex.

We have learned from Freud that there are several ways of getting out of the Oedipus complex; more specifically, the great question for what follows in the history of the psyche, and therefore for the history of the whole culture, is indeed not only how one gets into the Oedipus complex but how one gets out of it. In a relatively late essay, "The Passing of the Oedipus Complex,"

Freud introduces the concept of the destruction or demolition of the Oedipus complex, the parallels to which in the two other registers we will point out shortly. In the Freudian register it is an economic concept, just like repression, identification, sublimation, desexualization. It is concerned with the fate of the instincts, the reworking of their depth distribution.

But let us understand the destruction carefully. It is insofar as it structures the psyche that the Oedipus complex is destroyed as a complex. We can come to understand the relation between the destruction (of the complex) and the structuration (of the psyche) in the following way: the stake involved in the dissolution of the Oedipus complex is the replacement of an identification with the father which is literally mortal—and even doubly mortal, since it kills the father by murder and the son by remorse—by a mutual recognition, where difference is compatible with similarity.

The recognition of the father: that is what is at stake. There will be other examples of it in the two registers that we will consider further on. In particular, it will be the task of a history of figures to set up the mediations—of having, of power, of valuing, and of knowing—which articulate this structuring destruction. This is not the task of psychoanalysis. But it is its task to spot the trace of these mediations in the instinctual reshufflings at the level of a history of desire and of pleasure. In the successful Oedipus complex, if we may express it thus, desire is rectified in its most profound avowal of omnipotence and immortality; what is destroyed is the economy of all or nothing. The proof par excellence in this respect is the power to accept the father as mortal and, finally, to accept the death of the father, just as his immortality was only the fantastic projection of the omnipotence of desire. It is in terms of this meaning of mortality that there will be articulated a representation of fatherhood distinct from physical begetting and less attached to the very person of the father. Begetting is a matter of nature, fatherhood of designation. It is necessary that the blood tie be loosened, be marked by death, in order that fatherhood be truly instituted; then the father is father because he is designated and called father.

Mutual recognition, reciprocal designation: with this theme we touch on the frontier that is common to psychoanalysis and to a theory of culture. We enter psychoanalysis by the concept of instinct, at the boundary line between biology and psychology; we leave it by other limit-ideas, at the boundary line between psychology and the sociology of culture. Identification is such a concept, and Freud exerts himself to repeat that he has not resolved the problem that such a concept introduces. To resolve it will require a change of field.

But before changing field, it is crucial to take into consideration the third theme, which, if I may say so, sets the tone—the psychoanalytic tone—for what precedes. This third theme is this: in a certain respect, the Oedipus complex is insurmountable. In a certain respect—or rather in several senses.

In the sense, first of all, of repetition: psychoanalysis has remained attentive to the regressions, to the new paths of the Oedipal conflict, to the revivals of the archaic complex occasioned by new "object choices." On a number of occasions Freud has written that new choices of sexual objects are based inescapably on the model of the primary fixations. Everything in Freudianism tends to a certain pessimism with respect to the capacity for sublimation, as if the Oedipus complex condemned the psychic life to a sort of running-in-place, indeed, of perpetual recommencement. In this sense the Oedipal heritage is indeed a destiny. It is certain that the principal weight of Freudian doctrine leans to this side; it is to this notion of repetition that the concepts of latency and return of the repressed are attached, which, as we know, hold the decisive, if not exclusive, role in the interpretation of the religious phenomenon. Freud remained attached to it in an obstinate fashion from *Totem and Taboo* to *Moses and Monotheism.*

But, if the Oedipus complex were nontranscendable in this sense only, there would remain but one alternative for understanding not only religion but all the facts of culture where a certain sublimation is expressed: it would be necessary either to disregard them, by attributing them without further ado to the return of the repressed, or to attempt to inscribe them outside the field of the Oedipus complex, in some sphere that is nonlibidinal and free of conflict. But what we said above about the structuring function of the Oedipus complex permits us to risk another sense of its nontranscendability, another sense of its repetition, according to which it is by the same Eros, the same instinctual depths, that we are impelled toward new constellations of objects and new instinctual organizations. What psychoanalysis teaches us, then, is this: we do not have to deny our desire; we can unmask it and recognize it. Agape is nothing else than Eros. It is by the same love that we love the archaic objects and those that the education of desire discloses to us. There is only one economy of desire, and repetition is the great law of this economy. It is therefore within this single economy of repetition that we must regard as identical and different the neurotic organizations of desire and the nonneurotic organizations; the transfiguration of the father in culture and in religion is the same thing, and not the same thing, as the return of the repressed: the same thing in the sense that everything continues to take place in the field of the Oedipus complex; not the same thing to the degree that our desire, by renouncing omnipotence, assents to the representation of a mortal father whom it is no longer necessary to kill but who can be recognized.

If such is indeed the future of the Oedipus complex, we understand that all of psychic life can be interrogated in relation to the Oedipus complex and that there is no place, as Father Pohier has stated emphatically, "to institute religion outside the field structured by the Oedipus complex."

It is this same dialectic of repetition that we are going to find again, in an analogous mode, in the field of the phenomenology of the spirit. But before taking leave of psychoanalysis, we should understand that it is the same reality that is going to be interrogated, in a different perspective. In leaving psychoanalysis, we do not mean that it has missed half or two-thirds of the human reality; we willingly believe that nothing human is foreign to it and that it apprehends the totality truly, but under an angle of vision that is limited by its theory, by its method, and, above all, by the analytic situation itself. As Leibniz put it concerning the vision of the monad, psychoanalysis sees the whole, but from one point of view. That is why it is the same elements, the same structures, and especially the same processes which return in the two other fields but in another perspective.

II. The Father Figure in a Phenomenology of the Spirit

THE SECOND "FIELD" we are taking into consideration is the one in which is deployed and delimited the method I have called, on several occasions, "concrete reflection." The method is reflective, in that it is concerned with a repetition of the acts, operations, and productions in which the self-consciousness of humanity is constituted. But the reflection is concrete, in that it attains to subjectivity only by the long detour of the signs that subjectivity has produced from itself in the works of culture. The history of culture is, even more than the individual consciousness, the great matrix of these signs. But philosophy is not limited to a chronology of their production; it attempts to order them in intelligible series which permit us to sketch out an itinerary of consciousness, a path on which an advance of self-consciousness occurs. This procedure is neither psychological nor historical; it imposes on the psychological consciousness—in itself too short— the detour through the texts of a culture in which the self is documented; and it imposes on event-oriented historicity the constitution of a meaning which is a true work of the concept. It is this work of meaning which constitutes the philosophical character of reflection and of the interpretation in which reflection is invested.

These brief remarks on method suffice to establish the difference in level between concrete reflection and the economy of desire. But more noteworthy than the difference in methods is the homology of the structures and processes which are encountered there. This is what the privileged example of the father is going to demonstrate.

Let us then begin our "second voyage," as Plato put it!

No one will be surprised that here I take as my guide Hegel's philosophy of spirit, just as I did in *Freud and Philosophy*.[1] But I hope to go further, particularly beyond phenomenology properly so called, whose insufficiency Hegel has pointed out in the *Encyclopaedia;* that is why I shall look for only one impulse, one primary starting point in the *Phenomenology of the Spirit.* If we pursue this—in effect the movement which leads from consciousness to self-consciousness—by way of the experience of the restless and unlimited life, everything seems to happen as in Freud; as in Freud, self-consciousness is rooted in life and desire. And the history of self-consciousness is the history of the education of desire. As with Freud also, desire is first of all infinite, extravagant:

> And self-consciousness is thus only assured of itself through sublating this other, which is presented to self-consciousness as an independent life; self-consciousness is *Desire.* Convinced of the nothingness of this other, it definitely affirms this nothingness to be for itself the truth of this other, negates the independent object,

1. Paul Ricoeur, *Freud and Philosophy: An Essay on Interpretation,* trans. Denis Savage (New Haven: Yale University Press, 1970).

and thereby acquires the certainty of its own self, as true certainty. . . .[2]

We could once more interpret in strictly Oedipal terms the first phases of duplicated reflection or of the doubling of self-consciousness. The father and the son, is this not a history of the doubling of consciousness? Is it not also a struggle to the death? Yes, but only up to a certain point. For it is important that the educative dialectic, for Hegel, is not that of father and son but rather that of master and slave. It is this which has a future and which—let us say it immediately—gives a future to sexuality. It would appear to me absolutely fundamental that the movement of recognition originates in another sphere than fatherhood and sonship. Or, if one prefers, fatherhood and sonship enter into the movement of recognition only in the light of the master-slave relation. That is what I had in mind in the introduction, when I said that it is from the other figures of the cultural field that the figure of the father draws its dynamism and its capacity for symbolization.

Why this privilege of the master-slave relation? Above all, because it is the first which incorporates an exchange of roles: "the action of one," says Hegel, "is the act of the one as well as of the other" (p. 230). As unequal as the roles are, they are reciprocal.

But above all, the winning of mastery proceeds by way of the risk of one's own life; the master has staked his life and thus has shown himself to be more than life: "it is only by the risk of life that we preserve freedom." It would appear retrospectively that the cycle of birth and death, to which natural fatherhood and sonship belong—begetting and being begotten—is closed on itself: the growth of the children is the death of the parents. In this sense, natural fatherhood and sonship remain caught in the immediacy of life, in what Hegel would call, in his Jena period, "life of the kind that does not yet know itself." For that life, "nothingness does not exist as such." This is what the master inaugurates by risking his life. Now, as we have said with Freud, the great challenge is to renounce the vital immortality of desire, to accept the death of the father and one's own death. This is

2. G. W. F. Hegel, *The Phenomenology of Mind*, trans. J. B. Baillie (New York: Humanities Press, 1964), p. 225. [All page citations for this and subsequent quotations are to this volume. Throughout this book we have translated Ricoeur's *"esprit"* (Hegel's "Geist") as "spirit" rather than "mind," and in harmony with this the title of Hegel's work appears in the text as *The Phenomenology of the Spirit.*—Ed.]

precisely what the master does: what Hegel calls the supreme test by way of death, the conquest of the independence of spirit with respect to the immediacy of life. What Hegel describes here is therefore quite precisely what Freud has called sublimation and desexualization.

Finally, and above all—and now we pass immediately to the side of the slave—the dialectic of master and slave encounters the category of labor: if the master is raised above life by the risk of death, the slave is raised above formless, unshapen desire by the rude schooling of thingness—in Freudian language, by the reality principle. Whereas extravagant desire would suppress the thing, the slave is rubbed raw by the real:

> [He] takes up a negative attitude to things and cancels them; but the thing is, at the same time, independent for him, and, in consequence, he cannot, with all his negating, get so far as to annihilate it outright and be done with it; that is to say, he merely works on it (p. 235).

A *Bildung* is set in motion; in "forming" (*bilden*) the thing, the individual is formed himself. "Labor," says Hegel, "is desire restrained, and checked, evanescence delayed and postponed . . . ; labor shapes . . ." (p. 238).

Thus the *Phenomenology of the Spirit* presents a dialectic between desire and labor for which Freud has designated only the empty mold by speaking of the dissolution of the Oedipus complex. This dialectic permits the introduction of fatherhood itself into a process of recognition; but the recognition of the father and the son takes place by the double mediation of the mastery of men and things and the conquest of nature by labor. This is why the *Phenomenology of the Spirit* no longer fits neatly with psychoanalysis—or with the father and the son—beyond the turning from life to self-consciousness. For it unfolds henceforth in the great empty interval which stretches between the dissolution of the Oedipus complex and the final return of the repressed on the higher levels of culture. For the economy of desire, this great interval is the time of subterranean existence, the period of latency. For the *Phenomenology of the Spirit*, this time is filled in by all the other nonparental figures which build human culture. We must extend this great interval boundlessly and multiply the intermediary thresholds. I have mentioned the whole first threshold, that of the savage struggle for recognition. I shall mention only one other, a much later one—at least for a genesis of meaning—that by which two wills, struggling for possession, enter into a contractual relation. I choose this moment, which is omitted from the *Phenomenology of the Spirit* and which opens the *Philosophy of Right*,[3] because it constitutes the fundamentally nonparental relation, starting from which fatherhood can be rethought.

The contract repeats the dialectic of master and slave but on another level; desire is still implied in the moment of the taking of possession; the arbitrary will is as extravagant there as vital desire: there is nothing, indeed, which it cannot in principle appropriate, make its own: "man's right to appropriation bears on everything" (*Philosophy of Right,* § 44). Confronted by another arbitrary will, my will must compromise: this is the contract. And what is noteworthy about the contract is that another will mediates between my will and the thing and that a thing mediates between two wills. Thus is born, from the negotiation between wills, a juridical relation to things: this is property; and a juridical relation between persons: this is the contract. The moment whose constitution we have just briefly reviewed defines the juridical person, the subject of right.

Now, we can very well say that neither fatherhood nor sonship could take on a consistency beyond simple natural generation if they were not mutually bound together, one in relation to the other, not only as two self-consciousnesses, as in the dialectic of master and slave, but as two wills, objectivated by their relation to things and by their contractual ties. I say two wills purposely. The word "will" should stop us, for it is unknown to Freud. We understand why: the will is not a category of the Freudian "field"; it does not relate to an economy of desire; not only can one not find it there, but one ought not to look for it there, under pain of committing a *category mistake,* a mistake concerning the laws of the field considered. The will is a category of the philosophy of spirit. It takes shape only in the sphere of right, in the broad sense which Hegel gives to it, one which is broader than the juridical order, since it extends from abstract right to moral conscience and to political existence. Prior to formal right there is not yet a person or respect for the person; and this abstract right must be taken for what it is: not only along with the idealism of the contract but along with the realism of property. There is no *Personenrecht* which is not a *Sachenrecht.* As in the dialectic of master and slave, things are the interme-

---

3. G. W. F. Hegel, *The Philosophy of Right,* trans. T. M. Knox (New York: Oxford University Press, 1942).

diaries. Thus the reality principle continues to educate the pleasure principle. Hegel did not hesitate to say that my body is mine —that I possess a body—only subsequent to a relation of right, that is, of contract and of property: "as person, I possess my life and my body, like other things, only insofar as it is my property"; and he adds: "I possess the members of my body, my life, only so long as I will to possess them. An animal cannot maim or destroy itself, but a man can" (§ 47);[4] to the degree that I can give up my life, it belongs to me. Thus the body is taken into possession, *in Besitz genommen,* by the spirit.

The conclusion now imposes itself: if the person is posterior to the contract and to property, if even the relation to the body is posterior to these, then the same holds for the mutual recognition of father and son; it is as free wills that they can now confront each other. The passage from an exclusive identification to a differential identification—an enigma that is not resolved in the dialectic of desire—is effected in the dialectic of the will (§§ 73–74).

Let us stop here. The point we have reached is what Hegel calls independence: independence with respect to desires and to life, independence with respect to the other. Independence with respect to desires, Hegel calls self-consciousness; independence with respect to the other, Hegel calls the person. It appears that at this point we have dissolved kinship into nonkinship.

This is not the case.

For the second time, we are going to see true kinship reinstated, beyond the simple continuity of generations, by the mediation of nonkinship.

At what level, in fact, can the properly familial *bond* be inscribed? Not before but after, long after, the dialectic of wills, which has left only proprietors in league, subjects of independent rights, facing one another—persons, certainly, but stripped of all concrete bonds. In two short remarks, Hegel has alerted us to this. First, with respect to the right of persons (§ 40): "[whereas] in Kant, family relationships are the *jura realiter personalia,*" Hegel expressly excludes family relations from the sphere of abstract right; "further on," he says, "it will be shown that the substantial basis of family relationship is rather the sacrifice of personality." Second example: after having declared (§ 75) that the two parties to a contract are "immediate self-subsistent persons," he remarks: "to subsume marriage under

---

4. [Wording slightly altered.—TRANS.]

the concept of contract is thus quite impossible; this subsumption—though shameful is the only word for it—is propounded in Kant." These two remarks quite agree with each other, as is attested by the double horrified reference to Kant. And indeed, in the ascending dialectic, we must look for the family relation quite beyond abstract right; we must leap beyond the *Moralität* which posits a subjective and moral will, i.e., a subject capable of a purpose for which he takes responsibility, in short, a *schuldig* subject, accountable for an action which can be imputed to him as the fault of his will. Yes, it is necessary to pass through all that density of the mediations of abstract right and morality to reach the spiritual and carnal kingdom of *Sittlichkeit,* the ethical life. Now the threshold of this kingdom is the family. Let us understand this precisely: there is a father because there is a family, and not the reverse. And there is a family because there is *Sittlichkeit,* and not the reverse. It is necessary first, therefore, to posit this spiritual and living bond of *Sittlichkeit* in order to rediscover the father. What characterizes this bond is that it envelops its members in a relation of belonging which is no longer voluntary and which in this sense repeats something of the immediacy of life. This famous repetition, which has occupied us in Freud, is signaled in Hegel by a word: the word "substance"; the family relation, we said above, has for its "substantial basis . . . the sacrifice of the personality." Equivalently (§ 144), the family is a concrete totality, which recalls organic totality, but only after having traversed the abstract mediations of right and of morality. It demands "the abandonment of the personality"; the individual is there bound anew, caught in a network, in a system of felt, rational, intelligible determinations: "the substantial order," says Hegel, "in the self-consciousness which it has thus actually attained in individuals, knows itself and so is an object of knowledge" (§ 146); and again: "It is mind living and present as a world, and the substance of mind thus exists now for the first time as mind (§ 151). *Sittlichkeit* is the individual surmounted in the concrete community. That is why the family does not proceed from a contract.

It is against this background of *Sittlichkeit* that the father figure returns. And he returns by way of that concrete community that Hegel calls "the immediate substance of spirit" (§ 158). He returns as master, of course, but primarily as a member. As member of . . . ; that is, "not as an independent person" (§ 158). Moreover, to be recognized by way of the *Sittlichkeit* of the living family community, the father can be recognized only as the spouse of the spouse. What I first recognize in the substance of the family community is what marriage establishes. Let us compare this point with Freud. To recognize the father is to recognize him with the mother. It is to renounce the possessing of one through killing the other. It is to accept the father's being with the mother and the mother's being with the father. Thus, sexuality is recognized—the sexuality of the couple that has begotten me; but it is recognized as the carnal dimension of the institution. This reaffirmed unity of desire and spirit is what makes the recognition of the father possible.

Or rather, the recognition of fatherhood, for in this astonishing text on the family the father as such is never mentioned. What is mentioned are the Penates, that is, the representation of fatherhood in the absence of a father who is dead. The *sittlich* spirit—the spirit of the concrete community—is itself extricated only from the exterior diversity of its appearances, hence freed from its support in individuals and their interests; the spirit of the ethical community "emerges in a shape for representative thinking and has been revered as Penates, etc.; and in general it is in this spirit that the religious character of marriage and the family, or *pietas*, is grounded" (§ 163). In this sense the family is the religious element, but not yet the religious as Christian: it is the religious of the Penates. Now what are the Penates? They are the dead father raised to a representation; it is when he is dead, when he is absent, that he passes into the symbol of fatherhood. It is a symbol in a double sense: first as a signification of the ethical substance; then, as the tie which binds the members, in accordance with another meaning of the word symbol; for it is before the Penates that every new union is contracted: "instead of continually reserving to itself the contingency and caprice of bodily desire, it removes the marriage bond from the province of this caprice, surrenders to the substantive, and swears allegiance to the Penates" (§ 164, note).

Let us end our "second voyage" here. What is its result? The analysis we have just completed is homologous with the preceding one. It is homologous only, because these are two quite distinct discourses. The figure appears first in the framework of an economy of desire, second in the framework of a spiritual history. This is why the relations of one framework to the other are not one-to-one relations. The figures which separate the world of desire from its repetition in the concrete community correspond rather to the great apparent silence of the instincts which Freud calls the latency period. But the two frameworks present analogous articulations. The chief articulation is that of the repetition of the initial figure in the terminal figure—the Penates—beyond all juridical and moral mediations. We can now say: from phantasm to symbol; put differently, from non-recognized fatherhood, mortal and mortifying for desire, to recognized fatherhood, which has become the tie between love and life.

III. The Dialectic of Divine Fatherhood

The third field in which we now undertake to discern the structure of fatherhood is that of "religious representation."

I take the word "representation" in the sense which Hegel gives it continually, whenever he speaks of religion, not only in the *Phenomenology of the Spirit* but in the *Encyclopaedia* and in the *Lectures on the Philosophy of Religion:* "Representation" is the shaped [*figurée*] form of the self-manifestation of the absolute. I am equally in accord with saying that the investigation of religious representation no longer relates to a phenomenology properly speaking, that is, to the sequence of the figures of self-consciousness. It is no longer a matter of self-consciousness but of the deployment, in representation, of speculative thought about the divine as such.

Contrariwise, I am less in accord with saying with Hegel that the reign of representation can be surmounted in a philosophy of the concept, in an absolute knowledge. Absolute knowledge can only be the never-achieved aim of representation itself. This question is inseparable from the definition of religion. For my own part I feel myself closer to Kant finally—to the Kant of *Religion within the Limits of Reason Alone*—than to Hegel and would gladly, like Kant, define religion by the question: What can I hope for?

This place given to hope is not unconnected with the status of representation in general and with the representation of the father in particular. If representation can never be discarded, this is because religion is constituted less by faith than by hope. For if faith falls short in comparison with vision, and hence representation in comparison with the concept, hope is in excess by comparison with knowing and acting. It is of that excess that there cannot be any concept—but always only representation. The question will be to know whether the schema of fatherhood does not connect also with this theology of hope. We can see what is at stake in this third course.

I now propose, like Father Pohier,[5] to take up again the problem of God "the Father," in the Judeo-Christian tradition. But my method will be somewhat different from his. I shall not take theology for my guide, but exegesis. Why exegesis rather than theology? Exegesis has the advantage of remaining on the level of representation and of delivering up the very process of representation, its progressive constitution. In deconstructing theology right to its original representative elements, exegesis plunges us directly into the interplay of the designations of God, it ventures to deliver up to us their originary intention and proper dynamics. I like to say that the philosopher, when he reflects on religion, should have for his partner the exegete rather than the theologian. Another reason for having recourse to exegesis rather than theology is that it invites us not to separate the figures of God from the forms of discourse in which these figures occur. By form of discourse I understand the narrative or the "saga," the myth, the prophecy, the hymn and psalm, wisdom literature, etc. Why this attention to the forms of discourse? Because the designation of God is in each case different according to whether the narrator mentions him in the third person, as the agent in a great deed, such as the Exodus from Egypt, or whether the prophet announces him as the one in whose name he speaks in the first person, or whether the believer addresses God in the second person in the liturgical prayer of the cult or in solitary prayer. Now theology itself, when it strives to be biblical theology, is too often content with extracting from all these texts a conception of God and man and of their relations from which the specific traits that pertain to the forms of discourse have been removed. We shall not ask, then, what the Bible says about God by way of theological abstraction but how God occurs in the various discourses which structure the Bible.

Such being the method, what does it achieve?

Well, the finding that is most important and at first glance most confusing is that, in the Old Testament (we reserve judgment on the New Testament), the designation of God as father is quantitatively insignificant. Specialists in Old and New Testament scholarship are in agreement in emphasizing—and at first being surprised at—this great reserve limiting the use of the

5. [Works by Fr. Pohier and other authors mentioned but not footnoted in the text will be found in the Bibliography at the end of the book.—TRANS.]

epithet "father" in the writings of the Old Testament. Marchel and Jeremias count less than twenty instances in the Old Testament.[6]

It is this reserve that will concern us first. I would like to set it in relation to the hypothesis that has guided me throughout this work, namely, that the father figure, before making its return, must in a certain way be lost, and that it can return only as reinterpreted by means of other figures—figures that are nonparental, nonpaternal. The refinement which leads from the phantasm to the symbol requires—on the three levels which we have considered, the instinctual level, the level of cultural figures, the level of religious representations—a sort of reduction of the initial figure by means of the other figures.

The initial figure, on the level on which we now place ourselves, is well known. All the people of the Near East designate their gods as father and even invoke them by the name of father. This appelation is not simply the common property of the Semites; comparative history of religions teaches us that it is found in India, China, Australia, Africa, and among the Greeks and Romans. All men used to call God their father—this is the initial given; it is even an immense banality, which, as such, is quite insignificant. Here it is like the positing of the Oedipus complex on the instinctual level. Entering into the Oedipus complex is the common datum; what is important is the consequence, whether it is neurotic or not; it is the dissolution of the Oedipus complex and its return. Here, likewise, the fact of the designation of God as father is still nothing; it is the meaning attached to this designation which creates the problem. Or rather, it is the meaning process, for it is the process which contains the schema of fatherhood.

Now, exegesis of the Old Testament shows us that the reserve of the Hebrews with respect to the designation of God as father is the counterpart of their positive manner of apprehending Yahweh as the sovereign hero of a singular history, punctuated with acts of salvation and deliverance, of which the people of Israel, taken as a whole, is the beneficiary and witness. It is here that the categories of discourse intervene and that their incidence in the naming of God is decisive. The first kind of discourse in which the biblical writers tried to speak of God is the narrative. The acts of salvation and deliverance are avowed by

6. W. Marchel, *Dieu-Père dans le Nouveau Testament* (Paris: Cerf, 1966); J. Jeremias, *Abba* (Göttingen, 1965).

means of the "saga," which recounts the dealings of Yahweh with Israel.

This narrative has as its center of gravity the avowal of the Exodus from Egypt; this is the act of deliverance which institutes the people of Israel as a people. The entire theological work of the schools of writers to whom we owe the Hexateuch consisted in ordering the fragmentary tales, of sometimes varied and disparate origin, within the intervals of this great narrative and in extending this back to the great ancestors and even to the myths of creation, which are thus taken into the gravitational space of the avowal of the historical faith of Israel and receive from it a very specific historicization. This joining of the kerygmatic confession to the form of the narrative governs the theological aspect which dominates the Hexateuch and which Gerhard von Rad calls "the theology of historical traditions," to which he opposes "the theology of prophetic traditions," which we shall rediscover shortly with the return of the father figure. It is this theology of historical traditions which is the crucible of the first biblical representations of God. Now, in this first structure—that of the narrative—Yahweh is not in the position of father. If we complete the exegetical method of von Rad by the structural analysis of the tales, derived from Propp and the Russian formalists and applied in France by Greimas and Barthes, we will say that the dominant categories here are those of action and agent, that is, of the hero defined by his function in the narrative. More precisely, the analysis of the action into hierarchized segments causes the appearance, corresponding to the logic of the narrative, of an interplay of personages or agents. The whole theology of traditions consists in articulating the ultimate agent, Yahweh, the principal and collective agent, Israel, taken as a unique historical personage, and various individual agents, with Moses in the top rank, in a dialectic which is never reflected on but is simply narrated. It is this dialectic of actions and agents that is the dramatic support of the theology of the Hexateuch.

In this dialectic of actions and agents, the relation of fatherhood and sonship is nonessential. If there is a father, it is Israel itself: "My father was an Aramaean . . . , etc.," and Yahweh is "God of our fathers" before being father. Likewise, the dialectic of action is deployed on the scale of a people and a history. If the relation of agents will, in a second instance, be able to enter into the category father-son, it will be because it has first been initiated in another category. Which category?

As we know, the theology of the Hexateuch rests on the reinterpretation of the great tales of the acts of Yahweh and Israel, beginning with the relation of the Covenant. Moreover, it must be said immediately: covenants. These are not first and primarily represented as covenants of kinship; on the contrary, it is the Covenant which gives meaning to kinship before this latter adds its own note (we shall see what). It is not necessary, in fact, to interpret the Covenant by fatherhood but by beginning with the clauses and roles which the Covenant develops and articulates; and these can be interpreted within neither the categories of kinship nor juridical categories. In his studies on the Hexateuch, von Rad shows how an original theology of the Covenant is constituted little by little, through a multiplicity of covenants—the covenant with Noah, the covenant with Abraham, he covenant of Sinai—and through different interpretations of these covenants—covenant of one pole, covenant of unequal poles, reciprocal covenants. The Priestly Document (source P) articulates this theology around three themes: Israel will be constituted as a people; Israel will receive the gift of land; Israel will enter into a privileged relation with God. The theology of the Covenant is at the same time a theology of the promise. This point is clearly crucial for fatherhood, which will be able to be reinterpreted on the basis of the third theme of the Covenant: "I shall be your God."

But before reintroducing fatherhood, we must still consider three points, and first the role of the Torah, of instruction, of the law, in this constitutive genesis of meaning. If Israel has a privileged relation with Yahweh, it is because it has the Law: Yahweh is the prime agent, Yahweh is the active pole of the covenant, Yahweh is the one who gives the law. And, here again, it is Israel taken as a whole, as an individual and collective personage, which is the *vis-à-vis:* "Hear, O Israel, I *am* the Eternal, your God, etc."

A final point, before introducing the father figure: it is crucial that Yahweh be designated by a name before being designated as father. In certain psychoanalytic contexts, it is fashionable to speak of the name of the father. But we must distinguish, if not, indeed, dissociate. The name is a proper name. Father is an epithet. The name is a connotation. Father is a description. It is essential for the faith of Israel that the revelation of Yahweh be raised to that terrible level where the name is a connotation without denotation, not even that of the father. Let us reread the story of the burning bush (Ex. 3:13–15): "[If] they say to me,

What is his name [of the God of your fathers], what shall I say unto them? And God said unto Moses: *I am that I am, Ehyeh, asher ehyeh"*; and in the remainder of the text "I am" becomes the subject: "You shall say to them: *I am* hath sent me unto you." This revelation of the name is central to our reflection. For the revelation of the name is the dissolution of all anthropomorphisms, of all figures and figurations, including that of the father. The name against the idol. All nonmetaphoric sonship, all literal descent, is thus reduced. This dissolving action of the theology of the name has been masked for a long time by efforts at harmonization with Greek ontology, as if "I am that I am" were an ontological statement. Is it not necessary, rather, to understand it in an almost ironic sense: what I am, I am for me; but you have my fidelity and my guidance: "You will say to them: *I am* hath sent me unto you"?

This reduction of the idol, and therefore also of the paternal figure, in the theology of the name should not be lost from view when we consider the stories of the Creation. It is noteworthy that on this occasion God is not designated as father and that a specific verb—*bara*—is used to tell about the creative act; any trace of begetting is thus eliminated. The Creation—a mythic theme borrowed from surrounding peoples and introduced tardily and with infinite prudence—is not a piece of paternal theology; it is rather reinterpreted on the basis of the theology of historical traditions and is placed as a preface to the history of the acts of salvation, as the first act of foundation. It is not therefore because he is a father that he is a creator. The theology of the Creation will be, rather, the key to the reinterpretation of the father figure when this latter will return. We must say the same about the qualification of man in the Creation narrative of the priestly school (Gen. 1–2); there it is said that man has been created in the image and likeness of God. The word son is no more pronounced than the Creator is called father. It is rather sonship that will be able to be reinterpreted on the basis of this relation of similitude (in addition, corrected, doubtless, by that of resemblance, which reestablishes the distance); this similitude raises man above created things and institutes him as master and controller of nature. The theology of the name is here denied in no way; we should say, rather, that it is the name without image and without idol which is given as image of the very transcendence of man.

Thus the evolution of the father figure toward a superior symbolism is dependent on other symbols, which do not belong to the sphere of kinship: the liberator of the Hebraic primitive "saga," the lawgiver of Sinai, the bearer of the Name without image, and even the Creator of the Creation myth, none of which has anything to do with kinship. We could even say, in a way that is scarcely paradoxical, that Yahweh is not primarily father; on this condition, he is also father.

It was indeed necessary to take this route; it was necessary to go to what one could call the zero degree of the figure—of the figure in general, of the paternal figure in particular—to be able to designate God as father.

Now—but only now—we can speak of the return of the father figure, that is, interpret, on the level of the biblical text, the designation—not explicit but at the same time very significant—of God as father. This journey of the representation of God corresponds, on the biblical level, to the return of the repressed on the instinctual level or to the institution of the family as a category, following the institution of abstract right and moral consciousness, in the philosophy of the spirit.

This repetition of the father figure itself presents a significant progression, which we can set down schematically as follows: first the designation *as* father, which is still a description in the sense that linguistic analysis gives to this word; then the declaration *of* the father; and finally the invocation *to* the father, which is properly the address to God as father. This movement terminates only in the Lord's Prayer, in which the return of the father figure and the recognition of the father are completed.

We see very well how the designation of God as father proceeds from the other designations of Yahweh in the Covenant; the key here is the relationship of election. Israel has been chosen among the peoples; Yahweh is completely devoted to this people; they are his concern. This election is equivalent to adoption; thus Israel is a son, but it is a son only by a word of designation. By the same stroke, fatherhood itself is entirely dissociated from begetting.

What does the representation of fatherhood add, then, to the historical categories which determine it? If we consider the infrequent occurrences of the designation of God as father, it would appear that it always happens at a moment when the relation in some way exteriorized by the story—Yahweh is *He*—is interiorized. I take the word "interiorize" in the sense of *Erinnerung*, which is both memory and interiority—recollection. Entry into *Erinnerung* is at the same time entry into feeling; the affective connotations are, moreover, extremely complex, ranging from sovereign authority to tenderness and pity, as if the father were also the mother. Thus fatherhood is deployed in a vast range of feelings: "feelings of dependence, of necessity, of protection, of trust, of gratitude, of familiarity" (Marchel, p. 33): ". . . O foolish people and unwise? is not he thy father that hath gotten thee? hath he not made thee and established thee?" (Deut. 32:6). God, who has only a name, who is only a name, receives a face, at the same time as that figure achieves its movement from phantasm to symbol.

It is thus that the designation is inflected toward invocation, but without quite crossing the threshold: "He shall cry unto me, Thou art my father, my God, and the rock of my salvation"; this is not yet an invocation. Nowhere else in the Old Testament is Yahweh invoked as father; the appellations of Jeremiah 3:4 and 19, which we shall consider below, are not invocations, Marchel notes, but simple statements that God pronounces about himself through the voice of the prophets.

What is signified by this incomplete movement toward invocation of the father, which I have called the declaration of the father? Here we must take into account the distinction, evoked earlier, between the two forms of discourse, the story and the prophecy, and the two theologies that are attached to them, the theology of historical traditions and the theology of prophetic traditions, to use von Rad's terms. Indeed, if we scrutinize the texts where God is named father, it would appear that these are the prophetic texts: Hosea, Jeremiah, and the third book[7] of Isaiah, to which we can add the Deuteronomy derived from prophetic contexts. What does this tie between the name of father and prophecy signify? Prophecy marks a break both in the form of discourse and in the theological intention: the story tells the acts of deliverance with which Israel has been favored in the past. Prophecy itself does not tell, but announces, in the performative mode of the oracle; the prophet announces in the first person, in the name of God in the first person. And he announces what? He announces something other than what has been avowed in the framework of the great recounting: first, the exhaustion of this very history, its imminent ruin, and, from its ruin, a new Covenant, a new Zion, a new David. We understand henceforth that, in the prophetic texts, Yahweh is not only designated as father but is declared to be the father (Marchel, p. 41);

7. [Biblical scholars refer to a group of chapters in the book of Isaiah as the "third Isaiah," as the literary and historical evidence points to multiple authors.—Ed.]

and this declaration of God as father would appear inseparable from the direction toward the future that prophecy contains. Three times Jeremiah pronounces: "I am a father for Israel, you shall call me my father and you shall not be separated from me." If we follow the suggestion that prophecy is turned toward and looks for the fulfillment to come, toward the eschatological banquet, is it not necessary to go so far as to say that the figure of the father is itself entailed by this movement and that it is not only the figure of the origin—the God of our fathers, within the realm of the ancestor—but the figure of the new creation?

It is on these terms that the father can be recognized.

Not only is the father no longer in any way an ancestor, but he is indiscernible from the spouse, as if the figures of kinship burst forth and changed places; when the prophet Hosea reinterprets the Covenant, he sees God much more as a spouse than as a father. All the metaphors of fidelity and infidelity, of evil as adultery, are metaphors of a conjugal nature, as are also the feelings of jealousy, of wounded tenderness and the appeal to come back. Jeremiah again says: "and I said, Thou shalt call me, My father; and shalt not turn away from me. Surely as a wife treacherously departeth from her husband, so have ye dealt treacherously with me, O house of Israel" (Jer. 3:19–20). By means of this strange mutual contamination of two kinship figures, the shell of literality of the image is broken and the symbol is liberated. A father who is a spouse is no longer a progenitor (begetter), nor is he any more an enemy to his sons; love, solicitude, and pity carry him beyond domination and severity. To this reversal in the relations of feelings the magnificent text of the "third" Isaiah testifies: "thou art our Father" (Isaiah 64:8).

In the phrase "thou art our Father," we are at the threshold of invocation. Again it is with that modesty which makes the invocation appear in a sort of indirect language, as in Psalm 89:26: "He shall cry unto me, Thou art my father, my God, and the rock of my salvation."

In the New Testament, the movement of the return of the father figure is completed by the invocation of Jesus: *Abba.* Again it is necessary to understand the audacious and unprecedented character of this invocation by setting it against the background of the whole Gospel. If we take into consideration the whole of the Gospel and not some isolated quotations, we must acknowledge that the New Testament retains something of the reserve and modesty of the Old Testament. If John includes more than one hundred occurrences of the designation of God as father,

Mark includes only four, Luke fifteen, and Matthew forty-two. This is to say that the designation of God as father is initially rare and results from a later expansion, which must not be unrelated to the permission given by Jesus to call God father. But first of all, we must admit that fatherhood has not been the initial category of the Gospels; the melodic theme of the Gospels, as we see in Mark, is the coming of the kingdom, the eschatological notion par excellence. Here, as in the Old Testament, it is because there is the Covenant that there is fatherhood; more exactly, the kindgom which is coming, preached by the evangelical kerygma, is the inheritor of the new economy announced by the prophets. It is on the basis of this category of the kingdom that we must interpret the category of fatherhood. Eschatological royalty and fatherhood remain inseparable right into the Lord's Prayer; this begins with the invocation of the Father and is continued by the "petitions" concerning name, kingdom, and will which are understandable only in the perspective of an eschatological fulfillment. Fatherhood is thus placed in the realm of a theology of hope. The Father of the invocation is the same as the God of the preaching of the kingdom, into which one enters only if one is like a child. Thus the figure of the father, inseparable from the preaching of the kingdom, relates, as Jeremias puts it, to the *sich realisierende Eschatologie.*

Put back into this perspective of eschatological preaching, the title of father stands out in a special way, at the same time that sonship receives a new meaning, as we see in the words of Jesus that include the expression "My Father." Let us read Matthew 11:27, which contains the core of the future Johannine theology. A unique relation of mutual knowledge, of recognition, constitutes henceforth true fatherhood and true sonship. "All things are delivered unto me of my Father: and no man knoweth the Son, but the Father; neither knoweth any man the Father, save the Son, and he to whomsoever the Son will reveal him."

It is against this background that we can understand the Lord's Prayer: *Abba,* which we could translate by "dear father." Here is completed the movement from designation to invocation. Jesus, in all probability, was addressing himself to God in saying *"Abba."* This invocation is absolutely unprecedented and without parallel in all the literature of Jewish prayer. Jesus dares to address himself to God as a child to his father. The reserve to which the whole Bible testifies is broken at this precise point. The audacity is possible because a new time has begun.

Far, therefore, from the addressing of God as father being

easy, along the lines of a relapse into archaism, it is rare, difficult, and audacious, because it is prophetic, directed toward fulfillment rather than toward origins. It does not look backward, toward a great ancestor, but forward, in the direction of a new intimacy on the model of the knowledge of the son. In the exegesis of Paul, it is because the Spirit witnesses our sonship (Romans 8:16) that we can cry *Abba*, Father. Far, therefore, from the religion of the father being that of a distant and hostile transcendence, there is fatherhood because there is sonship, and there is sonship because there is community of spirit.

To complete the constitution of this paradigm of fatherhood according to the spirit, we still have to say how *death*—the death of the son and eventually the death of the father—is inserted into this genesis of meaning. We recall in what terms Freudian psychoanalysis poses the problem: on the level of the phantasm, there is a death of the father, but it is a murder; this murder is the work of omnipotent desire, which dreams of itself as immortal; it gives birth, by the interiorization of the paternal image, to a complementary phantasm, that of the father immortalized beyond the murder. This is the phantasm which returns, through the murder of the prophet, in Hebraic religion. As to Christianity, it invents a religion of the Son in which the Son plays a double role: on the one hand, he expiates, for us all, the crime of having killed God; but, at the same time, by taking over the guilt, he becomes God at the side of the father and thus replaces the father, providing an outlet for the resentment against the father. Freud concludes: Christianity, offspring of a religion of the father, becomes a religion of the son.

That the death of Christ can be inscribed in the lineage of the offspring of the phantasm of paternal murder, that it adds to this phantasm the additional trait of realizing, at the same time, the vow of submission to the father and that of rebellion of the son, does not create any misgivings for us who admit that the Oedipal structures constitute a level of instinctual articulation for the entire life of man. But the question is to know what sort of repetition is thus effected by the death of the Just One in Christianity and doubtless already in the prophetic theme of the "Suffering Servant," which Freud did not take into consideration.

Now, psychoanalysis offers us perhaps a second way. Another meaning of the death of the father—we have already suggested it—belongs to the nonneurotic outcomes of the Oedipus complex; this is the counterpart of the mutual recognition between father and son in which the Oedipus complex may be resolved happily. If it is true that the omnipotence of desire is the source of the projection of an immortal father, the rectification of desire occurs through acceptance of the father's mortality.

The philosophy of basic cultural figures helped us to take one step further in that direction. The true kinship bond, we said with the *Philosophy of Right* of Hegel, is that which is established on the level of *Sittlichkeit*, of the concrete ethical life; now this bond raises fatherhood above the contingency of individuals and is expressed in the representation of the Penates; the death of the father is thus blended into the representation of the bond of fatherhood which dominates the sequence of the generations. This death has no further need of being a murder; it is only the suppression of particularity and of the "exterior diversity of appearances" (§ 163) which the establishment of the spiritual bond implies.

There is, therefore, somewhere a death of the father which is no longer a murder and which belongs to the conversion of the phantasm into the symbol.

My hypothesis is that the death of the Just Sufferer leads to a certain meaning of the death of God which corresponds, on the level of religious representations, to what has begun to appear on the two other levels of symbolization. This death of God would be situated in the extension of the noncriminal death of the father and would achieve the evolution of the symbol in the sense of a death by compassion. A *dying for* would come to take the place of a being *killed by*. As we know, the symbol of the Just One who offers his life is rooted in Jewish prophetism and finds its most pathetic lyrical expression in the chants of the "Suffering Servant" of "second" Isaiah. Certainly the "'Suffering Servant" of Isaiah is not God; but if Freud is correct in holding the murder of the prophet—of Moses, first, and then of every prophet who plays the role of Moses *redivivus*—to be a reiteration of the murder of the father, then we can certainly say that the death of the Suffering Servant belongs to the cycle of the death of the father. The Just One is killed, certainly, and thereby the aggressive impulse against the father is satisfied by means of the offspring of the archaic paternal image; but at the same time, and this is the essential point, the meaning of the death is reversed: by becoming "dead for another," the death of the Just One achieves the metamorphosis of the paternal image in the direction of a figure of kindness and compassion. The death of Christ stands at the end of this development: it is as an oblation that the Epistle to the Philippians celebrates it in its liturgical hymn: "He humbled himself, . . . obedient unto death" (Phil. 2:8).

Here is completed the conversion of death as murder into death as offering. Now this meaning is so much beyond the expectation of natural man that the history of theology abounds in purely punitive and penal interpretations of the sacrifice of Christ which make Freud entirely right, so tenacious is the phantasm of the murder of the father and the punishment of the son. For my part, I would believe that the only truly evangelical Christology is one that would take entirely seriously the word of the Johannine Christ: "No one takes my life. I give it."

Is it not, then, this death of the son which can furnish us the final schema of fatherhood, to the degree that the son is also the father? As we know, this last development, initiated only in Scripture—in particular, in the text of Matthew that we have seen above—belongs rather to the epoch of the great trinitarian and theological interpretations. It is at the outer limits of competency of an exegetical method of the kind I have practiced here. I shall say two words about it, nevertheless, in relation to Freud and to Hegel.

Freud indeed was right to say that Jesus "by taking sin onto himself has himself become God at the side of the father and is thus set in his place"; but if Christ is here the Suffering Servant, does he not reveal, in taking the place of the father, a dimension of the father to which death by compassion belongs primordially? In this sense, we could speak truly of the death of God as the death of the father. And that death would be at the same time a murder on the level of the phantasm and of the return of the repressed, and a supreme abandonment, a supreme dispossession of self, on the level of the most advanced symbol.

This is what Hegel has seen perfectly. Hegel is the first modern philosopher to have adopted the formula "God himself is dead" as a fundamental proposition of the philosophy of religion. The death of God for Hegel is the death of separated transcendence. We must shed an idea of the Divine as Wholly Other to reach the idea of the Divine as spirit immanent in the community. The cruel words, as Hegel put it, the cruel words "God himself is dead," are words not of atheism but of true religion, which is a religion not of God above but of the Spirit among us.

But these words can be uttered on different levels and thus take on different meanings. With Hegel himself they resonate on two levels. They are first of all the words of "the unhappy consciousness," which, seeking to attain absolute and immutable certitude of itself, drives this certitude into the beyond. Hegel recalls this at the beginning of his chapter on revealed religion, in the recapitulation of anterior figures. Here are the terms in which he recounts that "total loss":

> we see that this "unhappy consciousness" constituted the counterpart and the complement of the perfectly happy consciousness, that of comedy. . . . It is consciousness of the loss of everything of significance in this certainty of itself, and of the loss even of this knowledge or certainty of itself—the loss of substance as well as of self; it is the bitter pain which finds expression in the cruel words, "God is dead" (*The Phenomenology of the Spirit*, p. 752).

But the unhappy consciousness is still the tragic consciousness; as such, it belongs to the presuppositions of revealed religion and corresponds to the end and general collapse of the ancient world; it is not on the level of the concept of revealed religion, in which, Hegel says, the spirit is going to know itself under the form of spirit. According to this concept, it is spirit itself that alienates itself:

> Of this spirit, which has left the form of substance behind, and enters existence in the shape of self-consciousness, we may say, therefore—if we wish to use terms drawn from the process of natural generation—that it has a real mother but a potential or implicit father. For actual reality, or self-consciousness, and implicit being in the sense of substance are its two moments; and by the reciprocity of their kenosis, each relinquishing or "emptying" itself of itself and becoming the other, spirit thus comes into existence as their unity (*ibid.*, p. 756).

And, a little further on:

> Spirit is known as self-consciousness, and to this self-consciousness it is directly revealed, for it is this self-consciousness itself. The divine nature is the same as the human, and it is this unity which is intuitively apprehended" (pp. 759–60).

It is in this movement of manifestation as alienation that death takes on its ultimate meaning, not only as death of the son, but as death of the father. First, death of the son:

> The death of the Divine Man, *qua* death, is abstract negativity, the immediate result of the process which terminates only in the universality belonging to nature . . . . Death then ceases to signify what it means directly—the non-existence of *this* individual—and

becomes transfigured into the universality of the spirit, which lives in its own communion, dies there daily, and daily rises again (p. 780).

Thus death itself changes meaning on each level of actualization of spirit; like Freud, Hegel speaks of transfiguration, but in the sense of a dialectic which passes several times by the same point, on different levels. We must also say that the final meaning that the death of the son is capable of assuming is the key to the final meaning that the death of the father is in its turn capable of receiving, by a sort of remodeling of paternity along the lines of sonship.

The death of the mediator is death not merely of his *natural* aspect, of his particular self-existence: what dies is not merely the other casement, which, being stripped of essential Being, is *eo ipso* dead, but also the abstraction of the Divine Being. The death of this pictorial idea implies at the same time the death of the abstraction of Divine Being, which is not yet affirmed as a self. That death is the bitterness of feeling of the unhappy consciousness, when it feels that God Himself is dead (pp. 781–82).

The formula of the unhappy consciousness is thus reassumed, only it no longer pertains to unhappy consciousness but, rather, to the spirit of community. What is sketched here could be a theology of the weakness of God, like that which Bonhoeffer envisaged when he said: "Only a weak God can bring help." If this theology were possible, the analogy would be complete between the three levels which we have traversed: between psychoanalysis, philosophy of spirit, and philosophy of religion. The final theme, for each of these three disciplines, would be the inclusion of the death of the father in the final constitution of the symbol of fatherhood. And this death would no longer be a murder but the most extreme abandonment of self.

In conclusion, let me make a brief balance sheet of the questions that are resolved and those that are not resolved. Among the resolved questions I shall count the following points:
1. The comparison between the first analysis, in the field of desire, and the last one, in the field of religious symbols, causes a sort of analogy to appear between the instinctual organizations and the chain of symbolic figures of faith. Moreover, this analogy bears less on structures than on processes; its discovery would appear susceptible of engendering a spirit of equity, as we say, between psychoanalysis and religion. Certainly, nothing is

settled for all that; and everything remains open and even unde-cided at this stage of reflection. In any event, the right of psycho-analysis to deal with the religious phenomenon remains complete: all the analyses of our third part are inscribed in the "field" of instinctual formations; in a certain way, the history of the divine names belongs to the adventures of the libido. This conclusion ceases to surprise us if we remain attentive to the diversity of ways out of the Oedipal crisis and to the species of discontinuous continuity which reconnects the organizations of the nonneurotic outcome to those of the neurotic outcome. This is why the notion of the return of the repressed must remain quite open and problematic. Conversely, psychoanalysis does not have the power to reduce the meanings of the religious sphere or to deprive them of their proper sense, whatever be their de-gree of libidinal investment. In this respect we can reproach Freud, above all in *Moses and Monotheism,* with having wished to proceed directly to a psychoanalysis of the believer without making the detour of an exegesis of the texts in which his faith is documented.

But this first conclusion is of less interest to me today than the following ones. After all, the armistice which it proposes expresses at best the diplomatic virtues of a good arbiter in the war of the hermeneutics. I will emphasize, rather, the second and the third conclusions.

2. The second conclusion is this: the center of gravity and the pivot of the whole investigation is the phenomenology and the philosophy of the spirit developed in the second part; there lies the philosophical strength of the analysis. The two other panels are connected with this central panel in the direction, on the one hand, of what I called an archaeology and, on the other hand, in the direction of a teleology, which points toward a the-ology of hope without, however, necessarily implying it. Remove this middle panel and the analysis is undone or destroys itself in insoluble conflicts; many confrontations between psychoanalysis and religion are badly directed and badly controlled for lack of this philosophical instrument and the mediation exercised by what I call concrete reflection.

3. My third conclusion is, in my view, even more important; it bears on the precise result of this investigation, namely, the schema of fatherhood. If I resume the summary description given in the introduction, it would appear that it is enriched in some important traits. In my working hypothesis I laid emphasis on the passing from phantasm to symbol, on the role of figures

other than kinship in the emergence of the symbol, and, finally, on the return of the initial phantasm in the terminal symbol. The triple analysis to which this process of symbolism has been submitted has brought to light traits which give us much to think about. First, the retreat of physical generation in favor of a word of designation; then, the replacement of a doubly destructive identification by the mutual recognition of father and son; finally, the access to a symbol of fatherhood detached from the person of the father. It is perhaps this last trait which is the most exacting for thought, for it introduces not only contingency but death into the building-up of the symbol. We saw something of this on the instinctual level, with the understanding of the death of the father and the death of desire; then, on the level of basic cultural figures, with the Hegelian theme of the family community reassembled under the sign of the Penates; finally, on the theological level, with the "death of God" in one or another of the meanings that this theme is susceptible of assuming. This link between death and the symbol is what has not yet been sufficiently thought out.

With this last remark we have already moved into the area of unresolved problems. It is on this point that I shall finish. One fundamental problem remains in suspense. What does the distribution into three fields, which has governed this analysis, signify? I see very well that they are delimited by different methodologies: an economics, a phenomenology, and a hermeneutics. But one cannot hide indefinitely behind this kind of response, which avoids the crucial question, namely, what about the realities themselves? For, finally, economics is an economics of desire, phenomenology a phenomenology of spirit, hermeneutics an exegesis of religious figures. How are desire, spirit, and God connected? Put differently, what is the reason for the analogies of structure and process among the three fields considered? What that question demands of the philosopher is nothing else but this: to undertake again, with renewed energy, the task assumed in the last century by Hegel, of a dialectical philosophy which would take up the diversity of the schemes of experience and reality into a systematic unity. Now, it is indeed with renewed energy that we must take up this task once again, if it is true that, on the one hand, the unconscious ought to be assigned another place than the categories of reflective philosophy and that, on the other hand, hope is destined to open what system tends to close up. That is the task. But who today could assume it?

Bibliography

Actes du Ier Congrès international de linguistique. (The Hague, 1928). Leyden, 1929.

L'Analyse structurale du récit. Communications, no. 8. Paris: Editions du Seuil, 1966.

Aristotle. *On Interpretation. Nicomachean Ethics.*

Augustine, Saint. *De doctrina Christiana. Contra Julianum. De libero arbitrio. De peccatorum meritis et remissione. Quaestiones VII ad Simplicianum. Retractiones.* Anti-Manichaean writings.

Barthes, Roland. "Introduction à l'analyse structurale des récits." In *L'Analyse structurale du récit.*

Bastide, R., Benveniste, E., Lévi-Strauss, C., et al. *Sens et usages du terme structure dans les sciences humaines et sociales.* The Hague: Mouton, 1962.

Benveniste, Emile. "La Forme et le sens dans le langage." In *Le Langage: Actes du XIIIe Congrès des sociétés de philosophie de langue française.* Neuchâtel: La Baconnière, 1967.

———. *Problems in General Linguistics.* Trans. Mary E. Meek. Miami Linguistics Series, no. 8. Coral Gables: University of Miami Press, 1971.

Bonhoeffer, Dietrich. *Letters and Papers from Prison.* Ed. Eberhard Bethge. English trans. Rev. and enlarged ed. (Original title: *Prisoner for God.*) New York: Macmillan, 1972.

Bultmann, Rudolf. *Faith and Understanding.* Trans. Louise P. Smith. New York: Harper & Row, 1969.

———. *The Gospel of John: A Commentary.* English trans. Philadelphia: Westminster Press, 1971.

Bultmann, Rudolf. *Jesus Christ and Mythology*. Ed. Paul Schubert. English trans. New York: Scribner's, 1958.

――. *Jesus and the Word*. Trans. Louise P. Smith and Erminie Huntress. New York: Scribner's, 1934.

――. *The Theology of the New Testament*. English trans. New York: Scribner's, 1970.

Carroll, John B. *The Study of Language: A Survey of Linguistics and Related Disciplines in America*. Cambridge, Mass.: Harvard University Press, 1953.

Cassirer, Ernst. *The Philosophy of Symbolic Forms*. Vol. I: *Language*. Vol. II: *Mythical Thought*. New Haven: Yale University Press, 1953; 2d ed., 1955.

Chenu, M. D. *La Théologie au XIIe siècle*. Paris, 1957.

――. *Nature, Man, and Society in the Twelfth Century: Essays on New Theological Perspectives in the Latin West*. Abridged ed. Trans. Jerome Taylor. Chicago: University of Chicago Press, 1968.

Chomsky, Noam. *Cartesian Linguistics*. New York: Harper & Row, 1966.

――. *Current Issues in Linguistic Theory*. New York: Humanities Press, 1964.

――. *Syntactic Structures*. New York: Humanities Press, 1957.

Communications, no. 8. See *L'Analyse structurale du récit*.

Confession de foi de la Rochelle. Ed. R. Mehl. Coll. "Les Bergers et les Mages." 1959.

Dilthey, Wilhelm. "Die Entstehung der Hermeneutik." *Gesammelte Schriften*, Vol. V.

Dodd, C. H. *The Bible Today*. Cambridge, Eng.: At the University Press, 1946; 2d ed., 1960.

Dufrenne, Mikel. *Le Poétique*. Paris: Presses Universitaires de France, 1963.

Ebeling, Gerhard. "Hermeneutik." In Vol. III, *Religion in Geschichte und Gegenwart*. 3d ed., 1959.

Eliade, Mircea. *Patterns in Comparative Religion*. Trans. Rosemary Sheed. New York: Sheed & Ward, 1958.

Enuma Elish. See Pritchard, James B.

Feuerbach, Ludwig. *Manifestes philosophiques*. French trans. Paris: Presses Universitaires de France, 1960.

Fichte, Johann G. *Fichtes Werke*. Ed. Immanuel H. Fichte. 11 vols. Berlin: De Gruyter, 1971.

Frege, Gottlob. "Über Sinn und Bedeutung." In *Philosophical*

Writings. Trans. P. Geach and M. Black. Oxford: Basil Blackwell, 1960.

Freud, Sigmund. *The Complete Psychological Works of Sigmund Freud*. English trans. Ed. James Strachey. London, 1927–31.

Gardiner, Sir Alan H. *The Theory of Speech and Language*. Oxford: Clarendon Press, 1932; 2d ed., 1951.

Godel, R. *Les Sources manuscrites du "Cours de linguistique générale" de Ferdinand de Saussure*. Geneva and Paris: Droz-Minard, 1957.

Greimas, A. J. "Eléments pour une théorie de l'interprétation du récit mythique." In *L'Analyse structurale du récit. Communications*, no. 8. Paris: Editions du Seuil, 1966.

————. *La Sémantique structurale*. Paris: Larousse, 1966.

Guillaume, G. *Temps et verbe*. Champion, 1965.

————. *Langage et sciences du langage*. Nizet, 1964.

Guiraud, P. *La Sémantique*. Paris: Presses Universitaires de France, 1962. ("Que sais-je.")

Hegel, G. W. F. *The Phenomenology of Mind*. Trans. J. B. Baillie. New York: Humanities Press, 1964.

————. *The Philosophy of Right*. Trans. T. M. Knox. New York: Oxford University Press, 1942.

————. *Lectures on the Philosophy of Religion*. Trans. Speirs and Sanderson. 3 vols. London: Routledge & Kegan Paul.

————. *Précis de l'Encyclopédie des sciences philosophiques*. French trans. Paris: Vrin, 1952.

Heidegger, Martin. *Being and Time*. Trans. John Macquarrie and Edward Robinson. New York: Harper & Row, 1962.

————. *Erläuterungen zu Hölderlins Dichtung*. Frankfort a.M.: Klostermann, 1954.

————. *Gelassenheit*. Pfullingen: Neske, 1959.

————. *Holzwege*. Frankfort a.M.: Klostermann, 1953.

————. *Introduction to Metaphysics*. Trans. Ralph Manheim. New Haven: Yale University Press, 1959.

————. *On the Way to Language*. [*Unterwegs zur Sprache*.] Trans. Peter D. Hertz and Joan Stambaugh. New York: Harper & Row, 1971.

Hesnard, A. *L'Oeuvre de Freud*. With a Preface by Maurice Merleau-Ponty. Paris: Payot, 1960.

Hjelmslev, Louis. *Essais linguistiques*. Copenhagen, 1959.

————. *Language: An Introduction*. Trans. Francis J. Whitfield. Madison: University of Wisconsin Press, 1970.

————. *Prolegomena to a Theory of Language*. Trans. Francis J. Whitfield. Madison: University of Wisconsin Press, 1961.

Humboldt, W. von. *Über die Verschiedenheit des menschlichen Sprachbaues und ihren Einfluss auf die geistige Entwickelung des Menschengeschlechts* (1836). Bonn: F. Dümmlers Verlag, 1967.

Husserl, Edmund. *Cartesian Meditations: An Introduction to Phenomenology*. Trans. Dorion Cairns. The Hague: Nijhoff, 1960.

———. *The Crisis of European Sciences and Transcendental Phenomenology: An Introduction to Phenomenological Philosophy*. Trans. David Carr. Evanston, Ill.: Northwestern University Press, 1970.

———. *Formal and Transcendental Logic*. Trans. Dorion Cairns. The Hague: Nijhoff, 1969.

———. *Ideas: General Introduction to Pure Phenomenology*. [*Ideen I.*] Trans. W. R. Boyce Gibson. New York: Macmillan, 1931.

———. *Logical Investigations*. Trans. J. N. Findlay. 2 vols. New York: Humanities Press, 1970.

———. "The Origin of Geometry." Appendix VI in *The Crisis*, trans. Carr.

Hyppolite, Jean. *Genesis and Structure of "The Phenomenology of the Spirit."* Trans. John Heckman and Samuel Cherniak. Evanston, Ill.: Northwestern University Press, forthcoming.

Ihde, Don. *Hermeneutic Phenomenology: The Philosophy of Paul Ricoeur*. Evanston, Ill.: Northwestern University Press, 1971.

Jakobson, Roman. *Essais de linguistique générale*. Paris: Editions de Minuit, 1963.

———. "Principien der historischen Phonologie." *Travaux du Cercle linguistique de Prague*, Vol. IV (1931).

———. *Selected Writings*. Vol. I: *Phonological Studies*. Vol. II: *Word and Language*. New York: Humanities Press, 1971.

Jeremias, Joachim. "Abba." *Untersuchungen zur neutestamentlichen Theologie und Zeitgeschichte*. Göttingen, 1965. English trans., *The Prayers of Jesus*. Studies in Biblical Theology, 2d ser., no. 6. Naperville, Ill.: Alec R. Allenson, 1967.

Jonas, Hans. *Gnostic Religion*. Boston: Beacon Press, 1963.

Kant, Immanuel. *Critique of Practical Reason*. Trans. L. W. Beck. New York: Liberal Arts Press, 1956.

———. *Critique of Pure Reason*. Trans. Norman K. Smith. New York: St. Martin's Press, 1929.

———. *Religion within the Limits of Reason Alone*. Trans. Theodore M. Greene and Hoyt H. Hudson. New York: Harper Torchbooks, 1960.

Kierkegaard, Søren. *Fear and Trembling.* Trans. Walter Lowrie. Princeton: Princeton University Press, 1941.

——. *Post-scriptum aux miettes philosophiques.* French trans. Paris: Gallimard, 1938.

——. *Repetition: An Essay in Experimental Psychology.* Trans. Walter Lowrie. New York: Harper Torchbooks.

——. *Traité du désespoir.* French trans. Paris: Gallimard, 1932.

Lacan, Jacques. *The Language of the Self: The Function of Language in Psychoanalysis.* Trans. Anthony Wilden. Baltimore: Johns Hopkins University Press, 1968.

Leenhardt, M. *Do Kamo: La Personne et le mythe dans le monde mélanésien.* Paris: Gallimard, 1947.

Leeuw, Gerardus van der. *Religion in Essence and Manifestation: A Study in Phenomenology.* Trans. J. E. Turner. London: Allen & Unwin, 1938. Rev. ed., 2 vols., New York: Harper, 1963.

Lévi-Strauss, Claude. *Elementary Structures of Kinship.* English trans. Ed. Rodney Needham. Boston: Beacon Press, 1969.

——. "Introduction à l'*Oeuvre de Marcel Mauss*." In Marcel Mauss, *Sociologie et anthropologie.* Paris, 1950.

——. *The Savage Mind.* English trans. Chicago: University of Chicago Press, 1966.

——. *Structural Anthropology.* Trans. Claire Jacobson and Brooke Grundfest Schoepf. New York: Basic Books, 1963.

——. *Totemism.* Boston: Beacon Press, 1963.

——. *Le Totémisme aujourd'hui.* Paris: Presses Universitaires de France, 1962.

Lubac, M. de. *Exégèse médiévale: Les quatre sens de l'Ecriture.* 4 vols. Paris: Aubier, 1959–64.

Marchel, W. *Dieu-Père dans le Nouveau Testament.* Paris: Cerf, 1966.

Martinet, André. *Elements of General Linguistics.* Trans. Elisabeth Palmer. Chicago: University of Chicago Press, 1964.

Merleau-Ponty, Maurice. *Phenomenology of Perception.* Trans. Colin Smith. New York: Humanities Press, 1962.

——. *Signs.* Trans. Richard C. McCleary. Evanston, Ill.: Northwestern University Press, 1964.

——. *The Visible and the Invisible.* Ed. Claude Lefort. Trans. Alphonso Lingis. Evanston, Ill.: Northwestern University Press, 1968.

Moltmann, Jürgen. *The Theology of Hope*. Trans. J. W. Leitch. New York: Harper & Row, 1967.

Nabert, Jean. *Elements for an Ethic*. Trans. William J. Petrek. Evanston, Ill.: Northwestern University Press, 1969.

———. *Essai sur le mal*. Paris: Presses Universitaires de France, 1955.

———. *L'Expérience intérieure de la liberté*. Paris: Presses Universitaires de France, 1924.

———. "La Philosophie reflexive." *Encyclopédie française* XIX, 19.04-14–19.06-3.

Nietzsche, Friedrich. *Beyond Good and Evil*. Trans. Walter Kaufmann. New York: Random House, 1966.

———. *On the Genealogy of Morals*. Trans. Walter Kaufmann. New York: Random House.

———. *Joyful Wisdom*. Trans. Thomas Common. New York: Macmillan, 1924.

———. *Thus Spake Zarathustra*. Trans. Walter Kaufmann. New York: Viking Press, 1966.

———. *The Will to Power*. Trans. Walter Kaufmann. New York: Random House, 1967.

Ogden, C. K., and Richards, I. A. *The Meaning of Meaning*. London: Routledge & Kegan Paul, 1923; 2d ed., 1946.

Ortigues, Edmond. *Le Discours et le symbole*. Paris, 1962.

Peirce, Charles Sanders. *Collected Papers*. Ed. Charles Hartshorne and Paul Weiss. 8 vols. Cambridge, Mass.: Harvard University Press, 1931–35.

Pelagius. *Pelagius's Expositions of Thirteen Epistles of Saint Paul*. English trans. Ed. Alexander Souter. 3 vols. Cambridge, Eng.: At the University Press, 1922–31.

Pépin, J. *Mythe et allégorie: Les Origines grecques et les contestations judéo-chrétiennes*. Paris: Aubier, 1958.

Plinvale, G. de. *Pélage: Ses écrits, sa vie, et sa reforme*. Paris: Payot, 1943.

Plotinus. *Enneads*. Trans. Stephen McKenna. New York: Pantheon, 1957.

Pohier, J. M. "La Paternité de Dieu." In *L'Inconscient*, no. 5. Paris: Presses Universitaires de France, 1968.

Pritchard, James B. *Ancient Near Eastern Texts Relating to the Old Testament*. Princeton: Princeton University Press, 1950; 3d ed., 1969.

Puech, Henri-Charles. "Der Begriff der Erlösung im Manichaeismus." *Eranos-Jahrbuch*, 1936.

——. *Le Manichéisme, Civilisations du sud.* S.A.E.P., 1949.

——. "Les Nouveaux écrits gnostiques." *Coptic Studies,* 1950.

Quispel, Gilles. "La Conception de l'homme dans la gnose valentinienne." *Eranos-Jahrbuch,* 1947.

——. *Gnosis als Weltreligion.* Zurich: Orego Verlag, 1951.

——. "L'Homme gnostique (la doctrine de Basilide)." *Eranos-Jahrbuch,* 1958.

Rad, Gerhard von. *Old Testament Theology.* New York: Harper & Row.

——. *Theology of the Old Testament.* Vol. I: *Theology of the Historical Traditions of Israel.* Trans. D. M. G. Stalker. Edinburgh: Oliver & Boyd, 1962.

Rapaport, David, ed. *The Organization and Pathology of Thought.* New York: Columbia University Press, 1951.

Richardson, W. J. *Heidegger: Through Phenomenology to Thought.* The Hague: Nijhoff, 1963.

Ricoeur, Paul. *Freud and Philosophy: An Essay on Interpretation.* Trans. Denis Savage. The Terry Lectures. New Haven: Yale University Press, 1970.

——. *The Symbolism of Evil.* Trans. Emerson Buchanan. Boston: Beacon Press, 1969.

Rottmayer, Dom O. *L'Augustinisme.* French trans. Mélanges de Sciences religieuses, 1949.

Saussure, Ferdinand de. *Course in General Linguistics.* Trans. Wade Baskin. New York: Philosophical Library, 1966.

Schleiermacher, F. *Hermeneutik.* Ed. Heinz Kimmerle. Heidelberg: Carl Winter Universitätsverlag, 1959.

Spinoza, Benedict. *Ethics.* Trans. James Gutmann. New York: Hafner, 1949.

Trubetzkoy, N. "La Phonologie actuelle." *Psychologie du langage.* Paris, 1933.

——. *Principes de phonologie.* French trans. Paris: Klincksieck, 1949; 2d ed., 1957.

Ullmann, Stephen. *The Principles of Semantics.* New York: Philosophical Library, 1957.

Urban, Wilbur M. *Language and Reality: The Philosophy of Language and the Principles of Symbolism.* London: Allen & Unwin, 1939; 2d ed., 1961.

Index

This index was prepared with the collaboration of Richard W. Coté.

[507]